Every state in the world has undertaken human rights obligations on the basis of UN treaties. Today's challenge is to enhance the effectiveness of procedure and institutions established to promote the accountability of governments under the treaties. The six treaty bodies that monitor and evaluate state policies and practices play a vital role, but the whole system has been stretched almost to breaking point. It is under-funded, many governments fail to report or do so very late or superficially, there is a growing backlog of individual complaints, broad reservations have been lodged by many states, and the expertise of committee members has been questioned.

This volume contains detailed analyses of the strengths and weaknesses of the system, written by many leading participants in the work of the treaty bodies. Their recommendations provide a blueprint for far-reaching reform of a system of major importance for the future of international efforts to protect human rights.

Philip Alston is Professor of International Law and Co-Director of the Academy of European Law at the European University Institute, Florence.

James Crawford is Whewell Professor of International Law and Director of the Lauterpacht Research Centre for International Law, University of Cambridge.

D0555658

THE FUTURE OF
UN HUMAN RIGHTS TREATY
MONITORING

EDITED BY

PHILIP ALSTON AND
JAMES CRAWFORD

CAMBRIDGE
UNIVERSITY PRESS

PUBLISHED BY THE PRESS SYNDICATE OF THE UNIVERSITY OF CAMBRIDGE
The Pitt Building, Trumpington Street, Cambridge CB2 1RP, United Kingdom

CAMBRIDGE UNIVERSITY PRESS
The Edinburgh Building, Cambridge, CB2 2RU, UK http://www.cup.cam.ac.uk
40 West 20th Street, New York, NY 10011-4211, USA http://www.cup.org
10 Stamford Road, Oakleigh, Melbourne 3166, Australia

© Cambridge University Press 2000

This book is in copyright. Subject to statutory exception and to the provisions of relevant
collective licensing agreements, no reproduction of any part may take place without
the written permission of Cambridge University Press.

First published 2000

Printed in the United Kingdom at the University Press, Cambridge

Typeset in 10.5/13.5pt Minion   [GC]

A catalogue record for this book is available from the British Library

Library of Congress Cataloguing in Publication data

The future of UN human rights treaty monitoring / edited by Philip
Alston and James Crawford.
p.   cm.
ISBN 0 521 64195 0 (hardback). – ISBN 0 521 64574 3 (paperback)
1. Human rights.   2. United Nations–Commissions.   I. Alston,
Philip.   II. Crawford, James, 1948–   .
K3240.4.F88   2000
341.4'81–dc21   99-34665   CIP

ISBN 0 521 64195 0 hardback
ISBN 0 521 64574 3 paperback

CONTENTS

A · The UN human rights monitoring system in action

B · National influences and responses

C · Regional and sectoral comparisons

TABLES

FIGURE

APPENDICES

CONTRIBUTORS

Philip Alston is Professor of International Law at the European University Institute at Florence and was Chairperson of the UN Committee on Economic, Social and Cultural Rights for eight years (1991–1998). He is also a Global Visiting Law Professor at New York University, Editor of the *European Journal of International Law*, and co-director of the Academy of European Law, Florence. He is the author of a series of reports commissioned by the United Nations on the reform of the human rights treaty system.

Roland Bank has been a research fellow at the Max-Planck-Institute for Comparative Public Law and International Law in Heidelberg, Germany, since 1998. His doctoral thesis is on international mechanisms to combat torture and he has published broadly on this issue.

Michael Banton has been a member of the Committee on the Elimination of Racial Discrimination since 1986 (Rapporteur, 1990–1996 and Chairperson, 1996–1998). A Justice of the Peace since 1966, he served on the Royal Commission on Criminal Procedure, the Royal Commission on Civil Disorders in Bermuda, and on the Ethnic Minorities Advisory Committee of the Judicial Studies Board. Professor of Sociology in the University of Bristol from 1965 to 1992, he has been President of the Royal Anthropological Institute and is the author of some twenty books.

Daniel Bodansky is a Professor at the University of Washington School of Law in Seattle. He is a former Chair of the American Society of International Law's Interest Group in International Environmental Law, co-editor-in-chief of the International Law and Policy series published by

Kluwer Law International, and an advisory board member of the *Yearbook of International Environmental Law.*

Mara R. Bustelo is a staff member of the Office of the High Commissioner for Human Rights, in Geneva, working for the Committee on the Rights of the Child. She has degrees from the University of Completense in Madrid and the Fletcher School of Law and Diplomacy in Boston and previously worked at the European University Institute in Florence. Her most recent publication is *The EU and Human Rights* (co-editor) published in English in 1999 by Oxford University Press and forthcoming in French by Bruylant. The chapter for this volume was written while she was at the EUI and has since been updated.

Andrew Byrnes is an Associate Professor of Law and Director of the Centre for Comparative and Public Law in the Faculty of Law at the University of Hong Kong, where he teaches in the areas of international law, public law and human rights. He has written on international human rights law, in particular in relation to women and human rights, and the UN treaty bodies. He has worked closely with local and international human rights groups raising Hong Kong issues before the UN treaty bodies.

Antônio Augusto Cançado Trindade is Professor of International Law at the University of Brasilia and at the Rio-Branco Institute, Judge and currently President of the Inter-American Court of Human Rights, and former Executive Director of the Inter-American Institute of Human Rights in Costa Rica (1994–1996). He has also worked as Legal Adviser to the Brazilian Ministry of External Relations (1985–1990). His books include *The Application of the Rule of Exhaustion of Local Remedies in International Law*, Cambridge, 1983, and *Treatise on International Human Rights Law*, 3 vols, Fabris ed., 1997–1999.

Andrew Clapham is Associate Professor of Public International Law at the Graduate Institute of International Studies in Geneva and, until recently, was the Representative of Amnesty International at the United Nations in New York. His books include *Human Rights in the Private Sphere*, Oxford, 1993.

James Crawford is Whewell Professor of International Law and Director of the Research Centre for International Law, University of Cambridge. He is a member of the UN International Law Commission, and is co-editor of the Cambridge University Press series, Cambridge Studies in International and Comparative Law.

John Dugard is Professor of Public International Law at the University of Leiden in the Netherlands and Emeritus Professor at the University of the Witwatersrand, South Africa. He is a member of the UN International Law Commission and a Senior Counsel at the South African Bar. His books include *Human Rights and the South African Legal Order*, Princeton, 1978, *Recognition and the United Nations*, Cambridge, 1987, and *International Law. A South African Perspective*, Kenwyn, 1994.

Elizabeth Evatt was the first Chief Judge of the Australian Family Court, and subsequently President of the Australian Law Reform Commission. She was previously a Member and Chairperson of the Committee on the Elimination of Discrimination against Women and is currently the Vice-Chairperson and was previously the Rapporteur of the UN Human Rights Committee.

Anne Gallagher is a staff member of the Office of the High Commissioner for Human Rights in Geneva and a doctoral candidate at the University of Lund in Sweden. Previously she was a Lecturer in Law at the Australian National University.

Stefanie Grant is the Deputy Director of the Lawyers' Committee for Human Rights in New York City. She was previously Director of Research for Amnesty International, and has practised as a solicitor in the UK.

David Harris is Professor of Public International Law at the University of Nottingham and former member of the Council of Europe's Committee of Independent Experts on the European Social Charter. His books include *Cases and Materials on International Law* (5th edn) London, 1998, *The International Covenant on Civil and Political Rights and United Kingdom Law*, Oxford, 1995, *The Law of the European Convention on Human Rights*, London, 1995 and *The Inter-American System of Human Rights*, Oxford, 1998.

Yuji Iwasawa is Professor of International Law in the Department of International Relations at the University of Tokyo. He holds an LLM from Harvard and an SJD from the University of Virginia. He is Rapporteur of the Committee on Human Rights Law and Practice of the International Law Association. His most recent book is *International Law, Human Rights,* *and Japanese Law: The Impact of International Law on Japanese Law*, Oxford, 1998.

Gerison Lansdown is the director of the Children's Rights Office which exists to promote the fullest possible implementation of the UN Convention on the Rights of the Child in the United Kingdom. She has lectured and published widely on children's rights both nationally and internationally, and is a leading commentator on the Convention on the Rights of the Child.

Scott Leckie is Executive Director of the Centre on Housing Rights and Evictions (COHRE). He has worked for various international organisations including the Office of the High Commissioner for Human Rights, the UN High Commissioner for Refugees, the UN Development Programme, the UN Centre for Human Settlements and the Council of Europe, and has participated in all sessions of the UN Committee on Economic, Social and Cultural Rights since 1988. His next book will address housing and property restitution issues for refugees and internally displaced persons.

Michael O'Flaherty is Chief of the Human Rights Section of the United Nations Mission in Sierra Leone. His former positions with the UN have included Secretary of the Committee on the Elimination of Racial Discrimination, Expert Advisor of the Office of the High Commissioner for Human Rights to the High Representative for Implementation of the General Framework Agreement for Peace in Bosnia and Herzegovina, and initiation of the field offices in Bosnia of the Commission on Human Rights Special Rapporteur for former Yugoslavia. His most recent publications include, *Human Rights and the UN: Practice Before the Treaty Bodies*, London, and *Post-war Protection of Human Rights in Bosnia and Herzegovina* (ed., with G. Gisvold), The Hague, 1998.

Martin Scheinin is Professor of International Law at the University of Helsinki and a member of the UN Human Rights Committee. He has written extensively on economic and social rights and on the role of human rights norms in domestic law. His most recent publication is *International Human Rights Norms in the Nordic and Baltic Countries*, The Hague, 1996.

Markus Schmidt is a staff member of the Office of the High Commissioner for Human Rights and currently the secretary of the UN Working Group on Arbitrary Detention. He previously was responsible for UN treaty-based complaints mechanisms. His publications include *Common Heritage or*

Common Burden? . . . The US Position on Deep Sea-bed Mining under the Law of the Sea Convention, Oxford, 1989.

Craig Scott is Associate Professor in the Faculty of Law, University of Toronto. Prior to joining the faculty, he served as law clerk to the former Chief Justice of the Supreme Court of Canada, Brian Dickson. He teaches and researches generally in the fields of public international law and private international law, specialising in the place of international human rights law in both these fields. He also works on the doctrine and theory of constitutional rights protection and has been closely involved in three major cases dealing with the interface of international law and Canadian law decided by the Supreme Court of Canada in recent years. He is editor of a volume called *Torture as Tort: Comparative Perspectives on the Development of Transnational Human Rights Litigation* to be published by Hart Publishing in mid-2000.

Henry Steiner is Jeremiah Smith, Jr. Professor of Law and the Director of the Harvard Law School Human Rights Program at Harvard University. He is also Chair of the University Committee on Human Rights Studies. Steiner has written on a broad range of human rights topics, and is co-author (with Philip Alston) of *International Human Rights in Context*, Oxford, 1996.

Eric Tistounet is an official in the Office of the UN High Commissioner for Human Rights in Geneva. A graduate of the University of Strasbourg and the Université Paris I Panthéon-Sorbonne, he began his career in the Directorate of Human Rights of the Council of Europe. After joining the UN Centre for Human Rights in 1987, he held several positions within the International Instruments Branch and more recently served as Secretary of the Human Rights Committee. Since February 1998, he has worked in the High Commissioner's Front Office responsible for external relations.

EDITORS' PREFACE

In human rights terms the twentieth century yielded a valuable legacy of internationally agreed standards and the creation of a set of institutional arrangements designed to monitor compliance with those standards. But the overriding challenge for the future is to develop the effectiveness of those monitoring mechanisms. Many of the most important standards have been incorporated into the six 'core' United Nations human rights treaties. They are the two International Covenants dealing respectively with civil and political rights and economic, social and cultural rights; two anti-discrimination conventions dealing with racial discrimination and discrimination against women, and conventions against torture and on the rights of the child. A separate supervisory body has been set up in relation to each of these treaties and it is those 'treaty bodies' that form the focus of the present volume.

Their work is important, and the system as a whole has great potential. However, there are major challenges confronting the human rights treaty regime. The problems facing each of the committees individually are exacerbated by declining support for multilateralism in general and constant budgetary pressures on international organisations. In addition there is deep-seated ambivalence on the part of many governments when it comes to the strengthening of mechanisms which might enhance their accountability for compliance with their international human rights obligations.

This volume contains detailed analyses of the strengths and weaknesses of the system, written by many of the leading participants in the work of the treaty bodies. Their recommendations add up to a blueprint for far-reaching reform of the system. Earlier versions of the papers were presented at a conference in Cambridge, organised jointly by the Lauterpacht

Research Centre for International Law at the University of Cambridge, and the European University Institute, Florence, in March 1997. All the papers have since been revised and updated. Many debts have been incurred along the way. The project was funded by the Ford Foundation and special thanks are due to Margo Picken and Larry Cox for their strong support. The organization of the conference was undertaken with great skill and energy from Florence by Mara Bustelo. Without Glen Howard's efficient support at every step the conference in Cambridge and the administration of the project would have been infinitely more difficult. James Heenan assisted greatly in the editing of the papers and in bringing the project to fruition. Finally, Frances Nicholson was a superb copy-editor and Finola O'Sullivan at Cambridge University Press oversaw the project from start to finish with constant support and encouragement.

In relation to matters of style, we have, for the reader's convenience, systematically used the standard acronyms to refer to each of the treaties and, when the commonly used acronym for the Committee is similar or even identical, we have added the word Committee to avoid confusion (the Convention on the Elimination of All Forms of Discrimination Against Women becomes 'CEDAW' and the Committee established under it becomes 'the CEDAW Committee'). Similarly, although the usage of the term 'Chairperson' or 'Chairman' varies from one committee to another, we have standardised the usage to refer to 'Chairperson' throughout the volume.

Philip Alston
Florence

James Crawford
Cambridge

TABLE OF TREATIES

TABLE OF CASES

International bodies

INTERNATIONAL CRIMINAL TRIBUNAL FOR THE
FORMER YUGOSLAVIA

Regional bodies

EUROPEAN COMMISSION OF HUMAN RIGHTS

EUROPEAN COURT OF HUMAN RIGHTS

EUROPEAN COMMITTEE OF SOCIAL RIGHTS (FORMERLY
COMMITTEE OF INDEPENDENT EXPERTS)

National courts

CANADA

NAMIBIA

ABBREVIATIONS

In a field full of acronyms they cannot be avoided, only made less confusing. We use the following abbreviations for the various conventions, the full titles of which are given here, although the short title is used within the text. The committees are referred to by the addition of the word 'Committee' to the relevant Convention abbreviation (thus CAT Committee). The only exception is the Human Rights Committee, for which the now standard abbreviation HRC is used.

ACABQ	Advisory Committee on Administrative and Budgetary Questions (within UN)
ACHR	American Convention on Human Rights
ACLU	American Civil Liberties Union
AJIL	*American Journal of International Law*
BULRev	*Buffalo University Law Review*
BYbIL	*British Yearbook of International Law*
CAT	Convention against Torture and other Cruel, Inhuman or Degrading Treatment or Punishment
CEDAW	Convention on the Elimination of All Forms of Discrimination against Women
CERD	Convention on the Elimination of All Forms of Racial Discrimination
CESCRC	Committee on Economic, Social and Cultural Rights
CHR	Commission on Human Rights
CIDH	Comisión Interamericana de Derechos Humanos (IACHR)

CIE	Committee of Independent Experts (under ESC)
CITES	Convention on International Trade in Endangered Species of Wild Fauna and Flora
CPG	Central People's Government (China)
CPT	Committee for the Prevention of Torture
CRC	Convention on the Rights of the Child
CRDU	Children's Rights Development Unit
DLR	*Dominion Law Reports*
EASC	Election Appeals Sub-Commission (in Bosnia and Herzegovina)
ECHR	European Convention for the Protection of Human Rights and Fundamental Freedoms
ECOSOC	Economic and Social Committee
EHRLR	*European Human Rights Law Review*
EHRR	*European Human Rights Reports*
EJIL	*European Journal of International Law*
EMEP	Cooperative Programme for Monitoring and Evaluation of the Long-Range Transmission of Air Pollutants in Europe (under LRTAP)
EPG	Eminent Persons Group
ESC	European Social Charter
ESCR	Economic, Social and Cultural Rights
ETS	European Treaty Series
FAO	Food and Agriculture Organisation
GA	General Assembly
GAO	General Accounting Office (USA)
GAOR	General Assembly Official Record
GFA	General Framework Agreement for Peace in Bosnia and Herzegovina
GTZ	Gesellschaft für Technische Zusammenarbeit
HKLJ	*Hong Kong Law Journal*
HKPLR	Hong Kong Public Law Reports
HRC	Human Rights Committee
HREOC	Human Rights and Equal Opportunity Commission (Australia)
HRLJ	*Human Rights Law Journal*
HRQ	*Human Rights Quarterly*
IACHR	Inter-American Commission of Human Rights

ICCPR	International Covenant on Civil and Political Rights
ICESCR	International Covenant on Economic, Social and Cultural Rights
ICJ	International Court of Justice
ICLQ	*International and Comparative Law Quarterly*
IFAD	International Fund for Agricultural Development
IFOR	Implementation Force (NATO-led force in Bosnia and Herzegovina)
IHRR	*International Human Rights Reports*
ILA	International Law Association
ILM	*International Legal Materials*
ILO	International Labour Organisation
ILR	*International Law Reports*
IUCN	International Union for the Conservation of Nature
IWC	International Whaling Commission
JPO	junior professional officer (within UN)
Komnas HAM Komisi	Nasional Hak Azasi Manusia (Indonesian Human Rights Commission)
LCHR	Lawyers' Committee for Human Rights
LRTAP	Long-Range Transboundary Air Pollution Convention
MLF	Multilateral Fund (of Montreal Protocol on Substances that Deplete the Ozone Layer)
NAFTA	North American Free Trade Agreement
NethILR	*Netherlands International Law Review*
NGO	non-governmental organisation
NmSC	Namibian Supreme Court
NZLR	*New Zealand Law Reports*
OAS	Organization of American States
OASTS	Organization of American States Treaty Series
OEA	Organizacion de los Estados Americanos (OAS)
OECD	Organisation for Economic Cooperation and Development
PC	Privy Council
RUD	Reservations, Understandings and Declarations
SAR	Special Administrative Region (of China)

TEAP	Technological and Economic Assessment Panel (under Montreal Protocol)
TRAFFIC	Trade Records Analysis of Fauna and Flora in Commerce
UDHR	Universal Declaration of Human Rights
UN	United Nations
UNDP	United Nations Development Programme
UNESCO	United Nations Educational, Scientific and Cultural Organisation
UNFPA	United Nations Population Fund
UNHCHR	United Nations High Commissioner for Human Rights
UNHCR	United Nations High Commissioner for Refugees
UNICEF	United Nations Children's Fund
UNIFEM	United Nations Development Fund for Women
UNTS	United Nations Treaty System
USC	United States Code
USSR	Union of Soviet Socialist Republics
Virginia JIL	*Virginia Journal of International Law*
WEOG	Western European and Others Group (one of five regional UN groupings)
WHO	World Health Organisation
YJIL	*Yale Journal of International Law*
YLJ	*Yale Law Journal*
ZSC	Zimbabwe Supreme Court

1

THE UN HUMAN RIGHTS TREATY SYSTEM: A SYSTEM IN CRISIS?

JAMES CRAWFORD*

A. The evolution of the United Nations treaty system

In 1945, almost for the first time, the United Nations Charter announced the idea of human rights as real rights at the universal level.[1] That required the development of substantive human rights standards, a process commenced with the Universal Declaration of Human Rights in 1948 and substantially extended through the two International Covenants in 1966, the Racial Discrimination Convention in the same year, and a large number of other instruments, general or specific in scope. All this has been in addition to the development of human rights standards and structures at regional level.

The articulation of new universal standards and new treaties has not ceased (although norm fatigue and avoiding the most obvious forms of duplication must, presumably, mean that it will become progressively more selective). But the need for their implementation remains, as much for the older standards and treaties as for the newer. Here the approach adopted at the universal level in 1966 had the following features:

(1) the establishment of specialist bodies charged with the oversight of treaty performance, each concerned with a specific treaty;
(2) regular reporting obligations for states parties, on the assumption that the examination of reports would lead to a dialogue between each state and the relevant treaty body, and to progressive improvements in compliance, associated with limited reliance on state-to-state or individual complaints procedures;

---

* My thanks to James Heenan for his very helpful research assistance in the preparation of this chapter.
[1] See UN Charter, articles 1, 55.

(3) the absence of decision-making powers of a judicial or quasi-judicial character vested in the treaty bodies.[2]

This was in contrast with the regional systems in Europe and the Americas, in which:

(1) the development of regional standards relied much more on the adoption of protocols to a single basic treaty, with the corollary that only a single institution or set of institutions remained involved;
(2) there was much more emphasis on individual complaints procedures as the basic supervisory tool, with the possibility of state-to-state complaints but little or no reliance on periodic reporting;
(3) the supervisory bodies dealing with such complaints had judicial or at least quasi-judicial powers: they could make decisions and even award compensation.

These contrasts were the result of deliberate decisions, and there were reasons – for the most part, good reasons – for them. But as time has gone

---

[2] The language of the relevant provisions is not that of judicial determination. For example, Convention on the Elimination of All Forms of Racial Discrimination (CERD), article 9 (2) states that the Committee 'may make suggestions and general recommendations' based on state reports received. See also International Covenant on Civil and Political Rights (ICCPR), article 40 (4); Convention on the Elimination of All Forms of Discrimination against Women (CEDAW), article 21 (1); Convention against Torture (CAT), article 20 (4) (authorising the Committee to make 'comments and suggestions' to states parties regarding well-founded allegations of systematic torture); Convention on the Rights of the Child (CRC), article 45 (d). Even under the Optional Protocol to the ICCPR, article 5 (3), the Human Rights Committee shall simply 'forward its views' to the state party and individual concerned. In *Wellington District Legal Services Committee v. Tangiora* [1998] 1 NZLR 129, the New Zealand Court of Appeal held that the Human Rights Committee is not '[a]ny administrative tribunal or judicial authority' within the meaning of the Legal Services Act 1991 since (a) it is not called a court (cf. the International Court of Justice (ICJ)) or a tribunal (cf. the UN Administrative Tribunal); (b) the process set out in the Optional Protocol is exiguous and not that expected of a judicial body or tribunal; and (c) the wording of the Protocol is not the language of a binding obligation, as is the case with other bodies set up to resolve disputes of an international character. See generally D. McGoldrick, *The Human Rights Committee. Its Role in the Development of the International Covenant on Civil and Political Rights* (Oxford: Clarendon Press, 1994), paras. 2.21–2.22. As to the nature of the Committee on Economic, Social and Cultural Rights, established by Economic and Social Committee (ECOSOC) Res. 1985/17 subsequent to the adoption of the International Covenant on Economic, Social and Cultural Rights (ICESCR) itself, see M. C. R. Craven, *The International Covenant on Economic, Social and Cultural Rights. A Perspective on its Development* (Oxford: Clarendon Press, 1995), pp. 56–7.

on the contrasts have grown even sharper. At the regional level, we have seen the consolidation of institutions, with increasing emphasis on their judicial or quasi-judicial character;[3] at the universal level, there has been a proliferation of bodies, and a certain decline, or at the least a failure to develop, complaints procedures as distinct from reporting. Despite a relative decrease in the resources available at the universal level, the proliferation of instances has continued, with a host of special procedures and personnel dealing with particular problems, thematic or geographic, as well as the establishment in 1994 of a United Nations High Commissioner of Human Rights (UNHCHR). At the regional level, by contrast, the original institutions have largely retained their central roles, and the problems of coordination and avoiding duplication are far less.

No doubt the contrast can be overdrawn, and it is not a simple case of regional success stories set against universal decay. As the chapters which follow show, the United Nations human rights treaty system has its own record of successes. It must also be stressed how rapidly the UN human rights treaty body system has developed, in parallel with the treaties themselves. The first such body, the Committee of the International Convention on the Elimination of All Forms of Racial Discrimination (CERD), first met in January 1970. By 1991 there were six treaty bodies; a seventh, the Migrant Workers' Committee, is envisaged. Participation in the treaties themselves has grown exponentially, as Table 1 shows.

During this period the treaty bodies have developed and consolidated methods of considering reports, have pioneered and developed the institution of general comments, have developed forms of coordination with each other and (to a lesser extent) with other human rights institutions, especially UN High Commissioner for Human Rights (UNHCHR), have increasingly involved non-governmental organisations in their work, and generally have sought to keep up with a greatly increased workload. If the system is in difficulty, this is to a large degree a product of its success in attracting the participation and involvement of states and of other bodies. But the fact remains that the system *is* in difficulty, a difficulty characterised by some as crisis.

---

[3] Especially with the 1994 adoption by the Council of Europe of Protocol 11 to the European Convention on Human Rights, and the eventual abolition of the European Commission on Human Rights.

Table 1.1 *Participation in UN human rights treaties*
(as at 1 December 1998)

Treaty	Date of adoption	Time to enter into force (number of parties required)	Time to reach 100 parties	Present number of parties
CERD	21 Dec 1965	3 yr 1 m (27)	12 yr 10 m	151
ICESCR	16 Dec 1966	9 yr 1 m (35)	14 yr 10 m	138
ICCPR	16 Dec 1966	9 yr 3 m (35)	15 yr 1 m	140
Optional Protocol	16 Dec 1966	9 yr 3 m (10)	—————	92
CEDAW	18 Dec 1979	1 yr 9 m (20)	10 yr 7 m	162
CAT	10 Dec 1984	2 yr 6 m (20)	11 yr 6 m	110
CRC	20 Nov 1989	11 m (20)	2 yr 1 m	191

Notes: Acronyms for the UN human rights treaties are CERD – Convention on the Elimination of Racial Discrimination; ICESCR – International Covenant on Economic, Social and Cultural Rights; ICCPR – International Covenant on Civil and Political Rights; CEDAW – Convention on the Elimination of Discrimination against Women; CAT – Convention against Torture; CRC – Convention on the Rights of the Child.

B. Symptoms of success: Crises of the treaty system

Details will be provided in the chapters which follow, but the following summary gives some indication of the character of these difficulties and of their extent.

1. CORROSIVE EFFECTS OF THE BACKLOG IN STATE REPORTING

The first and most obvious issue is the huge backlog in state reports due under the various treaties. The progressive deterioration can be seen from Table 2.

There is, however, no provision which enables delinquent states to be censured, other than by committees noting the delays in their annual reports, and by repeated and so far ineffectual calls on the part of the General Assembly.

2. DELAYS IN PROCESSING REPORTS AND COMMUNICATIONS

A second symptom is the delays presently experienced within the committees, whether it takes the form of delay between the date of submission of a

Table 1.2 *Overdue reports under UN human rights treaties (as at 1 December 1998)*[4]

Treaty	Number of parties		Parties with overdue reports		Total overdue reports
	1993	1998	1993	1998	1998
CERD	119	151	65	124	390
ICESCR	115	138	64	97	134
ICCPR	132	140	112	97	145
CEDAW	118	162	78	134	245
CAT	71	110	36	72	105
CRC	126	191	59	124	141

report and the date of its consideration, or (in the case of the committees which deal with individual petitions or communications) delay between their submission and their consideration by the committee.

In confronting these delays the committees are in a dilemma: they must give sufficient attention to individual reports and communications, whatever their source, while at the same time the number of states parties and of communications has increased and is increasing. Some committees (e.g. CERD) simply increase the number of reports considered at a session, but beyond a certain point this strategy will break down; moreover state representatives who have travelled to the meeting of a committee to discuss a report are entitled to a degree of attention: a system based on 'constructive dialogue' has to allow time for that dialogue even if the state is generally in compliance with the treaty. The underlying fact is that none of the committees has received any sustained increase to its regular meeting time, and no such increases can be expected. Moreover it is difficult to make use of intersessional time, because committee members are not paid for intersessional work (even if their other commitments left them time to do it); moreover problems of communication and lack of internet access for many members make intersessional work difficult and cumbersome.

It needs to be stressed that these unacceptable delays are occurring at a time when many reports are overdue. If all states were to report on time,

---

[4] Adapted from Alston, Final Report (E/CN.4/1997/74) 14.

the delays in dealing both with reports and individual communications would become extreme: it is not too much to say that the system, established to oversee state compliance, depends for its continued functioning on a high level of state default.[5] As to individual complaints procedures, the delays are even less excusable. Arguably the reason the Human Rights Committee is not itself in breach of the spirit of article 14 of its own Covenant through the delay in dealing with communications is, precisely, its non-judicial character.[6]

3. RESOURCE CONSTRAINTS

One possible solution to such problems is, quite simply, a substantial increase in the resources available. If the principle of state reporting and periodic review is right, as has been repeatedly asserted, then the first step must surely be to allow to all the committees the time, resources and staff to deal efficiently with the backlog, at the same time examining on the basis of other available materials the record of compliance in states whose reports are seriously overdue. But no informed observer believes that any substantial injection of resources for the system as a whole is likely. Recent limited improvements experienced by the Committee of the Convention on the Rights of the Child (CRC) are so far the exception rather than the norm. This alone raises serious questions of sustainability.

Resource constraints, identified in the chapters which follow, have a number of different features.

---

[5] Alston estimated that as at 1996, somewhere between seven and twenty-four years, approximately, would be required to review all state reports overdue, if they were to be submitted forthwith: ibid., p. 17. The only exception was the CRC (four years), which only commenced operations in 1991 and thus had less time to develop a backlog. By December 1998, however, 141 state reports were overdue in respect of the CRC.

[6] In *Prosecutor v. Tadic*, 105 ILR 419, the Appeals Chamber of the International Criminal Tribunal for the Former Yugoslavia held that the 'due process' requirements laid down in ICCPR, article 14 (1), European Convention for the Protection of Human Rights and Fundamental Freedoms (ECHR), article 6 (1) and American Convention on Human Rights (ACHR), article 8 (1) do not apply to proceedings conducted before an international tribunal (at para. 42). Notwithstanding this, the Chamber concluded that such a tribunal 'must provide all the guarantees of fairness, justice and even-handedness, in full conformity with internationally recognized human rights instruments' (at para. 45). Note, however, that the requirement that any hearing take place 'within a reasonable time', embodied in both ECHR, article 6 (1) and ACHR, article 8 (1), does not form part of ICCPR, article 14 (1).

Secretariat/personnel constraints

Committee secretariats are understaffed and underpowered. A handful of people (less than the number of support staff in a standard department in a medium-sized university) has to staff the six committees.[7] The number is hardly more than twice the number of persons in the secretariat of the European Social Charter.[8] This acute staff shortage is exacerbated by such factors as the over-specialisation of staff (each person only works for a single treaty body), leading to gaps in expertise available to the system as a whole (e.g. the lack of Russian-speaking lawyers despite the growing number of communications in that language). Recruitment of short-term interns does not resolve the problem.[9]

Other financial constraints

In certain cases acute lack of funds has led to the cancellation of sessions (e.g. CERD). More generally there are complaints at restrictions on documentation, constraints arising from the lack of or delays in translation,[10] the absence of funds for field visits to member states (cf. CERD's missions), for cooperation between treaty bodies (e.g. joint or thematic working groups), or for attendance of members at other committees' sessions.

Limited technology

The United Nations cannot provide access to internet or email for committee members, although this is by far the cheapest and most efficient way to develop texts and generally to consult outside of sessions. The UNHCHR website is a good, though overdue, first step, but by no means all UN human rights material is available electronically. Better use of databases would help redress the problem of lack of a corporate memory within committees.

4. PROCEDURAL ISSUES

There are no doubt inherent problems with a system for human rights protection based essentially on self-criticism and good faith. The system

---

[7] See Leckie, *infra*, chapter 6.   [8] See Harris, *infra*, chapter 16.
[9] See Schmidt, *infra*, chapter 22; Evatt, *infra*, chapter 21.
[10] See Evatt, *infra*, chapter 21.

encourages states to view compliance only in the context of a rather sporadic reporting procedure, with a lack of follow-up mechanisms for both periodic reports and communications. On the other hand a more selective approach by committees, focusing only on serious breaches which are suspected or have come to notice, would give rise to complaints of selectivity: there is, as Scott Leckie notes, a continuing concern not to alienate states parties whose cooperation is assumed and is necessary for the idea of constructive dialogue to work.[11] To some extent these constraints are inbuilt, but the contrast drawn by Daniel Bodansky with the environmental bodies (e.g. under the Climate Change Convention), with their use of state visits, *ad hoc* teams, wide dissemination of views etc., suggests that improvements can nonetheless be made.[12]

5. PROBLEMS OF COMMUNICATIONS PROCEDURES

Henry Steiner's review of the Human Rights Committee's communications procedure shows the problems inherent in 'mandatory jurisdiction'. There is no correlation between the general level of complaints (or for that matter their complete absence) and the state of human rights compliance in a given country. For example the 'death row' phenomenon is highlighted in one country, or one region, but not in others where it may be just as prevalent. To avoid the Committee becoming a 'fourth instance', some discretionary element may need to be introduced at the stage of admissibility (such as most final appellate courts exercise within national systems). But the tendency is the other way; the Committee normally telescopes admissibility and merits, and it is reticent to develop criteria for admissibility which would inevitably reduce the focus on the individual and – except in clear cases of individual injustice – would tend to focus on systemic considerations. But the communications procedures are themselves so occasional, overall and for most countries, as to raise questions about their underlying rationale. As Steiner points out, over the twenty years from 1977 to 1997, the Committee had issued views in only about 260 cases, and its capacity to process communications is estimated at around thirty communications per year. If every state party to the Optional Protocol were to generate only one communication per year, the backlog would soon

---

[11] See Leckie, *infra*, chapter 6. See also O'Flaherty, *infra*, chapter 20.
[12] See Bodansky, *infra*, chapter 17.

become intolerable. A more differentiated and selective approach to communications seems necessary.

6. COMPOSITION OF COMMITTEES

Many members of the treaty bodies have given dedicated, and largely unremunerated, service. But the electoral process (like most such processes within the UN) is haphazard and takes limited account of qualifications. Vote trading between unrelated UN bodies is so common as to be unremarked. This is of course part of a broader problem. UN electoral processes are no doubt irreducibly political, but there has been no effort to distinguish between the political properly so-called and the purely venal. Some form of scrutiny of candidates for minimum qualifications could bring great dividends in terms of the quality of membership, but there is for the time being no prospect that the electorate of state party representatives will adopt such a step.[13] There may, however, be room for non-governmental organisations (NGOs) to have some informal input into the electoral process, something presently lacking.

7. PROBLEMS WITH RECENT OR PROPOSED REFORMS

Some of the reforms that have been adopted, or that are proposed, carry their own costs, as Markus Schmidt demonstrates in his analysis of the disadvantages of Plans of Action.[14] In addition to being quite costly to implement (the budget for the CRC plan is about $1.25 million annually), they rely on voluntary contributions from states parties. If these are not pledged or paid in time, the plan may have to be reduced in scope, shortened or simply abandoned. More fundamentally, they shift the emphasis from financing of treaty body activities through the regular UN budget to financing from outside, and could thereby open the door to influence-peddling.

---

[13] One of the difficulties is that major reform is extremely difficult to achieve, and tinkering is unlikely to help. Still, there are steps in the right direction in other bodies, which may provide precedents in terms of any long-term restructuring. For example, the new electoral process for judges of the European Court of Human Rights requires governments to nominate several candidates who are then subject to a form of scrutiny; cf. also the prohibition of re-election of judges, under the Rome Statute of the International Criminal Court, 17 July 1998 (A/CONF.183/9) article 36 (9) (a) (which, if extended to the treaty bodies, would require longer and staggered terms of office).

[14] See Schmidt, *infra*, chapter 22.

8. LIMITED POLITICAL SUPPORT FROM STATES

The underlying problem is no doubt the limited will of the states parties to improve the system. There is a view that inclusion of more states parties is to be preferred to the integrity of the treaty, and this manifests itself in the lack of reaction by many states to questionable reservations, to overdue or inadequate reports and even to failures of compliance.[15] For those dedicated to the application of universal human rights standards the position can appear a depressing and even dispiriting one. As against this, however, certain comments should be made.

First of all, the 'system' (the committees and their secretariats, the member states) is capable of responding strongly on occasion. For example, when North Korea purported to withdraw from the International Covenant on Civil and Political Rights (ICCPR), the position taken by the United Nations as depositary, by the Human Rights Committee (HRC) itself, and by member states was that it could not validly do so,[16] and it continues to be treated as a member *malgré lui*.[17] The response by many states, at least in Europe, to the United States reservation with respect to the imposition of the death penalty on juveniles was also strong and consistent.[18]

Secondly, the attitude of member state governments is almost bound to be different from that of the committees, with their specific mandate to encourage compliance with their own treaty. Governments confronted with a wide range of problems and having only limited (possibly contracting) resources are likely to respond routinely and in a lower key to what are seen as routine requirements of an established system. They are certainly not

[15] See e.g. Banton, *infra*, chapter 3.

[16] In response to an attempted withdrawal by the Democratic People's Republic of Korea from the ICCPR, the Secretary-General ruled that 'a withdrawal from the Covenant would not appear possible unless all States Parties to the Covenant agree with such a withdrawal': C.N.467.1997.TREATIES-10, 12 November 1997. The Human Rights Committee (HRC) agreed (HRC, General Comment 26 (61), adopted by the Committee at its 1631st meeting, 8 December 1997), as did a number of governments.

[17] The position under the Optional Protocol is of course different: article 14 specifically allows withdrawal and this option has been taken up recently by Barbados and by Trinidad and Tobago in response to the many death penalty communications brought against them. See N. Schiffrin, 'Jamaica Withdraws the Right of Individual Petition Under the International Covenant on Civil and Political Rights', 92 *AJIL*, 1998, p. 563.

[18] See the objections lodged by Belgium (5 October 1993), Denmark (1 October 1993), Finland (28 September 1993), France (4 October 1993), Germany (29 September 1993), Italy (5 October 1993), Netherlands (28 September 1993), Norway (4 October 1993), Portugal (5 October 1993), Spain (5 October 1993) and Sweden (18 June 1993).

inclined to encourage more rigorous scrutiny of their own human rights record, and problems in other countries tend only to obtrude on specific occasions, usually involving major incidents, trials or crises. The burden of day-to-day scrutiny is thus left to the committees. But the fact remains that the committees are attempting valiantly to square a vicious circle resulting from the proliferation of instruments, a huge increase in participation and static resources. Member state apathy at this situation is, certainly, a problem, whatever excuses or explanations may be offered.

C. The structure of this volume

Against this background, the chapters in this volume are organised in the following way. In **Section A**, the work of each of the six existing committees is reviewed by a knowledgeable observer or participant, as is the crucial work of NGOs in relation to the committees. The human rights treaty system acts, however, not for itself but in order to promote and monitor developments in the national systems parties to the treaties. Thus, the uneven, but by no means negligible, effect of the treaty system on national law and practice is reviewed in **Section B**. In a volume of this size, this review can only be highly selective, but the cases chosen (the Nordic states, Japan, South Africa, Hong Kong and the United States) range quite widely: from countries with strong institutions or traditions of human rights to countries struggling to establish them; from countries open, or at least opening, to international human rights influence to countries resolutely closed or closing. The *particularity* of this experience is in each case notable, resulting from particular historical circumstances and social and political developments, in contrast to the universality of values the treaty bodies claim to represent and foster.

Section C presents, for the purposes of illustration as well as contrast, the experience of state reporting under three distinct systems, two regional (the Inter-American System and the European Social Charter), one functional (under global environmental treaties).

Against this background of the treaty bodies in action, of a sample of the legal and social systems with which they interact, and of some other treaty systems from which they might learn, **Section D** surveys some of the common problems they are experiencing. Again it has been necessary to be selective: the themes chosen are those of duplication, diversity, focus, and the need for and the provision of resources. Of particular importance here is the question of focus. Are the treaty bodies to be seen as having a general mandate to deal with situations arising within the field of 'their' treaty, or are they better seen as specialist agencies performing a particular function of supervision in the context of a specific system of reporting? The experience of the treaty bodies confronted with widespread violations in Bosnia and Herzegovina raises that question in an acute form.

Finally, in the concluding **Section E** a comparison is undertaken of the approach generally shared by the contributors to this volume with an alternative approach which attributes relatively little importance to the universality of the system and instead advocates restricting participation in the treaty regime to those states which are deemed to be democratic.

A

THE UN HUMAN RIGHTS MONITORING
SYSTEM IN ACTION

2

INDIVIDUAL CLAIMS IN A WORLD OF MASSIVE VIOLATIONS: WHAT ROLE FOR THE HUMAN RIGHTS COMMITTEE?

HENRY J. STEINER*

A. Introduction

1. SETTING OUT THE PROBLEM

Individual claims against a state before a permanent international organ (committee, commission, tribunal, court) no longer stand out as stark exceptions to the usual patterns of international law, as anomalies that we struggle to fit within an established or even necessary order. The earlier questions – How can we understand this phenomenon within a system of state-to-state relations? How can it be reconciled with rooted premises of international law like state sovereignty? – have lost their salience as such claims have become more familiar, and as the premises have changed. An evolving theory and practice expressing different understandings of international law and relations readily make place for the individual, together with many types of non-state institutions, as essential actors and participants.

Individual claims are not yet commonplace, but neither are they rare. Undoubtedly the growth of the human rights movement over the last fifty years has had much to do with this changed incidence and perception. That movement – by which this chapter refers to governmental and intergovern-mental as well as non-governmental developments in human rights since

* The author is very grateful to several members of the Human Rights Committee and of the Secretariat staff for conversations over the last few years that have deepened his under-standing of the Committee's history and current work. The author has benefited from criticisms of an earlier draft of this article by Philip Alston, Makau Mutua and Lewis Sargentich, but the analysis and proposals herein are of course his sole responsibility.

1945 – has taken a vital step beyond the historical analogies by authorising claims by individuals against the very state of their nationality. Several universal human rights treaties empower an individual to initiate against the state some kind of process before a treaty organ that allows for the consideration and disposition of a claim of violation of a right declared in the treaty. Each of the three regional human rights regimes – the African, European and Inter-American systems – also provides in one way or another for such complaints.

Such a burst of committees, commissions and courts poses basic questions. What powers and procedures are appropriate for the international organ concerned? What relation should exist between that organ and the national legal and political system out of which a case arises? What paths can an individual benefiting from a favourable international decision follow in order to influence the state to comply with it? More broadly, what purposes should such forms of international dispute resolution between individuals and their states of nationality serve? What goals should give direction to these innovative processes? Are there generally valid answers to these last questions, or will answers necessarily vary with context?

This chapter addresses the latter questions about purposes, goals and context. It does so not abstractly, by viewing the great range of international organs and procedures as a group, but concretely by addressing the so-called communications procedure of the most significant body created by a universal human rights treaty: the Human Rights Committee (hereafter the Committee or HRC), established by article 28 of the International Covenant on Civil and Political Rights (hereafter the Covenant or ICCPR).[1] The Optional Protocol[2] institutes a system of complaints against states parties by individuals who claim that they are victims of violations by such states of rights set forth in the Covenant. The Protocol gives the Committee competence to consider a complaint – referred to in the Protocol as a 'communication' – and to 'forward its views' about whether or not there has been a violation to the individual and the state concerned.

As of December 1999, ninety-five of the 144 parties to the ICCPR were also parties to the Protocol. Their combined population amounts to well over one billion people. These states can be placed at many points on a spectrum ranging, over the last decade, from those committing relatively

---

[1] GA Res. 2200A (XXI), UN Doc. A/6316 (1966), 999 UNTS 171.
[2] 999 UNTS 171. A Second Optional Protocol, GA Res. 44/128, concerning abolition of the death penalty, is not discussed in this chapter.

modest violations of human rights to those practising systemic, massive and severe violations. A selection of parties including Algeria, Argentina, Bosnia and Herzegovina, Canada, the Democratic Republic of the Congo, France, Germany, Peru, and the Russian Federation well illustrates this range.

The Committee here exercises a challenging, indeed puzzling, jurisdiction. Do the Covenant and Protocol provide authoritative answers, or even helpful guidance, to the questions about purposes and goals? Alternatively, do the HRC's more than two decades of work under the Protocol – both the Covenant and Protocol entered into force in 1976 – give satisfactory answers?

The two treaty texts are sparse and unrevealing on these issues. No more can be said for the records of the drafting sessions within the United Nations organs, beyond the inevitable stress (leading to both support and opposition) on the Protocol's most striking feature of empowering individuals to seek international relief.[3] Moreover, although the idea of individual claims appeared early in the United Nations drafting process, the Protocol itself was drafted only at a late stage and produced correspondingly less debate.[4] Over two decades, neither deliberations by the Committee about the communications procedure nor the views that it has issued under the Protocol have sought to identify and assess the purposes that the procedure might serve.

During the sharp ideological conflicts from the 1950s to 1980s when the two treaties were drafted and ratified and when the Committee began to function, it was inevitable that compromises over incompatible points of view took the form of terse and ambiguous provisions about institutional purposes and powers whose language lay unexplored. But in the post-Cold War context, holding to the Committee's historical course without questioning its assumptions and without reflecting on institutional purposes simply obscures the important choices that lie before the Committee and the states parties.

This chapter characterises the Committee's work under the Protocol as a form of adjudication and identifies several purposes that this adjudicatory scheme could serve. It argues that the Committee could make its most

---

[3] See D. McGoldrick, *The Human Rights Committee: Its Role in the Development of the International Covenant on Civil and Political Rights*, Oxford, 1991, chapters 1 and 4 on the drafting of the Covenant and Protocol, particularly pp. 3–10 and 120–4; M. Nowak, *CCPR Commentary: UN Covenant on Civil and Political Rights*, Kehl/Strasbourg/Arlington, 1993, sections on article 40 (p. 545) and the Protocol (p. 647), particularly pp. 647–51.

[4] See McGoldrick, *supra*, note 3, at pp. 123–4; Nowak, *supra*, note 3, at p. 651.

significant contribution to the ICCPR and the human rights movement by concentrating on expounding the ICCPR – that is, exploring and explaining it, justifying its own decisions, and acting as a deliberative body seeking to illuminate and advance understanding of the Covenant rather than to apply it summarily case by case. The Committee would thereby facilitate a dialogue about its content with states, other international organs, and nongovernmental actors participating in the movement. The goal of dialogue would reinforce similar goals of the two other principal activities of the Committee: criticising the reports on implementation of human rights that states parties must periodically file with the Committee, and issuing general comments that interpret provisions of the Covenant. Such a shift in emphasis would enable the Committee to play a more influential role and a complementary one in relation to other universal institutions of the human rights movement.

2. RECONSIDERING INSTITUTIONAL STRUCTURE AND PURPOSES

These proposals would require a significant revision of the Committee's mode of work under the Protocol. For reasons developed below, their realisation could well require an amendment to the Protocol itself, a time-consuming and complex process under its article 11. The proposals are not then modest and interstitial, suitable for full realisation within a year or two. But neither are they radical, in the sense of uprooting the present mandate and structure of the Committee and reinventing it from scratch.

The proposed goal of the Committee under the Protocol would build on two decades of work that have contributed in important ways to the human rights movement. Above all, the Committee has transformed what was a novel and in some ways radical mandate into one that now appears conventional. As recently as fifty years ago, sober state officials from all parts of the world would have viewed the Committee's three principal activities as absurdly impractical, as too threatening to state sovereignty to be acceptable. Today many states continue to resist one or another of the Committee's requests or acts as unauthorised or as unjustifiably interfering in their internal affairs. But these now familiar activities are well instituted, and broadly viewed in the international community as unremarkable components of the human rights movement. To have made the exceptional routine in merely two decades, and in the process to have further instituted the new discourse of human rights, are no small accomplishments.

Nonetheless, the Committee can rest on these achievements only at the risk of becoming increasingly marginal to the human rights movement. Two decades of work on its three major activities have left only modest marks on the development of the ICCPR. Nor has that work succeeded in persuading states to end systematic abuses. The Committee can do better. Its leading role among human rights treaty bodies gives it a special capacity to develop civil and political rights, and a special responsibility to attempt to do so.

In contemplating serious institutional change, the Committee would not be discarding a tried and valued institutional structure. Its structure, like that of many of the new human rights institutions, was problematic from the start. The burst of energies, the idealism and imagination that generated treaties and created their implementing organs necessarily pushed the architecture of international institutions in novel directions. The architects would have found no adequate and convincing models to realise the novel goals of the young human rights regimes. The institutions had no *necessary* character, no *traditional* form or functions. Their structure could not be derived from some self-evident or reigning theory of international law or institutions – in the way, for example, that the institutions of a state newly become democratic might naturally reflect tried and valued notions such as the separation of powers.

The architecture was rather invented to fit the moment, to express the compromises between divergent viewpoints and draw into the treaties as many states as possible. Hence the different treaty institutions, as well as the UN organs provided for in the UN Charter, had a contingent character that distinguished them from most norms of the treaties. As times changed and new situations developed, there was little reason to reconsider the rules against torture, discrimination, or censorship, but much reason to reconsider the adequacy of institutions.

The structure and powers of these institutions were serious matters, for the treaty organs could readily be understood to threaten states more than the norms themselves. Ratification of a treaty that declared human rights norms could be advantageous to a state unlikely to honour its commitments. That state now formally participated on the side of the angels in a developing international discourse, and in a relatively costless way. A profound cynicism, a contempt directed not only to the content of the norms but also to their inefficacy, informed many such ratifications. Anchoring norms in institutions, however, raises the cost of joining. Institutions make rights more effective by threatening or taking actions that may lead a state to comply. Institutions with real power cut to the bone of sovereignty. No wonder that intense fights over the provisions creating the new institutions became the rule.

Some human rights institutions have evolved in significant ways through internal decisions made by the organs of the relevant treaty. Take for example the expansion of powers of the UN Commission on Human Rights through its decisions and those of its supervisory body Economic and Social Council (ECOSOC), both organs provided for by the UN Charter.[5] Other institutions turned to formal amendment, such as the current reform of the institutional structure of the European human rights system through a new protocol.[6] The HRC has revised its processes over the two decades of its life, particularly with respect to its internal mode of operation.[7] The revisions have been helpful, but their reach is limited and, even in their entirety, they do not respond adequately to the concerns and circumstances motivating this chapter. This chapter urges a bolder course.

B. Structure and functions of the HRC

1. PRINCIPAL ACTIVITIES

The Committee's mandate confines its work to matters covered by the ICCPR and its protocols. That work amounts primarily to determining whether and how states are implementing the rights declared in those instruments. At the same time, the Committee forms part of a complex

---

[5] Consider the development of the so-called 1235 and 1503 procedures of the UN Commission on Human Rights, described in P. Alston, 'The Commission on Human Rights', in *The United Nations and Human Rights: A Critical Appraisal* (ed. P. Alston), Oxford, 1992, p. 126 at pp. 144–81. Consider also the striking evolution of the Inter-American Commission on Human Rights as described in C. Medina, *The Battle of Human Rights: Gross, Systematic Violations and the Inter-American System*, Boston, 1988, chapter 4.

[6] Protocol No. 11 to the European Convention on Human Rights, ETS 155, which entered into force 1 November 1998.

[7] See generally T. Buergenthal, 'Human Rights Committee', in *The United Nations and Human Rights: A Critical Appraisal* (ed. P. Alston), 2nd edn, Oxford, 1999. The innovations from the time of the Committee's start of operations include: the 'concluding observations' now adopted by the Committee as a collegial assessment of a state's human rights record in connection with the state's submission of a periodic report; the appointment from among Committee members of a rapporteur and working group to study a state report; and the appointment of Special Rapporteurs for new communications under the Protocol and for follow-up procedures to determine if states have complied with views directed to them.

structure of international human rights organs, both universal (some formed under the UN Charter and some under human rights treaties) and regional. Its role under the ICCPR and its role as one part of an international system are in some measure complementary and interdependent. Although concentrating on the Committee's activities under the Protocol, this chapter gives attention to the broader framework by relating its proposals for the Committee's work to the powers and purposes of other institutions.

Part IV of the Covenant together with the Protocol set forth the Committee's organisation and functions.[8] Its eighteen members, who must be nationals of states parties, 'shall be persons of high moral character and recognised competence in the field of human rights'. The states parties who elect the members are to consider 'the usefulness of the participation of some persons having legal experience'. Members 'serve in their personal capacity'. In the language of the United Nations, they are therefore 'experts' rather than representatives of governments. Serving in their 'personal capacity' requires them to exercise an independent judgment in their decisions as Committee members rather than follow their governments' instructions.

The Committee performs three principal activities: reviewing state reports and responding to them through its collegial 'concluding observations'; issuing so-called General Comments directed to all states parties that clarify states' obligations and interpret the substantive provisions of the Covenant; and handling communications under the Protocol. These distinct activities – performed at different times in different settings, their output communicated to different states parties in different ways – can readily be understood to serve distinct purposes. But the three interact pervasively in the work of the Committee and can most usefully be considered as closely related, interdependent activities. The first two of the three activities described below therefore enter the argument for revision of the Committee's work under the optional Protocol.

(a) State reports

Article 40 of the ICCPR requires states parties to 'submit reports' on measures taken to 'give effect' to the rights declared by the ICCPR, and 'on the progress made in the enjoyment of those rights'. The reports are to

---

[8] The provisions in this paragraph are set forth in article 28 of the ICCPR.

'indicate the factors and difficulties, if any, affecting the implementation' of the ICCPR. The Committee is instructed to 'study' these reports, and to transmit 'its reports, and such general comments as it may consider appropriate', to the states. Discussions of the reports between Committee members and the representatives of reporting states take place at public meetings. Since 1992, the Committee has followed the practice of deciding in closed sessions on concluding observations about each state report. These observations, ranging from strong criticism to compliments, are worked out by consensus and express the views of the Committee as a whole. They are sent to the state concerned and become public documents.

(b) General comments

As noted, article 40 authorises the Committee to transmit to states 'such general comments as it may consider appropriate'. This terse phrase has experienced a life of its own. It is clear that general comments address states parties as a whole rather than an individual state's report. There is less agreement over their content and purpose, both of which have evolved significantly over the two decades. The accumulated general comments range from spelling out the internal procedures of the Committee or requiring states to include certain information in their periodic reports, to making general interpretations of the substantive provisions of the Covenant, such as those on non-discrimination[9] or political participation.[10]

(c) Communications

The bulk of this chapter examines the Committee's role in implementing the Protocol, which is devoted exclusively to communications. The Protocol speaks in a guarded language and leaves great lacunae that suggest the political compromises in its formulation. Its principal terms – 'communications' rather than complaints, 'views' rather than decisions or opinions – express a cautious strategy in defining the Committee's functions and powers by distancing the Protocol from the more direct and forceful language generally used to describe adjudication.

---

[9] General Comment No. 18 (thirty-seventh Session 1989), UN Doc. HRI/Gen/1/Rev. 1 at 26 (1994).

[10] General Comment No. 25 (fifty-seventh Session 1996), UN Doc. CCPR/C/21/Rev. 1/Add. 7 (1996).

Under article 1 of the Protocol, the Committee is to 'receive and consider communications' from individuals who claim to be victims of violations by a state party of any of the rights declared in the ICCPR. Within six months of being advised of a communication, the challenged state must submit to the Committee written explanations clarifying the matter. Article 3 provides that a communication is to be held inadmissible if it constitutes 'an abuse of the right of submission' or if it is 'incompatible with the provisions of the Covenant'. Under article 5 the Committee is not to consider a communication unless it has determined that the same matter is not being examined under another international procedure, and that the complaining individual has exhausted all available domestic remedies that are not unreasonably prolonged.

The Committee examines communications in closed meetings, with the aid of the Secretariat staff and of working groups composed of its members. The Protocol instructs it to consider the communications 'in the light of all written information made available' to it. To the present, the Committee has not sought to supplement written submissions with oral argument by the parties, let alone oral testimony of witnesses.

As spare as the Protocol is with respect to process, it is even leaner in its provisions about the disposition of a communication that is found admissible. The Committee must decide whether the state party has violated a right secured under the ICCPR. It is instructed to 'forward its views to the State Party concerned and to the individual'. No text defines the form or status of these 'views' – hortatory, recommendatory or binding – or refers to remedies.

It seems apparent that communications were feared by many states as the most imposing or potentially threatening of the Committee's several powers. Individual complaints were not included in the early drafts of the ICCPR prepared in the Commission on Human Rights, but rather were introduced at a relatively late stage by the Third Committee before approval by the General Assembly. The entire procedure was distanced from the ICCPR and relegated to a protocol.

This special concern, however, may not have been justified. The Committee's functions with respect to periodic state reports (a duty of states upon their ratification of the ICCPR without any requirement of further special consent) were surely as innovative and as threatening to a traditional conception of state sovereignty. But international adjudication seems to raise special and acute fears. Unlike the Committee's reactions to state reports, it could lead to an order (in the Committee's case, not a legally binding one) requiring the state to take concrete action. Moreover, the Protocol might have been viewed as a prelude to a broader and disquieting transformation of international law.

2. COMPROMISE IN PROVIDING FOR THE THREE ACTIVITIES

As an original matter, the drafters of the Covenant and Protocol might have empowered the Committee to perform different functions, or clearly defined the purposes of its three activities. Surely they could have used more forceful language. For example, the governing instruments might have authorised the Committee to 'apply' the ICCPR to states parties in specified ways, to 'enforce' the rights declared in the ICCPR through specified procedures, to 'implement' or 'develop' the ICCPR, or more broadly to 'expound' or 'elaborate' it through its reactions to states' reports, general comments, and decisions about communications.

One way out of this morass was to say as little as possible, and to say even that cautiously. Consider article 40's anaemic descriptions of processes and functions. States' periodic reports are to be transmitted to the Committee 'for consideration'. The Committee is instructed to 'study' them and to 'transmit' its 'reports' and 'such general comments as it may consider appropriate' to states parties. The Committee submits to the General Assembly its 'annual report' on its activities. As for communications, the Committee is to 'receive and consider' them, including 'examining' them in closed meetings. It is to 'forward its views' to the parties involved. Somewhat more affirmatively, the Preamble to the Protocol does refer to 'implementation' of the Covenant.

All this hardly constitutes a battle cry to marshal all forces and lead the human rights movement forward. The stronger characterisations of the Committee's role that were imagined above find little support in the pallid language of the treaty texts. Contrast the verbs defining the Committee's functions with the strength and directness of the ICCPR's description in article 2 of the duties of states to individuals. A state party 'undertakes to respect and to ensure' the declared rights, to 'take the necessary steps . . . to give effect' to these rights, to 'ensure' effective remedies and 'ensure' that competent authorities 'enforce such remedies when granted'.

The drafters of the ICCPR knew then how to speak forcefully, just as later treaties like the Convention on the Elimination of All Forms of

Discrimination against Women (CEDAW) boldly impose on states a range of duties not only to respect and protect individual rights but also to promote the cultural change necessary for their realisation.[11] Anchoring the norms in a potent international institution would sharply raise the level of states' anxiety. The states opted for a classical compromise: ambitious norms demanding deep change in state behaviour, coupled with a fragile institution of doubtful effectiveness in applying them.

C. The challenge of the ICCPR

The Committee's three activities do not touch violations of other human rights treaties or customary law. Given the breadth of the ICCPR and the large number of its states parties, these are not significant limitations for civil and political rights. That breadth is reflected in the five principal categories of individual rights declared in the ICCPR that may come before the Committee through communications:

(i) individual physical integrity, expressed primarily through rights protecting against such state conduct as killings, torture or arbitrary detention;

(ii) procedural regularity and fairness required in judicial proceedings and when the state deprives an individual of liberty, as by arrest and imprisonment;

(iii) equal protection norms, applied to racial, religious, gender and other categories;

(iv) freedoms of belief, advocacy and association, as described in the ICCPR's articles on the practice of religion, the press, and assembly and associations, qualified by clauses that limit such freedoms for reasons such as national security, public order or morals; and

(v) the right to political participation through voting in elections and taking part in the conduct of public affairs.

Several articles in the Covenant stand outside this classification, such as the right of peoples in article 1 to self-determination (which in the opinion of the Committee cannot be the foundation of an individual communication),

---

[11] 1249 UNTS 13; GA Res. 34/180, 34 UN GAOR Supp. (No. 46), UN Doc. A/34/46, at p. 193 (1979). See particularly article 2 (states parties 'agree to pursue by all appropriate means and without delay a policy of eliminating discrimination . . .') and article 5 (states parties 'shall take all appropriate measures: (a) To modify the social and cultural patterns of conduct of men and women . . .').

the enjoyment under article 27 by members of minorities of their own religion, language and ethnic culture, and family-related rights under article 23.

Two decades of debate over these rights in national and international settings – involving state executives, legislatures, and courts, as well as scholars, non-governmental organisation (NGO) activists, and inter-governmental organs – underscore the difficulties in applying them. Most of these difficulties are common to rights discourse generally, similar to problems confronting state courts and other organs. The breadth of provisions in instruments like the ICCPR and state constitutions, these provisions' pervasive significance for the character of a society, their majestic ideals expressed in solemn prose, all exaggerate the problems of indeterminacy and susceptibility to different meanings that inhabit language and law generally. Inevitably such basic rights generate conflicts among themselves (privacy and free speech, fair trials and free press, equal protection and religious freedom), or with governmental tasks like the protection of national security. Adjudication must work out not only the meanings and boundaries of the individual rights, but also the expanding duties of states to respect, protect and promote them.

The international rather than national context for the elaboration of human rights intensifies such characteristic problems. International law has long stated many norms that grow out of state conduct and correspond closely with most states' interests and behaviour (diplomatic immunities, exclusive territorial control, rules of navigation). But human rights instruments, together with related international law developments such as peace-keeping norms and the contemporary humanitarian law of armed conflict, shatter that correspondence. For most states, these treaties represent more aspiration than achievement. Their ideals are not embedded in but, to the contrary, tower above state behaviour. Their stance is deeply critical, their aim transformative.[12]

International adjudicatory organs are inevitably sensitive to this gap, and to the tensions that it generates. Relative to, say, courts in states within the liberal and democratic traditions, they often enjoy only precarious political support.[13] Their room for bold decision-making is correspondingly limited,

---

[12] See generally M. Koskenniemi, *Apology and Utopia*, Helsinki, 1989; and M. Koskenniemi, 'The Politics of International Law', 1 *EJIL*, 1990, p. 4.

[13] The degree of political support varies with the human rights regime. Despite occasional problems, the regional European system is at the high-support end of the spectrum, for

at least for decision-making that criticises and regulates state conduct.[14] Moreover, to a far greater degree than in national contexts, international human rights organs confront formidable differences in culture and tradition that have given rise to arguments between the proponents of universalism and of cultural relativism. The ICCPR, after all, ranges from consensual norms about torture (violated in fact in many states, however) to highly disputed norms about subjects like gender or religious equality, limitations on freedoms of speech or association, sexual and family matters, and political participation. Such is the Covenant's challenge to the Committee, one that underscores the difficulty and necessity of deciding on the purposes that should inform the communications procedure.

D. Communications and views

1. THE COMMITTEE AND ADJUDICATION

The communications procedure assumes that the issues put before the Committee were or could have been raised and disposed of in state judicial or administrative proceedings. The Protocol thus requires the exhaustion of local remedies that were reasonably available to the complaining individual.

the judgment of the European Court of Human Rights is to be 'transmitted to the Committee of Ministers, which shall supervise its execution'. Article 54 of the European Convention for the Protection of Human Rights and Fundamental Freedoms (ECHR), 213 UNTS 221, ETS 5; and article 46 of Protocol No. 11, *supra*, note 6. The Committee of Ministers consists of the foreign ministers or their deputies of the member states of the Council of Europe. The situation of the HRC, as indicated below in the text, differs radically.

[14] The situation differs between the regional and universal regimes, and indeed among regional regimes. The European Court of Human Rights, *supra*, note 13, addresses a relatively homogenous group of states within the liberal and democratic tradition, and enjoys a correspondingly greater freedom of action and sense that its judgments will be complied with. Nonetheless, principles that animate its own decision-making, such as the margin of appreciation, express in part a sensitivity to the concerns and cultural–political differences among the states parties, a sensitivity that may grow with the recent expansion of states parties to include many from eastern Europe. See generally H. Steiner and P. Alston, *International Human Rights in Context: Law, Politics, Morals*, Oxford, 1996, at pp. 631–6. The Inter-American Court of Human Rights, whose governing provisions appear in chapter VIII of the American Convention on Human Rights, OASTS 36, OAS Off. Rec. OEA/Ser.L/V/II.23, doc.21, rev. 6 (1979), addresses a more troubled and varied group of states and lacks as much assurance of political support. These factors have not, however, prevented it from issuing some leading human rights judgments that have been deeply critical of state behaviour. See, e.g., *Velásquez-Rodriguez Case*, Ser. C, No. 4 (1988).

But in no sense are the proceedings before the Committee an appeal from or otherwise a continuation of state judicial or other proceedings. They are independent, *de novo*, even to the point of differences in party structure. Although the Committee now states in its views the appropriate remedies for a violation, it does not remand the case or otherwise direct the views to a state organ. Rather, it transmits the views to the state party itself. As is typical of international human rights organs engaged in adjudication, the Covenant and Protocol create no organic link between the state and international systems.[15]

The distinctions between these independent proceedings and the traditional forms of adjudication or structures of courts are clear enough. Consider first the criteria for membership. Article 28 of the ICCPR requires that Committee members be persons of 'recognised competence in the field of human rights', and merely suggests consideration by the states parties of the 'usefulness' of including some persons 'having legal experience' (although in fact most members have been practising lawyers, judges or prosecutors). During the long gaps between its three annual sessions of three weeks each, the eighteen members generally return to their primary work: the academic, professional and other positions on which their careers and earnings depend. Although they are required to 'serve in their personal capacity' rather than as state representatives, some members throughout the Committee's history have simultaneously held appointive office in their own states' governments. Other salient differences from courts and judges appear. Staggered four-year terms can lead to periods of substantial and rapid turnovers in membership.[16] Even during Committee sessions, two

---

[15] Contrast the jurisdiction of the European Court of Justice created by the Treaty Establishing the European Community (Common Market) under article 177 of that treaty. That article grants the Court jurisdiction to give 'preliminary rulings' on matters including the Treaty's interpretation, and the validity and interpretation of acts of Community institutions. It states: 'Where such a question is raised before any court or tribunal of a Member State, that court or tribunal may, if it considers that a decision on the question is necessary to enable it to give judgment, request the Court of Justice to give a ruling thereon.' Article 177 is not an 'appeals' procedure leading to affirmation, reversal, remand with instructions, and so on. The Court does not 'decide' the case. It interprets rather than applies the relevant provision of the treaty. The state court then continues the proceeding in the light of the opinion of the Court of Justice. Unlike the human rights organs, article 177 thus creates an organic link between the state and community systems involving mutual co-operation and a shared jurisdiction. See generally J. Steiner, *Textbook on EEC Law*, 3rd edn, London, 1992, pp. 285–305.

[16] The period 1994–1996 is illustrative, if somewhat exceptional. Five new members were elected in each of two successive elections, and one member resigned and was replaced.

other and very different activities (reacting to state reports, issuing general comments) absorb most of the members' time.

The Committee has accepted only written information from the parties, although the Protocol's provision for such information in article 5 (the Committee is to consider communications 'in the light of all written information made available to it' by the parties) need not be read to bar oral proceedings.[17] All meetings in which the Committee examines communications are closed, and the pleadings are treated by the Committee as confidential[18] (although the subsequent views give detailed accounts of them). The Committee Secretariat prepares the first draft of a proposed view, which it submits to a Committee member who has been appointed case rapporteur for that view. The member may revise the draft, which is then submitted to a pre-sessional Working Group of members. That group, after any revision, will in turn present the draft view to the full Committee. All eighteen members participate in the effort to achieve a consensus, but any member unable to join the consensus may write a concurring or dissenting opinion.[19] The Protocol is silent about the legal effect of its views on states, and about remedies. All these provisions contrast sharply with characteristic requirements for judges and judicial process – for example, those set forth in Protocol No. 11 to the European Convention on Human Rights.[20]

Despite its atypical features and despite the Committee's radical differences from a court, the communications procedure amounts to a distinctive

Hence a committee of eighteen members found itself at the end of this process with eleven new members over a two-year period.

[17] See T. Opsahl, 'The Human Rights Committee', in Alston (ed.), *supra*, note 5, at pp. 369, 427.

[18] See Buergenthal, *supra*, note 7, at Section V(A).   [19] Ibid.

[20] For example, article 21 of Protocol No. 11, *supra*, note 6, states that judges 'must either possess the qualifications required for appointment to high judicial office or be jurisconsults of recognised competence'. While holding judicial office, they 'shall not engage in any activity which is incompatible with their independence, impartiality or with the demands of a full-time office . . .'. Under article 23, the judges are elected for six-year periods, one half of the judges being renewed every three years. Article 38 provides that, once an application is declared admissible, the Court is to 'pursue the examination of the case . . . and if need be, undertake an investigation . . .'. Under article 40, hearings (absent exceptional circumstances) are public, as are all documents deposited with the Registrar. In the event that a violation is found, article 41 instructs the Court to 'afford just satisfaction to the injured party'. Under article 46, states parties 'undertake to abide by the final judgment of the Court', and the judgment is transmitted to the Committee of Ministers, *supra*, note 13, which is to 'supervise its execution'.

form of adjudication. In essence, a collegial body of independent experts decides a claim of violation of the ICCPR in favour of one or the other party, by applying norms that it interprets to facts that it either accepts from the state proceedings or that it independently finds or assumes. It reaches a conclusion accompanied by a suggestion of appropriate remedies for any violation that it transmits to the parties.

Over two decades, the Committee has interpreted the Covenant and Protocol so as to bring communications closer to a typical system of adjudication. For example, it has taken the position that absence of a provision in the Protocol describing views as 'binding' cannot mean that a state may freely choose whether or not to comply with them. Views carry a normative obligation for states to provide the stated remedies, an obligation that stems from provisions of the Covenant and Protocol.[21] It is indeed unclear whether an amendment to the Protocol making views binding would improve the historically spotty record of compliance.[22] The problem stems less from uncertainty over the formal effect of the views than from unyielding attitudes of the recalcitrant states, the gross and systematic violators.

---

[21] See F. Pocar, 'Legal Value of the Human Rights Committee's Views', *Canadian Human Rights Yearbook*, 1991–1992, p. 119. Views issued by the Committee that impose obligations on a state party now include a clause to the effect that a state, by becoming a party to the Protocol, 'has recognised the competence of the Committee to determine whether there has been a violation of the Covenant or not and that, pursuant to article 2 of the Covenant, the State party has undertaken to ensure to all individuals within its territory . . . the rights recognised in the Covenant and to provide an effective and enforceable remedy in case a violation has been established . . .'. Consequently the Committee requests from the state party, within ninety days of the issuance of views, information about what measures it has taken to give effect to those views. See, e.g., para. 13 of *Eustace Henry and Everald Douglas v. Jamaica*, Communication No. 571/1994, UN Doc. CCPR/C/57/D/571/1994.

[22] See the discussion arguing that the views carry a 'normative and institutional' legitimacy and a 'justifiable expectation' of compliance, together with advocacy of an amendment to the Protocol to give them binding effect, in Buergenthal, *supra*, note 7, in Section V (C). Nowak, *supra*, note 3, takes a different position, arguing that since there is in any event so little possibility of sanctions, one can doubt the significance of the fact that the views are not binding. He refers to the international reputation secured by the Committee that imparts great 'moral authority' to views that find a state party in violation of the Covenant (ibid. at pp. 710–11). An account of recent follow-ups of views by the Committee to determine whether they had been implemented by states, appearing in Section VIII of the 1997 Report of the Human Rights Committee, GAOR Supp. No. 40 (A/52/40), indicates that many requests for information received no reply and that many replies that were received were unsatisfactory.

2. PURPOSES OF ADJUDICATION

What purposes might the Committee serve through the communications procedure? Consider preliminarily a basic purpose of adjudication that informs many national legal systems. The availability of dispute resolution through courts constitutes an essential condition for the non-violent conduct of affairs, for protection against abuse by government or others, for the application of systems of law that are vital to property or commerce – in short, for the functioning of modern states. Within at least politically liberal and market-oriented economies, it forms part of that set of ideas and ideology collectively referred to as the rule of law. The core meaning of that elastic concept stresses the significance for personal security, for freedom, and for the conduct of affairs of a system of rules of reasonable generality and determinacy, an independent judiciary equally open to all, and application of those rules by the judiciary in an impartial and predictable manner.[23]

Of course the Committee cannot serve any such purpose. It is not part of a state system, indeed not even connected to state judiciaries through formal links like appeals, remands, or certified questions. Its subject-matter competence is confined to adjudication about violations of rights declared in the ICCPR. In any event, it can handle only a small number of cases. Within national legal systems, the closer analogies to the Committee's work are found not in appellate courts of general jurisdiction, but rather in the distinctive constitutional courts in European and other states that have developed as part of the human rights movement.

The Committee might, however, serve any or all of three purposes associated with adjudicatory bodies: (a) doing justice in the individual case within its jurisdiction and to that extent vindicating the rule of law; (b) protecting rights under the Covenant through deterrence and related behaviour modification; and (c) expounding (elucidating, interpreting and explaining) the Covenant so as to engage the Committee in an ongoing, fruitful dialogue with states parties, non-governmental and intergovernmental institutions, advocates, scholars and students.

---

[23] For a classic exposition of the role and character of the rule of law, see F. Hayek, *The Road to Serfdom*, Chicago, 1944. For modern approaches, see M. Radin, 'Reconsidering the Rule of Law', 69 *BULRev* 1989, p. 781, and F. Sejersted, 'Democracy and the Rule of Law', in *Constitutionalism and Democracy* (eds. J. Elster and R. Slagstad), New York, 1988, p. 131.

(a) Individual justice and the rule of law

The treaty texts and the historical practice of the Committee in writing views give some support to the argument that vindicating individual rights declared in the Covenant is a primary purpose of the Protocol. Even the barest of views that merely states the Committee's conclusion about violation and a suggested remedy achieves that goal. Whether the state party will comply with such views poses a vital but distinct issue. At least the Committee has done its best to realise this basic purpose.

The idea that justice in the individual case – or vindication of the rule of law in this special field of adjudication – constitutes the principal purpose of the Protocol finds further support in the fact that the jurisdiction of the HRC to decide the dispute is mandatory. Provided that the criteria for admissibility are met, the Protocol does not authorise the HRC to exercise discretion about whether to accept a communication, even if it believes the communication to raise no issue of importance.

Such a mandate expresses a grand and noble ideal. The HRC offers hope to wronged individuals after state processes have failed. The humblest and most remote peasant who has been deprived of rights under the ICCPR can secure a remedy (or at least a view suggesting a remedy). This is indeed a striking vision, a deep aspiration of the human rights movement – though not the deepest, which would have the states themselves respect rights so as to make recourse to international procedures unnecessary. When the suggested remedy would save a defendant from execution after a trial violating procedural rights, and when the state party honours that remedy, one can hardly overstate the significance and the satisfaction of vindicating the rule of law by achieving justice in the individual case under international law.[24]

But the ideal is as unrealisable as it is noble. Statistics tell why.[25] As of August 1997, twenty years after the Committee began its work under the Protocol, 765 communications involving fifty-four states parties had been registered with the Committee.[26] Of this number, 263 had led to the issuance of views under the Protocol. In 199 of these cases, the Committee

---

[24] See p. 47, *infra*.

[25] The statistics in this and the following paragraphs appear in Section VII(A) of the 1997 Report of the Human Rights Committee, *supra*, note 22.

[26] Of this total, 168 cases came from Jamaica and seventy-nine from Uruguay. The highest number of views decided in favour of petitioners, about 50 per cent of the total of such views, were directed against those two states.

found violations of rights – an annual average of ten such views, although the number of communications filed and of views written rose significantly over this period. Another 242 communications were found inadmissible, while 115 were discontinued or withdrawn. There remained to be disposed of forty-five communications that had been declared admissible, and 100 that were pending at the pre-admissibility stage.

Some Committee members have estimated that time exists under present procedures for the Committee to issue a maximum of ten views a session, hence about thirty a year. Under this estimate, the Committee today faces a backlog of three or more years. Even if recent and proposed time-saving changes in the Committee's procedures are taken into account – joining the issue of admissibility to the merits rather than issuing a separate earlier opinion,[27] the use of panels of members for deciding cases that would only exceptionally be fully reviewed on the merits by the entire membership[28] – the number of views that could be issued at each session is unlikely to increase substantially.

A striking contrast emerges between the Committee's limited capacity and the potential demand on its services. Almost two-thirds of the states parties to the ICCPR have ratified the Protocol. Well over a billion people inhabit those ninety states, which include many with a record of brutal and systematic human rights violations. When measured against these facts, as well as the likelihood of more ratifications of the Protocol, even thirty views written annually would offer slender support for the rule of law.

What makes the statistics so alarming is less the fact of a backlog of several years (itself typical of many state judiciaries and of other international organs such as the European Court of Human Rights) than the very modest caseload producing that backlog, even taking into account the gradual increase in the number of communications submitted annually to the HRC.[29] Views could not realistically keep pace with a sharp increase. Over the three most recent sessions described in the 1997 Annual Report, only twenty-four views were issued.[30]

---

[27] See paras. 470–1 of the Committee's 1997 Annual Report *supra*, note 22.

[28] See the description of the present procedures in Buergenthal, *supra*, note 7, Section V(A).

[29] Para. 462 of the Committee's 1997 Annual Report *supra*, note 22 explains the growing number of communications submitted to the Committee by the increased number of parties to the Protocol and 'better public awareness of the procedure'. It notes that, for various reasons, this increase is not fully reflected in the number of cases annually registered under the Protocol, 'which has remained constant at 40–50 each year'.

[30] Ibid. at para. 458.

It is difficult to imagine the consequence if a state like India, with a vast population and a tradition of resort to courts on constitutional issues, accepted the Protocol. Indeed, the consequences could be remarkable if the communications procedure became better known and more easily utilisable by the present states parties. This might well occur if non-governmental human rights organisations increased their efforts to publicise the Protocol and regularly assisted victims in submitting communications. Some basis for prediction can be found in the exceptional number of cases originating in two countries where the Protocol was relatively well known and which experienced serious and systematic human rights problems – Uruguay in the early years of the Committee, and Jamaica in recent years.[31]

As states parties and familiarity with the Protocol grow, should one anticipate an annual submission of 500 communications (a tenfold increase)? Or 5,000, or 50,000? For states with systematic breakdowns of the rule of law in which there are no genuine remedies to exhaust, the Committee could become by default the 'court of first instance' in whole fields like ordinary crimes or political activities or ethnic violence. One can question whether the communications procedure has thus far survived only because of the relatively meagre resort to it,[32] and even question whether it is wise to foster a broader recourse. Would not the promise of that procedure be illusory and ultimately disheartening to its intended beneficiaries, even apart from uncertainty about their states' compliance with Committee views that might be issued many years later in their favour?

The problems in a mandatory jurisdiction to decide all admissible communications go beyond the mismatch between statistics and resources. The Committee acts alone under the Protocol. It does not benefit from the deliberations, findings and conclusions of another international organ that

---

[31] J. Möller, 'Recent Jurisprudence of the Human Rights Committee', *Canadian Human Rights Yearbook 1991–92*, p. 79, reports that seventy of the first 144 registered communications came from Uruguay. The communications from Jamaica have frequently involved criminal trials in which the death penalty was imposed, and have been prominent over a number of years. Para. 458 of the Committee's 1997 Annual Report (*supra*, note 22) indicates that over the three sessions preceding the Report, the Committee adopted views in twenty-four cases, half of which originated in Jamaica. See note 26, *supra*.

[32] It is understandable that few communications would originate in states that were parties to an effective regional system such as the European human rights system, for individual complainants might prefer to invoke the help of the regional institutions. For an indication of the attitudes of such states toward the ICCPR and the ECHR, see the comments in paras. 83, 86, 88 and 100 of the Second Periodic Report of Austria to the Human Rights Committee, UN Doc. A/47/40 (1994), Supp. No. 40, at p. 26.

first hears a case, in contrast, hitherto, with the European Court of Human Rights and, still, the Inter-American Court of Human Rights. No trusted institution, such as the commissions in the two regional regimes, plays a preliminary role in sorting out the facts and proceedings within a state, coming to a decision, and deciding whether to request review of the decision by the Committee.[33] The aggrieved individual alone makes the decision to invoke the Committee's jurisdiction.

In such circumstances, it is not simply the lack of screening that poses a difficulty, but also the vexing problems of fact-finding. Those problems become more intense in cases originating in states that inspire distrust in the light of their human rights records. Concern about the accuracy of accounts of events and proceedings within a state will be inescapable. The HRC may be reluctant to rely on the facts found below, as well as on a state's assertions in the pleadings. But it can do little to overcome this discomfort. From the start of its operations, it has been without means of finding facts for itself on such vital issues as whether a confession was coerced, or whether the assassin of a political opponent was linked to the army. It is unlikely to introduce investigative procedures now.

The HRC has developed ways of handling some of these situations. It has benefited the petitioner by shifting the burden of proof or using presumptions – for example, when a state fails to reply to a petitioner's detailed charges or rests with a general denial, or fails to produce evidence that is within its control.[34] Accepting the petitioner's account of the facts in these circumstances – perhaps an account of torture – makes the case unproblematic and leads to the obvious conclusion of a violation. But in other contexts, the Committee may have no satisfactory option. For example, a government that is known to suppress forcibly its political opposition may deny allegations of an opposition press that its agents burned the press building and may offer a detailed contradictory account. In these circumstances, the Committee may find it difficult to accept the petitioner's

---

[33] See Sections III and IV of the ECHR, *supra*, note 6, and chapters VII and VIII of the American Convention on Human Rights, *supra*, note 14. Protocol No. 11 to the ECHR, *supra*, note 6, abolished the Commission when it became effective in 1998.

[34] See the discussion in McGoldrick, *supra*, note 3, at pp. 147–9. For a typical situation, see *El-Megreisi v. Libyan Arab Jamahiriya*, Communication No. 440/1990, UN Doc. CCPR/C/ 50/D/440/1990 (1994) (state fails to provide requested information or otherwise cooperate and therefore violates its obligations under article 4(2) of the Protocol to investigate in good faith the allegations of its violation of the ICCPR; Committee accepts petitioner's 'undisputed facts' and finds in his favour).

account of facts. A refusal on its part to find facts one way or the other may hardly appear neutral to a petitioner whose claim has thereby been deprived of its foundation.[35]

(b) Protecting rights: Deterrence and other behaviour modification

Doing justice in the individual case looks backward, correcting a historical wrong by providing an appropriate remedy or sanction and thereby vindicating the rule of law. By contrast, the protection of rights through adjudication is forward-looking. Judicial judgments make a better world more likely because of their effects in deterring potential violators, and encouraging them to modify behaviour to make it more consistent with the legal order.

Attributing such a utilitarian goal to adjudication by the Committee rests on some standard assumptions: many states parties will be aware of the Committee's jurisprudence, will take into account in their future behaviour the likelihood and severity of remedial action required of them by adverse views, and will consequently modify their behaviour to avoid these undesired acts by complying with the ICCPR (abstain from torture, investigate reported crimes, administer an electoral system with integrity). Deterrence theory may also rest on the assumption that states will try to avoid the injury to reputation (so-called 'shaming') that may stem from the submission of many communications against them and related publicity.

The Committee's views are, however, inept instruments to achieve greater protection of rights by all states. To start with, the goal of behaviour modification is compromised by the small number of views issued and by the threat of a mounting backlog. The great majority of the views receive little if any publicity, and even the more noteworthy among them tend to be discussed only in a few specialised professional journals.[36] Moreover, the

---

[35] Other international human rights organs have confronted such problems, and on occasion have worked out ingenious solutions. See, e.g., the *Velásquez Rodriguez* decision of the Inter-American Court of Human Rights, Ser. C, No. 4 (1988). The question posed was whether Honduras had violated the American Convention on Human Rights through its responsibility for the disappearance of a political opponent of the regime. It denied responsibility. In finding a violation of the Convention, the Court drew upon a systematic practice and pattern of Honduras in carrying out or tolerating disappearances, and found that the disappearance of Velásquez fell within this practice.

[36] The situation is slowly changing in a few states like Australia, Canada and Finland, where the Committee's views are becoming more widely disseminated through media such as the Internet. Still, the views fall well behind the publicity accorded many decisions of, say, the European Court of Human Rights.

remedies now suggested in the views – compensation, release of prisoner, legislative change – do not threaten state interests sufficiently to bring about prompt compliance. The Committee has no authority to act punitively against the offending state, or impose any sanctions. Indeed, another of the Committee's activities, examining and collectively reacting to the periodic reports of states parties about their implementation of the ICCPR, might prove far more effective in inducing changes in behaviour.[37]

Even assuming that views were formally binding on states, the Committee is powerless to assure compliance with them. Its only recourse is to advise UN organs through its annual reports about the delinquent states. The Committee has not sought to put pressure on states by requesting the help of the General Assembly or the Security Council. Neither of those bodies, nor the UN Commission on Human Rights, is likely to treat states' failure to honour views as reason to take serious action. The Committee lacks the formal political support enjoyed by the European Court of Human Rights through the role of the Committee of Ministers in assuring compliance with its judgments.[38]

Other institutions in the universal human rights movement, as well as states themselves, are better equipped to persuade an offending state to change its conduct. The techniques are familiar: public discussion of a state's offensive conduct in the General Assembly or Commission on Human Rights followed by sharp condemnatory resolutions; well publicised reports of working groups or rapporteurs appointed by an international organ to investigate violations; restrictions on aid or trade imposed by a state or group of states or pursuant to a decision of the Security Council; and so on. The differences between the Committee and such institutions, as well as between it and established national judiciaries that enjoy political support for their judgments, reinforce the argument that the Committee cannot realise this traditional purpose of adjudication.[39]

These observations about deterrence and enforcement should not be understood to contrast a weak Committee with human rights institutions of exemplary effectiveness. There is no sharp polarity. Political organs of

---

[37] See p. 51, *infra.*   [38] See note 13, *supra.*

[39] Commentators on the Committee have generally been more favourable than the text above in their assessment of the communications procedure. See, e.g., Nowak, *supra,* note 3, at p. 648: 'Despite the strong scepticism voiced by many States . . . the individual communications procedure has developed into one of the most important procedures for the international protection of human rights.'

the human rights movement such as the UN Commission on Human Rights struggle with inadequate legitimacy and power, while even the regional human rights courts in the Americas and in Europe face instances of round disobedience.[40] All here is comparative, a matter of degree in the often feeble world of human rights protection or enforcement. But compared with other human rights institutions, the Committee fares poorly. It should play to its strengths.

(c) Expounding the Covenant and opening a dialogue

The views written over two decades have created a considerable and important body of doctrine related to the ICCPR. But the doctrine is little reported or organised outside the Committee's internal documents such as Annual Reports, and a handful of scholarly articles and books.[41] Only occasionally do views figure in a discursive way in judicial opinions of state courts.[42]

---

[40] Compare C. Tomuschat, 'Quo Vadis, Argentoratum? The Success Story of the European Convention on Human Rights – and a Few Dark Stains', 13 *HRLJ*, 1992, p. 401: 'However numerous and bold the decisions of the Strasbourg bodies may be, it has recently emerged that especially their implementation lacks sufficiently effective safeguards.' Tomuschat stresses the failure of the Committee of Ministers to discharge its functions under the Convention effectively, as with respect to enforcement of the Court's judgments.

[41] Comprehensive substantive descriptions of the Committee's views appear in chapters 5–12 in McGoldrick, *supra*, note 3, and in the section on the Protocol starting at p. 647 in Nowak, *supra*, note 3. For descriptions of more recent views, see M. Nowak, 'The Activities of the UN Human Rights Committee: Developments from 1 August 1992 to 31 July 1995', 16 *HRLJ*, 1995, p. 377; and the Committee's 1997 Annual Report *supra*, note 22, paras. 486–516.

[42] In states within regional systems that have generated a good volume of caselaw of a regional court, limited citation of views of the Committee is not surprising. Within the states parties to the ECHR, individuals might understandably prefer recourse to regional remedies, formerly involving in the first instance the European Commission, but since November 1998 when Protocol No. 11 came into effect, involving the European Court itself. See note 6, *supra*. For an illuminating discussion of relationships between the ICCPR and the ECHR, and of choices of petitioners about which avenue of relief to pursue, see R. Higgins, 'Ten Years on the UN Human Rights Committee: Some Thoughts Upon Parting', 1996 *European Human Rights Law Review*, pp. 570, 573–6. Courts of states that are parties to the ICCPR sometimes refer to views of the Committee without expressing any sense of their particular status or relevance in resolving an issue, perhaps an issue that arises under domestic constitutional law. See, e.g., *Catholic Commission for Justice and Peace in Zimbabwe v. Attorney-General*, Judgment No. S.C. 73/93 (Supreme Court of Zimbabwe, 1993), where the Court (after drawing on opinions of courts in several other states and opinions of the European Court of Human Rights) quoted from both a Committee view on whether long detention on death row could amount to 'cruel, inhuman, or degrading treatment', and from a dissenting opinion to that view. It indicated tersely its agreement with the dissent.

Only rarely do they summon attention and provoke comment outside formal legal circles. The production over two decades of views of this character, however valuable for the relatively small number of individual beneficiaries, has not made a significant contribution to the normative development of the human rights movement.

Expounding a constitution or basic law-making treaty is a different business. It requires judges to use appropriate cases to elucidate the instrument that they are applying, to interpret and explain it. Committee members must employ such cases to probe the basic purposes of the Covenant, to show its significance for the life and needs of the peoples it is meant to serve. Such an understanding of the role of opinions will often require acknowledgement of the difficulties in reaching a judgment, the consideration of alternative grounds, and some form of justification for the decision reached. In the novel and vexing cases, it will always require reasoned argument rather than the terse and opaque application of norm to facts. The Committee must act as a deliberative body that is sensitive to the legitimate and immense possibilities of its role in the human rights movement.

Given the significance and complexity as well as the range of the issues that come before it under the Protocol, the Committee is inevitably engaged in the development of the Covenant: confronting its ambiguities and indeterminacy, resolving conflicts among its principles and rights, working out meanings of its grand terms through consideration of the object and purposes of the Covenant, or through recourse to methods of interpretation other than the teleological, such as *travaux préparatoires*, the contextual analysis of a provision within the broader structure of the treaty, or attention to trends in legal and moral thought.

To expound the ICCPR is to make this process explicit, to confront openly the dilemmas before the Committee in deciding the more troubling communications. The Committee fails to expound, and therefore to realise what should be a major purpose of the communications procedure, when its considerations in reaching a decision remain covert, secreted within formal opinions that merely state rather than argue towards conclusions. In so acting, the Committee wastes a unique opportunity to make the ICCPR a better known, more significant and persuasive instrument, and thereby to add strength to the universal human rights movement.[43]

---

[43] The suggested purpose of expounding the ICCPR and the related proposals about the writing of views have not figured much in the legal literature about the Committee's work

The Committee could at the same time explore questions of influence and perspective among adjudicatory institutions applying human rights treaties. No formal lines of authority or patterns of deference exist among organs created by different universal and regional human rights treaties. Nonetheless, one can foresee the evolution of a more integrated international system that would only benefit from heightened interaction among its parts. The Committee could be more attentive in its views to opinions of other international organs and state courts interpreting the ICCPR that might be helpful for understanding the issues before it. Opinions of the European Court of Human Rights could serve to illuminate differences between the cultural assumptions in regional and universal regimes, despite the similarity in the provisions of the governing instruments for these two regimes. The Committee could draw on decisions of state courts that interpreted and applied the Covenant or that explored the same issue posed by a communication in order to explore the similarities or differences between perspectives of state and international institutions. Views could systematically inquire whether the Committee should look to laws of states to resolve certain matters, or whether it should regard state law only as suggestive while interpreting the ICCPR in the light of its purposes within an international human rights system.

In undertaking these tasks, the Committee would serve the larger purpose of illuminating and developing international human rights law as a whole. To some degree, it could overcome the fragmentation of the international system that stems from having each treaty served by its own organ and interpreted within many state systems, while at the same time observing the formal boundaries of its authority under the Covenant and Protocol.

under the Protocol. Such opinions as authors have expressed include starkly different assessments. See, e.g., Opsahl, *supra*, note 17, who says (at p. 427): 'The views are not reasoned in great detail, but sufficiently to explain the Committee's understanding and application of the Covenant.' Buergenthal, *supra*, note 7, makes brief suggestions in Section VII (C) about norm-setting by the Committee and its 'quasi-judicial' role. He stresses the importance of interpretation and application of the Covenant by the Committee 'in an objective and legally sound manner' that is 'perceived as being culturally neutral and legally beyond reproach. To satisfy this requirement the Committee may have to spell out in greater detail the legal reasons justifying its decisions . . .'. Not every communication will invite the kind of argument here urged. Many that have come before the Committee permit the more or less automatic application of a well understood norm to undisputed facts (say, a clear torture case), and thus a terse opinion. This chapter's concern is with cases that raise important and vexing issues, and that therefore merit argument.

(i) What the Committee's views could achieve

Despite its stark differences from courts, the Committee could contribute to the international adjudicatory processes that elaborate human rights law in the same manner as do opinions of the European and Inter-American Courts of Human Rights. The Committee's jurisdiction under the Protocol finds distant analogies in the human rights cases before the constitutional courts of states in Europe and elsewhere such as South Africa, and in the appellate courts with a broader jurisdiction that exercise the power of judicial review in countries like the United States. All these courts rule on the consistency of a state's executive and legislative action with the supreme law of a treaty or constitution. Of course the Committee lacks the formal authority and prestige of these other institutions and influences the general discourse of human rights correspondingly less. But that gap can be significantly narrowed.

To one or another degree, all these courts serve the two purposes earlier sketched: achieving justice in the individual case, and deterrence. But they do more. There can be no doubt of the significance for other courts, for legislatures and executive officials, for the legal profession and for the general public of their major opinions that expound the constitutions or law-making treaties before them. Such opinions are not put to the side as matters of dry law settling this or that dispute. Rather, they provoke discussion and reflection, praise and criticism. They inform and stimulate an ongoing legal, political, and moral debate on human rights issues. They become part of a rich and varied dialogue. They educate.

The argument behind this chapter's proposals is simple and straightforward. For reasons earlier developed, the Committee cannot achieve the purpose of doing justice in the individual case and vindicating the rule of law in states parties to the Protocol. It cannot effectively realise the purpose of strengthening protection for human rights through deterrence. It is, however, admirably situated to make a substantial contribution to the human rights movement through its views under the Protocol. Views that develop and illuminate the Covenant would move the Committee closer in its achievements to the prestigious and influential courts noted above.

The institutional status of the Committee could enhance the influence of its views. It is not that they would carry some formal, defined authority with respect to the interpretation and elaboration of the Covenant. Neither the Covenant nor Protocol assigns a particular weight to the views – at the extreme, say, by describing views as authoritative interpretations of the Covenant that states parties should follow. Nonetheless, the ICCPR makes the Committee its exclusive organ. Each of the Committee's three principal activities concern only that instrument. No other international organ is as dedicated to the application and development of this vital treaty, and hence as well situated to assume a principal responsibility for expounding it. Courts in national legal systems that incorporated the ICCPR as domestic law could not make as strong an institutional claim for international attention to their interpretations.

Two significant changes in the Committee's mode of functioning under the Protocol would be necessary for realising these proposals: breaking with the historical pattern and style of writing views, and moving from a mandatory to a discretionary jurisdiction.

(ii) Reconsidering the character of the views under the Protocol
The purpose of expounding the ICCPR would require the Committee to reconsider the views' organisation and content. The capacity of the Committee to produce views meeting the more demanding criteria proposed in this chapter depends on factors such as the quality of its membership, internal reorganisation (including the use of panels in the first instance to decide communications), and the time, Secretariat staff and financial resources available to it (during a period of great fiscal stringency in the UN). Throughout its life, the Committee has included a great range of members, from the exceptionally able to the mediocre, from the dedicated to the detached. The politics of nominations of members by states and elections to the Committee by the states parties permit no optimistic prediction about achieving a membership of a uniformly high level. But prospects for moving toward this goal should improve if the Committee gained more reputation in the world. One might well observe a causal relationship between greater effectiveness and respect, and greater responsibility by states in selecting members.

The road for the Committee would not be easy, for the track record is disappointing. Throughout the Committee's life, views have been written in a form that could not be called user-friendly. Rather than highlight issues and argument, they too frequently frustrate the reader because of their rigid structure and excessive information, the disjunction between most of this information and the conclusions of the Committee, the terse statement of these conclusions, and the sheer lack of readability. The process by which views are drafted[44] contributes to this discouraging picture. Committee members ought to become involved in a case before the Secretariat produces a first draft, if only to instruct the Secretariat of the directions that the view is to follow. Members rather than the Secretariat should make the initial substantive decisions. Moreover, the very effort to reach consensus has sapped the views of strength. According to some Committee members, this process has often purged the conclusions of controversial matter on which members differ. Since members have long had the authority to write concurring or dissenting opinions, it is difficult to understand why a vote on a draft opinion should not displace the elaborate, time-consuming, and perhaps debilitating search for consensus.

The upshot is that views are uninspiring documents, whatever their audience: state governments, other intergovernmental organs, courts or jurists, advocates, students, or (an important category) journalists. They hardly summon the human rights community to debate and dialogue. They fail to educate their readership adequately about the ICCPR in particular or about human rights in general.

These formulaic presentations go well back in the Committee's history. Responsibility for them lies not with the Secretariat staff lawyers (some of whom are of the highest competence) who prepare the first drafts of the views, but with the Committee as a whole that initially imposed and now retains this style. Consider the typical view. It lacks an introduction putting the case in some broad context and alerting the reader to the issues that the Committee has found to be relevant. Rather, it starts with detailed descriptions of legal arguments and assertions of facts made by the parties, set forth more or less in the chronological order of the pleadings from the time of registration of the communication to the proceedings on admissibility and the merits. Most of this material turns out to be irrelevant to the Committee's conclusions, as many of the parties' arguments fall by the wayside.

Views would gain in power and influence if the Committee undertook to carve its own path through the mass of information and argument offered by the parties. The Committee's narrative account could organise that information and identify the relevant issues as the Committee saw them. The foundation would then be laid for the Committee to expound the ICCPR: confrontation of the difficulties in the case, argument involving justification and explanation for the decision reached.

[44] See p. 29, *supra*.

While retaining the traditional forms, a certain number of views have come closer to meeting the suggested criteria. The conclusions are somewhat more ample and exploratory, and in several instances a range of concurring and dissenting opinions has further illuminated the issues. Frequently, these individual opinions have probed more deeply than the opinion for the Committee, perhaps because released from some implicit collegial obligation to be terse and closed.

Not surprisingly, these more exploratory views do not involve routine matters or turn on controverted questions of fact, but rather examine significant issues that are new to the Committee. They have addressed diverse topics, including gender discrimination affecting indigenous peoples,[45] the charge that long stays on death row constitute cruel or inhuman treatment,[46] the argument that a state that abolished capital punishment cannot extradite to a state in which such punishment is possible,[47] and the question whether a statute imposing criminal penalties for Holocaust-denial violates free speech.[48] Such opinions, particularly the useful exploration of issues by the several opinions in the last noted *Faurisson* case, could serve as points of departure toward a different style of opinion.

One could challenge these suggestions for change in the form and content of views by arguing that they reflect the approaches of only a few legal cultures, such as that of the United States, and hence are inappropriate for an international organ. Such an objection would have rested on stronger ground when the human rights movement began a half century ago. There are two replies.

First, the Committee's present style was not inspired by an effort to follow any existing international model, or to reflect a consensus among many states of what would be an appropriate style, structure and content for opinion writing. Nor are the views modelled on the opinions of other international organs such as the International Court of Justice or the regional human rights courts. The Protocol gives no guidance. The present practice is invention rather than necessity. The Committee's persistence in

---

[45] *Lovelace v. Canada*, Communication No. R.6/24/1977, UN Doc. A/36/40, Supp. No. 40.

[46] *Johnson v. Jamaica*, Communication No. 588/1994, UN Doc. CCPR/C/56/D/588/1994 (1996).

[47] *Charles Chitat Ng v. Canada*, Communication No. 469/1991, UN Doc. CCPR/C/49/D/469/1991 (1994).

[48] *Faurisson v. France*, Communication No. 550/1993, UN Doc. CCPR/C/58/D/550/1993 (1996).

holding to this odd construction hardly rests on careful deliberation or a revered tradition.

Second, whatever its force in earlier periods, the argument is no longer justified. Sharp differences among regions and legal cultures, often reflecting different conceptions of law and of the role of courts, continue to characterise opinion writing. But the last half century has witnessed a considerable change, a drawing together of states that once had little in common in this respect. Contemporary opinions of the constitutional courts in many European states[49] and of the European and Inter-American Courts of Human Rights, often engage in extensive argument and justification. That is, they expound the constitutions and treaties before them, and receive the professional and public attention appropriate to their substantial contributions to an understanding of human rights.[50]

(iii) Discretionary jurisdiction

The writing of views that possess the suggested characteristics requires that the Committee husband its energies under the Protocol, to allow more time to research and reflect on an issue, and to write. The Committee would have to allocate time to cases meriting exploration for the development of the Covenant, rather than depend on the flow of registered communications. These requirements would be difficult to satisfy in light of the overload of cases before the Committee and the prospects for its increase.

What then can be done to enable the Committee to establish some control over its caseload and the allocation of its time? The flexible criteria for admissibility – failure to exhaust domestic remedies, incompatibility of

---

[49] See decisions of constitutional courts of several European states at pp. 170, 215–24, 260–71, 586–605, and 615–22 in M. Cappelletti and W. Cohen, *Comparative Constitutional Law: Cases and Materials*, Indianapolis, 1979.

[50] The illustrations are too numerous and well known to require citation. Opinions of the European Court have been widely drawn on by the judiciaries of states parties to the ECHR, particularly in the majority of parties that have incorporated the Convention into their domestic legal systems. See R. Bernhardt, 'The Convention and Domestic Law', in *The European System for the Protection of Human Rights* (eds. R. St. J. Macdonald, F. Matscher and H. Petzold), Boston, 1993, p. 25. It is instructive to compare opinions that each deal with the criminalisation of homosexual conduct and the right to privacy: the Committee view, *Toonen v. Australia*, Communication No. 488/1992, UN Doc. CCPR/C/50/D/488/1992 (1994); and the opinions of the European Court of Human Rights in *Dudgeon v. United Kingdom*, Ser. A, No. 45, 4 *EHRR*, 1981, p. 149, and *Norris v. Ireland*, Ser. A, No. 142, 13 *EHRR*, 1989, p. 186.

the communication with the ICCPR, abuse of the right of submission – are surely susceptible to an application that could amount to a covert control of caseload.[51] Alternatively, various reforms now being discussed or recently instituted would expedite the disposition of communications that are found admissible – for example, examination of communications through panels, or the joining of admissibility to the merits in the writing of views. Perhaps a summary docket could be created to dispose tersely of communications decided by reference to earlier views. But none of these measures is likely to achieve a reduction in the number of communications that would be sufficient to permit the kind of opinion writing urged in this chapter.

Achieving that reduction could then require amending the Protocol to make the jurisdiction of the Committee (in whole or in substantial part) discretionary rather than mandatory. Opening the process toward amendment poses some risk. It could backfire by providing a fruitful opportunity for states intent on weakening the Committee to introduce amendments with this effect. Ongoing advocacy by some groups in Latin American states to amend provisions governing the Inter-American Commission and the Court on Human Rights, and thereby weaken those institutions, illustrates the risk. It must be measured against the possible gain, in the light of existing political circumstances.

Operating under a discretionary jurisdiction, the Committee might be able to issue twenty to thirty views a year, an ample number for making significant contributions to the understanding and development of the Covenant, and for stimulating thought and dialogue with diverse actors. In so different a system, the Committee would necessarily develop criteria for selection of communications. Such criteria might, for example, lead to rejection of cases where the case turned on controverted matters of fact that the Committee was not in a good position to resolve. They could disfavour cases raising issues that had been settled in prior views or that were not of general significance. The criteria might give priority to emergent issues affecting many states. The Committee might decide to handle a group of related problems, such as issues of criminal procedure or free speech, over several sessions.

---

[51] Nowak, *supra*, note 3, at p. 666, observes that under the pressure of its increasing workload, the Committee 'interprets the admissibility requirements more broadly', and in a series of cases, declared communications inadmissible because of 'non-substantiation of allegations' or lack of a 'claim' under article 2 of the Protocol.

Two illustrations may be helpful for determining such criteria. Protocol No. 11 to the European Convention for the Protection of Human Rights and Fundamental Freedoms (ECHR) provides that any party to a case decided by a Chamber of the Court may in exceptional cases request referral of the case to the Grand Chamber. The request is to be accepted if the case 'raises a serious question affecting the interpretation or application of the Convention', or raises 'a serious issue of general importance'.[52] The Judicial Code of the United States gives the United States Supreme Court (with minor exceptions) discretion whether to review any case decided by a federal or state court – even cases of the highest significance, involving the constitutionality of federal or state statutes, that had previously been subject to mandatory jurisdiction.[53] The Court's criteria for exercising discretion in favour of review include a decision by a state or federal court on 'an important question of federal law that has not been, but should be, settled by this Court'.[54]

These illustrations involve referrals or appeals relating to cases that, in one instance, were decided by a Chamber of the same court and, in the other, by a state or federal appellate court in the same country. If the Protocol provided for a discretionary jurisdiction, the Committee could have no such assurance that the earlier decision had been decided with integrity by a reputable court. The stakes are higher, in the sense that denial of review might quash the only hope of petitioners who lacked any possibility of achieving justice in their own state (a situation that might continue if a petitioner eventually benefited from a favourable view that the state refused to enforce).

Such an objection to a discretionary jurisdiction has considerable force.[55] This chapter earlier referred to the strong sense of satisfaction of the Committee in doing justice in the individual case, and used as an illustration the invalidation of a conviction and sentence of death after a trial whose procedures violated the ICCPR. The surrender of automatic review, not simply in cases of capital punishment but also of torture and other gross and

---

[52] Article 43 of Protocol No. 11, *supra*, note 6.   [53] See 28 U.S.C. §§ 1254, 1257.

[54] Rule 10 of the Rules of the United States Supreme Court.

[55] Compare Nowak, *supra*, note 3, who refers at pp. 667–8 to provisions governing the European and Inter-American Courts of Human Rights that had 'a filtering function with regards to the merits of a case in order to relieve the burden on the two Courts of Human Rights . . . An analogous provision in the Optional Protocol would be inappropriate for the simple reason that the Committee is the only organ entrusted with decision-making possibilities.'

systematic abuses, in order to marshal the time and energy to expound the Covenant in appropriate cases might appear not only unjustified but heartless, remote, and sadly academic.

The proposal is less harsh than such an objection suggests. The present mandatory jurisdiction cannot realise the general purpose of providing justice in the individual case and vindicating the rule of law.[56] Hence the Committee's historical approach to the communications procedure has veiled a more productive approach for the cause of human rights. More-over, the proposed discretionary jurisdiction could take many forms. It could give the Committee discretion for the great range of cases but require decisions on the merits in a specific category of cases, perhaps capital punishment cases. Deciding on the precise criteria for review, including a decision whether any categorical exception to a discretionary jurisdiction, could by its sheer volume undermine the new approach, and requires deliberation by the Committee on substantive and statistical matters.

(iv) The Committee's mandate as a 'legal' institution
The half century of the universal human rights movement has been charac-terised principally by standard setting through treaties such as the ICCPR and by institution building. The processes for drafting treaties and declara-tions have often involved the kind of extensive and thoughtful debate that one would expect in deliberative bodies. The same elements of reflection, analysis and reasoned argument cannot be said to characterise much of the discussion of state violations in international organs like the General Assembly or UN Commission on Human Rights. Public debate about violations of human rights has been dominated by brutal facts on the ground and by the turbulent politics of seeking support for a resolution or attempting more forceful international responses to those facts. Outside the highly developed regional regime in Europe and to a lesser extent in the Americas, there has been no sustained public discourse about human rights of a more legal character, a discourse that would depend more on the ongoing contributions of institutions like courts than on, say, politicised and polemical exchanges about issues like cultural relativism or democracy that often arise in the context of debates about violations.

---

[56] Of course the objection described above to discretionary jurisdiction could take an extreme form by granting the impossibility of doing justice in a systematic way, but nonetheless asserting that even one life saved over time justifies the Committee's current practice.

This chapter's proposals imagine such a discourse. An international movement now understood in most parts of the world as either the raw politics of life or as moral ideals remote from that life (or both) would have a better opportunity to develop its legal dimension through that most 'legal' of all processes, adjudication. The Committee could fill a gap by becoming a truly deliberative body in the image of many state constitutional courts.[57]

It is well suited to do so. In varying degrees, all three of the Committee's activities point toward a characterisation of it as more a 'legal' body (the ideals of the rule of law: independent and impartial members, limited discretion, norm-to-fact decision-making) than a 'political' body (the facts of politics: power, pressure, bargaining, compromise). A comparison with the UN Commission on Human Rights bears out this understanding of the Committee. It consists of independent experts, while state representatives participate in the work of the Commission. To a large extent, the Committee's agenda escapes its control, determined as it is principally by the filing of state reports and of communications, while the Commission's agenda turns on the political influence of states, patron–client relationships, internal voting blocs, and other factors related to power and bargaining. The Committee has no authority to impose sanctions and a limited ability to exert pressures against states, while the Commission has discretion to take a range of more or less threatening actions (investigations, reports, resolutions, publicity). The Committee holds itself aloof from the political and power relations and strategies within the UN, whereas the Commission fully engages in that process.

The proposal for rethinking the communications procedure would draw on and strengthen the Committee's 'legal' character. It does so partly because this path corresponds with the present deep conception and nature of the Committee. As important, within the larger purpose of encouraging complementary roles for universal human rights organs of different compositions and capacities, it makes sense for this Committee to develop the legal side of the human rights movement.

---

[57] Some advocates of human rights might entertain little hope for reform proposals for the Committee, doubting that such proposals can significantly heighten the Committee's effectiveness. Whatever the political likelihood of success, they might instead press for a larger reconstruction, as by urging a full-time Universal Court of Human Rights serving the ICCPR and other treaties with adequate numbers of judges and staff, better process, links to state judiciaries, binding judgments, and connections with UN political organs that would back judgments.

E. Relation between proposals and other activities of the Committee

Revision of the communications procedure would better integrate the three activities of the Committee, thereby lending more force to its work as a whole. Periodic reports of states offer the easier illustration. Sharp criticisms of the reporting process have stressed the failure of many states (disproportionately those with bad records) to file reports, or the filing of late or inadequate reports.[58] The inadequacy stems from the continuing tendency of serious violators to stress their exemplary if illusory law on the statute books, to the exclusion of the abuse and rampant illegality described in the reports of intergovernmental organisations and NGOs. Moreover, like the views themselves, the reporting process has been least effective where most needed – that is, in changing the behaviour of gross and systematic violators.

From another perspective, the Committee's work on reports has achieved a great deal. A mere half century ago, the notion that states would submit periodic reports on their compliance with and implementation of the ICCPR to a body of eighteen experts drawn from all parts of the world would have been considered fanciful. After two decades, such reporting and the collegial reactions of the Committee to those reports – all public documents – have become a relatively non-contentious, familiar practice. That practice has surely reinforced the sense of the 144 states parties that a broad array of sensitive and politically contentious internal matters have become international concerns routinely subjected to international scrutiny. For states taking the reporting requirement seriously, the very pre-paration of the report reinforces the internationalisation of treaty norms. In all such respects, state reporting has helped to institute more deeply in national and international fora this relatively new discourse of human rights.

The most significant change in reporting over the two decades has been the 1992 decision of the Committee to adopt comments, after the discus-sion of a report with the state representative, 'reflecting the views of the Committee as a whole'. These 'concluding observations' displaced the prior practice of relying exclusively on comments by individual Committee members during the discussions with the state representatives.[59] They are intended to provide a 'general evaluation' of the report. The Committee

---

[58] See, e.g., Buergenthal, *supra*, note 7, Section III(C) on Delinquent State Reports.
[59] Ibid., Section III(A).

lacks authority under the ICCPR to issue a binding order to the state. It reaches no formal 'judgment' of violation, and includes only 'suggestions and recommendations' in its concluding observations.[60]

The concluding observations employ norm-to-fact reasoning in deciding whether the state has committed violations. In most cases, surely in the reports of gross violators of human rights, these conclusions do not require complex interpretation and argument: a state closes a press, or discriminates against women, or tortures prisoners. Only rarely do the recommendations in the concluding observations – and then principally for states with strong records of compliance – raise difficult issues of interpretation or deal with questions of conflicts among rights. That is, the Committee cannot be said to be expounding the ICCPR in significant ways through its concluding observations. Moreover, it relies on consensus in drafting the observations, a process promoting compromise and more guarded criticism. The reporting process therefore serves a different primary purpose from that proposed for views.

Of course the Committee seeks to induce state action through its observations. They are public documents, transmitted to the UN and now widely available – though like the views, not widely enough known to a larger public or commented on outside official circles. What publicity they do enjoy can damage a state's standing in the international community and bring about changes in conduct through 'shaming' and material self-interest. Moreover, the Committee's observations may become part of political debate within the state involved, as a local political opposition and NGOs draw on them to provoke public discussion and make demands on the government. In fields such as women's rights many concluding observations have stressed that the Committee's work has likely influenced internal political processes.

In urging greater compliance with the ICCPR, the Committee has acted in a careful, measured way. While criticising and recommending, it also compliments the state for what it has achieved and may recognise obstacles to greater compliance. The process takes on the aura of a conversation, albeit an often difficult one, described by the Committee as a process of 'constructive dialogue' rather than as a discrete moment of third-party judgment and demand for compliance.[61] This approach of the Committee

---

[60] Concluding observations are set forth in the Committee's Annual Report. Observations directed to fourteen states appear in the Committee's 1997 Annual Report, *supra*, note 22.

[61] The term 'constructive dialogue' has become one of art, much repeated in this context. See, e.g., Nowak, *supra*, note 3, at p. 562.

obviously complements the dialogic role proposed for the Committee's activity under the Protocol. A sharper tone and less formulaic style of presentation in the concluding observations could stir in some states a greater sense of urgency to do the necessary, and to that extent would represent progress. But tougher observations are unlikely to influence serious violators like Iraq or Nigeria that have remained impervious to all the Committee's work.

General comments raise more complex issues, partly because their character has changed so significantly over two decades. In recent years they have assumed the character of broad interpretations of provisions of the ICCPR. Typically each general comment addresses a particular article – for example, political participation, or privacy, or non-discrimination.[62] These comments carry no formal authority to bind states parties, although the status of the Committee under the Covenant gives them a special claim for attention. Rather like views under the Protocol, their influence will rest primarily on the quality of their argument, and on the degree to which they expound the Covenant in a serious, probing and illuminating way.

As a method of expounding the ICCPR, views have a great advantage over general comments. They are contextual. They grow out of concrete controversies and facts that can enrich the discussion, set boundaries to an opinion, and lend a reality to the Committee's argument and decision. General comments proceed more abstractly, except to the extent that they can be said to grow out of or even codify earlier views and concluding observations about state reports. Hence they encounter related problems of appropriate scope and authority. The best among them have succeeded not only in presenting the Committee's position about an issue in an ordered way, but also in advancing thought about a difficult matter. They have served to encourage debate about the Covenant, and thereby to spread and deepen its relevance to the human rights movement.

To advance these goals, and to draw states more deeply into its work, the Committee could alter the present procedures for formulating general comments. Discussion now takes place within closed sessions of the

---

[62] General comments up to 1992 are set forth in UN Doc. HRI/GEN/1, 4 September 1992, at pp. 1–34. Two more recent general comments of a more probing and challenging character are General Comment No. 24 (on issues relating to reservations made upon ratification or accession by states parties to the ICCPR or the Optional Protocols thereto), CCPR/C/21/Rev.1/Add.6, 2 November 1994; and General Comment No. 25 (on the right to political participation), CCPR/C/57/CRP.2/Add.2, 15 July 1996, Annex V.

Committee, and comments are issued without advance warning. The Committee could revise this procedure and issue a draft of a proposed general comment. Together with intergovernmental and non-governmental organisations, states would be invited to submit comments; there could be a public hearing. Such a procedure would both give the Committee more presence and encourage dialogue, thereby drawing general comments closer to the goals of the Committee's other two activities. To be sure, the Committee would have to be sufficiently strong to resist pressures from powerful states who opposed certain provisions in the draft comment, and to follow its own best judgment after receiving a range of opinions.

F. Conclusion

In a world rich in human rights norms and ideals but wanting in political will and enforcement of those ideals, the universal institutions have played a modest role. It is true that the norms are not loose and floating, but anchored in the institutions. This constitutes a solid achievement of the first half century of the human rights movement. We are much better off having our institutions, whatever their inadequacies, than resting with declarations and law-making treaties that lack permanent human rights organs. They give us a start. We can exploit the politically possible to work towards a next half century that will give international institutions and processes greater capacity to aid peoples.

The Committee will here have its role. It has a long way to go to become a significant actor in the universal human rights movement. The relatively modest improvements in its functioning over two decades give no cause for complacency. But they do suggest that serious change may be possible through strong will and advocacy of the Committee – by internal reforms to the extent possible, and through UN organs and the states parties if treaty amendment is essential.

This chapter builds on that hope. It looks to the Committee not as a forum for resolving major disputes or putting great pressure on states, but as a deliberative body playing a more legal role with energy and conviction. By expounding the ICCPR and spurring dialogue about it, by enriching and instituting more deeply the discourse of human rights, the Committee can best contribute to the massive work of the next fifty years.

3

DECISION-TAKING IN THE COMMITTEE ON THE ELIMINATION OF RACIAL DISCRIMINATION

MICHAEL BANTON

When the Committee of the Convention on the Elimination of All Forms of Racial Discrimination (CERD) has to take decisions in connection with state reports submitted under article 9 of CERD, it encounters problems that do not arise when it is dealing with individual communications under article 14. This chapter begins by contrasting the ways in which the Committee sets about its work under these two articles.[1] It notes that state reports, and the consideration of them, sometimes introduce issues that are marginal to the Convention and which observers might consider political rather than legal. The Committee then has to exercise a delicate judgment when deciding where the line should be drawn. Its difficulties in reaching decisions on such issues reflect the difficulties of decision-taking in the United Nations as a whole.

Under article 14 of the Convention a state may make a declaration that it recognises the competence of the Committee to receive and consider communications from individuals or groups of individuals within its jurisdiction claiming to be victims of a violation by that state of one or more rights set forth in the Convention. If the Committee finds a violation of the Convention, the state should revise its law or practice in the light of the Committee's opinion. The Committee has considered ten communications. It does so in private session, but in the author's experience it has nonetheless approached its task judicially. That the decisions of courts are enforced by the states that establish them gives their proceedings a different character. There are still significant parallels. This chapter discusses the process by which a treaty body's decisions are reached rather than the status of these decisions.

---

[1] Prof. Rüdiger Wolfrum kindly contributed critical comments on an earlier draft of this chapter.

Most of the Committee's time is spent not on article 14 communications but on reports submitted under article 9. Each state party has undertaken to submit every two years a report on the legislative, judicial, administrative or other measures which it has adopted to give effect to the provisions of the Convention. The Committee reports annually to the United Nations General Assembly. It may make suggestions and general recommendations based on the examination of the reports and information received from the states parties. It has also to transmit any comments received from the states parties. In performing this task the Committee has, from the time of its first meeting in 1970, sought to act judicially, arguably with increasing success. But it has not succeeded to the extent that it now succeeds with respect to article 14.

A. The changing context

Three factors in particular have influenced the rate at which the Committee, in performing its tasks under article 9, has become a more judicial body: changes in the conception of racial discrimination; the reduction in tensions between states; and the increased willingness of states to accept a degree of international oversight of their domestic policies in this field. Each of these factors has affected the sorts of persons states nominate for election to the Committee, the outcome of elections, members' conceptions of their duties, and the processes of decision-taking within the Committee.

There are other factors which are bound to influence any international treaty body, but which operate as constants rather than as variables. One is size: a committee of eighteen cannot reach decisions as easily as a bench of three judges, but as an international body it has to be relatively large. Another is language: in committee meetings not all members are able to speak in their mother tongue. Interpretation, which is provided between Chinese, English, French, Russian, Spanish, and – when required – Arabic, tends to slow the process of reaching a shared understanding.

No less important is the question of accountability. A bench of judges or magistrates in a national court acts within a unitary system such that without compromising the principle of judicial independence, their senior colleagues and peers can reward or sanction them according to their discharge of closely-prescribed duties. In any committee set up by a body like a governmental department or a university, members are part of a structured system with a host of rules, notions of rank, and informal expectations that constrain their conduct. Those who drafted the Convention introduced the new implementation procedure of state reporting, the examination of reports, and then a further report to the General Assembly. Governments were bound to be suspicious of a proposal to create a novel kind of body with the power to oversee the actions of sovereign states. The new body was made to appear less threatening by being given the familiar designation 'committee', although it was quite unlike most committees. A treaty body like the Committee resembles an assembly of eighteen kings and queens. All members are equal, and behind their sentiments about their equality lies the doctrine of the sovereign equality of states, even if members are not state representatives. Formally speaking, they are restrained by little more than the solemn declaration made after election that they will perform their duties 'honourably, faithfully, impartially and conscientiously'. Yet they cannot, for six weeks of the year, slough their national identities as snakes slough their skins.

In the election of the Committee consideration has to be given to 'equitable geographical distribution and to the representation of the different forms of civilisation as well as of the principal legal systems'. States parties have reached an understanding whereby the seats on the Committee are to be divided between the United Nations' five regional groups. Within the Committee there is a system of rotation of office whereby every two years members from the next regional group in line propose a new chairperson for election.

When dealing with petitions under article 14 of the Convention, the Committee, like a national court, benefits from the prior refinement of issues and from the adversarial nature of the proceedings. If the petitioner is legally represented there will be a systematic account of the facts alleged, of the relevant national law, and an argument that some part or parts of the Convention have been breached; there will be a legal argument from the state designed to clarify the issues and perhaps a response from the petitioner to the state's submission. If the petitioner is not legally represented the secretariat helps in the process of refining the issues to be put before the Committee, which has then simply to adjudicate on them.

When evaluating reports submitted under article 9 of the Convention, any adversarial relationship (and it is only notional) is that between the states parties as a whole and the state whose report is under consideration. Each state has promised the others that it will fulfil specified obligations. These other states have appointed the Committee to work for them in verifying the fulfilment of these obligations, but circumstances vary so much from one state to another that when examining reports under article 9, the Committee has itself to identify the issues for examination. The history of its activities under this article can be written as the story of how over the past twenty-seven years the Committee has progressively identified and refined issues in dialogue with states parties. To this extent it has some inquisitorial features. The influence upon this trend of the three factors mentioned above can be summarised as follows.

First, those who drafted the Convention assumed that racial discrimination was a social pathology caused by either colonialism or the dissemination of doctrines of racial superiority. It was specific to particular sorts of society and a particular historical era. Almost all the states which acceded in the early years believed that it was *other* states which practised racial discrimination. In their eyes, therefore, accession had no implications for their domestic policy; rather it specified objectives for their foreign policy. Consequently they nominated diplomats, foreign policy specialists, for election to the Committee. Of the eighteen Committee members first elected, ten were serving diplomats, one was a retired diplomat, four were law professors and three were judges.[2] When the Convention was first opened for signature in 1966 the procedure for states to report on the discharge of their treaty obligations was novel. One of the Committee's priorities in the 1970s was to explain to state delegations that their governments were legally obliged to have in force legislation against racial discrimination even if it was only of a preventive character. States were unaccustomed to being held accountable in this way and were often suspicious. In these circumstances it was an advantage that the Committee included so many diplomats. Since those days there has been a gradual change in the conception of racial discrimination, which is now more generally seen as just one ground of a universal tendency for people to be treated differently because of their 'race, colour, sex, language, religion, political or other opinion, national or social origin, property, birth or other status' as expressed in article 26 of the ICCPR. It is therefore a normal rather than a pathological social feature. This has drained some of the emotion from the charge of racial discrimination, as compared with the earlier tendency to see any reference to racism as accusatory.

---

[2] M. Banton, *International Action against Racial Discrimination*, Oxford, 1996, pp. 50–62, 99–112.

Second, international tensions affected views of the issues which the Committee had to address. The 1960s and 1970s were the era of decolonisation, something recalled in the Convention's fourth preambular paragraph and the subject of a task imposed upon the Committee under article 15. Action against apartheid was so high a priority that the Committee stretched its mandate to order to invite states to report on the status of their diplomatic, economic and other relations with racist regimes in southern Africa. The tensions also affected conceptions of the Committee's role. Some members cited the requirement that part of Committee's report be 'based on the examination of the reports and information received from the States Parties'[3] to contend that evidence obtained from personal experience or submitted by non-governmental organisations was inadmissible. The reduction in inter-state tensions was reflected in the results of the 1988 election to the Committee. Since then it has been easier to obtain agreement on the nature of issues before the Committee.

Third, states may have their own views about the issues and do not regard the Committee as having any kind of jurisdiction to define them. For example, in the drafting process of the Convention no consideration was given to the application to Asian societies of the definition of racial discrimination as covering distinctions based on 'descent, or national or ethnic origin'. Does the reference to descent cover Hindu castes, or is it, as the Government of India believes, a synonym for race?[4] With respect to such matters the Committee is unlikely to be perceived as acting as a judicial body when there is so little agreement about the nature of the issues.

The number of diplomats with UN experience who have been members has had an abiding influence upon the Committee's procedures. It always seeks to reach decisions by consensus. It avoids taking votes because it has so little power to bind anyone to the result. Once a procedure has been agreed it can be easy to reach decisions about new matters of a similar kind, but when new issues arise the procedures to which diplomats are accustomed may absorb a lot of the Committee's scarce time without producing results. For example, at its forty-seventh session the Committee discussed a letter from a Turkish ambassador to the Special Rapporteur on Racism and Xenophobia concerning his discussions with the Committee, a letter which included what many members regarded as disparaging remarks. Since the

---

[3] Article 9.2 of the Convention.
[4] UN Doc. CERD/C/299/Add.3 (Fourteenth Report of India), paras. 7–8.

letter was only copied to the Committee it was not necessary to react to it, but, because it touched on the susceptibilities of the diplomat members of the Committee, much time was wasted on it.[5]

B. The Committee's meetings

Since the Committee's first year, the number of states parties has grown from forty-one to 154, and its tasks have increased in many respects, but it has continued to meet for just two sessions a year, each of three weeks. There are two three-hour meetings each day. Of the thirty meetings possible in one session, twenty-two are allocated to the consideration of new state reports; two to the review of the implementation of the Convention in states whose reports are overdue by five years or more; two to the prevention of racial discrimination, including early-warning and urgent procedures; and four to other business, including individual communications. These figures are approximate and may vary from session to session.

At its fifty-first session in August 1997 the Committee considered ten new state reports, the positions of five 'overdue' states and of four states under the category of early warning and urgent procedures, and four individual communications. Although the number of incoming reports has been increasing, the Committee has not allowed any backlog of unconsidered reports to build up. In relation to new reports, the procedure is for the leader of the state delegation to introduce the report, then the discussion of it is opened by the Committee member who has been designated Country Rapporteur, followed by contributions from other members and replies from the delegation. The willingness of other members to allow the Country Rapporteur to speak for them and to refrain from speaking themselves has meant that this stage in the consideration of a report is normally completed within five hours. After hearing the delegation's replies, the Committee passes to the next report, providing an interval during which the Country Rapporteur, assisted by a member of the Secretariat, drafts a set of concluding observations which are later presented for adoption by the Committee as a whole. In accordance with article 9.2 of the Convention, a state may submit its comments on the concluding observations for inclusion in the Committee's annual report to the General Assembly.

[5] See UN Doc. CERD/C/SR 1100:1–39 for initial discussion; the available records do not give an adequate representation of the time taken over this or the eventual agreement on a letter to the Special Rapporteur.

The suggestion that Committee members behave like eighteen kings and queens may seem less outrageous if account is taken of irregularities in attendance. It is not unusual for a member to be absent for part of a meeting or even for several days, perhaps leaving Geneva to deal with governmental business elsewhere, but no one knows because the member need not tell the chairperson of the absence or the reasons for it. There is no question of the member having to seek anyone else's permission for this. The Secretariat may note the absence and check this against the member's claim for sub-sistence expenses, but whether or how this is done is not the business of the Committee. On one occasion the Committee was considering the Country Rapporteur's draft concluding observations on a state report when it had to break for lunch. After lunch the Committee resumed its consideration of the draft although the Country Rapporteur was not present. Later the chairperson said to this member that it was difficult to imagine what duties at this time could have overridden his duties to the Committee. The member was enraged, and could not accept that he was accountable to the chair-person. A member's absence from a whole or a substantial part of a session is mentioned in the Committee's annual report and this may be noted by states parties if the member is nominated for re-election.

The present practice is for the Committee at the last meeting of a session to determine which reports it will consider at its next session. It is left to the chairperson to fit them into the time available and to avoid any embar-rassment to a delegation that is kept waiting because Committee members have overrun the time allocated for the previous report. In any treaty body members may speak at what their colleagues consider excessive length; others expect the chairperson to regulate this, if necessary over the objections of the members concerned. At the Committee's fiftieth session members disliked the chairperson's reminding the meeting that another delegation was shortly due, complaining that 'the Committee is not a railway station'. In another treaty body the chairperson tried holding up yellow and red cards like a football referee, but the objections were forceful. The Committee's Rule 37 allows a chairperson to propose time limits on speeches but any such proposal is likely to start a discussion that will consume more time than could be saved by its adoption. The one effective time constraint is that imposed by the interpreters who simply leave their booths if a meeting overruns by ten minutes. All too often a member who agrees with others on the general principles believes that the particular instance that concerns him or her is an exception to the rule.[6] It is not unknown for a judge to speak unnecessarily in order to display his or her expertise, and it does sometimes appear as if a member is speaking simply because nothing has been heard from him or her for a while, or simply to be awkward or to delay a decision. But even when members are privately critical of something a colleague has said, and occasionally criticise one another's statements in front of a delegation, they close ranks whenever a state delegate criticises an individual member.

A major problem is that of questions irrelevant to implementation of Convention obligations. In March 1997 the Committee considered the tenth and eleventh periodic reports of Iraq. Introducing the report, the representative of the reporting state referred to reports by the UN Children's Fund (UNICEF) and the World Health Organisation (WHO) on the catastrophic consequences of the health situation for children. The Country Rapporteur, Mr Wolfrum, referred to the report of the Special Rapporteur of the Commission on Human Rights on the situation in Iraq[7] according to which the authorities had refused to issue ration cards to some Kurds and Marsh Arab tribes in the governorate of Basra. He expressed doubt about the non-discriminatory character of the current distribution of food and medicines. CERD member Mr Aboul-Nasr said that the reports referred to 'the difficulties which the country was facing because of the unjust sanctions which had been imposed on the Iraqi people' and agreed with the representative's statement that a 'slow genocide' was under way. CERD member Mr van Boven remarked on the 'unjust penalty' imposed on the Iraqi population and said 'it would be useful for the Committee to determine whether children belonging to specific ethnic groups were particularly affected by the shortage of food and medicines'. CERD member Mr de Gouttes endorsed Mr Aboul-Nasr's proposal that the immediate implementation of the 'oil-for-food' agreement should be recommended. CERD members Mr Aga Shahi, Mr Ahmadu and Mr Lechuga Hevia spoke to similar purpose. Three other members addressed different matters. Replying to questions, the state representative insisted that all children in Iraq suffered deprivation equally. Mr Aboul-Nasr supported him in this, maintaining that the allegations about the inequitable distribution of medicines were an excuse for destabilising the situation.[8] This exchange of views is

---

[6] For recent discussions of possible time limits for speeches see UN Docs. CERD/C/SR. 1088:50, 1165:46–58 and 1214:12 and 24.

[7] UN Doc. E/CN.4/1995/61.   [8] UN Doc. CERD/C/SR.1203–4.

recounted here because some observers might consider that some of those members who spoke after Mr Wolfrum strayed beyond the Committee's mandate. Had the chairperson intervened to voice an opinion that the boundary of relevance had been crossed, the only result would have been an unproductive debate that would have made the atmosphere even more difficult.

When the Committee discussed the draft concluding observations on the report of Iraq, some of these differences reappeared. Although the draft had been the subject of much prior consultation, four hours were spent on further amendments and argument. Paragraph 14 read:

> The Committee recommends that Iraq comply with the relevant Security Council resolutions calling for the release of all Kuwaiti nationals and nationals of other States who might still be in detention, and to provide all information available on missing individuals of such States.

It was argued that as the preamble to the Convention places it within the broader framework of human rights instruments such a recommendation could be justified; most members were unconvinced by this argument but were unwilling to vote against the proposition, which was therefore carried on the votes of the minority of the members voting. Believing this an unsatisfactory conclusion, some members wished to reconsider the decision but their motion failed to secure the necessary two-thirds majority. After so much discussion, members were tired of the matter.

By comparison with most national committees, treaty bodies are characterised by the weakness of the chairperson's power. The Committee's Rule 17 stipulates that 'in exercising his functions as Chairman, the Chairman shall remain under the authority of the Committee'. The chairperson has no special influence with respect to decisions of substance, though considerable influence over a decision, for example, as to which agenda item shall be taken next. The weakness of the chairperson's powers and of the very limited influence of the secretariat are both associated with the relative lack of refinement of the issues for decision. Committee members have to take responsibility for the drafting of all texts and to provide precise instructions for any drafting by a member of the secretariat. Since the issues are more clearly defined in connection with decisions about Article 14 communications it is possible to delegate more drafting work to the secretariat concerning them than with matters relating to Article 9 reports.

C. Decisions

A review of the reports and summary records[9] of the Committee since 1986 (the year the author joined the Committee) may be instructive. Between then and the end of 1996 the Committee adopted fifteen general recommendations. The history of some of these is instructive. In March 1993 the author introduced a draft general recommendation to make it clear that article 3 of the Convention was directed against all forms of racial segregation and not just apartheid.[10] After discussion, the author produced revised drafts but it seemed so difficult to get agreement that hope was almost given up when in 1995, on the third attempt, it suddenly went through, perhaps because it had by then been possible to get a large number of members to join as co-sponsors.[11] Another draft general recommendation was proposed by Mr Wolfrum to clarify certain obscure passages in article 5.[12] That draft, after further revision, was also adopted on its third submission in 1995; it came up for reconsideration at a time when one of the members who had expressed most doubts happened to be absent.[13] One of the obstacles to agreement on such matters is that some members are unwilling to work on drafts beforehand and voice objections only when proposals are tabled; sometimes one or two of them may be able to exercise a power of veto.

In the course of a discussion members often succeed in reconciling and synthesising the apparently opposed views of previous speakers, so that the latest speaker comes nearest to presenting a consensus view which may then be adopted by the chairperson as the view of the Committee. Decision-taking is also influenced by the sense that time is pressing. Towards the end of a session members are more inclined either to settle their differences or to postpone any decision to the following session. For example, at the last meeting of its fifty-first session, the Committee had to draw up its agenda for the next session. Seventeen recently received reports were awaiting consideration. How many should it schedule? Should it take them in order of receipt, as had been the established practice? The Committee decided that the order of receipt would not be its sole criterion. It would prioritise initial

---

[9] The summary records of the public meetings of the Committee for 1986–1994 run to 2,698 pages. Those for 1994–1997 have not yet been finalised and paginated and are still subject to correction.

[10] Banton, *supra*, note 2, pp. 159–60, 201–2.

[11] UN Docs. CERD/C/SRs 969:45–59, 1078:36–49, 1125.

[12] Banton, *supra*, note 2, pp. 209–10.

[13] UN Docs. CERD/C/SRs 1081:20–39, 1120:1–15, 1147:7–22.

reports over periodic reports, reports submitted after long delays and reports from countries where there were important developments. With the
aid of a ballot it selected twelve. This was a radical departure from previous
practice, and would have evoked much discussion had it been proposed
earlier in the session. By further deciding to consider the position in twelve
states whose reports were overdue, and in four states under its procedures
for the prevention of racial discrimination, the Committee forced itself to
keep abreast with the inflow of new work.

Apart from general recommendations, the Committee took thirty-three
formal decisions during the years 1986–1996. One of these put to rest a
long dispute about the sources members might draw upon in connection
with article 9. Eight dealt with non-legal matters (the financing of the Committee, the venue for meetings, the aim of universal accession, and the UN
Decade against Racism and Racial Discrimination). Nine decisions were
requests to states for information. In 1994 the Committee adopted new
measures for the prevention of racial discrimination, including the giving
of early warning; one decision was about the procedure to be followed, and
there have since been nineteen decisions about situations in particular
states. The problems of identifying and refining a legal issue within the
Committee's mandate were magnified with the adoption of prevention
procedures. Consider, for example, the Committee's resolution on Bosnia
and Herzegovina.[14] This re-emphasised 'that any attempt to change or to
uphold a changed demographic composition of an area against the will of
the original inhabitants, by whatever means, is a violation of international
law' and included seven other components. At the instigation of the then
chairperson, a former diplomat, it was followed by explanations of vote in
accordance with the practice of the General Assembly and provided for by
the Committee's Rule 54. General Assembly resolutions are often important as rhetoric, which explains why explanations of vote are allowed, but it
is doubtful if they are appropriate to a treaty body.

At the invitation of the Government of the Federal Republic of
Yugoslavia (Serbia and Montenegro) the Committee sent a three-member
mission in 1993 to 'help promote a dialogue for a peaceful solution of
issues concerning respect for human rights in Kosovo, in particular the
elimination of all forms of racial discrimination . . .'. A visit took place in
November–December of that year. Subsequently Croatia invited the

---

[14] Decision 2(47) of UN Doc. A/50/18, see note 3 for Explanations Of Vote.

Committee to send one of its members on mission, while another single-member mission to Guatemala has recently taken place.[15] The delegation of Burundi at the fifty-first session also raised the possibility of a mission to that country.

Many decisions are taken without their being formulated as resolutions. For example, the Committee has long been concerned about overdue reports, but felt constrained by the requirement that its report be 'based on the examination of the reports and information received from the States Parties'.[16] If no report or information had been received, it had little or no basis for action. It first decided to deal with overdue periodic reports by re-examining the last report received, then, when this procedure proved acceptable, it reported that it would review implementation of the Convention in states whose initial reports were seriously overdue on the basis of other information submitted to UN bodies. It did not regard the General Assembly as empowered to authorise action that was not authorised by the Convention, but concluded that it would be safer for it to act in this way if the General Assembly was supportive.[17] In acting for the prevention of racial discrimination, including its use of early-warning and urgent procedures, the Committee followed a similar course.[18]

In 1973 the Committee adopted a general recommendation inviting states to include in their article 9 reports 'relevant information on the demographic composition of the population' and this was embodied in the

[15] See UN Doc. A/48/18 para. 546 for the invitation and UN Doc. A/49/18 paras. 21–5 for the outcome. For the mission to Croatia see UN Doc. A/49/18 paras. 26–9. For the invitation from Guatemala see UN Doc. A/50/18 para. 320.

[16] Article 9.2 of the Convention.

[17] Action on overdue periodic reports was discussed: UN Docs. CERD/C/SR 903:25 and 909; reported in UN Doc. A/46/18 para. 27, and commended in GA Res. 47/79 which '[w]elcomes the innovatory procedures adopted by the Committee for reviewing the implementation of the Convention in States whose reports are overdue and for formulating concluding observations on State party reports'. Action on overdue initial reports was discussed: SR 1167; the proposed action was reported in UN Doc. A/51/18 para. 22; then GA Res. 51/80 para. 4 '[c]ommends the Committee on its working methods, including its procedure for reviewing the implementation of the Convention in States whose *initial* and periodic reports are overdue . . .' (italics added).

[18] For the Committee's discussion of prevention, see UN Doc. CERD/C/SRs 960, 974, 979; its decision was reported in UN Doc. A/48/18 paras. 15–19; General Assembly resolutions starting with 47/79 have commended its innovation, including 50/137 which in para. 5 'commends the Committee for its continuous efforts to improve its contribution to the prevention of racial discrimination, including early-warning and urgent procedures, and welcomes its relevant decisions and action thereon'.

introductory portion of the Committee's reporting guidelines. When the guidelines were modified in 1992 to introduce a uniform guideline covering reports under other treaties, this passage was overlooked. It took a long time to get it reinstated because many Committee members assume that such information is to be collected in periodic population censuses. Several African states have concluded that collecting such information in this way is divisive and contrary to their policies of nation-building, but Committee members believe they can find ways around this difficulty. The first proposals to modify the guidelines in order to restore the 1973 request were blocked by a Committee member who objected to anything that implied a criticism of reporting states. When it was tabled for the fourth time in 1994, the proposal was adopted, perhaps because this member was not present.[19]

In 1991 the Committee agreed that in future its comments on state reports would lead to 'Concluding observations' expressing a collective view of the whole Committee.[20] This is helping to refine the issues. It has also resulted in agreement on certain formulations. For example, since some members wish to encourage states to make declarations under article 14 while others believe that this is a matter for states themselves and not one on which Committee members should comment, a set phraseology was agreed to avoid re-opening the issue. Committee members who are nationals of a reporting state do not normally participate in the consideration of their own state's reports, but in 1996 the members from China and India were so perturbed about the observations on their states' reports that they wished to record their dissent, and the Committee found an acceptable way of recording this.[21]

Decisions have also been taken on matters internal to the Committee, like proposed amendments to rules of procedure, and on matters relating to other UN bodies, for example representation at World Conference on Human Rights, participation in Decades for Action against Racism and Racial Discrimination, comments on draft model legislation against racial discrimination, views on the report of the independent expert on enhancing the long-term effectiveness of the UN human rights treaty bodies, and involvement in the now annual meetings of persons chairing UN human rights treaty bodies.

---

[19] See, e.g., UN Docs. CERD/C/SRs 1194:56, 61 and 64; 1199:33–52.

[20] Banton, *supra*, note 2, pp. 147–50.

[21] UN Doc. CERD/C/SR 1179:60–91; UN Doc. A/51/18 para. 21. Note also comments of the Government of India in Annex IX.

Over the period 1988–1997 the Committee has been able to reach more decisions. The prime reason is that changes in international relations and continuity in membership have permitted a growth in trust (two of the current members are in their sixth term of office, and two in their fifth; the average member is in his or her third term). However, there can still be difficulties in securing consensus even over comparatively minor matters. For example at the forty-sixth session, in preparation for a joint meeting with the Sub-Commission on Prevention of Discrimination and Protection of Minorities, Committee members Mr Banton and Mr van Boven were asked to draft for the benefit of Sub-Commission members a text about the work of the Committee in order to inform the discussion. This they did, and the chairperson proposed to transmit it to the Sub-Commission.[22] After some Committee members objected to formulations in the text, the chairperson abandoned it without bringing it back to the Committee, since the text would have appeared as the work of two persons on behalf of the Committee. It is remarkable that other members, having asked two colleagues to produce the document, should have been unwilling to allow it to go forward.

D. The principle of the ratchet

The human rights enterprise has from its origin been a continuing struggle and the difficulties that the Committee experiences in reaching decisions often reflect similar difficulties in the General Assembly and elsewhere within the United Nations. The struggle centres on the principle of the ratchet. A group of states takes an initiative, secures agreement on a particular form of words or course of action, and then tries to use this as a foundation for another step forward whenever opportunity offers. Once a form of words has been accepted it can be used again or moved up a notch; this is the function of rhetoric in official conferences. Similarly, once a procedure for reaching decisions has been established, it can usually be employed again, but securing agreement on a new procedure can be very time-consuming.

The Convention was a remarkable initiative in its time, driven by the imperatives of policies directed against colonialism and apartheid, and attempting to use the institutions of the United Nations to pursue ends that most states saw as irrelevant to their domestic responsibilities. Those who drafted it were not confident that many states would become parties to the

---

[22] The summary records do not report this adequately. UN Doc. CERD/C/SR 1102:54 refers to the planned transmittal of the text.

Convention and refrained from taking steps that might discourage potential adherents. An early commentator suspected that states had misconceived the significance of the reporting requirement, believing it 'the most innoc-uous of implementation techniques'.[23] The Committee's experience suggests this was correct. If states did act in error, circumstances have now changed so much that no state is likely to backtrack and denounce the Convention.

The Human Rights Committee maintained, in paragraph 17 of its General Comment No. 24 on reservations, that human rights treaties are not a web of inter-state exchanges of mutual obligations like other treaties, and that the mandate of their monitoring bodies requires them to take the lead within their fields.[24] For its part the Committee's new procedures for the implementation of the Convention have been commended by the states meeting as members of the General Assembly, while the Assembly's resolutions on 'Effective implementation of international instruments on human rights' have regularly supported the proposals of the meetings of persons chairing the human rights treaty bodies. The initiatives have almost always come from the treaty bodies themselves. So if the ratchet is to be given another turn and the rule of law extended a little further, the treaty bodies must advance feasible proposals for improving the reporting process; experience suggests that delegations in the General Assembly are likely to view them sympathetically.

E. Dialogue with reporting states

The examination of state reports is part of a wider structure represented in Figure 1.

The process whereby states' reports are examined is represented in the dimension A–B of the figure. The persons whose rights are to be protected through the Convention are represented at point C. Their experiences and views may be advanced by NGOs. Some members of treaty bodies are suspicious of NGOs, but most members feel they have a duty to those whose rights are to be protected as well as to the reporting state.[25] Point D

---

[23] T. Buergenthal, 'Implementing the UN Racial Convention', 12 *Texas International Law Journal*, 1977, p. 189.

[24] General Comment No. 24 (fifty-second Session, 1994), 'General comment on issues relating to reservations made upon ratification or accession to the Covenant or the Optional Protocols thereto, or in relation to declarations under article 41 of the Covenant'. UN Doc. HRI/GEN/1/Rev.3 (1997) p. 42.

[25] See, e.g., UN Docs. CERD/C/SRs 1194:56, 61 and 64; 1199:33–52.

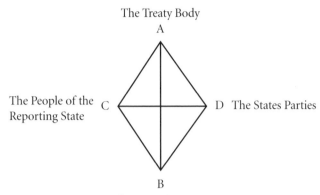

Figure 3.1. *The Examination of State Reports by the Committee on the Elimination of Racial Discrimination*

represents the states parties as a collective, either meeting separately or as members of the UN General Assembly when debating human rights issues. At point D, discussion of the reporting process should include consideration, or the lack of it, of action on the treaty body's report on the discharge of their obligations by the reporting states.

Starting at point A, it should be noted that the Committee has itself given the ratchet a few turns by its general recommendations, such as No. XIX on segregation and No. XXIII on the rights of indigenous peoples. Without such stimuli states might not have perceived the relevance of the Convention to the matters in question. There has been a progressive improvement in the questioning of delegations and a parallel improvement in state implementation of the Convention.

The Committee frequently reviews its methods of work to meet changing circumstances. It has been suggested that, like certain other treaty bodies, the Committee might convene an inter-sessional working party to prepare the dialogue and to notify the reporting state of the issues to be raised. At present a country rapporteur may prepare a list of questions in advance for circulation to the state and to Committee members, but most of the members who serve as country rapporteurs prefer, for varied reasons, not to do this. The Committee has decided against any inter-sessional working party, one objection being that it could interfere with the equality of Committee members.[26] The suggestion that treaty bodies could help ease

[26] UN Docs. CERD/C/SR 1027:62–80 and 1029:51–66.

70

the reporting burden by asking states for specially-tailored or thematic reports is less relevant to the most specialised committees, that is, the CERD Committee and that established under the Convention against Torture, though the former has been moving in this direction.

While the Committee's proceedings could be accelerated by the prior circulation of written proposals, it should not be forgotten that members receive no payment for the work they do on behalf of the Convention. They have no research or secretarial assistance. Most work hard outside meetings, and many work on Committee tasks in between sessions, but conditions are particularly difficult for those who live in countries with poor communications. Delays in translating documents are another source of difficulty. Many members lack access to sources of information complementary to state reports. The most practical assistance would be to enable them to use the Internet in their home countries. Many members are in full-time employment; some hold positions which give them access to much information but which also limit their opportunities to undertake extra work.

As to point B in Figure 1, the concerns of states parties were expressed in the Commission on Human Rights (CHR). CHR resolution 1995/92, paragraph 8(d) urged the treaty bodies to consider ways of reducing the reporting burden on states, including 'considering the utility of single comprehensive reports and of replacing periodic reports with specifically tailored reports and thematic reports'. The Committee would not be concerned if a state's reports under several treaties were consolidated in a single report provided there was no decline in the standard of reporting and such a change did not call into question the two-year reporting cycle. Because ethnic conflicts can escalate very quickly, they may require quick responses. While the Committee is empowered to seek 'further information' from states parties, there is always the possibility that if some member proposes that the Committee seeks such information from state X, some other member may object that it did not take similar action in respect of state Y. In such circumstances discussion of the application of the principle of the equality of states can be so time-consuming as to amount to a kind of veto. Because the Convention requires two-yearly reporting it is much easier to point out to a state that its nth report is due by a particular date and then request that this deadline be met. With states that give occasion for less concern the Committee can show a little diplomatic blindness to the two-year requirement.

The examination of periodic reports has so far been the prime means for overseeing implementation of the Convention, though in future it may be possible to rely more upon the receipt of individual communications to draw attention to any deficiencies. Yet that future must be quite distant, to judge from the small number of communications so far received and the low proportion of states parties that have made the necessary declaration under article 14. Of the 144 states parties to the ICCPR at 3 December 1999, ninety-five had ratified the Optional Protocol to permit individual petitions. Yet at the same time, of the 155 parties to the Convention only twenty-eight had made the equivalent declaration under article 14.

Point C in Figure 1 has hitherto been the least important of the four points. Only in the 1990s has the Committee started to receive any significant inflow of information from national NGOs commenting upon state reports. They have been assisted by the founding, in 1993, of the Anti-Racism Information Service, which collates information from various sources and feeds it to Committee members. Members now sometimes meet with NGO representatives before a state report is considered. So in the terms of Figure 1, relations between points A and C have strengthened a little, but NGOs have not been allowed to develop the adversarial relationship C–B. In several recent instances the press in the reporting state has publicised any differences between the government and the Committee, which can be seen as a line of pressure A → B → C → B, supplementing A → B.

The main problems lie at point D in Figure 1, in the relations between the state parties. Should they not, as a collective, take more interest in the body they have established to work on their behalf? Perhaps because they did not wish to discourage states from ratifying the Convention, those who drafted it made no provision for action against states which failed to pay their assessments or submit reports. Even in the years 1986–1990 and 1992, in which the Committee was enabled to meet for only half the scheduled number of weeks, the states parties did not consider suspending the right to participate in the elections of those states whose failure to pay was so seriously restricting the Committee's ability to do its work. One of the few occasions when the states have acted multilaterally was when, for reasons of inter-state politics, they decided to exclude Yugoslavia (Serbia and Montenegro) from their meeting. Despite appeals from the meetings of persons chairing UN human rights treaty bodies, endorsed by the General Assembly,[27]

---

[27] GA Res. 49/178, para. 6.

the meetings of state parties every two years do nothing to reinforce the Committee's efforts.

Some diplomats from states committed to the better observance of human rights fear that if the states parties were to get together more effectively, they might take decisions suiting the convenience of those states which dislike scrutiny of their records. They might try to disengage the ratchet and move it back. No governments have chosen to use the procedures for negotiating inter-state disputes which are available under the treaties. Most concentrate upon their relations with the Committee, and if sometimes they feel that they have been treated rather roughly, this is often because they have not studied the Committee's dealings with states in circumstances comparable to their own.[28]

F. Productivity

Among the six human rights treaty bodies the Committee is unique in exercising four functions: (a) examining reports; (b) reviewing implementation when reports are overdue; (c) deploying preventive procedures; and (d) issuing opinions on individual communications. How well is it managing?

As to the examination of reports, most of these are considered within six months of receipt unless the state requests deferment. The mandate of the Committee is more limited than that of the HRC, and the Committees established under the International Covenant on Economic, Social and Cultural Rights (ICESCR), the Convention on the Elimination of All Forms of Discrimination against Women (CEDAW) and the Convention on the Rights of the Child (CRC), so it should be able to consider more reports. But it also has, rather more than these other committees, to tackle issues on the frontier between law and politics which can excite much discussion. As to states overdue with their reports, many states respond to the review procedure by expediting the submission of overdue reports, while the governments of many states which fail to do so are currently in so poor a condition that they are quite unable to meet reporting requirements of any

---

[28] In 1986 the Committee considered a periodic report from Bulgaria at a time when that government was using force in its attempts to assimilate its Turkish minority. Because of the controversy, diplomats from some other missions attended the proceedings. Since that year the Committee has met only in Geneva. Mission staff rarely attend except in preparation for their own countries' appearance before the Committee.

kind. It may therefore be concluded that the Committee is fully in control of its reporting process. With respect to preventive procedures, it should be recalled that at the World Conference on Human Rights in 1993 there were complaints that the United Nations was stirred into action only after massive human rights abuses had taken place. The treaty bodies were identified as being unique in the UN system in their potential to exercise a preventive function. Since so many of the conflicts that have occasioned gross losses of human life have had an ethnic dimension, the Committee has a special responsibility. It is making slow but steady progress with its innovatory procedures. As to individual communications, these are a smaller part of the work of the Committee than of the HRC, while the ICESCR, CEDAW, and CRC Committees do not at present have any provision of this kind.

In addition the Committee's reporting cycle is laid down in the Convention and could be altered only by an amendment adopted by two-thirds of the states parties. By August 1997 only twenty-two states had formally accepted the amendments to article 8.6 adopted at the 1992 meeting of states parties (and which it is in their financial interest to accept). Treaty amendment is a very slow process.

A treaty body is effective to the degree to which it attains its objectives. It is efficient to the degree to which it attains its results with the minimum expenditure of resources. A treaty body's product in the examination of state reports consists of its concluding observations and the effect they have upon the reporting state's delegation in explaining the treaty's requirements and cultivating improved implementation within that state. Examples of petty inefficiencies are easily identified. At times members speak at excessive length. Some repeat the observations of colleagues, ask irrelevant questions or take time to supply information which does not contribute to the concluding observations. These could be reduced by improvements to working practices, but to some extent they are inherent in international organisations founded on the equality of states.

The Committee's members are conscious that if they cannot streamline their working methods, then either they will have to allow a backlog of unconsidered reports to accumulate or they will have to seek additional meeting time. Some present members might not be able to continue serving if there were three sessions per year instead of two, and they fear that any such change would have an unwelcome effect upon the range of persons available for nomination at election time. It has been suggested that one of the present regular sessions should be extended to four weeks, but many members already find a three-week session difficult. If the Committee, like its sibling committees, cannot improve its productivity by the further division of labour states might decide to reduce their workload by transferring some of their functions to professional staff.[29]

States may well expect the treaty bodies to coordinate their activities more closely and to promote efficiency as well as effectiveness. With an eye to this possibility and in the interests of the Committees themselves, the Committee has suggested 'that the meeting of persons chairing human rights treaty bodies might establish norms about the meeting times each treaty body needs to fulfil its mandate, and note whether individual treaty bodies meet norms of performance'.

G. A living instrument

The Committee is entering upon a new era which will require new decisions. As has been noted, the Convention had its origins in the particular concerns of the early 1960s but it need not be put into storage along with the International Convention on the Suppression and Punishment of the Crime of *Apartheid* and the International Convention Against *Apartheid* in Sports. The apartheid regimes in Southern Africa may have come to an end but the break-up of the former Yugoslavia and the current conflicts in the Great Lakes region of Africa show that discrimination on the basis of race, ethnic or national origin remains a threat to international order. 'Ethnic cleansing' is a new and complex horror. It is the task of the Committee, in dialogue with delegations, to see that the Convention is applied to mitigate new kinds of abuses of human rights.

---

[29] A small team of legally-qualified advocates-general could be appointed to the staff of the Office of the UN High Commissioner for Human Rights. On receipt of a state report the advocate-general would conduct a preliminary examination, correspond with the reporting state in order to clarify the issues which at present are the subject of oral questioning, and prepare a report for the treaty body. An eighteen-member treaty body would divide into three chambers for the purpose of examining state reports and would draft concluding observations for submission to a plenary meeting of the treaty body. Such a change would not require any amendment of treaties. It would initially require additional resources but there would no longer be any need for pre-sessional working parties. One session of a treaty body should be able to complete the examination of three times as many state reports, so there should be savings in the longer term. The judicial aspect of the role of committee members would be strengthened. For a survey of the chamber system employed in the reporting system under the European Social Charter, see the chapter by David Harris in this volume.

In 1993 the Committee expressed its concern about 'ethnic cleansing' in Bosnia and Herzegovina and that 'partition along ethnic lines in that country could encourage groups elsewhere who were unwilling to respect the territorial integrity of States . . . The Committee strongly supported the principle of multi-ethnic societies and States'.[30] In its General Recommendation XXI it emphasised that in accordance with the Declaration on Friendly Relations[31] none of its actions 'shall be construed as authorising or encouraging any action which would dismember or impair, totally or in part, the territorial integrity or political unity of sovereign and independent States'. 'Ethnic cleansing' is contrary to article 3 of the Convention which prohibits segregation. Article 3 applies both to state policies and to interpersonal behaviour, where however the issues are not always simple. For example, under English law when, on a parent's request, a child was removed from a school because there were too many immigrant pupils in the class, it was the moved child who was held to have been segregated.[32] In its General Recommendation XIX the Committee has advised that the prohibition in article 3 covers patterns of segregation that arise in residential districts and in schools as a result of preferences exercised by private persons. Such patterns, which are often taken for granted, are of increasing importance in industrial societies. The Committee's General Recommendation XXII draws the attention of states to the relevance of the Convention to the rights of refugees, while General Recommendation XXIII likewise outlines its relevance to the rights of indigenous peoples. A draft recommendation on criteria to be used in state reporting about minorities will be considered shortly.

The Convention's definition of racial discrimination is based on that to be found in the International Labour Organisation (ILO) Convention on Discrimination in Occupation and Employment.[33] It is well adapted to the regulation of relations in the workplace, as when deciding whether an individual has been treated less favourably on the ground of his or her ethnic origin, but it offers little guidance to its application in some of the circumstances which the Committee has to address.

---

[30] UN Doc. A/48/18 paras. 468–9.
[31] Declaration on Principles of International Law Concerning Friendly Relations and Co-operation of States in Accordance with the Charter of the United Nations (1970), GA Res. 2625.
[32] R. v. Cleveland County Council, The Times, 25 August 1992.
[33] 1958 ILO Convention (No. 111) on Discrimination (Occupation and Employment).

The problem in distinguishing a group based upon ethnic origin is that in practice most large groups that continue from one generation to another are distinguished on several dimensions, possibly including culture, language, religion, nationality and political interests as well as ethnic origin. In its General Recommendation VIII the Committee advised that the identification of persons as members of racial or ethnic groups 'shall . . . be based upon self-identification by the individual concerned'. Individuals in South Asia often identify themselves with groups that are known by proper names or by the names of religions or castes, rather than by the signs which distinguish ethnic groups in Africa, Europe or North America. The Government of India acknowledges that castes and tribes are social systems based on descent, but maintains that the Convention's use of 'descent' refers to 'race'. The Committee has taken a different view. Likewise, when the report of Bangladesh was considered in 1992, the Committee described groups in the Chittagong Hill Tracts as ethnic minorities. The representative of the government disputed the application of the Convention to his country's circumstances, maintaining that there could be no racial discrimination in Bangladesh 'since there was but one mixed race', making it a 'post-racial society'.[34]

In 1995 the Committee reported that, in several of the situations being considered under its procedures for prevention (notably the situations in Chechnya, Chiapas and Algeria), 'members were uncertain whether the ethnic elements in the apparent tensions were sufficient to bring the situation within the scope of the Convention. It was concluded that the Committee should first request further information from the State party and decide later whether the Convention had any bearing on the situation in question'.[35] There have been comparable arguments about whether the conflict in Israel is political or is influenced by differences in ethnic or national origin.

These two problems were combined in the recent contention of the leader of the delegation of Burundi when he insisted that the conflict in his country was political in origin, and not ethnic, because the political leaders responsible for it had been politically motivated. He maintained that the conflict had created 'artificial' ethnic groups which in their nature did not correspond to a scientific and biological definition of an ethnic group.[36]

---

[34] For the dialogue with Bangladesh, see Banton, *supra*, note 2, pp. 292–7.
[35] UN Doc. A/50/18 p. 6.   [36] UN Doc. CERD/C/SR 1238.

This argument touches on conceptual problems which as yet have not been clarified. Elsewhere it has been argued that the identification of 'direct discrimination' (purposive discrimination in the terms of the Convention's article 1.1) turns on motivation, whereas the availability of a remedy for 'indirect discrimination' (or 'discrimination in effect' in the terms of the Convention) turns on the objective characteristics of the protected class.[37] An ethnic group is founded upon a shared consciousness, not upon biological distinctiveness. To apply the Convention it is essential to focus on its definition of racial discrimination, and not on attempting to characterise conflicts. It will take some time before the implications of the definition adopted in 1965 are generally appreciated.

In the new era the Committee's task, in dialogue with states parties, will be to apply the Convention to circumstances that were not contemplated in the drafting process, and to do so without attempting to exercise any 'creeping jurisdiction'. The processes whereby issues are refined and decisions reached will continue to be central to the movement to extend the rule of law.

[37] M. Banton, *Discrimination*, Buckingham, 1994.

4

THE COMMITTEE ON THE ELIMINATION OF DISCRIMINATION AGAINST WOMEN AT THE CROSSROADS

MARA R. BUSTELO

A. Introduction

Among the treaty bodies set up to monitor the implementation of the key international human rights instruments, the Committee of the Convention on the Elimination of Discrimination against Women has long been the least visible one for the international human rights community. Having started its work in 1982, it is only since the mid-1990s that a number of developments have provided greater opportunities for the Committee to increase its impact and visibility both within and outside the United Nations human rights treaty system.

The Convention on the Elimination of All Forms of Discrimination against Women (CEDAW) was adopted by the General Assembly of the United Nations on 18 December 1979,[1] and entered into force on 3 September 1981. As of 9 December 1999, there were 165 states parties to the Convention,[2] making it the second most widely accepted international human rights treaty after the Convention on the Rights of the Child (CRC), whose own success could be seen as helping to set the scene for increased attention to less traditional areas of human rights concern.

---

[1] GA Res. 34/180, 1249 UNTS 13. For a discussion of the process leading to the adoption of the Convention see Noreen Burrows, 'The 1979 Convention on the Elimination of All Forms of Discrimination against Women', 32 *NethILR*, 1985, pp. 49–57. For a recent review of the content of the Convention, see Andrew Byrnes, 'The Convention on the Elimination of All Forms of Discrimination against Women', in *Human Rights of Women – International and African Perspectives*, (eds. W. Renteln, D. Gierycz, M. Nowak and G. Oberlietner), Zed Books, London, 1998.

[2] http://www.un.org/Depts/Treaty/ accessed on 18 December 1999.

The Committee on the Elimination of Discrimination against Women was established by the provisions of article 17 of the Convention. The Committee has twenty-three members, experts who serve in their personal capacity, although they are nominated and elected by states parties with due regard to equitable geographical distribution. A principle meant to guarantee the representation of different forms of civilisation and the principal legal systems, the political imperatives of elections based on such mechanisms have not spared the CEDAW Committee any more than any other UN expert body. In terms of ensuring a reasonable store of expertise among its members, the Committee enjoys the advantage of having the largest membership of the United Nations human rights treaty bodies; it should be pointed out that since its establishment all of its experts have been women, with a single exception.[3]

The main function of the Committee is the consideration of the reports submitted by states parties within one year of ratification or accession, and thereafter every four years or whenever the Committee requests.[4] The Committee can also formulate suggestions and general recommendations based on its examination of reports and information received from states parties.[5] Suggestions are usually directed at the United Nations system, and general recommendations to states parties. The Convention enables the Committee to invite United Nations specialised agencies to submit reports for its consideration, and these agencies are entitled to be represented during its sessions. There are no explicit provisions relating to participation by non-governmental organisations (NGOs).[6]

Of all the developments that may affect significantly the role and functions of the Committee, it is important to keep in mind that the Convention itself made no provision for a communications procedure. However, on the basis of work by an open-ended working group of the Commission on the Status of Women (CSW) which met annually from 1996 to 1999, an Optional Protocol was adopted by the Commission on 12 March 1999

---

[3] The exception is Mr Johan Nordenfelt, Sweden, who served on the Committee from 1982 to 1984.
[4] CEDAW, article 18.   [5] CEDAW, article 21.
[6] CEDAW, article 22. For a more detailed discussion of the ways in which the Committee has interpreted these provisions, see below the sections dealing with the relationship with specialised agencies and bodies and with NGOs.

and by the General Assembly on 6 October 1999.[7] It provides both for the submission of individual complaints to the Committee and for a procedure under which the Committee can inquire into serious and systematic violations of the Convention. The Optional Protocol requires ten ratifications in order to enter into force. That event will begin a marked expansion of the Committee's current role.

The rest of this chapter considers the unique characteristics of the CEDAW Committee, as well as approaches that could increase the capacity of the Committee to identify measures required to eliminate discrimination against women and provide guidance to states parties in this respect, and to monitor the implementation of those measures. Many of the approaches discussed are already embodied in the practices of other treaty bodies. The Committee is now seriously considering some of these practices, which have been frequently addressed since its twelfth session under a regular agenda item entitled 'ways and means of expediting the work of the Committee'.[8] However, it is important that it continue to examine its working methods critically. That the Committee started introducing a significant amount of changes from the mid-1990s provides clear illustration of the improved perspectives for significant change. The Committee would be well advised to continue to set aside an even more significant part of future sessions to the discussion of improvements in its working methods.

B. Location and servicing

During the years since its first session in 1982, the CEDAW Committee has been seen both by commentators and by its own members as the 'poor relation' of the treaty bodies, left outside the mainstream of human rights work within the United Nations and neglected by the international human rights community. The CEDAW Committee, whose secretariat is not provided by the Office of the High Commissioner for Human Rights, has, unlike all other treaty bodies, always been serviced both technically and

---

[7] GA Res. 54/4. The text is contained in an annex to the resolution. The Optional Protocol was opened for signature on 10 December 1999.

[8] Report of the Committee on the Elimination of Discrimination against Women (twelfth session), General Assembly, Official Records, Forty-eighth session, Supplement No. 38 (A/48/38), para. 632.

substantively by the Division for the Advancement of Women, which also services the Commission on the Status of Women, the intergovernmental body which drafted the Convention. Also, unlike other treaty bodies, the Committee's sessions have never been held at the Centre for Human Rights (now the Office of the UN High Commissioner for Human Rights) in Geneva. Until 1993, when the Division for the Advancement of Women was relocated to United Nations Headquarters in New York from the United Nations Offices in Vienna, the Committee met alternately in Vienna and New York. Since its thirteenth session in 1994, Committee sessions have always been held in New York; this dual geographical shift has assisted the work of the Committee, increasing its visibility within the United Nations system.

The distinction that has the clearest impact on the work of the Committee is that, alone among the human rights treaties, the Convention sets a specific limit on the Committee's meeting time. Article 20 provides that the Committee shall normally meet annually for no more than two weeks. The rapid rate of ratification proved that expansion of that meeting time was unavoidable; from 1990, a pre-sessional working group of the Committee started meeting to review periodic reports[9] and shortly afterwards the General Assembly started to allow the Committee to meet on an exceptional basis for an extra week per annum. In an effort to eliminate the need for such continuous exceptions, the states parties to the Convention adopted in May 1995 an amendment to article 20, providing that the CEDAW Committee shall normally meet annually but that the duration of its meetings would be determined by a meeting of states parties, subject to the approval of the General Assembly. Entry into force of the amendment is subject to its acceptance by a two-thirds majority of states parties.[10] By late 1996, less than ten states parties had accepted the amendment and, at its fifty-first session in 1996, the General Assembly approved another increase in additional meeting time for the Committee (for an interim period, pending entry into force of the amendment), allowing it to meet

---

[9] See Report of the Committee on the Elimination of Discrimination against Women (ninth session), General Assembly, Official Records, forty-fifth session, Supplement No. 38 and corrigendum (A/45/38 and Corr. 1), paras. 28–31.

[10] A/Res/50/202 (1995), see Report of the Secretary-General to the General Assembly on the Convention on the Elimination of All Forms of Discrimination against Women, including the text of the proposed amendment to article 20 of the Convention, UN Doc. A/50/346.

for two three-week sessions annually, each preceded by a one-week pre-sessional working group.[11]

The different servicing arrangements for the Committee, and its geographical separation from the other United Nations human rights treaty bodies, has meant that the Committee's jurisprudential approach and practices have developed, to a large extent, with little reference to the approach and practices of other treaty bodies. While this is not of itself necessarily problematic, the Committee has in practice been harshly judged for being out of step with its sister bodies, with critics suggesting that its intellectual and practical development has been slow in comparison. The Committee itself has been highly sensitive to these charges. From 1992, it argued that its sessions should be held in Geneva, and should be serviced by the then Centre for Human Rights, so that it could interact more closely with the other treaty bodies.[12] The Committee's views in this regard were supported by the meeting of persons chairing human rights treaty bodies.[13] Nonetheless, in early 1996, the Secretary-General of the United Nations informed the Committee's chairperson that, although he had sympathy with the considerations that had motivated the Committee's views, it would continue to be serviced by the Division for the Advancement of Women so as to provide a strong and unified programme for the advancement of women within the United Nations. At the same time, the Secretary-General assured the Committee that renewed efforts would be made to ensure close collaboration between the Division for the Advancement of Women and the then Centre for Human Rights.[14]

Although the decision of the Secretary-General with regard to the CEDAW Secretariat has not been the last word on the matter,[15] it seems clear that the Committee will continue to be serviced by the Division for

---

[11] GA Res. 51/66. By late 1999 only twenty-two states had accepted the amendment.

[12] Decision 14/II, Report of the Committee on the Elimination of Discrimination against Women (fourteenth session), General Assembly, Official Records, fiftieth session, Supplement No. 38 (A/48/38).

[13] Report of the Fifth Meeting of Persons Chairing Human Rights Treaty Bodies, A/49/537.

[14] Secretary-General's letter to the chairperson of the CEDAW Committee, 8 February 1996, quoted in 'Ways and Means of Expediting the Work of the Committee', Report by the Secretariat, CEDAW/C/1997/5, para. 3.

[15] The seventh meeting of persons chairing the human rights treaty bodies regretted that the Committee's wishes had not been complied with and noted that they 'share the Committee's view that the Committee cannot function properly if its secretariat is physically separated from the secretariat of all the other human rights treaty bodies': A/51/482, para. 46.

the Advancement of Women for the foreseeable future. However, clarification of this issue and the strengthening of the CEDAW Secretariat during 1996 through the establishment of a Women's Rights Unit in the Division, combined with the increase in the Committee's meeting time, has opened the door to a strengthened role for the Committee. The adoption of an Optional Protocol to the Convention in October 1999 enhances these possibilities.

C. Consideration of reports

The primary responsibility of the Committee is the consideration of states parties' reports. By August 1999, and after twenty-one sessions, it had considered initial reports from 101 states parties, second reports from seventy-one, third reports from forty-six, and fourth periodic reports from sixteen states parties. In addition it has considered five reports on an exceptional basis. At the same time, there were in August 1999 forty-nine reports submitted by states parties awaiting consideration by the Committee. As with the other human rights treaty bodies, non-reporting is a significant problem, and 226 reports were already overdue by August 1999. Of these, fifty-three states parties had yet to submit an initial report; as of August 1999, seventy-four reports were more than five years overdue, including twenty-nine initial reports.[16]

During its lifetime, the Committee has considered the reports of up to thirteen states parties per session. In many cases, states parties have chosen to put forward more than one report for review. At its fourteenth session in 1995, the CEDAW Committee decided that consideration of an initial report required up to three meetings, each of three hours duration. It also decided that each periodic report, which had already been considered by the pre-sessional working group, should be reviewed over a meeting and a half. Accordingly, it decided that it would review implementation of the Convention in up to a maximum of eight countries at each of its sessions, although these states parties could put forward more than one report for

---

[16] 'Status of submission and consideration of reports submitted by States parties under Article 18 of the Convention on the Elimination of All Forms of Discrimination against Women as at 1 August 1999', in Report of the Committee on the Elimination of Discrimination against Women (twentieth and twenty-first sessions), General Assembly, Official Records, fifty-third session, Supplement No. 38 (A/54/38/Rev.1), Annex V.

combined review. From 1995, the Committee has scheduled the reports of eight states parties for consideration at each session, though during the fifteenth and sixteenth sessions, in 1996 and 1997, the Committee considered a ninth country on an exceptional basis, and only seven countries were considered at the twentieth and twenty-first sessions in 1999.

The Committee's decision to limit the consideration of reports to eight states parties per session, despite the growing backlog of reports awaiting consideration, attracted criticism from several states parties, a number of which openly suggested that the backlog was more the result of poor working methods than of the limited meeting time of the Committee. Some of these critics suggest that the Committee's wide interpretation of its mandate to include, *inter alia*, discussion of the cycle of United Nations World Conferences, has diverted it from its primary task of report consideration. Conscious of these criticisms, and concerned that the General Assembly's approval of its additional meeting time might be fragile, the Committee scheduled ten reports for consideration at its seventeenth and eighteenth sessions in July 1997 and January 1998 respectively. The Committee revisited this decision during its seventeenth session in July 1997, agreeing that although a list of ten states parties would be proposed, it would normally take up only eight for review at each session. It is to be noted that even if the Committee were to consider ten reports per session and even if no further reports were received, on the basis of two sessions per year it would take the Committee roughly ten years to work through the backlog of reports awaiting consideration, assuming states parties were precluded from presenting combined reports. While it might be possible for the Committee to reduce its backlog by considering more reports at each session, this would inevitably affect the quality of report review. Most states parties' reports are lengthy and detailed and, in most cases, the Committee is also provided with extensive updating information by states parties shortly before the consideration of their reports, or during the meetings at which the report is reviewed.

While the constructive dialogue between the Committee and states parties should be detailed enough to provide the state party with sufficient guidance for the practical implementation of the Convention, it is crucial for the Committee to consider methods of reducing the report backlog. First, because the eventual entry into force of the Optional Protocol allowing complaints under the Convention will place the Committee under even greater time constraints. Second, because the backlog also serves as a disincentive to those states parties whose reports are overdue. Many states parties are well aware that there may be a wait of up to three years before the Committee considers their reports, and that it will, at that time, be necessary to submit additional information to ensure that their reports are updated.

Like some of the other human rights treaty bodies, the Committee has not developed effective strategies to address the problem of its backlog. At its sixteenth session in 1997, it took a formal decision encouraging states parties to combine up to two reports.[17] During discussions leading to this decision, several Committee members objected to states parties combining more than two reports, although it had previously considered consolidations of up to three reports, including the combined initial, second and third periodic reports of Saint Vincent and the Grenadines which had been considered by the Committee during that same session. These members suggested that although combined reports would lead to reduced backlog, states parties would largely be evading their reporting obligation.

However, other members of the Committee have proposed increasing efforts to combine reports; for example, when states parties' reports are selected for consideration at subsequent sessions, they could also be invited to submit the report selected as well as their next periodic report, if that report is already or nearly overdue.[18] This approach would not only reduce the Committee's backlog, but also address the need to provide up-to-date information, particularly in the cases where domestic conditions have changed significantly since the preparation and submission of the report. Updates are usually extensive and often as substantial and substantive as the states parties' reports. An additional problem is that, although generally prepared in written form, the updating material is introduced to the Committee by an oral presentation of the representative of the relevant state party at the time its report is introduced. Thus, although updates usually contain vital and important information, they do not become United Nations documents, which means that the distribution and accessibility

---

[17] Report of the Committee on the Elimination of Discrimination against Women (sixteenth and seventeenth sessions), General Assembly, Official Records, Fifty-second Session, Supplement No. 38 (A/52/38/Rev.1), Part I, Decision 16 (III).

[18] 'Ways and Means . . .', *supra*, note 14, para. 24.

of the information they contain rarely reaches beyond members of the Committee and the Secretariat.[19]

Implementation of this proposal, which essentially means that the update usually necessary would become the state party's next periodic report, would reduce some of the Committee's backlog and would also reduce the workload of states parties; it may be facilitated by the 1999 change in the timing of the pre-session. More fundamental changes in the Committee's approach to reporting will however be needed to enable it to deal with the backlog of reports and still ensure that its review of states parties' reports is sufficiently rigorous to promote full and effective implementation of the Convention.

At their eighth and ninth meetings in 1997 and 1998, the chairpersons of human rights treaty bodies suggested that, while the current practice of requiring comprehensive initial reports from states parties should be maintained, periodic reports could be focused and address only a limited range of issues which would be identified by the relevant Committee in advance of the preparation of the report.[20] The chairpersons pointed out that this would reduce the need for lengthy reports, minimise duplication, help eliminate long delays between the submission and the examination of reports, enable problem areas to be dealt with in depth and facilitate follow-up of concluding comments, both for the state party and for the Committee concerned. The CEDAW Committee will consider the practice of other Committees in this regard. Its pre-sessional working group could identify a limited number of specific issues, pertinent to the individual state party. A report would be requested in relation to these issues, and the Committee would then conduct its dialogue on the basis of that detailed, but targeted or tailored report. The burden imposed on states parties would be reduced, making way for a clearer focus for the dialogue between the Committee and states parties, which would allow more in-depth consideration of areas of particular interest or concern. This clearer and

[19] In his final report on enhancing the long-term effectiveness of the United Nations human rights treaty system, Philip Alston drew attention to the problem of what he called 'ephemeral and unrecorded documentation' which is effectively lost: 'Effective Functioning of Bodies established pursuant to United Nations Human Rights Instruments', E/CN.4/ 1997/74, paras. 55 and 56.

[20] Report of the Eighth Meeting of Persons Chairing the Human Rights Treaty Bodies, A/52/507, para. 35; Report of the Ninth Meeting of Persons Chairing the Human Rights Treaty Bodies, A/53/125, paras. 30 and 31. The Human Rights Committee is considering a similar approach: CCPR/C/61/MET.1, paras. 18–25.

more tailored focus would also avoid the perception that the Committee has a list of issues that it discusses with all states parties, irrespective of their level of development or specific domestic problems. The response to the list of questions and issues identified at the pre-session could be counted, if the information provided is adequate, as the next report; the responses would then be translated and become an official UN document, facilitating distribution and availability of the information provided.

A more targeted approach should be facilitated by the CEDAW Committee's decision to adopt the practice of the Committee on Economic Social and Cultural Rights and the Committee on the Rights of the Child whose pre-sessional working groups meet at the session prior to that at which the state party's report will be considered.[21] For years, the pre-session group of the Committee on the Elimination of Discrimination against Women, which has the task of preparing a list of issues and questions to guide the review of periodic reports only, met immediately before the session at which the reports are considered by the full Committee. States parties presenting periodic reports were, therefore, in the unenviable position of preparing responses to a large number of questions posed by the pre-sessional working group on reports which were to be considered by the Committee one or two weeks after the questions had been received. Indeed, states parties were sometimes faced with up to one hundred and twenty, usually detailed, questions to respond to in the presentation of their reports during the session.

At its sixteenth session in 1997, the Committee started considering a proposal to have its pre-sessional working group convened at the end of the session prior to the one at which selected states parties would report, in order to provide states parties with the Committee's questions well in advance.[22] Practical difficulties made it impossible for the Committee to move swiftly to this pattern of work. At its eighteenth session, in January 1998, it again suggested such a change, identifying the twentieth session in January 1999 as the session at which this change would be initiated, and at

---

[21] In its *Overview of the Reporting Procedures* (CRC/C/33, 24 October 1994), the CRC points out 'the principal purpose of the working group is to identify in advance the most important issues to be discussed with representatives of States. The intent is to give advance notice to the States parties of the principal issues which might arise in the examination of their reports . . . the possibility for government representatives to prepare in advance their answers to some of the principal questions is likely to make the discussion more constructive' (para. 8).

[22] Report of the CEDAW Committee (sixteenth and seventeenth sessions), *supra*, note 17, Part I, sixteenth session, Suggestion 16 (II).

the nineteenth session, it decided that the pre-sessional working group for the twenty-first session would accordingly meet as a third working group during and after the twentieth session.[23]

The move to this work pattern will help to give the Committee a frame-work in which to address issues that, in view of the individual circum-stances of each state party, pose the greatest challenge to implementation of the Convention. The Committee must, however, exploit the possibilities created by this new pattern of work. Some critics, including several Com-mittee members, have suggested that the practice of posing many detailed questions to states parties, rather than a limited number of deep and focused questions, fails to identify the diverse factors that impede imple-mentation of the Convention in individual states parties. Maintenance of such a practice would mean that the time lag between the pre-session and the consideration of the state party's report will only provide more time for the state party to prepare detailed responses. During the twentieth session, in 1999, the Committee did recommend to the pre-sessional working group that it concentrate on major issues and trends and that it limit the total number of issues and questions identified; the pre-session working group and the Committee agreed to set a limited number of questions and issues (under fifty). The Committee also recommended that the list of issues and questions be sent to states parties within two weeks of the con-clusion of the working group and that they be encouraged to submit written answers no later than four weeks after their receipt.[24] Such changes in approach, if successfully implemented, could have a significant impact on the work of the Committee.

Any guidelines relating to the pre-sessional working group would need to address the obligations of the other members of the Committee with regard to its work. The pre-sessional working group of the Committee consists of four members, each drawn from a different regional group. Up until its seventeenth session, each Committee member was required to submit questions relating to the periodic reports to be considered prior to the meeting of the pre-sessional working group. These questions were compiled by the Secretariat into a report designed to assist the working

---

[23] Report of the Committee on the Elimination of Discrimination against Women (eight-eenth and nineteenth sessions), General Assembly Official Records, fifty-third session, Supplement No. 38 (A/53/38/Rev. 1), Part I, eighteenth session, Suggestion 18/I, and Part II nineteenth session, Decision 19/1.

[24] Report of the CEDAW Committee (twentieth and twenty-first sessions), *supra*, note 16, Part I, twentieth session, paras. 409–14.

group as it drew up the list of issues and questions. At its seventeenth session, the Committee decided that, while all members of the Committee should feel free to submit questions, a group of three Committee members, including the designated country rapporteur, would be assigned primary responsibility for the preparation of questions with regard to each report, to assist the pre-sessional working group's deliberations. In addition, each country rapporteur was requested to submit a written statement introducing the main issues relating to implementation of the Convention in the state party whose report she had been assigned to study.[25] This change, which represents a clear division of responsibility amongst members, was expected to provide improved conditions for consideration of reports. However, the approach may need to be revisited now that the pre-sessional working group is meeting at the session prior to the one scheduled for consideration of reports. Having reached that point, the Committee examined the approach of other treaty bodies, including the Human Rights Committee, where the country rapporteur assumes the lead responsibility for providing a draft list of issues and questions to the pre-sessional working group. Indeed, the Committee requested that the Secretariat provide such draft lists in advance of the meeting of the pre-sessional working group to the country rapporteur, and experience proved the value of this approach.[26]

Currently, and unlike the practice of other treaty bodies, the pre-sessional working group reviews periodic reports only. It does not review initial reports, in order to encourage a relationship of trust between the Committee and a new state party which the Committee believes might otherwise be jeopardised by the pre-sessional working group's review of its initial report. Some observers question whether the pre-sessional working group's review has such potential to imperil the relationship between the Committee and the state party and point out that other human rights treaty bodies take a different view. The CEDAW Committee might need to reconsider this question, though if the pre-sessional working group's review does become more issue-based and targeted, the relationship between a new state party and the Committee could be more vulnerable to the impact of such a review.

---

[25] Report of the CEDAW Committee (sixteenth and seventeenth sessions), *supra*, note 17, para. 469.

[26] See Decision 19/III, in Report of the CEDAW Committee (eighteenth and nineteenth sessions), *supra*, note 23, Part II nineteenth session.

The CEDAW Committee hesitated longer than other treaty bodies over the adoption of a structured pattern for review of states parties' reports during its meetings. Initial reports are considered over a period of up to three meetings, with the state party providing an often lengthy introduction. Led by the country rapporteur, individual Committee members make general observations on the report and orally pose questions from the floor. The state party responds to these questions at a meeting several days later during the same session, again orally, but usually also providing written answers for the Committee. Committee members are at liberty to ask follow-up questions, to which the state party usually undertakes to respond in its next report. As periodic reports have been reviewed by the pre-session group and questions have already been posed by this group, these reports are reviewed over a shorter period of up to one and a half meetings of the Committee. The state party orally addresses the questions that have been posed by the pre-sessional working group, but, again, usually provides its responses also in written form. Committee members are free to pose further oral questions to states parties submitting periodic reports. Generally, a number of these are briefly responded to by representatives of the state party.

Beyond posing questions based on successive articles of the Convention, and requiring the Committee member designated as the country rapporteur to introduce the report in a ten-minute closed session, the Committee has developed no formal *modus operandi* for constructive dialogue with states parties, although there is some *ad hoc* specialisation among Committee members. Limited efforts in this direction include the decision, taken at its eighteenth session in 1998, to adopt the suggestion of the eighth chairperson's meeting[27] that, in the interests of time, the task of expressing welcome and appreciation to representatives of reporting states should be entrusted solely to the chairperson of the Committee and not repeated by other members.[28] The Committee also agreed that greater efforts should be made by members to avoid replication of questions posed to representatives by other members. The current structure of the dialogue appears unsatisfactory to both Committee members and states parties. Detailed questions are posed, but there is a significant amount of repetition and a limited number of pointed questions or targeted suggestions for future action. In particular, the current practice for review of initial reports, when

[27] A/53/507, para. 57.
[28] Report of the CEDAW Committee (eighteenth and nineteenth sessions), *supra*, note 23, Part I, eighteenth session, para. 439.

Committee members take up to one and a half meetings posing oral questions, which are then answered by the representatives of the state party some days later, appears to provide limited opportunity for real dialogue. At its twentieth session, the Committee did recommend that states parties presenting periodic reports should be prepared to engage in open dialogue with the Committee, including providing immediate answers to questions.[29]

As for the pre-sessional working group, the review of reports by the Committee itself would be enhanced if the Committee were to succeed in increasing its focus on country-specific issues and problems and if it were to develop a formalised practice of specialisation. At its sixteenth session in January 1997, the Committee agreed that members should identify those areas in which they wished to concentrate at the next session. Members who wished to specialise in the same area would be encouraged to communicate with each other prior to the following session so that thematic questions in their designated area could be developed.[30] In practice, there has been little evidence of efforts to implement this procedure.

Strategic preparation by the Committee for the review of each report is also needed. The country rapporteurs nominated by the Committee to focus on particular states parties' reports should be made widely known. Efforts are being made by the Secretariat and others to provide them with assistance to identify the key issues relating to Convention implementation in the countries to which they are assigned. Building on the approach adopted by the seventeenth session for review of periodic reports, other Committee members might be assigned to prepare specific articles for review, and requested to submit these questions in advance to a sub-group of the Committee. This sub-group could review the questions for focus and harmonisation prior to formal consideration of the report by the Committee.

The Committee could build on its practice of requiring the country rapporteur to present an introductory report on the condition of women in the relevant state party to the Committee in private session. Following this introduction, time should be devoted to the preparation of a strategy for constructive dialogue, with individual members raising issues they wish to discuss. The Committee should also consider the approach of the Human Rights Committee, and impose a time limit on the interventions of

---

[29] Report of the CEDAW Committee (twentieth and twenty-first sessions), *supra*, note 16, Part I, twentieth session, para. 408.

[30] Report of the CEDAW Committee (sixteenth and seventeenth sessions), *supra*, note 17, para. 371.

members, as it has already done for the oral presentation of states parties updating their written reports, where the Committee recommended at its twentieth session that sixty minutes should be the limit.[31]

The Committee should also consider its current reporting guidelines, which are too vague and general, and could mislead states parties into thinking that a descriptive review of legislation and policy is sufficient. In this regard, the Committee could consider the extensive guidelines formulated by the Committee on the Rights of the Child, particularly for periodic reports, which aim to provide detailed advice to reporting states.[32] At its sixteenth session in January 1997, the Committee did decide that guidelines should be formulated to guide states parties on the oral presentation of periodic reports and that these should become part of the Committee's overall reporting guidelines,[33] but there has been no progress in the preparation of the proposed guidelines.

D. Country rapporteurs and concluding comments

The CEDAW Committee started formulating concluding comments in respect of the reports of states parties at its thirteenth session in 1994. This practice was introduced by the Committee to provide concrete suggestions for the implementation of the Convention, to make its work more accessible to government policy-makers, civil servants and non-governmental organisations, and to bring its practice into line with other human rights treaty bodies. The procedures initially set for the formulation of concluding comments were reflected in the report of the Committee's thirteenth session.[34]

---

[31] Report of the CEDAW Committee (twentieth and twenty-first sessions), *supra*, note 16, Part I, twentieth session, para. 407.

[32] CRC/C/58, 20 November 1996.

[33] Report of the CEDAW Committee (sixteenth and seventeenth sessions), *supra*, note 17, para. 370.

[34] Report of the Committee on the Elimination of Discrimination against Women, (thirteenth session) General Assembly, Official Records, forty-ninth session, Supplement No. 38 (A/49/38), paras. 813–16. At the time, the procedure relied on the designation by the chairperson, for each report, of two members of the Committee to draft concluding comments to be considered for adoption by the Committee. To the extent possible, at least one of those rapporteurs are to be from the region of the reporting state. For second and subsequent reports, they should consult with the members of the pre-sessional working group. The drafts are to be considered in closed meetings of the Committee scheduled periodically during the session, but at least one per week, and, once agreed, the concluding comments are to be incorporated into the Committee's report on the consideration of the state party's report.

In its decision 15/III,[35] the Committee agreed to revise the structure of its report, again to bring it into line with those of other treaty bodies. Dispensing with a lengthy description of the constructive dialogue, the Committee agreed that the presentation of states parties' reports would be reflected in the report of the Committee by a brief summary of the state party's presentation, followed by the Committee's concluding comments and recommendations. The concluding comments, accordingly, represent the most visible output of the Committee. Their visibility has been enhanced by the establishment of the web sites of the Division for the Advancement of Women and the Office of the High Commissioner for Human Rights, both of which incorporate comprehensive coverage of the work of the CEDAW Committee.[36]

The Committee's concluding comments, which average four to six pages in length, are adopted in closed meetings. They largely follow the pattern of the early concluding observations of the Human Rights Committee and initially consisted of five sections, recently merged into four: introduction; positive aspects, addressed in the order of the articles of the Convention; factors and difficulties affecting implementation of the Convention; and a section identifying the principal areas of concern in the state party, addressed in order of importance. The final part of the comments, now merged with the section on concerns, deals with recommendations and suggestions and aims to provide concrete suggestions from the Committee with regard to the problems identified in the comments.[37]

The quality of the CEDAW Committee's concluding comments reflects the quality of the review of states parties' reports and the ability of the Committee to identify strengths and weaknesses in Convention implementation in individual states parties in a limited amount of time. At present, the Secretariat prepares a summary of the state party's introduction of the report, which it sends to that state party for comment. It also provides

---

[35] Report of the Committee on the Elimination of Discrimination against Women (fifteenth session), General Assembly, Official Records, fifty-first session, Supplement No. 38 (A/51/38), p. 1.

[36] Division for the Advancement of Women, http://www.un.org/womenwatch/daw; Office of the High Commissioner for Human Rights, http://www.unhchr.ch.

[37] Decision 16/1 of the Sixteenth Session: Report of the CEDAW Committee (sixteenth and seventeenth sessions), *supra*, note 17, Part I, sixteenth session. The Committee revised the format of its concluding comments at its seventeenth session, ibid., Part II, seventeenth session, para. 471.

the Committee member who is charged with the preparation of the draft concluding comments with points, arranged in the Committee's agreed format for comments, which she might wish to consider in the preparation of the comments. The designated country rapporteur then prepares the comments in close consultation with the main rapporteur. The introduction to the comments may be based on the information the country rapporteur has gained through a study of the country prior to the session, but the balance of the comments reflects the views of the Committee expressed during the presentation of the report.

The importance of high quality concluding comments, incorporating specific recommendations has been emphasised in various fora.[38] Although the concluding comments of the Committee are improving in quality, they remain uneven in length, detail and calibre. Partly to address concerns over the need to increase coherence and specificity, and partly as a response to similar pressures throughout the treaty bodies, the Committee decided, at its nineteenth session in 1998, to follow the emerging trend in other treaty bodies of combining concerns with suggestions and recommendations.[39] At that session the Committee also adopted a new set of procedures and format to be followed for the elaboration of concluding comments, basically continuing to rely on the role of the country rapporteur, with the support of the Secretariat, for the preparation of the concluding comments, while following a consistent format in the content of each section and striving to ensure some consistency and balance between the concluding comments adopted for different states parties.[40]

As concluding comments are adopted at the session during which the report is considered, their formulation is governed by strict time constraints, which intensify as the session progresses. The content of the comments is also governed by the information available to Committee members, and particularly to the country rapporteur. Quality could be enhanced by greater involvement of the Secretariat in the drafting of the comments, as well as by participation of NGOs and other UN system entities. Draft comments could also be prepared by the country rapporteur

---

[38] Report of the Ninth Meeting, *supra*, note 20, para. 32.

[39] This approach was approved by the ninth meeting of persons chairing the human rights treaty bodies, ibid.

[40] Report of the CEDAW Committee (eighteenth and nineteenth sessions), *supra*, note 23, Part II, nineteenth session, para. 397.

prior to the session at which the report is considered, as long as careful attention is given to the need to make adjustments in the light of the presentation of the report and its review by the Committee. There is no reason in principle, however, for the Committee to adopt its comments at the session at which the country report is considered. Indeed, the concluding comments relating to the reports of several states parties considered at its thirteenth session were adopted at the fourteenth session, although some concern was raised on this court by both the states parties involved and the Committee's Secretariat. If the standard pattern were, however, preparation and discussion of the concluding comments at the session at which the report was considered with a view to adoption at the next session, comments could be of improved quality and oversight by the Committee of state party implementation would be enhanced. The state party might be invited to reappear before the Committee at that session both to receive the concluding comments and to address any questions left over from its reporting at the prior session.

In the context of limited meeting time, and given the accumulating backlog of reports to be reviewed, resource constraints will probably make the adoption of such an approach impossible, given its budgetary implications. As another alternative, the pre-session working group, which will be meeting at the session prior to that at which the report will be considered, could be charged with the preparation of draft concluding comments for both initial and periodic reports. It could be assisted in its task by the Secretariat, NGOs and others.

E. General Recommendations

By its twentieth session in 1999, the CEDAW Committee had formulated twenty-four general recommendations since its establishment. Early general recommendations were short and narrowly focused. As the Committee developed, they became more sophisticated and lengthy, with the Committee in 1991 deciding on a long-term programme of work to produce general recommendations on substantive matters covered by the Convention. Since that decision the Committee has adopted four substantial General Recommendations – General Recommendation No. 19 (1992) concerning violence against women, General Recommendation No. 21 (1994) on equality in marriage and family relations; General Recommendation No. 23 (1997) relating to women in public life; and General Recommendation

No. 24 (1999) on women's health.[41] The General Recommendation concerning women and health could not be finalised at its nineteenth session in June/July 1998, partly because the Committee chose to devote some of the available time to the adoption of a statement on the issue of reservations as a contribution to the commemoration of the fiftieth anniversary of the Universal Declaration of Human Rights.[42]

The CEDAW Committee's production of general recommendations has been hampered by the limitation on its meeting time and the long period between sessions. As a result, its more ambitious recommendations have taken up to three years to produce. At its seventeenth session in July 1997, the Committee adopted a new, more structured approach to the preparation of General Recommendations, allowing it to take advantage of the expertise of members and the input possible from the UN system and NGOs. The new process consists of three stages. First, a general discussion and exchange of views on the subject of the proposed general recommendation takes place at an open meeting of the Committee. Specialised agencies and other United Nations bodies, as well as non-governmental organisations, are encouraged to participate and to submit informal background papers. Second, a member of the Committee and the Secretariat draw the results of the discussion into an initial draft. This draft is discussed at the next session by a working group of the Committee, which is entitled to invite resource persons and NGOs to participate in its discussions. A revised draft is compiled and distributed to all experts before the next session, which considers the draft with a view to its approval.[43]

The CEDAW Committee's new approach to the formulation of general recommendations, which encourages wide UN system and NGO input, promises to improve the quality of general recommendations. The Committee's general recommendations until 1997 were more programmatic

---

[41] General recommendation 23 (sixteenth session), Report of the CEDAW Committee (sixteenth and seventeenth sessions), *supra*, note 17, pp. 61–70; General recommendation 24 (twentieth session), Report of the CEDAW Committee (twentieth and twenty-first sessions), *supra*, note 16, pp. 3–7.

[42] The Committee's statement built on its own views as reflected in General Recommendations Nos. 20 and 21, as well as on the concerns expressed by other treaty bodies, the International Law Commission and the World Conference on Human Rights, held in Vienna in 1993, and Fourth World Conference on Women, held in Beijing in 1995. See Report of the Committee (eighteenth and nineteenth sessions), *supra*, note 23, Part II nineteenth session, paras. 1–25.

[43] Report of the CEDAW Committee (sixteenth and seventeenth sessions), *supra*, note 17, para. 480, p. 127.

than the general comments/recommendations of its sister bodies. At this point in its development, the Committee had to consider whether its general recommendations should be more in line with those of other treaty bodies, which elaborate the content of convention norms. The Committee should also review its existing recommendations, and perhaps, like other treaty bodies, including the Human Rights Committee, revise some of its early recommendations or combine several recommendations that address similar themes.

The ninth chairpersons' meeting[44] suggested that all treaty bodies consider drawing on the general recommendations and comments of other human rights treaty bodies and even that they consider issuing joint recommendations on relevant areas.[45] This would ensure consistency of interpretation of human rights obligations across treaty bodies and ensure that the gender mainstreaming mandate of the Vienna and Beijing Conferences is fully pursued where the treaty bodies are concerned. In line with these suggestions, the CEDAW Committee adopted at its nineteenth session a statement on 'the indivisibility of civil and political rights and economic, social and cultural rights and the centrality of gender awareness to the enjoyment of those rights', for 'consideration and possible adoption' by at least two of the other treaty bodies, the Human Rights Committee and the Committee on Economic, Social and Cultural Rights.[46]

F. Mainstreaming the work of the CEDAW Committee

The Committee's status as the 'poor relation' of the treaty bodies has been aggravated by its isolation from other international human rights bodies. Its reports are submitted through the Economic and Social Council (ECOSOC) to the General Assembly and transmitted to the Commission on the Status of Women for information;[47] but the Commission has only very recently taken account of the Committee's work in its own programme.[48]

---

[44] Report of the Ninth Meeting, *supra*, note 20, para. 34.   [45] Ibid., paras. 35 and 36.

[46] See Report of the CEDAW Committee (eighteenth and nineteenth sessions), *supra*, note 23, Part II nineteenth session, paras. 407–8.

[47] CEDAW, article 21.

[48] It is of interest to note that at its fiftieth anniversary celebrations on 10 March 1997, the Secretary-General pointed to the drafting of the Convention as the crowning achievement of the Commission, a sentiment agreed with by all other speakers at the event. At the following session, CSW made decisions relating to CEDAW. See, for example, agreed

There has been no institutionalised mechanism of cooperation and co-ordination between the Committee and the Commission on Human Rights and its Sub-Commission on Prevention of Discrimination and Protection of Minorities. Except for the chairpersons' meetings, in which the Committee has participated since the chairpersons' second meeting, there has been no formal mechanism of coordination between it and the other treaty bodies and no formal connections with the non-conventional human rights mechanisms. Awareness of the need to step up efforts to mainstream gender issues into the work of other human rights bodies led, among other initiatives, to the holding of an informal discussion on the issue during the 1998 session of the Commission on Human Rights and of a workshop in May 1999.[49]

In the absence of formal linkages with the intergovernmental, treaty-based and non-conventional human rights mechanisms, *ad hoc* strategies have been initiated. The chairperson of the CEDAW Committee usually attends at least some of the sessions of the Commission on the Status of Women and the Commission on Human Rights and has occasionally attended the Sub-Commission. In respect to the treaty bodies, since 1994, CEDAW Committee members have been nominated by the Committee to serve as 'contact persons' or 'focal points' in relation to individual treaty bodies, and to report on their activities and working methods to the Committee's plenary session. The CEDAW Secretariat seeks to provide the Committee with the output of the other treaty bodies in a timely manner, particularly in the 'ways and means' report; at the same time, the CEDAW Secretariat makes concerted efforts to ensure that the output of the Committee is made known to its sister bodies. The Office of the High Commissioner for Human Rights tries to ensure that parallel efforts are made as part of the provision of Secretariat support to the other treaty bodies, both to provide them with information about the work of the CEDAW Committee and to facilitate information on the output of the other treaty bodies to the Committee.

More recently, meetings have taken place between the CEDAW Committee and members of other treaty bodies. In late 1996, members of the

conclusions on the human rights of women, paras. II.4, III.2, III.3, III.11 (CRP.II) and the resolution 11 relating to follow-up of the Fourth World Conference on Women: E/CN.6/1998/L.11, para. 8.

[49] See Report of the fifty-fourth session of the Commission on Human Rights, E/1998/23, paras. 207–12.

CEDAW Committee and the Committee on the Rights of the Child met in Cairo at a meeting organised by the UN Children's Fund (UNICEF) to discuss working methods and other areas of mutual concern. Also in 1996, the Division for the Advancement of Women, the Office of the High Commissioner for Human Rights and the United Nations Population Fund (UNFPA) hosted a roundtable of human rights treaty bodies on human rights approaches to women's health, with a focus on women's reproductive and sexual health rights at Glen Cove, New York. Participants included several members of each treaty body, representatives of UN specialised agencies and other entities, and NGOs. The Glen Cove Roundtable was the first occasion, outside the chairpersons' meetings, at which members of all the treaty bodies met to discuss a substantive human rights issue. The success of the Roundtable, which made concrete recommendations with regard to the treaty bodies,[50] suggests that such meetings should be a regular feature of the future programme of these bodies. Nonetheless, limited resources and, to a certain extent, institutional jealousies, continue to impose constraints on the effort to increase collaboration with other treaty bodies.[51]

The CEDAW Committee must continue its efforts to forge linkages with other parts of the human rights framework of the UN, both to enhance its own work practices and to contribute to the declared gender mainstreaming mandate.[52] As well as continuing to appoint Committee members, whose identity should be made public in the annual report, to act as focal points, the Committee should actively monitor the progress made by each treaty body towards implementation of the chairpersons' recommenda-

[50] Glen Cove Roundtable, 'Briefing Note and Final Recommendations of the Roundtable of Human Rights Treaty Bodies on the "Human Rights Approach to Women's Health with Focus on Reproductive and Sexual Health Rights"', Glencove, 9–11 December 1996, WHG/97/3/8.

[51] For example, UNICEF organised in 1998 an NGO Consultation on the issue of violence against women and children, which was partly designed to contribute to the effort to promote collaboration between the CEDAW Committee and the Committee on the Rights of the Child. Organised in Geneva and timed to coincide with the nineteenth session of the Committee on the Rights of the Child, it gathered several members of both Committees, yet succeeded mainly in creating tension between both groups, as the interaction focused less on possible venues for collaboration and more on the perceived strengths and weaknesses of the relevant provisions of each Convention.

[52] Report of the Seventh Meeting of Persons Chairing the Human Rights Treaty Bodies, recalling the conclusions of their sixth meeting with regard to gender mainstreaming, A/51/482, para. 58.

tions on the integration of gender perspectives into their work. Means to facilitate the participation of CEDAW Committee members at the sessions of other treaty bodies, and vice versa, should be explored, as should attempts to encourage states parties to nominate past CEDAW Committee members to other UN human rights treaty bodies and vice versa. There are several examples where former CEDAW Committee members have served as experts on other treaty bodies, demonstrating the value of ensuring that the expertise gained by serving on one such body is inherited by another.

Except in the case of the Special Rapporteur on Violence against Women, its Causes and Consequences, the CEDAW Committee has yet to consider seriously linkages with the extra-conventional human rights mechanisms – the human rights special procedures system, consisting of special and thematic rapporteurs, representatives, experts and working groups. The Committee is, nonetheless, aware that there is increasing interaction between the chairpersons' meetings and the meeting of human rights special procedures.[53] It has also taken account of recommendations by the chairpersons that, where appropriate, the treaty bodies should take a more active role in supporting, suggesting topics for, and cooperating in the preparation of studies by the Sub-Commission on Prevention of Discrimination and Protection of Minorities, as well as by special rapporteurs and other experts appointed by the Commission on Human Rights. The CEDAW Committee has noted the suggestion that 'special rapporteurs and other experts whose work is of direct relevance to the activities of a particular treaty body could schedule their visits to the United Nations in connection with the meeting of the treaty bodies concerned in order to have direct cooperation on issues of mutual concern'.[54]

The Committee should nominate a representative to attend the meetings of the special procedures with the object of creating formal links between the Committee and those non-conventional mechanisms with mandates relating to issues which are of concern to the Committee. These would include the special rapporteurs on torture and other cruel, inhuman or degrading treatment or punishment, on internally displaced persons, on

---

[53] Report of the Third Meeting of the Special Rapporteurs/Representatives/Experts and Chairmen of Working Groups of the Special Procedures and the Advisory Services Programme of the Commission on Human Rights, E/CN.4/1997/3; Report of the Seventh Meeting, *supra*, note 52.

[54] Ibid., para. 53.

religious intolerance and on sale of children, child prostitution and child pornography. Presumably, a similar approach should be used for the special rapporteur on the right to education appointed in 1998.[55] Such contacts will be facilitated by efforts to schedule the meetings of the special rapporteurs so as to coincide with meetings of the treaty bodies.

The Committee has made a bigger effort to forge a strong relationship with the Special Rapporteur on Violence against Women. The mandate of the Special Rapporteur was defined by the Commission on Human Rights in its resolution 1994/45 and was extended for a further three years by the Commission in 1997.[56] Despite the fact that the Committee repeatedly requested the High Commissioner for Human Rights to facilitate the presence of the Special Rapporteur at all CEDAW Committee sessions, the Special Rapporteur was able to attend only a short part of one (the fourteenth) session of the CEDAW Committee between 1995 and 1998, possibly because of resource constraints. Nonetheless, the Committee and the Special Rapporteur are trying to ensure that their work is coordinated and mutually enhancing. To encourage her attendance at CEDAW Committee sessions, thus setting the stage for future cooperation, the Committee needs strategies to ensure that the Special Rapporteur considers attendance at its sessions valuable. At the twentieth session, in 1999, the Special Rapporteur met with the Committee in closed session, to discuss the need for increased collaboration and for further opportunities to explore matters of mutual concern in a structured way. Issues that the Committee and the Special Rapporteur may collaborate on include trafficking in women, and could also include discussion of the Committee's General Recommendation No. 19, and the impact of measures which have been implemented to address various forms of violence against women in states parties to the Convention. The Special Rapporteur agreed to brief the Committee periodically and to provide briefing material as well as information on states parties to be considered by the Committee. Agreement was also reached on providing information to the Committee on country missions; the Special Rapporteur could involve individual

---

[55] The matter was discussed by Working Group I on ways and means of expediting the work of the Committee at the eighteenth session, in January 1998; see Report of the CEDAW Committee (eighteenth and nineteenth sessions), *supra*, note 23, Part I, eighteenth session, paras. 434–5. It is of interest to note that the special rapporteur on religious intolerance addressed the eighteenth session of the CEDAW Committee and undertook to maintain links with the Committee, ibid., paras. 473–6.

[56] Human Rights Commission, Res. 1997/44.

Committee members in these country missions. This would benefit the Committee and be advantageous to the Special Rapporteur, particularly in those cases where her mission is to the home countries or countries of residence of Committee members. More formal methods of work would facilitate collaboration, but informal agreements and arrangements will provide a valuable starting point.

G. CEDAW Committee linkages with the UN system

Article 22 of the Convention provides that the Committee may invite specialised agencies of the United Nations to submit reports for considera-tion by the Committee on the implementation of the Convention in areas falling within the scope of their activities. At its fifteenth session, the Com-mittee encouraged specialised agencies and other UN bodies to involve themselves more fully in its work by requesting them to continue providing it with reports that focus on the implementation of the Convention in areas falling within the scope of their activities. The Committee also welcomed reports that referred to the states parties under consideration.[57]

Since its first session, UNESCO, the World Health Organisation (WHO), the International Labour Organisation (ILO) and the Food and Agriculture Organisation (FAO) have regularly contributed written submissions to the CEDAW Committee. The International Fund for Agricultural Develop-ment (IFAD), the UN Development Programme (UNDP), the UN Development Fund for Women (UNIFEM) and UNFPA, and the UN High Commissioner for Refugees (UNHCR) and the Bretton Woods institutions have not, as yet, contributed such reports to the Committee. At its four-teenth session, the Committee instituted the practice of designating focal points from amongst its members responsible for developing links with those bodies. During that session, a number of heads of agencies, including UNFPA and UNIFEM, addressed the Committee during plenary meetings. This practice became a regular feature of Committee sessions.

At its seventeenth session in July 1997, the CEDAW Committee's pre-sessional working group decided to follow the practice of other treaty bodies, including the Human Rights Committee, the Committee

---

[57] Report of the CEDAW Committee on the Elimination of Discrimination against Women, General Assembly, Official Records, Fifty-first Session, Supplement No. 38 (A/51/38), para. 340.

on Economic and Social Rights[58] and the Committee on the Rights of the Child,[59] and invited representatives of specialised agencies and other entities to provide oral information in relation to the periodic reports before it. The pre-sessional working group concluded that the practice was a valuable one and recommended that the Committee adopt it as the usual practice for its future sessions. The Committee adopted this recommendation in Decision 18/I.[60] To provide a similar opportunity for involvement in the consideration of initial reports, the Committee also decided that representatives of specialised agencies and bodies should be invited to meet with the Committee in a closed meeting.[61]

While their reports are becoming more focused and country-specific and their oral information is already useful, several United Nations agencies have requested the Committee to provide greater guidance to bodies which wish to contribute to its work. The Committee should formulate guidelines for this purpose, particularly in light of Decision 18/I. These guidelines should also address input required from agencies with field operations.

H. NGO involvement in the CEDAW Committee's work

The 1993 World Conference on Human Rights recognised the important role played by non-governmental organisations in the effective implementation of all human rights instruments.[62] The sixth chairpersons' meeting reiterated this theme, pointing to the vital role of NGOs in supplying the treaty bodies with documentation and other information on human rights developments.[63] At their seventh meeting, the chairpersons went so far as to encourage NGOs to take an active role in 'critically examining the work of the treaty bodies so that more effective performance by treaty bodies as a whole, as well as by individual experts' could be achieved.[64]

Since its establishment, the CEDAW Committee has enjoyed strong support from international and national NGOs. NGOs have voluntarily provided Committee members, both individually and collectively, with

---

[58] HRI/MC/1996/2.   [59] CRC/C/33, para. 11.
[60] Report of the CEDAW Committee (eighteenth and nineteenth sessions), *supra*, note 23, Part I, eighteenth session, Decision 18/I. Participating agencies and bodies included the Office of the High Commissioner for Human Rights, UNESCO, UNDP, UNIFEM, UNFPA, ILO and UNICEF; see ibid., paras. 18 and 20.
[61] Ibid., Decision 18/II.   [62] Vienna Declaration and Programme of Action, para. 52.
[63] A/50/505, para. 23.   [64] A/51/482, paras. 35 and 36.

information relevant to the consideration of states parties' reports and for other purposes. The International Women's Rights Action Watch (IWRAW), which was established at the NGO Forum of the Nairobi Women's Conference in 1985 specifically to monitor the work of the CEDAW Committee, has provided country-specific information to the Committee on a regular basis. In cooperation with the Commonwealth Secretariat, IWRAW has produced a guide for NGOs on reporting under the Convention.[65] Other international and national NGOs from a number of countries have also contributed information.

NGOs have also provided input for general recommendations. In 1992, the International League for Human Rights and IWRAW hosted a conference on violence against women as a contribution to the preparation of General Recommendation No. 19.[66] The International Human Rights Law Group and other NGOs co-hosted the meeting which developed the Maastricht draft as a possible model for an optional protocol for the Convention which formed the basis of the CEDAW Committee's Suggestion No. 7 outlining the elements for such a protocol. NGOs have also examined the working methods of the Committee and hosted general and specific briefings for Committee members. Since 1986, IWRAW has held an annual meeting in January which focuses on the work of the CEDAW Committee and in 1996, in collaboration with the Jacob Blaustein Institute for the Advancement of Human Rights and UNIFEM, it hosted a one-day colloquium relating to the Committee's working methods.[67]

Neither the Convention, nor the Committee's rules of procedure provide for NGO participation in the Committee's sessions. At its sixteenth session, in its report on 'ways and means' the Committee had before it an analysis of the practice of other human rights treaty bodies with respect to NGO participation,[68] which suggested several models for the Committee's consideration. The ensuing discussion revealed that although members found NGO information helpful and wished that reports could be more

---

[65] Jane Connors and Andrew Byrnes, *Assessing the Status of Women: A Guide to Reporting under the Convention on the Elimination of All Forms of Discrimination against Women*, Commonwealth Secretariat and IWRAW, 1995.

[66] International League for Human Rights, *Combatting Violence against Women*, New York, March 1993.

[67] Report of the Colloquium of the International Women's Rights Action Watch and the Committee on the Elimination of Discrimination against Women, New York, 13–14 January 1996.

[68] CEDAW/C/1997/5, paras. 28–48.

focused, timely, and available in all working languages of the United Nations, there were mixed feelings with regard to formalised relations between NGOs and the Committee. During the sixteenth session, however, an affiliate of IWRAW, IWRAW (Asia/Pacific), in collaboration with UNIFEM, organised a training session for NGOs, facilitating the attendance of national NGOs from states parties reporting to that session. The training session was extremely successful, with CEDAW Committee members finding interaction with the representatives of national NGOs useful. This, combined with the Committee's past experience of the value of NGO input, led the Committee to decide that NGO involvement in its work should be welcomed cautiously, but in such a way as to ensure that the independence of experts was not compromised. The Committee decided that from its seventeenth session, the Secretariat should facilitate an informal meeting of NGOs with the Committee outside the Committee's regular meeting time. During such meetings NGOs would be invited to provide country-specific information on the states parties whose reports were before the Committee.[69]

The Committee's decision at the sixteenth session represented a watershed in its relationship with NGOs, and provided the basis for more fundamental developments at its seventeenth and eighteenth sessions. The Committee's decision at its seventeenth session to increase NGO involvement in the formulation of general recommendations has already been described. It is likely that, as the new process for preparation of general recommendations becomes routine, the Committee, like other human rights treaty bodies, including the Committee on Economic, Social and Cultural Rights and the Committee on the Rights of the Child, will hold open discussion days, focusing on the content of rights in the Convention or cross-cutting themes.[70]

During its eighteenth session in January 1998, the CEDAW Committee reached a decision with regard to NGO involvement in the reporting process that moved well beyond its tentative decision at the sixteenth session. Taking advantage of the second IWRAW (Asia/Pacific)/UNIFEM training

---

[69] Report of the CEDAW Committee (sixteenth and seventeenth sessions), *supra*, note 17, Part I, sixteenth session, Decision 16/II. For a summary of the discussions leading to this decision, see para. 362.

[70] See for example, Summary Records of the Committee on Economic, Social and Cultural Rights, E/C.12.1993/SR.42, on the discussion regarding minimum core content and non-discrimination dimensions in the right to health, in which numerous NGOs took part.

programme and the presence of representatives of national NGOs in New York, the pre-sessional working group invited those representatives, as well as those of other NGOs, including those working at the international level, to attend its meetings and provide it with country-specific information on those states parties which were being considered by the working group. The experience proved to be fruitful, with the pre-sessional working group gaining insights which enhanced its work. On the recommendation of this group, the Committee plenary decided that representatives of national and international NGOs would, in future, as a matter of course, be invited to provide country-specific information on states parties whose reports are being reviewed by the group.[71]

Therefore, NGOs are part of the Committee's formal process of preparing general recommendations, and formally part of the pre-sessional working group preparation for the review of periodic reports. In 1999, at its twentieth session, the Committee also agreed that NGOs should be able to present country-specific information to the Committee meeting in a working group of the whole; thus, the Committee will hear from NGOs during a plenary informal meeting (with interpretation), in addition to their participation in the pre-sessional working group.[72] The Secretariat will continue to facilitate informal briefings of the Committee by NGOs outside the Committee's regular meetings, while more informal contacts between NGOs and individual Committee members, and the Committee as a whole, will be maintained.

The increased opportunities for NGO involvement in the work of the Committee raise a number of issues, not least of which is the role of the Secretariat in facilitating that involvement. The Committee on Economic, Social and Cultural Rights, for example, has directed its Secretariat to notify NGOs of the growing opportunities that exist for NGO contribution during sessions of the Committee. It has also requested its Secretariat to send copies of reports pending consideration to a range of national NGOs in the countries concerned and provide the chairperson of the Committee with a list of those NGOs to whom pending reports have been sent at least two months prior to each session. The current financial and human resource constraints of the UN Secretariat are well-known, yet, to

---

[71] See Report of the CEDAW Committee (eighteenth and nineteenth sessions), *supra*, note 23, Part I, eighteenth session, Decision 18/I, and paras. 19–20.

[72] See Report of the CEDAW Committee (twentieth and twenty-first sessions), *supra*, note 16, Part I, twentieth session, Decision 20/I.

some extent, these can be addressed by greater use of modern information technology, and the employment of interns and research fellows. Certainly, the Division for the Advancement of Women can use its Internet sites to inform NGOs and to post electronic versions of states parties' reports; more structured and regular outreach activities would have significant resource implications for the Secretariat and would thus require policy changes.

Responsibility for exploiting the new opportunities NGOs have for participating in the work of the CEDAW Committee lies to a large extent with the NGOs themselves. They should consider the model of the NGO Group for the Convention on the Rights of the Child, which coordinates NGO participation in the work of the treaty body established under that Convention,[73] and has been an important element in strengthening that body. The formation of a similar coordinating group for the CEDAW Committee could be achieved in a number of ways, including at the behest of an individual NGO or group of NGOs, or even with the assistance of UNIFEM, as a development of the IWRAW (Asia/Pacific)/UNIFEM CEDAW training programme.

The CEDAW Committee also faces increased responsibilities as a result of its increased openness to NGO input. The Committee has frequently requested that NGO documents be more timely and focused and available in the working languages of all Committee members. It is up to the Committee to clarify its requirements of NGOs, perhaps by formulating simple guidelines for this purpose.

I. Conclusion

The Committee on the Elimination of Discrimination against Women has now reached an important juncture in its work offering opportunities for increased impact and visibility. It has examined a substantial number of initial and subsequent reports, adopted the practice of formulating concluding comments, and adopted more than twenty general recommendations, a number of which provide important clarification of the obligations imposed by the Convention. The uncertainty surrounding its Secretariat has been resolved with the decision to keep it within the UN

---

[73] Laura Theytaz-Bergman, 'NGO Group for the Convention on the Rights of the Child' in *Monitoring Children's Rights* (ed. E. Verhellen), Kluwer International, 1996, pp. 537–40 at pp. 537–8.

Division for the Advancement of Women, its servicing strengthened and, for the foreseeable future, it is assured of two annual sessions.

The Committee also faces challenges that hamper its capacity to realise fully its own potential. At the forefront of these challenges is the issue of reservations. The Convention is plagued by a large number of substantive and far-reaching reservations which go, as one commentator has suggested, 'to the heart and soul of both values of universality and integrity'[74] in international human rights law generally, and in that relating to women in particular. The CEDAW Committee has actively pursued the issue of reservations, but has attracted little support from states parties to the Convention, or from the UN system.[75] As part of its commemoration of the fiftieth anniversary of the Universal Declaration of Human Rights, CEDAW decided to formulate a written statement on reservations.[76]

It is clear that the Committee has now started to reflect in a serious fashion on its working methods. It has decided to hold its pre-sessional working group at the session prior to that at which reports are to be considered and it is trying to give greater focus to the lists of issues and questions; it is also actively encouraging the participation of the wider UN system and NGOs in the work of the pre-sessional working group. The Committee has shown itself eager to improve its practices relating to report consideration and to enhance its concluding comments. It is also seeking to devise means of forging strong links with other parts of the UN human rights system and the UN system generally. At this point, it is too early to know if these changes will bring about the improvements in the quality of the report review process and in the formulation of concluding comments that they are intended to produce. At the same time, the Committee must

---

[74] Rebecca J. Cook, 'Reservations to the Convention on the Elimination of All Forms of Discrimination against Women', 30 *Virginia Journal of International Law*, 1990, pp. 643–716 at p. 644.

[75] Ibid.; Belinda Clark, 'The Vienna Convention Reservations Regime and the Convention on the Elimination of All Forms of Discrimination against Women' 85 *AJIL*, 1991, p. 281; Liesbeth Lijnzaard, *Reservations to UN Human Rights Treaties – Ratify or Ruin?*, Martinus Nijhoff, Dordrecht, 1995, pp. 298–370; J. P. Gardner (ed.) *Human Rights as General Norms and a State's Right to Opt Out*, British Institute of International and Comparative Law, London, 1997, chapters 4 and 5.

[76] Report of the CEDAW Committee (sixteenth and seventeenth sessions), *supra*, note 17, Part II, seventeenth session, para. 483. On the adoption of the statement, see note 37 above and accompanying text. Note that the statement relied more extensively on the work of the Special Rapporteur of the International Law Commission than on General Comment No. 24 of the Human Rights Committee (CCPR/C/21/Rev.1/Add.6 (1994)).

continue to take stock of its working methods, to observe the innovations adopted by other treaty bodies, and to identify measures that can bring about further enhancement of its capacity to monitor the implementation of the Convention.

Unfortunately, while recent improvements to working methods should increase the quality of the work carried out by the CEDAW Committee, they are unlikely to have an impact on the problem of the accumulating backlog of reports awaiting review by the Committee. Further expansion of limited meeting time is unlikely in the near future, whether following the entry into force of the amendment to article 20 or under the current regime of interim exceptions approved by the General Assembly. The Committee will have to continue discussing other possibilities, perhaps focusing on expansion of its current practice in connection with the possibility of combining reports, or on asking for reports to deal with a more limited range of issues.

In addition, like other treaty bodies, the CEDAW Committee urgently needs to develop techniques to encourage states parties to report, and to do so in a timely fashion. Several Committees have adopted the policy of reviewing the situation in those states parties whose reports are seriously overdue in the absence of reports. At their ninth meeting, the chairpersons made clear that there is a strong basis, in both law and policy, to support the consideration of a state party in the absence of a report, once repeated requests have failed to persuade a state party to honour its obligation to report.[77] Other treaty bodies, in particular the Committee on Economic, Social and Cultural Rights have already found that the scheduling of such a review can in many cases be the incentive needed to encourage states parties to submit a long overdue report.

The CEDAW Committee now faces both challenges and opportunities that should not be minimised. At one time the least known of all human rights treaty bodies, the CEDAW Committee now has a large following, both within the United Nations and civil society. Further strengthening of the Convention will follow the adoption in 1999 of a communications mechanism, which will allow individuals to complain to the Committee of violations of the Convention and entitle the Committee to investigate serious and systematic violations. But, to exploit these and other new opportunities allowing it to maximise the efficiency and efficacy of its

---

[77] Report of the Ninth Meeting, *supra*, note 20, paras. 25–8.

work, the Committee must develop a permanently self-critical attitude and continue to re-examine its working methods. It must go on introducing necessary changes, in its search for more productive ways to promote implementation of the Convention, and to advance the fight against the discrimination still faced by women – though to different extents and in different ways – in every one of the states parties to the Convention.

5

THE REPORTING PROCESS UNDER THE
CONVENTION ON THE RIGHTS OF THE CHILD

GERISON LANSDOWN

A. Introduction

The Convention on the Rights of the Child (CRC) was adopted by the UN General Assembly in November 1989. It entered into force in September 1990 and by December 1999 had been ratified by 191 states. Only the United States of America and Somalia have as yet failed to ratify it. As such it has achieved the unprecedented record of becoming a virtually universally accepted human rights treaty within only eight years of its adoption. The CRC establishes an international monitoring mechanism through the creation of the ten-member CRC Committee, elected by states parties. The Committee held its first meeting in 1991, and began its first scrutiny of states parties' reports in 1993. The CRC requires that the Committee meet annually. However, following a request of the Committee in 1994, made in view of the volume of work associated with the number of ratifications, it has since 1995 met three times a year.[1] Each session comprises a three-week period for scrutiny of states parties' reports with an additional week at each session for the pre-sessional working group.

The CRC imposes on states parties an obligation to report to the Committee initially two years after ratification and subsequently every five years. The reporting obligation is contained in article 44, which also requires states parties to make these reports widely available in their own countries. The purpose of the reports is to provide the Committee with sufficient information to allow it to develop a comprehensive understanding of the implementation of the CRC in every state party. This comprehensiveness is

---

[1] Report of the 5th session of the Committee on the Rights of the Child, UN Doc. A/49/41.

113

understood to relate not only to all the areas covered by the CRC, but also to the situation of all children within the jurisdiction of the state.

In order to guide governments in the preparation of their initial reports, the Committee has adopted General Guidelines regarding the form and the content of these reports.[2] The guidelines are intended to provide a clear indication of the nature and depth of information required, and also to impose some degree of uniformity on the production of reports. More detailed guidelines have also been produced by the Committee for the production of periodic reports by states parties.[3]

B. Reporting as a process

The guidelines for initial reports (and subsequent guidelines on periodic reports) recall that the process of preparing the report 'offers an important occasion for conducting a comprehensive review of the various measures undertaken to harmonise national law and policy with the CRC' and should be one that 'encourages and facilitates popular participation and public scrutiny of government policies'. In other words, the process is intended to promote social mobilisation and encourage government officials, non-governmental organisations (NGOs) and others to work collaboratively to realise children's rights. It recognises that the fundamental aim of the international monitoring mechanism is to strengthen the national capacity to monitor children's rights and not to replace it.[4] Accordingly, reporting by governments is perceived as part of a process rather than a formal and isolated activity. It is intended as a means through which governments acquire a greater understanding of the rights of children, the extent to which they are being respected and the strategies needed to be developed in order to meet their obligations to children. It is in this spirit that the CRC requires that governments publish their reports within their country. Similarly, the Committee's guidelines recommend that the summary records of the state party's dialogue with the Committee together

---

[2] General Guidelines regarding the form and content of initial reports to be submitted by States parties under article 44, paragraph 1(a) of the CRC, UN Doc. CRC/C/5.
[3] General Guidelines regarding the form and content of periodic reports to be submitted by States parties under article 44, paragraph 1 (b) of CRC, UN Doc. CRC/C/58.
[4] M. Pais, 'The CRC on the Rights of the Child', in United Nations, *Manual on Human Rights Reporting*, UN Doc. HR/PUB/91/1 (Rev.1)(1997).

with the concluding observations be published. This recognition of the national dimension to the international reporting process is innovative, and is linked to the ultimate purpose of enhancing respect for the rights of children. The emphasis given to the national component of monitoring was recognised by the 1993 World Conference on Human Rights in Vienna as a model to be followed.[5]

C. A thematic structure for reports

The guidelines lay down a thematic structure for reporting under the CRC. Instead of the more usual systematic article-by-article approach, the guidelines group the articles of CRC into the following broad themes:

- general measures of implementation;
- definition of the child;
- general principles;
- civil rights and freedoms;
- family environment and alternative care;
- basic health and welfare;
- education, leisure and cultural activities; and
- special measures of protection.

The complete thematic structure is set out in the Appendix at the end of this chapter.

The rationale of the Committee in developing this thematic approach is that the CRC embodies the rights of children to survival and development and to protection, as well as their civil and political rights. The grouping of articles within thematic clusters was devised to promote greater understanding amongst governments of the holistic nature of the Convention. Two particular benefits have resulted from their use.

1. IMPLEMENTATION

The first thematic cluster of articles relates to government obligations to introduce general measures of implementation. Drawing together the obligations has lent them greater focus. It has enabled the Committee to assess how the CRC has been used as an overall framework for action, and how its

---

[5] UN Doc. A/CONF.157/23,11.E, para. 89.

philosophy can be understood as a tool for change. The relevant obligations in the CRC include the duty to undertake all measures to harmonise legislation and policy with the principles of the CRC (article 4), to publish and make widely available the report within the country (article 44.6), and to make the CRC widely known to both adults and children (article 42). In the course of analysing states parties' reports on the measures taken to ensure implementation, the Committee has identified clearly strategies and structures which need to be introduced. Scrutiny of these structures is as important as scrutiny of compliance with the individual rights. The Committee's recommendations favouring inter-ministerial committees, independent monitoring mechanisms, interdepartmental cooperation at national and local level, child impact statements, annual reports to parliament, dialogue with NGOs and dissemination of the Committee's findings are consistent with a commitment to strategic implementation.[6] The recommendations have been valuable in supporting the arguments of NGOs that without effective structures at governmental level, the rights, needs and interests of children will never be properly addressed.[7] Children lack autonomy, lack the vote, are in a situation of political and economic dependency, with high levels of need for public services (health, education, etc), and are particularly vulnerable to the impact of those services. The emphasis placed by the Committee on effective measures of implementation has been influential in prompting initiatives in many countries to address their specific needs.

2. UNDERLYING PRINCIPLES

The guidelines identify four underlying principles which must be considered in the scrutiny of compliance with all other rights. These relate to non-discrimination (article 2), the best interests of the child (article 3), the rights to life, survival and development (article 6), and the right of children to participate in decisions affecting them (article 12). In considering, for example, the rights of refugee children (article 22), or the right of children to the best possible health (article 24), a thorough examination of the four underlying principles must be made. In this way the Committee has highlighted the indivisibility of the rights embodied in CRC and encouraged a

---

[6] See, e.g., Concluding Observations for Poland, UN Doc. CRC/C/15/Add.31, the United Kingdom, UN Doc. CRC/15/Add.34 and Jamaica, UN Doc. CRC/C/15/Add.32.

[7] See, e.g., R. Hodgkin and P. Newell, *Effective Government Structures for Children*, London, 1996.

holistic approach to children in respect of legislation, policy and practice. The introduction of the concept of article 12 as an underlying principle, for example, has also given considerable force to the recognition of children as active participants in matters of concern to them, rather than being merely the objects and recipients of adult concern.

There are, however, some difficulties with the imposition of the themes. Many of the articles do not fall neatly into one or other of the categories constructed by the Committee. For example, article 19 (the right to protection from all forms of violence) is placed in the section headed 'Family environment and alternative care'. The obligation on states to adopt all measures to abolish traditional practices prejudicial to the child (article 24.1) is located under 'Basic health and welfare'. The guidelines thus construe the right to respect for the physical integrity of the child as a social right of concern within the family or as a health matter, whereas one could equally argue that it is a fundamental civil right and should be so expressed. Similarly, article 23 (embodying the rights of disabled children) is located within the theme 'Basic health and welfare', a grouping which would appear to confirm disability as a medical matter. Yet there is an equally powerful case to be made for the explicit recognition that the right of disabled children to the 'fullest possible social integration', as required by article 23, is a basic civil right. By including it under health and welfare, the Committee is failing to challenge traditional models of viewing disabled children as 'problems' requiring individual intervention, rather than as people entitled to but denied equal respect and for whom social change is required to overcome direct and indirect discrimination. In short, it re-affirms the medical rather than the social model of disability. Article 2 is identified as an underlying principle but it could also be argued that its injunction that governments undertake measures to ensure that all the rights in the Convention apply to all children without discrimination could equally and usefully be categorised as a general measure of implementation.

One of the strengths of the CRC is its integration of civil and political with social, economic and cultural rights, and its implicit assertion of the indivisibility of those rights. The Committee has stressed that all the rights are inter-related and that each is equally important and fundamental to the dignity of the child. However, the clustering does, to some extent, work against that inter-relatedness. For example, the right to protection from economic exploitation and work which is likely to be harmful to the child's social development (article 32) is grouped under 'Special protection measures'. However, it also needs to be considered in relation to the right to education and the right to play (articles 28 and 31), listed under 'Education, leisure and cultural activities'. Again, rights in relation to adoption which are grouped in 'Family care and alternative environments' must address the child's right to preservation of identity which comes under 'Civil rights and freedoms', and also the right to respect for the child's culture, language and religion which is located under 'Special protection measures'. There is a concern that as a consequence of clustering, governments and NGOs may make connections only between the rights that fall within the same cluster, and may thus develop a narrower interpretation of the principles than is necessary for the full implementation of the CRC.

The Committee has now produced guidelines for periodic reports which require a more rigorous process of reporting from governments.[8] The first periodic reports were examined in October 1997.[9] The guidelines contain very detailed questions which indicate the standards against which law, policy and practice can be monitored for compliance. They should enable the Committee to identify much more effectively where governments fail to provide sufficient information and where there are gaps in legislation necessary to protect the rights of children. The questions will also require governments to be more explicit about the implementation and monitoring of any legislative programme. NGOs too will be expected to produce their reports in accordance with the guidelines, and the rigour they impose should prove useful in promoting more effective monitoring of CRC. The guidelines for periodic reports continue to follow the thematic approach to reporting. It could be argued that having established the importance of relationships between groups of articles in the guidelines for initial reports, it might have been better to revert to an article-by-article system for the longer term.

D. The role of NGOs in the reporting process and its benefits

Article 45 of the CRC states that the Committee can request submission of reports from the UN Children's Fund (UNICEF) and other UN bodies on areas falling within the scope of their activities. It can also invite these and other competent bodies, including NGOs, to provide it with expert

---

[8] *Supra*, note 3.
[9] Committee on the Rights of the Child, Report of the sixteenth session, CRC/C/69.

advice on areas falling within their respective mandates. The Committee has responded to this unique provision by actively encouraging NGOs to submit 'alternative' reports which provide the Committee with a fuller and often more critical analysis of the state of children's rights in a given country. Article 45 also emphasises the need for close cooperation between the Committee as the international monitoring body and other bodies active in the field of children's rights. It affirms the work of the Committee as a dynamic process, as a catalyst for action.[10]

At the end of each session of the Committee, a week is allocated to consideration of the questions to be addressed to the states parties which are due to appear at the next session. This pre-sessional working group meets in private, no government representatives are allowed to attend and no public record of the discussion is produced. NGOs, and in particular national coalitions of NGOs, which have submitted written reports are invited to attend the pre-sessional working group meetings. A three-hour session is allocated to each country report. At these sessions NGOs are invited to comment on the government report and the process of its production (including how much NGOs were consulted in its preparation), and to identify major issues of concern with regard to breaches of children's rights. UN agencies are also invited to attend and to contribute. Following this discussion, the Committee writes to the state party with a list of questions on which it seeks written answers in advance of the government appearing before it. The government delegation then appears before the Committee at the next session for a total of nine hours, after which the Committee produces concluding observations which include detailed recommendations for government action.

There are significant advantages to this procedure. Having had access to the evidence of NGOs, the Committee is better placed to identify inconsistencies between the interpretation given by the state party of children's rights and the realities on the ground. Its examination of government delegations can be more critical, more focused and better targeted in the following ways.

(i) Through the identification of key issues of concern by the NGOs, the Committee is provided with many of the central questions which need to be raised with the delegation.

---

[10] Pais, *supra*, note 4.

(ii) NGOs will often provide a more critical perspective on issues of implementation. It is a common feature of the concluding observations of the Committee that government reports lack information on the implementation of legislation documented. In the case of the United Kingdom, for example, the Government observed that in respect of article 12 (the right of children to be heard in proceedings concerning them) children were entitled under the general law to make representations if permanently excluded from school. In fact, children have no rights under the applicable legislation to do so. Only parents are given the right to appeal and to be present at the appeal hearing. Any decision as to whether or not children can appear is in the discretion of the appeal panel.[11]

(iii) An alternative report will often highlight significant gaps in the government report and provide access to information not otherwise available to the Committee. For example, in the report of the United Kingdom, article 27 (the right of children to an adequate standard of living for their proper development) was addressed merely by documenting the range of social security benefits available to families. No reference was made to the growing situation of social inequality in the United Kingdom with its harmful impacts on children's well-being, the growing problem of homelessness, and the inadequacy of benefit levels to provide children with a proper standard of living. The fact is that growing numbers of children are living in families dependent on those benefits. Similarly, with regard to article 28 (the right to education), the Government merely outlined the formal legislative provision by which education is provided free of charge to all children between the ages of five and sixteen. It failed to address the growing problem of school exclusions, the evidence of discriminatory admissions procedures in respect of black and other minority ethnic groups, and the increasing dependence of many schools on voluntary donations from parents, causing a widening of inequality between schools. The alternative report was able to expose and highlight these concerns.[12]

Encouraging NGOs to submit reports has promoted the creation of national coalitions presenting information on behalf of the national NGO body as a whole. The information produced in such reports is likely to be

[11] Initial report of the United Kingdom, UN Doc. CRC/C/11/Add.1.
[12] Children's Rights Development Unit, *UK Agenda for Children*, London, 1994.

more authoritative and comprehensive than the report of a single NGO and thus of considerably more value to the Committee. It avoids duplication of evidence presented to the Committee and provides for greater consistency in its presentation. It also enables the Committee to gain a sense of priorities among the concerns raised. The presence of NGOs at the pre-sessional working groups gives the Committee an opportunity to assess the validity or strength of any claims of breaches, and to feel more confident in relying on those claims in pursuing concerns with government delegations. The active involvement of NGOs in the process of reporting enhances their capacity and commitment to serve as advocates in the follow-up to concluding observations. Overall, this promotes the Committee's concern to see the reporting obligation as a process with a national dimension.

Significant benefits at a national level also flow from the open and receptive approach of the Committee to NGOs in the reporting process. From the United Kingdom's experience, it is possible to identify a number of positive outcomes.[13] For example, a small office of which the author is a member, the Children's Rights Development Unit (CRDU), was established to coordinate the production of an alternative report. This actively engaged a wide range of NGOs, and created an impetus for monitoring compliance with the CRC. In the United Kingdom, and probably in many other countries, the language of human rights does not inform the practice of most professionals working with children. 'Need' and 'welfare' are much more familiar concepts. By participating in the production of the report to the Committee, many professionals were encouraged to go beyond identifying problems that exist for children, and to begin to evaluate those problems against a framework of principles and standards with the status of international law. The CRC introduced a new language and understanding to perceptions of what is happening to children in the United Kingdom. It provided an opportunity for children's organisations to engage in dialogue about the concept of children's rights and to consider the legislative, policy and practice implications of the CRC. It also encouraged them to scrutinise their own practice against the principles and standards of the CRC.

The CRDU used the production of the NGO report as an opportunity to disseminate information about the CRC and its implications for children;

---

[13] See UNICEF, *A Model for Action: The Children's Rights Development Unit*, Florence, 1996, for a more detailed analysis of this experience.

the level of knowledge about the CRC in particular, and children's rights in general, was very limited in the United Kingdom. During the production of the report, members of the CRDU were regularly invited to speak at conferences for the purpose of promoting understanding of the implications of the CRC for the work of professionals in a number of related fields – education, health, child care, residential care, play, and welfare rights. There was a growing demand for information, interpretation and explanation. In other words, the process of producing the report served as a tool for promotion as well as for monitoring within the United Kingdom. Over 1,600 copies of the alternative report were sold, which indicates the level of interest provoked by the process. The number of countries where NGO coalitions have been developed and have contributed alternative reports suggests that this experience has not been unique to the United Kingdom.[14]

The emphasis by the Committee on national NGO coalitions encouraged people in the United Kingdom to work collaboratively, strengthening the legitimacy, breadth and credibility of the report, not only in the eyes of the Committee but domestically as well. Traditionally, NGOs do not find it easy to work in this way, and there are particular difficulties in the United Kingdom because of the complexity of the relations between England, Scotland, Wales and Northern Ireland in terms of governmental responsibility for children. However, organisations could see the strength of the case for an integrated approach, both as a means of rationalising the work and of producing an outcome from the Committee which would be useful.

The awareness of both the CRC and the international monitoring process achieved through the collaborative production of the NGO report also served to raise interest in the findings of the Committee. There was considerable media attention on the process and the publication of the concluding observations achieved front page headlines in the national press. The CRDU disseminated the findings widely and encouraged many children's advocates to press for implementation of the Committee's concluding observations.[15] Thus the critique of the Government by the Committee has begun to enter the public domain, at least to a limited degree.

---

[14] See, for example, International Save the Children Alliance Working Group on the CRC on the Rights of the Child, *Monitoring the CRC on the Rights of the Child at the National Level: The Experiences of Some National Coalitions*, Geneva, 1996, paras. 5.1–5.10.

[15] Children's Rights Office, *Making the CRC Work for Children: Explaining the History and Structure of the UN CRC on the Rights of the Child and its Application in the UK*, London, 1995.

E. Issues of concern in relation to the reporting process

There is no doubt that the Committee has been creative in developing its working methods and in turn has begun to influence other treaty bodies. There are, nevertheless, aspects of the process which merit further consideration.

The Committee always follows the structure of the guidelines for their examination of government representatives, which means that key issues of concern appearing at the end of the guidelines are often given inadequate attention. In the case of the United Kingdom for example, this meant that the issue of youth justice was given insufficient scrutiny with the consequence that the Government dismissed the findings of the Committee on the grounds that it had not given the Government adequate time to clarify the nature of the current and proposed legislation relating to young offenders. The Government therefore argued that the Committee recommendations were invalid.[16] No time at all was spent on the rights of children seeking asylum, an issue of considerable concern in the NGO report.[17] In theory, the pre-sessional working group provides the opportunity for the Committee to identify where it should focus its questions to government delegations. In practice, however, the value of this session for developing a strategic approach to an examination of a government's representative is not always exploited. Perhaps there is a case for the Committee to ascertain more thoroughly in advance the specific issues it wishes to address in each thematic cluster of rights.

Another aspect is the absence of country rapporteurs. Initially, a country rapporteur was appointed for each report but this practice has now been abandoned for a number of years. The reason given was that the rapporteurs were sometimes subjected to pressure from governments seeking to influence the concluding observations. Accordingly, there has been no individual Committee member with responsibility for providing a focus to the discussion, either at the pre-sessional working group stage or during the examination of the state party's report. A rapporteur would ensure that the relevant papers had been read and that the key issues were properly addressed. All members have the responsibility to brief themselves for each session, but given their workload, it is unrealistic to expect every member

---

[16] See, e.g., Written Parliamentary Answer, House of Commons, Hansard, Col. 784, 26 April 1995.
[17] UN Doc. CRC/C/SR.206, 3 July 1995.

to be have read all the relevant documentation in respect of every country report. The lack of a country rapporteur has detracted from the Committee's effectiveness. It is therefore to be welcomed that at the twenty-first session of the Committee it was agreed to reintroduce a system of appointing country rapporteurs.[18]

There is a broad consensus amongst participating NGOs and the Committee members that the pre-sessional working group has been of significant benefit. It provides an opportunity to subject concerns raised by NGOs to more rigorous scrutiny, and to test the validity of any critical observations. In respect of the United Kingdom, it enabled the Committee to see how the critique of the CRC's implementation was related to the general state of children's rights in Britain. There is a clear commitment from the Committee that these sessions should continue. However, there are a number of concerns.

First, the pre-sessional working groups take place at the end of the full session of the Committee. The Committee members are often tired and there are often too few members present. For NGOs who have made considerable efforts to be present, often at significant financial cost, the absence of Committee members indicates a disappointing lack of interest in the evidence they have prepared. Second, the procedure of pre-sessional working groups is rather formal in character. Some Committee members have commented that a more effective dialogue might be achieved through a more open discussion as distinct from the formal question/answer format.

After four years of these sessions, with the first round of periodic reports now examined and a number of new members on the Committee, it is time to review the procedure. For example, should the pre-sessional working group take place at the beginning of each session rather than at the end? Should it take place at another time of year with only a limited number of members of the Committee? Does the evidence of breaches of children's rights submitted in these sessions sufficiently guide the process of examining the government delegations? The aim of the pre-sessional working group is to provide an alternative source of evidence of the state of children's rights in a given country in order to help the Committee to undertake an effective scrutiny of the government's record in implementing

---

[18] Committee on the Rights of the Child, Report on the twenty-first session, CRC/C/87, July 1999.

CRC. What working methods would be most effective in ensuring that that aim is satisfactorily achieved?

A further concern is the volume of work faced by the Committee. The CRC is a victim of its own success and the demands placed on it as a result are inordinate. In 1993 the World Conference on Human Rights recommended that 'the Committee should be enabled expeditiously and effectively to meet its mandate especially in view of the unprecedented number of ratifications and subsequent submission of country reports'.[19] The UN has developed a Plan of Action to provide additional resources for the Committee in the Office of the UN High Commissioner for Human Rights (UNHCHR). Five new posts have been created, providing considerable additional support for members. It is to be hoped that with this support, it will be easier for the Committee to manage the volume of papers and evidence and thereby to operate with greater effectiveness in its scrutiny of governments in the reporting process. There is also a proposed amendment to the CRC from Costa Rica, tabled at the states parties' meeting in December 1995, to increase the membership of the Committee from ten to eighteen. To be accepted, the proposal needs the approval by the General Assembly of the UN and ratification by a two-thirds majority of states parties. It was approved by the General Assembly in December 1995.[20] As of January 1998, fifty-two states had notified the Secretary-General of their acceptance of the amendment, 120 being needed before it comes into force.[21]

There is now a one- to two-year backlog of initial reports waiting to be examined. When the first round of periodic reports became due in 1997, the problem was compounded. The backlog will grow, despite the increase in meetings from two to three a year and a decision taken by the Committee at its twenty-first session to increase the numbers of states parties' reports considered at each session to eight.[22] Delay also creates problems for governments and NGOs. If produced on time, their reports are likely to be considerably out of date by the time the examination actually takes place. Furthermore, the delay undermines the credibility of the reporting process and serves as a disincentive to report.[23] These delays need urgent

---

[19] *Vienna Declaration and Programme of Action* adopted by the World Conference on Human Rights, Vienna, 25 June 1993, UN Doc. A/CONF.157/24.

[20] GA Res. 50/155 (21 December 1995).

[21] Sixth meeting of states parties, 18 February 1997, UN Doc. CRC/SP/22.

[22] *Supra*, note 18.

[23] See 'Final Report on Enhancing the Long-term Effectiveness of the United Nations Human Rights Treaty System'.

consideration. One of the strategies for tackling the backlog, under consideration by the Committee, has been the possibility of redefining periodicity under the terms of article 44 such that periodic reports will be considered to be due five years after receipt of the previous report, rather than five years after the previous report was actually due. However there is serious concern, certainly amongst NGOs, that such an interpretation of the reporting obligations would be a retrograde step which would serve to reward governments failing to meet deadlines, and indeed could well encourage them to do so.

A final concern arises from the comparative newness of the process. The development by the Committee of detailed measures against which to monitor compliance with the CRC's principles and standards is obviously far from complete. Inevitably, in some areas the development of indicators is less advanced than in others. For example, little attention has yet been given to the full implications of articles 13–16 (the rights to freedom of expression, religion, conscience, thought, association, and to privacy as they relate specifically to children's lives). Comparatively little attention has been given to article 23 (the rights of disabled children) and the implications of the principle of non-discrimination as it affects this vulnerable group. Clearly, the process of developing explicit indicators of compliance must be evolutionary. But it is important to ensure that each article in the CRC is considered as of equal value and significance and that no area of rights is neglected. The Committee has decided to prepare general comments with a view to promoting further implementation and to assist states parties in their reporting obligations, but none to date have been produced.[24] There is a degree of urgency now that this work should begin.

F. Conclusion

The success of the CRC has exceeded all expectations and the role of the Committee in contributing to the understanding and implementation of children's rights has not been insignificant. The Committee has been faced with a unique challenge in monitoring an international treaty that, within eight years of its adoption by the UN, has acquired near universal support. It has responded to that challenge with the introduction of many innov-

---

[24] Rule 73 of the *Rules of Procedure*, adopted by the Committee at its twenty-second meeting, 15 October 1991.

ative working methods. It has sought to enhance understanding of the indivisibility of the human rights of children, has strengthened the relationship between the international and national monitoring systems; and has engaged NGOs as critical actors in promoting and monitoring children's rights. However, if the Committee is to capitalise on its commitment to innovative working methods, it must be prepared to review those methods regularly, and to draw on the shared experience of those who have participated in the reporting process. The test of its value as a monitoring body will be its capacity to provide rigorous interpretation and analysis of the principles and standards embodied in the CRC coupled with a dynamic communication with governments, UN agencies and NGOs to translate those principles into action. Review and evaluation of its own work will be as important to its success as its examination and critique of the implementation of CRC in the field.

Appendix, chapter 5
Thematic Structure of General Guidelines for Reporting on the Convention on the Rights of the Child

General measures of implementation:

Article 4	The duty to take all possible measures to ensure implementation of the CRC.
Article 42	The duty to make the principles of the CRC widely known to children and adults.
Article 44.6	The duty to make countries' reports on progress towards implementation widely available.

Definition of the child:

Article 1	The CRC applies to everyone under the age of eighteen years.

General principles:

Article 2	Non-discrimination.
Article 3	Best interests of the child.
Article 6	The right to life, survival and development.
Article 12	Respect for the views of the child.

Civil rights and freedoms:

Article 7	Name and nationality.
Article 8	Preservation of identity.
Article 13	Freedom of expression.
Article 17	Access to appropriate information.
Article 14	Freedom of thought, conscience and religion.
Article 15	Freedom of association and of peaceful assembly.
Article 16	Protection of privacy.

Article 37(a)	The right not to be subjected to torture or other cruel, inhuman or degrading treatment.

Family environment and alternative care:

Article 5	Parental guidance.
Article 18	Parental responsibilities.
Article 9	Separation from parents.
Article 10	Family reunification.
Article 19	Violence, abuse and neglect.
Article 27(4)	Recovery of maintenance.
Article 20	Children deprived of a family environment.
Article 21	Adoption.
Article 11	Illicit transfer and non-return.
Article 25	Periodic review of placement.
Article 39	Physical and psychological recovery and social reintegration

Basic health and welfare:

Article 6	Right to life, survival and development
Article 18	Child care services and facilities.
Article 23	Disabled children.
Article 24	Health and welfare.
Article 26	Social security.
Article 27	Standard of living.

Education, leisure and cultural activities:

Article 28	Education.
Article 29	Aims of education.
Article 31	Leisure, recreation and cultural activities.

Special measures of protection:

(a) Children in situations of emergency –

Article 22	Refugee children.
Article 38	Children in armed conflicts.
Article 39	Physical and psychological recovery and social reintegration.

(b) Children in conflict with the law –

Article 40	The administration of justice.
Articles 37 (b), (c) and (d)	Children deprived of liberty including imprisonment, detention or placement in custodial settings.
Article 37 (a)	Sentencing of juveniles, in particular, the prohibition of capital punishment and life imprisonment.

(c) Children in situations of exploitation –

Article 32	Economic exploitation.
Article 33	Drug abuse.
Article 34	Sexual exploitation and abuse.
Article 35	Sale, trafficking and abduction.
Article 36	Other forms of exploitation

(d) Children belonging to a minority or indigenous group –

Article 30	Right to respect for culture, language and religion.

6

THE COMMITTEE ON ECONOMIC, SOCIAL AND
CULTURAL RIGHTS: CATALYST FOR CHANGE
IN A SYSTEM NEEDING REFORM

SCOTT LECKIE

A. Introduction

The state reporting process under the international human rights treaty regime has been subjected to a barrage of criticism in recent years, much of it justified.[1] Some commentators have suggested fundamental reform, some that the entire system should be abolished.[2] While this is too drastic a conclusion at present, there is much room for improvement within existing structures. Indeed throughout the 1990s the treaty bodies have made serious efforts to close some of the more gaping holes in the reporting process. Overall, the system is improving in important ways. This is true of several treaty bodies, but most notably the Committee of the International Covenant on Economic, Social and Cultural Rights (ICESCR). The Committee has developed new mechanisms and given expansive interpretations to the ICESCR and its own rules of procedure with a view to securing greater compliance by states parties. It has done so in a way which encourages, and indeed often results from, the efforts of third parties, in particular non-governmental organisations (NGOs).[3]

Owing to its restricted powers (particularly when contrasted with independent national judicial or quasi-judicial institutions), the Committee

---

[1] See, for instance, 'Effective Implementation of International Instruments on Human Rights, Including Reporting Obligations Under International Instruments on Human Rights', UN Doc. A/CONF.157/PC/62/Add.11/Rev.1.

[2] For a particularly severe critique, see A. Bayefsky, 'Making the Human Rights Treaties Work', in *Human Rights: An Agenda for the Next Century* (eds. L. Henkin and J. Hargrove), Washington DC, 1994, p. 264.

[3] On the Committee and ICESCR, see M. Craven, *The International Covenant on Economic, Social and Cultural Rights: A Perspective on its Development*, Oxford, 1995.

can only be expected to have a limited impact upon the actual enjoyment of human rights in countries over which it has occasional supervisory jurisdiction. This is true no matter how far the Committee may improve its methods of work or how intensively it may strive to address serious human rights infractions. Nonetheless, bodies such as the Committee can have an effect, especially where they respond openly to information provided by NGOs within or outside the context of the state reporting process. In such cases the Committee can provide an impetus for the fuller realisation of domestic human rights objectives. The Committee has gained growing support due to its openness to alternative information sources and its willingness, on occasion, to accept the credibility and reliability of this information, even when it contradicts reports or other representations by states parties.

This shift towards diversifying the sources of information has not only resulted in improved decision-making processes but also in a growing awareness of impediments that are deeply ingrained in the whole human rights treaty monitoring regime. These 'built-in defects' – many of which were included in the UN treaty system by states parties at the outset – will continue to restrict the Committee's impact at the national level unless it can develop more imaginative ways of overcoming them.

B. Overcoming the built-in defects

Given the nature of states and state interests, the treaty body reporting system is always liable to be circumvented or manipulated by states intent on skirting their legal obligations. Some of these imperfections can be avoided by the treaty bodies. But, even assuming the implementation of realistic or politically possible reforms, the system remains a strange one. How can it be, a lay observer might ask, that the procedures for securing compliance with major human rights treaties hinge upon a system that makes governments entirely responsible for reporting on themselves, once every five years, subject to soft questioning for a few hours by cautious committees, elected by those very governments, and with almost no like-lihood of serious censure or real sanctions?

The UN human rights treaty regime can improve guidelines on states' reports, reinforce the requirements for their submission, develop pro-cedural innovations and generally improve the reporting system. But the problems of a system grounded essentially on self-criticism and dependent almost entirely upon good faith will remain. Commentators have sought to defend the reporting procedures by focusing on the positive functions that can be served if states are willing to take their obligations seriously.[4] But officials entrusted with reporting responsibilities often admit privately that they are much more concerned with fulfilling as quickly as possible, and with the least possible effort, the unwanted, boring and burdensome task of reporting than they are with using the reporting process as a means of determining treaty compliance and working towards improvement.

There are also states which view the array of obligations stemming from human rights treaties solely through the lens of the reporting process. These states apparently perceive that merely through the preparation and presentation of a report and the appearance by a state party delegation before a committee, they have fulfilled their obligations under the treaty concerned. Considering the small number of people who will have read a state report, and the very limited impact such reports have in influencing governmental behaviour in directions conducive to the enjoyment of human rights, one can understand why states might find it convenient to see matters in this way.

In short, the failure of many states to submit reports, on time or at all, the frequent presentation of reports of poor quality, the failure by states to follow reporting guidelines established by the relevant committee, the overlapping of reporting obligations and the reluctance by states to use the reporting process as a means of divulging particular problems or short-comings typify the system as it now stands.

The uneven quality of the membership of the treaty bodies represents another defect of the system.[5] Although committee members are meant to serve in their personal capacity and to be 'experts with recognised competence in the field of human rights',[6] both the terms 'personal' and 'expert' have been flexibly interpreted. Membership of treaty bodies is loaded with foreign ministers, serving or retired ambassadors and other officials. Yet

---

[4] According to Philip Alston, the primary functions of the reporting process include: (i) the initial review function; (ii) the monitoring function; (iii) the policy formulation function; (iv) the public scrutiny function; (v) the evaluation function; (vi) the function of acknowledging problems; and (vii) the information exchange function. P. Alston, 'The Purposes of Reporting', in *Manual on Human Rights Reporting*, New York, 1991 at p. 14. These sentiments are more or less reflected in General Comment No. 1 of the Committee, UN Doc. E/1989/22, Annex III.

[5] See the discussion in chapter 19 below.

[6] Economic and Social Council, Res. 1985/17 (28 May 1985).

these monitoring bodies are meant to represent the cornerstone of the UN human rights system. To be effective, treaty bodies should consist of independent experts with long-term appointments rather than politicians concerned to secure re-election or avoid displeasing their fellows at home. If national supreme courts were stacked with persons who had worked their entire professional lives for the government, questions would be raised as to their independence, impartiality, objectivity and as to the values underlying the separation of powers. It is time these questions were put at the international level.

The treaty bodies base much of their interaction with states parties on the notion of 'constructive dialogue'. While such a system need not be overly 'diplomatic' nor lack exchanges of substance, too often the effect is to undermine prospects for wider and more serious analyses, even of flagrant human rights violations. There is a marked tendency by some members of the treaty bodies to refrain from outright criticism in the interests of state sovereignty, or of not alienating states parties. When the legality of governmental practices is considered by national courts, the state is not treated in a deferential manner, nor do the courts use tender language to avoid offending the state. While the analogy between national judicial systems and the international mechanisms for monitoring human rights cannot be taken very far, the attitudes often manifested within treaty bodies smack not so much of a pragmatic balancing of interests designed to find the truth and to suggest ways of making positive changes in policy and law, as of an inherent pro-government bias, to the detriment of the rights of the individuals concerned.

Linked to the notion of constructive dialogue is the frequent adoption of 'concluding observations' which are so general as to lose any realistic hope of being taken seriously. The concluding observations often focus rather selectively on particular human rights issues.[7] One reason for this, and perhaps the most important, is the minimal level of resources devoted to the UN human rights treaty regime. Presently only seventeen persons are entrusted with all secretarial, administrative, support and research tasks associated with all six treaty bodies. They are expected to provide detailed

---

[7] For instance, 'The Committee draws the attention of the authorities to the need to eliminate discrimination of any kind in the exercise of the rights set forth in the Covenant, especially the right to housing', UN Doc. E/C.12/1996/6, para. 317. While statements of this type are clearly important, more substantial comments, such as the suggestion of possible ways of eradicating discrimination and so forth, would inevitably achieve more.

back-up support to each of the treaty bodies and to have information or access to information about compliance with the particular treaties by all states parties. In the case of the Committee on Economic, Social and Cultural Rights (ESCR), the Covenant for which has been ratified by 142 states, the 'secretariat' consists of one professional staff person working half-time, supplemented in 1999 by one additional professional funded by voluntary contributions by a few governments. If the international community is serious about securing compliance with and proper monitoring of the human rights treaties, massive reinforcement of the staff allocated to the treaty bodies is required. By contrast, the monitoring system under the European Social Charter (with only twenty-two ratifications) has a staff of ten.

These are just some of the more obvious deficiencies afflicting the UN human rights treaty system. But they have not discouraged an increasing number of individuals from pursuing claims through the treaty bodies. In a number of cases many of the hurdles just discussed have been overcome and helpful decisions have been secured. These results would not have been possible without the active participation of NGOs, which have also increased support for the treaty bodies and given them renewed credibility.

C. State reporting as a basis for NGO action

NGO participation in the treaty bodies' processes is a relatively new phenomenon. As far as the ESCR Committee is concerned, NGO involvement has significantly increased the availability of alternative sources of information, facilitating the adoption of some forceful concluding observations. When NGOs feel that pronouncements by the treaty bodies may serve some practical purpose in defending rights, the reporting process can provide encouragement to internationalise what may be otherwise local and even isolated human rights problems.

It is not necessarily the state report itself which tends to mobilise NGO involvement, but rather the prospect that the committee will adopt a position critical of rights practices within a particular country. Thus when seeking to influence the outcome of committee deliberations, most NGOs spend only a limited amount of time analysing their own government's report, preferring instead to prepare alternative reports and other documents which more accurately describe the situation. In turn, this information has often been strongly reflected in concluding observations adopted by the committee.[8] Alternative reports can draw attention to inaccuracies and distortions in a governmental report; they can provide new information and offer ideas for more appropriate policies and legislation. The preparation of alternative reports can also act as a catalyst in the emergence of new coalitions and movements between previously unconnected groups. This has taken place, for example, in the Dominican Republic, Panama, the Philippines and Israel. The emergence of such alliances can lead to greater reliance on international human rights standards as a basis for demands on the state, and give new meaning to otherwise neglected or under-used legal texts. This is particularly true in the case of groups and NGOs not traditionally working in the human rights area.

In the case of the ICESCR, NGO reports have often laid the groundwork for what Craven calls an '*ad hoc* complaints procedure', through which the Committee has initiated action in response to NGO-derived information.[9] Through the imaginative use of supervisory powers, the Committee has produced an interesting and innovative jurisprudence. In such contexts, its concluding observations have sometimes achieved a level of detail and analysis more commonly associated with judicial bodies. This is true, for example, with the Committee's treatment of the housing rights provisions in article 11(1) of the ICESCR, to which it has devoted much attention.[10]

---

[8] See, for instance, 'A Report to the UN Committee on Economic, Social and Cultural Rights on Housing Rights Violations and the Poverty Problem in Hong Kong', November 1994, prepared by the Society for Community Organisation and the Hong Kong Human Rights Commission; 'Housing for All? Implementation of the Right to Adequate Housing for the Arab Palestinian Minority in Israel: A Report for the UN Committee on Economic, Social and Cultural Rights on the Implementation of Article 11(1) of the United Nations Covenant on Economic, Social and Cultural Rights', April 1996, prepared by the Arab Coordinating Committee on Housing Rights, Israel (ACCHRI); and 'El Derecho a la Vivienda en Mexico', March 1994, prepared by Casa y Ciudad, Cenvi, Copevi and Fosovi.

[9] M. Craven, 'Towards an Unofficial Petition Procedure: A Review on the Role of the UN Committee on Economic, Social and Cultural Rights', in *Social Rights as Human Rights: A European Challenge* (eds. K. Drzewicki, C. Krause and A. Rosas), Turku/Åbo, 1994, p. 91.

[10] On the Committee and the right to housing, see: H. Steiner and P. Alston, *International Human Rights in Context: Law, Politics, Morals*, Oxford, 1996, pp. 316–22; and S. Leckie 'The UN Committee on Economic, Social and Cultural Rights: Towards an Appropriate Approach', 11 *HRQ*, No. 4, 1989, p. 522.

1. THE DETERMINATION OF VIOLATIONS OF THE ICESCR

While the determination of violations of a treaty[11] should be an essential element of any human rights monitoring procedure, determinations by the Committee that a state party had violated any particular right guaranteed by the ICESCR were long in coming. It was not until 1990 that the Committee first declared a state party to have violated its housing rights obligations under the Covenant.

> The information that had reached members of the Committee concerning the massive expulsion of nearly 15,000 families in the course of the last five years, the deplorable conditions in which the families had had to live, and the conditions in which the expulsions had taken place were deemed sufficiently serious for it to be considered that the guarantees in article 11 of the Covenant had not been respected.[12]

A year later it adopted a similar formula with respect to Panama, stating that 'evictions carried out in this way not only infringed upon the right to adequate housing but also on the inhabitants' rights to privacy and security of the home'.[13] Since that time, the Committee has issued further findings of violations, although it has generally been cautious in making such determinations.[14]

---

[11] See *The Maastricht Guidelines on Violations of Economic, Social and Cultural Rights*, adopted on 26 January 1997, 20 *HRQ*, No. 3, 1998, p. 691; and S. Leckie, 'Another Step Towards Indivisibility: Identifying the Key Features of Violations of Economic, Social and Cultural Rights', 29 *HRQ*, No. 1, 1998, p. 81.

[12] Dominican Republic, UN Doc. E/C.12/1990/8, para. 249.

[13] '[T]he justification for the action carried out by the Panamanian and United States forces in Tocumen, San Miguelito and Panama Viejo in early 1990, which affected over 5,000 persons, was unacceptable under the terms of the Covenant as a ground for forcibly removing people from their homes. During the actions concerned, a large number of houses were demolished, in spite of the affected persons having lived in the area for more than two years. Additionally, these evictions had not been accompanied by legal eviction orders': UN Doc. E/C.12/1991/4, para. 135.

[14] 'The Government itself acknowledges that planned forced evictions may affect up to 200,000 families, and that the Government has identified only 150,000 relocation sites. Such a situation would not be compatible with respect for the right to housing. If these estimates are correct a very significant number of persons currently threatened with eviction will not receive adequate resettlement. Such a situation would not be compatible with respect for the right to housing': Philippines, UN Doc. E/C.12/1995/18.

2. URGING THE ADOPTION OF NEW LEGISLATION

In addition to declaring that violations of the ICESCR have occurred, the Committee has encouraged a number of states to adopt new legislation designed to promote the domestic implementation of the Covenant. Two examples illustrate the Committee's attempts at helping to shape national laws with a view to promoting compliance with the housing rights norms:

> The Committee requests the Government to apply existing housing rights provisions in the Constitution and for that purpose to take such measures to facilitate and promote their application. Such measures could include: (a) adoption of comprehensive housing rights legislation; (b) legal recognition of the right of affected communities to information concerning any Governmental plans actually or potentially affecting their rights; (c) adoption of urban reform legislation which recognizes the contribution of civil society in implementing the Covenant and addresses questions of security of tenure, the regularization of land ownership arrangements, etc.[15]

> The Committee also urges the Government seriously to consider the embodiment into domestic law of the right to housing.[16]

While more detailed guidance from the Committee regarding the content of such legislation might have been useful (considering the broad range of issues linked to domestic housing rights legislation), the very suggestion that states adopt legislation provides a basis for action by local human rights groups, and can initiate popular processes in support of such legislation.

3. URGING THE REPEAL OF LEGISLATION

On the basis of NGO information as to the negative impact of certain laws, particularly presidential decrees, the Committee has explicitly requested states to repeal laws deemed inconsistent with the ICESCR. For example, in 1995 the Committee urged that the Philippines Government give

> consideration . . . to the repeal of Presidential Decrees 772 and 1818 and recommends that all existing legislation relevant to the practice of forced evictions should be reviewed so as to ensure its compatibility with the provisions of the Covenant.[17]

[15] Dominican Republic, UN Doc. E/C.12/1994/20.
[16] Hong Kong, UN Doc. E/C.12/1994/20.   [17] Philippines, *supra*, note 14.

In the same year, the Committee informed the Government of the Dominican Republic that 'Presidential decrees 358–91 and 359–91 are formulated in a manner inconsistent with the provisions of the Covenant' and urged the Government 'to consider the repeal of both of these decrees within the shortest possible time frame'.[18] Both states responded to the Committee's comments. In the Philippines, hearings were held by a Senate Committee to consider the repeal of Decree 772, and the Decree was repealed shortly thereafter. In September 1996, on the fifth anniversary of the adoption of decree 358–91, the recently elected President of the Dominican Republic announced on national television the repeal of the decree. If implemented the decree would have resulted in the eviction of over 100,000 urban poor dwellers.

4. ENCOURAGING IMPLEMENTATION OF LEGISLATION

The Committee also makes regular appeals to states to implement and apply existing laws which are favourable to the enjoyment of economic, social and cultural rights. With respect to Belgium, the Committee expressed . . .

> concern at the adequacy of the measures taken to actually enforce that [housing rights] constitutional provision. The Committee urges the Government to more intensively apply existing laws allowing the Government to requisition properties and housing left unoccupied by owners.[19]

Again, the Committee specifically asked the Government of the Philippines to

> promote greater security of tenure in relation to housing in accordance with the principles outlined in the Committee's General Comment No. 4 and . . . take the necessary measures, including prosecutions wherever appropriate, to stop violations of laws such as R. A. 7279 [The Urban Development and Housing Act, 1992].[20]

5. ENCOURAGING PREVENTIVE ACTION TO AVOID VIOLATIONS OF THE COVENANT

The provision of information by NGOs concerning possible or pending violations of the ICESCR has occasionally produced comments by the

---

[18] Dominican Republic, *supra*, note 15.   [19] Belgium, UN Doc. E/C.12/1994/20.
[20] Philippines, *supra*, note 14.

Committee intended to prevent potential infringements. This has occurred particularly in relation to planned forced evictions. For instance:

> The Committee notes with concern a statement attributed to the Commissioner for Environment and Physical Planning . . . that the owners of 'shanties have no moral justification to ask the state government to renew their houses for them'. If correct, such a statement could easily be taken to be inconsistent with the provisions of the Covenant which, in the view of the Committee, require that forced evictions cannot take place unless alternative arrangements are in place to ensure respect for the right to adequate housing of those affected.[21]

With respect to mass pending evictions in the Dominican Republic, the Committee requested that state . . .

> to suspend any actions which are not clearly in conformity with the provisions of the Covenant, and . . . to provide additional information . . . as a matter of urgency.[22]

In the latter case, the government decided to refrain from the planned forced evictions. In the former, over one million Nigerians remain threatened by a huge eviction plan in Nigeria's largest city.[23]

6. URGING THE IMPLEMENTATION OF NGO-DEVISED HOUSING PLANS

In recognition that certain aspects of development are best guided by the efforts of those holding direct stakes in the process, the Committee has urged a state to take full account in its housing policy of proposals by NGOs which, if carried out in full, 'would have positive effects on well over 100,000 persons'.[24] In the case *La Cienega-los Guandules* in Santo Domingo (Dominican Republic), a slum whose inhabitants were under constant threat of eviction, the Committee pointed out to the Government that it . . .

---

[21] Letter from the Chairperson of the Committee on Economic, Social and Cultural Rights to the Government of Nigeria, 10 December 1996.

[22] Dominican Republic, UN Doc. E/C.12/1991/4, para. 330. See also the concluding observations on Mexico which stated that: 'The Committee urges the State party to desist from policy measures that lead to large-scale evictions': UN Doc. E/C.12/1993/3.

[23] Social and Economic Rights Action Centre, *Forced Evictions in Lagos, Nigeria*, Lagos, 1997.

[24] Dominican Republic, *supra*, note 15, para. 328.

should also give careful consideration to implementing alternative develop-ment plans for the area, taking full account of plans developed by non-governmental and community-based organizations.[25]

According to local NGOs and community-based groups, this brief men-tion by the Committee resulted in a major volte-face by the Government of the Dominican Republic, which has fully involved the community sector in urban development efforts and has begun implementing alternative plans for one of the capital city's largest slums.

7. RECOMMENDING THE SUBSTANTIVE PROVISION OF RIGHTS

It is often presumed that UN treaty bodies can only make general observa-tions about the human rights situation in any given country, and that decisions urging states parties to carry out major alterations in law, policy and practice are necessarily the exception rather than the norm. The ESCR Committee, however, has often recommended that states parties ensure the provision of specific services necessary for the realisation of the rights in question. In this manner, the Committee has displayed a clear willing-ness to suggest that states parties make every effort, in accordance with the 'maximum of available resources', to fulfil the positive obligations arising from the provisions of the ICESCR. The following examples are illustrative:

> The Committee is concerned that the right to security of tenure is not enjoyed by all tenants in Canada ... The Committee recommends the extension of security of tenure to all tenants and draws the attention of the State party to its General Comment No. 4 on the Right to Adequate Housing.[26]

> The Committee recommends the speedy adoption of policies and measures designed to ensure adequate civic services, security of tenure and the avail-ability of resources to facilitate access by low-income communities to afford-able housing. The Committee also recommends the increased construction of rental housing . . .[27]

> The Committee recommends that the Belgian authorities take appropriate measures to promote investment programmes and encourage, in particular, the construction of low-cost rental housing.[28]

---

[25] Dominican Republic, *supra*, note 15.   [26] Canada, UN Doc. E/C.12/1993/3.
[27] Mexico, *supra*, note 22.   [28] Belgium, *supra*, note 19.

The Committee urges the Government to take immediate steps, as a matter of high priority, to eradicate the phenomenon of 'cage homes', and to ensure that those currently living in such accommodation are provided with adequate and affordable rehousing.[29]

The Committee considers that, when relocating evicted or homeless persons or families, attention should be paid to the availability of job opportunities, schools, hospitals, health centres, and transport facilities in the areas selected.[30]

8. RECOMMENDING SPECIFIC POLICY MEASURES

The Committee has also requested that states adopt and implement specific policies within the context of the housing rights provisions of the ICESCR. For instance:

The Committee recommends that the State party develop and implement urgently a comprehensive housing policy.[31]

The Government should ensure that forced evictions are not carried out except in truly exceptional circumstances, following consideration of all possible alternatives and in full respect of the rights of all persons affected. The Committee urges the Government to extend indefinitely the moratorium on summary and illegal forced evictions and demolitions and to ensure that all those under threat in those contexts are entitled to due process.[32]

(a) The need to establish new national institutions

In recognition of the importance of local mechanisms designed to promote, implement and monitor progress with respect to housing rights, the Committee has suggested to several states that they establish new national housing institutions. For instance:

The Committee, in view of the problems in the housing sector, which are still considerable, urges the Government to establish an official, nationwide Commission on Housing, comprised of representatives of Government, non-governmental organizations and other relevant groups.[33]

The Government should consider the establishment of an independent body legally responsible for preventing illegal forced evictions, and for

---

[29] United Kingdom (Hong Kong), *supra*, note 16.   [30] Philippines, *supra*, note 14.
[31] Nicaragua, UN Doc. E/C.12/1993/3.   [32] Philippines, *supra*, note 14.
[33] Belgium, *supra*, note 19.

monitoring, documenting and reviewing any ongoing or planned forced evictions. The Presidential Commission on the Urban Poor could also be given an enhanced mandate to protect housing rights, and to collect accurate and reliable indicators and statistics relating to urban problems such as homelessness, forced evictions, the numbers of those relocated, and the number of squatters.[34]

(b) The obligation to monitor compliance

Finally, in response to information received from NGOs, the Committee has repeatedly asked states to provide it with information previously withheld:

> The Committee is concerned by the housing situation in the Republic of Korea and considers that it has not been given adequate information on the subject, especially with regard to unsuitable housing, the number of homeless people and forcible evictions. It notes that, according to international non-governmental sources, 720,000 persons were evicted on the occasion of the Olympic Games in Seoul and that no information has been provided on their subsequent situation, while 16,000 are said to have been evicted since February 1992. Lastly, according to national non-governmental sources, 4,000 evictions took place in 1994. Despite the Committee's concerns, there has been no response to its questions or, more generally, to problems relating to the right to housing.[35]

> The Committee urges the State party to improve its monitoring of the problem of inadequate housing and to develop more active and focused measures to improve the situation. In this connection, it draws the attention of the State party to the provisions of its General Comment No. 4 (1991).[36]

As these examples show, tangible results can emerge from the Committee, despite the superficiality of the formal process of state reporting and the other obstacles to the Committee's effective operation.[37] When NGO involvement is substantial and sustained, the Committee activities have led to laws being repealed, large-scale threatened violations being prevented and, overall, to an enhancement in the stature of community-based groups.

---

[34] Philippines, *supra*, note 14.   [35] South Korea, UN Doc. E/C.12/1995/18.

[36] United Kingdom, UN Doc. E/C.12/1995/18.

[37] See also chapter 5 of this volume by G. Lansdown, subheading 'The role of NGOs in the reporting process and its benefits', and chapter 8 by A. Clapham.

In the Dominican Republic, for instance, the large-scale evictions of the late 1980s and early 1990s which resulted in more than 200,000 dwellers losing their homes have effectively stopped. A presidential decree manifestly incompatible with the provisions of the ICESCR was repealed. Homeless families and communities have been relocated and rehoused in accordance with the Committee's requests, and various new institutional frameworks established. All this points to a more responsive attitude by governments to the ICESCR which in turn has resulted from increased international attention to the domestic human rights situation. Arguably, these and other favourable outcomes had far less to do with the reports of the state party (which have always been of low quality), than with information given by NGOs and systematic follow-up. In cases such as these, the government reporting process acted as a window of opportunity for NGOs to air their grievances before the international community and for the Committee to act upon them.

D. Two modest ideas for improving the current UN treaty system

The positive steps described above have taken place within the confines of a system which is still very much in need of repair. While the Committee has made considerable progress much remains to be done. Of numerous suggestions put forward for improving the UN treaty system, two warrant particular attention here.

1. DIGITALISE THE REPORTING SYSTEM

Although the Office of the UN High Commissioner for Human Rights (UNHCHR) now has its own website and is now fully computerised, both the application of, and access to, computer technology could be greatly improved. Greater use of available information technology throughout the treaty system would increase the efficiency, consistency and capabilities of the treaty monitoring process. Some of the ways digitalisation could proceed include:

(a) A formal request by the High Commissioner to all states parties to submit their reports in electronic form. All states, regardless of the level of current economic development, have the capacity to do so. Once states' reports are received electronically they should be immediately entered into a UN Treaty Body Country Database which would be permanently posted on the Internet. Information in the country data base would be key-worded and searchable. The contents of the database would then be used as the basis for electronically examining the report in question and would be accessible to any Internet user. The database would contain all relevant information as it relates specifically to the treaty system, including, but not limited to:

(i) copies of all states' reports;
(ii) copies of previous concluding observations by the monitoring body involved and by other monitoring bodies;
(iii) any other information placed in the database by independent sources, suitably acknowledged; and
(iv) accessible descriptions of the reporting process, the relevance of the treaty in question and other information for persons not already involved in the human rights field.

(b) The complete absence of computers in the meeting rooms of the treaty bodies illustrates how far the UN has to go in the context of information technology. The High Commissioner could request that two meeting rooms (possibly rooms IX and XI in the United Nations *Palais des Nations* in Geneva) be set aside for the use of treaty bodies. The treaty bodies would always meet in these rooms, but the space would be available for other UN activities. Each position on the table would have a computer screen and keyboard installed with Internet access, allowing Committee members direct access to the country database mentioned and any other sources or sites relevant to the country concerned.

Each treaty body should create its own website (in addition to the High Commissioner's site) which would enable a much broader range of people to submit information and alternative reports than is currently the case. Instead or in addition to the current 'country-file' system, digitalising the reporting process and the human rights monitoring process generally would make the system substantially more democratic, accountable and transparent than is currently the case. Treaty body members should have access to comprehensive computer training.

2. MORE SYSTEMATIC AND INTENSIVE SECRETARIAT FOLLOW-UP

Following the consideration of a report, each committee secretariat should prepare (or coordinate the preparation of) country follow-up documents, to be available within twelve months of the release of the concluding observations. Systematically following up previous recommendations and suggestions of the treaty bodies will assist in maintaining institutional memory and promote treaty compliance. While some committees offer detailed concluding observations, there is no apparatus for determining whether they are actually complied with. Waiting five years to discover what has or has not been done is far too long. The vagueness and generality of many of the recommendations and suggestions issued to date could be addressed through more intensive secretariat involvement.[38]

Issuing concluding observations certainly represents an improvement over earlier outcomes of the supervisory process. This method would have a greater impact were it to include a sixth category entitled 'Violations of the Treaty', elaborating, in a more judicially-oriented manner, each violation found and making specific recommendations for the steps required to redress any violations.

E. Conclusions

There can be no doubting that significant improvements have been made within the global human rights treaty regime. Important elements of the system, which were viewed as unrealistic only a few years ago, are now widely accepted. The system, once inaccessible and almost entirely ineffectual, has grown substantially to the point where on occasions, it can make a real difference in the lives of real people. Nevertheless, these minor successes have produced a form of counter-reaction in the form of criticisms by some states and cautious attitudes by the treaty bodies. This has occurred at a time when rather than caution, sterner measures grounded in human rights law would have been a more appropriate response.

---

[38] In other words, 'Law X should be repealed immediately due to its incompatibility with the terms and objectives of the treaty' is much more likely to receive some form of response from a state party than a phrase such as 'The Committee is concerned about Law X'.

7

COUNTRY-ORIENTED PROCEDURES UNDER THE CONVENTION AGAINST TORTURE: TOWARDS A NEW DYNAMISM

ROLAND BANK

A. Introduction

When negotiations for a convention aimed at combating torture took place in the early 1980s, the time was not yet ripe for the introduction of a treaty monitoring system based on preventive inspection visits to places of detention. Such a proposal, submitted by Costa Rica during the negotiations and based on a proposal by Jean Jacques Gautier, failed to gain strong support. The idea thus remained operative only at the regional level in the framework of the Council of Europe.[1] It was not until 1992 that the (still ongoing) drafting process for a system of on-the-spot inspections at the UN level was initiated. Rather than adopting this novel mechanism, the 1984 Convention against Torture (CAT) kept to traditional supervisory techniques. As with other treaties, such as the International Covenant on Civil and Political Rights (ICCPR), states parties to the CAT are obliged to report regularly on their efforts to implement the substantive provisions of the Convention (article 19). These reports are then considered by the CAT Committee, a body established to oversee implementation of the Convention. In addition, the CAT provides for procedures for examining complaints submitted by states parties (article 21) or by individuals (article 22). Adoption of these procedures by states parties is optional, as is the case for the ICCPR and its Optional Protocol. In addition to these well-known monitoring mechanisms, the CAT contains an entirely new inquiry provision (article 20), which permits the CAT Committee to conduct an inquiry whenever it receives 'well-founded indications that torture is being

---

[1] The European Convention for the Prevention of Torture (ETS 126) entered into force on 1 February 1989.

systematically practised in the territory of a State Party'. States parties, however, may opt out of article 20 upon signature, accession or ratification, but not after having accepted the procedure.

Whereas procedures for state complaints have thus far been insignificant in the practice of the CAT Committee,[2] a rising number of individual complaints has been addressed to this treaty body. The overall number, however, cannot be considered to be very high, with only sixty-seven cases brought during the first ten years of the procedure's operation.[3] The CAT Committee's jurisprudence has developed a noteworthy profile in the area of protection against expulsion, return and extradition (article 3 CAT), guaranteeing a high level of protection, particularly in comparison to the jurisprudence of the European Convention on Human Rights (ECHR).[4] As a violation of article 3 CAT was claimed in the majority of cases, it is not surprising that almost all of these complaints were directed against states of the Western world.[5]

Having given this very brief overview of the procedures with which the CAT Committee is entrusted, this chapter will focus on the country-oriented mechanisms established under CAT, namely, the state reporting and inquiry procedures. As drafting is still under way for an Optional Protocol to the Convention, the aim of which is to establish a visiting system (which will be a landmark in the UN human rights supervisory system), the

---

[2] This irrelevance may to some extent be due to the complicated design of the procedures. Of more importance seems to be the problem of potential complainants refraining from applying to the CAT Committee because of diplomatic considerations. Similarly, a state complaint within the European Convention for the Prevention of Torture is considered an 'unfriendly act' (cf. M. Villiger, *Handbuch der Europäischen Menschenrechtskonvention*, Zürich, 1993, p. 110). However, the ten complaints which have been examined under the respective provisions of the ECHR show that interests such as those concerning national minorities might overrule such diplomatic courtesies.

[3] As of May 1997. Cf. UN Doc. A/52/44 (Annual Report of the Committee Against Torture), para. 273.

[4] For a comparison of the jurisdiction of the ECHR organs under article 3 ECHR and of the practice of the CAT Committee under article 3 CAT, see W. Suntinger, 'The Principle of Non-Refoulement: Looking to Geneva rather than to Strasbourg?', 49 *Austrian Journal of Public and International Law*, 1995, pp. 203–25.

[5] In addition, this state of affairs may be partly explained by the fact that the states that have accepted the individual complaints procedure tend to be more democratic. However, some of the states that have recognised the competence of the CAT Committee under article 22 of the Convention (e.g. Algeria and Turkey) are known for tolerating the widespread practice of torture.

existing instruments for monitoring the performance of states parties in implementing the Convention will continue to play the key role for some time to come. How have these procedures functioned in practice? What are their flaws and how can they be overcome?

B. The state reporting procedure

The state reporting procedure, which has become the classical monitoring mechanism for UN treaty bodies, is also the central instrument under the CAT.[6] As with other treaty bodies, this procedure has come up against several problems with regard to both the quantity of state reports and the readiness of states parties to fulfil their obligations by submitting state reports on time. The poor quality of certain state reports and of discussions by the CAT Committee of some reports have been the subject of criticism and have most likely contributed to the low impact of the Committee's work.[7] In recent years, however, the system of state reporting to UN treaty bodies has undergone significant change. These developments suggest a more dynamic interpretation of the treaty bodies' mandates in the future. The following analysis reflects on these changes and considers options for further improvement.

1. QUANTITATIVE ASPECTS

During the CAT Committee's first twelve years of operation it has examined an enormous number of state reports. Each year the Committee has held two sessions, each of which lasted for two weeks, during which five to seven reports have been discussed by the Committee with representatives of the state party concerned. As at 9 December 1999, the CAT had been ratified or acceded to by 118 states. Bearing in mind that states parties are required to submit an initial report within one year of the entering into force of the Convention in that country and are then obliged to produce a periodic report every four years, the amount of time presently allotted for

---

[6] As indicated by the number of meetings concerned with this procedure. For instance, the CAT Committee dedicated thirteen out of nineteen meetings of the seventeenth session and fifteen out of eighteen meetings of the eighteenth session to the discussion of state reports, cf. Annual Report of the Committee Against Torture, UN Doc. A/52/44, paras. 23, 26.

[7] Cf. R. Bank, 'International Efforts to Combat Torture and Inhuman Treatment: Have the New Mechanisms Improved Protection?', 8 *EJIL*, 1997, pp. 613–37 at p. 633.

sessions of the Committee seems very modest. It hardly seems adequate for discussions of state reports, let alone for dealing with additional matters.

As has been the experience of other treaty bodies, the CAT Committee faces a widespread reluctance on the part of states parties to submit reports on time: as at 9 May 1997, thirty-two first periodic reports, thirty second periodic reports and twenty-one third periodic reports were overdue.[8] In response to this poor level of compliance with treaty obligations, the Committee lists in its annual report those states parties whose reports are late. In addition, a reminder system is now well established, with notifications sent by the UN Secretary-General and by the chairperson of the CAT Committee. Given, however, that this system has been in place for some years, one might readily doubt its effectiveness in enhancing compliance with reporting obligations.

The problem of long-term non-compliance of states parties with their reporting obligations has led to a debate on the possibility of discussion of the Convention's implementation in such countries in the absence of a report. The Committee has recently considered this option, but concluded that the Convention only allows for the Committee to discuss actual reports. A counter-argument may be put forward on the basis of the concept of implied powers,[9] but only if interpreted very extensively. It could be argued that the general task of supervising implementation of the Convention, as constituted by the different procedures, implies a power independent of the submission of a state report. However, the centrality of the state report to the whole CAT procedure, together with the lack of textual support in the Convention, does not support the option of Committee discussion in the absence of such a report. Yet, given that the established practice of treaty bodies is to extend discussions beyond the actual contents of state reports, it seems overly formalistic to allow comprehensive discussions of the implementation of the Convention with states parties that have delivered flimsy and superficial state reports but to completely rule out the possibility of discussion in those cases where a state report has been overdue for several years. The Committee has, nevertheless, decided to continue with the condition that discussion can only take place with states parties that have delivered their reports. It will however seek to encourage the filing of state reports by feeding information received from

[8] Cf. UN Doc. A/52/44 (Annual report of the CAT Committee), para. 20.
[9] Cf. A. Byrnes, 'The Committee against Torture', in *The United Nations and Human Rights: A Critical Appraisal*, (ed. P. Alston), Oxford, 1992, pp. 509–46, at p. 530.

non-governmental organisations (NGOs) to those governments that have failed to fulfil their reporting obligations.

Notwithstanding the unsatisfactory level of compliance with reporting obligations, the Committee is not in a position to examine submitted reports promptly. Indeed, it faces a significant backlog. Until the time of the Annual Report of 1997, reports were regularly examined in the next but one session after submission.[10] The situation, however, seems to be worsening due to the increasing numbers of state reports. Of the state reports discussed during the twentieth session of the Committee, held in May 1998, only the initial reports of Sri Lanka and Kuwait had been submitted not more than one session before, while the other reports had been submitted more than two sessions earlier. Thus, the period of time between submission of a report and its discussion has increased to seventeen months in some cases.[11]

The problem of work overload has been addressed recently, with the result that the Committee now meets for a session of three weeks rather than two: the twentieth session in May 1998 was extended to three weeks, which enabled the Committee to review ten (instead of the usual six or seven) state reports. The UN High Commissioner for Human Rights announced that she would support additional three-week sessions as required.[12] This would at least prevent an increase in the backlog of state reports to be examined.

2. PERFORMANCE IN DISCUSSING STATE REPORTS

As is the case with other treaty bodies, discussion of state reports with representatives of the state party concerned is conducted according to a set

[10] During the eighteenth session of the Committee (April/May 1997), the following periodic reports were examined: third periodic reports of Ukraine (submitted in June 1996), Mexico (submitted in June 1996), Denmark (submitted in July 1996), and Sweden (submitted in August 1996); the second periodic report of Paraguay (submitted in July 1996); and the initial report of Namibia (submitted in August 1996).

[11] During the twentieth session of the Committee (May 1998), the following periodic reports were examined: initial reports of Sri Lanka (submitted in October 1997), and Kuwait (August 1997); second periodic reports of Germany (December 1996), Guatemala (February 1997), France (December 1996), Israel (February 1997), New Zealand (February 1997), Norway (February 1997), Peru (January 1997); and the third periodic report of Panama (May 1997).

[12] Cf. UN Department of Public Information, Press Releases, 'Committee Against Torture Concludes Twentieth Session', 22 May 1998.

procedure. At the beginning of each discussion, the government delegation has the opportunity to introduce the state report. Committee members then pose their questions to the delegation, which gives its responses at a second meeting, usually held later the same day. One Committee member serves as country rapporteur and another as co-rapporteur, their role being to prepare an in-depth discussion of the report and to put forward the first questions.

While the quality of state report discussions by the CAT Committee has varied in the past, the following shortcomings have frequently been noted:[13]

- lack of depth in oral inquiries (in particular, structural problems under-pinning a problematic observation were often not addressed);
- failure to address the most significant problems in a country under consideration (even to the extent that, for instance, a state party with a known record of police brutality and important gaps in safeguards was suggested as a model for other states parties);[14]
- repetition of questions by different Committee members;
- lack of cohesion (no visible concept of interpretation of the Convention and even contradictory remarks by different Committee members);
- questions indicating a misunderstanding of the CAT by individual Committee members;
- lack of differentiation between different risk groups, for instance, between ordinary and terrorist suspects;
- premature praising of governments' efforts;[15]
- vague questions inviting evasive answers; and
- failure to insist on exhaustive answers in cases of wrong, incomplete or unsatisfactory responses.

Some of these faults have been remedied to a certain extent in recent years. In particular, it is now much less likely that the Committee will rely solely on its own resources to examine acute problems of states parties under

---

[13] For evidence see Bank, *supra*, note 7, pp. 621–33.

[14] Cf. CAT/C/SR.27, 36 (discussion of the initial report of France). In contrast, the Committee for the Prevention of Torture (CPT) concluded that persons arrested by the police in France ran a non-negligible risk of being ill-treated, cf. CPT Rapport France (CPT/Inf (93)2), para. 11.

[15] For instance, the United Kingdom received the appreciation of the CAT Committee for the modernising of buildings and equipment in the prison system without having considered the significant increase in the prison population which at least partly countered the material progress achieved. Cf. Bank, *supra*, note 7, p. 628.

consideration. It makes considerably greater use of NGO information, including explicit references to NGO reports during discussions. This is evident in recent state report discussions. In contrast to the discussion of its initial report, the examination of France's second periodic report addressed the issue of police brutality[16] and basic safeguards for arrested persons.[17] Similarly, the Committee's discussion of Germany's second periodic report took up the question of police maltreatment of foreigners.[18] Nevertheless, certain serious problems continue to escape the Committee's attention, as seen in the latter case where the issue of detention conditions for foreigners awaiting deportation was not raised.[19]

In more general terms, it may be noted that the discussions of the CAT Committee have become more cohesive and improved in quality since the introduction of the system of 'Concluding observations'. It would appear that questions are now being posed with a view to drawing possible conclusions and recommendations. This has given discussions a visible direction.

However, it seems that most of the other problems continue to hamper the Committee's effectiveness. A glance at the Summary Records of the 1998 spring session brings to light various examples of the shortcomings discussed above, though possibly fewer than in previous years. Questions put to the delegations were sometimes as vague as an enquiry into whether the law in the country under review was in complete accordance with article 3 CAT.[20] Other questions confused issues by failing to make proper differentiations: for instance, not clearly distinguishing between penal,

---

[16] Cf. CAT/C/SR.320, para. 32, with reference to a report of Amnesty International. However, it may be doubted whether a single question constitutes an appropriate inquiry into such a problem.

[17] Cf. CAT/C/SR.320, paras. 27, 39, 40.   [18] Cf. CAT/C/SR.328, paras. 15, 19.

[19] The main targets of criticism include the duration of such detention (maximum eighteen months), absence of efforts to overcome language barriers, the splitting up of families into different centres (cf. *Süddeutsche Zeitung* 10/11 December 1994), substandard material conditions and the high risk of suicide (cf. Deutscher Caritasverband, *Erfahrungsbericht zur Situation von Asylsuchenden und Flüchtlingen in Deutschland*, Freiburg-im-Breisgau, 1994, 13 ff.; Pro Asyl, *Weggesperrt zum Abtransport. Abschiebehaft in Deutschland*, Karlsruhe, 1995.) Both court officials and police officers have described detention conditions as inhuman on several occasions (cf. Bank, *supra*, note 7; R. Bank, *Die internationale Bekämpfung von Folter und unmenschlicher Behandlung auf den Ebenen der Vereinten Nationen und des Europarates*, Edition Iuscrim, Freiburg-im-Breisgau, 1996, 244, footnotes 66–8).

[20] Cf. CAT/C/SR.328, para. 12 (discussion of the second periodic report of Germany).

disciplinary and compensatory procedures,[21] or addressing different issues in one question.[22] One also finds inconsistencies in comments by different Committee members: for example, one Committee member congratulated the German Government for its contribution to the UN Fund for the Victims of Torture, while the next member demanded an increase in this contribution.[23] Committee members also persisted in demanding state action which, however, is not required under the Convention, such as insisting on incorporation of the definition of torture according to article 1 CAT into national law.[24] In various instances some explanation would have been called for to justify the link between the Convention and certain issues – including asylum policy,[25] permissible reasons for arresting suspects,[26] training of medical personnel in recognising signs of torture in order to treat refugees properly.[27] Further, the Committee once again failed to focus

---

[21] Cf. CAT/C/SR.328, para. 13 (discussion of the second periodic report of Germany).

[22] CAT/C/SR.330, para. 15, (discussion of second periodic report of Peru): 'M. Zupancic asked if the victims of acts of torture could benefit from legal aid and if there are any programmes for the rehabilitation of victims, and also educational programmes aimed at members of the armed forces and police, bearing specifically on the prohibition of torture, in the broadest sense, and on respect for human rights.' (editor's translation).

[23] Cf. CAT/C/SR.328, paras. 20 and 23 (discussion of the second periodic report of Germany).

[24] Cf. CAT/C/SR.320, para. 21 (discussion of the second periodic report of France). The obligations of member states are contained in articles 2–16 CAT whereas article 1 CAT does not require implementation by member states.

[25] Cf. CAT/C/SR.320, para. 23 (discussion of the second periodic report of France).

[26] Cf. CAT/C/SR.320, para. 39 (discussion of the second periodic report of France). The Convention does not contain any rules relating to permissible reasons for detaining individuals. Furthermore, other treaties distinguish between the prohibition of torture and inhuman or degrading treatment on the one hand and permissible reasons for a deprivation of liberty on the other (cf. articles 3 and 5 ECHR or articles 7, 9 and 10 ICCPR). While it may be worth considering detention ordered for certain reasons as constituting at least inhuman or degrading treatment, this step would require well-founded argumentation.

[27] Cf. CAT/C/SR.328, para. 21 (discussion of the second periodic report of Germany). This comment was linked to article 10 CAT by the respective Committee member. Article 10 is indeed concerned with training of medical personnel but refers to training on the *prohibition* of torture and of professionals dealing in any form with *persons deprived of their liberty*. Both aspects generally do not apply to asylum seekers in Germany. It may be arguable that the training mentioned by the Committee member is relevant for securing the rehabilitation of torture victims (article 14 CAT – which is unclear, however, as to whether it also applies to torture victims having suffered ill-treatment in another state) or as an important piece of evidence in favour of granting protection against expulsion and deportation under article 3.

on unsatisfactory answers, be they incomplete[28] or incomprehensible.[29] Finally, the Committee did not display a clear concept of its expectations. For instance, in the case of France, the Committee first emphasised that the period allowed for detainees to be held without any outside contact should be as short as possible to prevent ill-treatment in police custody, but it then failed to react to the delegation's answer that access to a lawyer would only be granted after twenty, thirty-six or seventy-two hours.[30]

While several of these criticisms can be attributed to lack of attention on the part of individual members during sessions or to insufficient individual preparation for discussions,[31] others maybe have their origins in structural deficiencies.

A lack of conceptualisation may account for the sometimes low level of cohesion, the undifferentiated approach taken in Committee members' inquiries and certain misinterpretations of the Convention. To date, the most important initiative taken to establish a certain consistency in questions raised by individual Committee members on different articles of the Convention was a summary of the most frequently asked questions put together by the secretariat several years ago. Apart from this exercise there has been only one remarkable attempt to ascertain systematically what the CAT Committee expects from states parties in terms of fully implementing the Convention. While the CAT Committee, in contrast to the Human Rights Committee (HRC), does not have an explicit power publicly to address all states parties with 'general comments', it has been argued that such a competence would be implied in the task of monitoring and encouraging improved implementation of the Convention.[32] Indeed, the CAT

---

[28] Cf. CAT/C/SR.321, para. 25 (discussion of the second periodic report of France). The government delegation only responded to the use of weapons by the *gendarmerie*. Questions regarding the *gendarmerie* were related to overlaps with police competences, whether protection is the same for persons apprehended by the *gendarmerie* and those arrested by the police, and how decisions on competence are taken.

[29] Cf. CAT/C/SR.321, para. 27 (discussion of the second periodic report of France). The government delegation reported that the *gendarmerie* was instructed in international humanitarian law. It is not clear how far international law relating to armed conflicts is relevant for the *gendarmerie*.

[30] Cf. CAT/C/SR.320, para. 39 and CAT/C/SR.321, para. 23 (discussion of the second periodic report of France).

[31] For a criticism levelled by former Human Rights Committee member T. Opsahl against the procedures for selecting HRC members (which may also apply to the selection of CAT Committee members), see T. Opsahl, 'The Human Rights Committee', in Alston, *supra*, note 9, p. 369, at p. 374.

[32] Cf. A. Byrnes, *supra*, note 9, pp. 509–46, at 530.

Committee has adopted and published one 'general comment' on article 3.[33] More generally, the Committee is not prevented from drawing up its 'general comments' internally so as to establish guidelines for requirements under each article which could then underpin the discussions of state reports.

A further factor which may contribute to the inadequate quality of questions is the modest investment of time and energy in the systematic preparation of discussions. The Committee as such does not programme its discussion of individual state reports. The country rapporteurs may consult each other prior to the meeting, but this does not seem to be standard practice. The only initiative taken in this regard is the compilation of materials received from NGOs, other UN bodies or the Council of Europe in folders which are available for consultation by Committee members. A thorough preparation for discussions would require that Committee members receive comprehensive information well in advance. In turn, all material presented would need to be analysed, relating it to the Convention and highlighting areas of concern and possible remedies. Given that this type of analysis would require considerable commitment of resources, and would include regular updating of information, the secretariat would be best qualified to take on the responsibility. Such analyses could be distributed to the Committee members in written form before sessions. Additionally, Committee members could be briefed on the country situation – on the basis of the analytical paper – by the secretariat or country rapporteur shortly before the discussion to ensure that all Committee members are fully informed and aware of the main areas of concern. However, a thorough preparation of this nature would definitely call for increased staffing of the secretariat.

This type of in-depth preparation could also help to streamline procedures for the discussion of state reports by creating thematic clusters of concern. Moreover, it would enable the country rapporteur to formulate and send complex questions in advance to the state party concerned, a practice similar to that of the 'list of issues' discussed by the HRC in relation to state reports. This would allow government delegations to prepare their answers to questions more thoroughly, rather than having only the time between the morning meeting (when questions are posed) and the afternoon meeting (when answers are given).

---

[33] General Comment on the implementation of article 3 of the Convention in the context of article 22, Report of the Committee against Torture, UN Doc. A/53/44, Annex IX.

3. PERFORMANCE IN THE FORMULATION OF 'CONCLUDING OBSERVATIONS'

As noted, CAT's provisions on the state reporting procedure are virtually identical to those of the ICCPR. However, the possibility, set down in the Convention, of formulating concluding remarks on every state report discussion marked a significant step forward. Indeed, the CAT contains an express provision for 'general comments' on each state report (article 19(3)). In contrast, at the time the CAT was adopted, the HRC interpreted the corresponding provision in the ICCPR (article 40(4)) as permitting 'general comments' only in cases where they are addressed to all parties to the Covenant. Despite strong criticism, the HRC did not take the opportunity of drawing up its own reports on specific state report discussions. Thus, it was most likely that the CAT Committee was the first UN body to react with specific comments on each and every state report.[34]

Nonetheless, the practices of the two committees have developed along similar lines. In its early days, individual HRC members voiced their concern about a state party at the end of each discussion. The CAT Committee, too, restricted itself to comments by individual members, refraining from consensus evaluations. Practice in both the HRC and the CAT Committee has since tended in the direction of substantive criticisms issued by the committees as a whole, with the result that each committee now uses a system of committee-level evaluations of each state report discussion. This evaluation system comprises comments in various categories of concern, including: positive aspects; factors and difficulties impeding the implementation of provisions of the Convention or the Covenant; subjects of concern; and recommendations. This dynamic interpretation of CAT and the ICCPR has breathed new life into state reporting procedures, especially by providing for concrete recommendations on the part of the treaty bodies.

However, the question thus arises whether such a degree of specificity in the Committee's recommendations is compatible with the Convention, which explicitly allows for '*general* comments' on each report (article 19(3)). There seems to be consensus that the phrase 'general comments' in the CAT is to be interpreted in the same way as in the ICCPR, except that the CAT Committee may also issue such comments on individual state

---

[34] Cf. M. Nowak, 'The Implementation Functions of the UN Committee Against Torture', in *Fortschritt im Bewusstsein der Grund- und Menschenrechte. Festschrift für Felix Ermacora* (eds. M. Nowak, D. Streurer and H. Tretter), Kehl/Strasbourg/Arlington, 1988, p. 525.

reports.[35] General comments of the HRC have been interpreted in such a way as to allow for matters concerning the implementation of the Covenant to be addressed and for the giving of (non-binding) interpretations of the Convention.[36] Treaty interpretation necessarily involves a certain specificity or particularity. Accordingly, the term 'general' is to be understood as being in contrast to the idea of comments on specific cases.[37] However, the Committee's practice has tended to give a very narrow interpretation to the notion of 'specific', occasionally commenting on specific instances of physical violence in certain places and designating them as 'cruel and degrading treatment'.[38] With this interpretation of the phrase 'general comments', the Committee has paved the way for the further development of 'Concluding observations'. In turn, this could lead to the development of a jurisprudence dealing with issues or practices which are not specifically addressed in the Convention.

The Committee has published a considerable number of useful comments, with a view to expressing its concerns clearly and making recommendations to tackle problems raised. These comments are increasingly referred to by NGOs. However, given that the Committee's conclusions and recommendations should be clear, specific, accurate and reflect the actual discussion, the 'Concluding observations' issued during the CAT Committee's 1998 spring session continue to reveal an array of shortcomings.

(a) Clarity and specificity

While some recommendations issued by the Committee are sufficiently clear and precise, others lack clarity or fail to indicate concrete measures to be taken. The Committee frequently recommends the need to 'intensify'[39] or 'strengthen'[40] efforts, to take 'all the means that are

---

[35] Cf. J. H. Burgers and H. Danelius, *The United Nations Convention against Torture*, Dordrecht, 1988, pp. 158 ff; M. Nowak, *CCPR Commentary*, Kehl/Strasbourg/Arlington, 1993, para. 51.

[36] Cf. ibid. paras. 53, 55.   [37] In this sense see also Byrnes, *supra*, note 9, at p. 529.

[38] CAT/C/NZE (Concluding observations on the second periodic report of New Zealand), para. 7.

[39] CAT/C/GUA (Concluding observations on the second periodic report of Guatemala), para. E.1.

[40] CAT/C/SRI (Concluding observations on the initial report of Sri Lanka), para. 24; CAT/C/ NOR (Concluding observations on the third periodic report of Norway), para. 7; CAT/C/ NZE (Concluding observations on the second periodic report of New Zealand), para. 9.

necessary',[41] to pay 'further legislative attention'[42] or 'apporter la plus grande attention possible'[43] to particular problems, without further specifying which measures should be taken or which legal gaps should be filled. Such vague appeals to states parties are very likely to be ignored. This is all the more true for recommendations which request states parties to 'continue' their efforts in relation to particular issues that have already been quite comprehensively addressed, such as occurred, for instance, with the German authorities' translation of an information brochure on detainees' rights into twenty-three languages.[44]

Further instances of a failure to give concrete guidelines to states parties on how to rectify a particular problem or how to meet the requirements of certain treaty obligations can be found. Examples where recommendations have not been sufficiently directive include the introduction of safeguards for refugee security,[45] the limiting of permits to carry firearms to 'strictly indispensable cases',[46] or the review of administrative detention practices 'in order to ensure its conformity with article 16'.

As the impact of the Committee's conclusions also depends on the perceptions of public opinion and interest groups able to lobby for relevant reforms in their country, it is most desirable that 'Concluding observations' be formulated in such a way that they may be understood without reference to other material. However, some conclusions and recommendations cannot be deciphered without reading the Summary Records. In one conclusion, for instance, the CAT Committee refers to certain laws which impair the independence of the judiciary without, however, indicating the elements relevant to this diagnosis.[47] On another occasion, the Committee points to 'certain omissions' in a law implementing the Convention.[48] For

---

[41] CAT/C/SRI (Concluding observations on the initial report of Sri Lanka), para. 24; CAT/C/GER (Concluding observations on the second periodic report of Germany), para. 14, and similarly CAT/C/GUA, para. E.5.

[42] Cf. CAT/C/GER (Concluding observations on the second periodic report of Germany), para. 15.

[43] CAT/C/FRA (Concluding observations on the second periodic report of France), para. 16.

[44] Cf. CAT/C/GER (Concluding observations on the second periodic report of Germany), para. 17.

[45] Cf. CAT/C/PAN (Concluding observations on the third periodic report of Panama), para. D.2.

[46] CAT/C/GUA, para. E.3 (translation from Spanish by the author).

[47] Cf. CAT/C/PER (Concluding observations on the second periodic report of Peru), para. 12.

[48] Cf. CAT/C/SRI (Concluding observations on the initial report of Sri Lanka), para. 17.

both of these examples, interested persons or NGOs would have to consult the Summary Records in order to ascertain the meaning of the comment.

Finally, recommendations which merely echo the text or contents of the Convention[49] cannot be considered strong incentives for states parties to undertake concrete measures. While it may be worthwhile emphasising that a state party is not fulfilling its obligations under the Convention, it will always be more helpful if concrete proposals on how to comply better with the requirements of the treaty are given.

(b) Reflection of discussion in the 'Concluding observations'

As the discussion of a state report with representatives of the state party concerned is a central element of the whole reporting procedure, 'Concluding observations' should reflect only those issues which have been properly addressed during the discussion. Conclusions and recommendations could otherwise create harmful misunderstandings or impair the credibility of comments. The Committee's 'Concluding observations' do not always meet these requirements. In one case, for instance, the Committee included a concern in its conclusions about allegations of police ill-treatment after the issue had been raised by only one question (which sought comments on reports by Amnesty International).[50] There have even been instances of issues being highlighted in the conclusions as subjects of concern without their having been discussed at all with the state party.[51]

At the same time, it seems equally desirable that all issues raised in the discussion and mentioned as 'subjects of concern' in the 'Concluding observations' be included in the recommendations. Once again, this has not always been the case and the Committee has at times voiced its concern on certain issues without addressing them in its recommendations.[52]

Moreover, the Committee may dilute the convincing force of a recommendation if counter-arguments against the proposed measure are put

[49] Ibid., para. 21, which is echoing article 12 CAT.
[50] Cf. CAT/C/FRA (Concluding observations on the second periodic report of France), para. 13 and CAT/C/SR.320, para. 32.
[51] Cf. CAT/C/GER (Concluding observations on the second periodic report of Germany), para. 7. The point made concerned exculpation from a criminal accusation of torture by superior order that was in the eyes of the Committee not categorically excluded. Cf. ibid., para. 14 on the length of investigations of police ill-treatment.
[52] Cf. CAT/C/PAN (Concluding observations on the third periodic report of Panama), para. D.2.

forward during the discussion by the government delegation and are not challenged by the Committee. For instance, despite the German Government's argument that police officers did not wear personal identification for reasons of protecting themselves against reprisals, the Committee simply recommended 'wear[ing] a form of personal identification'.[53]

Finally, conclusions and recommendations can of course reflect the superficiality of a discussion. By way of example, in the 'Concluding observations' on Kuwait's initial report, the Committee did not note any concerns other than the absence of a crime of torture and its recommendations were confined to the typical quest to encourage the state party to accept procedures under articles 20–22 of the Convention and to introduce a crime of torture into the criminal code. Yet, Amnesty International has recently criticised the Government's failure to address many human rights violations committed during the period of martial law immediately following the occupation by Iraq. Violations cited include torture and the precarious human rights situation of foreign nationals and stateless persons.[54] This issue was not addressed during the course of the Committee's discussion. Similarly, problematic topics touched on during the discussion, such as the question of police detention exceeding four days on the basis of a police investigator's order (for a period of unspecified maximum duration),[55] did not give rise to any critical remarks on the part of the Committee and were consequently not reflected in the conclusions.

(c) Correctness

Clearly, conclusions and recommendations should reflect an accurate understanding of the relevant legal rules in the state party under discussion as well as of the Convention itself. However, there have been instances of conclusions containing substantial errors. In the 'Concluding observations' on the second German report, for example, the Committee displayed a fundamental misunderstanding of the principle of proportionality. As explained by the government delegation,[56] this principle limits the powers

---

[53] Cf. CAT/C/GER (Concluding observations on the second periodic report of Germany), para. 18.
[54] Amnesty International, *AI Report: State Injustice: Unfair Trials in the Middle East*, March 1998.
[55] Cf. CAT/C/SR.335 Add.1, paras. 22, 24.
[56] Cf. CAT/C/SR.329, para. 7.

of the state rather than, as the Committee interpreted it,[57] opening the way to the possibility of an arbitrary reduction of the rights of arrested persons.

In some cases, it remains a mystery as to how certain recommendations relate to treaty obligations. For instance, while there is no obligation for states parties to introduce into domestic law a definition of torture according to article 1 CAT, the Committee persists in recommending this measure.[58] Such a recommendation is even more surprising in those cases where it is directed to a state which had outlined in its report that the treaty forms part of the country's legal system.[59] In addition, erroneous reference to treaty articles may occasionally be observed.[60]

While some of these shortcomings could be effectively addressed by means of the same measures proposed above to improve the quality of discussions, others pertain to specific problems in the drafting process of 'Concluding observations'. To date, the Committee has issued its conclusions and recommendations, as a rule, immediately after the end of the discussion, allowing only about one hour for drafting. In its spring 1998 session, the Committee took the decision to give more time in the future to the drafting of concluding remarks, publishing them one or two days after the conclusion of discussions. Given the complex and significant nature of the drafting process, this development can only be welcomed.

Finally, a secretariat which has been accorded an important role in the preparation of discussions, as suggested above, could also take on an enhanced role in relation to the drafting of 'Concluding observations'. To date, the secretariat has been asked for advice only on an *ad hoc* basis.[61]

---

[57] Cf. CAT/C/GER (Concluding observations on the second periodic report of Germany), para. 11.

[58] Cf. CAT/C/ISR (Concluding observations on the second periodic report of Israel), para. 12.

[59] Cf. CAT/C/FRA (Concluding observations on the second periodic report of France), para. 9. Reference to France's monistic system had been made in CAT/C/17/Add.18, para. 2 ('In the French legal system, which is monistic, "Treaties or agreements duly ratified or approved shall, upon their publication, have an authority superior to that of laws, subject, for each agreement or treaty, to its application by the other party" (Constitution, article 55). This primacy naturally applies in the case of the Convention and is binding on the legislature, executive, administration and judiciary.') and in CAT/C/SR.320, para. 22.

[60] A wrong reference is given in the Concluding observations on Peru's report, which recommends taking appropriate measures to ensure indemnity, reparation and rehabilitation to victims while referring, among others, to article 6 CAT (concerning detention of persons suspected of having committed a torture crime). Cf. CAT/C/PER, para. 16.

[61] Interview with the Secretary of the CAT Committee, Alessio Bruni.

An upgraded secretariat could be entrusted with drafting the 'Concluding observations', which would then be revised by the Committee plenary.

4. FOLLOW-UP ON RECOMMENDATIONS

The crucial point for assuring that state reporting procedures actually have an impact lies in the follow-up procedures. Governments will not be very motivated by the recommendations of an international monitoring body, such as the CAT Committee, if these are not reinforced by subsequent pressure to implement the recommendations. However, the systematic approach of issuing recommendations at the end of each state report discussion has not been matched to date in relation to follow-up questions. Until recently, the Committee made no effort, either regarding the 'General guidelines for periodic reports' or the discussion of periodic reports, systematically to urge states parties to respond to each recommendation issued at the conclusion of the previous state report discussion. The 'General guidelines' contained only a request for information on 'any new measures taken' and 'any new developments' as well as for 'any information requested by the Committee during its consideration of the preceding report'.[62] This allowed states parties to focus on CAT-positive measures, if any, without requiring a reaction in the event of non-implementation of recommendations. There was thus no need for states parties to demonstrate that they had given careful consideration to the CAT Committee's recommendations. The Committee even took more seriously states parties' compliance with the 'General guidelines' than their responses to recommendations: a state report which examined one-by-one almost all the recommendations, without complying with the guidelines, gave rise to criticism.[63]

Similarly, Committee members do not systematically pick up on recommendations left unanswered in periodic reports. While some recommendations may be referred to by individual Committee members in the subsequent discussion, there is no systematic review of reactions to recommendations. Therefore, it is not surprising that some recommendations

---

[62] CAT, General Guidelines for periodic reports (UN Doc. No. CAT/C/14).

[63] Cf. CAT/C/SR.330, para. 10 (discussion of the second periodic report of Peru). The Government's report (cf. CAT/C/20/Add.6) addressed each of the CAT Committee's recommendations on Peru's initial report (cf. UN Doc. A/50/44, para. 73). The reaction of the Committee member who then criticised general non-compliance with the 'General guidelines' raises the question of why the Committee does not enumerate the information missing and request concrete information by the delegation on these issues.

receive no follow-up at all, even though they have not been adequately addressed by the state party.[64]

These shortcomings have been resolved for the 'General Guidelines for periodic reports'. In its spring 1998 session the Committee revised the 'General guidelines', inserting a third section headed 'Compliance with the Committee's conclusions and recommendations'.[65] States parties are thus requested to report on their reactions to the Committee's recommendations. It remains to be seen whether this amendment will be used to introduce a systematic review of responses to the Committee's recommendations during the state report discussions. In order to ensure this, it would be helpful if every discussion began with a review of reactions to recommendations, a task which should be entrusted to the country rapporteur. This would enable the Committee to establish a dialogue on issues that have raised the need for recommendations and, if necessary, to provide further arguments in favour of requested changes. The follow-up examinations could also be outlined in a special sub-paragraph of the 'Concluding observations' issued after a state report discussion. At the present time, the performance of states parties in implementing recommendations of the Committee is occasionally referred to in the 'Concluding observations',[66] but usually it is not addressed at all.

Considering the period of time which may elapse between one state reporting procedure and the next (four years in the case of regular submission of state reports), one may question whether the present system provides for an appropriate dialogue, particularly for those countries where severe problems have been brought to light. In order to guarantee an ongoing follow-up of recommendations, it would be helpful if governments were asked to write a report on the implementation of recommendations within a certain, short period of time (for instance, one year or less) on a systematic basis, at least in respect of certain grave situations. Such further reporting could be based on the power of the Committee to request 'other reports' in addition to initial and periodic reports (article 19(1)). This rule allows the Committee also to engage in an ongoing dialogue with states

---

[64] For instance, during the discussion of the second state report of Peru (CAT/C/SR.330 and 331) the Committee did not follow-up on the recommendation on the country's initial report to 'intensify' programmes for the rehabilitation of victims of torture (cf. UN Doc. A/50/44, para. 73(g)). The report of the Peruvian Government set out possibilities for compensation (cf. CAT/C/20/Add.6, para. 83 ff.).

[65] CAT/C/14/Rev.1.   [66] Cf. CAT/C/ISR, para. 10.

parties on specific questions in between the periodic submission and discussion of full state reports. In order to prepare the information received as follow-up reports for the Committee's sessions, a member of the CAT Committee should be designated 'Special Rapporteur for follow-up on recommendations'. Introduction of the use of special reports for follow-up purposes would require a fundamentally different approach in the Committee as it has so far been quite reluctant to request additional reports from states parties.[67]

Furthermore, the effectiveness of follow-up procedures could be significantly enhanced through the establishment of fact-finding mechanisms to give an overview of the implementation of recommendations. The assistance of NGOs could be sought, requesting them to submit specific information on the implementation of recommendations by governments. Similarly, the Special Rapporteur on Torture could be asked at an informal level to take note of the extent of implementation of the CAT Committee's recommendations during visits to those countries which are states parties to the CAT. In addition, the practice of the HRC presents the possibility of fact-finding missions to states parties on an invitation basis. To date, this option has only been taken up in one case when the HRC was invited to make a follow-up visit, during which it reviewed the measures taken in response to the 'final views' adopted by the Committee under the individual complaints procedure.[68] Similarly, proposals have been made to provide for follow-up visits within the framework of the ICCPR state reporting procedure,[69] although unfortunately no action has yet been taken.

Clearly, such a mechanism would only be worthwhile for follow-up on recommendations involving a certain complexity and with implications extending beyond the legislative level. For instance, a recommendation to introduce a specific crime of torture into penal law does not require a follow-up visit, as the government's response can readily be reviewed in the course of the subsequent state report or through a special report, as suggested above. In contrast, recommendations which address complex matters, such as a pattern of impunity, may also imply a number of problems requiring resolution at the practical level. In such cases, a follow-up mission may serve as a means of increasing the impact of recommendations.

---

[67] The only exception being Israel, see text at note 74, below.

[68] Cf. UN Doc. A/50/40 (Annual Report of the Human Rights Committee), paras. 557 ff.

[69] Cf. UN Doc. A/48/40 (Annual Report of the Human Rights Committee), para. 18 and Annex X, para. 8.

5. REACTIONS TO DRAMATIC CHANGES OR HIGH-RISK SITUATIONS IN A STATE PARTY

A rapid and firm response on the part of the Committee to critical situations involving a high risk of torture or ill-treatment or to reports of a dramatic deterioration of human rights conditions in a state party, including incidences of torture, would certainly seem to be desirable. However, this aim would appear to be incompatible with the traditional approach in state reporting procedures of emphasising periodicity. This was indeed the reason why other treaty monitoring bodies, such as the HRC, restricted themselves for a long time to requesting periodic reports. This approach may be viewed as helpful in allowing states parties to appear before a treaty body independently of complaints about its human rights situation. In this way, it is argued, the procedure remains free from the slightest accusatory nature. In the past, this encouraged states who had refused to cooperate with other organs, such as the Commission on Human Rights, to agree to present a report to a treaty body.[70]

However, since the beginning of the 1990s the view that such an attitude was far too passive in cases of gross violations of human rights has gained stronger ground. As a result, the HRC decided to abandon strict periodicity in its reporting procedures.[71] In response to the massive violations of human rights in the former Yugoslavia, the HRC requested the governments of Bosnia and Herzegovina, Croatia and the Federal Republic of Yugoslavia to submit short reports on specific questions within one month. The respective states complied with this request and it was thus possible to discuss the reports at the beginning of November 1992.[72] Several reports of this type have since been requested, including from Angola, Burundi, Haiti and Rwanda.

---

[70] Cf. V. Dimitrijevic (1993), 'The Monitoring of Human Rights and the Prevention of Human Rights Violations Through Reporting Procedures', in *Monitoring Human Rights in Europe: Comparing International Procedures and Mechanisms* (eds. A. Bloed *et al.*), Dordrecht, 1993, p. 1 at p. 15.

[71] The first step in this direction had been taken in 1991 when the HRC urged Iraq (April) and the Federal Republic of Yugoslavia (November) to transmit their periodic reports in time and to answer certain questions on their human rights situations which had recently deteriorated.

[72] Cf. UN Doc. A/48/40 (Annual Report of the Human Rights Committee), paras. 311–32 (Bosnia and Herzegovina), 333–62 (Croatia) and 363–89 (Federal Republic of Yugoslavia (Serbia and Montenegro)). Cf. Boerefijn, 'Towards a Strong System of Supervision: The Human Rights Committee's Role in Reforming the Reporting Procedure under Article 40 of the Covenant on Civil and Political Rights', 17 *HRQ*, 1995, pp. 766–93.

In contrast to the HRC, the CAT Committee has rarely made use of the option of requesting special reports from governments, although the CAT provides for 'such other reports as the Committee may request' in addition to periodic state reports.[73] It appears that this policy will be pursued, as the CAT Committee recently indicated that it would only consider asking for special reports in 'extraordinary circumstances'.[74] To date, the Committee has only invited the Israeli Government to submit a special report on a decision of the Supreme Court of Israel. The Supreme Court had declared lawful the use of physical pressure by Israeli security services during interrogations of suspects of terrorist acts, with a view to obtaining from them information which would prevent the perpetration of criminal acts in the future. Such a practice was deemed to be incompatible with the provisions of the Convention.[75] The CAT Committee set a time limit of approximately two months for submission of this report, which was almost adhered to,[76] so as to allow for an examination of the report during the following session of the Committee.[77]

Why has the CAT Committee made such little use of the possibility of requesting special reports in urgent situations? One factor could be that it was not considered feasible to request a special report in those cases where the HRC had already sought one, at least in relation to states which are parties to both the ICCPR and CAT. However, this consideration would only make sense in those situations where the HRC report and the subsequent discussion addressed torture-related issues in such a way as to make further examination by the CAT Committee redundant. Another possible reason could relate to the existence of the inquiry procedure under article 20 CAT for cases of a dramatic deterioration of human rights. A decision on the part of the CAT Committee to initiate an inquiry which remains *confidential* until publication of the results would seem to exclude the possibility of requesting at the same time a special report under the state reporting procedure which is entirely *public*. This said, given that the inquiry procedure applies to only extremely serious and systematic violations

---

[73] Article 19(1) CAT.

[74] DPI – Press release, 'Committee Against Torture to Request "Timely" Report from Egypt Following Amnesty International Charges of Abuses by Security Forces', 20 May 1998.

[75] Cf. UN Doc. A/52/44 (Annual Report of the CAT Committee), para. 24 f.

[76] The CAT Committee had set a deadline for 31 January 1997. The Israeli Government submitted a first response on 6 December 1996 and its final (revised) report on 17 February 1997.

[77] For results see UN Doc. A/52/44 (Annual Report of the CAT Committee), paras. 253–60.

of human rights and that the article 20 procedure has produced a very small output,[78] it would appear that there is room for a more extensive use of the reporting procedure through the request of special reports.

This system of requesting special reports in response to serious situations of human rights violations could be made more effective through the empowering, by the CAT Committee, of its chairperson to request such reports between sessions after consultation with the other Committee members. Such a provision has been introduced into the Rules of Procedure of the HRC.[79] Given the importance of this type of initiative, it can hardly be argued that the chairperson alone is entitled to make such decisions in order 'to promote compliance with the Convention', as a general power of the chairperson is formulated in Rule 17 paragraph 2 of the CAT Committee's Rules of Procedure.[80] Hence, the Committee's Rules of Procedure should be amended accordingly.

C. Inquiry procedure

Under article 20 CAT, the Committee may carry out and conclude an inquiry on the existence of a systematic practice of torture in a state party. In order that such an inquiry be initiated the Committee must have received well-founded information on incidents of torture which amount to a systematic practice. Relevant information must be provided to the state party concerned before an inquiry can be formally opened (in the light of the information and the reaction of the state party). During later stages of the procedure the Committee is bound to seek the cooperation of the target state. Apart from this condition, the Committee may freely choose its methods of examination.

This procedure can be applied in respect of the great majority of states parties, despite the option, upon ratification or accession, of 'opting out' of the inquiry procedure under article 28 CAT. Currently, only thirteen states parties have maintained their reservation to article 20.[81] Nevertheless, the

---

[78] See text at note 80, below.

[79] Cf. Human Rights Committee, Rules of Procedure (UN Doc. No. CCPR/C/3/Rev.5) Rule 66 para. 2: 'In the case of an exceptional situation when the Committee is not in session, a request may be made through the Chairperson, acting in consultation with the members of the Committee.'

[80] Committee Against Torture, Rules of Procedure (UN Doc. No. CAT/C/3/Rev.2).

[81] As of 16 June 1999, the following states had opted out of article 20 CAT: Afghanistan, Bahrain, Belarus, Bulgaria, China, Cuba (the Cuban Government had declared that the first

results achieved from the inquiry procedure since the Convention entered into force on 26 June 1987 is anything but impressive. Only two inquiries – in respect of Turkey and Egypt – have so far been concluded and published. Moreover, only in one case (that of Turkey) was the Committee able to conduct a visit to the target state in the course of an inquiry.

1. THE QUALITY OF THE PUBLISHED REPORTS

The published summaries of the reports on Turkey and Egypt differ significantly.[82] The report on Turkey begins by outlining the development of the procedure and then goes on to examine in its conclusions the relevant legal rules, allegations received during the inquiry, and places of detention run by the Ministry of the Interior and the Ministry of Justice. In contrast, the conclusions of the Committee's report on Egypt are concerned to a large extent with the credibility of allegations received. While it is self-evident that an inquiry report which includes information collected during a fact-finding visit will be more detailed, this does not explain the absence of a thorough examination of the relevant legal rules in the Egypt report. Instead, the Committee only commented in general terms on some of the deficiencies in the repressive reaction to atrocities committed, without a word on preventive measures. So too in the report's recommendations, safeguards against ill-treatment are only referred to in relation to their supervision by an independent investigative body. Apart from these comments, the general nature of the published summary of the inquiry on Egypt does not allow for a close analysis of its quality, if not to say that the small amount of information included therein is in itself a shortcoming.

As noted, the summary of the Turkey report is much more detailed and informative. The main criticism that should be voiced is that the CAT Committee seems to restrict its perception of a widespread practice of torture to persons arrested in connection with terrorist activities. In contrast, the Committee for the Prevention of Torture has emphasised in its Public Statements on Turkey that a widespread practice of torture is also found in

---

three paragraphs of article 20 would only be applicable to Cuba with the consent of the Government), Indonesia, Israel, Kuwait, Morocco, Poland, Saudi Arabia and Ukraine.

[82] See 'Summary Account of the Results of the Proceedings Concerning the Inquiry on Turkey', in Report of the Committee Against Torture, A/48/44/Add.1 (1993), 4 *IHRR* 227 (1997); 'Summary Account of the Results of the Proceedings Concerning the Inquiry on Egypt', UN Doc. A/51/44 (Annual Report of the CAT Committee), pp. 30–6.

investigations of ordinary criminal offences.[83] Another point of criticism needs to be raised in relation to the CAT Committee's final statement, in which it congratulates the Turkish Government for having acted upon a number of its recommendations without mentioning that there had been no response at all to other recommendations and that the most problematic structures of emergency legislation and state security issues had not been improved.

2. FOLLOW-UP ON RECOMMENDATIONS

In relation to follow-up on inquiry reports and recommendations, the Committee, in the absence of any indication in the Convention empowering it to take specific follow-up measures, has not assumed an active role. It is thus dependent on the initiative of the target state as to whether or not that state responds to recommendations.

In the case of Turkey, the Committee has been informed by the Turkish Government of measures taken in relation to some of the recommendations. These measures were considered in the summary of the inquiry report published one year after the conclusion of the inquiry.

In contrast, the inquiry report on Egypt does not contain similar information, as the Government evidently had not submitted any substantial response. Action taken by the CAT Committee during its spring 1998 session shows that it intends to use the state reporting procedure for follow-up on recommendations issued in its inquiry report on Egypt. After having reviewed information submitted by Amnesty International on continuing instances of ill-treatment of detainees by Egyptian security forces, the Committee sent a letter to the Government urging a timely submission of its third periodic report and stressing that it should contain an account of its implementation of the Committee's recommendations as contained in the inquiry report.[84] The use of the reporting procedure for follow-up on inquiry recommendations also implies the possibility of requesting a special report in which the country can react to the Committee's conclusions. This option has not been applied in the Egypt case, the Committee arguing that the concept of special reports should be restricted to 'extraordinary circumstances'.[85] It is difficult to imagine, however, how 'extraordinary' a

---

[83] Cf. CPT Public Statement on Turkey (CPT/Inf (93)1), CPT Second Public Statement on Turkey (CPT/Inf (96)34).
[84] Cf. DPI Press Release, *supra*, note 73. [85] Cf. ibid.

situation must be if persisting reports that the Committee's recommendations are being ignored in a situation as grave as that described in the
inquiry report on Egypt do not suffice.

3. THE LIMITATIONS AND POTENTIAL OF THE INQUIRY PROCEDURE

The reasons for the extremely small number of concluded inquiries during
the thirteen years of the Committee's existence may be found in the highly
problematic preconditions for the initiation of an inquiry and the stigmat-
ising effects of this procedure. An inquiry can only be initiated on the basis
of reliable information containing well-founded indications of a systematic
practice of torture. This means that the Committee may open an inquiry
under article 20 CAT when there is a very high likelihood that extremely
serious violations of human rights are taking place, violations which cannot
be qualified as individual cases (as opposed to a *systematic* practice).[86] Thus,
the very fact of opening an inquiry is embarrassing for a state party,
although it is protected by the confidentiality of the proceedings until the
inquiry is over. After the conclusion of an inquiry, the CAT Committee
may decide to include a summary of the results in its annual report. Thus,
many target states have a strong interest in obstructing the course of such
an inquiry. Moreover, the fact that the Committee has to seek the target
state's cooperation at every stage of the procedure creates ample opportunities for obstruction on the part of target states, especially as they are
not bound by a reciprocal obligation to cooperate. One possible way of
obstructing an inquiry is for a target state to declare a vague consent for the
Committee to visit its territory and then to repeatedly delay the issue of a
formal invitation.

---

[86] The CAT Committee has outlined its interpretation of the term 'systematic practice' (UN
Doc. A/48/44/Add.1, para. 39): 'The Committee considers that torture is practised systematically when it is apparent that the torture cases reported have not occurred fortuitously
in a particular place or at a particular time, but are seen to be habitual, widespread and
deliberate in at least a considerable part of the territory of the country in question. Torture
may in fact be of a systematic character without resulting from the direct intention of a
Government. It may be the consequence of factors which the Government has difficulty in
controlling, and its existence may indicate a discrepancy between policy as determined by
the central Government and its implementation by the local administration. Inadequate
legislation which in practice allows room for the use of torture may also add to the systematic nature of this practice.'

The visits carried out by the Special Rapporteur on Torture illustrate the impact of these factors on the obstructive attitude of many target states, as these are also dependent on the invitation of a government. In twelve years of operation to December 1997, the special rapporteur has managed to carry out nineteen visits.[87] It cannot be argued that the CAT Committee's lack of success is due to the fact that the countries visited by the special rapporteur were not accessible to the CAT Committee, since the majority of these countries are states parties to CAT and have not opted out of article 20.

The successful practice of visits established by the Special Rapporteur on Torture, together with the small likelihood of receiving further invitations for visits as part of an article 20 CAT inquiry, leads to the conclusion that the Committee should not focus on basing its inquiry results on fact-finding visits. Indeed, the Egypt inquiry, which was formally concluded in May 1996 after several failed attempts to receive approval for a visit,[88] represents a positive development. In this case, NGO information formed the main basis of the Committee's conclusion that torture was being practised systematically. This approach, which is fully in line with CAT regulations, allows the Committee greater independence from the lack of cooperation on the part of a state party.[89]

However, no further inquiries have been concluded since the Egypt inquiry came to a close three years ago. This indicates the need for a more active approach in taking up the inquiry procedure option. Indeed, the two published inquiries took between two-and-a-half (Turkey) and three years (Egypt)[90] to be concluded and a further year (Turkey) or one-and-a-half

---

[87] Visits have been conducted to Argentina, Colombia and Uruguay (1987); Peru, Turkey and Republic of Korea (1988); Guatemala and Honduras (1989); Zaire and the Philippines (1990); Indonesia and East Timor (1991); the former Yugoslavia (1992, together with the country rapporteur); Rwanda (together with the country rapporteur); the Russian Federation and Colombia (joint mission with the Special Rapporteur on extralegal, summary and arbitrary executions) (1994); Chile (1995); Pakistan and Venezuela (1996); and Mexico (1997).

[88] *Supra*, note 81.

[89] In this regard, problems then arise in respect of Rule 80 of the CAT Committee's Rules of Procedure. Rule 80 stipulates that the Committee should first decide whether or not the carrying out of a visit is *necessary* for the conduct of the inquiry and only subsequently seek an invitation of the target state. This seems to weaken the observations of the Committee in those cases where they are concluded without having paid a visit to the target state.

[90] These dates refer to the period between the first consideration of information indicating a systematic practice of torture and the conclusion of the inquiry. The period between the

years (Egypt) to be published. Given the gravity of the situations in these countries, as well as the general concept of the inquiry procedure relating to serious and systematic human rights violations, such periods must be considered excessive. While part of the delay may be due to government obstruction, another part of the problem may be the overly cumbersome proceedings of the Committee. One relevant factor here, as noted in the published summary of the Egypt inquiry, is that most of the measures taken to carry out the procedure were based on express decisions of the Committee. This means that the minimum amount of time between two subsequent steps of an inquiry is six months, i.e. the time between two sessions. Moreover, decisions which could have been taken at the same time were in fact spread over subsequent sessions. For instance, instead of making the decision to request NGOs to provide additional information and at the same time resolving to set up an informal working group with the task of submitting the information collected to the government for its observations, these decisions were made at separate sessions and thus involved time lapse of six months. Furthermore, after having considered the information for eighteen months, the Committee did not consider itself in a position to combine the formal decision to open an inquiry with the decision to request the Egyptian Government to agree on a visit. Finally, lengthy negotiations with the Government on the question of a visit resulted in a postponement of the deadline for a possible visit.

In this context it may be recalled that the CAT Committee has to allow for reactions by the target state to information on a systematic practice of torture before an inquiry can be formally opened (article 20(1) and (20)(2)). Moreover, the Committee is obliged to seek the state party's cooperation at every stage of the procedure (article 20(5)). However, in view of the seriousness of situations that might warrant a special inquiry, the Committee should vigorously push the proceedings ahead and should be allowed to set short time limits without violating the cooperation requirement.[91] Furthermore, streamlining the procedure, especially by avoiding

---

formal decision to open an inquiry and its conclusion may be shorter. Whereas the report on Turkey does not contain any reference to a formal opening of an inquiry, the report on Egypt indicates that the inquiry was opened formally only one-and-a-half years after the first consideration of relevant information.

[91] With regard to the initial observations of the target state's government, the Committee's Rules of Procedure (Rule 76, para. 2) provide for the setting of a time-limit. However, it is not made clear whether the Committee will proceed if the time limit is not observed.

delays due to cumbersome decision-making staggered over different sessions, should help to produce more effective results. In particular, the establishment of an informal working group responsible for some of the necessary steps in the procedure, including the search for NGO information and for observations by the government during the preliminary phase of a *particular* inquiry, would prevent delays resulting from inefficient scheduling of sessions. An even more significant step would be the setting up of a 'bureau' consisting of the chairperson and the two vice-chairpersons, who would be responsible for all arrangements deemed necessary between sessions during the preliminary phase of *any* inquiry. Moreover, once an inquiry has formally been opened, the government should be asked immediately for an invitation to carry out a visit; or at least the Committee members entrusted to undertake the inquiry should be empowered to make such a request.

D. Conclusions

As has been shown, the country-oriented monitoring procedures of the CAT have undergone significant changes during recent years. In particular, state reporting has been enhanced through the introduction of a system of detailed 'Concluding observations' issued by the CAT Committee after the discussion of each state report. In addition, the increased use of NGO information has enabled the Committee to lead more informed discussions with states parties presenting their reports. Furthermore, initial measures have been taken to provide for follow-up on recommendations issued in response to state reports. Finally, new opportunities have been opened up in the framework of the inquiry procedure by the Committee's conclusion of an inquiry without having conducted a visit. This has given the Committee a more effective tool with which to confront obstructive tactics used by target states.

Despite these constructive steps, important problems remain to be resolved and the considerable potential inherent in the existing procedures is yet to be explored. In particular, the quality of debates needs to be raised, the follow-up on recommendations should be improved, and possibilities for a more effective response by the Committee to patterns of serious human rights violations needs to be developed. In order to achieve such improvements, a more dynamic interpretation of the mandate would be necessary, including fundamental changes in the functioning of the secretariat and in the Committee's understanding of its role and purpose.

To start with the role of the secretariat, one part-time professional is entrusted with the task of supporting the Committee in monitoring the implementation of the Convention in the 118 states parties. The Committee can only be effective and incisive in discussions of state reports if it is well informed by the secretariat. It would not be possible – both in terms of time dedicated to the Committee's work and in terms of practicality – for Committee members to remain up to date on developments in all 118 states parties. The systematic collection of materials, and their preparation and analysis to serve as a sound basis for a state report discussion, can only be expected from a professional and adequately staffed secretariat. This type of thorough preparation for discussions would also justify according an enhanced role to the secretariat in the process of formulating appropriate and informed conclusions and recommendations at the end of each discussion.

The other fundamental change proposed here – a shift in the Committee's self-perception from a passive to an active role – encompasses a broad range of issues, for which the Convention does allow for active measures. While it may be arguable whether the CAT provides for the possibility of discussions on its implementation in a state which has not submitted a report, the option of requesting special reports could be applied more frequently to improve the Committee's performance in responding to urgent situations as well as to facilitate the monitoring of governments' reactions to recommendations. The Committee has also approached its functions in an unnecessarily passive manner in relation to the conceptualisation of requirements under different articles of the Convention. There is no reason why the CAT Committee should not establish what it expects from states parties under each article. The results of such decisions could be published as 'general comments' of the CAT Committee addressed to all states parties. Even if the Committee chose not to publish these comments, the discussion and clarification at the internal level would be extremely valuable for the examination of state reports.

Similarly, inquiries under article 20 would be more effective if the CAT Committee took a more active approach. As noted, procedures should be streamlined so that conclusions may be reached more rapidly. This would require a Committee which seeks the cooperation of the target state, while at the same time driving the inquiry forward as quickly as possible by placing a greater emphasis on efficiency than on (waiting extended periods for) invitations for visits.

These proposed changes are consistent with the idea of the state reporting and inquiry procedures becoming less differentiated than they have been until now. The inquiry procedure would no longer be the only procedure called upon to respond to dramatic changes and serious violations in states if special reports were more extensively used in such situations. Moreover, if inquiries are increasingly concluded in the absence of a visit, they will tend to become another procedure based on third-hand information and documents rather than on the Committee's actual fact-finding activities. Considering that on-the-spot inspections usually provide a better source of information for issuing qualified comments, the failure of the inquiry procedure to date is regrettable. Nevertheless, the embarrassing aspects of the inquiry procedure under article 20 CAT will continue to make visits very unlikely in the future. It would therefore seem that inquiries without visits are the only possible means of avoiding the obstruction of target states. Indeed, a comparison with the successful practice of the Special Rapporteur on Torture suggests that it is more likely that an invitation will be received on an *ad hoc* basis independent from an inquiry procedure. This observation also favours the rethinking of fact-finding visits as a means of monitoring implementation of recommendations made pursuant to the discussion of a state party's report.

8

UN HUMAN RIGHTS REPORTING PROCEDURES: AN NGO PERSPECTIVE

ANDREW CLAPHAM[1]

A. Introduction

This chapter is written from the perspective of a large international non-governmental organisation (NGO): it seeks to share some of the experiences which Amnesty International has had with the UN treaty bodies. Amnesty International operates in several different contexts within the UN system. The organisation works with the political bodies (the Security Council, General Assembly and Commission on Human Rights), as well as with the various agencies, expert bodies, and field operations.

The first thing that strikes one when considering the use made of the treaty bodies by NGOs is the 'splendid isolation'[2] of the treaty bodies from the rest of the UN system. The treaty bodies are considered by some to be the heart of the human rights system, and the treaty bodies see themselves as the hub around which others should circle. The reality is that the treaty bodies are becoming more and more peripheral to the UN system and need to reach out to establish new links. In preparing this chapter the author spoke to two former UN officials who had headed UN human rights field

[1] The author would like to thank Liz Hodgkin, Nick Howen, Mariana Katzarova, Martin MacPherson, Guadaloupe Marengo, Florence Martin and Wilder Taylor, who all provided useful contributions for this piece. The opinions expressed are personal and do not necessarily represent the formal position of Amnesty International.

[2] This phrase is apparently originally attributable to Sir George Foster (1828–1904) who used it in a speech in the Canadian House of Commons on 16 June 1896 to describe the position of Britain in Europe: 'In these somewhat troublesome days when the great Mother Empire stands splendidly isolated in Europe', Official Report of the Dominion of Canada, 1896 volume 41 col. 176. The speech was reported in *The Times* of London under the heading 'splendid isolation' on 22 June 1896. (Details from the *Oxford Dictionary of Quotations*, Oxford, 1996.)

operations. Neither ex-director could remember having had any contact or use for the treaty bodies. They considered the treaty bodies irrelevant for the 'real' human rights work which was being performed in the country. This chapter will highlight the need for new links to the treaty bodies and will put forward a series of suggestions for a more integrated approach to human rights monitoring in the UN system.

B. Positive experiences with the reporting procedures

The first impression of most outsiders attending a meeting of one of the UN human rights treaty bodies is that the human rights inquiry one might have expected has been replaced by a strange diplomatic ritual. Government representatives explain all the things that the government has been doing to fulfil the requirements of the treaty, and the expert members of the treaty body then pose gently worded questions which imply that certain issues are being ducked. Often the officials sent to answer the questions are unable to respond to the questions but are particularly able at talking around the subject in a lengthy and uninformative response.

If this were the whole story NGOs would have given up on the treaty bodies some time ago. There is scope for NGOs to use the treaty bodies to achieve positive results; but to get such a positive return requires considerable investment. Rather than present a blueprint for NGO participation, the next section looks at some recent examinations of states' reports and describes the positive use made by NGOs of the opportunities available under the current arrangements for examining state reports.

1. THE PERUVIAN BILLS TO PARDON PRISONERS UNJUSTLY CONVICTED OF TERRORISM OR TREASON

Since 1994 at least seven bills have been filed before the Peruvian Congress aiming to address the problem of prisoners falsely charged and convicted of terrorism-related offences. In order to increase the pressure on President Fujimori to finalise solutions for the problem of 'innocent prisoners', Amnesty International sent the President an open letter and produced a report for the upcoming meeting of the Human Rights Committee (HRC).[3]

---

[3] Amnesty International, International Secretariat, *Offices of the Ombudsman and Ministry of Justice prepare legislative bills to pardon prisoners unjustly convicted of terrorism or treason*, AI Index AMR 46/18/96, 16 July 1996.

The Coordinadora Nacional de Derechos Humanos, an independent organisation which brings together forty-seven non-governmental human rights groups in Peru, became associated in lobbying the HRC. The lobby of the Coordinadora concentrated on two amnesty laws which granted a general amnesty to military, police or civilian personnel who face a complaint or conviction in relation to events related to the fight against terrorism in the period between May 1980 and June 1995.[4] The amnesty law is not reviewable by any judicial authority.[5]

The day after the publication of the Amnesty International report, the members of the HRC were invited to meet with the Coordinadora and an Amnesty International researcher. The UN secretariat arranged a meeting room in the *Palais des Nations* in Geneva to discuss the background to the issues raised by examination of Peru's report. Fifteen of the eighteen Committee members attended the briefing. Such a briefing serves a number of purposes. First, the Committee members can raise any queries they have about the reports sent to them by the NGOs. These may be questions of clarification or they may relate to misgivings Committee members may have about the research methodology or agenda of the NGOs. Second, the briefing provides an opportunity to exchange documentation such as translations of the relevant laws and draft legislation. This can be invaluable as the treaty bodies have no real resource facilities for finding such materials. Third, it can provide background and stimulation for the Committee members.

As a result of this briefing the HRC's members repeatedly referred to the Amnesty International material during the review of Peru's report and asked for a response from the Minister of Justice who was presenting the report. Rather than address the issues in the report and the Committee's concerns, the Minister chose to question the use of information provided by Amnesty International and suggested that those labelled by Amnesty International as 'prisoners of conscience' and 'political prisoners' were in fact simply terrorists. The end result of this 'constructive dialogue' was that the preliminary observations of the HRC reflected Amnesty International's concerns, and that some positive steps were taken by the Peruvian

[4] Law No. 26479, article 1, 'Normas Legales', *Diario Oficial El Peruano*, 15 June 1995. For an English translation see Amnesty International, *Peru: UN Experts Condemn Amnesty Laws*, AI Index AMR 46/20/96, 5 August 1996, Appendix 1.

[5] Law No. 26492, article 2, 'Normas Legales', *Diario Oficial El Peruano*, 2 July 1995. For an English translation see Amnesty International, *supra*, note 4, Appendix 2.

Government in response to the Committee's questions and observations.[6] But the limits of the power of recommendations by the HRC were illustrated by the Government's rejection of the experts' recommendations that the 'faceless judges' be abolished.[7] Less than three months after the HRC's Preliminary Observations urged the Government to abolish the system of 'faceless judges' and ensure public trials for all defendants, Peru's Congress passed Law No. 26671.[8] This law extended the use of 'faceless judges' for another year. When the HRC finally concluded its examination of Peru's report it was forced to 'deplore' the fact that Peru had done nothing with regard to its preliminary observation and had extended the use of 'faceless judges'. The Committee expressed 'profound concern at this situation,

---

[6] See preliminary observations in UN Doc. CCPR/C/79/Add.67, 25 July 1996, para. 9, which state in no uncertain terms that the application of the amnesty laws mean that Peru is in violation of the Covenant: 'Such an amnesty prevents appropriate investigation and punishment of perpetrators of past human rights violations, undermines efforts to establish respect for human rights, contributes to an atmosphere of impunity among perpetrators of past human rights violations, and constitutes a very serious impediment to efforts undertaken to consolidate democracy and promote respect for human rights and is thus in violations of article 2 of the Covenant. In this connection the Committee reiterates its view, as expressed in its General Comment 20(44), that this type of amnesty is incompatible with the duty of States to investigate human rights violations, to guarantee freedom from such acts within their jurisdiction, and to ensure that they do not occur in the future.' See also paras. 10, 21 and 23. In para. 23 the Committee urges the Government to investigate allegations of summary executions, disappearances, cases of torture and ill treatment, and arbitrary arrest and detention and suspend personnel from office pending the outcome of such investigations. For some of the positive steps see Amnesty International, *Peru: Government Persists in Retaining Unfair Trial Procedures*, AMR 46/25/96, December 1996 at p. 8, which details how in the month following the preliminary observations, August 1996, the Congress passed a law creating an *ad hoc* Commission charged with proposing to the President that prisoners awaiting trial on false charges of terrorism benefit from a right to clemency and those who had been convicted be pardoned and released. According to Amnesty International: 'By 15 November 1996, 74 prisoners unjustly accused of terrorism-related offences had been released, following a review of their cases by the *ad hoc* Commission.' Ibid., p. 8.

[7] According to the Centre for the Independence of Judges and Lawyers (a component of the International Commission of Jurists) the 'faceless justice system' has been criticised on, *inter alia*, the following grounds: the identity of judges, prosecutors, and even witnesses remains anonymous; the court proceedings are summary and secret; only the defendant and his or her attorney may be present; and the defendant has inadequate access to court files and no possibility of cross-examining anonymous witnesses. Press Release, 16 October 1997.

[8] For more detail see Amnesty International, *Peru: Government Rejects Recommendation by UN Human Rights Experts to Abolish 'Faceless Judges'*, AMR 46/22/96; and *Peru: Government Persists in Retaining Unfair Trial Procedures*, supra, note 6.

which undermines the judicial system and will once again lead to the conviction of innocent persons without a proper trial'.[9]

On 15 October 1997 the law eventually lapsed and was not renewed. This meant the effective abolition of the civilian 'faceless judges' system used to try cases of 'terrorism', even if some concern remains about 'faceless judges' in the military courts.[10] The HRC clearly played a role in consolidating the pressure for the abolition of this system. By presenting the arguments in terms of international treaty obligations the Committee was able to put forward an irrefutable case for abolition. This is an important use of the treaty bodies; statements emanating from a UN treaty body can not be easily dismissed as just 'support for terrorism'. Moreover the appeal to legal obligations, rather than humanitarianism, colours how Peru is seen in the international community. A sense that the Government is prepared to violate its treaty obligations will be a poor advertisement for prospective trading or business partners.

2. THE FIRST REPORT OF THE UNITED STATES AND THE ISSUE OF THE EXTRATERRITORIAL SCOPE OF THE ICCPR

In the period leading to the presentation of the first report of the United States to the HRC in March 1995,[11] a number of NGOs prepared reports on the shortcomings of the United States Government with regard to their treaty obligations under the International Covenant on Civil and Political Rights (ICCPR).[12] Again, briefings were organised by NGOs. Obviously many organisations were concerned by the reservations and declarations made by the United States; this concern was reflected in the questions and observations of Committee members.[13] But these briefings also gave NGOs

---

[9] UN Doc. CCPR/C/79/Add.72, para. 11.

[10] The Centre for the Independence of Judges and Lawyers welcomed 'the abolition of the civilian faceless justice system' but expressed concern that this abolition might not extend to the military courts which used the system to try cases of 'treason'. Press release, 16 October 1997.

[11] See UN Doc. A/50/40 (1995), paras. 266–304.

[12] For example, Amnesty International, *United States of America – Human Rights Violations: A Summary of Amnesty International's Concerns*, AI Index AMR 51/25/95, March 1995. The United States' report is contained in UN Docs. CCPR/C/81/Add.4 and HRI/CORE/Add.49.

[13] See chapter 14 of this volume; W. Schabas, 'Invalid Reservations to the International Covenant on Civil and Political Rights: Is the United States Still a Party?', 21 *Brooklyn Journal of International Law*, 1995, pp. 277–325.

the chance to remind the expert members of the Committee of their consistent case-law that the ICCPR needs to be interpreted as having extraterritorial effect.[14] The issue was particularly relevant at the time due to the interdiction of Haitian refugees on the high seas and recent interventions of the United States in Somalia and Haiti, as well as the prospect of a United States military presence in Bosnia and Herzegovina.

In the presentation of its report the United States consistently rejected any interpretation which would extend the ICCPR extraterritorially. Yet the Committee in its final comments makes its position clear regarding the international legal obligations on the United States:

> The Committee does not share the view expressed by the Government that the Covenant lacks extraterritorial reach under all circumstances. Such a view is contrary to the consistent interpretation of the Committee on this subject, that, in special circumstances, persons may fall under the subject matter jurisdiction of a State Party even when outside that State's territory.[15]

Ironically the expert on this topic, Professor Buergenthal, did not take part in the proceedings as he is himself from the United States.[16]

Other issues raised specifically by NGOs and subsequently incorporated into the Committee's questioning and comments included: the then imminent changes in sentencing laws which were to lead to severe overcrowding in prisons; the criminalisation of sexual relations between adult consenting partners (in some states); and the lack of effective measures to ensure that indigent offenders are represented by competent counsel. The HRC was given a series of well prepared non-governmental reports dealing with matters not addressed in the Government's reports and with several obvious problems regarding compliance with the Covenant.

The examination was held in New York and national NGOs therefore had a remarkable opportunity to work with the Committee members. The NGO briefings were particularly detailed and related to complex areas of law and policy. Although some issues were pursued by the Committee,

---

[14] See T. Meron, 'Extraterritoriality of Human Rights Treaties', 89 *AJIL*, 1995, pp. 78–83. See in particular the communication under the Optional Protocol: *Saldías de López v. Uruguay*, UN GAOR, thirty-sixth session, Supplement 40, UN Doc. A/36/40 (1981) at p. 176.

[15] Concluding Observations, 10 March 1995, CCPR/C/79/Add.50 also in Annual Report of the HRC to the General Assembly (1995) A/50/40 paras. 266–304 at para. 284.

[16] T. Buergenthal, 'To Respect and Ensure: State Obligations and Permissible Derogations', in *The International Bill of Rights* (ed. L. Henkin), New York, 1981, pp. 72–91.

the examination inevitably remained at a certain level of generality. This highlights the obvious, but rarely mentioned, fact that most Committee members are unlikely to be experts on the legal systems and factual situations they are examining. In some cases a chance sighting of a newspaper article can form the basis for a whole line of questioning. The examination of the United States' report highlights the need for Committee members to be exposed to a wide range of alternative sources of information before any meaningful examination of a country report can be undertaken. It seems absurd that, in many cases, the Committees only have the official government report and no supplementary information or critique. In the case of the United States' report, NGOs were able to raise questions of law, current violations of the ICCPR, and future problems, none of which could be found in the official report.

Whether or not the United States Government will change any of its law or practice to comply with the recommendations of the HRC remains to be seen. What was useful for NGOs was that this process established benchmarks with which to judge the record of the United States Government in this field. This is an important use of the treaty body reporting procedures by the NGOs; without the reporting mechanism there would have been no interpretation of the United States' reservations or reaffirmation of the territorial scope of the Convention. Such authoritative interpretation can help form the legal basis of continuing non-governmental criticism of government action and inaction.

3. SPREADING THE WORD AT THE NATIONAL LEVEL FOLLOWING THE CAT COMMITTEE'S EXAMINATION OF THE RUSSIAN FEDERATION'S SECOND PERIODIC REPORT

Prior to the November 1996 meeting of the Committee of the Convention Against Torture (CAT), Amnesty International prepared a long unpublished briefing paper and issued a report entitled: 'Russian Federation: Comments on the Second Periodic Report submitted to the United Nations Committee Against Torture'.[17] In an unusual step Amnesty International also distributed a detailed letter in Russian to a number of Russian NGOs encouraging participation in the upcoming examination. Four of

---

[17] AI Index EUR 46/46/96.

these organisations submitted their own reports to the CAT Committee and one NGO sent a representative to the meeting.[18]

As a result of these briefings the questions of the CAT Committee members reflected the concerns of the NGOs, and the Committee's own views included the major areas of preoccupation of the human rights organisations. The media interest surrounding the hearings included a Russian radio station which transmits its broadcasts throughout the Russian prison system. Moreover, the CAT Committee gave permission for the question and answer session to be recorded. Amnesty International transcribed the session for use by Russian NGOs in their follow-up campaigns. When the twelve-member Russian Federal Government delegation met with the Amnesty International researcher it was apparent that they felt caught off-balance by the extensive use of the non-governmental material and there was some anger at the use of these reports. However the encounter became the basis for an agreement for future exchanges of information.

This episode highlights another use to which the reporting procedure can be put by NGOs: enticing government officials and local NGOs into a closer examination of the treaty body recommendations. Without such a symbiotic follow-up at the national level the recommendations are more than likely to remain a dead letter. Retaining links with the local media and interested non-governmental sectors during the hearing is a useful way of encouraging effective follow-up. Strategic non-governmental cooperation can effectively pierce the membrane which so often seals off the international discussion of human rights from the national reality.

4. WORKING WITH THE MEDIA DURING THE EXAMINATION OF THE UNITED KINGDOM'S RECORD ON TORTURE, INHUMAN AND DEGRADING TREATMENT IN NORTHERN IRELAND

As the United Kingdom prepared to defend its record on Northern Ireland before the CAT Committee, NGOs alerted the media to the upcoming examination. In contrast to the previous example concerning the Russian Federation (where the media was used to raise consciousness at the national level with regard to the procedures for complaint and the work of local

---

[18] The Moscow Centre for Prison Reform sent a representative, the other three organisations which submitted reports were *Novy Dom*, International Protection Centre, and the Organisation of Soldiers' Mothers of St Petersburg.

organisations), here the media attention simply galvanised the debate and drew public attention to the Government's breaches of its international obligations.

In November 1991, in the weeks prior to the examination of the United Kingdom's report by the CAT Committee, an article appeared in *The Guardian* newspaper reporting that Amnesty International would be informing the Committee about ill-treatment of prisoners in Northern Ireland. This prompted a flurry of interest in the United Kingdom media and the meeting was covered in some detail by the British Broadcasting Corporation (BBC) and *The Guardian*. The presence of the media in the Committee room during the examination increased the pressure on the Committee members to ask probing and difficult questions. It also heightened the sense of occasion. Media reports appeared in *The Independent, The Guardian, The Irish Times, Irish News*, and the international wire services on consecutive days. The BBC and Channel 4 also covered the meetings.

According to Amnesty International, allegations of ill-treatment in Northern Ireland's detention centres dropped off dramatically after the CAT Committee's session. In the words of a member of the Amnesty International secretariat: '[i]t's not because ten experts sat in a room talking about Northern Ireland. It's because of all the publicity before and after the CAT session.'

This method of enhancing accountability and improving the human rights situation is dependent on several factors. First, the success was due in part to the hard work and perseverance of the rapporteur nominated by the CAT Committee (in this case Professor Peter Burns). Because the rapporteur had digested the briefs and was prepared to ask difficult questions based on actual facts rather than the usual legal clarifications, the session came alive. Second, local NGOs and lawyers had presented detailed casework to the Committee. Organisations such as the Committee on the Administration of Justice, the Howard League for Penal Reform, and Charter 88 provided information. This meant that the Committee had detailed up-to-date information from sources which could not be easily discounted or discredited by the government.[19] Third, the government

---

[19] At the time of the second periodic report in 1995 nineteen non-governmental submissions were made to the Committee: see H. Gowan, 'The United Kingdom's Second Periodic Report under the UN Torture Convention', 1 *European Human Rights Law Review*, 1996, pp. 34–6.

in question has to be sensitive to national criticism and vulnerable to media commentary. When some of these components are missing, governments may escape scrutiny, even though there may be serious problems.

By way of comparison it is worth considering the CAT Committee's 1991 examination of Australia's report. Despite the fact that the report of the Australian Royal Commission of Inquiry into Aboriginal Deaths in Custody had been published earlier that year and had found that there were 'glaring deficiencies' in the standard of care afforded to many of the deceased, the Committee hardly touched on this issue. There was no written or oral briefing from NGOs and few experts had knowledge or expertise on issues relating to aboriginal rights and the situation in Australia.

5. DISSEMINATING DETAIL ON THE EXAMINATION OF SRI LANKA IN THE CONTEXT OF LEGISLATIVE DEBATE

Mention has already been made of the poor dissemination of reports and the conclusions of the treaty bodies at the national level. Some international human rights organisations have in recent years sought to stimulate interest among national NGOs and the national media by distributing commentaries on the examination of country reports. Where there is a serious national debate concerning proposed legislation, the comments of a human rights treaty body may provide a framework for determining the legality of any proposals.

The debate on the emergency legislation in Sri Lanka provided an opportunity for such a discussion. Although one should not overstate the potential of such a process, some small changes were brought about as a result of the HRC's questions. With regard to the discrepancies between provisions of certain Sri Lankan presidential directives and the national emergency regulations, some problems were ironed out. These small advances can be attributed to the non-governmental input and the Committee's subsequent questions.[20]

---

[20] Amnesty International, *Sri Lanka: Under Scrutiny by the Human Rights Committee*, ASA 37/21/95. Prior to the examination Amnesty International published *Sri Lanka: Security Measures Violate Human Rights*, ASA 37/12/95. For the detailed discrepancies, see Amnesty International, *Sri Lanka: Appeal for Full Implementation of Commitment to Human Rights*, ASA 37/15/95.

6. REQUESTS FOR SPECIAL REPORTS AND ISRAEL'S 1997 SPECIAL REPORT ON TORTURE

In November 1996 the Supreme Court of Israel lifted an interim injunction which had been issued against the security services ordering them to abstain from the use of any physical pressure throughout the interrogation of Mohammed Hamdan. The Court concluded:

> After reviewing the classified material presented to us, we are satisfied that the Respondent does indeed have in his possession information on which a clear suspicion can be based that the Petitioner possesses extremely vital information, the immediate disclosure of which will prevent a terrible disaster, will save human lives, and will prevent the most serious terrorist attacks. Under these circumstances, we are of the opinion that there is no justification to continue with the interim injunction . . . Needless to say the cancelling of the interim injunction is not tantamount to permission to use interrogation methods against the petitioner which are against the law. With regard to this matter, we have not been given any information regarding the methods of interrogation which the Respondent wishes to use and we are not taking any stand regarding them.[21]

The CAT Committee reacted immediately by stating that it took the view that 'the decision reportedly taken by the Supreme Court of Israel is contrary to the conclusions of the Committee'.[22] The CAT Committee had concluded in 1994 that the Landau Commission report which permitted 'moderate physical pressure' was completely unacceptable. Amnesty International wrote to the CAT Committee to suggest urgent action by the Committee. The Committee wrote two days later to the Permanent Representative of Israel inviting Israel to submit a special report as a matter of urgency on the question of the decision taken by the Supreme Court. The Committee suggested that the report reach them in time to be considered in the April-May 1997 session.[23]

Israel sent a report intended to clarify 'Israel's interrogation policies and practices and in particular the . . . decision of the Supreme Court'.[24] Although this report addressed some of the decisions taken by the Supreme

---

[21] *Mohammed Hamdan v. The General Security Service*, decided 14 November 1996, annexed to the special report of Israel, UN Doc. CAT/C/33/Add.2/Rev.1, 18 February 1997.

[22] UN Doc. HR/CAT/96/28, 19 November 1996.

[23] Article 19(1) CAT provides for states parties to submit 'such other reports as the Committee may request'.

[24] UN Doc. CAT/C/33/Add.2/Rev.1 at para. 1.

Court it was not considered satisfactory by the CAT Committee. The CAT Committee concluded in its draft annual report that, because the Israeli report did not deny the allegations of NGOs that certain physical interrogation techniques were being used in a way that cumulatively amounted to torture, the Committee would have to assume these allegations to be correct.[25] It also expressed its concern that the decision of the Supreme Court concerning the use of physical pressure had the effect of legitimising certain interrogation techniques at the domestic level. The Committee went on to recommend that '[i]nterrogations applying the methods referred to above and any other methods that are in conflict with the provisions of Articles 1 and 16 of the Convention cease immediately'.

---

[25] UN Doc. CAT/C/XVIII/CRP.1/Add.4, 11 April 1997, at paras. 131–5:

131. The information provided by Israel in its special report and in the opening statement of its representatives was essentially a reiteration of its position described in the initial report, namely that interrogation, including the use of 'moderate physical pressure' where it is thought that interrogatees have information of imminent attacks against the State which may involve deaths of innocent citizens, is lawful if conducted in accordance with the 'Landau rules'. These rules permit 'moderate physical pressure' to be used in strictly defined interrogation circumstances.

132. It is the position of Israel that interrogations pursuant to the 'Landau rules' do not breach prohibitions against cruel, inhuman or degrading treatment as contained in article 16 of the Convention against Torture and do not amount to torture as contained in article 1 of the Convention.

133. However, the methods of interrogation, described by non-governmental organisations on the basis of accounts given to them by interrogatees, which appear to be applied systematically, were neither confirmed nor denied by Israel. The Committee, therefore, must assume them to be accurate. These methods include: (1) restraining in very painful conditions, (2) hooding under special conditions, (3) sounding of loud music for prolonged periods, (4) sleep deprivation for prolonged periods, (5) threats, including death threats, (6) violent shaking, and (7) using cold air to chill; and are in the Committee's view breaches of article 16 and also constitute torture as defined in article 1 of the Convention. This conclusion is particularly evident where such methods of interrogation are used in combination, which appears to be the standard case.

134. The Committee acknowledges the terrible dilemma that Israel confronts in dealing with terrorist threats to its security, but as a State party to the Convention against Torture Israel is precluded from raising before this Committee exceptional circumstances as justification for acts prohibited by article 1 of the Convention. This is plainly expressed in article 2 of the Convention.

135. The Committee is also concerned that the effect of the Hamdan decision [*supra*, note 21] by the Israeli Supreme Court dissolving the interim injunction was to allow some of the interrogation practices, referred to above, to continue and to legitimize them for domestic purposes.

This use by the CAT Committee of NGO material for the purposes of placing a burden of proof on the government shows how influential NGOs can be for the reporting procedure. The stand taken by the CAT Committee was widely reported in the media; it makes the important point that CAT outlaws torture in all circumstances and that no defence of 'necessity' can ever be countenanced.

Other treaty bodies have requested special reports in the context of internal armed conflict. Some NGOs have pointed to the futility of asking for reports when the country has descended into all-out civil war. However some interesting opportunities for NGOs arose in the context of the former Zaire (report requested by the Committee of the Convention on the Elimination of Discrimination against Women (CEDAW)) and the former Yugoslavia (report requested by the HRC). Although there is a sense that turning to the human rights treaty bodies in times of crisis is a way of avoiding more meaningful action, there remains a case for calling for special reports in response to a particular phenomenon or decision.

C. Negative experiences with the reporting procedures and abuses of the system

1. SCHEDULING AND EVASION

Meetings of the UN treaty bodies are nearly always scheduled for an uninterrupted three hours (10 a.m.–1 p.m., 3–6 p.m.). The effect of these set pieces is often soporific. No other performances continue uninterrupted in this way. Opera, films and football matches all break to allow the audience and players time to recuperate and refresh themselves. This may seem a trivial point, but the real issue is that there is little chance for the Committee members to confer during the questioning, nor is there a chance for NGOs to discuss the 'dialogue' with the experts. Often the experts read a non-governmental report and examine a government on the allegations. Too often there is no opportunity for representatives from NGOs to explain to experts why the responses have skirted the issue or to discuss what follow-up questions might be useful. Rescheduling the meeting to allow for a series of breaks would probably result in better levels of concentration for all concerned, as well as creating opportunities for consultation amongst the experts and NGOs.

Another problem with the examination of the states parties' reports is the formulaic way in which the examination is organised. The question and answer session takes place over one or two days and follows more or less the same format each time. The government presents its report orally and members of the Committee ask questions one after the other. The government responds to the questions. Often there is little time for follow-up questions or re-questioning where responses have been inadequate. Many government delegates have gleaned the importance of providing long-winded and evasive answers in order to ensure that little time is left for further probing or challenges from the Committee members. The present author once witnessed one government delegation successfully keep the floor for over two hours, ensuring that no time was left at the end to challenge any of its responses.

2. GOVERNMENTAL EXPERTS AND THE EXPERTISE OF GOVERNMENTS

The states parties to the treaties elect the experts sitting on treaty body committees at biannual meetings. Too often experts are elected who do not have the time or incentive to study the reports of the government and the non-governmental information that is sent to them prior to examinations. The current arrangements, whereby experts have insufficient help from the secretariat in the preparation of the questions and digestion of the non-governmental material, mean that many experts arrive for the meetings straight from their normal job. Nearly all are in full time employment doing something else, and have inadequate time to spend preparing for the meetings.

Although several members of the treaty bodies can be considered real experts in the fields in question, there is hardly any examination of the actual 'expertise' of the experts by the states parties at the time of their election. There are a number of problems in this context. First, some candidates do not have the relevant background to qualify as an expert, or a potential expert, on the obligations contained in the treaty in question. Second, several successful candidates are actually working for their government (or are even members of their government). Third, the elections are simply part of the bigger set of elections that take place in and around the UN. Votes for a member of the Committee of the Convention on the

Rights of the Child (CRC) are traded, for example, for votes for a member of the Tribunal on the Law of the Sea.

There is definitely a new role here for NGOs. NGOs have so far failed to acquire the curriculum vitae of the candidates and to expose those who are unqualified to serve as 'impartial' experts 'in a personal capacity'.[26] A coordinated approach should result in better geographical representation, as well as the non-election of those experts who are clearly going to labour under a conflict of interest. However, in the long term the author's preferred solution is the professionalisation of the treaty bodies so that members give up all other commitments, are paid as full-time professionals, and are elected for a single term of seven years.

With regard to the expertise of the government representatives, too often they are badly briefed or unable to answer the Committee's questions. In some cases the state party simply asks the Permanent Representative to the United Nations to present the report. While this is perfectly satisfactory in some cases, in other cases it leaves even the casual observer with the distinct impression that the ambassador has no intention of communicating any views and observations back to the government in any meaningful way. The examination by the treaty body is seen as an irritation in the working week. This sparse attention to the importance of the 'dialogue' in turn acts as a disincentive for the expert members to study the social, economic, and legal structure of the state under examination. The resulting dialogue sometimes takes the form of gentle encouragement to the state party to take their reporting obligation more seriously. The only external result is often simply a set of public comments and views which reflect the encouragement given by the Committee. In this context national NGOs can ask the government probing questions at the time of the preparation of the report so as to ensure that the government delegation includes persons with relevant expertise and authority. Through this sort of scrutiny one might

---

[26] For example the ICCPR states in article 28:

> (2) The Committee shall be composed of nationals of States Parties to the present Covenant who shall be persons of high moral character and recognized competence in the field of human rights, consideration being given to the usefulness of the participation of some persons having legal experience.
>
> (3) The members of the Committee shall be elected and shall serve in their *personal capacity*. (Emphasis added.)

Article 38 states in part: 'Every member of the Committee shall, before taking up his duties, make a solemn declaration in open committee that he will perform his functions impartially and conscientiously.'

even encourage better dialogue at the national level between the government and the interested non-governmental sectors.

D. Suggestions for reform

1. BETTER PROCEDURES FOR NGO PARTICIPATION

This chapter has presented the perspective of one particular NGO, Amnesty International. But from a general NGO perspective the reporting to the treaty bodies could be greatly enhanced through the adoption of a few simple procedures to ensure that NGOs find it worthwhile to invest time and resources in assisting the treaty bodies. The CRC Committee has already adopted procedures whereby NGOs can informally address the Committee on country issues at pre-sessional working group meetings. The Committee of the International Covenant on Economic, Social and Cultural Rights (ICESCR) has made provision for non-governmental briefings to the whole Committee on thematic issues and NGO position papers on country reports are circulated as official UN documents.[27]

These are important advances, but from the perspective of NGOs, participation is not an end in itself. The real issue is what use the Committees make of this information as well as of information containing NGO perspectives on thematic issues. So far the committees have made good use of NGO input in their questioning. The challenge is to take the results of the questions and the Committee's conclusions and make them relevant for the public discussion on human rights, as well as for the UN's larger projects to promote and protect human rights in the field. There are signs here of recent progress in bridging this gap between the private world of the Committee room and the discussion in the public sphere regarding the record of various countries with regard to human rights.

In the 1996 meeting of the chairpersons of the treaty bodies there was a brief discussion concerning the need to attract greater attention to the work of the treaty bodies. It was decided that the treaty bodies should allow

---

[27] See for example UN Doc. E/C.12/1997/NGO/1, 1 October 1997, 'Written statement by the Committee on the Administration of Justice (United Kingdom) and the International Federation of Human Rights, a non-governmental organization in consultative status (category II)' distributed by the UN Secretary-General in accordance with Economic and Social Council Res. 1988/4.

NGOs to attend the regular press conferences which are given at the end of each session, and that individual treaty bodies may also consider a separate NGO briefing at the end of their sessions.[28]

In addition to more meaningful interaction with NGOs during and after the examination of state reports, there are other dimensions to non-governmental participation in the process. It has often been suggested by the treaty bodies that governments should consult with NGOs in the preparation of their reports and later ensure wide dissemination of the report at the national level.[29] However, governments are uneasy about full consultation before the report is finalised. For example Peter Thomson, an official who has been involved in the preparation of the reports by the Australian Government, sees limits to the consultation process with NGOs:

> Another issue is that of timing. When should the consultation take place – prior to the drafting, or once the report has been drafted but not finalised? The former would allow a greater opportunity for the consultation to be used to identify issues which NGOs would wish to see incorporated in the report. The latter would provide a greater opportunity for NGOs to critique the entire report. Doing both, albeit desirable, would add to delays and the costs of the process.[30]

By the same token NGOs too have to consider the utility of critiquing a government report at all stages. What may be needed in this context is a mind shift so that governments and NGOs see the reporting process as an opportunity to discuss differences and improve national structures for the protection of human rights. The reporting moment gives the dialogue

---

[28] A/51/482, 10 October 1996, para. 38.

[29] The ICESCR Committee has suggested that by consulting with NGOs in the preparation of their reports and through its wide dissemination at the national level 'the preparation of the report, and its consideration at the national level can come to be of at least as much value as the constructive dialogue conducted at the international level between the Committee and representatives of the reporting State': General Comment No. 1, UN Doc. HRI/GEN/1/Rev.1 at p. 44. The CEDAW Committee has recommended that where national human rights commissions have been established they 'should be associated with the preparation of reports and possibly included in government delegations in order to intensify the dialogue between the Committee and the State Party concerned': General Recommendation XVII, UN Doc. HRI/GEN/1/Rev.1 at p. 70. For more detail on the usefulness of consulting with NGOs during the preparation of the governmental report, see L. Wiseberg, 'Human Rights Information and Documentation' in United Nations, *Manual on Human Rights Reporting*, UN Doc. HR/PUB/91/1 (Rev.1) (1997), pp. 45–61.

[30] P. Thomson, 'Human Rights Reporting from a State Party's Perspective', in *Towards an Australian Bill of Rights* (ed. P. Alston), Canberra, 1994, pp. 329–64 at p. 354.

between the government and the sectors of civil society a focus; the examination by a Committee need not necessarily always be the setting for a show-down. Of course NGOs are by definition distinct from government, but now that several governments are more familiar with the role of the treaty bodies and the scope of the reporting procedure, there may be more room for governments to work with national organisations to find solutions to some of the problems highlighted in the context of the reporting procedure.

2. MORE ATTENTION TO THE GENDER DIMENSION

One of the clearest complaints by NGOs has been the Committee members' ignorance of gender issues and their failure to take gender into account either in their questions on the reports, or in their elaboration of General Comments. Of course the exception to the rule in this context is the CEDAW Committee, but even this committee has failed in the past to examine the Comments of the other Committees in order to attempt to inject a gender perspective into the evolving interpretation of international human rights law.[31]

The failure of the other treaty bodies to take full cognisance of women's rights is well known. Andrew Byrnes has pointed out that the HRC's Comment on privacy omits any reference to women's control over their bodies, and that the Comment on the right to life fails to mention the implications for the rights to access to abortion.[32] The more recent General Comment on torture, cruel, inhuman or degrading treatment or punishment makes no reference to the preventive measures which can be taken to tackle rape and sexual abuse of women.[33] Although the chairpersons' meetings have repeatedly recommended that the treaty bodies 'fully integrate gender perspectives into their pre-sessional and sessional working methods',[34] it seems unlikely that this will happen until greater gender expertise is injected into the Committees, either through the election of new members or through proper consultations with non-governmental experts.

---

[31] See A. Byrnes, 'The "Other Human Rights Treaty Body": The Work of the Committee on the Elimination of Discrimination Against Women', 14 *YJIL*, 1989, p. 6.
[32] Ibid.   [33] See General Comment No. 20, article 7, forty-fourth session, 1992.
[34] Report of the seventh meeting of persons chairing human rights treaty bodies, UN Doc. A/51/482, 10 October 1996, para. 58.

In order to examine the issue of respect for women's human rights the treaty bodies will need to focus much more on state *inaction*. A plethora of violations of women's rights occurs in the private sphere. Although the state's responsibility for these violations extends into the private sphere under the state's treaty obligations, this inaction by the state will inevitably be absent from the state's reports.[35] In order to illuminate the state's failure to act in this sphere, greater attention will have to be paid by the treaty bodies to women's organisations who detail and report on the status of women and the disadvantages women face due to structures which reinforce inequality.

3. COMPARATIVE ADVANTAGE *VIS-À-VIS* OTHER UN ACTION

One problem for NGOs is that time spent preparing reports for the treaty bodies and monitoring their meetings is time spent away from other work. So far the treaty bodies have not always demonstrated why NGOs should consider that time spent with them is time well spent. The opportunities for human rights work within the UN system are increasing. At a time when some states are presenting their third or fourth quinquennial reports the procedure before the treaty bodies can seem a little stale. The five-year space between examinations and the tardiness of so many reports leads to a lack of immediacy and relevance which is unattractive to NGOs. By contrast, the chance to break new ground in the context of a field operation, an operational agency such as the UN Children's Fund (UNICEF), or programmes such as the UN Development Programme (UNDP) or the UN Development Fund for Women may bring greater rewards for NGOs, particularly for national organisations working on the ground. Large projects aimed at 'democratisation' or 'good governance' organised through specialised agencies such as the World Bank may provide huge opportunities for improving human rights in the relevant country.[36] These concrete operational activities are proving more and more attractive to NGOs as

---

[35] On the need for private organisations to highlight state responsibility for abuses in the private sphere, see A. Clapham, *Human Rights in the Private Sphere*, Oxford, 1994, chapter 9.

[36] See generally Boutros Boutros-Ghali, *An Agenda for Democratization*, New York, 1996, and 'Report of the Secretary-General: Support by the United Nations System of the Efforts of Governments to Promote and Consolidate New or Restored Democracies', UN Doc. A/51/512, 18 October 1996.

they plan their work with the UN. Part of the attraction is obviously the fact that many of the projects for training, education and development are subcontracted out to NGOs by the donors and agencies. The treaty bodies have no such operational activity or material resources and, rather than representing partners for cooperation, sometimes leave NGOs with an impression of dull diplomatic debate.

With regard to opportunities for publicity and political action, other UN bodies such as the Commission on Human Rights, the General Assembly and the Security Council are now more amenable to straightforward condemnations of violations of human rights and humanitarian law. In addition, the 1990s has seen a series of international conferences, summits, and special sessions of the General Assembly. NGOs from around the world have found that these occasions have provided useful platforms for policy discussion and for encouraging political commitments from states. In contrast to the slow, rather legalistic work of the treaty bodies, these *ad hoc* meetings have become very appealing for NGOs from very different sectors.[37] The vast majority of NGOs are now concentrating on the special sessions of the General Assembly which have been scheduled to follow up the recent series of world conferences: environment (1997), disarmament (1997), social development (2000) and children (2001). NGOs cannot normally address meetings of the General Assembly, but a decision of the General Assembly in April 1997 ensured that NGOs would be able to address the plenary session on follow-up to the Rio Conference on the environment. NGOs are increasing their demands for greater access to UN meetings and more and more UN bodies and organs are now actually inviting NGOs to participate in their work. Even members of the Security Council have met to discuss humanitarian issues in the Great Lakes with the relief and development NGOs Oxfam, CARE and Médecins sans Frontières. In September 1997 the Secretary-General of Amnesty International met the members of the Security Council at a special meeting organised by one of the members (Portugal) to discuss the Security Council's work and issues of human rights and armed conflict. On the other hand the treaty bodies have not been a focus of NGO demands.[38]

---

[37] See 'Beyond Beijing – NGO Participation at the UN Fourth World Conference on Women: Report on Barriers to Access, with Recommendations for Change', October 1996 (joint NGO report). Available at gopher: //gopher.igc.apc.org:5000/00/int/hrw/general.

[38] In a review of the work of human rights organisations at the UN and the future possible direction of this work, Felice Gaer outlines a number of different opportunities for NGO

From the NGO perspective, the treaty bodies remain splendidly isolated and disconnected from the mainstream discussion and activity relating to human rights around the world. NGOs can provide the bridge to that larger world but will need to be convinced of the efficacy of investing time and money in preparing briefs and participating in the work of the treaty bodies. Secretary-General Kofi Annan's reform programme of July 1997 included the outline of a new policy demanding that human rights be a cross-cutting issue in the other four core missions of the UN (humanitarian assistance, development, economic and social issues, and peace and security).[39] This imperative has reverberated around the UN system, but most agencies and programmes are still in the dark as to how to 'mainstream' human rights in their work. Rather than expecting the agencies and UN programmes to come to their meetings, the treaty bodies need to start to reach out to the UN's agencies, conferences, and field operations. But as long as the expert members of the treaty bodies remain part-time *pro bono* panelists, without staff and resources, this will remain an unlikely prospect. In the short term these connections are still most likely to be made by NGOs seeking to reinforce the legal basis for the UN's field work on human rights.

4. A RADICAL SUGGESTION FOR A SUSTAINABLE SYSTEM: A PERMANENT PROFESSIONAL TREATY BODY

Many of the problems referred to above could be tackled by a concerted effort to take NGOs more seriously in the context of the examination of reports under the treaty body regime. But the system itself is under increasing strain. According to Philip Alston's final report as UN independent expert on the effective functioning of the treaty bodies, one of the premises on which his report is based is that

action and suggests that the governmental opposition to NGO participation in the political bodies is to be contrasted with the 'friendly' attitude of the experts in the treaty bodies: F. Gaer, 'Reality Check: Human Rights NGOs Confront Governments at the UN', in *NGOs, the UN and Global Governance* (eds. T. G. Weiss and L. Gordenker), Boulder, 1996, pp. 51–66. The fact that NGOs may have concentrated on access to intergovernmental meetings rather than closer cooperation with the treaty bodies may reflect a certain desire for international recognition as global voices. However, the political acceptance of NGOs as legitimate participants in international meetings and discussions would suggest that the climate would be propitious for the elaboration or consolidation of procedures for better NGO participation in the work of the treaty bodies.

[39] 'Renewing the United Nations: A Programme for Reform', UN Doc. A/51/950 (1997).

the present system is unsustainable and that significant reforms will be required if the overall regime is to achieve its objectives. This is a function of several developments including the immense expansion of the human rights treaty system in a period of less than two decades, the expanding reach and increasing demands of regional human rights systems, the proliferation of reporting obligations in other contexts, especially in the environmental field, and increasing pressures upon Governments and the United Nations system to reduce their budgetary outlays and streamline their programmes. The treaty bodies cannot, and nor should they seek to, remain immune to these pressures.[40]

On the one hand, the increasing number of states parties means that the treaty bodies will have to meet more often or fall further behind in their examination of reports. On the other hand, governments are becoming overwhelmed by the plethora of reporting expected of them as they become party to more and more treaties. Many of the reporting obligations are of a general and overlapping nature and it would make sense to start to move towards a system of consolidated reports.[41] But the more fundamental issue is how the members of the committees will be able to give sufficient time and energy to this human rights work when they act either on a *pro bono* basis, or with an honorarium of US$3,000 per annum.[42] As Philip Alston pointed out in his final report, the increasing work of the treaty bodies means that

> members of the treaty bodies would be required to spend between one third and one half of their time in Geneva or New York. . . . [C]ommittee membership will be feasible only for governmental officials paid by their national authorities (a situation unlikely to guarantee either independence or expertise), academics subsidised by their governments (since in today's climate of budget cuts and a user-pays approach most universities are

---

[40] Report requested by the UN General Assembly in Resolution 48/120 of 20 December 1993, UN Doc. E/CN.4/1997/74, 7 March 1997, para. 10.

[41] See the recommendation of Philip Alston in his final report at para. 90 (UN Doc. E/CN.4/1997/74), and the more detailed suggestions in his interim report on his updated study at paras. 167–73, UN Doc. A/Conf.157/PC/62/Add.11/Rev.1, 22 April 1993.

[42] '[M]embers of the Human Rights Committee, the Committee on the Elimination of Discrimination Against Women and the Committee on the Rights of the Child will receive US$3,000 per year (apart from their daily allowance) and others (members of the Committee on Economic, Social and Cultural Rights, the Committee on the Elimination of Racial Discrimination and the Committee Against Torture) will receive nothing (apart from the same allowances).' Final report of Philip Alston, UN Doc. E/CN.4/1997/74, 7 March 1997, para. 84. For reform proposals on this issue see E. Evatt, chapter 21 of this volume, subheading 'Resource implications of these reforms'.

unlikely to be prepared to subsidise international service for half the year) or retirees.[43]

We are clearly facing 'governmentalisation' of the membership of the treaty bodies, with little prospect of this bringing greater expertise or rigour to the examination of governments' reports.

One radical solution would be to create a permanent professional treaty body which would conduct examinations of states' reports under the different treaties. In some cases these might be consolidated reports, in other cases states could still report under a single treaty. This is presented here as a goal or ideal. As has been pointed out many times by Alston, steps can already be taken to move in this direction without adopting a new treaty. Treaty bodies could meet so that their examinations overlap. The timing of states' reports to the treaty bodies could be harmonised to streamline their reporting obligations. Cross-treaty-body working groups could be established that would examine themes which are cross-cutting and of particular relevance in the context of any one state party report. Once states saw the advantages of such arrangements there could be momentum for radical changes in the system and eventually in the treaties themselves.

Such a reorganisation would have a number of advantages. First, by recruiting experts who would give up their normal employment, one would increase the level of commitment and expertise. In order to prevent these posts becoming over-politicised there should be terms of say, seven years, which would be non-renewable. There would therefore be a reduced incentive to go easy on governments in order to ensure re-election. A clear condition concerning independence from any of the arms of government should be built into the procedure.

Second, by concentrating the work into a single permanent body one could start to pool the experience across the treaty bodies so that an expert secretariat is developed to service and assist the new single treaty body. By focusing on one body, one would be able to enhance the visibility of the treaty body work and attract greater press interest. Only if the media come to know the body, and the key officials and members working for it, will one ever achieve serious coverage of this aspect of the UN's work.

Third, we have already seen how some treaty bodies are starting to feel their way in the context of action taken outside the regular context of reports. Treaty bodies have called for special reports and intervened in

[43] Ibid.

cases of imminent execution or deportation.[44] In order to exploit the opportunities for involvement fully, there needs to be a way for NGOs, UN agencies and others to communicate with the treaty body at any time. By creating a permanent body one would enhance the existing opportunities to activate procedures and ensure timely *démarches* by the treaty bodies. (In the current stage of development of the treaty bodies, the prospects for involvement may depend on whether the particular treaty body chairperson can be tracked down at home or work.) One could also envisage hearings by working groups of the new body taking place in the actual states whose report is under consideration.

Lastly, in order for treaty body work to be better integrated into the rest of the UN work on human rights, there must be full-time officials able to travel and meet with those involved in the other programmes. Placing the treaty bodies on a professional permanent footing would pave the way for proper interaction with the UN's programmes in the fields of electoral assistance, post-conflict peace-building, and human rights monitoring. There is now a chance to place the human rights treaty bodies at the heart of the UN system. Without such radical changes the treaty bodies will remain in 'splendid isolation'.

---

[44] On the prospects of even greater preventive and urgent procedures, see 'Prevention of Racial Discrimination, Including Early Warning and Urgent Procedures: Working Paper Adopted by the Committee on the Elimination of Racial Discrimination', UN Doc. CERD/ C/1993/Misc.1/Rev.2.

B

NATIONAL INFLUENCES AND RESPONSES

9

MAKING HUMAN RIGHTS TREATY
OBLIGATIONS A REALITY: WORKING WITH
NEW ACTORS AND PARTNERS

ANNE GALLAGHER

A. Introduction

This chapter takes, as its fundamental premise, the view that implementation of and compliance with international human rights treaties are ultimately national issues – a reality which is often lost on those of us working at the international level. International and even regional human rights mechanisms are simply inaccessible to the vast majority of the world's population. At the end of the day, individual rights and freedoms will be protected or violated because of what exists or what is lacking within a given state or society, and not because of what is said or done within the United Nations *Palais des Nations* in Geneva. The ability of a state to discharge its responsibilities in the area of human rights effectively will depend predominantly on the strength of its domestic institutions. It is for this very simple reason that the worth of the United Nations human rights treaty system can best be measured by reference to its ability to encourage and cultivate national implementation of, and compliance with, international human rights standards. This is the only valid test of that system's relevance and effectiveness.

It follows that the work of the treaty bodies themselves should be heavily weighted towards encouraging and facilitating the development of national systems and processes which support and defend protected rights. The identification of those domestic mechanisms which play a critical role in ensuring (and in obstructing) compliance with human rights treaty obligations should not be especially difficult or controversial. Human rights are best protected in societies governed by the rule of law and by a representative, accountable government. The protection of human rights also presupposes an adequate standard of living for all persons; an impartial, accessible and independent judiciary; efficient, professional and disciplined law enforcement; a free and responsible press and a vigorous civil society. The existence of specialised bodies charged with identifying and remedying violations in the civil, political, economic, social and cultural spheres can supplement these basic systems and processes or otherwise provide additional protection.

This study represents a preliminary attempt to explore the relationship which exists (or should exist) between the international human rights treaty system and certain key national partners. The chapter is divided into two parts. The first examines in detail the capacity of one particular type of national structure, the independent human rights institution, to impact upon compliance with international treaty norms. National human rights institutions have been selected to illustrate the chapter's central thesis because of their increasing number; because of the responsibility which they are usually given, under national law, to monitor implementation of and compliance with international human rights treaties; and because of their potential to 'democratise, de-politicise and decentralise international human rights standards'.[1] The second part explores and evaluates the role which the international human rights treaty regime is presently playing in the strengthening of domestic infrastructures (such as human rights institutions and law enforcement agencies) through, *inter alia*, the vehicle of international technical assistance. The possibility of developing a substantive role for the various committees in the formulation and delivery of human rights-oriented technical assistance is examined in this context.

B. National institutions and the international human rights treaty system

National human rights institutions can be defined for present purposes as independent entities which have been established by a government under the constitution or by a law and entrusted with specific responsibilities in terms of the promotion and protection of human rights. Institutions of this kind have now been set up in a large number of countries including Australia, Cameroon, Canada, Ghana, India, Indonesia, Latvia, Liberia,

---

[1] Statement of the representative of the National Human Rights Commission of India to the fifty-second session of the United Nations Commission on Human Rights, 10 April, 1996 (copy on file with the author).

Mexico, New Zealand, the Philippines, South Africa, Sri Lanka, Uganda and Zambia. The new constitutions of Ethiopia, Fiji, Malawi and Thailand all require the creation of specialised human rights commissions. Constitutional amendments which will permit the establishment of a human rights commission in Papua New Guinea are before parliament. In December 1996, a conference on setting up an independent human rights institution in the United Kingdom was organised, based on a commitment to such a body in the Labour Party's election platform. During 1996, 1997 and the first part of 1998, the Governments of, *inter alia*, Bangladesh, Cambodia, Georgia, Moldova, Mongolia and Nepal have all taken concrete steps towards establishing independent human rights institutions.

Supporters of the trend towards establishing national human rights institutions believe that these bodies have the capacity to narrow the gap between the international system and governments on the one hand, and civil society on the other. They argue that the national character of such institutions enables them to de-mystify universal principles and translate them into practical measures at the level where it most matters.[2] They also claim that national institutions can facilitate the implementation of international human rights standards in a way which accommodates national peculiarities and which respects cultural, religious and ethnic diversity, and in a more informed and sensitive manner than any international body.[3] This view is considered and evaluated below.

1. STRUCTURE, FUNCTION AND THE POLITICAL DIMENSION

In practice, all national institutions falling within the above definition are either 'quasi-judicial' or 'administrative' in nature, in the sense that they are neither judicial nor law-making. Unlike the more traditional ombudsman offices, (which focus primarily on overseeing fairness and legality in public administration)[4] human rights institutions are usually involved in

---

[2] Ibid.

[3] See further, Brian Burdekin and Anne Gallagher, 'The United Nations and National Human Rights Institutions', 1 (2) *Quarterly Review of the United Nations High Commissioner for Human Rights*, spring 1998.

[4] The traditional ombudsman model is not concerned with human rights except insofar as this relates to their principal function of administrative oversight. However, some of the more recently created ombudsman offices, especially those in Eastern Europe and Latin America 'defensor del pueblo', have been given specific human rights protection mandates – sometimes in relation to rights set forth in constitutions or other national

one or more specific functions directly related to the protection and promotion of human rights. These commonly include an advisory function (with regard to government policy and practice on human rights); an educative function (oriented towards the public); and what may be termed an impartial investigatory function. Differences between institutions are often related to differences in the weight given to particular functions. The focus of some ranges across a broad spectrum of rights while others are restricted to the promotion of a particular right or the protection of a particular vulnerable group. In certain countries the constitution will provide for the establishment of an independent human rights body. More often, such institutions are created by legislation. While some institutions are linked, in one way or another, to the executive branch of government, the actual level of independence which they enjoy depends upon a number of factors including composition, financial basis and the manner in which they operate.

By definition, national institutions are creations of government. The decision of a government to establish an institution can be motivated by disparate factors, not necessarily related to protection and promotion of human rights. Motives are often revealed in the structure of a particular body and the measure of independence which has been granted or denied. A government taking the matter of human rights seriously will generally be willing to vest an institution with significant responsibilities and to provide it with the powers and resources necessary to discharge those responsibilities fully. This strength will naturally carry through to the institution's work and a widely supported, properly resourced institution is likely to be an effective one. At the other extreme, a government which engages in systematic human rights violations will not be interested in creating an institution which is capable of interfering with its ability to exercise control through coercion. In a few clear-cut cases, institutions are established as no more than a cynical public relations exercise and can therefore become a convenient facade behind which an insincere government will attempt to

---

legislation. This issue of definition is further complicated by the fact that the functions implied in these designations are not always reflected in the work of institutions so categorised. An 'ombudsman' for example, may be engaged in a broad range of promotional and protective activities generally recognised as characteristic of a human rights commission (the Polish Ombudsman is a good example). Another entity, identified as a 'human rights commission' may be operating predominantly within the sphere of public administration. This is the case of the Mexican Human Rights Commission.

shield itself from criticism or attract foreign aid.[5] Identification of such cases is not particularly difficult. Sham institutions will be rendered impotent through denial of resources or substantive powers, or both.

In an increasing number of instances however, even hardened critics have been surprised by the ability of certain human rights institutions to take on a life of their own, distancing themselves from both the government and from the mixed motivations which lay behind their establishment. The Human Rights Commissions of India and Indonesia are examples of this phenomenon, and particularly relevant in the present context given the ambivalent attitude of many Asian states towards the international human rights treaty system. Both were set up in 1993 by governments which had come under heavy external criticism for their poor human rights performance.[6] Both suffer certain structural weaknesses.

In the case of the Indonesian Commission (*Komisi Nasional Hak Azasi Manusia* or Komnas HAM), the body was established (and is therefore vulnerable to dissolution) by presidential decree. Its mandate and powers are not clearly defined; there are no legal safeguards in place to protect its integrity and independence; and it is yet to be provided with adequate resources.[7] Despite these weaknesses, *Komnas HAM* quickly began to demonstrate an independent streak which earned it community support,

---

[5] This possibility was raised in the context of Liberia where a local human rights group recently expressed the hope that this country's Human Rights Commission, (created by parliament in October 1997) 'will not be a government surrogate to conduct public relations to attract foreign aid': *Liberian President Signs Human Rights Bill*, Reuters, 28 October 1998.

[6] The Indonesian Commission's Vice-Chairperson is on record as stating that this body was formed 'because of the need to enhance goodwill with the international community'. M. Darusman, 'Human Rights and International Cooperation', Keynote speech, reproduced in *Report of a Symposium on Human Rights in the Asia-Pacific Region*, organised by the Japanese Ministry of Foreign Affairs and the United Nations University, 20–21 July 1995 at p. 94. When introducing the Human Rights Commission bill to the Indian parliament, the Minister of Home Affairs explained that, while the human rights embodied in the two International Covenants are protected by the Constitution, '. . . there has been growing concern in the country and abroad about issues relating to human rights', Lawyers' Committee for Human Rights, *India: The Human Rights Commission Bill*, 1993 at p. 2.

[7] See further, Human Rights Watch Asia, *The Limits of Openness: Human Rights in Indonesia and East Timor*, 1994, at pp. 122–34; Amnesty International, *Indonesia and East Timor: When Will the Commission Take Action?*, AI Index ASA 21/10/96, February 1996. See also, M. Talwar, 'Indonesia's National Human Rights Commission: A Step in the Right Direction?', 4 *Human Rights Brief* (Centre for Human Rights and Humanitarian Law, Washington College of Law), winter 1997, p. 1 at p. 19.

government disapproval and international approbation.[8] Its actions (particularly in relation to controversial cases including the July 1996 riots in Jakarta and human rights violations in East Timor) have been said to act as 'a brake on the abuse of power' by Indonesian authorities.[9] In the case of the Indian Commission, the legislative act establishing this body has been criticised for failing to include additional sources of international human rights law (other than the two Covenants) and for shielding military and para-military forces from the Commission's investigative jurisdiction.[10] Once again however, international and local scepticism has been found to be somewhat misplaced. Since 1993, the Indian Commission, now with

---

[8] On the positive international reaction to the work of the Commission see, for example, Talwar, ibid., at pp. 19, 21; Human Rights Watch Asia, *Indonesia*, Vol. 7, No. 15, November 1995 at p. 26; Human Rights Watch Asia, *supra*, note 7; and US State Department, *Indonesia Country Report on Human Rights Practices for 1996*, Washington. The latter states: 'The Indonesian National Human Rights Commission, despite limited resources, and occasional government pressure and intimidation, vigorously undertook investigations and publicised its independent findings and recommendations'. On the equally positive reaction of the Indonesian public see Sri Wahyuni, 'Human Rights Commission, Last Avenue of People's Hope', *Jakarta Post*, 6 December 1996 at p. 4. On the distinctly unenthusiastic response of the Indonesian Government, see, for example, 'Rights Body Warned Over its Mission', *Jakarta Post*, 5 December 1996 at p. 1. Note that the Indonesian Armed Forces have called on the Commission to define the scope of its authority 'to reduce potential conflicts with the government': 'Rights Commission Needs Definition', *Jakarta Post*, 7 December 1996 at p. 2.

[9] P. Bowring, 'Despite July's Upheavals, Indonesia Won't Erupt', *International Herald Tribune*, 24–25 August 1996; see also K. Richburg, 'Indonesian Panel Faces Toughest Test, Human Rights Commission Likely to Blame Government for July Riots', *Washington Post Foreign Service*, 6 October 1996. See also: 'Jakarta: Authorities Blamed', *Independent on Sunday*, 13 October 1996; the 1996 US State Department Report, *supra*, note 8; Amnesty International, International Secretariat, *Indonesia: Irian Jaya: National Commission on Human Rights Confirms Violations*, AI Index ASA 21/47/95, November 1996; and Amnesty International, *Indonesia: Arrests, Torture and Intimidation: The Government's Response to its Critics*, AI Index ASA 21/70/96, November 1996 at pp. 10–14 and Appendix I. For a more recent (and very critical) review of the functions and performance of the Indonesian Commission, see South Asia Human Rights Documentation Centre, 'A Critique of the National Human Rights Commission of Indonesia', in *National Human Rights Institutions in the Asia Pacific Region (Report of the Alternate NGO Consultation on the Second Asia-Pacific Regional Workshop on National Human Rights Institutions)*, March 1998 at pp. 35–42.

[10] See further, Lawyers' Committee for Human Rights, *supra*, note 6; P. Sebastian, 'Protection of Human Rights: One More Ornamental Commission?', *Economic and Political Weekly* (India), 23 October 1993 at pp. 2327–8; and Amnesty International, *India: Submission to the Human Rights Committee Concerning Implementation of the Articles of the International Covenant on Civil and Political Rights*, AI Index ASA 20/27/97, July 1997 at pp. 79–80.

several hundred staff, has developed a solid reputation for taking on the government and is now a focal point for human rights advocacy in that country.[11]

2. THE CONNECTION BETWEEN NATIONAL INSTITUTIONS AND THE INTERNATIONAL HUMAN RIGHTS TREATY SYSTEM

While national institutions are not yet recognised as separate players in the international human rights arena, their influence is increasingly being felt. Milestones include substantive references in the Vienna Declaration and Programme of Action which emerged from the 1993 World Conference on Human Rights[12] and the 'Paris Principles' on the optimal structure and functioning of national institutions, endorsed that same year by the UN General Assembly.[13] In 1994 an International Coordinating Committee of National Human Rights Institutions was established. Through the

[11] See US State Department, *India Country Report on Human Rights Practices for 1996*, Washington, (referring to the role of the Commission in addressing both patterns of abuse and specific violations, as well as fostering human rights education in schools and among the police and security forces). See also Amnesty International, *supra*, note 10 (acknowledging the important role which the Indian Commission has played in 'monitoring human rights violations, in raising concerns on a broad range of human rights issues and in furthering human rights education'). But cf., South Asia Human Rights Documentation Centre, 'National Human Rights Commission of India', in *National Human Rights Institutions in the Asia Pacific Region (Report of the Alternate NGO Consultation on the Second Asia-Pacific Regional Workshop on National Human Rights Institutions)*, March 1998 at pp. 7–34 (criticising the Indian Commission for, *inter alia*, insufficiencies in its enquiry process and a 'scattered' approach to human rights education and training).

[12] In its final document: 'The World Conference on Human Rights reaffirms the important and constructive role played by national institutions for the promotion and protection of human rights, in particular in their advisory capacity to the competent authorities, their role in remedying human rights violations, in the dissemination of human rights information and education in human rights . . . The World Conference on Human Rights encourages the establishment and strengthening of national institutions, having regard to the "Principles relating to the status of national institutions" and recognising that it is the right of each State to choose the framework which is best suited to its particular needs at the national level.' *Vienna Declaration and Programme of Action* adopted by the World Conference on Human Rights, Vienna, 25 June 1993, UN Doc. A/CONF.157/24 (Part 1, para. 36).

[13] *Principles Relating to the Status of National Institutions*, GA Res. 48/134 (1993), annex, reprinted in *National Human Rights Institutions: A Handbook on the Establishment and Strengthening of National Institutions for the Promotion and Protection of Human Rights*, United Nations Centre for Human Rights, Professional Training Series No. 4, 1995.

Coordinating Committee, human rights institutions are lobbying for a special status which will enable them to participate as separate entities in the work of the Commission on Human Rights and other UN fora.[14]

Despite these developments, national human rights institutions and the international human rights treaty system have had very little direct contact with each other. Unlike non-governmental organisations (NGOs), national institutions seldom provide the treaty bodies with independent information. Representatives of national institutions are rarely present during the 'constructive dialogue' and, even then, only in the somewhat problematic role of 'adviser' to the official delegation. At the domestic level, many institutions operate in total isolation (and often, in near-total ignorance) of their international counterparts. Many do not participate in the process of preparing reports, even when a responsibility to do so can be inferred from their establishing legislation. Few have yet taken it upon themselves to disseminate, debate or follow up on reports produced by the state or on the resulting observations made by the treaty bodies.

For their part, the treaty bodies have paid little attention to human rights institutions in their analyses of states parties' reports. When an institution does exist in the country under review, its legislative basis, structure, functioning or activities are rarely examined[15] and are never the subject of

---

[14] The Commission on Human Rights has sought the views of governments on the question of national institutions' status in international human rights fora. These views are contained in UN Doc. E/CN.4/1996/48 and UN Doc. E/CN.4/1997/41. During the 1996 session, the Bureau of the Commission ruled that, for this session (and in the absence of any objections from the relevant national delegation), national institutions would be given the floor immediately after all categories of states (states members of the Commission, other states members of the UN and states having observer status). This arrangement was continued in 1997. In 1998, the Chairperson of the Commission went even further – noting publicly that as a reflection of their independence, the national institutions addressing the Commission on the relevant agenda item would be doing so from a special section of the floor set aside for this purpose and not from the seat of their government delegations. The Commission itself has subsequently confirmed this arrangement and reiterated the importance of independent national institutions being able to participate in an appropriate manner and in their own right in meetings of the Commission and its subsidiary bodies, CHR Res. 1997/49, para. 16.

[15] One very recent exception is provided by the Human Rights Committee's consideration of India's third periodic report. In its concluding observations, the Committee 'regrets that the National Human Rights Commission is prevented by Clause 19 of the Protection of Human Rights Act from investigating directly complaints of human rights violations against the armed forces, but must request a report from the central government. The Committee further regrets that complaints to the Commission are subject to a one-year time-limit, thus preventing the investigation of many alleged past human rights violations.'

in-depth consideration. Recommendations to states parties on the desirability of establishing such institutions are uncommon. The rare suggestions made in this direction are characterised by a breadth and generality which calls their usefulness into serious question.[16] With only two exceptions, the treaty bodies have not used the vehicle of general comments or recommendations to promote the establishment of independent national institutions.[17]

The Committee recommended 'that these restrictions be removed, and that the National Human Rights Commission be authorised to investigate all allegations of violations by agents of the state. It further recommends that all States within the Union be encouraged to establish Human Rights Commissions', UN Doc. CCPR/C/60/IND/3, (1997) at para. 22.

[16] In the context of examining the report of Zambia, for example, the HRC recommended that 'appropriate institutions be set up in order to effectively promote the observance of human rights', UN Doc. CCPR/C/79/Add.62 (1996) at para. 20. In relation to Burundi, the Committee of the Convention on the Elimination of Racial Discrimination (CERD) has recommended that the Government request assistance from the Office of the UN High Commissioner for Human Rights (UNHCHR) in, *inter alia*, 'the establishment of a national institution for the protection of human rights', the Committee, forty-fourth session, UN Doc. A/49/18 (1994) at para. 50. The Committee of the Convention on the Rights of the Child (CRC) tends to be slightly more specific – its standard recommendation being that the state party under review establish an overall national mechanism mandated to ensure continuing supervision and evaluation of implementation of the Convention, or even an 'ombudsman for children'. See, for example, sixth session, UN Docs. CRC/C/15/Add. 22 at para. 17 (Chile); CRC/C/15/Add. 54 at para. 24 (Guatemala); and CRC/C/15/Add. 40 at para. 29 (Sri Lanka).

[17] The first exception is provided by the CERD Committee's General Recommendation XVII concerning 'the establishment of national institutions to facilitate the implementation of the Convention', in which the Committee:

1. . . . *Recommends* that States parties establish national commissions or other appropriate bodies, taking into account, *mutatis mutandis*, the principles relating to the status of national institutions annexed to Commission on Human Rights resolution 1992/54 of 3 March 1992, to serve, *inter alia*, the following purposes: (a) To promote respect for the enjoyment of human rights without any discrimination, as expressly set out in article 5 of the International Convention on the Elimination of All Forms of Racial Discrimination; (b) To review government policy towards protection against racial discrimination; (c) To monitor legislative compliance with the provisions of the Convention; (d) To educate the public about the obligations of States parties under the Convention; (e) To assist the Government in the preparation of reports submitted to the Committee on the Elimination of Racial Discrimination;

2. *Also recommends* that, where such commissions have been established, they should be associated with the preparation of reports and possibly included in government delegations in order to intensify the dialogue between the Committee and the State party concerned.

Reprinted in *Compilation of General Comments and General Recommendations Adopted by the Human Rights Treaty Bodies*, UN Doc. HRI/GEN/1/Rev.2 (1996).

The functions commonly assigned to human rights institutions (as summarised in the previous section), clearly indicate the links which exist – or should exist – between these bodies and the human rights treaty system. In some cases, the connection is a fundamental one, the mandate of several national institutions being specifically framed in terms of the international instruments. The Australian Human Rights and Equal Opportunity Commission (HREOC), for example, was created by the same legislative act which incorporated the International Covenant on Civil and Political Rights (ICCPR) into domestic law.[18] HREOC is the implementing agency not only for the ICCPR but also for the Convention on the Elimination of Discrimination against Women (CEDAW), the Convention on the Rights of the Child (CRC) and the Convention on the Elimination of Racial Discrimination (CERD). For the purposes of the work of the Indian Commission, 'human rights' are defined with specific reference to the rights '. . . guaranteed by the Constitution or embedded in the International Covenants . . .'[19] Human rights are defined under the law establishing the Latvian Human Rights Office to include those rights protected in, *inter alia*, the Constitution and 'international human rights treaties which are binding for Latvia'.[20]

Framing a national institution's mandate with reference to the international human rights instruments has direct practical consequences. The work of each of the above institutions, whether it be in relation to education about human rights, advising government or investigating violations, must be undertaken with reference to, and in accordance with, international human rights treaty standards. The inclusion of references to international human rights treaties in the mandate of a national institution is of special significance in relation to countries which follow the 'non self-executing'[21]

The second and more recent exception is provided by the ICESCR Committee which in its General Comment No. 10 of 1998 noted that National Institutions have a potentially crucial role to play in promoting and ensuring the indivisibility and interdependence of all human rights. The general Comment also identified ways in which National Institutions could work to protect and promote economic, social and cultural right. UN Doc. E/1999/22 - E/C.12/1998/26, Annex V).

[18] Human Rights and Equal Opportunity Commission Act, 1986 (Cth).
[19] Protection of Human Rights Act (1993) at Section 2 (d). The Act defines 'International Covenants' as the ICCPR and the International Covenant on Economic, Social and Cultual Rights (ICESCR).
[20] Law on the Latvian Human Rights Office, article 1(1).
[21] Whether because, as in Australia, treaties generally need to be implemented by legislation in order to have legal effect in national law, or because, as in the United States, human rights treaties would be considered non self-executing.

theory of treaty law. In such instances, the national institution may be able to cover, at least partially, the gap which is often left by states parties failing to pass the necessary incorporating legislation.[22]

While the effect may be similar, not all constitutional or legislative provisions establishing human rights institutions refer specifically to the international instruments. The Constitutions of both Malawi[23] and South Africa[24] incorporate most of the rights protected in the human rights treaties to which those countries are parties. The human rights commissions established under the respective constitutions are both empowered to protect and investigate violations of these protected rights.[25] The connection between the mandate of other national institutions and the treaty system, while less direct, is still evident. The principal objective of the Indonesian Commission, for example, is to 'help develop a national condition which is conducive to the implementation of human rights in conformity with the United Nations Charter and the Universal Declaration of Human Rights'.[26]

The majority of independent human rights commissions are explicitly assigned a monitoring role *vis-à-vis* international human rights treaties. The Philippines Human Rights Commission is a constitutionally entrenched body with the function to, *inter alia*, 'monitor the Philippine Government's compliance with international treaty obligations on human rights'.[27] A specialised Human Rights Instruments Monitoring Division has been established for that purpose. The constitutional provision

[22] But cf. H. Charlesworth, 'Australia's Split Personality: Implementation of Human Rights Treaty Obligations in Australia', in *Treaty-making and Australia: Globalization Versus Sovereignty* (eds. P. Alston and M. Chiam), Sydney, 1995, p. 129 at pp. 136–7 (arguing that the limited powers accorded HREOC prevent that institution from providing the right to an effective remedy which is guaranteed under article 2 (2) of the ICCPR).

[23] Constitution of the Republic of Malawi, chapter III, Fundamental Principles, and chapter IV, Human Rights.

[24] Constitution of the Republic of South Africa, 1996, Act 108 of 1996. For a detailed examination of chapter 3 of the Constitution (sections 7–35) entitled 'Fundamental Rights' see A. Steenkamp, 'The South African Constitution of 1993 and the Bill of Rights: An Evaluation in Light of International Human Rights Norms', 17 *HRQ*, 1995, at pp. 101–26.

[25] Malawi, Constitution: article 129, see generally chapter XI; South Africa Constitution, section 184.

[26] Presidential Decree No. 50, Year 1993 [regarding] the National Commission on Human Rights.

[27] Constitution of the Republic of the Philippines, section 18, article XIII (1987). Note however, that the Commission is only empowered to investigate violations involving civil and political rights despite the fact that this country is party to both International Covenants.

establishing the Human Rights Commission of Uganda stipulates that this body is to 'monitor the Government's compliance with international treaty and convention obligations on human rights'.[28] One of three Sub-Commissions established under the Indonesian Commission's founding decree is charged with 'examination of human rights instruments',[29] presumably with a view to ratification. The proposed law to alter the Constitution of Papua New Guinea states that the functions of the Human Rights Commission will include monitoring compliance with existing international human rights instruments and making recommendations as to the desirability of that country becoming bound by any international instrument on human rights.[30]

The monitoring function assigned to national institutions often includes responsibility for ensuring compliance of national laws and practices with the state's international treaty obligations. The Latvian Human Rights Office, for example, is charged with 'carry(ing) out an analysis of Latvian legal norms to determine their compliance with international human rights treaties which are binding on Latvia'.[31] The Indian Commission is required to 'study treaties and other international instruments on human rights and make recommendations for their effective implementation',[32] as well as to 'review the safeguards provided by or under the Constitution or any law . . . for the protection of human rights and recommend measures for their effective implementation'.[33] One of the Standing Committees established by the South African Human Rights Commission is charged with, *inter alia*, assessing legislation against constitutionally protected rights as well as international human rights instruments.[34] HREOC is empowered to examine federal or territorial legislation to determine whether or not it is inconsistent with, *inter alia*, the ICCPR, CRC, CEDAW and CERD.[35] The New Zealand Human Rights Commission, in accordance with its mandate to keep national laws under review, recently undertook a comprehensive

---

[28] Constitution of Uganda, article 52(h).
[29] Presidential Decree No. 50, Year 1993 [regarding] the National Commission on Human Rights.
[30] Proposed law to alter the Constitution (*Constitutional Amendment (Human Rights Commission)*), articles 220C (c) and (d), National Gazette No. G82 of 2 October 1996.
[31] Law on the Latvian Human Rights Office, article 2(7).
[32] Protection of Human Rights Act, 1993 at section 12(f).   [33] Ibid., at section 12(d).
[34] Human Rights Commission of South Africa, *Annual Report, 1995–1996* at p. 6.
[35] Human Rights and Equal Opportunity Commission Act, 1986 (Cth), section 11.

survey of all legislation with a view to ascertaining its conformity with that country's human rights treaty obligations.[36]

Other aspects of the work normally undertaken by national institutions provide additional evidence of the connection which should be acknowledged to exist between these bodies and the international human rights treaty system. All national human rights institutions are entrusted with a promotional and educative role which is usually defined in terms of: (i) informing and educating about human rights; (ii) fostering the development of values and attitudes which uphold these rights; and (iii) encouraging action to defend these rights from violation. While promotional and educative strategies vary significantly, most institutions are involved in the collection, production and dissemination of human rights information materials relevant to their mandate.[37] This often includes translation and dissemination of the international instruments, as well as the preparation of simplified texts for children and the general public. Some national institutions play a valuable role in educating different groups about international and domestic human rights standards. In the case of the Indian and Philippines Commissions this has involved the elaboration and implementation of large-scale specialised training programmes for law enforcement and security personnel. Other common target audiences for such professional training include the legal profession, public officials, the media and non-governmental human rights and community organisations.

One of the most important functions with which a national institution can be entrusted is the investigation and resolution of human rights violations. In addition to acting as a powerful disincentive to violative behaviour, the existence of a mechanism with the capacity to investigate abuses and to provide relief to victims is in accordance with states parties' obligations under each of the international human rights treaties to give effect to protected rights and, by either explicit or implicit consequence, to ensure the provision of an effective remedy for violations. In many parts of

---

[36] Information provided by staff of the New Zealand Human Rights Commission to the first Asia-Pacific Regional Workshop of National Human Rights Institutions, Darwin, Australia, 8–10 July 1997. The New Zealand Government has, however, taken strong exception to the Commission's work on this project and has even indicated its intention of disregarding its findings. Human Rights Commission, *Annual Report*, Wellington, 1997 at pp. 45–6.

[37] For examples of human rights education strategies employed by national institutions see the presentations of the Canadian, Indian and Philippines Commissions to the Seminar on Human Rights Education and National Institutions, New Delhi, 16–17 February 1996 (report on file with the author).

the world, the most obvious source of redress for human rights violations – the courts – remain inaccessible to large sectors of the population. The establishment of a mechanism which permits the quick, informal, inexpensive and effective resolution of human rights complaints can therefore serve as a clear indication of a government's commitment to human rights and of a genuine willingness to take international human rights treaty obligations seriously. The nature (and, of course, the quality) of the investigatory function varies enormously between institutions. Differences exist in relation to the object and subject matter of admissible complaints, to powers granted in regard to conducting an investigation and providing remedies, and to the procedures by which a complaint may be resolved.[38] In their capacity as alternative dispute resolution mechanisms, human rights institutions are often empowered to encourage the settlement of complaints by conciliation instead of, or before launching, a formal investigation.[39]

Some human rights institutions are able to initiate their own investigations or public enquiries without the need to receive a formal complaint or invitation from a governmental agency. This power can be extremely important and far-reaching. Children, women, the poor, the homeless, the mentally or physically incapacitated, prisoners, and members of religious, ethnic and linguistic minorities are all, by virtue of their unequal status, especially vulnerable to human rights abuses. It is these same vulnerable

---

[38] Some institutions (such as the South African Commission, the Latvian Office and the proposed Papua New Guinea Commission) are able to consider any situation involving an alleged violation of rights which are protected by the constitution or other laws. Often, only public officials or agencies are permissible objects of investigation and specific restrictions are frequently imposed which operate to prevent investigation into sensitive areas including security and law enforcement. Other institutions (including both the Australian and New Zealand Commissions) are empowered to investigate allegations of violations committed by *any* public official as well as by private individuals and even by corporations. A few national institutions can make their own determinations following investigation of a complaint. Many others must refer their findings and recommendations to a higher body for approval or further action.

[39] Conciliation will involve bringing the parties together in an effort to ascertain the facts of the case and to effect a mutually acceptable resolution. This procedure has proved to be especially successful when applied to complaints regarding allegations of discrimination. Conciliation will often obviate the need for a formal investigation which can be both expensive and time-consuming. It is usually less confrontational in procedure and effect and, for this reason, is particularly useful in situations where securing a change in attitude or behaviour is considered more important than punishing a violation. In many countries, conciliation may also be considered a more culturally sensitive way of resolving human rights complaints than adversarial proceedings.

groups which are the ones most likely to be unaware of their rights and of the mechanisms which exist to protect these rights. Even where knowledge does exist, victims of human rights violations often do not have advocates to act on their behalf and may be extremely reluctant to approach a court – let alone an international body – in order to lodge a formal complaint. A national institution with the capacity to initiate its own investigations can make a significant contribution to ensuring that vulnerable groups are given a public voice and that human rights violations, wherever they occur, become a matter of general knowledge and concern. In the same way, violations of economic, social and cultural rights are more likely to be brought out in the open through the mechanism of a self-initiated public enquiry than through a regular complaints procedure.[40] In this connection, it has been argued that national human rights institutions, with their accessibility and flexible working methods, provide a rational alternative to the legalistic and litigation-oriented procedures of courts, which have thus far been unable to contribute substantially to the effective realisation of economic, social and cultural rights.[41]

3. STRENGTHENING THE RELATIONSHIP BETWEEN NATIONAL INSTITUTIONS AND THE HUMAN RIGHTS TREATY SYSTEM

Independent human rights institutions are, in a very real sense, the logical national collaborators of the treaty bodies. The general failure to recognise this reality has prevented both sides from drawing strength from the other. While the elaboration of a comprehensive strategy for strengthening the relationship between these two actors is beyond the scope of this present study, a number of preliminary observations may, nevertheless, be useful.

First, the treaty bodies and their various support networks must recognise the role which national institutions can play (and often are playing) in

---

[40] HREOC, for example, has conducted two major enquiries (on homeless children and on the mentally ill) with a strong economic, social and cultural rights perspective. The enquiry into homeless children led to approximately AU$100 million being allocated by federal and state governments to social and other services for this particularly vulnerable group. See Brian Burdekin, 'National Human Rights Commissions – National and International Perspectives', paper presented for the 1996 Commonwealth Meeting of Ministers, (copy on file with the author) at p. 3.

[41] See further, M. Gomez, 'Social Economic Rights and Human Rights Commissions', 17 *HRQ*, 1995, at pp. 155–69.

their own work of monitoring implementation and compliance. This role will be different for each committee and each state party. For this reason, the treaty bodies themselves must seek information on an existing institution and on the basis of this information, make their own judgments as to its possible usefulness. Ample standards are available which can assist the treaty bodies in separating independent institutions from government apologists. The treaty bodies could actively encourage the participation of genuine national institutions in the 'constructive dialogue' process.[42] Strong government objections are unlikely to arise, or if they did, could be countered with reference to the fact that the majority of such institutions have been created *by* governments and assigned a specific monitoring role *vis-à-vis* the international instruments themselves. The work of national institutions (particularly in relation to complaints and review of legislation to determine its consistency with treaty norms) can provide valuable background information for determining the progress of states parties in implementing their obligations. National institutions can also provide useful insights into laws, practices and traditions which impact upon a state's compliance with its obligations under human rights treaty law.

Consideration will need to be given to the practical dimensions of developing a role for national human rights institutions in the reporting process. Work which has already been done in relation to NGOs could usefully be adopted or applied. For example, the treaty bodies could instruct their secretariats to develop a database of national human rights institutions to be alerted to the scheduled review of states parties' reports. (At the moment this happens on an *ad hoc* basis.) Such a database could be used to ensure the distribution of reports to relevant national institutions prior to their consideration, with a view to encouraging their participation in the process, or at least the provision of supplementary information. As national institutions become integrated into the reporting and review process, an evolving expertise on the part of treaty bodies in relation to their structure

---

[42] *Ex post facto* encouragement, while not quite as valuable, is also important. In 1994, in the context of its consideration of Australia's report, the CERD Committee noted that: '[t]he opportunity given to the Social Justice Commissioner (Human Rights and Equal Opportunity Commission), who was independent from the Government, to provide information in reply to questions raised and comments made by members of the Committee was highly commended and considered to be an example to be followed by other reporting States', UN Doc. A/49/18 (1994) at para. 519. See also paras. 518, 526.

and functioning should, over time, be reflected in the committees' concluding observations, recommendations and general comments.

Any useful relationship cannot be too one-sided and efforts should therefore be made to bring the international human rights treaty system into the work of national institutions. Some institutions are able to contribute to the reporting procedure from the preparation side. Reporting is, of course, a government responsibility and care should be taken to ensure that this responsibility is not abdicated in favour of national institutions. Such bodies can, however, play an important role in providing information for inclusion in such reports and even in preparing 'shadow reports' if the institution believes these are warranted. National institutions are, along with NGOs, the logical vehicle for disseminating state parties' reports, as well as the results of a treaty body's examination of the reports. On a more general level, national institutions should be encouraged to take a leading role in educating the public about the international legal obligations which the state has undertaken and the institutions and processes which exist to enforce protected rights.

C. Strengthening national partners through technical cooperation

The previous section drew attention to the critical role which one type of national structure can play in the realisation of treaty-based human rights standards. The identification of key actors is, however, only one aspect of improving implementation and compliance. This second section of the chapter attempts to go a step further by considering the role which treaty bodies are presently playing – and could play – in the provision of practical assistance and support to states parties. It is interesting to note in this connection that the relevant instruments do not openly envisage a practical, advisory function for the human rights treaty bodies.[43] In spite of this, the notion of treaty bodies playing a helpful role, as opposed to an adversarial one, is not new. All committees have, over time and to a greater or lesser degree, evolved methods of work which emphasise gentle rebuke

---

[43] The HRC, for example, is to 'study the reports submitted by States parties' and 'transmit . . . such general comments as it may consider appropriate', article 40(4) ICCPR. The CERD and CEDAW Committees may both 'make suggestions and general recommendations based on the examination of the reports and information received from the States Parties', article 9(2) CERD and article 21 (1) CEDAW. See also CRC, article 45 (b); and CAT, article 19 (3).

over open condemnation, guidance over confrontation. The now-standard characterisation of discussion between states parties and the treaty bodies as 'constructive dialogue' embodies and confirms this approach. Another example is provided by the increasing number of 'recommendations for future action' being made by the treaty bodies in the context of their examination of states parties' reports.

1. WHAT ARE THE TREATY BODIES DOING?

'Recommendations for future action' almost invariably involve references (either explicit or indirect) to 'technical cooperation' or 'technical assistance'. These terms, as used by the treaty bodies, refer to the provision of external assistance and support to a state party for the purpose of strengthening key national structures and thereby improving implementation of and compliance with the relevant instruments. Only two of the major human rights treaties make specific reference to technical assistance or advice in the context of effective implementation of these respective instruments.[44]

From the point of view of the treaty bodies, the focal point for assistance to states has traditionally been the Technical Cooperation Programme of the Office of the UN High Commissioner for Human Rights (UNHCHR) (Technical Cooperation Programme).[45] Increasingly, however, attention is turning to the UN's major technical cooperation agencies and programmes such as the World Bank, the UN Development Programme (UNDP), the UN Children's Fund (UNICEF) and the International Labour Organisation

---

[44] The ICESCR permits the Economic and Social Committee (ECOSOC), and thereby the ICESCR Committee, to bring matters arising out of states parties' reports to the attention of relevant UN technical cooperation agencies (article 22). International action for the achievement of rights set forth in ICESCR includes methods such as 'the furnishing of technical assistance' (article 23). The CRC provides that the CRC Committee may transmit to the specialised agencies, the UN Children's Fund (UNICEF), and other competent bodies 'any reports from States Parties that contain a request or indicate a need for technical advice or assistance, along with the Committee's observations or suggestions, if any, on these requests or indications' (article 45 (b)).

[45] The major source of information on the Technical Cooperation Programme is the Secretariat's annual reports to the Commission on Human Rights. The reports of the Programme covering the years 1990–1998 may be found in the following documents: UN Docs. E/CN.4/1990/43 (1990); E/CN.4/1991/55 (1991); E/CN.4/1992/49 (1992); E/CN.4/1993/61 and Corr. 1 and Adds 1–2 (1993); E/CN.4/1994/78 and Corr. 1 and Adds 1–3 (1994); E/CN.4/1995/89 (1995); E/CN.4/1996/32 (1996); E/CN.4/1997/86 (1997) and E/CN.4/1998/92 (1998).

(ILO), the work of which, while only occasionally defined or implemented in terms of human rights,[46] can have a direct impact on the capacity of a state to implement its human rights treaty obligations.

An examination of recent treaty body recommendations for future action – the implementation of which would necessarily involve the provision of external assistance[47] – reveals that the overwhelming majority fall (in descending order of frequency) into the following categories: (i) professional training programmes in human rights (usually for the police and judiciary); (ii) preparation of reports; (iii) legislative review and incorporation of international instruments into national legislation; (iv) organisation of public awareness campaigns; (v) incorporation of human rights into educational curricula; (vi) data collection and analysis; (vii) establishment of national (monitoring, coordinating and investigatory) institutions; (viii) translation and dissemination of the international instruments; and (ix) reform of the judiciary and administration of justice system. In addition to making recommendations, several of the committees have both proposed and participated in various technical assistance missions. Both the CERD and CEDAW Committees have issued general recommendations

---

[46] UNICEF remains the principal exception to this generalisation. Several years ago UNICEF adopted a human rights approach to its technical cooperation activities, an approach which is firmly anchored to the provisions of both the CRC and CEDAW. See United Nations Children's Fund, 'Report of the Executive Director', UN Doc. E/ICEF/1997/10 (1997). See also UNICEF's Mission Statement adopted by its Executive Board in 1996, UN Doc. E/ICEF/1996/12/Rev. 1, decision 1996/1. While human rights are recognised in the rhetoric of many of the other development/technical cooperation agencies, this has yet to be translated into concrete actions. It is relevant to note, however, that in early 1998, UNDP also released a policy document: 'Integrating Human Rights with Sustainable Policy Development', United Nations Development Programme, 1998. The Policy Document represents a significant step forward in articulating at least a preliminary rationale and strategy for mainstreaming human rights into UNDP's activities. UNDP and OHCHR are currently developing a joint project which aims to operationalize the Policy Document. The project will address, inter alia, promotion of ratification as well as capacity development for reporting.

[47] The information contained in this and the following paragraph is from a background document entitled: *Recommendations for Advisory Services and Technical Cooperation by Treaty-Monitoring Bodies*, United Nations High Commissioner/Centre for Human Rights, August 1996. Note that the (very few) recommendations for technical assistance which have been made by the CEDAW Committee are *not* included in this compilation. This exclusion is clearly at odds with the public commitment of the Office of the UNHCHR to integrating the rights of women and a gender perspective into its work.

directed to all states parties urging them to take advantage, where necessary, of technical assistance for the preparation of reports.[48]

Distinct differences can be detected between the various committees in terms of both the nature and specificity of their recommendations and actions as well as the organisations or entities which they address. At the risk of over-generalisation, several observations can be made. The CRC Committee produces, by far, the most comprehensive (if usually standardised) recommendations, often covering at least several of the categories identified above. Unlike the other treaty bodies which largely restrict their recommendations for technical assistance to services provided by the Office of the UNHCHR, the CRC Committee often calls on the reporting state to seek assistance from a wide range of UN agencies including UNICEF, the ILO, the United Nations Educational, Scientific and Cultural Organisation (UNESCO), the Office of the UN High Commissioner for Refugees (UNHCR), and the UN Office for Drug Control and Crime Prevention. Apart from the CERD Committee's general recommendation on this subject,[49] most of the suggestions made concerning the establishment or strengthening of national human rights institutions have come from the CRC Committee. The majority of the recommendations of the Committee of the Convention Against Torture (CAT) concern, not surprisingly, the training of law enforcement officials. The Committees established under CERD, CEDAW and the International Covenant on Economic, Social and Cultural Rights (ICESCR) most often advise that assistance be provided in the preparation of the next report. The Human Rights Committee (HRC) makes a broader range of recommendations with particular focus on incorporation of ICCPR provisions into national law and training for professional groups.

2. A PRELIMINARY EVALUATION

It is not possible, in a chapter of this scope, to provide an adequate analysis of the performance of each treaty body with regard to its actions and

---

[48] The CERD Committee, General Recommendation X concerning technical assistance (adopted at the thirty-ninth session, 1991) and the CEDAW Committee, General Recommendation No. 11, 'Technical advisory services for reporting obligations', (adopted at the eighth session, 1989), both reprinted in *Compilation of General Comments and General Recommendations Adopted by the Human Rights Treaty Bodies*, UN Doc. HRI/GEN/1/ Rev.2 (1996).

[49] *Supra*, note 17.

recommendations for the strengthening of national structures. However, some preliminary observations are possible. First, the overwhelming majority of proposals and suggestions made to or about states parties are so broad as to be verging on the platitudinous. States parties are, for example, routinely urged to ensure that their public officials are given human rights training; that 'law reforms' be undertaken; that effective monitoring mechanisms be introduced; and that public information and education activities be strengthened. Recommendations for action often expose gaps and weaknesses in the committees' own information sources and it is only very occasionally that recommendations are made with enough specificity to enable their follow-up to be measured or evaluated.

Second, and perhaps most importantly, the pronouncements made by treaty bodies in relation to the strengthening of national structures reveal some basic misconceptions about the nature of technical cooperation and the capacity of the UN (particularly the Office of the UNHCHR) to deliver, as well as about the ways in which national mechanisms could or should be strengthened in order to enhance their ability to defend and promote protected rights. The views and recommendations of the treaty bodies in relation to national human rights institutions (see Section B.2 above) serve as a case in point. Another illustrative example is provided by the frequent suggestions of the treaty bodies that technical assistance be provided to law enforcement agencies.[50] With only one or two isolated exceptions, this sort of recommendation is invariably framed in very broad terms and is limited to the 'training' or 'sensitisation' of police officials in international human rights standards. Such proposals make the basic error of assuming that human rights violations by police officials are caused through ignorance, that teaching police officials about these standards will, in some obvious way, prevent future violations. This is overly simplistic and in fact it is often untrue. In the author's experience (of more than twenty such training programmes conducted in over a dozen countries in Africa, Europe and

---

[50] Recommendations with regard to training for law enforcement agencies are one of the most common type made by the treaty bodies (regularly in the case of the HRC, the CAT, CRC and CERD Committees; less frequently in the case of the CEDAW and ICESCR Committees). Note that the CERD Committee has also issued a general recommendation on the subject. See, The CERD Committee, 'General Recommendation XIII on the training of law enforcement officials in the protection of human rights' (adopted at the forty-second session, 1993) reprinted in UN Doc. HRI/GEN/1/Rev.2 (1996). The author acknowledges the contribution of Cees de Rover to the development of the views expressed in this paragraph.

Latin America), the majority of officials from the world's functioning law enforcement agencies are, along with their colleagues in the judiciary, familiar with the basic rules which have been enacted at both the international and national levels to safeguard individual rights and freedoms. What they lack is a capacity – or a willingness – to make the necessary transformation from theory to practical application. What many of these forces need – more than a lecture in human rights norms – is specialised skills training, adequate equipment and principled leadership. Human rights must become integrated into the fabric of a law enforcement organisation's structure and functioning – both in operations and in training. If the treaty bodies wish to make a substantive contribution to eliminating state violence and the resulting rights violations, they must take it upon themselves to learn about how the relevant forces are organised and how they operate. Understanding law enforcement organisation and practice is no more than a minimum prerequisite for giving useful advice. As a minimum the treaty bodies must know enough to ask the right questions to the right persons and to make recommendations which can be translated into identifiable, quantifiable actions, thereby providing at least some chance of affecting police attitudes and behaviour and, through this, the conduct of police operations.

3. SOME TENTATIVE RECOMMENDATIONS

There are a number of ways in which the treaty bodies could enhance their impact on the functioning of those national human rights structures which are identified as being key partners. The most obvious of these is for the various committees to improve the quality of their own 'recommendations for future action'. For a state party which is committed to upholding its treaty obligations but which lacks the internal capacity to do so, generalities are of little use. One way of moving from the general to the specific would be for the treaty bodies to improve their own information base. Current discussions on 'information' in this context tend to focus exclusively on NGOs. While an increase in the quantity and quality of NGO information flow to the treaty bodies is important, it should not be pursued to the exclusion of other sources. The two examples provided above are both relevant in this context. If a national human rights institution exists – or is said to exist – in a state under review, then the relevant treaty body must be aware of that institution's structure, functioning and achievements and be able to call on it to provide direct information. The treaty body could also use this opportunity to identify and address any problems which may have arisen in relation to the performance of the human rights institution. The 'real' intelligence on police behaviour will never be gleaned from a government report. Treaty bodies could explore the possibility of requesting the presence of key operational officials in government delegations and perhaps even the submission of detailed reports from different state agencies and departments.

Ultimately, of course, what states require is not just an opinion that certain laws, systems or practices need to be reformed, but the tools to make this happen. While the treaty bodies are not in a position to fulfil all needs, they could with some effort take the lead in ensuring that the required assistance is of sufficient quality and is channelled in the right direction. The first target of the treaty bodies' attention should be their institutional counterpart, the Technical Cooperation Programme run by the Office of the High Commissioner for Human Rights and which provides technical human rights-related advice and assistance to governments which request it. Unfortunately there presently exists a considerable gap between these two important components of the international human rights system. Recommendations of the treaty bodies all too often reveal an ignorance of the structure and capacities of the Programme as well as of specific activities and projects. For its part, the Technical Cooperation Programme has been allowed to develop without any input from the treaty bodies. One example is the near-total absence of any gender perspective in the programme,[51] a fact that has gone unnoticed by the CEDAW Committee.[52] Another consequence is a Programme which, in its present state, is functionally incapable of integrating economic, social and cultural rights. In relation to the latter situation however, continuing pressure from the relevant committee has recently resulted in plans for an evaluation and

---

[51] See further, A. Gallagher, 'Ending the Marginalization: Strategies for Integrating Women into the United Nations Human Rights System', 19 *HRQ*, 1997, p. 283 at pp. 294–309.

[52] The only recent reference which the CEDAW Committee has made to the Technical Cooperation Programme is a suggestion that 'the budget of the Centre for Human Rights of the United Nations secretariat for technical and advisory services [sic] be made available to promote the Convention and the work of the Committee'. 'Report of the Committee on the Elimination of Discrimination Against Women' (sixteenth session), UN Doc. A/52/38 (Part 1), 24 June 1997, p. 5 and § 373.

restructuring of the Programme with a view to integrating economic, social and cultural rights.[53] The CEDAW Committee may wish to become similarly informed and involved. On a more elementary level, treaty bodies should be kept informed about projects which have been, are being or may be implemented in countries under review, and be given a genuine (as opposed to symbolic) opportunity to provide substantive input.

The Technical Cooperation Programme is only a drop in the multi-billion dollar ocean of international development aid. Most such assistance – including that provided by the UN and its agencies – is designed, executed and evaluated in a human rights vacuum.[54] Mismanaged or ill-conceived development assistance projects which violate, endanger or fail to contribute to the realisation of fundamental rights are one well-documented result of this approach. Increasingly, major international technical cooperation agencies are turning their attention to national capacity-building through the strengthening of systems, processes and institutions. This can involve for example, assistance in the restructuring of a country's entire police force, judicial system or health-care sector. All too often, the human rights dimension of such activities goes unrecognised and a valuable opportunity to institutionalise international standards or otherwise promote their national implementation is thereby wasted. Of all the treaty bodies, only the ICESCR Committee has made a serious attempt to address directly the issue of human rights in international technical

[53] In its response to a paper prepared at its request by the secretariat ('Activities Undertaken so far Within the Advisory Services Programme and Proposals for the Type of Assistance that can be Envisaged for the Realization of Economic, Social and Cultural Rights', UN Doc. E/C.12/1994/W.P. 9 (1994)), the ICESCR Committee observed that while such rights had been included in a number of activities within the Technical Cooperation Programme, 'it was not possible to identify any single initiative which had focused exclusively or in any significant depth on these rights': UN Doc. E/1995/22 – E/E.12/1994/20 (1995) at para. 414. This matter was addressed at subsequent meetings, as well as at the 1996 Meeting of the Chairpersons of Treaty Bodies. Two projects – to review the Programme from an economic, social and cultural rights perspective and from a gender perspective – were developed by the secretariat in late 1996 and are currently under implementation. The relevant project documents are reproduced on the website of the Office of the UNHCHR (http://www.unhchr.ch).

[54] See, Human Rights Council of Australia, *The Rights Way to Development: A Human Rights Approach to Development Assistance*, Sydney, 1995, (which in addition to exploring this general tendency of international development cooperation to ignore human rights, makes a convincing case for placing development assistance policies within the internationally agreed human rights framework).

assistance.[55] The CRC Committee, through its growing relationship with UNICEF, is also developing an awareness of the way in which technical cooperation can be used to uphold the rights of the child. However, this is not enough. All treaty bodies should be fighting to ensure that the rights contained in their respective instruments are respected, protected and taken into account by UN agencies as well as by aid donor and recipient states parties. Of course, the political realities of the international aid system will not change overnight. As a first step, however, treaty bodies could resolve to inform themselves of the technical assistance process as it relates to their respective instruments, as well as of specific initiatives or projects involving their states parties as either donors or recipients. Current efforts by certain treaty bodies (notably the CRC and ICESCR Committees) to encourage the participation of relevant UN agencies in their work should be continued and expanded.

One final, difficult point which deserves to be raised in the present context concerns the composition of the treaty bodies. The world's human rights problems are presently being addressed, at the international level at least, by a group of (mostly male) lawyers and diplomats.[56] Unfortunately, the conditions laid down for membership of treaty bodies, while referring to equitable distribution on the basis of geography, civilisations, and legal systems, make no reference at all to sex, professional background or occupation. This has led to a situation where the so-called 'constructive dialogue' is often little more than a diplomatic exchange between government and legal elites who, for the most part, speak the same language – a language which is not well understood by those officials, private individuals, agencies and groups on whom the day-to-day burden of protecting rights invariably falls. Numerous other negative work practices can be traced, at

---

[55] ICESCR Committee, General Comment No. 2, 'International Technical Assistance Measures', (adopted at the fourth session, 1990) reprinted in *Compilation of General Comments and General Recommendations Adopted by the Human Rights Treaty Bodies*, UN Doc. HRI/GEN/1/Rev.2 (1996) at p. 93. In addition to making a number of general observations on the relationship between development and human rights, the ICESCR Committee's General Comment on this subject also proposes a number of specific actions which highlight the need for major technical cooperation agencies to take human rights into account in the formulation and implementation of projects. Also relevant is the ICESCR Committee's recent general comment on current UN efforts to unite its development cooperation work under a common conceptual and operational framework (UNDAF). The comment highlighted the need to ensure that international human rights standards are properly integrated into such an approach, E/1999/22, para. 516.

[56] On the composition of the treaty bodies in terms of gender, see Gallagher, *supra*, note 51.

least in part, to the homogenous composition of the treaty bodies and the delegations which come before them. These include the failure to identify appropriate national structures on which to focus attention and the failure to propose realistic solutions to genuine obstacles.

The human rights treaties are legal instruments and it is therefore difficult to argue against the need for lawyers to be involved in the process by which those same instruments are interpreted and applied. However, the relevance of treaty bodies and their work can only be enhanced by efforts aimed at bringing human rights practitioners into the treaty body process. This group is defined with reference to its ability to (i) provide *expert analysis* of situations; and (ii) influence human rights at the national level. It will thereby include those with either a background or current responsibilities in areas as diverse as military affairs, law enforcement, economics, journalism, health administration, social planning, etc. Effective participation does not always need to be at the membership level. The inclusion of practitioners on governmental delegations would immensely improve the quality, relevance and impact of the constructive dialogue. Composition does, however, remain a key issue and states parties must be actively discouraged from making (and accepting) self-serving nominations.

D. Conclusion

A more activist and informed approach on the part of the international human rights treaty system to its national partners will not come without a price. The critical shortages currently facing the treaty bodies and their secretariats in terms of both time and resources are well known. It is reasonable to suppose that, in the likely absence of any radical restructuring, the treaty bodies will not be able to increase the quality of their work substantially without making cuts in other areas. One way of achieving the necessary resource savings would be for the treaty bodies to consider prioritising their work. At the moment all states parties receive roughly equal attention, irrespective of their individual needs and capacities. While this approach is understandable in political terms – as well as in terms of the underlying objectives of the reporting process[57] – it conflicts with the

---

[57] This objective has been best formulated in terms of 'the principle of holding States accountable for non-compliance with their treaty obligations by means of an objective and constructive dialogue, on the basis of comprehensive information and inputs from all interested parties', UN Doc. E/CN.4/1997/74.

reality that certain states require (and some desire) more guidance and support than others. In connection with facilitating the strengthening of national structures, the treaty bodies could usefully consider identifying (even on an informal level) those states which are willing but which lack the necessary capacity to implement and ensure compliance with their international obligations. It is both just and appropriate that these states receive the greatest consideration and assistance.

Ultimately, the treaty bodies may come to the conclusion that attaining their basic objective (that is, to encourage and facilitate national implementation of and compliance with international human rights standards) will require a fundamental change in philosophy and approach. At present, tremendous energy is being channelled into the negative aspects of treaty implementation. There is ample evidence to support the contention that return on such investment remains depressingly low. Despite this reality, almost all discussion on 'reform' continues to focus on enhancing the capacity of the international human rights treaty system to deal with recalcitrant states. It might be more realistic to face the fact that certain categories of states are better left to the political and investigatory components of the international human rights system.[58] The expertise of the human rights treaty bodies could then be more productively and positively employed in working on a practical level, with cooperative governments and other key national partners in the difficult but essential task of strengthening human rights protection from within.

---

[58] This issue has been raised in the context of the recent practice of some committees of demanding exceptional reports from states parties in situations of great crisis characterised by massive human rights violations (the former Yugoslavia, the former Zaire, etc.). It can be convincingly argued that such a procedure is at odds with the nature of the reporting process and that it considerably overestimates the capacity of the committees to engage in useful preventive action in crisis situations.

10

DOMESTIC IMPLEMENTATION OF
INTERNATIONAL HUMAN RIGHTS TREATIES:
NORDIC AND BALTIC EXPERIENCES

MARTIN SCHEININ

A. Introduction

The domestic status of international human rights norms within various jurisdictions and constitutional settings is an old but continuing issue. Comparative studies, such as those by Andrew Drzemczewski,[1] Søren Stenderup Jensen,[2] or Jörg Polakiewicz and Valérie Jacob-Foltzer[3] explore the subject deeply. These studies deal with the domestic status of one specific human rights treaty, the European Convention on Human Rights (ECHR), and discuss only those states that at the time of writing were parties to the ECHR.

The present chapter focuses on the implementation of human rights treaties generally in the Nordic and Baltic countries.[4] It is thus concerned with a certain geographical region (the five Nordic and three Baltic countries) and with the full normative framework of international human rights, not only the two International Covenants of 1966 but also international human rights instruments other than treaties.

Within this overall setting, it proposes to ask whether incorporation of human rights treaties has advantages for the *actual* protection of human rights within a country. Here, the word 'incorporation' is used in a

---

[1] A. Drzemczewski, *The European Human Rights Convention in Domestic Law: A Comparative Study*, Oxford, 1983.

[2] S. Jensen, *The European Convention on Human Rights in Scandinavian Law*, Gylling, 1992.

[3] J. Polakiewicz and V. Jacob-Foltzer, 'The European Human Rights Convention in Domestic Law: The Impact of Strasbourg Case-law in States where Direct Effect is given to the Convention', 12 *HRLJ*, 1991, pp. 65–84 and 125–42.

[4] M. Scheinin (ed.), *International Human Rights Norms in the Nordic and Baltic Countries*. The Hague, 1996. For updates and related information, see http://www.abo.fi/instut/imr.

non-technical sense, referring to all methods of treaty implementation through which international treaty provisions become part of domestic law.[5] States very often apply a combination of more than one treaty implementation procedure. The fact that *some* treaties have formally been incorporated might lead to a general awareness of the relevance of international law and to the use of non-incorporated treaties as well, for instance in judicial reasoning.

B. Incorporation and the exhaustion of domestic remedies

It is evident that incorporation of a human rights treaty is relevant for human rights litigation: if a treaty is formally a part of the law of the land, judges are expected to apply its provisions, at least when they are invoked by a party. From the viewpoint of international monitoring bodies, a consequence is that the requirement to exhaust available domestic remedies[6] before filing an international petition might be interpreted more strictly in the context of a legal system where the treaty in question can be invoked in domestic courts.

One should, however, be careful with generalisations. This can be exemplified through a comparison of the cases *Hartikainen v. Finland* (Communication No. 40/1978)[7] and *A. and S. N. v. Norway* (Communication No. 224/1987),[8] both decided by the Human Rights Committee (HRC) under the International Covenant on Civil and Political Rights (ICCPR). The *Hartikainen* case involved Finland, where the ICCPR has been incorporated into domestic law through an act of parliament. Nevertheless, as Finnish courts have no power to examine the constitutionality of acts of parliament,[9] the applicants did not pursue any domestic remedies: they saw

---

[5] In this non-technical sense 'incorporation' covers, e.g., 'adoption' (monism) and the enactment of treaty-specific legislation giving the provisions of a named treaty the status of domestic law ('incorporation' in the technical sense). Of these and other treaty implementation methods see 'General Introduction', in Scheinin (ed.), *supra*, note 4.

[6] See, e.g., article 5(2)(b) of the (First) Optional Protocol to the International Covenant on Civil and Political Rights (ICCPR) and article 35(1) of the ECHR. On the interpretation under the latter of the requirement specifically to invoke the provisions of the Convention before domestic courts, see the cases of *Deweer v. Belgium* (27 February 1980, ECHR Series A No. 35, para. 26), *Van Oosterwijk v. Belgium* (6 November 1980, ECHR Series A No. 40, para. 39) and *Hentrich v. France* (22 September 1994, ECHR Series A No. 296-A, para. 33).

[7] Human Rights Committee, *Selected Decisions under the Optional Protocol* 1 (1985), UN Doc. CCPR/C/OP/1, pp. 74–6.

[8] UN Doc. A/43/40 (1988) pp. 248–9.

[9] See section 92 of the Constitution Act of 1919. The new Finnish Constitution that will enter into force on 1 March 2000 will have a clause that authorises courts to set aside an act of parliament in cases of manifest unconstitutionality. See Act No. 731 of 1999.

the case as involving a conflict between the ICCPR and a Finnish act of parliament. The Finnish Government agreed with the applicants that no domestic remedies were available, and the case was accordingly declared admissible by the HRC and decided on the merits.[10] In an almost identical case, the Norwegian applicants in *A. and S. N. v. Norway* followed the *Hartikainen* precedent and took their case to the HRC without exhausting domestic remedies. Although the ICCPR had not been incorporated into Norwegian law, the Government of Norway invoked the requirement that applicants exhaust domestic remedies. The Government presented convincing arguments for the ICCPR provisions being relevant in the interpretation of the Norwegian Constitution which, in contrast to that of Finland, allows judicial review. The case was declared inadmissible.[11]

C. The role of domestic courts as the keystone of international law

According to Benedetto Conforti,[12] the application of international law by municipal courts and other domestic legal operators is the keystone of international law itself. Like Pieter van Dijk,[13] he emphasises the role and the attitudes of the judiciary in determining the domestic effect of international law. For Conforti, more important than the characterisation of a legal system as 'dualistic' or 'monistic' is whether its judges are 'liberal' or 'conservative'.[14]

The Nordic and Baltic countries provide evidence for the view that the domestic role and effect of international human rights norms cannot be assessed in the abstract on the basis of a study of the written constitution of a country. What counts in the final analysis is whether the courts apply human rights norms in their substantive decisions. There is today a rich and rapidly growing case law of this kind on international human rights treaties in all five Nordic countries. In the Baltic states, the Lithuanian Constitutional Court and the Estonian National Court seem to be the only judicial authorities that so far have managed to develop some jurisprudence

---

[10] See, para. 5 of the HRC's final views in *Hartikainen*.
[11] See, paras. 4.5–4.6 and 6.2 on inadmissibility in *A. and S. N. v. Norway*.
[12] B. Conforti, *International Law and the Role of Domestic Legal Systems*, Dordrecht, 1993, p. 9.
[13] P. van Dijk, 'Domestic Status of Human Rights Treaties and the Attitude of the Judiciary', in *Progress in the Spirit of Human Rights* (eds. M. Nowak, D. Steurer, and H. Tretter), Kehl am Rhein, 1988, pp. 631–49.
[14] Conforti, *supra*, note 12, p. 26.

in the field. Some of the Nordic countries, for example Sweden and Finland, provide strong support for the contention that after the first steps are taken by domestic courts to build a human rights jurisprudence, the growth of case law can be very rapid.

The role of international human rights norms in a domestic case may be large even in countries where the 'dualistic' nature of the constitutional setting seems, prima facie, to bar the effective implementation of international law. Even prior to formal incorporation, the Norwegian and Icelandic Supreme Courts have shown their capability and willingness to give human rights treaty provisions priority in relation to domestic law, even in a substantive sense.[15] In relation to the principle of legality, such far-reaching interpretations are legitimate because of the uncontested axiological weight of human rights and through the courts' careful reasoning.

The existence of a system of individual complaints and of authoritative international bodies dealing with such complaints has greatly contributed to the success of the ECHR. The successful functioning of the European Commission and Court of Human Rights, and in particular the Court's judicial rulings, have gradually convinced the judiciaries of the states parties as to the legitimacy of human rights law *as law*, by any international or domestic standard. This success has not, however, come without sacrifices. A worrying side-effect of the judicial authority of the European Court of Human Rights is the fact that many domestic judges nowadays feel tempted to adopt a 'minimalist' or passive interpretation of the ECHR. Under this approach, it is sufficient to analyse existing case law by the European Court of Human Rights: if no precedent can be found, the Convention need not be applied. Of the Nordic countries, Denmark deserves attention on this point since the Danish Supreme Court seems to restrict itself to the passive application of the ECHR.[16] Similar trends may be identified in certain pronouncements by Norwegian and Swedish courts,[17] and at least one Finnish Supreme Court case might indicate a move towards a more passive position.[18] In the Finnish case, a defendant was denied free legal assistance as the majority in the Supreme Court, after analysing the case law of the European

---

[15] See the Norwegian cases Rt 1984, s. 1174 and Rt 1994, s. 610, and the Icelandic Supreme Court ruling 1992.174.

[16] See UfR 1989 p. 898 and UfR 1985 p. 181.

[17] See HD 1989: 28 published in NJA 1989 p. 131.

[18] Finnish Supreme Court ruling 1995: 7.

Court of Human Rights, came to the conclusion that free legal aid was not required by article 6 of the ECHR in the circumstances of the case.

The alternative is a more 'activist' or 'liberal' orientation by domestic judges, according to which it is also for the national judge to develop international human rights law by giving new answers to new questions. For such a creative approach to succeed it clearly is an advantage that international human rights law is pluralist in character: there is not only one human rights convention but a complex network of treaties drawn up within different international organisations and covering many situations that would fall outside the protection of any single convention taken alone. There are also other institutionalised practices of interpretation by international bodies than those that produce judicial case law. For instance, the concluding observations adopted by United Nations treaty bodies or the case law emerging from the application of the European Social Charter (ESC)[19] can be sources of inspiration for a creative judge at the national level.

In Finland, the Supreme Administrative Court has taken a liberal position in the interpretation of article 8 of the ECHR in expulsion cases (as exemplified by the cases *KHO 1993 A 26* and *KHO 1993 A 29*),[20] compared to the rather restrictive case law of the European Court of Human Rights on this point. The activist or liberal position of domestic judges, however, raises the problem of double standards as the same treaty provision may be interpreted differently by national and international courts. But the reason for the emergence of such double standards is not the activist role of domestic courts so much as the tendency of the European Court of Human Rights, and possibly other international human rights treaty bodies to apply the 'margin of appreciation' notion or similar doctrines limiting the scope of their review.

The 'minimalist' approach of domestic judges is not the only barrier to the effective realisation of international human rights norms through the

---

[19] The Council of Europe publishes compilations of the findings by the Committee of Independent Experts and the Governmental Committee, both acting under the ESC. See, *Case Law on the European Social Charter*, Strasbourg, 1982; *Case Law on the European Social Charter, Supplement*, Strasbourg, 1986; *Case Law on the European Social Charter, Supplement No. 2*, Strasbourg, 1987; and *Case Law on the European Social Charter, Supplement No. 3*, Strasbourg, 1993.

[20] The first-mentioned case concerned a Russian homosexual person whose 'private life' justified protection against expulsion. In the latter case, 'respect for family life' prevented the expulsion of an entire Estonian family.

operation of domestic courts. From the constitutional law of the United States we are familiar with certain 'drawback doctrines' that have the effect of barring access to courts or restricting the applicability of international norms in certain issues. In the Nordic and Baltic countries, by contrast, the 'act of state' doctrine or the 'political question' doctrine[21] do not appear to find support. Two other theoretical constructions, however, are of relevance in the context of Nordic and Baltic countries and seem to constitute at least potential threats to the effective implementation of human rights. These are the *lex posterior derogat legi priori* or 'last in time' rule and the doctrine of non-self-executing treaties.

Although Norway is a partial exception, the (largely dualist) Nordic countries have incorporated the ECHR into their law through an ordinary act of parliament. Though there exist some constitutional provisions modifying the situation in some of these countries, the starting point for courts and authorities is that international treaties incorporated through an act of parliament have the same hierarchical status as ordinary laws. This is also the position, at least prima facie, in Lithuania. Therefore, new legislation carries a potential threat to the applicability of human rights treaties. According to the *lex posterior* rule, new acts of parliament would supersede the provisions in such treaties unless the potential conflict can be resolved by interpretation.

However, even in countries where there is no explicit constitutional clause on the supremacy of international law, the *lex posterior* rule can be interpreted so as to include consideration of the intention of the domestic legislator. If the intention was not to supersede an earlier treaty-based norm, then this intention can be given effect by the courts declining to apply the later rule to the detriment of the country's international commitments. A later domestic act of parliament is to be given priority in relation to an incorporated human rights treaty only if parliament stated, when enacting the law in question, that it had the intention of deviating from the treaty. Through such a construction the constitutional setting based on the

---

[21] On these two doctrines, see R. Lillich, 'The Role of Domestic Courts in Promoting International Human Rights Norms', 24 *New York Law Review*, 1978, pp. 153–77; J. Smith, *The Constitution and American Foreign Policy*, St Paul, Minnesota, 1989, pp. 3, 75 and 134–7; and Conforti, *supra*, note 12, pp. 14–24. In short, the political question doctrine denies access to courts in issues that relate to the foreign policy of the country in question because it is not the judiciary's task to rule on foreign policy. The act of state doctrine, in turn, limits the power of courts to deal with cases that relate to measures undertaken by another sovereign state.

sovereignty of parliament can be maintained, while at the same time it is in practice highly unlikely that the courts would ever set aside a human rights treaty under the *lex posterior* rule.[22]

In Estonia and Norway it seems to be at least a possible precondition for the direct applicability of human rights treaties that the treaty provision is sufficiently clear and unambiguous. In a case before the Norwegian Supreme Court[23] this requirement was presented by the Court not as a condition for applicability in general but for setting aside Norwegian rules. This line of argument may be understood as referring to the doctrine of self-executing treaties.[24] In its extreme forms, this doctrine can seriously weaken the domestic role of international human rights norms since it simplifies the rich variety of legal issues encountered when applying international law to one single question: does the international provision have direct applicability or is it simply irrelevant for the judge? An understanding that legal norms are applicable in several ways and degrees (including their effect on the interpretation of other norms) helps to relativise the notion of 'direct applicability' and shows that a categorical distinction between 'self-executing' and 'non-self-executing' treaty provisions is impossible.[25] On the basis of existing case law, it seems that extreme versions of the doctrine are unlikely to find support in either the Nordic or Baltic countries. It is another matter that the formulation of a treaty provision might affect the *way* in which it is applied.

D. Broadening the scope of applicable rights:
social rights and 'soft law'

Extreme versions of the doctrine of self-executing treaties tend to limit the domestic applicability of international human rights to a traditional core of rights which have a long conceptual and judicial tradition in domestic

---

[22] A similar position is presented by B. Conforti, *supra*, note 12, p. 47.   [23] Rt 1994 p. 610.

[24] For the doctrine of self-executing treaties, see Y. Iwasawa, 'The Doctrine of Self-Executing Treaties in the United States: A Critical Analysis', 26 *Virginia Journal of International Law*, 1986, pp. 627–92; and T. Buergenthal, 'Self-Executing and Non-Self-Executing Treaties in National and International Law', 235 *Recueil des cours*, 1992-IV, pp. 303–400.

[25] For further elaboration of the argument see M. Scheinin, 'Direct Applicability of Economic, Social and Cultural Rights: A Critique of the Doctrine of Self-Executing Treaties', in *Social Rights as Human Rights: A European Challenge* (eds. K. Drzewicki, C. Krause and A. Rosas), Turku/Åbo, 1994.

jurisdictions. For many, 'freedom of expression' would be 'clear and precise' juridical language but 'the right to social assistance' something less self-evident.

The Nordic and Baltic countries are no exceptions to the general rule that 'traditional' civil and political rights tend to be more often applied by courts and other authorities than economic, social and cultural rights. Still, these countries provide evidence for the position that there are neither logical nor juridical obstacles to economic, social and cultural rights becoming applicable on the domestic plane. In Finland, the recent Bill of Rights reform of 1995 included economic and social rights in chapter two of the Constitution Act, some having a formulation that suggests justiciability before the courts.[26] As the new provisions entered into force only in August 1995, it is too early to judge whether the courts will apply the provisions on economic and social rights in their rulings.[27] What has been established already, however, is that section 15a on social assistance, social security and social welfare services has become one of the most often cited constitutional provisions in the assessment of the constitutionality of new government bills by the Parliamentary Committee for Constitutional Law.[28]

In countries where international treaties on economic and social rights are incorporated into domestic law – either directly under the constitution or as a consequence of a treaty-specific incorporating statute – these treaties may become enforceable by the courts. The ESC is an interesting example in this connection as its Appendix provides that 'the Charter contains legal obligations of an international character, the application of which is submitted solely to the supervision provided for in Part IV thereof'. Although this clause is sometimes understood as excluding domestic applicability of ESC provisions,[29] at least some of its provisions

---

[26] Finnish Constitution Act, as amended by Act No. 969 of 1995. See, in particular, section 13, para. 1 (right to education) and section 15a, para. 1 (right to social assistance and care). An English language translation of the new chapter two has been published in Scheinin (ed.), *supra*, note 4 at pp. 289–93.

[27] As the Finnish Constitution does not include the institution of judicial review of the constitutionality of acts of parliament, such application would, as a rule, be limited to 'constitution-friendly interpretation' and direct applicability in the absence of applicable ordinary legislation. See, however, note 9, *supra*.

[28] See, *inter alia*, Opinions No. 15 and 17 of 1995, as well as Nos. 17 and 34 of 1996.

[29] See, e.g. O. Kahn-Freund, 'The European Social Charter', in *European Law and the Individual* (ed. F. G. Jacobs), Amsterdam, 1976, p. 193.

have been applied by Netherlands[30] and German[31] courts. Before the Finnish Parliament gave its consent to the ratification of the ESC and passed an incorporating Act,[32] the Parliamentary Committee for Social Affairs and Health explicitly stated that a consequence of incorporation was that the provisions of the ESC became applicable in domestic courts and for administrative authorities.[33] These examples suggest that the possibility of treaty provisions on social and economic rights becoming justiciable at the domestic level is dependent on the constitutional framework into which the treaty provisions are incorporated. Treaty provisions may become 'self-executing' or directly applicable even against the actual intention of their framers.[34]

It is possible to go even further in demonstrating the possibilities for domestic applicability of international treaties on economic and social rights. In Sweden international treaties are usually not made part of domestic law through incorporation. They are internationally binding on the state but their domestic implementation is taken care of through the method of transformation, that is, through the harmonisation of relevant domestic laws by amendment. Still, we can find court cases in which reference is made to the ESC. In a ruling of 12 June 1991, the Swedish Supreme Administrative Court, after referring to the ESC, quashed the decision of a lower court and ordered social assistance benefits to be paid to two asylum seekers.[35]

One may go further and argue that even so-called 'soft law' may be of legal relevance. Norway is one example of a country where international human rights treaties, until 1999 without any formal status in the domestic legal system, have had considerable influence in the application of domestic

---

[30] L. Betten and T. Jaspers, 'The Netherlands', in *25 Years European Social Charter* (eds. A. Ph. C. M. Jaspers and L. Betten), Deventer, 1988, pp. 133–5.

[31] E.-M. Hohnerlein, 'Federal Republic of Germany', in A. Ph. C. M. Jaspers and L. Betten (eds.), *supra*, note 30, pp. 119–25.

[32] Section 1 of Act of Parliament No. 843 of 1991 reads: 'The provisions of the European Social Charter, made in Turin on 18 October 1961, and of its Additional Protocol are, as far as they fall within the domain of legislation, in force as they have been agreed upon.'

[33] Parliament of Finland, Social Affairs Committee, Opinion No. 14 of 1990.

[34] See also M. Pellonpää, 'Economic, Social and Cultural Rights', in *The European System for the Protection of Human Rights* (eds. R. St. J. Macdonald, F. Matscher and H. Petzold), Dordrecht, 1993, p. 858.

[35] 'It is to be added that Sweden has acceded to the European Social Charter according to which, i.a., a principle of equal treatment is valid in the field of social assistance.' (Case No. 4642–1989).

laws.[36] From Finland and some other countries we find decisions by the Ombudsman and other authorities (occasionally even by the courts) in which, for example, the human rights principles of certain documents of the Organisation for Security and Co-operation in Europe have been cited as affecting the outcome of legal reasoning. Such situations may be conceptualised by speaking of non-legal human rights instruments as 'standards' or 'yardsticks' that, formally speaking, are outside the realm of law but which still have an influence on argumentation, interpretation and decision-making inside that sphere. It is interesting to note that the Lithuanian Constitutional Court has from the beginning shown its willingness to reason by reference to international sources other than treaties, most often the 1948 Universal Declaration of Human Rights, classified by many authors as expressing rules of customary international law.

E. Constitutional protection of international human rights

The Estonian and Lithuanian Constitutions and the catalogue of fundamental rights inserted in 1998 into the Latvian Constitution all represent the transformation on the constitutional level of existing international human rights treaties. The same applies to the 1995 Finnish and Icelandic constitutional chapters on fundamental rights, and to the earlier chapter two of the Swedish Constitution Act. This line of development contributes to the harmonisation of international and constitutional protection of fundamental rights. One dimension of this harmonisation is the growing role of international human rights norms in the interpretation of domestic constitutional provisions.

In addition, constitution-makers attach growing importance to the need to secure the observance of international human rights through special clauses in their constitutions. Such clauses have recently been written into the Swedish (chapter 2, section 23), Norwegian (section 110c), Latvian (article 89) and Finnish (section 16a) Constitutions. In Estonia (articles 3 and 123) and in Lithuania (article 138) the constitutional guarantees for international human rights are achieved through general clauses on the domestic applicability and even supremacy of international treaties.

---

[36] On 21 May 1999, a Human Rights Act (Act No. 30 of 1999) was promulgated in Norway. Distinctive features of this incorporation act are that it includes a priority clause (section 3) and covers three treaties, the ECHR, the ICCPR and the International Covenant on Economic, Social and Cultural Rights (ICESCR).

In Sweden and Norway, the constitutional reference to either the ECHR (Sweden) or international human rights in general (Norway) affects the way in which the traditional, but rarely invoked, power of ordinary courts to examine the constitutionality of acts of parliament is exercised. Thus international human rights law can be used to examine whether or not a law is constitutional. In Finland, awareness and, finally, constitutional recognition of international human rights treaties has affected the use of domestic constitutional rights provisions in the legislative process. A turning point can be seen in Opinion No. 21 of 1994 of the Parliamentary Committee for Constitutional Law. In order to reduce expenses, a government bill[37] sought to introduce less generous rules for the calculation of maternity benefits than for paternity benefits. The Committee pronounced that such a proposal was in conflict with article 26 of the ICCPR and hence also the equality clause in section 5 of the Finnish Constitution.[38] The bill was subsequently withdrawn.

F. The principle of legality

The rule of law, or the principle of legality, has various facets. Many of these are of immediate relevance in the context of the domestic application of international human rights treaties. In the Nordic countries, particularly Denmark, the so-called 'rule of instruction' has been applied so that where domestic law gives or seems to give discretion to administrative authorities, international norms must be understood as limiting and guiding that discretion. This notion can be used legally to justify a requirement by ombudsmen and similar institutions that administrative authorities adhere even more faithfully to international human rights treaties than required by courts of law.

A traditional element in the legality principle, particularly strong in Norway, is that obligations or other burdens can only be placed on the individual by parliament. Hence, an act of parliament is always required to

---

[37] Government Bill No. 209 of 1994.

[38] At that time, the Constitution Act included a brief and general equality clause which until then had been interpreted as leaving the legislator a wide margin of operation with respect to differences in treatment. A new provision, including an independent non-discrimination clause formulated along the lines of article 26 of the ICCPR, was under consideration by Parliament and was subsequently affirmed as section 5 in the new Bill of Rights (Act No. 969 of 1995).

establish duties of private parties. A consequence is that there is a certain asymmetry in the law. Individuals are allowed to invoke a wider set of sources of law in relation to public authorities than the state is allowed to rely on against private parties.

As the origin of human rights lies in the protection of the individual against infringements by public authorities, the protection of human rights and the principle of legality very much support each other. Still, the principle of legality affects and even limits the applicability of human rights norms. This can be seen in relation to the concept of *Drittwirkung*, or the horizontal effect of human rights norms. Because the principle of legality requires parliament to pass an act before a human rights provision has legal consequences between private parties, *Drittwirkung* in human rights law mostly takes the form of *indirect* horizontal effect.

Against this background it is obvious that a certain contextuality is needed in applying human rights norms. The same treaty provision might be directly applicable for the benefit of an individual against the state but will require support of other domestic provisions before being capable of resolving a dispute between two private parties. Hence it can be said that the concepts of self-executing treaty provisions or 'direct applicability' are too general in nature to be useful in distinguishing between international human rights standards that are relevant for the domestic operator and those that are irrelevant.

In respect of some issues, like racial discrimination or torture, existing human rights treaties explicitly require states parties to penalise certain acts. But within a much broader area the duty of states to respect and ensure human rights includes the requirement to enact legislation preventing the violation of human rights by private parties. Hence, the domestic implementation of international human rights norms is never a matter for the judiciary only. The legislature, the administration and all branches of government have their own contribution to make.

G. Follow-up and implementation of the findings by international treaty bodies

Much of what has been said above illustrates how the existence and operation of an international court or other monitoring body is essential if the provisions of the human rights treaty in question are to acquire relevance, legal validity and concrete application in the domestic sphere. Judicial or quasi-judicial case law based on an international complaints procedure is a specific form of institutionalised practice of interpretation that is capable of convincing the domestic judge that human rights law is law. Other forms of institutionalised practices of interpretation may also be developed, for instance in the form of concluding observations or other findings resulting from a reporting process. A functioning international follow-up mechanism is one essential element in building the authority of any such institutionalised practice of interpretation. If concluding observations are meant to have an authoritative effect, then the treaty bodies themselves or the international community in general must pay attention to the follow-up measures related to the reporting process.

To illustrate the importance of follow-up, some experiences from Finland on the domestic implementation of cases decided by the HRC may be mentioned. The cases of *Vuolanne v. Finland* (Communication No. 265/1987)[39] and *Torres v. Finland* (Communication No. 291/1988),[40] both of which dealt with a violation of the requirement of court review of all forms of deprivation of liberty in article 9(4) of ICCPR, are important in two respects. First, subsequent to both, the Finnish Government introduced rapid amendments to the relevant domestic law which were approved by parliament without hesitation.[41] Second, although having to commence court proceedings, both victims were finally successful in seeking compensation for their respective human rights violations and some of their legal costs in Finnish courts.[42]

The cases of *Hartikainen et al. v. Finland* (Communication No. 40/1978) and *Järvinen v. Finland* (Communication No. 295/1988)[43] in turn show that even findings of non-violation may give rise to amendments in domestic law if a treaty body expresses concern over the contents of domestic legislation or of its implementation. After the HRC's views in *Hartikainen*, a secular alternative of '*Ethics*' to denominational religious instruction was

---

[39] UN Doc. A/44/40 (1989) pp. 249–58.
[40] UN Doc. A/45/40 (1990), vol. II, pp. 96–100.
[41] Government Bill No. 100 of 1989 and Act No. 374 of 1990 (*Vuolanne*), Government Bill No. 29 of 1990 and Act No. 408 of 1990 (*Torres*). In the latter case, the law was in fact amended before the HRC adopted its final views as it 'had become evident' that a conflict existed.
[42] KHO 1993 A 25 (*Torres*) and KHO 16 April 1996 No. 1069 (*Vuolanne*). Here, it must be noted that such a solution was reached only after several years of considerable hesitation by Finnish courts.
[43] UN Doc. A/45/40 (1990), vol. II, pp. 101–5.

introduced into the Finnish school curriculum.[44] The views in the *Järvinen* case were mentioned in a subsequent government bill as one reason to shorten the duration of alternative civilian service from sixteen to thirteen months, compared to military service of eight to eleven months.[45]

H. International reporting procedures and domestic human rights discourse

It is tempting to presume that the international reporting procedure under a human rights treaty is not so relevant in a country where the treaty in question has been incorporated into domestic law and the incorporation is duly reflected in the practice of courts and administrative authorities. This is, however, not a legitimate conclusion. The international reporting process may well be highly relevant in countries with a well-developed human rights culture exemplified by, *inter alia*, the use of human rights treaties by lawyers and judges, the systematic attention to international obligations in the legislative process, a functioning network of rights-oriented non-governmental organisations (NGOs) and consistent media attention on human rights issues.

At least in Denmark and Finland, NGOs have made systematic efforts to make use of reporting procedures by identifying issues of concern and bringing them to public and international attention. Both the judicial application of human rights treaties and the legislative process tend to focus on instances of 'negative obligations' stemming from human rights treaties, that is, instances where an actual or proposed action by public authorities endangers the enjoyment of certain liberties. Positive state obligations, whether they stem from civil and political rights or from economic, social and cultural rights, tend to be neglected in these processes. The periodic obligation of a state to report on the implementation of a specific human rights treaty allows a regular opportunity to draw attention to positive obligations not yet implemented or fully implemented by the state.

In the context of a human rights culture such as that in Finland, where international human rights treaties are, as a rule, incorporated, where

---

[44] The position that the views of the HRC were of relevance for the amendment of legislation is supported by Opinions Nos. 12 and 13 of 1982 by the Parliamentary Committee for Constitutional Law and the Committee files relating to these opinions.

[45] Government Bill No. 149 of 1991, p. 8.

courts of law and the Ombudsman quite often pay attention to human rights treaties and where the legislature also seeks to ensure compliance with international human rights obligations, the treaty-based reporting obligations may be seen largely as a continuing process which allows for a regular national audit of human rights and for a dialogue between the treaty body in question and civil society, rather than just the government. This cycle has four stages: the preparation of a government report, involving consultation with NGOs and other interested circles; the submission of the report and the preparation of one or more NGO commentaries; the consideration of the report by the treaty body; and the publication of the body's concluding observations. If NGO and media attention is directed to all four stages, the reporting process may form a continuing platform for a domestic human rights discourse.

If the development of such national human rights discourses is taken into consideration when the reform of the United Nations human rights treaty system is discussed, two arguments should be taken into account. First, the plurality of human rights treaties and treaty bodies is an asset, as it provides for different approaches to human rights and for emphasis on areas easily neglected in a complaints-based judicial approach to civil and political rights. Second, from the viewpoint of the continuing national process, what is needed is more coordination than consolidation. Five years is a long time span for an NGO activist participating in or a journalist following a single reporting process. If the treaty bodies and governments could regularise and coordinate the reporting cycles, one could reach a situation where each year a country would (a) submit a report under one treaty; (b) have a report considered under another treaty; and (c) under the remaining treaties, focus on other stages of the cycle: national pre-consideration discussion on the report and the preparation of NGO commentaries, and national post-consideration discussion of the concluding observations and the follow-up steps to be taken for their implementation.

11

THE DOMESTIC IMPACT OF INTERNATIONAL HUMAN RIGHTS STANDARDS: THE JAPANESE EXPERIENCE

YUJI IWASAWA*

A. Introduction

A prominent feature of contemporary international law is the growing interaction between international law and national law, and the area of human rights is no exception. Since the end of the Second World War, numerous treaties on human rights have been concluded and they have had significant impact on the domestic law of the contracting parties. International organisations, especially the United Nations, have adopted not only conventions but also declarations, standards, and principles on human rights. Although the latter are not binding on states, they often elaborate on the provisions in the conventions or further elucidate human rights principles. Human rights conventions often set up committees, commissions or courts to monitor their implementation by the contracting parties. These organs are 'international organisations' in a broad sense, and they perform more and more 'acts' of a legal character in discharging their monitoring functions. These acts may be judgments of courts of human rights, or more informal acts of monitoring bodies, such as decisions, reports, general comments, comments or views. In addition to the human rights conventions themselves, these acts have had a significant impact on the domestic law of states. While their impact within the framework of the

* An earlier version of this chapter was presented to the Second Trilateral (Japan-US-Canada) Symposium in 1996 and published in *Trilateral Perspectives on International Legal Issues: From Theory into Practice* (eds. T. Schoenbaum et al.), Irvington-on-Hudson, NY, 1998, p. 119. For more detailed discussion, see Y. Iwasawa, *International Law, Human Rights, and Japanese Law: The Impact of International Law on Japanese Law*, Oxford, 1998.

European system for the protection of human rights has been extensively analysed,[1] insufficient attention has been paid to their impact outside Europe.[2] In particular, the subject has been all but neglected in Japan.[3] The purpose of this chapter, then, is to analyse the domestic impact of acts of international organisations relating to human rights, with a focus on recent developments in Japan.

Article 98(2) of the Japanese Constitution provides that '[t]reaties concluded by Japan and established laws of nations shall be faithfully observed'. The prevailing view is that treaties concluded by Japan and customary international law have the force of law in Japan by virtue of this article. Treaties and customary international law are generally regarded as ranking higher than statutes but lower than the Constitution. Thus, treaties prevail even over a later inconsistent statute. The original draft of article 98(2) read:

---

[1] Cf., A. Drzemczewski, *The European Human Rights Convention in Domestic Law: A Comparative Study*, Oxford, 1983, pp. 260–325; J. Polakiewicz, *Die Verpflichtungen der Staaten aus den Urteilen des Europäischen Gerichtshofs für Menschenrechte*, Berlin, 1994; R. Bernhardt, 'Einwirkungen der Entscheidungen internationaler Menschenrechtsinstitutionen auf das nationale Recht', in *Staat und Völkerrechtsordnung: Festschrift für Karl Doehring* (eds. K. Hailbronner et al.), Berlin, 1989, p. 23; 'The European Convention on Human Rights: Institution of Review Proceedings at the National Level to Facilitate Compliance with Strasbourg Decisions', 13 *HRLJ*, 1992, p. 71; J. Polakiewicz and V. Jacob-Foltzer, 'The European Human Rights Convention in Domestic Law: The Impact of Strasbourg Case-Law in States where Direct Effect is given to the Convention', 12 *HRLJ*, 1991, pp. 65–84 and 125–42; G. Ress, 'The Effect of Judgments and Decisions in Domestic Law', in *The European System for the Protection of Human Rights* (eds. R. St. J. Macdonald et al.), Dordrecht, 1993, p. 801.

[2] Cf., T. Franck and G. Fox (eds.), *International Law Decisions in National Courts*, Irvington-on-Hudson, NY, 1996; C. Schreuer, *Decisions of International Institutions before Domestic Courts*, Dobbs Ferry, NY, 1981; T. Buergenthal, 'International Tribunals and National Courts: The Internationalization of Domestic Adjudication', in *Recht zwischen Umbruch und Bewahrung – Völkerrecht, Europarecht, Staatsrecht: Festschrift für Rudolf Bernhardt* (eds. U. Beyerlin et al.), Berlin, 1995, p. 687; H. Mosler, 'Supra-National Judicial Decisions and National Courts', 4 *Hastings International & Comparative Law Review*, 1981, p. 425.

[3] Hence at the Eighth International Congress of Comparative Law in 1970, the topic of 'The Legal Nature of Acts of International Organisations and International Courts and the Legal Status of Such Acts in Municipal Law' was discussed but no Japanese report was presented. See C. Dominicé, 'Swiss report', in *Recueil de travaux suisses présentés au VIIIe Congrès international de droit comparé*, Basle, 1970, p. 249; C. Economidès and A.-B. Papacostas, 'Greek reports', 23 *Revue hellénique de droit international*, 1970, pp. 225, 308; A.-Ch. Kiss, 'French report', in *Rapport français: VIIIe Congrès international de droit comparé*, Paris, 1970, p. 259; K. Skubiszewski, 'Polish report', in *Rapport polonais présenté au VIIIe Congrès international de droit comparé*, Warsaw, 1970, p. 194.

Treaties concluded or acceded by Japan, decisions of international organisations in which Japan has participated, and generally approved laws of nations
must be respected together with this Constitution.

It is not clear from the records why the reference to 'decisions of international organisations in which Japan has participated' was deleted from
the final version. Nothing in the records, however, seems to suggest that
the phrase was intentionally deleted to prevent decisions of international
organisations from having the force of law in domestic law.[4] If treaties
and customary international law have the force of law in Japan, it may be
understood that those resolutions of international organisations and judgments of international courts that are binding in international law also
have domestic legal force by the effect of article 98(2). This interpretation
conforms to the spirit of article 98(2) which requires residents and officials
of Japan faithfully to observe international law.[5]

In discussing acts of international organisations, it would be prudent to
make a distinction between abstract norm-creating acts and adjudicatory
acts in concrete cases.[6] Abstract norm-creating acts are acts in which organs
of international organisations – general assemblies or councils – formulate
rules designed to pursue the object of the organisation. Norm-creating acts
of international organisations, often called resolutions or regulations, are
usually hortatory and non-binding, as is the case with resolutions of the
United Nations General Assembly. Even though General Assembly resolutions – such as the 1948 Universal Declaration of Human Rights (UDHR)[7]
– are legally non-binding in themselves, they may be norm-creating in the
sense that they formulate rules in an abstract manner. On the other hand,
adjudicatory acts of international organisations are judgments or reports
of international adjudicatory organs – courts or commissions – in which
they make findings in specific cases. Views and interpretations which
international supervisory organs put forward in supervising compliance
with a treaty may be included in this category. Thus, general comments,

---

[4] See M. Atarashi, 'Kenpo 98 Jo 2 Ko Ritsuan Katei no Bunseki [An Analysis of the Drafting
Process of Article 98 Paragraph 2 of the Constitution]' (pt. 1), 1 *Gyosei Shakai Ronshu*,
1989, pp. 396, 395–91.

[5] Cf. K. Hirobe, 'Article 98 Paragraph 2 of the Constitution of Japan and the Domestic
Effects of Resolutions of the United Nations Security Council', 36 *Japanese Annual of
International Law*, 1993, pp. 17, 32.

[6] See Iwasawa, *supra*, initial asterisked note at pp. 103–22.

[7] Universal Declaration of Human Rights, adopted 10 December 1948, GA Res. 217A (III),
UN GAOR, 3rd Sess., pt. 1, p. 71, UN Doc. A/810 (1948).

comments, and views of committees established by human rights conventions fall within this category. Judgments of international courts are legally binding under international law, while views and comments of international supervisory organs are often not. Acts of international organisations relating to human rights – both norm-creating and adjudicatory – are often non-binding; exceptions include judgments of the European and Inter-American Courts of Human Rights and decisions of the Committee of Ministers of the Council of Europe. Those acts of international organisations that are non-binding on the international plane cannot be binding under domestic law.

B. Norm-creating acts of international organisations

The norm-creating act of an international organisation which has most often been invoked before Japanese courts is the UDHR. Since the UDHR is a resolution of the United Nations General Assembly, it is not legally binding in form. In the Preamble of the 1951 Peace Treaty with Japan, 'Japan . . . declare[d] its intention . . . to strive to realize the objectives of the Universal Declaration of Human Rights', and 'the Allied Powers welcome[d] the intention of Japan'.[8] Despite this apparent meeting of minds, it was not the intention of the United States to impose legal obligations on Japan.[9] Under the circumstances, Japanese courts have invariably rejected arguments based directly on the UDHR, stating that it is 'neither a treaty nor an international agreement', but 'a mere recommendation and lacks a legally binding character'.[10] The Japanese Government and most Japanese scholars also deny its binding character. It is true that the UDHR

---

[8] Treaty of Peace with Japan, 8 September 1951, 136 UNTS 46.

[9] E. Schwelb, *Human Rights and the International Community: The Roots and Growth of the Universal Declaration of Human Rights, 1948–1963*, Chicago, 1964, pp. 48–9.

[10] E.g., Judgment of 2 March 1989, Supreme Court, *Shomu geppo*, 35, pp. 1754, 1761; Judgment of 25 November 1983, Supreme Court, *Shomu geppo*, 30, pp. 826, 828; Judgment of 10 November 1986, Osaka High Court, Gyoshu, 37, pp. 1263, 1267; Judgment of 18 July 1986, Osaka High Court, *Hanrei taimuzu*, 627, pp. 113, 114; Judgment of 26 January 1981, Osaka High Court, *Hanrei jiho*, 1010, p. 139, 26 *Japanese Annual of International Law*, 1983, p. 125; Judgment of 30 March 1971, Tokyo High Court, Gyoshu, 22, pp. 361, 365, 16 *Japanese Annual of International Law*, 1972, p. 87, *ILR*, 59, p. 472; Judgment of 13 March 1968, Osaka High Court, *Hanrei taimuzu*, 221, p. 224; Judgment of 11 July 1978, Osaka District Court, *Shomu geppo*, 24, p. 1622, 24 *Japanese Annual of International Law*, 1981, p. 115; Judgment of 29 May 1996, Tokyo District Court, *Hanrei jiho*, 1577, p. 76; Judgment of 29 March 1977, Tokyo District Court, *Shomu geppo*, 23, p. 552.

was originally intended as a non-binding instrument. However, there is persuasive authority for the proposition that at least some provisions of the UDHR now represent customary international law.[11] Be that as it may, since the adoption and ratification by Japan of the two International Covenants,[12] the need to rely on the UDHR is less strong now than before, as long as the provisions of the UDHR are effectively reproduced in the Covenants. UDHR provisions which *have* often been invoked include article 14 on the right to asylum and article 15(2) on the right not to be deprived of one's nationality arbitrarily, neither of which has comparable provisions in the Covenants.

Arguments based on other acts of international organisations relating to human rights have been rejected summarily by Japanese courts. In 1989, the Supreme Court dismissed arguments based not only on the UDHR, but also on the 1971 Declaration of the Rights of Mentally Retarded Persons,[13] the 1975 Declaration on the Rights of Disabled Persons,[14] and the 1975 resolution of the Economic and Social Council (ECOSOC) on Prevention of Disability and Rehabilitation of Disabled Persons.[15] It ruled that 'being

---

[11] E.g., *Restatement (Third) of the Foreign Relations Law of the United States*, St Paul, 1987, §702; R. Lillich, *The Human Rights of Aliens in Contemporary International Law*, Manchester, 1984, p. 44; J. Humphrey, 'The Universal Declaration of Human Rights: Its History, Impact and Juridical Character', in *Human Rights: Thirty Years After the Universal Declaration* (ed. B. Ramcharan), The Hague, 1979, pp. 21, 36–7; L. Sohn, 'The Human Rights Law of the Charter', 12 *Texas International Law Journal*, 1977, pp. 129, 133–4. Some scholars have gone so far as to assert that the UDHR is customary international law *in toto*, e.g., M. McDougal, H. Lasswell and L. Chen, *Human Rights and World Public Order*, New Haven, 1980, pp. 274, 325–7, 338; A. Verdross and B. Simma, *Universelles Völkerrecht*, 3rd edn, Berlin, 1984, pp. 822–3. For further discussion on the binding character of the UDHR, see Y. Iwasawa, 'Amerika Saibansho ni okeru Kokusai Jinken Sosho no Tenkai: Sono Kokusaihoj no Igi to Mondaiten [International Human Rights Litigation before US Courts: Its Significance and Problems under International Law]' (pt. 1), 87 *Kokusaiho Gaiko Zassi*, 1988, pp. 160, 170–85.

[12] Both the International Covenant on Economic, Social and Cultural Rights (ICESCR) and the International Covenant on Civil and Political Rights (ICCPR) entered into force in Japan on 21 September 1979. Japan has not ratified the first Optional Protocol to the ICCPR nor made a declaration under article 41 of the ICCPR to recognise the competence of the Human Rights Committee (HRC) to receive communications from other states parties.

[13] Adopted 20 December 1971, GA Res. 2856 (XXVI), UN GAOR, 26th Sess., Supp. No. 29, UN Doc. A/8429 (1971), p. 93.

[14] Adopted 9 December 1975, GA Res. 3447 (XXX), UN GAOR, 30th Sess., Supp. No. 34, UN Doc. A/10034 (1975), p. 88.

[15] ESC Res. 1921 (LVIII), UN ESCOR, 58th Sess., Supp. No. 1, UN Doc. E/5683 (1975), p. 29.

expressions of the ideas of the United Nations or its organs, they do not have legally binding force on Member States'.[16] The 1966 International Labour Organisation (ILO)/UN Educational, Scientific and Cultural Organisation (UNESCO) Recommendation Concerning the Status of Teachers[17] has likewise been dismissed by the Supreme Court as not yet 'hav[ing] force as domestic law'.[18] The 1957 Standard Minimum Rules for the Treatment of Prisoners (SMR)[19] and the 1988 Body of Principles for the Protection of All Persons under Any Form of Detention or Imprisonment (1988 Body of Principles)[20] have frequently been invoked together with the International Covenant on Civil and Political Rights (ICCPR) in recent years, but they have been set aside, because 'they possess neither the force of treaties . . . nor the force equivalent to treaties as [standards for the interpretation of] the ICCPR or as customary international law'.[21] In 1996, the Tokushima District Court admitted that 'one cannot say that [the 1988 Body of Principles] has no effect on the interpretation of . . . the ICCPR', although it is still questionable that it constitutes a 'subsequent practice' as defined by article 31(3)(a) of the Vienna Convention on the Law of Treaties.[22] Acts of international non-governmental organisations (NGOs) have been invoked in some instances (for example, a resolution adopted at the nineteenth International Red Cross Conference held in New Delhi in 1957),[23] but the courts have dismissed arguments based on them because they have no 'force to bind states as a legal norm'.[24]

---

[16] Judgment of 2 March 1989, Supreme Court, *Shomu geppo*, 35, pp. 1754, 1761.

[17] Adopted 4 October 1966, 50 *ILO Official Bulletin*, 1967, p. 126.

[18] Judgment of 2 April 1969, Supreme Court Grand Bench, Keishu, 23, pp. 305, 311.

[19] ESC Res. 663 (XXIV) C, UN ESCOR, 24th Sess., Supp. No. 1, UN Doc. E/3048 (1957), p. 11.

[20] GA Res. 43/173, UN GAOR, 43rd Sess., Supp. No. 49, UN Doc. A/43/49 (1988), p. 297.

[21] Judgment of 19 May 1993, Sapporo High Court, *Hanrei jiho*, 1462, pp. 107, 117. See also Judgment of 10 August 1995, Tokyo High Court, *Hanrei jiho*, 1546, pp. 3, 14; Judgment of 14 April 1993, Sendai High Court, *Shomu geppo*, 40, pp. 930, 966; Judgment of 7 December 1993, Tokyo District Court, *Hanrei jiho*, 1505, pp. 91, 106; Judgment of 9 November 1992, Osaka District Court, *Hanrei jiho*, 1470, pp. 106, 119.

[22] Judgment of 15 March 1996, Tokushima District Court, *Hanrei jiho*, 1597, p. 115.

[23] Resolution No. XX adopted at the nineteenth International Red Cross Conference, in *International Red Cross Handbook*, 12th edn, Geneva, 1983, p. 650.

[24] E.g., Judgment of 11 November 1982, Tokyo District Court, *Hanrei taimuzu*, 490, p. 112; Judgment of 28 June 1979, Kobe District Court, *Shomu geppo*, 25, p. 2819; Judgment of 12 July 1977, Tokyo District Court, *Shomu geppo*, 23, p. 1283; Judgment of 25 December 1975, Tokyo District Court, *Shomu geppo*, 22, p. 574; Judgment of 28 July 1970, Nagoya District Court, *Shomu geppo*, 16, p. 1453; Judgment of 15 May 1969, Nagoya District Court, *Shomu geppo*, 15, p. 406.

Norm-creating acts of international organisations are usually not legally binding under international law. As such, they have no force of law in Japanese law. For that reason, Japanese courts have rejected arguments based directly upon them. However, they can have some effect upon domestic law. In particular, they can aid in the interpretation of human rights treaties as well as of domestic law. Although Japanese courts have rejected arguments based directly on the UDHR, in one case the Japanese Supreme Court used it as an aid in the interpretation of the Constitution, significantly broadening the protection of human rights under the Constitution. Article 14 of the Constitution provides that '[a]ll nationals are equal under the law and there shall be no discrimination in political, economic or social relations because of race, creed, sex, social status or family origin'. In 1964, the Supreme Court stated that 'although Article 14 . . . is targeted directly to Japanese nationals, its tenor must also be applied, by analogy, to aliens as well, in view of the fact that Article 7 of the [UDHR] provides that "[a]ll are equal before the law"'.[25]

C. Adjudicatory acts of international organisations

1. REPORTS OF ORGANS OF THE ILO

Reports of international supervisory organs are also often invoked before the courts. The ILO has an elaborate mechanism to supervise implementation of its conventions and recommendations.[26] Reports and views of the organs of the ILO have frequently been invoked before Japanese courts and their legal status has become a subject of controversy. In Japan, trade union rights of public employees are highly restricted; the right to strike is entirely prohibited. Japan is a party to two of the most important ILO conventions on trade union rights: the 1948 Convention No. 87 on Freedom of Association and Protection of the Right to Organise,[27] and the 1949 Convention No. 98 on the Right to Organise and Collective Bargaining.[28] Neither of

---

[25] Judgment of 18 November 1964, Supreme Court, Keishu, 18, pp. 579, 582.

[26] For details on the supervisory mechanism of the ILO, see, e.g., N. Valticos, 'Les méthodes de la protection internationale de la liberté syndicale', 144 *Recueil des cours de l'Académie de droit international*, 1975, p. 79.

[27] Adopted 9 July 1948, 68 UNTS 17 (entered into force 4 July 1950; for Japan on 14 June 1966).

[28] Adopted 1 July 1949, 96 UNTS 257 (entered into force 18 July 1951; for Japan on 20 October 1954).

these conventions, however, explicitly guarantees the right to strike to public employees. Nevertheless, ILO organs have often expressed views critical of the Japanese restrictions of trade union rights in their reports.[29] When Japan ratified the International Covenant on Economic, Social and Cultural Rights (ICESCR), Japan made a reservation on the right to strike. As a result, the ICESCR cannot be invoked to challenge the Japanese practice. Hence, special attention is placed upon the ILO conventions and the reports of the ILO organs.

In 1964, Japan agreed to an investigation and conciliation on the matter by the ILO Fact-Finding and Conciliation Commission on Freedom of Association. In 1965, the Commission issued a comprehensive and voluminous report (the 'Dreyer Report' after the Commission's chairperson) analysing in detail Japanese restrictions of trade union rights in the public sector. This was the first of only five cases ever dealt with by the Commission since its creation in 1950.[30] The Committee of Experts on the Application of Conventions and Recommendations and the Committee on Freedom of Association have also expressed views critical of the Japanese restriction of trade union rights. For example, in a report published in 1983, the Committee of Experts suggested that the general ban on strikes by public employees might violate Convention No. 87.[31]

---

[29] On Japan's prohibition of strikes by public employees, see, e.g., K. Sugeno, 'Public Employee Strike Problems and its Legal Regulation in Japan', in *Current Studies in Japanese Law* (ed. W. Gray), Ann Arbor, 1979, p. 1. For analyses of Japanese law in light of international labour standards, see, e.g., E. Harari, *The Politics of Labor Legislation in Japan: National-International Interaction*, Berkeley, 1973; M. Bobke, 'Arbeitskampf und internationales Recht: Die Rechtsordnungen Japans und der Bundesrepublik Deutschland im Lichte internationaler Normen', in *Law in East and West: On the Occasion of the 30th Anniversary of the Institute of Comparative Law*, Waseda University, Tokyo, 1988, p. 1029.

[30] 'Report of the Fact-Finding and Conciliation Commission on Freedom of Association Concerning Persons Employed in the Public Sector in Japan', 49 *ILO Official Bulletin*, 1966, Special Supplement No. 1. See generally, D. Yiannoupoulos, *La protection internationale de la liberté syndicale: La Commission d'Investigation et de Conciliation en matière de liberté syndicale de l'Organisation Internationale du Travail*, Paris, 1973; J. Nafziger, 'The International Labor Organization and Social Change: The Fact-Finding and Conciliation Commission on Freedom of Association', 2 *NYU Journal of International Law & Politics*, 1969, 1 at pp. 15–25; P. Vellas, 'L'évolution de la compétence contentieuse de l'Organisation Internationale du Travail et l'affaire de la liberté syndicale au Japon (16 juillet 1965)', *Droit social*, 1966, p. 622, *Droit social*, 1967, p. 357.

[31] 'Freedom of Association and Collective Bargaining: General Survey by the Committee of Experts on the Application of Conventions and Recommendations, Report of the Committee of Experts', International Labour Conference, 69th Sess. (1983), p. 63. See also, e.g.,

Paradoxically, Japanese courts have tended to rely on ILO reports in justifying restrictions on trade union rights. When they expand these rights, they do so solely on the basis of constitutional interpretation without mentioning the ILO reports.[32] In 1966, the Tokyo District Court declared that article 4(3) of the Public Corporation and National Enterprise Labour Relations Law, which required officers of a trade union to be employed in the undertaking in which the trade union recruited its members, was null and void because it conflicted with Convention No. 98.[33] The Court was able to take such a determined position because article 4(3) had been deleted in 1965 when Japan ratified Convention No. 87, and the ILO organs had expressed a view in their reports that this provision would conflict with article 2 of Convention No. 98,[34] although the Court did not mention these reports in the judgment.

In the same year, in a case concerning the right to strike, the Japanese Supreme Court rendered a decision favourable to public employees, holding that the restriction of the trade union rights of public employees must be limited to an absolute minimum.[35] The influence of the Dreyer Report was obvious,[36] although the Court made no reference to the Report in its judgment. In 1969, in the Tokyo Teachers' Union case, the Supreme Court expanded the trade union rights of public employees even further. Article 37 of the Japanese Local Public Service Law prohibited strikes by any local public employees, while article 61(4) imposed criminal sanctions for instigating unlawful strikes. The Court restricted the scope of these provisions, and acquitted the leaders of the Tokyo Teachers' Union accused of instigating unlawful strikes. The Court, however, dismissed elaborate arguments of

---

'Report of the Committee on Freedom of Association (222d)', 66 *ILO Official Bulletin*, 1983, Ser. B, No. 1, pp. 44–6.

[32] See also Shin-ichi Ago, 'The ILO's Supervision and Japan', 38 *Japanese Annual of International Law*, 1995, pp. 3, 16 (quoting the present author's assessment and agreeing with it).

[33] Judgment of 10 September 1966, Tokyo District Court, Rominshu, 17, p. 1042.

[34] E.g., 'Report of the Committee of Experts on the Application of Conventions and Recommendations, Report III (Part IV)', International Labour Conference, 43rd Sess. (1959), p. 56.

[35] Judgment of 26 October 1966, Supreme Court Grand Bench, Keishu, 20, p. 901, translated and reprinted in part in H. Itoh and L. Beer, *The Constitutional Case Law of Japan: Selected Supreme Court Decisions, 1961–70*, Seattle, 1978, p. 85.

[36] Y. Matsuda, 'Labor Relations among Public Employees after the Ratification of ILO Convention No. 87: The Development of Legal Doctrines', 10 No. 1 *Japan Labour Bulletin*, 1971, pp. 5, 6; M. and M. Handsaker, 'The ILO and Japanese Public Employee Unions', 7 *Industrial Relations*, 1967, pp. 80, 90.

the accused based on ILO reports. The accused argued, *inter alia*, that the provisions of the Local Public Service Law violated Convention No. 87 as well as customary international law. They invoked various recommendations, reports and observations of ILO organs as aids in the interpretation of Convention No. 87 and as evidence of customary international law. The Court dismissed these arguments without much comment and simply stated that 'the purpose of Convention No. 87 was not a guarantee of the right to strike', and held that there was no rule of customary international law that denied the prohibition of strikes by public employees.[37]

In 1973, the trend to expand the trade union rights of public employees was reversed. In the Agriculture and Forestry Trade Union case, the Supreme Court held that the prohibition of strikes by public employees was entirely constitutional due to their special status. In this judgment, the Supreme Court used the reports of the ILO organs selectively and referred only to those reports which tended to reinforce its conclusion. The Court referred to older reports of the Committee on Freedom of Association,[38] some parts of the Dreyer Report, as well as article 6 of Convention No. 98, to conclude that it was internationally recognised as acceptable to treat public employees differently from other employees.[39]

Such selective use of ILO reports was made again by the Tokyo High Court in 1986. Article 6 of Convention No. 98 provides that the Convention does not deal with the position of 'public servants engaged in the administration of the State' ('fonctionnaires publics' in the French text). The Tokyo High Court referred to certain reports of the Committee on Freedom of Association to interpret the phrase broadly, and concluded that it meant public employees in general and would include employees of

---

[37] Judgment of 2 April 1969, Supreme Court Grand Bench, Keishu, 23, pp. 305, 311.

[38] Case No. 60, Complaints Presented by the World Federation of Trade Unions . . . against the Government of Japan, 'Report of the Committee on Freedom of Association (12th)', Eighth Report of the ILO to the UN (1954), Appendix II, pp. 202, 211. Case No. 179, Complaints Presented by the General Council of Trade Unions of Japan . . . against the Government of Japan, 'Report of the Committee on Freedom of Association (54th)', 44 *ILO Official Bulletin*, 1961, pp. 274, 308.

[39] Judgment of 25 April 1973, Supreme Court Grand Bench, Keishu, 27, p. 547, Judgment upon Case of Violation of the National Public Service Law Providing Crime of Inciting Public Officials to Acts of Dispute (1976), reprinted in part in L. Beer and H. Itoh, *The Constitutional Case Law of Japan, 1970 through 1990*, Seattle, 1996, p. 244. See also Judgment of 21 May 1976, Supreme Court Grand Bench, Keishu, 30, p. 1178 (following the Agriculture and Forestry Trade Union judgment and disregarding the appellants' invitation to take accurate account of the development in the ILO).

national enterprises. The Court, however, refused to rely on ILO reports to question the validity of the prohibition of strikes by employees of national enterprises, declaring that reports and recommendations of ILO organs were not legally binding, and that the recommendation adopted by the Committee on Freedom of Association in Case No. 1151[40] did not reflect an established international standard.[41] In 1988 in another case, the Tokyo High Court proclaimed that 'interpretation of [ILO] conventions adopted in [opinions and reports of the Committee of Experts on the Application of Conventions and Recommendations, and the Committee on Freedom of Association] signifies no authoritative or judicial interpretation, and are not of a nature to bind the interpretation of law by domestic courts'. Despite the disclaimer, however, the Court did refer to the report of the Committee on Freedom of Association in Case No. 792 to strengthen its decision supporting the government's position.[42] Case No. 792 had been brought to the ILO Committee by the Japan Teachers' Union in connection with the strike at issue before the Court, and the report contained language which could support the government's contentions.[43]

In numerous other cases Japanese courts have dismissed arguments based on views and reports of ILO organs, saying that they are not legally binding. For example, in 1993, the Oita District Court stated:

[Reports and recommendations of ILO organs] do not bind the parties ... unless they amount to 'subsequent practice in the application of the

---

[40] Case No. 1151, Complaints Presented by the International Confederation of Free Trade Unions ... against the Government of Japan, 'Report of the Committee on Freedom of Association (218th)', 65 *ILO Official Bulletin*, 1982, Ser. B, No. 3, p. 82.

[41] Judgment of 14 August 1986, Tokyo High Court, *Rodo hanrei*, 481, p. 27.

[42] Judgment of 26 May 1988, Tokyo High Court, *Rodo hanrei*, 519, pp. 73, 76, affirmed, Judgment of 17 April 1990, Supreme Court, Keishu, 44, p. 169. See also Judgment of 20 November 1985, Tokyo High Court, *Rodo hanrei*, 466, p. 65 (another judgment in which the Court referred to the report of the Committee on Freedom of Association in Case No. 792 which was given in connection with the strike at issue, while dismissing a report of the Committee of Experts on the Application of Conventions and Recommendations as 'wishful opinion'); Judgment of 15 December 1978, Nagoya District Court, *Hanrei jiho*, 920, pp. 219, 222, 232 (referring in one part of the judgment to a report of the Committee on Freedom of Association, but declaring in another part that the Dreyer Report and the reports of the Committee on Freedom of Association did not affect the constitutionality of Japanese laws).

[43] Case No. 792, Complaints Presented by the General Council of Trade Unions of Japan (Sohyo), the Japanese Teachers' Union (Nikkyoso) ... against the Government of Japan, 'Report of the Committee on Freedom of Association (187th)', 61 *ILO Official Bulletin*, 1978, Ser. B, No. 3, p. 13.

treaty which establishes the agreement of the parties regarding its interpretation' as provided for in the Vienna Convention on the Law of Treaties. It is obvious that the views of [the ILO organs] fall short of it.[44]

In another case, the accused argued that views of ILO organs were standards for treaty interpretation by judicial organs, being 'established universal international labour standards (international case law)' and having 'automatic binding force (Selfexecuting) [sic]'. The Tokyo High Court denied that they formed 'international labour standards', adding that 'they, of course, cannot have automatic binding force'.[45] In 1985, the Fukuoka District Court admitted that article 37(1) of the Local Public Service Law prohibiting strikes by local public employees was inconsistent with views of ILO organs. The Court concluded, however, that the validity of article 37(1) was unaffected, because 'unratified conventions, recommendations, reports and the like fall neither within "treaties concluded by Japan" nor within "established laws of nations"'. The Court declared:

> [V]iews of various ILO organs . . . are nothing but calls to the governments to make arrangements in domestic laws in accordance with the object of the ILO Conventions. One cannot conclude that they have become sources of law as legally binding standards in interpreting and applying the Conventions, unlike a final decision of the International Court of Justice rendered in cases of doubts or disputes over the interpretation of a Convention (article 37(1) & (2) of the Constitution of the ILO).[46]

This dictum is noteworthy because it implied that a final decision of the International Court of Justice (ICJ) could become a binding interpretative standard for Japanese courts. However, not only was it *obiter dictum* but it was later overruled by the Fukuoka High Court when it affirmed the lower court's decision in 1991.[47]

---

[44] Judgment of 19 January 1993, Oita District Court, *Hanrei jiho*, 1457, pp. 36, 49.

[45] Judgment of 20 November 1985, Tokyo High Court, *Rodo hanrei*, 466, pp. 65, 78, 79.

[46] Judgment of 26 December 1985, Fukuoka District Court, *Shomu geppo*, 32, pp. 2145, 2179–80. For other cases in which the courts dismissed arguments based on reports of ILO organs, saying that they are not binding, see, e.g., Judgment of 24 November 1992, Fukuoka High Court, *Rodo hanrei*, 620, p. 45; Judgment of 15 November 1988, Tokyo High Court, *Rodo hanrei*, 532, p. 77; Judgment of 19 April 1990, Tokyo District Court, *Hanrei jiho*, 1349, p. 3; Judgment of 11 June 1982, Morioka District Court, *Rodo hanrei*, 397, p. 53.

[47] Judgment of 26 December 1991, Fukuoka High Court, *Rodo hanrei*, 639, p. 73 (overruling also the sentence in which the District Court explicitly admitted that article 37(1) of the Local Public Service Law was inconsistent with the views of the ILO organs), affirmed, Judgment of 8 April 1993, Supreme Court, *Rodo hanrei*, 639, p. 12.

2. GENERAL COMMENTS, COMMENTS, AND VIEWS OF COMMITTEES ESTABLISHED BY HUMAN RIGHTS CONVENTIONS

Major human rights conventions adopted under the auspices of the United Nations oblige states parties to submit reports on the implementation of the convention in their countries. Committees established by the conventions consider the report, and, based on the consideration of various reports submitted by the states parties, may adopt 'general comments' or 'general recommendations'. Members of the committees from socialist countries opposed critical evaluation of a report on the human rights situation of any particular country. The compromise achieved was the formulation of general comments addressed to all states, in which committees set out their interpretation of the substantive provisions of the convention, inspired by the consideration of state reports as well as the examination of cases under individual communication procedures.[48] With the gradual erosion of the East-West conflict, various steps were taken to depart from the compromise struck during the Cold War era. In 1992, committees began the practice of adopting country-specific 'comments' or 'concluding observations' at the end of the consideration of each state report. In the comments, committees critically evaluate the report and the human rights situation of the state concerned, making suggestions and recommendations.[49] In addition to the system of state reports, the ICCPR, the Convention on the Elimination of Racial Discrimination (CERD), the Convention against Torture (CAT), and the Convention on Migrant

---

[48] With respect to the ICCPR and CERD, see, e.g., D. McGoldrick, *The Human Rights Committee: Its Role in the Development of the International Covenant on Civil and Political Rights*, Oxford, 1991, pp. 89–96; J. Gomez del Prado, 'United Nations Conventions on Human Rights: The Practice of the Human Rights Committee and the Committee on the Elimination of Racial Discrimination in Dealing with Reporting Obligations of States Parties', 7 *HRQ*, 1985, p. 492; T. Opsahl, 'The General Comments of the Human Rights Committee', in *Des Menschen Recht zwischen Freiheit und Verantwortung: Festschrift für Karl Josef Partsch zum 75. Geburtstag* (eds. J. Jekewitz et al.), Berlin, 1989, p. 273. With respect to the ICESCR, see, e.g., M. Craven, *The International Covenant on Economic, Social and Cultural Rights: A Perspective on Its Development*, Oxford, 1995, pp. 87–92. With respect to the Convention on the Elimination of Discrimination against Women (CEDAW), see, e.g., A. Byrnes, 'The "Other" Human Rights Treaty Body: The Work of the Committee on the Elimination of Discrimination against Women', 14 *YJIL*, 1989, p. 1, at pp. 42–51.

[49] With regard to the HRC, see, e.g., M. Nowak, 'The Activities of the UN Human Rights Committee: Developments from 1 August 1989 through July 1992', 14 (Nos. 1–2) *HRLJ*, 1993, pp. 9, 11.

Workers[50] provide for a system of individual communications. The committees established under these conventions consider communications from individuals who claim to be victims of a violation by a state party of any of the rights set forth in the convention, and forward their 'views' to the state party and to the individual.[51] A view contains the committee's interpretations of the convention and a conclusion on whether or not the facts as found disclose violations of the convention.

As comments and views are addressed to a particular state, they are clearly adjudicatory in the sense indicated above. In contrast, general comments are addressed to all states parties. Nevertheless, since their formulation is based on the experience of the committees in considering state reports and examining specific cases under individual communication procedures, they may also be regarded as adjudicatory in a sense. In any event, general comments, comments, and views all contain significant interpretations of the conventions and carry considerable weight for their interpretation, even though technically they do not bind the states parties. In respect of the views of the Human Rights Committee (HRC), Kurt Herndl has maintained that 'it remains disputed whether the "views" of the HRC are legally binding in a formal sense . . . It is certain, however, that [they] are an authoritative ascertainment of law, and that each state party is obligated, by general international law, and particularly by the effect of the provisions of the ICCPR, to eliminate violations of the provisions.'[52] The CAT, the Convention on the Elimination of Discrimination against Women (CEDAW) and the Convention on Migrant Workers each have a clause allowing states parties to refer a dispute concerning the interpretation of the convention to the ICJ. In contrast, ICESCR, ICCPR and the Convention on the Rights of the Child (CRC) have no comparable provision. The committees established by these conventions are the only organs to which the enforcement and supervision of the convention have been entrusted. Under these latter

---

[50] International Convention on the Protection of the Rights of All Migrant Workers and Members of Their Families, adopted 18 December 1990, GA Res. 45/158, UN GAOR, 45th Sess., Supp. No. 49A, UN Doc. A/45/49 (1990), p. 261, yet to enter into force.

[51] See, e.g. R. Müllerson, 'The Efficacy of the Individual Complaint Procedures: The Experience of CCPR, CERD, CAT, and ECHR', in *Monitoring Human Rights in Europe* (eds. A. Bload et al.), Dordrecht, 1993, p. 25.

[52] K. Herndl, 'Zur Frage des rechtlichen Status der Entscheidungen eines Staatengemeinschaftsorgans: Die "Views" des Menschenrechtsausschusses', in *Völkerrecht zwischen normativern Anspruch und politischer Realität: Festschrift für Karl Zemanek zum 65. Geburtstag* (eds. K. Ginther et al.), Berlin, 1994, pp. 203, 212 (translation by the present author).

conventions, it is all the clearer that general comments, comments, and views of the committees carry great weight for their interpretation.

General comments, comments, and views of the committees have been invoked by parties in domestic courts in support of a particular interpretation of the convention. The South African Constitution of 1996 explicitly provides that '[w]hen interpreting the Bill of Rights a court . . . must consider international law' (section 39(1)).[53] Consequently, the Constitutional Court of South Africa has been generous in having regard to international human rights law.[54]

General comments adopted under the conventions ratified by Japan, particularly the ICCPR, have been invoked before Japanese courts. Japan has neither ratified the first Optional Protocol to the ICCPR nor made a declaration under CERD recognising the competence of the respective committees to receive communications from individuals. However, views given in cases not involving Japan can still be of significance as reflecting on the authoritative interpretation of the convention. In 1994, the Osaka High Court declared the following general principle:

> 'General comments' and 'views' [of the HRC] should be relied upon as supplementary means of interpretation of the ICCPR. Furthermore, contents of an international convention of a similar kind such as the European Convention on Human Rights and jurisprudence under it can also be treated as supplementary means of interpretation of the ICCPR.[55]

In 1996, the Tokushima District Court explained the rationale of the courts' referring to judgments of the European Court of Human Rights in interpreting the ICCPR as follows. A draft Covenant was used as a model in the drafting of the European Convention on Human Rights (ECHR). One

---

[53] See, e.g., T. Maluwa, 'International Human Rights Norms and the South African Interim Constitution 1993', 19 *South African Yearbook of International Law*, 1993–1994, p. 15.

[54] See J. Dugard, in this volume; M. Botha, 'International Law in the Constitutional Court', 20 *South African Yearbook of International Law*, 1995, p. 222. For cases in which courts in other countries referred to views of the HRC, see Judgment of 24 June 1993, Supreme Court, 14 *HRLJ*, 1993, p. 323 (Zimbabwe); *X. v. Board of the Industrial Association for Social Insurance for Hotel, Restaurant, Café, and Lodging House Businesses*, Judgment of 23 May 1991, Central Appeals Court, 23 *Netherlands Yearbook of International Law*, 1992, p. 436 (Netherlands); Judgment of 26 March 1982, BVerwG, 65, p. 188 (Federal Republic of Germany). Canadian courts made reference to views of the HRC on several occasions. See W. Schabas, *International Human Rights Law and the Canadian Charter: A Manual for the Practitioner*, Toronto, 1991, p. 50.

[55] Judgment of 28 October 1994, Osaka High Court, *Hanrei jiho*, 1513, pp. 71, 87, 38 *Japanese Annual of International Law*, 1995, p. 118.

cannot assume that the same interpretation is always valid under the ICCPR, since the contracting parties to the ECHR form only a part of the states parties to the ICCPR. However, as a 'relevant rule of international law applicable in the relations between the parties' within the meaning of article 31(3)(c) of the Vienna Convention on the Law of Treaties, a judgment of the European Court of Human Rights has certain weight in interpreting the ICCPR.[56]

The impact of general comments, comments, and views of human rights committees in Japan is now analysed by examining some cases where they have been invoked before the courts.

(a) Fingerprinting of aliens

The Osaka High Court made ample references to decisions of international bodies relating to human rights in interpreting the ICCPR in a notable judgment of 1994.[57] A Korean arrested for refusing to be fingerprinted filed a lawsuit in 1986, demanding compensation for the arrest which he claimed to be unlawful. Presumably in response to protests which had mounted inside and outside Japan, fingerprinting was abandoned for permanent resident aliens in 1993 and will be abandoned entirely in 2000. In its judgment of 1994, the Osaka High Court found the arrest to be unnecessary and unlawful, and ordered the Government and the judge who had issued the arrest warrant to pay damages. The Court found that the fingerprinting required for resident aliens in Japan violated neither article 7 (prohibition of degrading treatment) nor article 26 (non-discrimination) of the ICCPR. However the Court pointed out that the need to require fingerprinting of settled resident aliens had all but disappeared. It concluded that 'there was room to suspect' that the fingerprinting, in so far as it was applied to Koreans and Taiwanese in Japan, was contrary to articles 7 and 26, referring to general comments[58]

---

[56] Judgment of 15 March 1996, Tokushima District Court, *Hanrei jiho*, 1597, p. 115, modified, Judgment of 25 November 1997, Takamatsu High Court, *Hanrei jiho*, 1653, p. 117, 41 *Japanese Annual of International Law*, 1998, p. 87.

[57] Judgment of 28 October 1994, Osaka High Court, *Hanrei jiho*, 1513, p. 71, 38 *Japanese Annual of International Law*, 1995, p. 118, reversed, Judgment of 7 September 1998, Supreme Court, *Hanrei jiho*, 1661, p. 70.

[58] General Comment No. 20 (Article 7), in 'Compilation of General Comments and General Recommendations Adopted by Human Rights Treaty Bodies', UN Doc. HRI/GEN/1/Rev. 3 (1997) p. 31. General Comment No. 15 (The position of aliens under the Covenant), ibid., p. 19. General Comment No. 18 (Non-discrimination), ibid., p. 26.

and views[59] of the HRC, a report of the European Commission on Human Rights,[60] and a judgment of the European Court of Human Rights.[61]

(b) Children born out of wedlock

A general comment of the HRC together with its comments regarding the third report of Japan have been invoked before Japanese courts in cases involving children born out of wedlock. Japanese law treats children born out of wedlock differently from legitimate children for various purposes. These differences have faced serious challenges by international human rights law in the 1990s. While article 900 of the Civil Code provides that an illegitimate child's share of inheritance is half that of a legitimate child, article 24(1) of the ICCPR provides that '[e]very child shall have, without any discrimination as to . . . social origin, property or birth, the right to such measures of protection as are required by his status as a minor'. The Covenant's *travaux préparatoires*[62] indicate that the criterion of 'birth' in this provision refers to the distinctions between legitimate and illegitimate children,[63] but that the intention of the drafters was not to place illegitimate children in a completely equal position in all areas of law, especially in the law of inheritance.[64] Nevertheless, in General Comment No. 17 of 1989, the HRC requested states parties to indicate in their reports 'how legislation and practice ensure that measures of protection are aimed at removing all

---

[59] *Vuolanne v. Finland*, Report of the Human Rights Committee, UN Doc. A/44/40 (1989), p. 249. *Gueye et al. v. France*, Report of the HRC, ibid. at p. 189. *S. Aumeeruddy-Cziffra et al. v. Mauritius*, in 'Human Rights Committee Selected Decisions under the Optional Protocol', vol. 1, UN Doc. CCPR/C/OP/1 (1985), p. 67.

[60] East African Asians Cases, 36 *Collected Decisions of the European Commission of Human Rights*, 1973, p. 92.

[61] *Tyrer v. United Kingdom*, European Court of Human Rights, Series A, vol. 26.

[62] 'Annotations on the Text of the Draft International Covenants on Human Rights', UN GAOR, 10th Sess., Annexes (Agenda Item 28 II), UN Doc. A/2929 (1955), p. 62. Report of the Third Committee, UN GAOR, 17th Sess., Annexes (Agenda Item 43), UN Doc. A/5365 (1962), pp. 7–9. Report of the Third Committee, UN GAOR, 18th Sess., Annexes (Agenda Item 48), UN Doc. A/5655 (1963), p. 20.

[63] M. Nowak, *CCPR Commentary: UN Covenant on Civil and Political Rights*, Kehl/ Strasbourg/Arlington, 1993, pp. 52–3, 426–7, 429–32; A. Robertson, 'The United Nations Covenant on Civil and Political Rights and the European Convention on Human Rights', 43 BYbIL, 1968–1969, pp. 21, 40. Cf. E. Schwelb, 'Some Aspects of the International Covenants on Human Rights December 1966', in *International Protection of Human Rights (Proceedings of the 7th Nobel Symposium)* (eds. A. Eide and A. Schou), Stockholm, 1968, pp. 103, 119.

[64] Nowak, *supra*, note 63; Robertson, *supra*, note 63, at p. 40.

discrimination in every field, including inheritance, particularly as between
. . . legitimate children and children born out of wedlock', suggesting that
discrimination against children born out of wedlock was prohibited with
respect to inheritance as well.[65] The HRC thus adopted a progressive interpretation which was not necessarily commensurate with the intention of
the drafters.

In 1990, a child born out of wedlock brought a lawsuit, arguing article
900 was unconstitutional. The plaintiff invoked article 16(1)(d) CEDAW,
the 1972 ECOSOC Resolution on the Status of the Unmarried Mother,
article 25(2) of the UDHR, article 24(1) of the ICCPR, and article 2(1)
CRC. The Tokyo High Court dismissed the claim, without giving reasons,
in 1991.[66] In an epoch-making decision delivered in 1993, however, the
Tokyo High Court took an initiative to change society with the support of
international human rights law. In this case, another child born out of
wedlock challenged article 900, invoking, in addition to the above provisions, article 1 of the Declaration on the Rights of the Child, article 2(2)
CRC and General Comment No. 17 of the HRC. The child invoked General
Comment No. 17 as the 'authoritative interpretation' of the ICCPR. In
June 1993, the Tokyo High Court held that article 900 was contrary to
article 14 of the Constitution as unreasonable discrimination, using international human rights law as an aid in the interpretation of the Constitution.[67] Even though the Court made no reference to the general comment,
its impact is undeniable.

In October 1993, when the HRC considered the third report of Japan,
many members criticised the Japanese legal treatment of children born out
of wedlock.[68] After consideration, the HRC adopted comments in which
it expressed concern 'at the discriminatory legal provisions concerning

---

[65] General Comment No. 17 (Article 24, 1989), reproduced in 'Compilation of General
Comments', *supra*, note 58, at p. 24.

[66] Judgment of 29 March 1991, Tokyo High Court, *Hanrei taimuzu*, 764, p. 133, affirmed,
Judgment of 5 July 1995, Supreme Court Grand Bench, *Hanrei jiho*, 1540, p. 3.

[67] Judgment of 23 June 1993, Tokyo High Court, *Kominshu*, 46, p. 43. See also Judgment of
30 November 1994, Tokyo High Court, *Hanrei jiho*, 1512, p. 3.

[68] Japan Federation of Bar Associations (ed.), *Record of the Human Rights Committee
Meetings on the Third Periodic Report of Japan: Held at the Palais des Nations, Geneva, on
27–28 October 1993*, Tokyo, 1995, pp. 33, 37, 38, 39, 42, 46, 47–8, 54, 60–1, 81, 82, 83–4,
149, 150, 153, 156 (statements of Sadi, Mavrommatis, Pocar, Evatt, Chanet, Prado Vallejo,
Herndl, Aguilar Urbina, Dimitrijevic, Higgins, Ndiaye). Ibid. at pp. 29–30, 72–4, 86
(responses of the Japanese representatives).

children born out of wedlock. In particular, provisions and practices regarding the birth registration forms and the family register are contrary to articles 17 and 24 of the Covenant. The discrimination in their right to inherit is not consistent with article 26 of the Covenant', and recommended that 'the Japanese legislation concerning children born out of wedlock be amended'.[69] The Japanese Government did not amend article 900 of the Civil Code in 1993 when it ratified the CRC, arguing that the article was not contrary to article 2(2) which prohibits discrimination on the basis of the 'status' of a child's parents. However, the Government explained in the Diet in March 1994 that in view of the change of situation – referring to the judgment of the Tokyo High Court and the comments of the HRC in 1993 – the Ministry of Justice would ask an advisory council to the Ministry to review article 900 of the Civil Code.[70] The advisory council agreed in July 1994 to make the share of inheritance equal between legitimate and illegitimate children.

Despite such outspoken criticism of article 900, the Supreme Court held in 1995 that the article was compatible with article 14 of the Constitution. Of the ten justices constituting the majority four believed that even though article 900 was constitutional it should be revised; two of them referred specifically to articles 24 and 26 of the ICCPR and article 2(1) CRC. Five justices dissented, referring to the ICCPR and CRC to conclude that article 900 was discriminatory to children born out of wedlock and thus null and void.[71]

The different treatment of children born out of wedlock in the description of their relationship with their parents on a resident card was challenged in 1988. Parents of a child born out of wedlock challenged the practice by a city of describing their child on a resident card as simply 'a child' rather than 'the first girl', which would have been the case if she had been a legitimate child. The plaintiffs invoked articles 24, 26 and 17 ICCPR,

---

[69] 'Comments of the Human Rights Committee: Japan' Report of the Human Rights Committee, Vol. 1, UN GAOR, 49th Sess., Supp. No. 40, UN Doc. A/49/40 (1994), pp. 23, 25, 26.

[70] House of Representatives, Foreign Affairs Committee, 129th Diet, 4 March 1994, *Gaimuiinkaigiroku*, 1, p. 5; House of Councillors, Foreign Affairs Committee, 129th Diet, 29 March 1994, *Gaimuiinkai Kaigiroku*, 1, p. 10 (remarks of a Justice Ministry official). See also Homusho Minjikyoku Sanjikan Shitsu [Civil Affairs Bureau, Ministry of Justice], 'Kon'in Seido to ni kansuru Minpo Kaisei Yoko Shian [A Draft Outline on the Revision of the Civil Code concerning the System of Marriage]', 1050 *Jurisuto*, 1994, pp. 214, 221.

[71] Judgment of 5 July 1995, Supreme Court Grand Bench, *Hanrei jiho*, 1540, p. 3.

article 25(2) UDHR, article 2 CRC and article 16(1)(d) CEDAW. In 1991, the Tokyo District Court dismissed their claim. The Court found that the different treatment did not contravene the ICCPR.[72] In 1994, while the appeal was pending, the Ministry of Home Affairs decided to describe every child (not only a legitimate child, but also an illegitimate child and an adopted child) as 'a child' on resident cards. On appeal, the appellants invoked, in addition to the above provisions, a general comment of the HRC, the comments adopted by the HRC in 1993, the Declaration on the Rights of the Child, and recommendations of ECOSOC. In 1995, the Tokyo High Court found that describing an illegitimate child as 'a child' on a resident card was contrary to article 14 of the Constitution as unreasonable discrimination. The Court dismissed the damages claim for the reason that the mayor had not been negligent. However, after noting the 1993 comments of the HRC, the Court added that, if the mayor had used the description now, he would be negligent.[73]

(c) Compensation for war damages

Views of the HRC have been invoked in cases concerning compensation for war damages. Most Japanese laws which provide relief to those who were wounded or killed in the Second World War exclude aliens.[74] Some Korean residents in Japan who were conscripted, fought for Japan and were wounded in the Second World War sued the Japanese Government for compensation. The plaintiffs argued that the relief laws which exclude aliens were contrary to articles 2(2) and 9 ICESCR and article 26 ICCPR: in support of their arguments, they invoked a view of the HRC given in a case brought by former Senegalese soldiers against France. In that case, retired soldiers of Senegalese nationality who had served in the French army challenged a French law which granted lower pensions to them than to retired French soldiers. The HRC took the view that the different treatment constituted a violation of article 26 ICCPR.[75] The view had a significant impact on the courts. In 1994, the Tokyo District Court held that the 1952 Relief Law was contrary neither to the ICESCR nor to the ICCPR. The Court added,

---

[72] Judgment of 23 May 1991, Tokyo District Court, *Hanrei jiho*, 1382, p. 3.
[73] Judgment of 22 March 1995, Tokyo High Court, *Hanrei jiho*, 1529, p. 29, affirmed, Judgment of 21 January 1999, Supreme Court, *Hanrei jiho*, 1675, p. 48.
[74] See generally Iwasawa, *supra*, initial asterisked note, at pp. 176–8.
[75] *Gueye et al. v. France, supra*, note 59.

however, that 'the arguments of the plaintiff contain some points worth listening to'.[76] In 1995, in another case, the Osaka District Court held that the exclusion of aliens from the 1952 Relief Law 'was suspected to run counter to article 14 [non-discrimination] of the Constitution'.[77] In another case, plaintiffs invoked *Gueye et al. v. France*, arguing that the HRC's interpretation should be the standard for the application of the ICCPR. In 1996, the Tokyo District Court discussed *Gueye* in some detail, rejecting it as inappropriate for the present case because 'the nature of payment is different' and 'reasons and backgrounds for making distinctions on the basis of nationality are completely different'.[78] The Court thus implicitly admitted that views of the HRC could be of relevance in other cases.

(d) Prison conditions

A prisoner who had been sentenced to death and placed in a solitary cell sued the Japanese Government for compensation, arguing that he had suffered physical and mental anguish by the semi-transparent board covering his window. In 1995, referring to articles 14(2) and 7 of the ICCPR, a general comment of the HRC,[79] the Standard Minimum Rules, and the 1988 Body of Principles, the Tokyo High Court acknowledged that 'in principle, it was more in accord with international standards not to cover cell windows'. The Court, however, held that the act of covering the window in this case was a reasonable measure under the arrangement of buildings in the prison concerned and concluded that there was no defect in the establishment and management of public works, and that the government had no obligation to pay damages under the State Redress Law.[80]

D. Conclusion

Even though treaties and customary international law have the force of law in Japan, Japanese courts are wary of recognising the direct applicability

---

[76] Judgment of 15 July 1994, Tokyo District Court, *Hanrei jiho*, 1505, pp. 46, 53, 55, 38 *Japanese Annual of International Law*, 1995, p. 133.

[77] Judgment of 11 October 1995, Osaka District Court, *Hanrei taimuzu*, 901, pp. 84, 99.

[78] Judgment of 22 November 1996, Tokyo District Court, not yet reported.

[79] General Comment No. 20 (Article 7, 1992), reproduced in 'Compilation of General Comments', *supra*, note 58, at p. 31.

[80] Judgment of 22 May 1995, Tokyo High Court, *Hanrei taimuzu*, 903, p. 112, affirming Judgment of 28 March 1994, Tokyo District Court, ibid. at p. 114.

(self-executing character) of treaties and customary international law,[81] as international law overrides domestic statutes in Japan. Direct application, however, is only one effect international law can have on domestic law. Another important effect international law has on the national legal order is to aid in the interpretation of domestic law. International law may also be used by courts as evidence to support a conclusion reached through the interpretation of domestic law. Such indirect application of international law can be very effective; while reluctant to endorse the direct application of international law, courts may be more willing to use international law in this manner.

The legal character of the international instruments is not so important in indirect application, even though the instruments' authority as an aid in the interpretation of domestic law admittedly differs depending upon its legal character. The stronger its legal character, the greater its authority. Not only a binding treaty and customary international law, but also a non-binding international instrument can be used as an aid in the interpretation of domestic law. A treaty which has been signed but not yet ratified, a treaty which has not even been signed, a treaty which cannot be acceded to by the state concerned (for example, the ECHR for non-European countries), and a declaration adopted by the UN General Assembly can all be referred to in interpreting domestic law. Adjudicatory acts of international organisations may indicate authoritative interpretation of a treaty which has domestic legal force. Reports, comments, and views of the committees established by human rights conventions may elucidate the meaning of a convention. Any adjudicatory act could be used, as long as it helps to clarify the meaning of the convention. It need not have been given in a case involving the state concerned.

Even in dualist-oriented states in which treaties have no domestic legal force, such as the United Kingdom and Canada, international human rights instruments can be used at least as aids in the interpretation of domestic law. Courts in these countries refer to treaties, declarations adopted by the UN General Assembly, and various acts of international supervisory organs in interpreting domestic law. In the United Kingdom, the Judicial Committee of the Privy Council referred extensively to views and decisions of human rights bodies in *Pratt v. Attorney-General for*

---

[81] See Iwasawa, *supra*, initial asterisked note, at pp. 44–81. For the concept of direct applicability, see generally Y. Iwasawa, 'The Doctrine of Self-Executing Treaties in the United States: A Critical Analysis', 26 *Virginia JIL*, 1986, p. 627.

Jamaica in 1993.[82] Persons sentenced to death but held on death row for many years in Jamaica challenged the legality of the sentences. The Privy Council ordered the sentences to be commuted to life imprisonment, holding that 'in any case in which execution is to take place more than five years after sentence there will be strong grounds for believing that the delay is such as to constitute "inhuman or degrading punishment or other treatment"' as provided for in section 17(1) of the Jamaican Constitution.[83] In interpreting the Jamaican Constitution, the Privy Council referred extensively to a view of the HRC,[84] a decision of the Inter-American Commission on Human Rights,[85] and a judgment of the European Court of Human Rights.[86] Pointing out that the delay in issuing the warrant of execution was caused partly by a wish of the Governor-General to obtain the Attorney-General's advice on 'the legal status of decisions of human rights bodies', the Privy Council declared that although 'not of legally binding effect', the views of the HRC 'should be afforded weight and respect'.[87]

In Canada, even though treaties do not have the force of law, the courts frequently refer to international human rights instruments in interpreting the 1982 Canadian Charter of Rights and Freedoms. The International Covenants and the ECHR are the most often cited instruments, even though Canada is not a party to the ECHR and cannot become one. In addition to these treaties, various human rights instruments adopted by the United Nations, including the UDHR, and ILO conventions are often referred to by the courts in interpreting the Canadian Charter. Moreover, Canadian courts often refer not only to the text of the treaties but also to acts of the supervisory organs (such as the European Commission of Human Rights, the European Court of Human Rights, the HRC, and ILO organs) in interpreting the relevant treaty.[88] The question of the right to strike (by public employees) is particularly interesting because Japan has a similar problem. The Canadian Charter guarantees 'freedom of association' (section 2(d)). The question was whether the guarantee of freedom of association would

---

[82] *Pratt v. Attorney-General for Jamaica*, AC [1994] 2, p. 1; 14 *HRLJ*, 1993, p. 338 (PC). For further discussion on this case, see, e.g., Buergenthal, *supra*, note 2, at pp. 689–95.

[83] *Pratt v. Attorney-General for Jamaica*, ibid., at p. 35.

[84] *Pratt & Morgan v. Jamaica*, Report of the Human Rights Committee, UN GAOR, 44th Sess., Supp. No. 40, UN Doc. A/44/40 (1989), p. 222.

[85] The 'decision' was never published in the Commission's annual reports.

[86] *Soering v. United Kingdom*, European Court of Human Rights, Series A, vol. 161.

[87] *Pratt v. Attorney-General for Jamaica, supra*, note 82, at p. 1, 27.

[88] See Schabas, *supra*, note 54, Iwasawa, *supra*, note 11, at pp. 477–8.

include a guarantee of the right to strike. The Ontario High Court answered this question in the affirmative,[89] while other courts answered in the negative.[90] In 1987, the Supreme Court of Canada rejected the proposition without referring to international law.[91] In a dissenting opinion, Chief Justice Dickson stated that '[t]he Charter conforms to the spirit of this contemporary international human rights movement . . . The various sources of international human rights law – declarations, covenants, conventions, judicial and quasi-judicial decisions of international tribunals, customary norms – must, in my opinion, be relevant and persuasive sources for the interpretation of the Charter's provisions'. He then concluded that 'freedom of association' as provided in the Canadian Charter included the right to organise and the right to strike, referring to the International Covenants, Convention No. 87, and views of ILO organs.[92] Consequently, we are in an ironic situation, the impact of human rights conventions is much greater in Canada where treaties have no domestic legal force than in the United States where treaties do have domestic legal force. This irony is produced in large part by the declarations attached by the United States Government to human rights conventions that they are not self-executing in the United States.[93]

[89] *Re Service Employees' International Union & Broadway Manor Nursing Home*, DLR 4th, 4 (1983), pp. 231, 280–4 (Ont. H. Ct.). See also *Re Retail, Whole Sale & Department Store Union & Goverment of Saskatchewan*, DLR 4th, 19 (1985), p. 609 (Sask. CA).

[90] *Public Service Alliance of Canada v. The Queen in Right of Canada*, DLR 4th, 11 (1984), p. 337 (FCTD). *Re Public Service Employee Relations Act, Labor Relations Act and Police Officers Collective Bargaining Act*, DLR 4th, 16 (1984), p. 359 (Alberta CA). Cf. *Re Alberta Union of Provincial Employees & The Crown in Right of Alberta*, DLR 3d, 120 (1980), p. 590 (Alberta QB).

[91] *Re Public Service Employee Relations Act, Labor Relations Act and Police Officers Collective Bargaining Act*, DLR 4th, 38 (1987), p. 161 (Can.).

[92] Ibid. at pp. 184–92, 239 (Dickson and Wilson, JJ., dissenting). A communication was filed with the HRC by a Canadian in connection with the *Alberta Union* Case cited *supra*, note 90. The HRC held the communication inadmissible in 1986 because the freedom of association did not include the right to strike. 'Report of the Human Rights Committee', GAOR, 41st Sess., Supp. No. 40, UN Doc. A/41/40 (1986), p. 151. Chief Justice Dickson did not refer to this decision of the HRC. Another Justice of the Supreme Court of Canada later confirmed: 'Though speaking in dissent, his comments on the use of international law generally reflect what we all do.' Statement of Justice G. V. La Forest at the Canadian Council on International Law in 1988, cited in Schabas, *supra*, note 54, at p. 17.

[93] See generally L. Damrosch, 'The Role of the United States Senate Concerning "Self-Executing" and "Non-Self-Executing" Treaties', in *Parliamentary Participation in the Making and Operation of Treaties: A Comparative Study* (eds. S. Riesenfeld and F. Abbott), Dordrecht, 1994, p. 205.

12

THE ROLE OF HUMAN RIGHTS TREATY STANDARDS IN DOMESTIC LAW: THE SOUTHERN AFRICAN EXPERIENCE

JOHN DUGARD

South Africa, Namibia and Zimbabwe occupy a special place in the history of United Nations action to promote human rights. The perpetuation of white minority rule in these territories in a world order committed to decolonisation, self-determination and majority rule provoked a concerted response from the United Nations, which included economic sanctions and the toleration of military support to national liberation movements. United Nations action against Southern Rhodesia (as it then was) was premised on the denial of self-determination and the perpetuation of minority rule. The international status of South West Africa/Namibia and the failure of South Africa to honour the obligations contained in the Mandate for South West Africa provided the basis for United Nations action against South Africa. In South Africa itself racial discrimination, political repression, military intervention in neighbouring states and minority rule combined to justify United Nations intervention. But in all three cases there was a serious denial of human rights and most of the resolutions adopted by the General Assembly and the Security Council on these three territories castigated the government or the administering authority for its denial of human rights to the majority of the people. The action of the United Nations in the Southern African region can therefore legitimately be characterised as action taken to promote human rights.[1]

It is not surprising that when change came to these territories the national liberation movements involved in the negotiations that led to the

---

[1] See J. Dugard, 'Apartheid: A Case Study in the Response of the International Community to Gross Violations of Human Rights', in *International Human Rights Law: Theory and Practice* (eds. I. Cotler and F. D. Eliadis), Montreal, 1992, p. 301; L. Sohn, *Rights in Conflict: The United Nations and South Africa*, Irvington, NY, 1994.

establishment of new political orders should insist on constitutions that provided guarantees for human rights. After all the national liberation movements of Southern Africa (unlike the Palestine Liberation Organisation)[2] had conducted their international campaigns against white rule in Southern Africa in the name of human rights and self-determination. Ironically the authorities that had denied human rights to their people for so long likewise insisted on constitutional guarantees for basic rights as they saw in such guarantees a protection against the very practices in which they had engaged themselves. So it was that Zimbabwe and Namibia became independent under constitutions with a bill of rights protected by an independent judiciary. South Africa, when it abandoned apartheid and accepted majority rule, adopted a similar course.

A. A brief constitutional overview

1. ZIMBABWE

Zimbabwe became independent in 1980 with a Constitution that includes a justiciable Declaration of Rights. This Declaration follows the form of the Bill of Rights contained in other British independence-conferring constitutions. The influence of international human rights conventions is, however, clear. Consequently most of the rights contained in the International Covenant on Civil and Political Rights (ICCPR) are protected in Zimbabwe's Declaration of Rights. The Declaration of Rights is protected by a judiciary which, under the leadership of Chief Justices Fieldsend, Dumbutshena and Gubbay, has acquired a reputation for independence and courage.[3]

Zimbabwe is a party to the African Charter on Human and Peoples' Rights (African Charter), the Convention on the Rights of the Child (CRC) and since 1991 has been a party to the ICCPR, the International Covenant on Economic, Social and Cultural Rights (ICESCR), the Convention on the Elimination of Discrimination against Women (CEDAW) and the Convention on the Elimination of Racial Discrimination (CERD). It is not a party to the Convention against Torture (CAT), nor has it signed the Optional Protocol to the ICCPR.

---

[2] This may explain the failure of the Palestinian Authority in the West Bank and Gaza to concern itself with the promotion of human rights.

[3] See J. Hatchard, 'The Constitution of Zimbabwe: Towards a Model for Africa?', 35 *Journal of African Law*, 1991, pp. 79, 91.

Unlike the constitutions of Namibia and South Africa, that of Zimbabwe does not recognise the important role of international law in municipal law. Zimbabwe follows the common law approach to the relationship between international law and municipal law. Customary international law forms part of municipal law, but treaties require incorporation by statute.

2. NAMIBIA

The bitter dispute between South Africa and the United Nations over the former's claim to administer the mandated territory of South West Africa[4] came to an end on 21 March 1990 when Namibia became an independent state. The Constitution of Namibia[5] includes a justiciable Bill of Rights which shows the influence of the ICCPR and, to a lesser extent, the ICESCR. An independent judiciary is charged with the task of protecting the rights enshrined in the Bill of Rights by means of judicial review. The Constitution also contains a chapter dealing with Principles of State Policy, modelled on the Indian Constitution, which directs the state, *inter alia*, to promote the welfare of the people by progressively realising certain social and economic rights.[6]

The Namibian Constitution 'constitutionalises' the place of international law in municipal law. Article 144 provides:

> Unless otherwise provided by this Constitution or Act of Parliament, the general rules of public international law and international agreements binding upon Namibia under this Constitution shall form part of the law of Namibia.

Namibia is a party to the African Charter and became a party to the ICCPR, ICESCR and CAT in 1994, CEDAW in 1992, CRC in 1990 and CERD in 1982.[7] It is also a party to the Optional Protocol to the ICCPR.

---

[4] For a history of this dispute, see J. Dugard, *The South West Africa/Namibia Dispute*, Berkeley, 1973.

[5] For a comprehensive analysis of this Constitution, particularly from the perspective of international law, see 15 *South African Yearbook of International Law* (1989–1990). See, too, J. Hatchard and P. Slinn, 'Namibia: The Constitutional Path to Freedom', 17 *Commonwealth Law Bulletin*, 1991, p. 644.

[6] Chapter II (article 95).

[7] Obligations under CERD passed from the United Nations Council for Namibia to the Republic of Namibia at independence on 21 March 1990.

3. SOUTH AFRICA: THE 1993 AND 1996 CONSTITUTIONS

In 1993 twenty-six political groups assembled at Kempton Park, near Johannesburg, to draft a constitution to bring an end to the apartheid legal order. As these groups were in most instances unelected, and simply reflected the political realities of the time, it was considered inappropriate to confer on them the power to draft a final constitution. Instead the constitution which they fashioned in negotiations lasting some six months was to serve as an interim constitution, pending the drafting of a constitution by a democratically elected Constitutional Assembly. As the Interim Constitution represented a political compromise between rival groups, notably the National Party and the African National Congress, it was agreed at Kempton Park that the 'final' constitution would comply with thirty-four constitutional principles contained in a schedule to the Interim Constitution and that the Constitutional Court created by the 1993 Interim Constitution would be empowered to pronounce on the issue of compliance. This Interim Constitution approved at Kempton Park was duly endorsed by the last apartheid parliament and became the Constitution of the Republic of South Africa, Act 200 of 1993.

On 27 April 1994 the Interim Constitution came into effect to govern South Africa's first democratic elections.[8] The Parliament thus elected served the dual role of legislature and Constitutional Assembly. From January 1995 to May 1996 the Constitutional Assembly met regularly to draft the 'final' constitution in accordance with the thirty-four constitutional principles agreed upon at Kempton Park. A Draft Constitution was approved by the required two-thirds majority vote in the Constitutional Assembly on 8 May 1996 and forwarded to the Constitutional Court for certification. The Constitutional Court found fault with a number of provisions in the Draft Constitution[9] on the grounds that they failed to comply with the constitutional principles contained in the Interim Constitution, and referred the Draft Constitution back to the Constitutional Assembly. After these faults had been remedied by the Constitutional Assembly, the Constitutional Court gave its final approval to the Constitution

---

[8] For an account of the adoption of the Interim Constitution, see D. van Wyk, 'Introduction to the South African Constitution', in D. van Wyk et al., *Rights and Constitutionalism*, Oxford, 1995, p. 131.

[9] *In re: Certification of the Constitution of the Republic of South Africa*, 1996 (4) South African Law Reports [hereinafter SA] p. 744 (CC).

on 4 December 1996.[10] The new Constitution – the Constitution of the Republic of South Africa, Act 108 of 1996 – was signed into law by President Mandela on 10 December 1996.

Both the Interim Constitution and the 1996 Constitution contain a Bill of Rights which guarantees the rights protected by international human rights conventions.[11] Whereas the Interim Constitution is confined largely to civil and political rights, the 1996 Constitution extends its protection to both civil and political, and social and economic rights. This is a response to Constitutional Principle Two in the Interim Constitution which provides that 'everyone shall enjoy all *universally accepted* fundamental rights, freedoms and liberties'.[12] These rights are entrenched in the Constitution[13] and protected by a Constitutional Court with wide powers of judicial review over legislation and administrative action.[14]

Great care was taken to ensure that the Bill of Rights complies with international norms. Although the rights are formulated in simpler language than that found in most human rights conventions (in pursuance of a deliberate policy to make the Constitution accessible to the people), they are broadly modelled on their international counterparts. In part this was done in order to facilitate South Africa's accession to international human rights treaties. Moreover, some of the clauses in the 1996 Constitution refer expressly to international law. Section 37(4) provides that any legislation enacted in consequence of a declaration of a state emergency may derogate from the Bill of Rights only to the extent that, *inter alia*, the legislation 'is consistent with the Republic's obligations under international law applicable to states of emergency'. Section 35(3)(1) recognises the right 'not to be convicted of an act or omission that was not an offence under either national or international law at the time when it was committed or omitted'.

---

[10] *Ex parte Chairperson of the Constitutional Assembly; In re Certification of the Amended Text of the Constitution of the Republic of South Africa 1996*, 1997 (2) SA p. 97 (CC).

[11] See further on this subject, J. Dugard, 'The Influence of International Human Rights Law on the South African Constitution', 49 *Current Legal Problems*, 1996, p. 305; T. Maluwa, 'International Human Rights Norms and the South African Interim Constitution 1993', 19 *South African Yearbook of International Law*, 1993–1994, p. 14.

[12] Schedule 4 of Act 200 of 1993, italics added.

[13] Section 74(2) of Act 108 of 1996 provides that the Bill of Rights may only be amended by a two-thirds majority vote in the lower house (National Assembly) and by at least six of the nine Provinces in the upper house (National Council of Provinces).

[14] Sections 167 and 172 of Act 108 of 1996.

The clearest evidence of the desire to achieve harmony between South African and international human rights jurisprudence is provided by section 39(1) (previously section 35(1)) which declares that:

When interpreting the Bill of Rights, a court, tribunal or forum –
(a) must promote the values that underlie an open and democratic society based on human dignity, equality and freedom;
(b) must consider international law; and
(c) may consider foreign law.

This provision, together with section 233 which requires a court when interpreting legislation to 'prefer any reasonable interpretation of the legislation that is consistent with international law over any alternative interpretation that is inconsistent with international law', ensures that courts will be guided by international norms and the interpretation placed upon these norms by international courts and other institutions. Fears[15] that international human rights law in this context might be narrowly construed to cover only clear rules of customary law and those human rights conventions to which South Africa is a party have been dispelled. In one of its earliest decisions, in a case involving the constitutionality of the death penalty, the President of the Constitutional Court ruled:

In the context of section 35(1), public international law would include non-binding as well as binding law. They may both be used under the section as tools of interpretation. International agreements and customary international law accordingly provide a framework within which the Bill of Rights can be evaluated and understood, and for that purpose, decisions of tribunals dealing with comparable instruments, such as the United Nations Committee on Human Rights, the Inter-American Commission on Human Rights, the Inter-American Court of Human Rights, the European Commission on Human Rights and the European Court of Human Rights, and, in appropriate cases, reports of specialised agencies such as the International Labour Organisation, may provide guidance as to the correct interpretation of particular provisions of [the Bill of Rights].[16]

The Interim Constitution establishes a Human Rights Commission[17] and a Commission for Gender Equality[18] which, together with the courts of

---

[15] J. Dugard, 'The Role of International Law in Interpreting the Bill of Rights', 10 *South African Journal on Human Rights*, 1994, p. 208.
[16] *S. v. Makwanyane*, 1995 (3) SA p. 391 (CC) at pp. 413–14.
[17] Section 116 of Act 200 of 1993.
[18] Section 119 of Act 200 of 1993; section 185 of Act 108 of 1996.

the country (particularly the Constitutional Court), are required to promote respect for human rights. The Human Rights Commission is mandated to promote 'the observance of, respect for and protection of fundamental rights'; to 'develop an awareness of fundamental rights among all people of the Republic'; to make recommendations 'to organs of state at all levels of government' on the 'promotion and observance of human rights'; to investigate complaints about human rights violations; and to inform both Parliament and the provincial legislatures of any inconsistency between proposed legislation and the Bill of Rights, 'norms of international human rights law which form part of South African law' or 'other relevant norms of international law'.[19]

The procedures and powers of the Human Rights Commission were later prescribed in greater detail in the Human Rights Commission Act of 1994.[20] Consequently the 1996 Constitution simply recognises the role of the Human Rights Commission in promoting a democratic society without repeating the constitutional provision contained in the 1993 Interim Constitution.[21] The failure of the 1996 Constitution to repeat the direction to the Human Rights Commission to be guided by 'norms of international human rights law' in pointing out inconsistencies between legislation and human rights norms does not remove this standard.[22]

The South African common law – a blend of Roman-Dutch and English common law – adopts the monist approach to customary international law. Customary international law is part of South African law and courts are required to 'ascertain and administer' rules of customary international law without the need for proof of law.[23] The common law is given constitutional endorsement by section 232 of the 1996 Constitution which, in language substantially similar to the Interim Constitution, provides that '[c]ustomary international law is law in the Republic unless it is inconsistent with the Constitution or an Act of Parliament'.[24] Although the 1993 and 1996 Constitutions differ on the procedures for the

---

[19] Section 116 of Act 200 of 1993.   [20] Act 54 of 1994.   [21] Section 184 of Act 108 of 1996.

[22] Cf. R. Keightley, 'Public International Law and the Final Constitution', 12 *South African Journal on Human Rights*, 1996, p. 405.

[23] J. Dugard, *International Law. A South African Perspective*, Kenwyn, 1994, pp. 41–51; *South Atlantic Islands Development Corporation Ltd v. Buchan*, 1971 (1) SA p. 234 (C) at p. 238; *Inter-Science Research and Development Services (Pty) Ltd v. Republica Popúlar de Moçambique*, 1980 (2) SA p. 111 (T) at p. 124; *Kaffraria Property Co. (Pty) Ltd v. Government of the Republic of Zambia*, 1980 (2) SA p. 709 (E) at pp. 712, 715.

[24] See also section 231(4) of Act 200 of 1993.

incorporation of treaties into municipal law, both are essentially dualist in their approach.[25]

During the apartheid years South Africa rejected international human rights law and refused to sign any human rights convention. As a party to the United Nations Charter it was, however, subject to the obligations contained in articles 55 and 56 of the Charter to respect, *inter alia*, human rights.[26] However as the Charter had not been incorporated into domestic law, courts of the apartheid era refused to be guided by these provisions in their interpretation of the law.[27] In 1993, before the adoption of the Interim Constitution, the reformed National Party Government signed CEDAW, CAT and CRC. In 1994, the ANC-led government signed the ICCPR, the ICESCR and CERD. In 1995, CRC and CEDAW were ratified. In 1996 the African Charter was ratified. In 1998 CAT, CERD and ICCPR were ratified, leaving only the ICESCR unratified.

B. Common features and differences

Zimbabwe, Namibia and South Africa are all parties to the ICCPR. South Africa and Namibia are parties to CAT. Namibia alone is a party to the Optional Protocol to the ICCPR.

Although all three states are parties to the African Charter, this convention does not have effective monitoring procedures. Therefore, at this stage only Namibia is subject to scrutiny of its human rights record by means of individual petitions to the Human Rights Committee (HRC).

All three states have constitutions which, broadly, recognise the rights contained in the ICCPR, the European Convention on Human Rights (ECHR), the American Convention on Human Rights (American Convention) and the African Charter. Only the South African Constitution expressly directs courts to have regard to such conventions in the interpretation of its municipal law. On the other hand, the law of all three recognises customary international law as part of municipal law.

The constitutions of all three provide for judicial review of the rights contained in their respective constitutions and for the independence of

---

[25] Section 231(3) of Act 200 of 1993; section 231(4) of Act 108 of 1996. See further Keightley, *supra*, note 22 at p. 412.

[26] *Legal Consequences for States of the Continued Presence of South Africa in Namibia (South West Africa)*, ICJ Reports 1971, p. 12.

[27] *S. v. Adams; S. v. Werner*, 1981 (1) SA p. 187 (A) at p. 225; *S. v. Werner*, 1980 (2) SA p. 313 (W) at p. 328.

the judiciary. Perhaps more importantly, the judiciaries of all three have reputations for independence in practice.

Human rights NGOs established during the days of white minority rule continue to function, albeit with reduced funding from abroad, in all three states.

C. The impact of treaty-based human rights standards on domestic law

The people of Zimbabwe and South Africa receive no direct protection from international human rights conventions. Nevertheless they, together with Namibia, which is a party to the Optional Protocol, have benefited indirectly from the norms contained in these conventions as a result, first, of their incorporation into the constitutions of these countries and, secondly, of their application by municipal courts. In all three countries the courts have made frequent use of international human rights jurisprudence. The ECHR and the interpretation placed on its provisions by the European Commission and Court of Human Rights have received the most judicial attention. No doubt the accessibility of the decisions of the European Commission and Court, as well as the familiar method of judicial reasoning employed by these bodies, accounts for this favoured treatment. The ICCPR and the views of the HRC have also been considered on occasion. Other conventions have featured less prominently in judicial decisions.

In most instances courts have simply turned to international human rights law for guidance without explanation of the basis for recourse to this body of law. The similarity of the domestic provisions to those in human rights conventions provides an obvious justification. The presumption of statutory interpretation in favour of compliance with international law provides an additional justification. In the case of South Africa, both the 1993 and the 1996 Constitutions expressly instruct courts to have regard to international human rights law in their interpretation of the Bill of Rights. The extent to which courts have invoked international human rights law and the impact that this has had on domestic law appears from the following survey of judicial decisions in the three countries.

1. ZIMBABWE

The constitutionality of corporal punishment first gave the courts of Zimbabwe an opportunity to invoke international human rights norms. In

S. v. Ncube[28] the Zimbabwe Supreme Court held that the whipping of an adult offender violated the Declaration of Rights' prohibition on 'inhuman or degrading punishment'. It found support for this decision[29] in the judgment of the European Court of Human Rights in *Tyrer v. United Kingdom*.[30] Later it extended this ruling to the whipping of juveniles in *S. v. A Juvenile*.[31] In this case Dumbutshena CJ stated:

> Zimbabwe has a Constitution with a justiciable Bill of Rights. One of its provisions prohibits torture, or inhuman or degrading punishment or other such treatment. It is now possible for an accused person sentenced to a whipping to challenge the constitutionality of the punishment in terms of s. 15(1) [of the Zimbabwe Constitution]. An added advantage is that the Courts of this country are free to import into the interpretation of s. 15(1) interpretations of similar provisions in International and Regional Human Rights Instruments such as, among others, the International Bill of Human Rights, the European Convention for the Protection of Human Rights and Fundamental Freedoms, and the Inter-American Convention on Human Rights. In the end international human rights norms will become part of our domestic human rights law. In this way our domestic human rights jurisdiction is enriched.[32]

Again heavy reliance was placed on the decisions of the European Court of Human Rights holding corporal punishment to be an inhuman and degrading punishment.[33]

In *Catholic Commission for Justice and Peace in Zimbabwe v. Attorney General, Zimbabwe*[34] the Zimbabwe Supreme Court considered the question whether the fact that the appellants had spent several years on death row constituted 'inhuman and degrading punishment' within the meaning of section 15(1) of the Constitution of Zimbabwe. In holding that such treatment – known as the 'death row phenomenon' – violated the prohibition contained in section 15(1), and substituting sentences of life imprisonment for the sentences of death previously imposed on the appellants, Gubbay CJ was strongly influenced[35] by the decision of the European Court of Human Rights in *Soering v. United Kingdom*.[36]

---

[28] 1988 (2) SA p. 702 (ZSC).   [29] Ibid., at pp. 719–21.
[30] European Court of Human Rights, Series A, vol. 26, judgment of 25 April 1978.
[31] 1990 (4) SA p. 151 (ZSC).   [32] Ibid., at p. 155.
[33] Ibid., at pp. 156, 161, 167. In a dissenting judgment McNally JA considered and rejected the decisions of the European Court of Human Rights, pp. 170–3.
[34] 1993 (4) SA 239 (ZSC).   [35] Ibid., at pp. 261–3.
[36] European Court of Human Rights, Series A, vol. 161, judgment of 7 July 1989; 28 *ILM*, 1989, p. 1063.

Decisions of the HRC that failed to follow *Soering* were considered but not followed.[37] Although this judgment of the Zimbabwe Supreme Court was approved by the Privy Council[38] it was not well received by the Zimbabwe legislature which sought to reverse the decision by constitutional amendment.[39]

International human rights instruments, and the interpretation placed on them by monitoring bodies, have also been invoked in cases involving freedom of assembly,[40] freedom of speech,[41] prisoners' rights,[42] freedom of movement[43] and the margin of appreciation to be applied in the implementation of a social security scheme.[44]

2. NAMIBIA

The question of the constitutionality of whipping was also responsible for the Namibian Supreme Court's first recourse to international human rights norms. In *Ex Parte Attorney-General, Namibia: In Re Corporal Punishment*[45] the Namibian Supreme Court held that corporal punishment upon any person violated section 8(2)(b) of the Constitution's prohibition on inhuman or degrading treatment. In delivering the judgment of the Court, Mahomed JA stated:

> [T]he question as to whether a particular form of punishment authorised by the law can properly be said to be inhuman or degrading involves the exercise of a value judgment by the Court. It is however a value judgment which must be articulated and identified objectively, regard being had to

---

[37] 1993 (4) SA 239 at p. 264.
[38] *Pratt v. Attorney General for Jamaica* [1993] 4 All ER p. 769 (PC).
[39] Constitution of Zimbabwe Amendment Act 13 of 1993.
[40] *In Re Munhumeso*, 1995 (1) SA p. 551 (ZS) at p. 557 (European Court of Human Rights).
[41] *Retrofit (Put) Ltd v. Posts and Telecommunications Corporation*, 1996 (1) SA p. 847 (ZSC at pp. 856, 858, 860–1 (European Court of Human Rights and provisions of international human rights instruments).
[42] *Woods v. Minister of Justice, Legal and Parliamentary Affairs* 1995 (1) SA p. 703 (ZSC) at pp. 705–6 (European Court of Human Rights).
[43] *Rattigan v. Chief Immigration Officer, Zimbabwe*, 1995 (2) SA p. 182 (ZSC) at pp. 189 (Human Rights Committee) and 190 (European Court of Human Rights).
[44] *Nyambirai v. Social Security Authority*, 1996 (1) SA p. 639 (ZSC) at pp. 644–7 (European Court of Human Rights and international human rights instruments).
[45] 1991 (3) SA p. 76 (NmSC).

the contemporary norms, aspirations, expectations and sensitivities of the Namibian people as expressed in its national institutions and its Constitution, and further having regard to the emerging consensus of values in the civilised international community (of which Namibia is a part) which Namibians share. This is not a static exercise. It is a continually evolving dynamic. What may have been acceptable as a just form of punishment some decades ago, may appear to be manifestly inhuman or degrading today. Yesterday's orthodoxy might appear to be today's heresy. The provisions of art. 8(2) of the Constitution are not peculiar to Namibia; they articulate a temper throughout the civilised world which has manifested itself consciously since the Second World War. Exactly the same or similar articles are to be found in other instruments. (See for example art. 3 of the European Convention for the protection of Human Rights and Fundamental Freedoms; art. 1(1) of the German Constitution; art. 7 of the Constitution of Botswana; art. 15(1) of the Zimbabwean Constitution.) In the interpretation of such articles there is strong support for the view that the imposition of corporal punishment on adults by organs of the State is indeed degrading or inhuman and inconsistent with civilised values pertaining to the administration of justice and the punishment of offenders.[46]

As with the Supreme Court of Zimbabwe, the Court relied heavily[47] on the decision of the European Court of Human Rights in *Tyrer v. United Kingdom* outlawing corporal punishment.[48]

The following year in *Minister of Defence, Namibia v. Mwadinghi*[49] the Court stated that because the Namibian Constitution includes a Declaration of Fundamental Human Rights and Freedoms which are 'international in character', in their interpretation 'they call for the application of international human-rights norms'.

In *Kauesa v. Minister of Home Affairs*[50] the Namibian High Court examined the ECHR, the decision of the European Court of Human Rights in *Engel and Others v. Netherlands*,[51] the ICCPR, the American Convention, the Universal Declaration of Human Rights, the African Charter and CERD in its consideration of the limits of 'hate speech' under the Namibian Constitution.[52] O'Linn J stated that where the provisions of the Namibian Constitution were equivocal or uncertain as to their scope of application, the provisions of international conventions should at least be given considerable weight in interpreting and defining their scope.[53] On appeal, the

---

[46] Ibid., at pp. 86–7.   [47] Ibid., at pp. 88–90.   [48] *Supra*, note 30.
[49] 1992 (2) SA p. 354 (NmS) at p. 362.   [50] 1995 (1) SA p. 51 (Nm).
[51] European Court of Human Rights, Series A, vol. 22, judgment of 8 June 1976.
[52] 1995 (1) SA at pp. 75–6, 89, 91, 118–19.   [53] Ibid., at pp. 86–7.

Supreme Court likewise invoked support from international human rights instruments.[54]

In other decisions the courts of Namibia have reaffirmed the need to be guided by international rights norms.[55]

3. SOUTH AFRICA

(a) Before 1994

In the last decade of apartheid[56] human rights NGOs embarked on a pro-gramme of public education in the field of international human rights standards. First, arguments founded on international human rights norms were raised in support of challenges to the laws of apartheid. For example, in *S. v. Werner*[57] an unsuccessful attempt was made to persuade the Appel-late Division of the Supreme Court of South Africa to set aside the estab-lishment of separate residential zones for different races on the ground that this was in conflict with the human rights provisions in the United Nations Charter, which were binding on South Africa, albeit not incorporated into domestic law.

Second, seminars were held for judges and lawyers to introduce them to international human rights treaties and to suggest ways in which they might be implemented in domestic courts. In 1988 this strategy appeared to pay off when Judge Didcott, a regular participant in these seminars, invoked the ICCPR and the ECHR to support a finding that an indigent person might not be sentenced to a substantial jail term without counsel.[58] This reasoning was rejected by other courts[59] and simply ignored by the Appellate Division.[60] Unincorporated International Labour Organisation conventions dealing with unfair labour practices were, however, applied by

---

[54] *Kauesa v. Minister of Home Affairs*, 1996 (4) SA p. 965 (NmSC) at pp. 977–83 (European Court of Human Rights).

[55] *S. v. Tcoeib*, 1993 (1) SA Criminal Law Reports p. 274 (Nm) at p. 287; *Cultura 2000 v. Government of the Republic of Namibia*, 1993 (2) SA p. 12 (Nm) at p. 22.

[56] See J. Dugard (ed.) *The Last Years of Apartheid: Civil Liberties in South Africa*, New York, 1992.

[57] Reported as *S. v. Adams; S. v. Werner*, 1981 (1) SA p. 187 (A) at p. 225; *S. v. Werner* 1980 (2) SA p. 313 (W) at p. 328.

[58] *S. v. Khanyile*, 1988 (3) SA p. 795 (N) at p. 801. This decision was followed in *S. v. Davids; S. v. Dladla*, 1989 (4) SA p. 172 (N).

[59] *S. v. Rudman*, 1989 (3) SA p. 368 (ECD) at pp. 375–6; *S. v. Mthwana*, 1989 (4) SA p. 361 (N).

[60] *S. v. Rudman; S. v. Mthwana*, 1992 (1) SA p. 343 (A).

the Industrial Court[61] and the United Nations Standard Minimum Rules (SMR) were invoked as a guide to the interpretation of laws governing the treatment of prisoners.[62]

Third, academic lawyers started to attack the apartheid legal order on the basis that it violated international treaty standards, whereas before such attacks had been premised largely on violations of the rule of law.[63] This approach was fuelled by the appearance of the *South African Journal on Human Rights* in 1985.

Activities of this kind contributed substantially to the development of a human rights culture in South Africa. When political change came to South Africa in the early 1990s, lawyers who had played an active role in the anti-apartheid strategies outlined above were employed in the drafting of the Interim Constitution of 1993 and the 1996 Constitution. In part this explains why international human rights norms featured so prominently in the drafting of these instruments.[64]

One of the ironies of the new mood in South Africa in the early 1990s was that the courts of two of the unrecognised Homelands – Ciskei[65] and Bophuthatswana[66] – whose Constitutions included Bills of Rights, turned to international human rights instruments for guidance in the interpretation of their Constitutions. In the case of Ciskei this was made obligatory after 1991 by a constitutional provision which declared that:

> The general rules of public international law shall be an integral part of the law of Ciskei . . . And shall take precedence over the laws of Ciskei and shall directly create rights and duties for the people of Ciskei.[67]

---

[61] See D. Woolfrey, 'The Application of International Labour Norms to South African Law', 12 *South African Yearbook of International Law*, 1986–1987, p. 135.

[62] In *S. v. Staggie*, 1990 (1) SA Criminal Law Reports p. 669 (C) and *S. v. Daniels*, 1991 (2) SA Criminal Law Reports p. 403 the Court held that corporal punishment should not be imposed on convicted prisoners because it violated article 31 of the SMR.

[63] See J. Dugard, *Human Rights and the South African Legal Order*, Princeton, 1978.

[64] See R. Keightley, 'International Human Rights Norms in a New South Africa', *South African Journal on Human Rights*, 1992, p. 171; D. van Wyk et al., *supra*, note 8.

[65] *African National Congress (Border Branch) v. Chairman, Council of State of the Republic of Ciskei*, 1992 (4) SA p. 434 (Ck) at pp. 447, 449, 450; *Ntenteni v. Chairman, Ciskei Council of State*, 1993 (4) SA p. 546 (Ck) at pp. 554–5; *Bongopi v. Chairman of the Council of State, Ciskei*, 1992 (3) SA p. 250 (Ck) at p. 277; *Matinkica v. Council of State, Republic of Ciskei*, 1994 (4) SA p. 472 (Ck).

[66] *Nyamakazi v. President of Bophuthatswana*, 1992 (4) SA p. 540 (B) at pp. 564, 570, 579, 581–2; *Yates v. University of Bophuthatswana*, 1994 (3) SA p. 815 (B) at p. 846.

[67] Article 3.

Commenting on this provision, the Ciskei Supreme Court stated in *African National Congress (Border Branch) v. Chairman, Council of State of the Republic of Ciskei*[68] that it made 'a whole new sphere of law' applicable to Ciskei and obliged the Court 'to look at what has become known as "common standards of internationally agreed, and legally binding, rules collectively known as international human-rights law"'. Accordingly, the Court considered the Universal Declaration of Human Rights (together with a number of decisions of the European Court of Human Rights) in its interpretation of the fundamental rights contained in the Ciskei Constitution.

(b) After 1994

South African courts responded with surprising alacrity to the new legal order introduced by the Interim Constitution. Although a number of cases heard by the ordinary courts before the establishment of the Constitutional Court relied on decisions of the European Court of Human Rights,[69] it was the first major decision of the Constitutional Court, *S. v. Makwanyane*,[70] involving the constitutionality of the death penalty, that set the scene for the consideration of international human rights norms. Here the President of the Court, Mr Justice Chaskalson, made it clear that the Constitution required courts to have regard to the whole *corpus* of international human rights law, and not only to treaties to which South Africa was a party.[71] *In casu* he concluded, on the basis of article 6 of the ICCPR, article 4(2) of the American Convention, article 2 of the ECHR, and article 4 of the African Charter (which all qualify the right to life in the case of capital punishment), that 'capital punishment is not prohibited by public international law'.[72] This finding, which takes no account of the later Protocols to the

---

[68] *Supra*, note 65 at p. 444. See also at pp. 445–51.

[69] *S. v. Williams and Five Similar Cases*, 1994 (4) SA p. 126 (C) (constitutionality of corporal punishment: European Court of Human Rights at p. 139); *S. v. H.*, 1995 (1) SA p. 120 (C) (permissibility of homosexual acts; European Court of Human Rights at p. 127); *Shabalala v. Attorney General, Transvaal; Gumede v. Attorney General, Transvaal*, 1995 (1) SA p. 608 (T) (right of access to police docket; European Court of Human Rights at pp. 640–1); *De Klerk v. Du Plessis*, 1995 (2) SA p. 40 (T) (vertical application of Chapter 3 of the Constitution; several human rights conventions examined at pp. 47–8); *Government of the Republic of South Africa v. 'Sunday Times' Newspaper*, 1995 (2) SA p. 221 (T) (freedom of expression; European Court of Human Rights at p. 227); *Gardner v. Whitaker*, 1995 (2) SA p. 672 (E) (freedom of expression; European Court of Human Rights at p. 683).

[70] *Supra*, note 16.   [71] Ibid., at pp. 413–14.   [72] Ibid., at p. 414.

ICCPR and the European and American Conventions prohibiting the death penalty,[73] did not deter him from finding that the unqualified assertion of the right to life[74] in the South African Constitution led to a different conclusion. The President did, however, find support for the view that the death penalty is cruel and inhuman[75] in the judgment of the European Court of Human Rights in *Soering v. United Kingdom*[76] and the views of the HRC in *Kindler v. Canada*[77] and *Ng v. Canada*.[78]

Makwanyane was followed by *S. v. Williams*[79] in which the Constitutional Court found corporal punishment to be unconstitutional on the grounds that it violated section 11(2) of the Interim Constitution which provided that 'no person shall be subject to cruel, inhuman or degrading treatment or punishment'. After stating that '[i]n common with many of the rights entrenched in the Constitution, the wording of this section conforms to a large extent with most international human rights instruments',[80] the Court examined the jurisprudence of the HRC and the European Commission and Court of Human Rights on the corresponding provisions in these treaties. *Tyrer v. United Kingdom*[81] and *Campbell and Cosans v. United Kingdom*[82] featured prominently in the judgment.[83]

Subsequent decisions of the Constitutional Court have continued this practice. In *Ferreira and others v. Powell NO and others*[84] judges turned to international jurisprudence for guidance on the meaning of 'liberty' and 'security of person'; in *S. v. Rens*[85] the Court invoked a decision of the European Court of Human Rights on fairness in appellate proceedings; in *Coetzee v. Government of the Republic of South Africa*[86] international human rights norms were used to uphold a constitutional challenge to imprisonment for judgment debts; in *Bernstein v. Bester*[87] decisions of the European Court of Human Rights were considered in an examination of the right to privacy; and in *In re Gauteng School Education Bill 1995*[88] Sachs J examined

[73] Cf. the judgment of O'Regan J which does consider these protocols, ibid., at p. 505.
[74] Section 9 of Act 200 of 1993.
[75] See too the Opinion of Mahomed J, *supra*, note 16, at p. 493.   [76] *Supra*, note 36.
[77] UN Doc. CCPR/48/D/470/1991; View of 11 November 1993; 98 *ILR* p. 426.
[78] UN Doc. CCPR/49/D/469/1991; View of 7 December 1994; 98 *ILR* p. 479.
[79] 1995 (3) SA p. 632 (CC).   [80] Ibid., at p. 639.
[81] European Court of Human Rights, Series A, vol. 26, judgment of 25 April 1978.
[82] European Court of Human Rights, Series A, vol. 48, 1982.
[83] 1995 (3) SA p. 632 (CC) at pp. 640, 643, 645–7.
[84] 1996 (1) SA p. 984 (CC) at pp. 1035–6, 1085.   [85] 1996 (1) SA p. 1218 (CC) at p. 1225.
[86] 1995 (4) SA p. 631 (CC) at pp. 660–3.   [87] 1996 (2) SA p. 751 (CC) at pp. 790–2, 805.
[88] 1996 (3) SA p. 165 (CC) at pp. 190–204.

the practice of the League of Nations and the United Nations on minority rights in a challenge to the validity of an education bill by a minority group.

The constitutionality of South Africa's controversial amnesty legislation was challenged by the families of some of the best known victims of police brutality during the apartheid era, including the widow of Steve Biko, in *Azanian People's Organization (AZAPO) and others v. President of the Republic of South Africa and others.*[89] Here it was argued that section 20(7) of the Promotion of National Unity and Reconciliation Act,[90] granting amnesty from both criminal prosecutions and civil claims to members of the apartheid police responsible for killing anti-apartheid activists, violated section 22 of the Interim Constitution which provided that 'every person shall have the right to have justiciable disputes settled by a court of law'. In support of this challenge the applicants argued 'that the State was obliged by international law to prosecute those responsible for gross human rights violations and that the provisions of section 20(7) which authorised amnesty for such offences constituted a breach of international law'.[91] Unfortunately the Court, in finding that the amnesty legislation was constitutional, declined to examine the vexed question of whether norms of customary international law, generated by international human rights conventions, require a successor regime to prosecute and punish members of a previous regime guilty of egregious human rights violations.[92] This judgment stands in sharp contrast to earlier decisions of the Constitutional Court which show a ready willingness to be guided by international human rights law.

D. Conclusion

Although human rights would be more secure in Zimbabwe and South Africa if the individual enjoyed a right of petition to the HRC and other

---

[89] 1996 (4) SA p. 671 (CC). The judgment of the Cape Provincial Division in this case is reported in *Azanian People's Organization (AZAPO) and others v. Truth and Reconciliation Commission and others*, 1996 (4) SA p. 562 (C).

[90] Act 34 of 1995. [91] 1996 (4) SA p. 562(C) at p. 687.

[92] See in support of this view, D. Orentlicher, 'Settling Accounts: The Duty to Prosecute Human Rights Violations of a Prior Regime', 100 *YLJ*, 1991, p. 2537; K. Asmal, 'Victims, Survivors, and Citizens – Human Rights, Reparations and Reconciliation', 8 *South African Journal on Human Rights*, 1992, p. 491; M. Cherif Bassiouni, *Crimes Against Humanity in International Law*, Boston, 1992, pp. 503–8; *Impunity and Human Rights in International Law and Practice* (ed. N. Roht-Arriaza), New York, 1995, chapters 3 and 4.

supervisory committees, there can be little doubt that human rights are more effectively protected in these countries than in many countries which recognise a right of individual petition but provide inadequate safeguards in their municipal law. While international protective measures are important, it is essential, in the first instance, that municipal law provide legal protection to the rights contained in international human rights conventions. The experience of Zimbabwe, Namibia and South Africa illustrates this truth.

13

USES AND ABUSES OF THE TREATY REPORTING PROCEDURE: HONG KONG BETWEEN TWO SYSTEMS

ANDREW BYRNES*

The [third periodic report under the International Covenant on Civil and Political Rights (ICCPR)] was only drawn to the attention of the public when a visiting member of Amnesty International told the local media of its existence in August 1988.[1]

The tendency [on the part of non-govermental organisations (NGOs)], rather, has been to zero in on two or three issues to the exclusion of all else, and then for all the NGOs to do the same thing. So the result – and it was especially marked, I think, at the examination of the third periodic report of the United Kingdom – was that the United Kingdom was deluged with questions relating to Hong Kong and to the Northern Ireland terrorist provisions. Now the selection of one or two important issues, no matter how important . . . precludes a well-informed across-the-board examination. Important issues receive no attention.[2]

A. Introduction

As a dependent territory of the United Kingdom until its return to the People's Republic of China on 1 July 1997, Hong Kong benefited from the

* The author would like to thank Margarita Lacabe, Sarah Joseph, Sharon Ladin, Marsha Freeman, Jane Winter, Chris Ingelse, and Jeremy Croft, all of whom kindly provided him with information based on their own experiences with various reporting procedures. Research for this paper was also supported in part by a research grant made by the Hong Kong Research Grants Council (Hong Kong Treaty Project) and the Committee on Research and Conference Grants of the University of Hong Kong. The author is especially grateful to John Dean for his helpful comments on a draft of this chapter.
[1] J. Chan and K. Lau, 'Some Reflections on the Human Rights Committee's Hearing of the United Kingdom Second Report on Dependent Territories, held November 4–5, 1988 in Geneva', 20 *HKLJ*, 1990, p. 150, at p. 151 n. 8.
[2] R. Higgins, 'Foreword', in *The International Covenant on Civil and Political Rights and United Kingdom Law* (eds. D. J. Harris and S. Joseph), Oxford, 1995, p. xi, at p. xiv.

United Kingdom's participation in the six major United Nations human rights treaties, the implementation of which is subject to monitoring by committees of independent experts. While the United Kingdom did not always extend the treaties to Hong Kong at the same time as it ratified them in respect of its metropolitan territory, by the end of 1996 it had extended all six of the treaties to Hong Kong.[3]

This chapter examines the experience of reporting under the United Nations treaties in the period leading up to the resumption of Chinese sovereignty in July 1997, and seeks to evaluate the impact of that process on the protection of human rights in Hong Kong and to identify the reasons for that impact. It also briefly discusses the future of reporting under the treaties, now that Hong Kong has become a Special Administrative Region (SAR) of the People's Republic of China.

B. Human rights concerns and Hong Kong's return to China

From the mid-1980s the approaching resumption of sovereignty by China over Hong Kong gave rise to considerable concern about the continued enjoyment of human rights guaranteed by the treaties applicable to Hong Kong, most (though not all) of which were at the time protected under Hong Kong law and practice.[4] Despite the guarantee of a 'high degree of

---

[3] The International Covenant on Civil and Political Rights (ICCPR), the International Covenant on Economic, Social and Cultural Rights (ICESCR), and the Convention on the Elimination of Racial Discrimination (CERD) were extended to Hong Kong at the same time as the United Kingdom ratified them in respect of its metropolitan territory. The Convention against Torture (CAT), the Convention on the Rights of the Child (CRC), and the Convention on the Elimination of Discrimination against Women (CEDAW) were all extended to Hong Kong later than they were applied to the metropolitan territory. These delays were due in part to the Hong Kong Government's views and also the need, after the conclusion of the 1984 Sino-British Joint Declaration, to seek the approval of the Chinese Government to the extension of treaties that were intended to continue to apply to Hong Kong after 1 July 1997.

[4] While prior to July 1997 (and indeed after that date) many of the rights guaranteed by the human rights treaties have been protected under the general law of Hong Kong and, from 1991, by the Hong Kong Bill of Rights Ordinance (Cap 383), there were still several important areas in which Hong Kong law and practice fell short of international standards. It must also be recognised that a number of important statutory and constitutional reforms, which were intended to protect human rights directly or indirectly, were introduced relatively late in the period of UK rule over Hong Kong. Nevertheless, it is clear that even in colonial Hong Kong the level of legal protection and actual enjoyment of many human rights was considerably higher than that in China.

autonomy' embodied in the 1984 Sino-British Joint Declaration[5] and the Basic Law (which contains its own guarantees of human rights),[6] there was considerable concern that these might not be enough to ensure the continued enjoyment of those rights. As various efforts were undertaken to try to avoid any erosion of rights, many saw international monitoring of the situation as an important safeguard or, if necessary, an avenue to publicise any regression. While persuading other governments to monitor the situation in Hong Kong was seen as important, the United Nations treaty bodies (in particular the Human Rights Committee (HRC) and the Committee of the International Covenant of Economic, Social and Cultural Rights (ICESCR)) were seen as important fora for this continuing scrutiny of Hong Kong.

The impending change of sovereignty, and the threats some perceived it as posing, coincided with the due dates for the submission of a number of periodic reports under treaties which had been applicable to Hong Kong for some time,[7] as well as initial reports under two treaties just extended to Hong Kong.[8] As a result, in the period from November 1994 to March 1997, the human rights treaty bodies examined reports on Hong Kong on eight occasions.[9] This was unusual compared with the normal frequency of state party appearances before the supervisory bodies. Throughout this period NGO participation in the reporting procedure was, on the whole, active and extensive, both in Hong Kong and in Geneva. While the very intensity of the experience and the peculiarity of Hong Kong's political situation make the case in some respects atypical, aspects of the experience may be instructive.

This chapter examines the strategies used by NGOs in their utilisation of the reporting procedures under the various treaties, their influence on the process and substance of the reviews, and the impact of the review on government decision-making in Hong Kong. Twenty-five years ago many

---

[5] 1399 UNTS 36, 23 *ILM*, 1984, p. 1366, reproduced in *Public Law and Human Rights: A Hong Kong Sourcebook* (eds. A. Byrnes and J. Chan), Singapore, 1993, at p. 43.

[6] Basic Law of the Hong Kong Special Administrative Region, 29 *ILM*, 1990, p. 1511, reproduced in Byrnes and Chan, *supra*, note 5, at p. 81. See generally Yash Ghai, *Hong Kong's New Constitutional Law: The Resumption of Chinese Sovereignty and the Basic Law*, Hong Kong, 1997.

[7] The two Covenants and CERD.   [8] CAT and CRC.

[9] November 1994 (ICESCR Committee); October 1995 (HRC); November 1995 (CAT Committee); March 1996 (CERD Committee); October 1996 (CRC Committee); October 1996 (HRC); November 1996 (ICESCR Committee); and March 1997 (CERD Committee).

considered that NGO information would play no part in the public work of the committees; for many years there was disagreement over the manner in which such material could be made available to the committees and referred to in their discussions.[10] In the 1980s and 1990s, however, the fundamental importance of independent non-governmental information to the effective discharge of the treaty bodies' functions has been increasingly recognised,[11] and committees receive information and materials from NGOs, both informally and, where possible, formally.[12] While the review of state reports may once have involved only a dialogue between the committee and the state party, the importance of NGOs in the process has nowadays inserted a third interlocutor into the dialogue.

C. The background: Hong Kong and the treaty bodies prior to 1994

Hong Kong had, of course, been considered by the treaty bodies before the intensive activity of the 1990s. As the Convention on the Elimination of Racial Discrimination (CERD) had applied to the territory since 1969, and the two Covenants since 1976, the United Kingdom had already submitted reports which included material on Hong Kong and other dependent territories and which had been considered by the responsible supervisory body.[13]

---

[10] See, e.g., B. Graefrath, 'Reporting and Complaint Systems under Universal Human Rights Treaties', in *Human Rights in a Changing East-West Perspective* (eds. A. Rosas and J. Helgesen), London and New York, 1990, p. 290, at pp. 301–3.

[11] Though not without the occasional challenge: see International League for Human Rights, 'Sources of Information used by the Treaty Committees', a memorandum prepared for the Chairpersons of the Treaty Bodies, September 1990 (rebutting efforts to limit the power of treaty bodies to take into account non-governmental information in their review of reports).

[12] See generally the chapters on each of the treaty bodies in *The United Nations and Human Rights: A Critical Appraisal* (ed. P. Alston), Oxford, 1992; D. McGoldrick, *The Human Rights Committee: Its Role in the Development of the International Covenant on Civil and Political Rights*, Oxford, 1991, pp. 77–9; M. Craven, *The International Covenant on Economic, Social and Cultural Rights: A Perspective on its Development*, Oxford, 1995, pp. 75–6, 80–3; and International Law Association Committee on International Human Rights Law and Practice, *First Report of the Committee*, in International Law Association, *Report of the Sixty-Seventh Conference, Helsinki, 1996*, London, 1996, p. 336. For recent guides directed to NGOs see M. O'Flaherty, *Human Rights and Practice before the UN Treaty Bodies*, London, 1996, pp. 1–15 and British-Irish Rights Watch, *Human Rights, Human Wrongs: A Guide to the Human Rights Machinery of the United Nations*, London, 1996.

[13] For the details see A. Byrnes and J. Chan, *supra*, note 5, at pp. 243–4, 272–3, 284–5.

However, with the exception of the report examined by the HRC in 1988, the preparation of these reports passed almost completely unnoticed by the Hong Kong community (other than the officials involved in the preparation of material for inclusion in the report). Neither the reports nor their examination by the committees were given any publicity, before or afterwards; Hong Kong Government representatives were not included on the United Kingdom delegation, and Hong Kong NGOs were not involved in the hearings. In this manner passed the review of twelve reports under CERD (up to and including the 1994 hearing)[14] and four reports under the ICESCR.[15]

The HRC's hearings on Hong Kong were an exception to this trend. While there had been virtually no input from Hong Kong at the hearings on the initial report in 1979,[16] consideration of the second periodic report in 1988 attracted significantly more NGO interest. Although NGOs learnt about the submission of the report almost by accident,[17] a number of NGOs made submissions and attended the hearing.[18]

Consideration of the third periodic report in 1991 – the first occasion on which Hong Kong was considered by one of the treaty bodies after the crushing of the pro-democracy movement in the People's Republic of China in June 1989 – aroused even more interest both among NGOs and the community in general.[19] Once again the Committee was provided with a large volume of material by local NGOs,[20] a number of which attended

---

[14] Ibid., at pp. 284–5.

[15] Ibid., at pp. 272–3. The initial reports in respect of Hong Kong were submitted and considered by the Working Group of Governmental Experts as follows: articles 6–9, submitted in 1978 (UN Doc. E/1978/8/Add. 9) and considered in 1980 (UN Doc. E/1980/WG 1/SR 19); articles 10–12, submitted in 1981 (UN Doc. E/1980/6/Add. 25) and considered in 1981 (UN Doc. E/1981/WG 1/SR 16 and 17); and articles 13–15, submitted in 1982 (UN Doc. E/1982/3/Add. 16) and considered in 1982 (UN Doc. E/1982/WG 1/SR 21). The second periodic report in respect of articles 6–9 was submitted in 1984 (UN Doc. E/1984/7/Add. 20) and considered in 1984 (UN Doc. E/1984/WG 1/SR 14 and 17).

[16] See generally N. Jayawickrama, 'Hong Kong and the International Protection of Human Rights', in *Human Rights in Hong Kong* (ed. R. Wacks), Hong Kong, 1992, p. 120.

[17] See Chan and Lau, *supra*, note 1, at p. 151 n. 8.

[18] For a description of those involved and the role they played, as well as a general summary of the issues raised, see Chan and Lau, *supra*, note 1; Jayawickrama, *supra*, note 16, at p. 136.

[19] On this occasion, following criticism by the HRC of the Government's failure to distribute copies of the report widely in Hong Kong, the Hong Kong Government did publish the report in pamphlet form in English and Chinese, for presentation to the Legislative Council (LegCo) and general distribution, a practice which has regularly been followed since that time.

[20] See Hong Kong Bar Association, *Submission of the Hong Kong Bar Association to the UN Human Rights Committee on the Third Periodic Report of Hong Kong* (March 1991);

the hearings in New York,[21] and the issue of Hong Kong received what some considered a disproportionate share of the Committee's time.[22] The occasion attracted more media interest and put pressure on the Government to amend existing laws in a number of areas, a development given further impetus by the pending enactment of the ICCPR as a part of domestic law in the form of the Hong Kong Bill of Rights Ordinance (enacted in June 1991).[23]

At this time, several events contributed to an increased sense that many human rights issues needed urgent attention. They also gave rise to a perception that international standards and fora were potentially important for addressing these issues. They included the vividly remembered incidents of June 1989, the adoption in March 1991 of the Basic Law which was to be the constitution of the Hong Kong Special Administrative Region after 30 June 1997, the enactment of the Bill of Rights in June 1991, and the introduction in 1991 of the first directly elected seats in Hong Kong's Legislative Council. The focus at this stage was still overwhelmingly the field of civil and political rights, the ICCPR and the HRC; there was relatively little awareness of treaties other than the ICCPR and the possibilities that reporting under other treaties might afford for raising Hong Kong issues internationally.

Within four years the almost exclusive focus on the ICCPR had changed. The ICCPR and the HRC were still the best known of the international instruments and procedures among activists and government. But NGOs had become aware of the other treaties and had begun to use the review of

JUSTICE, *Human Rights in Hong Kong 1988–91: A Comment on the Third Periodic Report of Hong Kong under Article 40 of the International Covenant on Civil and Political Rights* (March 1991); *Report by the Hong Kong Council of Women on the Third Periodic Report by Hong Kong under Article 40 of the International Covenant on Civil and Political Rights* (1991); Amnesty International, *Summary of Amnesty International's Concerns in Hong Kong*, AI Index ASA 19/01/91 (February 1991); International League for Human Rights, *Ensuring Hong Kong's Rights Now and After 1997: Comments on the Report of the United Kingdom to the UN Human Rights Committee concerning Hong Kong* (March 1991).

[21] See Jayawickrama, *supra*, note 16, at p. 138.

[22] See Higgins, *supra*, note 2, at p. xiv, and D. J. Harris, 'The International Covenant on Civil and Political Rights and the United Kingdom: An Introduction', in Harris and Joseph, *supra*, note 2, p. 1, at p. 44.

[23] For the text of the Ordinance, see Byrnes and Chan, *supra*, note 5, at p. 218. See generally A. Byrnes, 'And Some Have Bills of Rights Thrust Upon Them: The Experience of Hong Kong's Bill of Rights', in *Promoting Human Rights Through Bills of Rights: Comparative Perspectives* (ed. P. Alston), Oxford, 1999, chapter 9.

reports under those treaties to raise a wide variety of issues, going beyond those raised under the ICCPR.[24]

Apart from Hong Kong's special situation and the resulting increased concern with rights issues, a number of factors contributed to this broader and more energetic use of the treaty bodies. These included increased interest by a number of grassroots organisations in the use of the international human rights discourse to bolster their work; the emergence of new human rights groups; the extension of further human rights conventions to Hong Kong; the increasing democratic and liberal element in Hong Kong's Legislative Council that saw in the reporting procedure an important opportunity to influence government policy; and the role played by academics in disseminating information and in providing fora for the critical examination of the reports submitted by the Government. These factors, combined with the receptivity of the treaty bodies to non-governmental input, to bring about a period of considerable activity and to put considerable pressure on the Government to respond to criticism of its policies.

D. Developments from 1994

This section describes the background to the hearings that took place before a number of the treaty bodies from November 1994 until November 1996.[25]

1. THE ICESCR COMMITTEE (NOVEMBER 1994)

The November 1994 hearings before the ICESCR Committee can be seen as a watershed in the process.[26] They are described here in some detail because

---

[24] There were, broadly speaking, two different types of concern with the reporting procedure. A number of groups were concerned to utilise each occasion to raise a number of the same issues. Other groups, such as those focusing on racial discrimination or children's rights were primarily concerned with thematic conventions. However, one of the developments was that these groups began to raise these issues not just under the convention that applied most obviously, but also under others.

[25] The author attended the hearings of all the treaty bodies described here, the only exception being the examination by the CERD Committee in March 1997 of the fourteenth periodic report in respect of Hong Kong.

[26] See generally A. Byrnes, 'Will the Government put its Money Where its Mouth is? The Verdict of the UN Committee on Economic, Social and Cultural Rights on Hong Kong's Human Rights Record', 25 *HKLJ*, 1995, p. 156.

in many respects they set the pattern for later hearings, and because they were important in defining the government's thinking on how to approach those hearings.

In November 1993, the United Kingdom Government submitted its second periodic reports under the ICESCR Committee in respect of Hong Kong. In early 1994, the Hong Kong Human Rights Commission,[27] in conjunction with the University of Hong Kong, organised a training session for local NGOs on the human rights mechanisms of the United Nations, in particular the reporting procedures. This workshop was intended to lay the basis for a loosely coordinated network of NGOs which would help ensure that the process of review of the Government's second periodic reports under articles 10–15 of the ICESCR would advance the issues with which they were concerned. One immediate result was the submission in June 1994 to the ICESCR Committee's pre-sessional working group of material from various NGOs, thus ensuring inclusion of those concerns in written questions submitted to the United Kingdom Government prior to the hearings scheduled for November 1994.[28]

Shortly afterwards, the Constitutional Affairs Panel of the Legislative Council, at the urging of NGOs, held hearings to examine the government report. After hearing submissions from a number of NGOs, it prepared a report of its own.[29] (Two members of the Panel subsequently attended the Committee's hearings in Geneva.) In October 1994, the Faculty of Law at the University of Hong Kong organised a seminar at which local experts in a number of areas were asked critically to review sections of the report. A member of the Committee who was the country rapporteur for the United Kingdom/Hong Kong was invited to participate in the seminar[30] and to

---

[27] A non-governmental coalition of a dozen or so groups involved in human rights work in a variety of fields.

[28] For the list of questions, see UN Doc. E/C.12/1994/WP.14, reproduced in *Bill of Rights Bulletin* (eds. A. Byrnes and J. Chan), vol. 3, no. 3, April 1995, Appendix B.

[29] *Submission of the Panel on Constitutional Development of the Legislative Council of Hong Kong to the United Nations Committee on Economic, Social and Cultural Rights on the Second Periodic Report on Hong Kong regarding Articles 10–15 of the International Covenant on Economic, Social and Cultural Rights*, July 1994.

[30] V. Bonoan-Dandan, 'The International Covenant on Economic, Social and Cultural Rights and the Work of the Committee on Economic, Social and Cultural Rights', paper presented at a seminar on Hong Kong and the Implementation of the International Covenant on Economic, Social and Cultural Rights, Faculty of Law, University of Hong Kong, 15 October 1994.

meet with various NGOs. A compilation of the papers presented at the seminar was provided to all members of the Committee.[31]

This preliminary work was followed by a strong representation of NGOs at the ICESCR Committee's session, as well as the provision of additional information by a number of NGOs. The NGOs made oral presentations (including the showing of video material on caged homes in Hong Kong) on the opening day of the session during the meeting set aside for NGO presentations, in the company of such other entities as the Government of Gibraltar. The provision of additional information to members during the discussion of the report with the United Kingdom Government, and further lobbying of the Committee in response to the additional material and oral answers provided by the Government, followed.

The United Kingdom Government had sent a sizeable delegation, with six of the nine members coming from Hong Kong, headed by the Solicitor-General. The delegation had provided a considerable amount of information in response to the Committee's questions, though there were fundamental differences of opinion between the Committee and the Government on a number of important issues.

Despite the Government's efforts, the concluding observations adopted by the Committee at the end of the session were sharply critical of the Government in many areas.[32] The detail and vigour of the criticism appears to have taken the Government by surprise;[33] its response was rather negative so far as suggestions relating to changes in laws or policies were concerned.[34] In a formal response, which took the form of a submission to the

---

[31] G. Edwards and A. Byrnes (compilers), *Hong Kong and the Implementation of the International Covenant on Economic, Social and Cultural Rights*, proceedings of a seminar held at the University of Hong Kong, 15 October 1994. Cf. M. Nowak, 'Die Durchsetzung der UNO Menschenrechtskonventionen in Österreich', in *70 Jahre Republik: Grund- und Menschenrechte in Österreich – Grundlagen, Entwicklung und internationale Verbindungen* (eds. R. Machacek, W. Pahr and G. Stadler), Kehl am Rhein, 1991, p. 703, at p. 718 (noting that after the publication of Austria's initial ICCPR report Amnesty International-Austria, the Austrian National Commission for UNESCO and the Austrian League for the United Nations held a symposium in Vienna at which the Austrian report was subject to critique).

[32] For the text of the concluding observations, see UN Doc. E/C.12/1994/19 (1994).

[33] This may have been due in part to the expectations created by the rather ineffectual review by the pre-sessional working group of the earlier reports under the ICESCR and the fact that this was the first occasion on which Hong Kong had been exposed to the developing practice of the treaty bodies of issuing concluding observations. The Government also took exception to the substance of most of the detailed criticisms.

[34] For details, see Byrnes, *supra*, note 26.

Constitutional Affairs Panel of the Legislative Council,[35] the administration essentially reiterated the positions already advanced before the ICESCR Committee, asserting that the Government was best placed to decide how the rights guaranteed by the Covenant should be implemented.

2. THE HUMAN RIGHTS COMMITTEE (OCTOBER 1995)

The lead-up to the examination of the fourth periodic report in respect of Hong Kong under the ICCPR saw a similar sequence of events. Following publication of the government report,[36] the Legislative Council held hearings, inviting NGOs to provide it with information. The University of Hong Kong again convened a seminar in which detailed critiques of the report were prepared by local experts and activists. This meeting was attended by two members of the HRC[37] invited to Hong Kong for that purpose; they also had the opportunity to consult with NGOs during their stay. The hearing itself – scheduled to deal only with Hong Kong – was well attended by NGOs, who provided a substantial body of written material to the Committee members. While the HRC, the UK/Hong Kong Government and NGOs were all in agreement about the need for the existing protections and international supervision to continue after 1997 (especially continued reporting under the Covenant),[38] the views of the Committee about the deficiencies of existing protections were fairly firmly stated in the concluding observations,[39] which reflected in important respects the arguments of the NGOs. Concerned about the implications of the transition for the continued implementation of the Covenant, the Committee requested the Government to submit a supplementary report by the middle of the following year.

---

[35] Appendix 1 to Legco Paper No. PL 81/94–95, 12 January 1995. The administration's response was considered by the Panel at meetings on 16 January and 16 February 1995.

[36] UN Doc. CCPR/C/95/Add. 5 (1995).

[37] Messrs Mavrommatis and Bhagwati. See *Hong Kong and the International Covenant on Civil and Political Rights*, proceedings of a seminar organised by the Centre for Comparative and Public Law, University of Hong Kong, 30 September 1995.

[38] On this topic, see N. Jayawickrama, 'Human Rights in Hong Kong – The Continued Applicability of the International Covenants', 25 *HKLJ*, 1995, p. 171; J. Chan, 'State Succession to Human Rights Treaties: Hong Kong and the International Covenant on Civil and Political Rights', 45 *ICLQ*, 1996, p. 928; and A. Byrnes, 'Hong Kong and the Continuation of International Obligations Relating to Human Rights after 1997', in *Hong Kong SAR: In Pursuit of Domestic and International Order* (eds. B. Leung and J. Cheng), Hong Kong, 1997, p. 135.

[39] UN Doc. CCPR/C/79/Add. 57 (1995).

3. THE CAT COMMITTEE (NOVEMBER 1995)

On the heels of the ICCPR Committee's hearings came the examination of the initial report of Hong Kong[40] under the Convention against Torture (CAT). This was contained in the second report of the United Kingdom under the Convention. Preparation for this hearing followed the earlier pattern of legislative hearings and a university-organised seminar in which a member of the Committee (the Country Rapporteur for the United Kingdom, Professor Peter Burns of Canada) spoke about its work, and local experts critiqued various aspects of the Government's report.[41] The Government responded positively to requests to facilitate visits by the member of the Committee to a number of prisons in Hong Kong, as well as to a refugee detention centre and also arranged other briefings.

Hong Kong NGOs attended the meeting of the CAT Committee and participated along with NGOs from the United Kingdom in an informal oral briefing. In view of the fact that the Committee was discussing both the UK itself and Hong Kong, less attention was given to Hong Kong issues than it would have received at a separate hearing. Nonetheless, there were a number of expressions of concern about the situation in Hong Kong.[42]

4. THE CERD COMMITTEE (MARCH 1996)

The thirteenth periodic report under CERD in relation to Hong Kong was submitted in August 1995.[43] Once again a seminar was organised around the work of the CERD Committee and critiques of the Government's report, with the participation of a member of the Committee who happened to be visiting Hong Kong.[44] The Home Affairs Panel of the Legislative Council considered the report, and dispatched one of its members to attend the meetings of the CERD Committee held in March 1996, at which

---

[40] UN Doc. CAT/C/25/Add. 6 (1995).

[41] *Seminar on Hong Kong and the UN Convention against Torture*, organised by the Centre for Comparative and Public Law, University of Hong Kong, 28 October 1995.

[42] UN Doc. A/51/44 (1996) at pp. 12–15. For further discussion of the hearing see *Bill of Rights Bulletin*, vol. 3, no. 4, December 1995, at pp. 20–3.

[43] UN Doc. CERD/C/263/Add. 7 (Part II) (1995).

[44] Professor Rüdiger Wolfrum of Germany. A summary of the proceedings of the seminar was forwarded to the members of the Committee: *Hong Kong and the International Convention on the Elimination of All Forms of Racial Discrimination*, seminar held at the University of Hong Kong, 11 November 1995.

the United Kingdom metropolitan report as well as that on Hong Kong were examined. While the NGO attendance from Hong Kong at this committee was less than at the other hearings, it seems that this was the first occasion on which Hong Kong Government and NGO representatives had attended a meeting of the CERD Committee. For almost the first time in the work of the Committee, members were provided with a great deal of information directly by NGOs. A dozen or more United Kingdom NGOs, together with four or five from Hong Kong, submitted written material. The Hong Kong Human Rights Monitor, the Legislative Council and the Indian Resources Group submitted reports, and the University of Hong Kong's Centre for Comparative and Public Law made a submission summarising the major concerns raised at the seminar on CERD held at the end of 1995.

The formal hearing before the Committee was preceded by an open meeting for NGOs to brief Committee members. Convened by the Country Rapporteur for the United Kingdom, Professor Theo van Boven of the Netherlands, the meeting was attended by six or seven Committee members, some thirty NGO representatives (including two from Hong Kong) and, intriguingly, representatives from the Hong Kong Government. The United Kingdom Government delegation consisted of ten members overall, five from the UK (one of whom was responsible for Hong Kong and the other dependent territories), and five from the Hong Kong Government. Thus six out of ten officials were covering Hong Kong.

The Committee's consideration both of the United Kingdom and of Hong Kong was fairly wide-ranging. It was critical of the situation in Hong Kong on a number of issues,[45] including the treatment of Vietnamese, the failure to enact legislation against racial discrimination, the situation of foreign domestic workers, and the nationality problems of ethnic minorities. While the Government once again undertook to study the conclusions, it did not undertake to comply with the recommendations, although subsequently some steps were taken, apparently stimulated in part by the hearings.[46]

---

[45] For a description of the hearing before the Committee, see *Bill of Rights Bulletin*, vol. 4, no. 1, June 1996, at pp. 25–31.

[46] Although the Government refused to enact legislation against racial discrimination (or to refrain from opposing a private member's bill on the subject), it did indicate it was prepared to undertake a consultation on racial discrimination to ascertain the extent of

5. THE CRC COMMITTEE (OCTOBER 1996)

By the time the Government submitted its initial report under the Convention on the Rights of the Child (CRC),[47] treaty body fatigue had begun to affect both NGOs and the Government. Nonetheless NGOs (in particular the Hong Kong Committee on Children's Rights, aided and encouraged by the Geneva-based NGO Group for the Convention on the Rights of the Child) and the Legislative Council showed interest in following the process closely. Hearings were once again held by the Home Affairs Panel,[48] a report was sent and members of the Council attended the hearings. No special seminar was organised, as the Hong Kong Committee on Children's Rights had organised a general seminar on the theme and had prepared a report analysing the situation of children in Hong Kong in light of CRC's provisions, a report which it updated for the review. Members of the HK Committee attended the pre-sessional working group to provide material, the first occasion a Hong Kong NGO had attended a pre-sessional meeting. A number of members of the HK Committee, as well as other NGOs, attended the session in October, briefing the CRC Committee on a range of issues, many of which were reflected in its questions and concluding observations.[49] The Government laid these observations before the Legislative Council, together with the administration's detailed response to them,[50] both of which were considered by the Home Affairs Panel.[51]

the problem and whether legislation or other steps were necessary to address it. That consultation paper was published in late February 1997 (see also note 62 below), shortly before the Government's next appearance before the CERD Committee. The result of the consultation was that the Government did not consider that legislative measures were necessary to address such racial discrimination as existed in Hong Kong.

[47] UN Doc. CRC/C/11/Add. 9 (1996).
[48] See LegCo Panel on Home Affairs, Minutes of Special Meeting held on Saturday, 25 May 1996, LegCo Paper No. CB(2) 1477/95–96; Minutes of Special Meeting held on Thursday, 6 June 1996, LegCo Paper No. CB(2) 1699/95–96; Minutes of Working Group Meeting held on Monday, 10 June 1996, LegCo Paper No. CB(2) 1827/95–96; Minutes of Working Group Meeting held on Wednesday, 26 June 1996, LegCo Paper No. CB(2) 2010/95–96. Many of the Legislative Council papers referred to in this chapter, from the 1995–96 session of the Council onwards, can be obtained though the website of the former Council: http://www.legco.gov.hk/yr97–98/english/former/former.htm.
[49] UN Doc. CRC/C/15/Add.63 (30 October 1996).
[50] LegCo Paper No. CB(2) 995/96–97 (05).
[51] See LegCo Panel on Home Affairs, Minutes of Meeting held on Friday, 24 January 1997.

6. THE HRC (OCTOBER 1996)/ICESCR COMMITTEE (NOVEMBER 1996)

As explained above, the HRC had asked in October 1995 for a supplementary report on Hong Kong by the end of May 1996. This report[52] was submitted more or less on time, permitting it to be reviewed at the autumn session of the Human Rights Committee. The third periodic report under the ICESCR,[53] the first report to treat all the substantive articles of the Covenant at one time, had been submitted in 1996 and was scheduled for review at the same time.

The Legislative Council held its now customary hearings on the supplementary report under the ICCPR[54] as well as on the third report under the ICESCR.[55] The Hong Kong Government decided to adopt local NGOs' own practice and itself invited two members of ICESCR Committee and two members of the HRC to Hong Kong for consultations. During their separate but overlapping visits the members of the two committees were treated to a strenuous programme of meetings with government officials and NGOs, which provided them with good exposure to the variety of views on the different issues.

The hearings before the two committees were quite different in character. The HRC limited itself to an examination of a number of transitional issues, the most important of which was the existence of a continuing obligation to report after 1997, which in its view was a clear obligation binding on China. While other matters were raised during the discussion,[56] this was the only substantive issue addressed in the Committee's concluding observations.[57] The HRC did nevertheless also request the United Kingdom Government to provide a report covering the period up to 30 June 1997, when British administration over Hong Kong would end.

The ICESCR Committee, on the other hand, had before it the first comprehensive report submitted in respect of Hong Kong.[58] Its examination

---

[52] UN Doc. CCPR/C/117 (1996).   [53] UN Doc. E/1994/104/Add. 10 (1996).

[54] LegCo Panel on Home Affairs, Minutes of Meeting held on Friday, 14 June 1996, LegCo Paper No. CB(2) 2039/95–96; Minutes of Meeting with the Administration on the Supplementary Report on Hong Kong under the ICCPR held on Friday, 21 June 1996, LegCo Paper No. CB(2) 289/96–97.

[55] LegCo Panel on Home Affairs, Minutes of Special Meeting held on Saturday, 6 July 1996, LegCo Paper No. CB(2) 1906/95–96.

[56] UN Doc. CCPR/C/SR 1536 (28 October 1996).

[57] UN Doc. CCPR/C/79/Add. 69 (8 November 1996).

[58] UN Doc. E/1994/104/Add. 10 (3 April 1996).

thus included a substantive discussion of all the rights guaranteed by the ICESCR as well as transitional issues including the obligation to report after 1997. The concluding observations of the Committee ranged broadly and were critical. While it came to a similar view about continuity of reporting as the HRC, the remainder of its observations were fairly critical of the situation in Hong Kong,[59] and it repeated a number of the criticisms it had made two years earlier.

Following the meetings of the committees, the concluding observations adopted by both were provided to the Legislative Council, together with the administration's detailed response to them;[60] these were considered by the Home Affairs Panel.[61]

7. THE CERD COMMITTEE (MARCH 1997)

By the time consideration of the fourteenth report under CERD was scheduled, the level of public interest in such proceedings had apparently diminished. However, issues of racial discrimination continued to remain on the domestic agenda, and the debate was stimulated by the Government's consultation exercise on racial discrimination,[62] following the enactment of sex and disability discrimination legislation. It was also stimulated by concern as to the possible impact of the coming change of sovereignty on racial minorities (such as those from South Asia who might be rendered stateless)[63] and foreign workers in Hong Kong. The Home Affairs Panel of the Legislative Council once again held hearings at which NGOs presented their views, and it met with the administration to discuss the reports.[64] The Council submitted a report of its own to the CERD Committee[65] and sent a delegation

---

[59] UN Doc. E/C.12/1/Add.10 (6 December 1996).

[60] LegCo Paper No. CB(2) 995/96–97 (06) (response to concluding observations of the HRC); LegCo Paper No. CB(2) 995/96–97 (07) (response to concluding observations of ICESCR Committee).

[61] See LegCo Panel on Home Affairs, Minutes of Meeting held on Friday, 24 January 1997.

[62] Home Affairs Branch, *Equal Opportunities: A Study of Discrimination on the Ground of Race – A Consultation Paper* (February 1997), available on the Internet at http://www.info.gov.hk/hab/topi_e.htm and mentioned in note 46 above.

[63] On 4 February 1997, the UK Government indicated that it would amend the law to enable British members of the ethnic minority community in Hong Kong only to apply for registration as British citizens.

[64] See LegCo Panel on Home Affairs, Minutes of Meeting held on Friday, 24 January 1997, LegCo Paper No. CB(2) 1150/96–97.

[65] LegCo Paper No. CB(2) 1250/96–97.

to attend the session,[66] at which metropolitan United Kingdom, Hong Kong and other dependent territories were considered. In its concluding observations[67] the Committee took up many of the same issues that it had raised a year earlier, to which the Government had done little to respond positively.

8. SUBSEQUENT DEVELOPMENTS UNDER BRITISH RULE

In the period leading up to the transfer of sovereignty on 1 July 1997, two supplementary reports were submitted by the United Kingdom, one under ICCPR[68] and another under CRC.[69] In neither case was a hearing by the responsible committee envisaged, though NGOs requested the committees to hold hearings, without success.

E. Using the products of the hearings

After each hearing the concluding observations adopted by the various committees were awaited with interest. Both government and NGOs

---

[66] House Committee, Minutes of 17th meeting held on Friday, 21 February 1997, LegCo Paper No. CB(2) 1317/96–97. There do not appear to have been other Hong Kong-based NGOs in attendance on this occasion.

[67] UN Doc. CERD/C/304/Add.20 (23 April 1997).

[68] 'Final Report by the United Kingdom of Great Britain and Northern Ireland in respect of Hong Kong under the International Covenant on Civil and Political Rights', 30 June 1997. This report was made available through the British Consulate General in Hong Kong from 1 July 1997. It was not distributed by the Hong Kong Government, nor was it made available on the Hong Kong SAR Government website, where previous reports had been posted, nor indeed on the British Consulate General's or Foreign and Commonwealth Office's websites. The explanation given for the Hong Kong Government's failure to distribute the document was that, as the report would not be finalised until its submission on 30 June 1997 and would be a British Government document, the 'HKSAR government – established on 1 July 1997 – would have no *locus* to distribute the report': LegCo Panel on Home Affairs, Minutes of Meeting held on Friday, 20 June 1997, PLC Paper No. CB(2) 101. This explanation seems rather formalistic and far from convincing, since with the advent of 1 July 1997, the Hong Kong SAR Government did not simply stop distribution of information about Hong Kong prepared by the United Kingdom Government, and it could simply have sought the agreement of the Central People's Government if that were felt necessary. The real explanation lies in the fact that a number of issues dealt with in the report were the subject of disagreement between the British and Chinese Governments (e.g., the repeal of parts of the Bill of Rights Ordinance, and amendments to laws relating to societies and assemblies), and the report sought to justify the British Government's view of these issues. For the text of the report see *Bill of Rights Bulletin*, vol. 4, no. 3, August 1997, Appendix D.

[69] UN Doc. CRC/C/11/Add.15 (16 June 1997).

scheduled press conferences. The concluding observations were brought to the attention of the Executive Council and other parts of government, as well as to members of the Legislative Council. While initially there was energetic follow-up in the Legislative Council, its vigour seems to have waned, in part as a result of the number and frequency of appearances before the treaty bodies and in part because many of the issues had been raised at earlier meetings and had already drawn a government response. Nonetheless, the legislature continued to keep up a general review function, holding hearings to review new reports and concluding observations, while individual members of the legislature have invoked committee conclusions in support of initiatives within the legislature.

Other NGOs drew on the committees' conclusions to support their claims for government action. Those pushing for comprehensive anti-discrimination legislation and the removal of wide-ranging exemptions in the Government's own legislation invoked the conclusions of the ICESCR Committee, the HRC and the CERD Committee on these issues. Calls to raise the minimum age for criminal responsibility from seven to ten gained additional support from the CRC Committee's comments on the matter. Efforts to persuade the Government to establish a fully independent police complaints body gained additional force from the comments of a number of committees, even though the Government's proposals fell short of the alternatives espoused by those committees.[70]

F. Assessment

The outcome of the various episodes of reporting – and in particular their cumulative effect – was largely positive in respect of the dissemination of knowledge in Hong Kong about the standards contained in the various treaties and how existing laws and policies compare to those standards.[71]

---

[70] There has been little or no use of the concluding observations in the courts as yet. One surprising omission in this regard was the failure by the Hong Kong Court of Appeal or either of the parties in *Lee Miu-ling v. Attorney General (No. 2)* to refer to the conclusions of the HRC that Hong Kong's system of functional constituencies was in violation of article 25 ICCPR: see (1995) 5 HKPLR 585; [1996] 1 HKC 124 (CA). The judge at first instance had held that even though the system was inconsistent with the guarantees under article 25, this was rendered unchallengeable by provisions of the Letters Patent which constitutionalised the arrangements.

[71] For a comparative perspective, see U. Kilkelly, 'The UN Committee on the Rights of the Child – An Evaluation in the Light of Recent UK Experience', 8(2) *Child and Family Law*

The increasing involvement of NGOs in briefing the committees improved the information base on which the committees undertook their review of reports on Hong Kong and spurred the Government to approach the reporting procedure with considerable professionalism and preparation. The participation by NGOs in the reporting process in Hong Kong and Geneva meant that the invocation of international human rights standards became part of their everyday work and gave additional legitimacy to their efforts; it was also of considerable benefit to the committees in their analysis of the situation and need for changes in Hong Kong. One consequence was that government officials had to become familiar with the standards affecting their work and to be able to respond to criticism formulated in those terms. A number of the objectives of a reporting procedure identified by some commentators[72] appear to have been significantly advanced, in particular promoting public scrutiny and discussion, and educating the Government to take account of human rights concerns in policy-making.

The reporting procedure was generally seen in Hong Kong both by government and most NGOs as an adversarial process, rather than as a cooperative venture between government and civil society (a model sometimes found, especially under CRC and the Convention on the Elimination of Discrimination against Women (CEDAW).[73] The Government's insistence that the report was that of the Government (and therefore for Government to formulate) limited NGO input to the content of the report and the process of drawing it up. For their part, many NGOs shared this view, considering that an advocacy or adversarial stance in relation to the Government's positions on many human rights issues was the most effective way of bringing about change in the contentious area of human rights. As a result, public debate around many controversial policy issues was increasingly focused and conducted in human rights terms.

Quarterly, 1996, p. 105; and M. O'Flaherty, 'The Reporting Obligation Under Article 40 of the International Covenant on Civil and Political Rights: Lessons to be Learned', 16 *HRQ*, 1994, p. 515.

[72] See ICESCR Committee, *General Comment No. 1*, UN Doc. HRI/GEN/1/Rev. 1 (1994), at p. 103; and P. Alston, 'The Purposes of Reporting', in United Nations, *Manual on Human Rights Reporting*, UN Doc. HR/PUB/91/1 (Rev. 1) (1997), pp. 19–24.

[73] See, e.g., the cases described in International Save the Children Alliance Working Group on the Convention on the Rights of the Child, *Monitoring the Convention on the Rights of the Child at the National Level: The Experiences of Some National Coalitions*, Geneva, 1996, paras. 5.1–5.10.

A number of factors contributed to the increased use and impact of the treaty reporting procedures during the period under review. A critical feature was that most of the organisations involved with the committees incorporated their participation in the reporting procedure into their over-all campaign at the domestic level. Thus, the Government's report and its review by the relevant committee was built into the domestic campaign of lobbying and critique, and the international forum provided a further opportunity for airing the issue and putting pressure on the Government to move in the direction urged. Housing rights (in particular the issue of so-called 'cage dwellers') and the need to ensure adequate oversight of police use of force were prime examples.

One factor contributing to the process was the role played by lawyers, especially academic international lawyers. The holding of seminars on a number of the Government's reports and the presence of members of the supervisory bodies at those seminars were important means of publicising the treaties and the review process locally. They provided opportunities to brief members of the committees, and helped the Government to identify the issues likely to be raised and to prepare its responses.

A more important factor was the increasing number of groups actively involved in the reporting procedure which, as a consequence, became more literate in international human rights discourse, deploying this regularly in their advocacy and analytical work in Hong Kong. Some were doing so for the first time; others more actively than before. These included women's groups and others campaigning for legislation against sex discrimination, those campaigning for legislation against discrimination on other grounds (such as age, race, and sexual orientation), groups working with children's rights, community-based organisations working with the socially disadvant-aged, ethnic minority groups, and newly formed human rights organisa-tions. This was in addition to those bodies that have been regularly involved in the process, such as the Hong Kong Bar Association, the Hong Kong Journalists' Association, JUSTICE, the (non-governmental) Hong Kong Human Rights Commission, and a number of international NGOs. That the Government thus faced analysis and critique of its policies from many community groups – not just from a small number of lawyers and 'human rights activists' – encouraged it to be more serious in its response.

While the level of activity around the reporting procedure increased significantly in the period under review, a more difficult question is whether the whole process had any meaningful impact on the enjoyment of human rights in Hong Kong. This is always a difficult question to answer, not just because many factors influence changes in law and practice but also because governments do not always identify the role that international scrutiny may have played in stimulating changes. In Hong Kong the difficulty was exacerbated by the 'China factor' and the concern on the part of the United Kingdom Government not to draw criticism from China for 'internationalising Hong Kong' or introducing major changes to law and policy in sensitive areas such as security and immigration immediately prior to 1 July 1997. Furthermore, an important dimension of the impact of such procedures is their longer-term impact on the culture of government. While a common initial reaction of governments is to respond to international criticism by defending present law and practice (e.g. by invoking the state's margin of appreciation or casting doubt on the supervisory body's ability to grasp the situation fully), the increased awareness of human rights standards and the incorporation of these into normal decision-making processes can nonetheless follow.

This pattern was evident in the case of Hong Kong. The Hong Kong Government was, on the whole, exemplary in its level of formal and procedural cooperation with the various treaty bodies in the period from 1991. Reports were prepared in a timely fashion and submitted on time (the few exceptions being largely due to delays in London). The reports were detailed, covering most of the issues. High-level and well-resourced delegations were sent to meet the committees, and they sought to provide detailed answers on the spot to questions. From early 1995 the Government published draft outlines of reports,[74] disseminated the reports itself in English

---

[74] The first occasion on which this was done was in early 1995, around which time the administration circulated a document entitled *An Outline of Topics to be Covered in the 4th Periodic Report Under the International Covenant on Civil and Political Rights*. This gave effect to the administration's undertaking to circulate such a document following the hearings of the ICESCR Committee in November 1994 (although this involved reneging on its original oral undertaking to the Committee to circulate draft reports for comment). The document set out under each article of the Covenant a brief description of the issues to be included in the report to the HRC, and was intended to give NGOs and other interested parties a chance to comment on the proposed report: for the text see *Bill of Rights Bulletin*, vol. 3, no. 3, April 1995, Appendix E. The practice has been followed with subsequent reports. NGO response has been mixed, with some NGOs pointing out gaps in the topics to be covered, while others have taken the approach that it is for the Government to draw up the report and only then should NGOs comment on it, on the basis that it is healthy to maintain the separate roles of 'poachers and gamekeepers' in this context (the phrase is that of Rosalyn Higgins, *supra*, note 2, at p. xiii).

and Chinese (in hard copy and later through its World Wide Web site), arranged for visits of committee members and cooperated with NGOs in similar visits, and considered at a high level the concluding observations of the committees. Continued NGO and Legislative Council pressure presumably encouraged the Government in these endeavours.

As to the substantive response to the many critical conclusions and recommendations of the various committees, the Government's record was less exemplary. While initially promising to 'consider seriously' suggestions made by the committees, as time went by the Government more frequently stated that it could not agree with the analysis of the committees and that the two parties would have to agree to disagree. The Government also became more aggressive in its own media strategy in relation to committee hearings, deploying its public relations machine to highlight the commendations of the committees, and to play down or attack any negative assessments.

Nevertheless, it appears that the reporting process did sometimes contribute to government action, whether in individual cases or through changes of policy. One notable case was that of Hai Ho-tak, a child born in 1987; both of his parents and his three siblings had the right of abode in Hong Kong. The child was unable to establish to the satisfaction of the Director of Immigration and the Immigration Tribunal that he had been born in Hong Kong (and thus had right of abode), and the Director of Immigration ordered his removal to China. An application for judicial review of the removal order failed[75] and he was deported. He was reported to be living in Canton with strangers. The Chinese authorities reportedly refused to consider his application for a one-way permit to Hong Kong (which would have allowed him to join his family permanently), on the ground that they had no proof that he was born on the mainland. In addition to a Hong Kong-based campaign, the case was taken up by the ICESCR Committee at its November 1994 session, when the Committee urged the Government to clarify the case and to permit the child to enter Hong Kong. He was eventually allowed to do so.[76]

If this incident is an example of the contribution of international pressure to the resolution of a case, it also reveals its limitations. While the Government was able to resolve this individual case, it did not respond in a

---

[75] *R. v. Director of Immigration, ex parte Hai Ho-tak* (1994) 4 HKPLR 324 (CA).
[76] *South China Morning Post*, 26 February 1995, p. 1.

307

similar way to the Committee's conclusion that the separation of children from parents (of which Hai Ho-tak's case was only one of many) was a violation of article 10 ICESCR, and that Hong Kong's immigration policy needed to be changed. While the individual case was resolved on humanitarian grounds, the general policy was not altered.

A similar outcome occurred in another case. The Office of the UN High Commissioner for Refugees in Hong Kong decided to encourage the remaining Vietnamese boat-people held in detention centres to return home by withdrawing the provision of secondary school education for children in the camps. The issue was taken up by ICESCR Committee at the instigation of NGOs and the Committee urged the Government to step in. Eventually the Government acted to remedy at least some of the deficiencies, providing funding for secondary education in the camps. At the same time the more general criticism and recommendations of the ICESCR Committee and other committees about the treatment of Vietnamese in the camps went unheeded.

It was disillusioning for some NGO activists to see clear pronouncements of the committees on important issues either rejected out of hand by the Government or simply ignored. Initial express rejection of such recommendations does not mean that they did not have a positive impact, and the NGOs no doubt recognised that hearings before the committees are just one component of a complex political process. Nevertheless, continuing intransigence on the part of a government in the face of strong pronouncements by a treaty body, and the inability of the international process to take the matter further, can lead to a loss of credibility of the treaty monitoring process. Expectations of the role of international obligations and the stature of the United Nations bodies may be exaggerated, but if NGOs come to the conclusion that, despite their proper and effective use of the reporting procedure, use of international procedures does not contribute concretely to the achievement of their goals, it will be difficult to persuade them to continue to put significant time and energy into using those procedures.

One must not, however, be too pessimistic. From the early 1990s there were significant advances in the formal legal protection of human rights in Hong Kong and much greater public discussion of rights issues. International scrutiny and criticism certainly played its part in helping to stimulate discussion and change in some areas. The longer-term effects are yet to be seen.

G. Problematic aspects of the reporting procedures in relation to Hong Kong

During the various episodes of reporting NGOs were influential in setting agendas, bringing to the attention of committee members the priority concerns. This was especially so on the occasions when a report on Hong Kong was the sole or main report under consideration, and Hong Kong NGOs did not have to compete for attention, for example with the many UK NGOs attending the hearings under CAT and CERD.

On the whole, Hong Kong NGOs were very satisfied with the openness of the various committees to their concerns and the willingness of many members to use NGO material in their questioning of the Government.[77] These very successes, however, may pose a danger to the effectiveness of the committees and the willingness of governments to cooperate. The impact of a committee's review in any case depends in large measure on the government's perception that the committee is impartial and fair in the issues it raises and the conclusions it adopts. A committee has to be seen not to be excessively dependent on or influenced by NGO views, a difficult balancing act in view of the importance of NGO information to their evaluation. On occasions the Hong Kong Government apparently felt that committee members paid too great a regard to the views of NGOs and did not give a full hearing to the Government's explanations.

A related aspect is the ability of NGOs to provide instant rebuttal of points made by the governments. Quite apart from the issue of impartiality, one danger of overuse of on the spot NGO information is that discussion of a particular issue can descend to a level of detail such that the larger issues may be obscured; the more detailed the focus, the less reasonable it may be to expect a government to respond on the spot. On a number of occasions, after providing the committees with a large body of detailed information, the Hong Kong Government faced the ironic consequence of being requested to provide ever more detailed answers to increasingly

---

[77] Perhaps the only recent exception was the HRC at its October 1996 review of the Hong Kong supplementary report. Only the night before the hearing were NGOs given a list of the issues to which the Committee wished to confine its examination, giving them little time to prepare and causing a certain frustration among those who had travelled all the way to Geneva at considerable expense to raise other issues as well. This feeling was exacerbated by the Committee's decision to address only one issue in its concluding observations, namely the obligation that passed from the United Kingdom to China to report under the Covenant in respect of Hong Kong.

specific questions on issues of seemingly minor importance, which would have challenged even the best prepared delegation. The instant rebuttal facilities that NGOs may be keen to provide may give government officials the feeling that they are engaged in an inquisition rather than a dialogue. This is not to say that evasive or incomplete answers should not be followed up with vigour: governments are usually skilled at not answering questions on difficult issues.

Another danger of excessive questioning is that the government may 'put up the shutters'. The UK/Hong Kong delegations generally sought to respond forthwith to issues raised, unlike many other delegations. Following one experience, doubts were raised as to whether the practice of seeking to respond on the spot was wise, in view of the snowballing effect it seemed to produce in terms of further, even more detailed questions. It would be unfortunate if a government which had sought to engage in a real dialogue with the committees were to become disenchanted with the process and to decide to take all questions on notice.

Another important feature of the use of the reporting procedure by NGOs is that some NGOs have consistently raised the same issue under several treaties.[78] This strategy has no doubt been a way of keeping the issue in the public eye and maintaining pressure on the government. It may also be justified substantively, given the overlapping coverage of the treaties in many respects. But the practice has raised concerns about the duplication of resources; part of the rationale for the creation of special subject treaties was that the issues covered by it could be examined in greater depth than under a treaty such as the ICCPR or the ICESCR Committee which covers the broad range of rights. In relation to Hong Kong, however, the most detailed discussion and strongest statements on issues did not necessarily come from the specialist bodies.[79]

A related development was that the Hong Kong Government's response on issues which were repeatedly raised became rigidly formulaic, limiting the possibility for genuine discussion and progress with any one of the committees. This was largely the result of the compressed time-scale within

---

[78] For example, the situation of Vietnamese in Hong Kong's detention centres has been raised under all five of the treaties (CEDAW was not applicable to Hong Kong until 14 October 1996); the laws regulating the conditions of stay of foreign domestic workers were raised under the ICCPR, the ICESCR, and CERD.

[79] See, e.g., the question of the need for an independent police complaints procedure which drew stronger recommendations from the HRC than it did from the CAT Committee.

which so many hearings were held in the years 1994 to 1997; there was too little time for the Government to rethink its position on some of these issues and to develop proposals for change, even if it was open to doing so in principle, which was by no means clear in many cases. The drawbacks – mainly the increasing rigidity of policy response – might not have been so pronounced had there been more time between the hearings. The need to discuss major policy changes with China was an ever-present factor.

H. Conclusion

There is no doubt that the reporting procedure under the human rights treaties played a helpful role in Hong Kong in increasing awareness of the applicable international human rights standards and the need to take them into account in formulating new laws and policies and reviewing old ones. That this role increased significantly over the period 1991–1997 was largely due to a fairly small group of committed activists, academics and legislators who, as well as taking part in the various reporting procedures themselves, acted as catalysts for broader public participation in those processes, and ensured significant use of the international outcomes at the domestic level.

A number of factors can be identified as significant in that process:

- the engagement of activist lawyers and academics in training on the work of the human rights treaty bodies and the organisation of public forums to discuss specific government reports;
- the developing interest of legislators in international human rights norms and the work of the treaty bodies, as evidenced in the holding of legislative hearings, the sending of representatives to hearings before the committees and the following up on the results of those hearings in the Legislative Council;
- a vigorous and active NGO movement, adept at applying its knowledge of international human rights norms and procedures, and the opportunities offered by the extension of additional treaties to Hong Kong, to achieve their specific goals in Hong Kong;
- the use of developing information technology by all parties – in particular increasing use of the World Wide Web – to disseminate government reports, NGO critiques and treaty body documents;
- a government willing to take the reporting procedure seriously by producing and disseminating high quality reports, sending well-prepared

delegations, and facilitating other initiatives to disseminate knowledge of the treaties;

- committees that have been highly receptive to the information provided by NGOs and willing to take up the opportunities both NGOs and government have offered to visit Hong Kong to view matters for themselves and to consult with many groups in Hong Kong (thus making it possible for many groups to become involved even if they were unable to come to Geneva for the hearings).

On the other hand, despite the high level activity in relation to Hong Kong in recent years, a number of areas gave rise to concern from the perspectives of the different parties involved:

- the somewhat intransigent and rigid attitude adopted publicly by the Government in response to committee criticism of a number of laws and government policies;
- the feeling on the part of government that on occasion it may not have received a completely fair hearing, or an evaluation which was sufficiently sensitive to the everyday business of governing; and
- duplication in the consideration of issues by various committees.

While the Hong Kong experience is plainly atypical in a number of respects, it nevertheless provides a useful case study of some of the factors that can contribute to active NGO participation in the reporting procedure, something that has certainly enhanced the work of the treaty bodies in relation to Hong Kong and contributed in turn to the importance of international human rights standards and their implementation in Hong Kong itself. Yet that is only part of the equation: it is in the political struggle at the national and local level that battles for human rights have to be won. International procedures of this kind can only contribute to that process.

I. Epilogue

British rule over Hong Kong ended at midnight on 30 June 1997 when Hong Kong became a Special Administrative Region of the People's Republic of China. That transformation had been awaited by many with apprehension about the continuation of the level of human rights protection which had evolved under British rule. How the substantive protection of rights could be maintained and how continued reporting on Hong Kong could be ensured was considered by each of the human rights treaty bodies in the lead-up to the change of sovereignty. With the exception of the two Covenants (to which China was not a party), there appeared to be no difficulty: China would report in respect of Hong Kong under the four conventions applicable to Hong Kong and to which China itself was already a party (CAT, CERD, CRC, CEDAW). The timing of these reports was not clarified, and it was not clear whether reports would be submitted according to the existing schedule or in accordance with the schedule applicable to China.

In relation to the two Covenants, prior to 1 July 1997 the question of reporting was a contentious one, with the United Kingdom insisting that China was obliged to submit reports, and China insisting that it was under no duty to do so.[80] Following the change of sovereignty, China announced that it would submit reports in respect of Hong Kong under the two Covenants and undertook to submit these in August 1998. Furthermore, China itself signed the ICESCR in late 1997 and the ICCPR in October 1998 (with ratification possibly following shortly afterwards). Eventually the question of the reporting obligation in respect of Hong Kong will lose relevance, as China itself will be under an obligation to report.

It appears that the Central People's Government (CPG) in Beijing has decided to permit the Hong Kong Government a fairly free hand in the preparation of reports, leaving that task in large part to the latter. It has, however, insisted that the reports be submitted to the United Nations through the Ministry of Foreign Affairs rather than directly by the Hong Kong Government. This was in essence the practice followed under British rule.

The process of preparation of reports and local scrutiny of them appears, in the short term at least, to be fairly similar to the experience under British rule. In its preparation of the first reports after 1 July 1997 the Hong Kong SAR Government followed the pre-1997 procedure, presumably having obtained the agreement of the CPG. The Hong Kong Government independently prepared a draft initial report on CEDAW in respect of Hong Kong and forwarded it to Beijing in October 1997. This report was submitted to the United Nations in September 1998 together with an update to China's third periodic report. The CEDAW Committee considered the reports of China (including Hong Kong) at its January 1999 session.

---

[80] See Byrnes, *supra*, note 38.

The standard procedure was followed in relation to the two Covenants. Consequent upon the Chinese announcement that it would report under the Covenants, the Hong Kong Government in March 1998 issued outlines of topics to be covered in the reports for public comment.[81] The reports were prepared by the Hong Kong Government and submitted by the Ministry of Foreign Affairs in December 1998. The Secretary for Home Affairs declared that there would be no changes made to the report by the CPG, an undertaking that could only have been made with the agreement of the central authorities.

Local scrutiny is also likely to follow established patterns. Since no reports had been submitted to the United Nations between 1 July 1997 and the middle of 1998, none had been laid for consideration before the Provisional Legislative Council (Hong Kong's legislature in the first year of Chinese sovereignty). Nor did the conclusions of the CERD Committee in March 1997 appear to have been considered by the Council. However, it seems likely that both the Government, and the Legislative Council will continue to follow the previous practice of encouraging parliamentary scrutiny of reports and that the Government will continue to inform the Legislative Council of any steps it proposes to take in response to the recommendations made by the treaty bodies.

Nevertheless, there are a number of factors which may impede the reporting procedures in relation to Hong Kong. Of concern to NGOs is that, if Hong Kong reports under some or all treaties are considered together with the report on mainland China (the issue of the cycle of reporting under some treaties is still not settled), Hong Kong will be overshadowed by the mainland and will receive relatively little attention from the treaty bodies. The autonomy of the Hong Kong Government to formulate its own responses to criticism by committees, and the possibility that the quality of the Hong Kong Government's reports and responses might put the CPG's performance in the shade, may also give rise to tension. In addition, the freedom of Hong Kong NGOs to criticise Hong Kong (and even the situation on the mainland) in international fora stands in stark contrast to the ability of mainland groups to do so. Whether such activities will draw criticism from the Hong Kong Government or from the CPG (directly or indirectly), and whether the ability of Hong Kong NGOs to engage in such work will be affected, remain to be seen. However, it will be difficult to roll

---

[81] See http://www.info.gov.hk/hab/new/index_e.htm.

back the established precedents and the existing expectations of the community and NGOs in this regard.

Thus, notwithstanding the change of sovereignty, international human rights standards and the reporting procedures are likely to continue to play a role in domestic debate and policy-making, in the general community, the legislature and the executive government of the Hong Kong Special Administrative Region.

14

THE UNITED STATES AND
THE INTERNATIONAL HUMAN RIGHTS
TREATY SYSTEM: FOR EXPORT ONLY?

STEFANIE GRANT

Participation by the United States in the international human rights treaty system has presented a number of difficult issues, both for itself and for the wider world. Taken separately, these issues are, perhaps, not unique; taken together and in the context of the United States' role on the international stage, they raise important questions. Because of its international role, and in particular the role played by the promotion of treaty-based human rights in United States foreign policy, it was perhaps natural to expect the United States to be equally engaged in ratifying and applying the human rights instruments at home. This has not been so, and the process – where it has taken place – has been slow and contradictory, and has excluded any dis-cussion of social and economic rights.

In its foreign affairs, the United States remains the friend and champion of the human rights treaty system, and within the United Nations it has played a leading part in the creation of the two *ad hoc* tribunals to prosecute genocide and other international crimes.[1] At home, however, the issue of treaty implementation and enforcement has been complicated by a number of factors: the breadth and character of the reservations made by the United States Senate on ratification; the complexity of the United States federal system; and the unique historical tradition of rights protection under the United States Constitution, which produces a reluctance to accept that international treaty obligations can be complementary and not threatening to US civil rights. There has also been a related unwillingness

---

[1] However, the USA, with China, Iraq and Libya, was one of only seven governments which voted against adopting the Rome Statute to create a permanent International Criminal Court in July 1998; 120 governments voted in favour.

on the part of the powerful civil rights community to look beyond the United States courts and legislature for civil and political rights protection. There are some signs that this attitude is beginning to change. The most significant is a recent Executive Order which was signed by President Bill Clinton in December 1998. The Order declares that 'it shall be the policy and practice' of the USA fully to respect and implement 'its human rights treaty obligations', and creates an inter-agency oversight and coordination mechanism.[2]

Nonetheless, popular distrust of the United Nations and populist opposition to United States acceptance of international standard-setting (both of which now coalesce around the Convention on the Rights of the Child (CRC)) continue to act as increasingly powerful disincentives to effective action on the part of the Executive and Congress in ensuring compliance with reporting duties and treaty implementation, especially at the state level. Nor has the Supreme Court sent a different signal: in the 1998 landmark *Breard* case, the Court reinforced the traditional unwillingness of US judges to apply international treaty law when it refused a request from the International Court of Justice to delay the execution of a Paraguayan national, convicted of murder, whose rights under a self-executing treaty had been denied.[3]

A. The issue of reservations

The issue which determines United States application of treaty norms, and increasingly lies at the centre of United States relations with the treaty body system, is however a legal one: the set of reservations attached by the United States Senate to each treaty ratification. Despite the fact that some of these reservations are widely regarded as invalid under international law, there is little realistic prospect of the Senate agreeing to the withdrawal or modification of any of them. In April 1995, when the time came for the Chairperson of the Human Rights Committee (HRC) to respond to a

---

[2] Executive Order 13, 107, 'Implementation of Human Rights Treaties', 10 December 1998, 34 *Weekly Comp. Pres. Doc.* 2459 (1998). See below, note 21.

[3] *Breard*, a Paraguayan national, had been systematically denied consular access rights under the Vienna Convention on Consular Relations; unlike the human rights treaties, the Vienna Convention is self-executing, and individuals may enforce their rights through US courts. See 'Agora:Breard', 92 *AJIL* 4, 1998, pp. 666–712; also Aceves, 'Litigation under the Vienna Convention', *ACLU International Civil Liberties Report*, 1998, pp. 6–13.

statement by the Legal Adviser to the United States State Department, which had in effect rejected the Committee's General Comment No. 24 on Reservations, he said that the United States and the Committee would have 'for the moment to agree to differ'. The question both for rights groups within the United States and for the treaty body system is how long that moment will last, and what can be done within the constraints of the present situation. The answer is different for the International Covenant on Civil and Political Rights (ICCPR) and for the Convention against Torture (CAT).

Although the legal effect of the Senate's reservations has been – in the words of the HRC – 'to ensure that the United States has accepted what is already the law of the United States', there is a growing awareness among domestic, as well as international, rights groups of the treaties' value: in setting a higher standard of rights protection, in providing a backstop against domestic erosion of rights, and in using the reporting system to identify areas of non-compliance around which public pressure can be organised.

In 1988, the Convention on the Prevention and Punishment of the Crime of Genocide was the first international human rights treaty to be ratified by the United States; it had waited for forty-one years after transmission to the Senate by President Truman in 1949. This was followed in 1992 by accession to the ICCPR and in 1994 to CAT and the Convention on the Elimination of Racial Discrimination (CERD).[4] Under article VI of the United States Constitution, treaties become the 'supreme law of the land', equivalent to federal statutes, and directly enforceable by the courts. But an exception to this general rule has been made in the case of the human rights treaties, whose legal status and impact are defined by the set of Reservations, Understandings and Declarations (RUDs) which the Senate has attached to each treaty on ratification. They have a precise legal function, but they also reflect the long-standing distrust of international human rights treaty-making which asserted itself in the 1950s, when treaties were seen by their opponents as a means of bringing to an end racial discrimination and segregation by international treaty.[5]

---

[4] See generally D. Stewart, 'U.S. Ratification of the Covenant on Civil and Political Rights: The Significance of the Reservations, Understandings and Declarations', 14 *HRLJ*, 1992, pp. 77–83.

[5] See L. Henkin, 'U.S. Ratification of Human Rights Conventions: The Ghost of Senator Bricker', 89 *AJIL* 2, 1995, pp. 341–50.

In the case of all three treaties – the ICCPR, CAT and CERD – the RUDs which the Senate attached to United States accession have reflected certain assumptions or 'principles', namely that:

(i) no treaty obligations should be undertaken that are inconsistent with the Constitution;

(ii) ratification should effect no change to United States law or practice where it fell below international standards;

(iii) treaties should be non-self-executing; and

(iv) implementation should be by states except for areas within the competence of the federal authorities.

By making each treaty non-self-executing, the United States has ensured that none of the adopted treaties gives individuals a right of action enforceable in United States courts.[6] Because the United States has not signed the ICCPR Optional Protocol, either, the HRC cannot oversee the Covenant's application in individual cases through the communications procedure.[7] In its domestic affairs, the United States is thereby in large part insulated against the impact of human rights treaty law.

The RUDs reflect a belief that – in the words of the State Department – 'in nearly every important respect, existing United States law and practice comply with the fundamental requirements of the Covenant'.[8] Where this is not the case, the RUDs expressly preserve United States law. Thus, a reservation to article 6(5) of the ICCPR allows the imposition of capital punishment, and execution, for offences committed by minors 'under existing or future law'.[9] By its reservation to article 7 of the same Covenant,

---

[6] The precise legal effect of the non-self-executing provision remains to be established. In the State Department's view, it 'does *not* affect or circumscribe the international obligations of the US ... [a]nd in no way restricts or limits the undertakings accepted by the United States under the Covenant. What the declaration makes clear is that the Executive Branch, acting in conjunction with the Federal legislature, will oversee domestic implementation of the Covenant, rather than the federal or state judiciaries': D. Stewart, *supra*, note 4. However, 'the declaration that a convention is non-self-executing is designed to keep [the United States'] own judges from judging the human rights conditions in the United States by international standards': Henkin, *supra*, note 5.

[7] Similarly, the United States has not made declarations under CERD or CAT to allow those treaty bodies to consider individual communications.

[8] Stewart, *supra*, note 4, p. 78.

[9] '(3) That the United States reserves the right, subject to its Constitutional constraints, to impose capital punishment on any person [other than a pregnant woman] duly convicted under existing or future laws permitting the imposition of capital punishment, including such punishment for crimes committed by persons below eighteen years of age.'

the United States binds itself only 'to the extent that "cruel, inhuman or degrading treatment or punishment" means cruel and unusual punishment' prohibited by the United States Constitution. Similar RUDs limit and blunt the legal impact of CAT.[10] In addition, and in response to the European Court of Human Rights' judgment in the *Soering* case,[11] the Senate went one step further by attaching an Understanding which expressly excludes application of that Convention to treatment which might be interpreted – as for example under the European Convention on Human Rights (ECHR) – as 'degrading treatment or punishment' but which is neither prohibited by the United States Constitution nor illegal in the United States.[12]

At the time of ratification, few[13] opposed accession on the basis of such a far-reaching package of RUDs, although it was clear that certain of the reservations, and the second underlying assumption outlined above – described by the Lawyers' Committee for Human Rights in its testimony as the 'principle that the United States would undertake to do only what it is already doing' – were incompatible with the Covenant's object. This view was confirmed by other states parties when the United States notified the United Nations of the terms of its accession. France, Germany, the Netherlands and other western European states parties made formal objections to two reservations, those in respect of capital punishment for crimes committed by those under the age of eighteen (article 6), and

---

[10] See generally *Message from the President of the United States* transmitting CAT to the Senate, Treaty Doc. 100–102, 100th Cong., 2d Sess. (1988). *Report together with Additional Views*, Convention against Torture and other Cruel, Inhuman and Degrading Treatment or Punishment, Senate Exec. Report 101–30, 101st Cong., 2d Sess., 30 August 1990.

[11] *Soering v. United Kingdom*, Series A, vol. 161, 1989, p. 34.

[12] '[T]he United States understands that international law does not prohibit the death penalty, and does not consider this Convention to restrict or prohibit the United States from applying the death penalty consistent with the Fifth, Eighth and/or Fourteenth Amendments to the Constitution of the United States, including any constitutional period of confinement prior to the imposition of the death penalty.' See Senate Exec. Report, *supra*, note 10, p. 26. '"[D]egrading treatment or punishment" has been interpreted, for example by the European Commission on Human Rights, to include treatment that would probably not be prohibited by the US Constitution and may not be illegal in the United States. In view of the ambiguity of the terms, the administration believes that US obligations under this article should be limited to conduct prohibited by the US Constitution.' *Report of the Senate Committee on Foreign Relations*, 30 August 1990.

[13] But see Lawyers' Committee for Human Rights, 'Statements on US Ratification of the CCPR', 14 *HRLJ* 3–4, 1992, pp. 125–9.

the definition of torture, cruel and inhuman treatment or punishment (article 7).[14]

B. ICCPR: The initial United States report to the HRC and the 1998 Executive Order

When the HRC reviewed the first United States report under the ICCPR in March 1995, the issue of reservations was prominent in its discussion with the United States delegation. The Committee's Concluding Comment, which followed hard on the heels of its November 1994 General Comment No. 24 on Reservations, found the reservations to articles 6(5) and 7 to be 'incompatible with the object and purpose of the Covenant',[15] a position which had been denied by the State Department Legal Adviser in his testimony. This remains a bitterly contested issue, which has produced a continuing political fallout. The fallout illustrates the depth of the opposition which exists to the notion of the United States submitting itself to any form of independent treaty supervision in this area.

The United States submitted a lengthy initial report[16] and was represented by a twenty-four-member delegation, led by John Shattuck, Assistant Secretary of State for Democracy, Human Rights and Labor, and formerly an officer of the American Civil Liberties Union (ACLU). In statements before the Committee, and in response to questions and comments, the delegation made a number of commitments: to review the RUDs; to undertake closer coordination between federal, state and local actors to increase states' awareness and implementation of the treaty and their involvement in the reporting process; to consider the establishment of an

---

[14] Human Rights Committee, 'Reservations, Declarations, Notifications and Objections Relating to the International Covenant on Civil and Political Rights and the Optional Protocols thereto: Note by the Secretary General', UN Doc. CCPR/C/2/Rev.4, 24 August 1994.

[15] 'The Committee regrets the extent of the State Party's reservations, declarations and understandings to the Covenant. It believes that, taken together, they intended to ensure that the United States has accepted what is already the law of the United States. The Committee is also particularly concerned at reservations to article 6, paragraph 5, and article 7 of the Covenant, which it believes to be incompatible with the object and purpose of the Covenant': CCPR/C/79/Add. 50, 6 April 1995.

[16] Human Rights Committee, 'International Covenant on Civil and Political Rights – Initial Reports of States Parties due in 1993: United States of America', UN Doc. CCPR/C/81/Add.4, 1994.

inter-agency working group at the federal level; and to review the possibility of designing a specific institution to investigate and report on complaints in order to encourage monitoring of United States law and practice. But follow-up has been slow and even the Civil Rights Division of the Justice Department has not yet become significantly involved in review and monitoring.[17]

Any prompt discussion about reviewing reservations became a political impossibility after the HRC's meeting in New York; the Chair of the Senate Committee on Foreign Relations, Senator Jessie Helms, inserted into the 1996–1999 State Department appropriations bill a funding prohibition intended to bar the Executive from undertaking any reporting activity to the HRC under article 40 ICCPR. The prohibition was accompanied by an inaccurate and damaging reference to General Comment No. 24.[18] As drafted, the prohibition would have continued until the President could certify to Congress that the HRC had both revoked General Comment No. 24, and 'expressly recognised the validity as a matter of international law' of all the United States RUDs to the ICCPR. While this strict prohibition did not survive the legislative process, and was never adopted by Congress, the Helms message can only have been a discouragement to vigorous action by State Department and other officials.[19] It is impossible to know the degree to which this political initiative was responsible for the Administration's three-and-a-half-year delay in following up on the Committee's recommendations and on its own commitments, and issuing the 1998 Executive Order. Given the direct and indirect power enjoyed by the Chair of the Foreign Relations Committee, its impact was certainly considerable.

---

[17] See J. Diller, 'Implementation of Human Rights Treaties within the United States', *ACLU International Civil Liberties Report*, February 1996, pp. 1–7; and Lawyers' Committee for Human Rights, *In the National Interest*, New York, 1996.

[18] 'The purpose and effect of General Comment No. 24 is to seek to nullify as a matter of international law the reservations, understandings, declarations, and proviso contained in the Senate resolution of ratification, thereby purporting to impose legal obligations on the United States never accepted by the United States.' S.1441, 104th Cong.,1st sess. #314 (1995).

[19] This opposition was again articulated by Senator Jessie Helms during UN negotiations of the proposed International Criminal Court in 1998. Expressing concern that an American citizen could come under the Court's jurisdiction 'even over the express objectives of the United States Government', Senator Helms warned Secretary of State Albright that any treaty which did not give the USA a veto on prosecutions 'will be *dead on arrival* at the Senate Foreign Relations Committee'. Helms is Chairman of the Senate Foreign Relations Committee. See *New York Times*, 27 March 1998.

The Executive Order tracks commitments made to the Human Rights Committee.[20] It requires 'executive departments and agencies' to 'respect and implement' US human rights treaty obligations, and to that end creates an Inter-Agency Working Group on Human Rights Treaties to provide 'guidance, oversight and co-ordination' on 'questions of implementation'. These include an annual review of reservations, the development of mechanisms to ensure that legislation proposed by the Administration conforms to US treaty obligations, and the monitoring of state laws.[21] This is an ambitious agenda, and one that has the potential to create a permanent structure for making international law relevant to human rights protection in the USA. The Executive Order is also an important first step towards changing US attitudes. Nevertheless, if the Inter-Agency Working Group is to be effective, even within its own terms of reference, it will need considerable political support from this and subsequent Administrations.

C. The Conaaaaavention against Torture

CAT presents a different experience to that of the ICCPR, and for a range of reasons the experience is seen as more positive by those in the USA who would use treaty law to expand domestic civil rights.

United States reservations do not constitute the same total barrier to implementing CAT as they have done in the case of the ICCPR, at least in relation to torture committed overseas. Unlike the ICCPR, United States

---

[20] See, too, specific recommendations made by the Lawyers' Committee for Human Rights, *In the National Interest*, 1996, pp. 61–8.

[21] The Group's functions include:
- coordinating the preparation of reports to treaty bodies, and responses to complaints submitted to the UN, the Organization of American States (OAS) and other international organisations;
- developing effective mechanisms to ensure that legislation proposed by the Administration is reviewed for conformity with treaty obligations, and that these obligations are taken into account in reviewing legislation under consideration by the Congress;
- developing 'recommended proposals and mechanisms for improving the monitoring of the actions by the various States, Commonwealths, and territories of the United States and, where appropriate, of Native Americans and Federally recognised Indian tribes, including the review of State, Commonwealth and territorial laws for their conformity with relevant treaties . . .';
- coordinating and directing 'an annual review of US reservations, declarations and understandings to human rights treaties, . . . in order to determine whether there should be consideration of any modification on relevant reservations, declarations and understandings to human rights treaties, or US practices or laws. . . .'. [Executive Order, section 4(c)].

courts have been given a defined role to play in applying those provisions of CAT which give national courts universal jurisdiction in respect of acts of torture committed in other countries, which create a duty to prosecute or extradite, and which bar *refoulement* (articles 3, 5, 6 and 7). Implementing legislation has been passed by the Congress which gives United States courts jurisdiction to prosecute acts of torture committed by non-nationals outside the United States, and award compensation to victims through civil proceedings under the Torture Victims Protection Act.[22] Pressure from the UN High Commissioner for Refugees (UNHCR), refugee lawyers and non-governmental organisations (NGOs) then focused on incorporation of the *non-refoulement* duty contained in article 3 of CAT,[23] and implementing legislation passed by the Congress in October 1998.[24]

In October 1999, the USA submitted its initial report to the Committee against Torture. The report is a serious and detailed review of US laws which effectively proscribe torture – despite the absence of a federal law criminalising the act of torture *per se* – and of the enforcement of constitutional bars on cruel and unusual punishment at the federal and state levels. The report acknowledges, albeit briefly, areas of concern and criticism including, for example, abuses by police, the effects of racial discrimination, and abuse in 'supermaximum' security facilities.[25]

The NGO community regards action on CAT as a priority, and sees the treaty as a new tool in a familiar area: litigation in United States courts on behalf of foreign torture victims. In this way, CAT is already acting as a

---

[22] The US Congress has enacted a criminal statute asserting jurisdiction over extraterritorial acts of torture (18 U.S.C. § 2340A), a civil statute providing for compensation for victims of acts of torture committed overseas (Pub.L.102–256, 12 March 1990, 106 Stat.73), and it has waived the foreign sovereign immunity of certain states for torture committed against US nationals (28 U.S.C.§ 1605(a)(7)).

[23] Article 3 creates an absolute bar to the forcible return of 'any person' to another state where 'there are substantial grounds' for believing they would be in danger of being subjected to torture. The protection is not limited to refugees, and there is no exception on the basis of serious crime or security.

[24] Sec. 2242(b) of the Foreign Affairs Reform and Restructuring Act of 1998.

[25] *US Department of State Initial Report of the United States of America to the UN Committee Against Torture*, 15 October 1999, http://www.state.gov/www/global/human_rights/. Assistant Secretary Harold Hongju Koh told the press that the report represented "the US Government's strong commitment to fulfilling its obligations under the Convention"; he noted a number of implementing statutes which had resulted from ratification. See http://www.state.gov/www/policy_remarks/1999/. A separate Annex to the Report addresses the issue of capital punishment "for informational purposes", while stating that the USA does not see capital punishment as within its reporting obligations.

catalyst and is leading to greater awareness by rights groups of the value of human rights treaties and giving treaty standards relevance in terms of United States domestic rights issues. This contrasts with NGO attitudes in the 1980s, which saw treaties only as the rights component of foreign policy. In two specific instances – prosecution and *non-refoulement* – CAT is welcomed by the civil rights community as a source of rights which are broader than those in the United States Constitution,[26] and as a legally effective human rights treaty in terms of the protection that United States law and courts can provide to torture victims.[27] The Lawyers' Committee for Human Rights is also pressing the Administration to take action to bring the United States into compliance with CAT, in relation to domestic law, including amending the 1994 statute making acts of torture committed in other countries a federal offence to include the same acts when committed *within* the United States.[28]

These developments are likely, in turn, to stimulate prisoners' rights groups – which grapple with deteriorating prison conditions, an unresponsive Supreme Court, and clear breaches of the international prohibition of 'cruel, inhuman or degrading treatment or punishment' – to begin to rely on international language, and to become more vigorous in seeking ways around those RUDs which replace the wider international norms and definitions with the lesser United States constitutional standard.

D. The future

The United States has also signed the Convention on the Elimination of Discrimination against Women (CEDAW), CRC and the International Covenant on Economic Social and Cultural Rights (ICESCR),[29] but none is

---

[26] See E. Massimino, 'Relief from Deportation under Article 3 of the United Nations Convention against Torture' in *1997–1998 Immigration and Nationality Handbook* (ed. P. Murphy), Washington, 1997, p. 467.

[27] See N. Dorsen, 'New Applications for International Law in US Domestic Law – the Case of Torture', *ACLU International Civil Liberties Report*, March 1997, pp. 1–3.

[28] Under US law as it currently stands, torture as such is proscribed only when it is committed outside the United States (18 U.S.C. § 2340 A). Torture committed inside the USA is prosecuted only under the general criminal law, e.g., as assault or under federal civil rights law, but these options are limited in scope by the definition of the elements of these crimes. See 2 *LCHR Advisor* 1, Spring 1998, New York.

[29] Prospects for action on the ICESCR are remote, and the obstacles to be overcome to secure ratification are even more formidable than for CRC. 'They arise essentially from the absence of clear agreement on values between the United States and the international

a likely candidate for ratification by the present Senate. Although the United States took an active part in drafting CRC, this treaty has come under direct political fire, with a number of conservative political and religious organisations orchestrating grassroots campaigns to demonstrate to Congress the strength of popular opposition.[30] It has also attracted outright opposition in the Senate. Five months after President Clinton signed CRC on 16 February 1995, Senator Helms, with support from nearly twenty senators, submitted a resolution to the Committee on Foreign Relations warning that 'if the President does attempt to push this unwise proposal [CRC] through the Senate, I want him to know . . . that I intend to do everything possible to make sure he is not successful'.[31] The Administration clearly heeded this warning and has made no attempt to secure ratification. The United States, with Somalia, is now the only UN member state which is not a party to CRC.

Despite this continuing failure to ratify these three human rights treaties, some advantages have flowed from the separate treaty regimes from a domestic standpoint. CAT has been protected from the political controversy between the Senate and the HRC over United States reservations to the ICCPR. The ICCPR has escaped the witch hunt now directed against CRC.

Until recently, human rights treaties have been kept on the outer margins of the United States civil rights map by the double constraint of the non-self-executing rule, and the inability of individuals to seek redress through the Optional Protocol to the ICCPR. But attitudes are changing.

---

community when it comes to the very concept of economic, social and cultural rights.' There is continued denial 'that there is any such thing as an economic, social or cultural right'. See P. Alston, 'US Ratification of the Covenant on Economic, Social and Cultural Rights', 84 *AJIL* 2, 1990, pp. 365–93.

[30] A bill entitled the Parental Rights and Responsibilities Act was introduced in Congress in 1995. It would have provided that 'no Federal, State or local government, or any official of such a government acting under color of law, shall interfere with or usurp the right of a parent to direct the upbringing of the child of the parent'. Efforts have begun in twenty-eight states to pass legislation or state constitutional amendments in similar terms.

[31] Senate Resolution 133 – Relative to the United Nations Convention on the Rights of the Child. S.Res.133, 104th Cong., 1st Sess., 141 Congressional Record 8400 (1995). The Chairman of the Senate Committee on Foreign Relations received over 5,000 letters opposing CRC, and only one in support: see A. Renteln, 'Who's Afraid of the CRC: Objections to the Convention on the Rights of the Child', 3 *ILSA Journal of Int'l & Comparative Law*, 1997, pp. 629–40. See also S. Kilbourne, 'United States Failure to Ratify the United Nations Convention on the Rights of the Child: Playing Politics with Children's Rights', *Transnational Law and Contemporary Problems*, 1996, p. 437.

As the Congress and the courts turn away from the civil rights activism of an earlier period, advocates – especially those engaged in prison reform and death penalty issues – are increasingly turning their attention to international norms. Organisations like the National Association for the Advancement of Colored People Legal Defense Fund now see linking the struggle for civil rights in the United States to the international human rights movement as a matter of necessity, and believe that international human rights law offers new weapons in the battle for civil rights, at a time when civil rights are under attack. As the United States expands use of the death penalty, the international treaties offer both an alternative ethic and a new legal authority.[32] The National Coalition to Abolish the Death Penalty – which now focuses on juvenile executions – sees international institutions as giving more hope for change than continued reliance on rights litigation under United States law in United States courts.[33]

The HRC's decision to review the United States report under the ICCPR at a meeting in New York rather than Geneva had a significant and positive effect on the perceptions of the many NGOs who were able to attend the sessions.[34] One consequence of the fiftieth anniversary of the Universal Declaration of Human Rights in 1998 has been a growth in pressure from the NGO sector on federal and state authorities to undertake effective

---

[32] See Stefanie Grant, 'Dialogue of the Deaf: New International Attitudes and the Death Penalty in America', 17 *Criminal Justice Ethics* 2, 1998, pp. 19–32.

[33] The National Coalition to Abolish the Death Penalty now places the ICCPR at the centre of its advocacy against the juvenile death penalty. Sixteen states retain the death penalty for offences committed by someone under the age of eighteen. Of these, Arkansas and North Carolina have a minimum age of fourteen, Louisiana and Virginia set the minimum age at fifteen and in Mississippi it is thirteen years of age. In 1997 fifty-eight persons were on death row awaiting execution for crimes committed when they were under the age of eighteen. There is pressure to reduce still further the death penalty eligibility age in some states. See *Washington Post*, Editorial, 'Executing Children', 14 April 1998. See also Human Rights Watch, *Modern Capital of Human Rights? Abuses in the State of Georgia*, New York, 1996.

[34] See generally A. Ginger, A. Wagley and R. Markfield, 'Nonprofits Have a New Role in Ensuring Human Rights in the United States', 30 *University of San Francisco Law Review* 2, 1996, pp. 427–76: 'The event was observed by a gallery full of representatives of NGOs from California to Maine, and by students from New York universities . . . Since returning from the Committee sessions . . . the Meiklejohn Civil Liberties Institute has made innumerable presentations on the new human rights treaties to other nonprofits including bar association conventions, city councils, coalitions of activists for affirmative action and against California Proposition 187, womens' groups preparing for the Beijing Conference on Women, UN Association meetings, university committees, religious bodies, a global network for cultural rights, and classrooms.'

review and monitoring of US laws and practice against international norms, on judges to learn this area of law, and on elected representatives to support the treaties. Law schools are increasingly including international human rights in their academic and clinical programmes, opening the door to its application by a new generation. There is also a growing recognition among international lawyers that in an increasingly interdependent world, the US cannot continue to stand aside from its international treaty obligations. This recognition was expressed editorially by the *American Journal of International Law* in these terms:

> US policies abroad depend on our being able to negotiate treaties and obtain compliance with them from our foreign counterparts. Some of these treaties require other countries to make drastic changes in their domestic legal systems . . . A reputation for playing fast and loose with treaty commitments can only harm our capacity to be a leader in the post-Cold War world.[35]

Meanwhile, until – and unless – the new direction signalled in the 1998 Executive Order becomes a reality, the prospects for any change in the United States Senate's attitude to international human rights law, or for any significant review of United States RUDs, are remote. While United States domestic groups are learning to use treaty law within the narrow limits set by the RUDs,[36] the challenge the latter present to the international system is enormous. Those states which seek to strengthen the treaty system must find a way to prevent United States' attitudes, as reflected in its reservations, from being used as an example and justification by countries which lack the rights protection provided by the United States Constitution.[37] It will not be easy.

---

[35] Detlev F. Vagts, 'Taking Rights Less Seriously', 92 *AJIL*, 1998, p. 462.

[36] See E. Massimino, 'Moving from Commitment to Compliance: Human Rights Treaties in US Law', *Georgetown Journal on Fighting Poverty*, No. 2, Summer 1998, pp. 263–6.

[37] Addressing the UN Human Rights Commission, the Chinese Ambassador rebuked the USA for tabling a resolution criticising China, commenting that the USA 'had ratified the International Covenant on Civil and Political Rights, with many reservations, fifteen years after signing it and had yet to ratify the International Covenant on Economic, Social and Cultural Rights. To demand prompt action from China on the Covenants was hegemonism or double standards.' See 'Summary Record of Commission on Human Rights', 23 April 1999.

C

REGIONAL AND SECTORAL COMPARISONS

15

REPORTING IN THE INTER-AMERICAN SYSTEM OF HUMAN RIGHTS PROTECTION

ANTÔNIO AUGUSTO CANÇADO TRINDADE

A. Human rights reports: legal basis, forms and objectives

By and large the international protection of human rights is undertaken through three basic procedures – petitioning, reporting and fact-finding, together with their variations. They operate either when invoked, as in the petitioning system, or on a periodic *ex officio* basis, as in the reporting system. These methods of protection cannot be seen in isolation; in practice, they may be related. For example, the petitioning and reporting systems may require, or bring about, *in loco* investigations. In its own way each system endeavours to coordinate actors and resources for the protection of human rights. Hence the petitioning system seeks to avoid duplication or conflict of jurisdiction and interpretation, the reporting system promotes standardisation and consolidation of guidelines, and the fact-finding system facilitates consultation and exchange of information.

Within the framework of the international protection of human rights, reports take a variety of forms. First, one may distinguish reports of states from reports of international organs. The expression 'reporting system' is normally used in reference to reports of states parties to human rights treaties which are made to the international supervisory organs established under those treaties. These reports can be periodic (i.e. regularly submitted in cycles), or submitted upon the request of the international organ concerned. Human rights reports *lato sensu* also encompass reports produced by international human rights supervisory organs. For example, besides producing the usual form of annual reports, the Inter-American Commission of Human Rights (IACHR) prepares reports, linked to its fact-finding function, on the human rights situation in certain member states of the

Organization of American States (OAS). The IACHR also prepares special reports on individual cases submitted to it.

Although reporting duties are explicitly provided for in each of the three regional human rights conventions in force, they have had a rather limited scope, especially when compared with the experience accumulated under United Nations instruments.[1] It has been at the global level of the United Nations, its specialised agencies (in particular the International Labour Organisation (ILO)) and the human rights treaty bodies that the reporting system has been most widely used.

Reporting obligations find their legal basis either in the human rights treaties or instruments or in the constituent instruments of the international organisations concerned, or in both. Reporting by states parties to human rights treaty bodies is intended to achieve a number of objectives:

(a) to provoke a comprehensive review of national legislation and administrative practices so as to ensure their conformity with international norms;
(b) to ensure that the state party monitors the human rights situation in an ongoing way and to enable it to demonstrate that it has done so on the basis of principled policy-making;
(c) to facilitate public scrutiny of governmental policies;
(d) to provide a basis on which to evaluate the progress achieved in the human rights situation;
(e) to enable states parties to develop a better understanding of the problems faced in realising human rights; and
(f) to facilitate an exchange of information among states parties with a view to developing a better understanding of the common problems encountered.[2]

The reporting system thus purports to promote and improve, at the domestic level, the implementation of international human rights obligations. In their operation, supervisory organs do not act as judicial or semi-judicial

---

[1] European Convention on Human Rights (ECHR), article 57; American Convention on Human Rights (ACHR), articles 42 and 43; African Charter on Human Rights and People's Rights, article 62. See also articles 21–24 of the European Social Charter (ESC).

[2] United Nations, *Report of the Committee on Economic, Social and Cultural Rights – Third Session* UN Doc. E/1989/22, 1989, pp. 87–9 (General Comment No. 1 (1989)); P. Alston, 'The Purposes of Reporting', in United Nations, *Manual on Human Rights Reporting*, UN Doc. HR/PUB/97/1 (Rev. 1) (1997), pp. 19–24.

organs. Rather, they assist states in complying with their international obligations and, to that end, in securing the fullest possible conformity of their domestic laws and administrative practices with human rights treaties.[3] Seen in this way, the system appears non-contentious in character. However, supervisory organs can establish whether and to what extent the human rights situations reported meet international obligations of protection and what measures are needed at the domestic level to improve the situation and bring the state in line with its international obligations.[4]

Opinions differ regarding the effectiveness of this method of human rights protection. Some argue that the reporting system is a method that, if properly used, is capable of providing an overall view of the human rights situation in a given country, a view which could not be achieved through the petitioning system, even though this system has been effectively used – at least in the inter-American system – to address cases of gross and systematic violations of human rights. Others argue more sceptically that it is precisely those countries with particularly serious human rights problems that tend to make insufficient disclosures in their reports, thus making evaluation more difficult. Bearing these preliminary points in mind, we turn our attention to human rights reports in the inter-American system of human rights protection.

B. Human rights reports in the inter-American system of protection

1. REPORTS OF STATES PARTIES TO THE AMERICAN CONVENTION ON HUMAN RIGHTS

Under the 1969 American Convention on Human Rights (ACHR) there is no periodic reporting system of the kind found, for example, under the United Nations human rights treaties.[5] However, two provisions of the

---

[3] United Nations, *Workshop on International Human Rights Instruments and Reporting Obligations: Preparation of Reports to United Nations Human Rights Treaty Bodies*, New York, 1992, pp. 9 and 18–26.

[4] F. Pocar and C. Bernard, 'National Reports: Their Submission to Expert Bodies and Follow-up', in *Manual on Human Rights Reporting, supra*, note 2, p. 37.

[5] Such as the International Covenant on Civil and Political Rights (ICCPR), the International Covenant on Economic, Social and Cultural Rights (ICESCR), the Convention on the Elimination of Racial Discrimination (CERD), the Convention on the Elimination of Discrimination against Women (CEDAW), the Convention on the Suppression and Punishment of the Crime of Apartheid, the Convention against Torture (CAT), and the Convention on Children's Rights (CRC).

ACHR have a bearing on the reporting duties of states parties, namely, articles 42 and 43. Article 43 provides that:

> The States Parties undertake to provide the Commission with such information as it may request of them as to the manner in which their domestic law ensures the effective application of any provisions of this Convention.

This duty, drafted in broad terms, is different from the obligations underlying the reporting system of the core conventions of the United Nations in the field of human rights.[6] Article 43 leaves to the IACHR the decision whether or not to request information from states parties. This information relates to a general duty enshrined in article 2 of the ACHR, which provides:

> Where the exercise of any of the rights or freedoms referred to in Article 1 is not already ensured by legislative or other provisions, the States Parties undertake to adopt, in accordance with their constitutional processes and the provisions of this Convention, such legislative or other measures as may be necessary to give effect to those rights or freedoms.

As a result, states parties to the ACHR are under the general obligation to adopt legislative measures and modify national laws so as to ensure that the ACHR is given effect in domestic law.

In recent years, both the IACHR and the Inter-American Court have begun to give indications of their preparedness to develop the potential of the general duty under article 2. Thus, in the *Amnesty Laws cases* of 1992 concerning Uruguay and Argentina, the IACHR concluded that the laws under review were incompatible with the ACHR in that they amounted to a denial of justice.[7] Subsequently, in the 1994 case of *Verbitsky v. Argentina* the IACHR explicitly stressed the extent of the general duty under article 2 with a view to giving effect to the rights it seeks to guarantee. In that case the Commission expressed its satisfaction with the culmination of a process of friendly settlement under which the respondent state removed the offence of contempt from national legislation.[8] For its part, the Inter-American

---

[6] ICCPR, ICESCR, CAT, CEDAW, CERD, and CRC.

[7] The laws under review were found to be in breach of articles 8, 25 and 1(1) of the Convention; cf. cases *Santos Mendoza et al. v. Uruguay*, and *Herrera et al. v. Argentina*, in OEA/CIDH, *Informe Anual de la Comisión Interamericana de Derechos Humanos 1992–1993*, Washington DC, 1994, pp. 162–74 and 42–53, respectively.

[8] OEA/CIDH, *Informe Anual de la Comisión Interamericana de Derechos Humanos 1994*, Washington DC, 1995, pp. 40–5.

Court, in its judgment of 17 September 1997 in the case of *Loayza Tamayo v. Peru*, ruled that certain decree-laws characterising the offences of *traición a la patria* (treason) and 'terrorism' were incompatible with article 8(4) of the ACHR incorporating the principle of *non bis in idem*.[9]

It is reassuring that the two supervisory organs of the ACHR have taken the first steps in this direction, but there is a long way still to go. In order to progress they will need, besides firm determination, to effect a considerable conceptual and jurisprudential development. The fact that they have not yet constructed their *jurisprudence constante* as to the general obligation of states parties to the ACHR to harmonise their domestic law with the relevant norms of the ACHR has a bearing on the current difficulty of determining whether states have to date complied with that general obligation. One is thus led to wonder whether the future development of case law under article 2 will prompt the IACHR to make greater use of its powers under article 43.

The second provision of the ACHR relating to reporting duties is article 42:

> The States Parties shall transmit to the Commission a copy of each of the reports and studies that they submit annually to the Executive Committees of the Inter-American Economic and Social Council and the Inter-American Council for Education, Science and Culture, in their respective fields, so that the Commission may watch over the promotion of the rights implicit in the economic, social, educational, scientific, and cultural standards set forth in the Charter of the Organization of American States as amended by the Protocol of Buenos Aires.

Despite its mandatory language, in practice article 42 has been ineffective. Regrettably states parties have never regarded this article as imposing upon them a legal duty, and despite recent efforts, the IACHR has not yet been

---

[9] *Loayza Tamayo v. Peru*, judgment on the merits of 17 September 1997, para. 68, and paras. 66–77. The Court had earlier pronounced upon the matter in general also in the exercise of its advisory competence. See fourteenth Advisory Opinion, on International Responsibility for the Promulgation and Enforcement of Laws in Violation of the Convention, 9 December 1994. For the treatment by the Court of this matter in the exercise of its competence in contentious cases, see *El Amparo* (Venezuela), judgment on reparations of 14 September 1996, resolution of interpretation of judgment of 16 April 1997, and dissenting opinions (in both) of Judge A. A. Cançado Trindade; *Caballero Delgado and Santana v. Colombia*, judgment on reparations of 29 January 1997, and dissenting opinion of Judge A. A. Cançado Trindade; *Genie Lacayo v. Nicaragua*, resolution of revision of judgment of 13 September 1997, and dissenting opinion of Judge A. A. Cançado Trindade.

able to explore the article's potential. In its report no. 90/90 of 3 October 1990,[10] the IACHR *inter alia* invoked article 42 in requesting the respondent state to incorporate into the annual reports referred to in the article, a chapter dealing with retirement and pension benefits, so as to enable a follow-up by the IACHR.[11] In urging the respondent state to submit this information in a report under article 42, the IACHR illustrated both the usefulness of the provision and how it can be used in a specific way rather than only in a general, even automatic, fashion. Had states parties always seen themselves as bound by the reporting obligation provided under article 42, it would not have been necessary for the IACHR to invoke it in the circumstances. Thus, article 42 has considerable potential, which has yet to be fully explored.

Article 42 can be extended to the domain of economic, social and cultural rights. As to the protection of these rights, a historical gap still prevails in the inter-American system, exemplified by article 26, the sole and broad provision on the matter in the ACHR. It is true that the 1988 Additional Protocol to the ACHR on Human Rights in the Area of Economic, Social and Cultural Rights (the San Salvador Protocol) opens up new possibilities in this area. For example, article 19(6) of the San Salvador Protocol contemplates the application of the system of individual petitions or communications as regulated by articles 44–51 and 61–69 of the ACHR to the right of association and trade union freedom (article 8(1)(a)) and the right to education (article 13). It also provides for the formulation by the IACHR of observations and recommendations concerning the situation of economic, social and cultural rights enshrined in the Protocol (article 19(7)).[12]

However, the San Salvador Protocol has not yet obtained the necessary ratifications for its entry into force. From its adoption in 1988 until mid-1999 ten states had ratified the Protocol,[13] leaving only one more ratification needed for it to enter in to force. Following the adoption of the San

---

[10] Case No. 9893 concerning Uruguay.

[11] OEA/CIDH, *Informe Anual de la Comisión Interamericana de Derechos Humanos 1990–1991*, Washington DC, 1992, p. 95, at pp. 81–95.

[12] For a study of the 1988 San Salvador Protocol, see e.g., A. Cançado Trindade, *La Cuestión de la Protección Internacional de los Derechos Económicos, Sociales y Culturales: Evolución y Tendencias Actuales*, San José, Costa Rica, 1992; A. Cançado Trindade, 'La question de la protection internationale des droits économiques, sociaux et culturels: évolution et tendances actuelles', 94 *Revue générale de droit international public*, 1990, pp. 913–46.

[13] Namely: Brazil, Colombia, Ecuador, El Salvador, Mexico, Panama, Paraguay, Peru, Suriname and Uruguay.

Salvador Protocol, article 42 of the ACHR for a time attracted attention as a possibility for protecting these rights.[14] For example, the 1991 Annual Report of the IACHR contained a section on the 'status of economic, social and cultural rights' in the hemisphere.[15] A similar section also appeared in the Commission's Annual Report for 1992–1993,[16] giving the impression of a trend towards closer attention to the situation of economic, social and cultural rights in member states, based on information obtained by the IACHR through the application of article 42. However, the IACHR Annual Reports for 1994, 1995 and 1996 no longer contain such a section, suggesting that this trend may have been halted.[17]

2. REPORTS OF THE INTER-AMERICAN COMMISSION ON HUMAN RIGHTS

Another group of provisions in the ACHR relate to reports prepared by the IACHR. Article 49 provides that, in the case of a friendly settlement of a petition or communication having been reached under article 48(1)(f), the IACHR is to draw up a report to be transmitted to the petitioner and to all states parties and then to the OAS Secretary-General for publication. Under article 49 such a report must contain a brief statement of the facts and of the solution reached but any party in the case may request and is

---

[14] A. Cançado Trindade, 'The Inter-American Human Rights Protection System', in *Recueil des cours – Textes et sommaires (XXVII Session d'enseignement)*, Strasbourg, 1996, pp. 257–8. Before the adoption of the San Salvador Protocol, the IACHR had to some extent taken account of the situation of some economic, social and cultural rights in certain Latin American countries (e.g., in its reports on El Salvador, 1978, and on Haiti, 1979). Furthermore, it acknowledged, in its Annual Report of 1979–1980, the 'organic relationship' between civil and political rights, and economic, social and cultural rights. The field was thus open for the next step, i.e., the preparation of an international instrument for the protection of the latter. Such work, initiated in 1982, culminated in the adoption in 1988 of the Additional Protocol to the ACHR in the Area of Economic, Social and Cultural Rights, mentioned above.

[15] OAS/CIDH, *Annual Report of the Inter-American Commission on Human Rights 1991*, Washington DC, 1992, pp. 287–304.

[16] OEA/CIDH, *Informe Anual de la Comisión Interamericana de Derechos Humanos 1992–1993*, Washington DC, 1994, pp. 233–52.

[17] In its report of 1996, aspects of the matter are only dealt with indirectly under other more specific topics such as the rights of indigenous peoples, of women, and of migrant workers and their families: see, OEA/CIDH, *Informe Anual de la Comisión Interamericana de Derechos Humanos 1996*, Washington DC, 1997, pp. 655–76 and 787–95.

REGIONAL AND SECTORAL COMPARISONS

entitled to receive 'the fullest possible information'. Friendly settlements were reached in several cases before the IACHR,[18] and in one case before the Court.[19]

Articles 50 and 51 of the ACHR also deal with reports by the IACHR. These two provisions have in the past caused difficulties in interpretation, most likely owing to their rather clumsy wording:

Article 50

1. If a settlement is not reached, the Commission shall, within the time limit established by its Statute, draw up a report setting forth the facts and stating its conclusions. If the report, in whole or in part, does not represent the unanimous agreement of the members of the Commission, any member may attach to it a separate opinion. The written and oral statements made by the parties in accordance with paragraph 1(e) of Article 48 shall also be attached to the report.

2. The report shall be transmitted to the States concerned, which shall not be at liberty to publish it.

3. In transmitting the report, the Commission may make such proposals and recommendations as it sees fit.

Article 51

1. If, within a period of three months from the date of the transmittal of the report of the Commission to the States concerned, the matter has not either been settled or submitted by the Commission or by the State concerned to the Court and its jurisdiction accepted, the Commission may, by the vote of an absolute majority of its members, set forth its opinion and conclusions concerning the question submitted for its consideration.

2. Where appropriate, the Commission shall make pertinent recommendations and shall prescribe a period within which the State is to take the measures that are incumbent upon it to remedy the situation examined.

---

[18] Report No. 1/93, of 3 March 1993 (cases nos. 10.288, 10.310, 10.496, 10.631 and 10.771, Argentina), in OEA/CIDH, *Informe Anual de la Comisión Interamericana de Derechos Humanos 1992–1993*, Washington DC, 1994, pp. 36–41; Report No. 22/94 of 20 September 1994 (*Verbitsky* case, No. 11.012, Argentina), in OEA, *Informe Anual de la Comisión Interamericana de Derechos Humanos – 1994*, Washington DC, 1995, pp. 40–5.

[19] In the *Maqueda* case (Argentina), the Court, having examined a friendly settlement reached by the parties, allowed the discontinuance and dismissal of the case, but reserved the right to reopen and continue the hearing should the settlement change in the future. Inter-American Court of Human Rights, Resolution of 15 January 1995, Series C, No. 18, pp. 15–26.

3. When the prescribed period has expired, the Commission shall decide by the vote of an absolute majority of its members whether the State has taken adequate measures and whether to publish its report.

These are possibly the most obscure provisions of the ACHR. If a serious revision of the Convention were ever undertaken, articles 50 and 51 would surely rank among the provisions most in need of reconsideration. The confusion centres on the number of reports contemplated by the two articles. The Inter-American Court, on the one hand, has indicated[20] that articles 50 and 51 refer to what have been described as two distinct reports, one of a preliminary character, the other definitive.[21] On the other hand, articles 46 to 48 of the IACHR's Regulations appear to proceed on the assumption that the report mentioned in article 50 is the same as that referred to in article 51.

It has recently been suggested that this ambiguity be resolved by amending articles 46 to 48 of the IACHR's Regulations so as to make it clear that two reports are contemplated by articles 50 and 51, and that they are distinct, both in the sense indicated above by the Inter-American Court, and as to the measures to be taken, even if their content may, depending on the conduct of the respondent state, end up being largely the same.[22] The essence of the problem lies in the fact that only the report mentioned in article 51[23] may be published, and not the report referred to in article 50. It is surprising that the confidential report under article 50 is transmitted only to the respondent state and not to the individual claimant, but this is what article 50(2) appears clearly to say. Whatever practical reasons may have prompted the drafting of article 50 in its present terms (and the *travaux préparatoires* of the ACHR often appear nebulous), this would appear to be an assault on fairness and equality of arms.

---

[20] See the Court's fifteenth Advisory Opinion (1997), its thirteenth Advisory Opinion (1993), its judgments of 1987 on preliminary objections in the *Honduran cases*, and its *obiter dicta* on article 51(1) of the Convention in its judgments on preliminary objections in the cases of *Neira Alegría* (1995) and *Cayara* (1993), concerning Peru.

[21] In its fifteenth Advisory Opinion, the court reaffirmed the finality of the report referred to article 51 of the ACHR save in certain specific circumstances set out in the Opinion.

[22] M. Ventura Robles, 'Los Artículos 50 y 51 de la Convención Americana sobre Derechos Humanos', in *La Corte y el Sistema Interamericanos de Derechos Humanos* (ed. R. Navia), San José, Costa Rica, 1994, pp. 553–69.

[23] As to the three-month period mentioned in paragraph 1 of article 51, the Court has indicated (*Neira Alegría, supra,* note 20, paras. 32–4) that, under certain circumstances, it can be extended.

3. THE RELATIONSHIP BETWEEN REPORTS, FACT-FINDING AND PETITIONS

As already pointed out, the different methods of international protection of human rights cannot be approached in isolation from each other. A reporting system, in the sense of those under UN human rights treaties, is virtually non-existent in the inter-American system and is a non-issue under the ACHR. Yet the ACHR does prescribe some reporting *duties*, which have in turn raised problems in practice as regards both states parties' reports under article 42 and the IACHR's reports under articles 50 and 51.[24]

In contrast to the very limited use of reports in the inter-American system, the IACHR has undertaken extensive fact-finding exercises, probably to a larger extent than any other international supervisory organ at least in so far as *in loco* observations are concerned. These are of particular significance as *in loco* investigations have in turn produced several major reports, such as that of the *in loco* investigation in Chile of 1974, the report on forced disappearances in Argentina of 1979, the report on the population of Miskito origin in Nicaragua of 1984, and the reports on Haiti of 1993–1994, among others.

The number of *in loco* investigations undertaken by the IACHR on the basis of article 18(g) of its statute has steadily increased through the years: in the 1960s and 1970s eleven missions took place; twenty-four in the 1980s; twenty-five in the first half of the 1990s. Thus, by the end of 1995 the IACHR had undertaken a total of sixty *in loco* investigations of general human rights situations in OAS member states.[25] Importantly, investigations are undertaken not only in respect of states parties to the ACHR but also of member states of the OAS. This is owing to the duality of functions of the IACHR, which is a supervisory organ of the ACHR as well as an OAS organ.[26]

---

[24] Under articles 42 and 50–51 of the Convention, respectively (see above).

[25] For an appraisal, see E. Vargas Carreño, 'Las Observaciones *in loco* Practicadas por la Comisión Interamericana de Derechos Humanos', in *Derechos Humanos en las Américas – Homenaje a la Memoria de C.A. Dunshee de Abranches*, Washington DC, 1984, pp. 290–305; E. Márquez Rodríguez, 'Visitas de Observación *in loco* de la Comisión Interamericana de Derechos Humanos y sus Informes', in *Estudios Básicos de Derechos Humanos* (eds. A. Cançado Trindade, G. Elizondo and J. Ordóñez), vol. III, San José, Costa Rica, 1995, pp. 135–44.

[26] On the IACHR's duality of functions see A. Cançado Trindade, 'Co-existence and Co-ordination of Mechanisms of International Protection of Human Rights (at Global and Regional Levels)', 202 *Recueil des cours de l'Académie de droit international de La Haye*, 1987, pp. 203–6.

The reports resulting from these missions have been instrumental in ascertaining the facts of a situation. Moreover, the publicity given to the reports has served to achieve certain of the objectives of a reporting system, such as the monitoring of human rights, public scrutiny of legislative measures and administrative practices, exchange of information and the fostering of a better understanding of the problems encountered.

Thus the reporting function of the IACHR is often related to its fact-finding function. Equally, it is often related to the petitioning system under the ACHR. Articles 48(1)(d) and 48(2) of the ACHR[27] allow the IACHR to pursue investigations with a view to verifying facts alleged in a petition or communication. This is distinct from an investigation of a general human rights situation, which is subject to the invitation or consent of the host state. In relation to the petitioning system, a lack of cooperation on the part of the respondent state with the fact-finding exercise of the IACHR could amount to a violation of the ACHR. Hence the IACHR's petitioning and fact-finding functions are each conducive to the eventual adoption of the Commission's reports under articles 50 and 51.

It has sometimes been suggested that petitioning systems cannot be effective to respond to gross violations of human rights, and that this task is better dealt with by governmental reporting. The inter-American experience suggests otherwise. Individual petitions or communications under the inter-American system, even in the early practice of the IACHR before the entry into force of the ACHR, have effectively addressed cases of gross and systematic violations of human rights. One need only recall the IACHR's handling of the so-called 'general' cases of the 1960s and 1970s. As a result of its decisions in these cases (and also in 'individual' cases), as well as in its *in loco* observations and its recommendations addressed to respondent states or formulated in its reports, changes have been introduced to national laws which violated human rights, and domestic remedies and procedures have been set up or amended so as to ensure the observance of human rights. The IACHR's decisions in 'general' cases have thus to a degree transcended the particular circumstances of these cases and the issue of redress to individual victims.

The same may be said of the first regional system of protection, that of the 1950 European Convention on Human Rights (ECHR) and its

---

[27] Article 48 of the Convention allows the IACHR to carry out an 'investigation' for the purposes of verifying the facts alleged in a petition or communication (paras. 1(d) and 2).

Protocols. Commencing with cases in the 1970s relating to 'legislative measures and administrative practices' in states parties, it was soon made clear that petitions under article 25 of the ECHR, even though motivated by the search for individual redress, could also contribute to securing respect for obligations of an objective nature incumbent upon states parties.[28] The role of the petitioning system should not therefore be underestimated. The experience of the inter-American system suggests that it should be considered in a historical perspective and through its relations with the reporting and fact-finding systems.

C. Concluding comments

The ACHR does not provide for any periodic reporting system of the kind found under UN human rights treaties and, given the features of the inter-American system of protection, the possibility of such reporting being developed along UN lines is unlikely. Rather, reporting in the system is divided between the reporting functions of the IACHR on the one hand, and reporting duties of states parties on the other.

The reporting functions of the IACHR (under the procedure set out in articles 50 and 51 of the ACHR) have been beset by uncertainties and misunderstandings. These problems could in the future be overcome by a definitive interpretation of the provisions or by a reconsideration of the problematic wording of articles 50 and 51, in any future revision of the ACHR. The reporting duties of states parties to the ACHR under articles 42 and 43 in their turn have not been fully complied with by states parties to date. This is regrettable, as these duties have considerable potential, which has so far remained virtually unexplored.

---

[28] H. Rolin, 'Le rôle du requérant dans la procédure prévue par la Commission européenne des droits de l'homme', 9 *Revue hellénique de droit international*, 1956, pp. 3–14, especially p. 9; C.Th. Eustathiades, 'Les recours individuels à la Commission européenne des droits de l'homme', in *Grundprobleme des internationalen Rechts – Festschrift für Jean Spiropoulos*, Bonn, 1957, p. 121; F. Durante, *Ricorsi Individuali ad Organi Internazionali*, Milan, 1958, pp. 125–52, esp. pp. 129–30; Karel Vasak, *La Convention européenne des droits de l'homme*, Paris, 1964, pp. 96–8; M. Virally, 'L'accès des particuliers à une instance internationale: la protection des droits de l'homme dans le cadre européen', 20 *Mémoires publiés par la faculté de droit de Genève*, 1964, pp. 67–89; H. Mosler, 'The Protection of Human Rights by International Legal Procedure', 52 *Georgetown Law Journal*, 1964, pp. 818–19.

Further developments on this matter are bound to occur as a new awareness grows within the inter-American human rights system of the extent of
the legislative obligations of states parties to the ACHR under article 2.
These legislative obligations complement the specific obligations relating to
each of the protected rights, as well as the general duty *to respect* the recognised human rights and *to ensure* their free and full exercise (article 1(1)).
It may well happen that a given national law, or else the *vacatio legis*, lies at
the root of a proven violation of human rights. Hence the obligation of the
state party concerned is to remedy this situation so as to put an end to
the violation and to avoid the possibility of further breaches occurring. The
duty of prevention is thus a basic component of the two general obligations
provided for in articles 1(1) and 2 of the ACHR.

One of the most reliable ways of measuring the effectiveness of a human
rights treaty is to consider its impact upon the domestic laws of the states
parties. This impact can be gleaned from legislative reforms made as a
consequence of the decisions of international supervisory organs and
which promote the harmonisation of national laws with the international
obligations. There is a great need in the inter-American system for a better
understanding of the wide scope of the conventional obligations of protection which encompass acts or omissions of the states parties through their
organs or agents in any of the three branches of government.

One of the key purposes served by a system of reporting by states parties
is to determine the conformity of their national legislation (and its application by judicial organs, as well as of administrative practices) with the
provisions of human rights treaties. Given the deficiencies of the reporting
system under the ACHR, the greater reliance on petitioning and fact-
finding is bound to continue. This being so, it is to be expected that in
exercising their petitioning and fact-finding functions, the two international supervisory organs will pay particular and close attention to compliance by states parties with their legislative obligations under the ACHR.

Other challenges present themselves, in particular the necessity of devis-
ing a procedure of follow-up for the decisions of the Inter-American Court
and the IACHR in order to secure compliance. There is also the need for
the case law of the Court and the Commission to develop the potential of
article 2 of the ACHR, as it has done over the last decade[29] with regard to
article 1(1). The general obligations of articles 1(1) and 2 complement each

---

[29] See the so-called *Honduran cases* (*Velásquez Rodríguez*, 1988, and *Godínez Cruz*, 1989).

other, besides strengthening the specific duties pertaining to each of the protected rights. The correction of the current jurisprudential imbalance should be one of the highest priorities of both the Court and the Commission. This is demanded by the rule of law and will benefit all those subject to the jurisdictions of states parties.

The operation of the inter-American system of protection shows the interrelatedness of the fact-finding, petitioning and reporting methods of the international protection of human rights. Despite the limited use of reporting, the extensive fact-finding missions undertaken by the IACHR and subsequent reports have served to achieve the objectives of the human rights reporting system itself. Likewise, the petitioning regime in the inter-American system has been effective in addressing cases of gross and systematic violations of human rights in addition to individual rights abuse.

The 'integrated vision' of human rights propounded at the two World Conferences on Human Rights (Teheran in 1968 and Vienna in 1993)[30] is today broadly accepted at the normative and conceptual level. The time has come for this 'integrated vision' to be advanced at an operational level by relating methods of implementation to each other, having regard to the complementary character of the mechanisms of protection at global and regional levels. Regional systems of protection, such as the inter-American, are surely to be approached in the light of the *universality* of human rights, and this has implications both on the normative and operational planes.

---

[30] For a comprehensive study, see, e.g., A. Cançado Trindade, *Tratado de Direito Internacional dos Direitos Humanos*, vol. I, Porto Alegre, Brazil, 1997, pp. 1–447.

16

LESSONS FROM THE REPORTING SYSTEM OF THE EUROPEAN SOCIAL CHARTER

DAVID HARRIS

The object of this chapter is to reflect upon the reporting system for the European Social Charter (ESC)[1] with a view to considering what lessons it may have for the reporting systems that operate under UN human rights treaties. This is not to suggest that the reporting system under the ESC is perfect or that, given its regional nature, it provides a good analogy in all respects for its UN equivalents. It is rather that the ESC reporting system is a well established system that has in some respects developed along different lines from those of UN reporting systems, and that some of its good features may be transferable to the universal level.

A. Reports

The ESC requires contracting parties (of whom there are currently twenty-five)[2] to submit periodic national reports relating to all of the ESC provisions they have accepted.[3] The first parties to the Charter have now reported for thirty years.

---

[1] ETS 35; 529 UNTS 89, adopted 1961, in force since 1965. In addition to the 1961 Charter, there is now a 1996 Revised European Social Charter, ETS 163. The Revised Charter, in force since 1999, replaces the substantive guarantee of the 1961 Charter for the parties to it; the system of supervision is the same for the two treaties. This chapter is expressed just in terms of the 1961 Charter for convenience.

[2] These are Austria, Belgium, Cyprus, Denmark, Finland, France, Germany, Greece, Hungary, Iceland, Ireland, Italy, Luxembourg, Malta, the Netherlands, Norway, Poland, Portugal, Romania, Slovakia, Slovenia, Spain, Sweden, Turkey and the United Kingdom. Romania and Slovakia are parties to the Revised Charter; France, Italy and Sweden are parties to both the 1961 and Revised Charters. The others are parties to the 1961 Charter only.

[3] The ESC is unusual in that it permits states to ratify it on an *à la carte* basis. They are required to accept at least ten of the nineteen articles of the ESC or forty-five of its seventy-two paragraphs.

The system works well in the sense that, although reports are commonly some months late and the information provided is not always complete, there has never been a case of a state not submitting a report.[4] Consequently, the Council of Europe has never been faced with anything like the problem that regularly faces UN treaty monitoring bodies of reports being many years overdue.

There are several reasons for the good reporting record of states under the ESC. The European states concerned are generally better equipped administratively and financially to prepare national reports and have greater experience of doing so than many developing states. The Council of Europe is composed of a relatively small and homogeneous group of states, the representatives of which meet regularly for many Council of Europe purposes. The result is a strong collegiate sense of obligation to comply with the undertakings that go with Council membership.

This general sense of obligation is reinforced in the case of the ESC by the fact that, in contrast with the arrangements within the UN system, states parties to the ESC play a central role in its system of enforcement through their membership of the Governmental Committee. The persons who sit on the Governmental Committee are civil servants who are responsible at some level for the submission of their state's national report. At Governmental Committee meetings, these individuals are subjected to questioning by their peers on the matter of compliance with their state's reporting obligations; the questioners may be concerned that others put as much effort into the preparation and submission of reports as the competent departments in their own governments do.

In addition the Governmental Committee has, on its own initiative, been active in developing a system of warnings for states that have submitted reports but have failed to provide the Committee of Independent Experts (CIE) with all the information that it needs to make a determination as to compliance.[5] In 1999 the CIE changed its name to the European Committee of Social Rights; the old name is used in this chapter for convenience. Members of the Governmental Committee have occasionally shown signs of irritation with states that have persistently, and in breach of their ESC reporting obligations, failed to supply the information requested by the CIE in earlier reporting cycles.

But it is not immediately evident that there are lessons to be learnt for the

---

[4] The worst case was in the 1980s when Iceland submitted its first report two years late.
[5] There is no provision in the ESC for such a system.

UN system from the experience of the ESC on this matter. UN supervisory procedures do not have the same small, homogeneous grouping of states and there are not – and arguably should not be – bodies with functions comparable to those of the Governmental Committee. Are there other, as yet untried, means within the UN system (possibly through the meetings of contracting parties to the human rights treaty concerned or in meetings of the Economic and Social Council) by which states might be encouraged to bring pressure to bear upon other states to achieve fuller and swifter reporting? The answer is far from clear.

The ESC requires states to submit national reports every two years on the Charter articles they have accepted, although the Committee of Ministers of the Council of Europe has decided that full biennial reports on non-core articles must be submitted only once every four years.[6] This contrasts with the practice of some UN treaty bodies which call for reports on a less frequent basis – in the case of the two Covenants at five-yearly intervals.[7] The question arises whether intervals as long as five years are too long. The preparation and presentation of reports concentrates the minds of those who prepare them and provides a focal point and opportunity for criticism of a state's human rights record by non-governmental organisations (NGOs) and others. The more often states are required to submit reports, the more frequently these factors come into play and the more up-to-date is the review and critique of a state's performance by a monitoring body. The experience at Strasbourg, where the CIE commonly requests states to provide further information on particular points of law or practice, suggests that two years to wait for a reply is long enough if the dialogue between the CIE and the reporting state is to be more than a stuttering, or even historical exercise.

As far as UN bodies are concerned, if their workload and secretariat resources were ever to permit it (which is not the case at present), a reduction of the current four- or five-year reporting cycle would be an improvement.

The ESC provides for two kinds of reports: the biennial reports on accepted provisions (article 21) and occasional reports on unaccepted

---

[6] Until the early 1990s, a full biennial report was required of parties on every ESC provision that they had accepted. This requirement was relaxed because of the workload for the supervisory organs. As of 1997, following a period of experimentation, parties are called upon to report biennially on the seven 'core' ESC articles (articles 1, 5, 6, 12, 13, 16, and 19 on the rights to organise, social security, etc.) and to report on other articles every four years: Decision of the Committee of Ministers, September 1996, reprinted in *European Social Charter: Collected Texts*, Strasbourg, 1997, p. 287.

[7] See article 40 ICCPR and UN Doc. A/36/40 Annex V as modified in UN Doc. A/37/40 (Decision on Periodicity); and UN Doc. E/1988/14.

provisions (article 22). So far contracting parties have been called upon on four occasions to submit reports under article 22. These reports provide an opportunity for the CIE to explain the meaning of particular provisions and to comment constructively on the difficulties that a state sees as standing in the way of its acceptance of them. Given that parties to all UN human rights treaties have to accept all of the provisions of the treaty in question, the ESC practice under article 22 may be most relevant in respect of treaty reservations made by parties to UN treaties. It is comparable to the review or questioning that a UN human rights treaty body might make of a state party's reasons for maintaining a reservation.

B. The Committee of Independent Experts

The task of assessing whether a party complies with its ESC obligations falls to the CIE. This is a body composed of just nine members.[8] They are elected by the Committee of Ministers of the Council of Europe from candidates put forward by the governments of member states. The process thus only involves states. The Protocol Amending the European Social Charter of 1991 (1991 Amending Protocol), which is not yet in force,[9] provides for the election of CIE members from a list of candidates nominated by the contracting parties, and by the Parliamentary Assembly of the Council of Europe, which is composed of members of the national parliaments of the member states.[10] This will provide a democratic element in the election process and may open the process up to more public scrutiny.[11]

---

[8] While the ESC provides for seven members (article 25.1) provision was made in the 1991 Amending Protocol (ETS 142) for an increase in membership to nine or more. Although the 1991 Amending Protocol is not yet in force, it was unanimously agreed that the membership should be raised to nine to cope with the increased workload of the CIE and to provide a better cross-section of knowledge of national law within its membership: Decision of the Committee of Ministers, March 1994, reprinted in *European Social Charter: Collected Texts*, Strasbourg, 1997, p. 239.

[9] Fourteen of the twenty-five parties have ratified the 1991 Amending Protocol, with ratification by all required for its entry into force. Even so, almost all of its provisions are being applied by unanimous agreement of the ESC parties. The new election rule is an exception.

[10] See revised article 25 of the ESC.

[11] The election of judges to the European Court of Human Rights has always been by the Parliamentary Assembly of the Council of Europe from a list of candidates nominated by member states. Under Protocol 11 to the ECHR (ETS 155), the Parliamentary Assembly conducts interviews of candidates (see the discussion of this procedure by Craig Scott in chapter 19). A similar practice would be beneficial in the election of CIE members.

Some mechanism by which the election of members to UN human rights bodies was not exclusively in the hands of the contracting parties would be welcome, although there is no forum comparable to the Parliamentary Assembly of the Council of Europe within the UN system that could play a similar part. True, the Sub-Commission on Promotion and Protection of Human Rights, although not composed of democratically-elected members, is designated as independent. But it would clearly not be acceptable to the states parties to human rights treaties to hand over their powers of election to that body.

A crucial requirement of any human rights monitoring body is its independence from governments and others. The CIE had this in mind from the very outset, when it insisted that its title should include the word '*independent*' to distinguish it from the many committees of governmental experts that function within the Council of Europe.[12] In practice, the CIE has lived up to its claim of independence. This was demonstrated in its early years when it at once set about interpreting and applying the substantive guarantees in the ESC in a rigorous way, an approach that it has maintained to the present.

The independence of such a body depends upon the independence of its individual members. This has not been a problem for the CIE. At present, it is composed of six law professors, an economics professor, a retired head of the Social Section of the French Conseil d'Etat and a national judge, none of whom currently hold posts that might be thought to compromise their independence. This is in line with the membership of the CIE during the whole of its history, which has generally not been such as to raise questions over its independence.

There might be a lesson, or a reminder, here for states parties to UN human rights treaties when, under the current election arrangements, they nominate or vote for candidates to the treaty bodies. It is commonly accepted that there is at present a spectrum of independence on these bodies. Some members concurrently hold positions with their government's delegation to the UN or other posts that, on a 'justice being seen to be done' basis, do not seem consistent with a requirement of independence from governments.[13]

---

[12] Article 25 of the ESC refers to the CIE as a 'committee of experts'.

[13] See, for example in respect of the Human Rights Committee, T. Opsahl, 'The Human Rights Committee', in *The United Nations and Human Rights: A Critical Appraisal*, (ed. P. Alston), 2nd edn, Oxford, 2000 forthcoming, pp. 369, 376.

The working methods of the CIE are characterised by the thoroughness with which it reviews each contracting party's performance in each reporting cycle. The CIE reaches a conclusion as to compliance with every ESC provision that the state has accepted. The result is the publication each year of a volume several hundred pages long, entitled *Conclusions of the Committee of Independent Experts of the European Social Charter* which contains the CIE's findings on compliance.[14] In contrast with UN human rights treaty bodies, the CIE does not limit itself to a consideration of serious problems. While it is commendable to tackle serious problems and perhaps to highlight them by being selective, it might be argued that a more thorough review of a state's law and practice in the area of a guaranteed right is preferable. But the adoption of such a comprehensive approach depends upon the time and resources available to the monitoring body.

Another, recently introduced feature of the working methods of the CIE that UN human rights bodies might study is the use of working groups or chambers. As the number of parties to the ESC has grown, the CIE has found itself under considerable pressure of time, as a part-time body, to conduct detailed examinations of the parties' compliance with all of their obligations in each biennial reporting cycle. One remedy[15] is the division of the CIE into two working groups for the examination of reports. This was tried for the first time in the working year 1995–1996, and expedited the work of the CIE considerably.[16] The arrangements presuppose that all final decisions are still taken by the plenary committee, to which matters of principle or difficulty are also referred. The use of working groups was suspended in 1996–1997 because of the election of an unusually large number of new CIE members who needed time to become familiar with ESC case law and the working methods of the CIE, but it was reintroduced in 1997–1998. Obviously, the use of working groups calls for sufficient

---

[14] The latest volume is *European Social Charter – Committee of Independent Experts – Conclusions XIV-2* (1998), 828 pp.

[15] Resort to working groups only became feasible when the size of the CIE was increased from seven to nine in accordance with the terms of the 1991 Amending Protocol. Working Groups with at most three or four members were not practicable.

[16] A further remedy would be to increase the number or length of meetings of the CIE: at present it usually meets for seven one-week sessions a year. For another remedy – the move to a partially four-year reporting cycle – see note 6 above.

secretariat staff to service the additional meetings, particularly if they are held at the same time.[17]

A further characteristic of the ESC reporting system is that it is almost entirely a written one. In nearly all cases, the CIE reaches its conclusions on the question of compliance solely on the basis of national reports and other written information and evidence presented to it by NGOs and others. The 1991 Amending Protocol, in a provision that has been implemented in practice even though the protocol is not yet in force, authorises meetings between the CIE and the representatives of a reporting state, at the request of either side, in order to assist in the examination of the report. Although such meetings have occurred and are likely to continue, they will probably remain the exception rather than the rule.

This is in strong contrast with the experience of UN human rights treaty bodies. As with the oral hearings that such bodies routinely conduct, the object of the ESC meetings is to provide an opportunity for a dialogue that will clarify a state's law and practice and establish its conformity with the state's treaty obligations or encourage reform in a constructive way. In practice, the meetings have so far produced mixed results, with both the CIE and the states concerned still learning how best to use the time. One further development has been that, with the consent of the states concerned (Finland and Portugal), a European Trade Union Confederation representative participated in two meetings held in 1997.

Another instructive aspect of the CIE's work in the examination of reports concerns the approach to standard setting. In the very first cycle of reporting, the CIE found that all seven reporting states had infringed at least one of the ESC provisions they had accepted and that altogether they were in breach of fifty-seven provisions. This alarmed the Governmental Committee, whose members, or their predecessors, had advised their governments that they could accept nominated provisions of the Charter without difficulty. It was, at least in part, as a reaction to the strong position taken by the CIE at the outset that the Governmental Committee took upon itself the task of spelling out its own, generally less demanding, interpretation of the Charter and, until the late 1980s, did not agree with the CIE that a party was in breach of the Charter in even a single case.

---

[17] The cost of additional interpreting facilities has been avoided by having one of the chambers composed of members who work in just one of the official Council of Europe languages, English or French.

Fortunately, this situation of confrontation has disappeared. The Governmental Committee has changed its perception of its function and become much more constructive in its approach. The lesson of this experience is that a monitoring body such as the CIE does well in its early years to act cautiously, gradually gaining the confidence of states. In a reporting system, such a body has the problem that it may be called upon straight away to interpret many of the treaty obligations it has to apply, as different problems arise from the multiple national reports submitted to it. It will not have the advantage that a body operating a petition system has of tackling in the early years just the small number of points of interpretation that arise in the first few cases. This problem was accentuated in the case of the ESC by the CIE's ambitious decision to give a ruling from the outset on a state's compliance with every obligation it had accepted.[18] Clearly, the CIE was correct at the beginning to interpret the ESC as it meant to continue: it would not have been credible to have re-interpreted a provision more rigorously later.[19] But what might have been desirable – and this has been the practice of the CIE more recently – would have been for it to have refrained from making determinations as to compliance until it was sure, following two or more cycles of reports, what the law and practice of a particular state was. The same, more measured approach can also give a state the opportunity to change its law ahead of time to avoid a foreseeable ruling against it.

One problem that the CIE has had to face when examining national reports has been that of the regression in the provision of social services by Western European states in the face of recession and increased costs resulting from medical advances and demographic and other changes. The question for the CIE has been whether to make allowance for these new circumstances or to insist that the necessary resources should continue to be made available within a limited budget. For example, article 12 (3) of the ESC requires states to 'endeavour progressively to improve' their social security systems. As evidence has mounted in national reports that all European states are feeling the need to cut back on social security provision rather than to 'improve' it, the CIE has given much time to considering

[18] UN human rights treaty bodies have created for themselves a similar (though less acute) problem with their practice of drafting General Comments that analyse and spell out in the abstract all the elements of the guarantee of a particular right.

[19] This is distinct from interpreting dynamic provisions so as to require states to improve their performance in the light of changed social expectations and practice.

whether some allowance can be made for the strain upon resources caused by the cost of medical services and the increasing number of older persons.[20]

C. The Governmental Committee

It might be thought odd to set the ESC up as an example in terms of the independence of the members of monitoring bodies, when one of the two central bodies in the ESC system is composed entirely of government representatives. Article 27 of the ESC provides for a Governmental Committee on which each of the contracting parties has a representative, usually a civil servant from the ministry responsible for the ESC. The function of the Governmental Committee is to 'examine' the conclusions of the CIE on the question of compliance. As mentioned earlier, until the 1990s, in conducting this examination the Governmental Committee saw itself as having the same competence to interpret and apply the ESC as the CIE. This led to disagreements between the two institutions which seriously affected the effectiveness and credibility of the ESC's supervisory system. But the 1991 Amending Protocol, in amendments that are already being implemented, established that it is for the CIE alone to interpret and apply the standards of the ESC to national reports.[21] The role of the Governmental Committee is instead to advise the Committee of Ministers, in the light of 'economic and social' considerations, on those breaches of the ESC (as determined by the CIE) that should be the subject of Committee of Ministers' recommendations to particular parties calling on them to bring their law and practice into line.

This involvement of governments at the heart of the supervisory process has the advantage that a state may take criticism by its peers (who may be thought by it better able to understand its problems and explanations) more seriously than condemnation by a body of experts who, although independent, may not be perceived as having the same understanding of the 'real world'. This is a point well worth making in the context of the ESC because the Governmental Committee has in the last few years taken its role very seriously and does make a significant number of proposals for Committee of Ministers' recommendations against states represented within its membership. Even so, the example is probably best not followed.

---

[20] See the general observations in CIE Conclusions 13–4, pp. 40–2, 143–4 and the negative conclusion in CIE Conclusions 14–1, pp. 560–5 (Netherlands).
[21] See amended article 24.

Within Europe, there is no such mediation by any governmental body under the European Convention on Human Rights (ECHR); the decisions of the independent European Court of Human Rights are accepted and implemented as the final word.

D. The Secretariat

The success of any human rights reporting system depends upon the secretariat provided in support. In this respect, the arrangements at Strasbourg for the ESC are considerably better than those available through the Office of the UN High Commissioner for Human Rights (UNHCHR) for the UN human rights treaty committees. In the case of the ESC, there is a permanent, full-time Secretariat composed of a secretary and, at present, five other lawyers, plus a documentalist and four secretaries. The Secretariat services both the CIE and the Governmental Committee. In the case of the CIE, it provides detailed analyses, along the lines of the Secretariat of the International Labour Organisation (ILO), concerning a state's compliance with its obligations. For this exercise, a Secretariat member is assigned to prepare a document in which a state's report on an ESC provision is summarised and commented upon, as is other relevant evidence from additional sources available to the Secretariat. The document ends with a draft conclusion prepared by the Secretariat which summarises the state's law and practice on the provision concerned and gives a reasoned conclusion as to whether it conforms with the Charter. The draft conclusion may be adopted by the CIE, with or without redrafting, or the CIE may reach a different conclusion on the question of compliance. Although redrafting is very common and the CIE by no means always agrees on the Secretariat's proposal on the question of compliance, the initial draft conclusion, which in many cases takes a great deal of time and effort on the part of the Secretariat, provides an invaluable basis for the CIE's discussion of the case and contributes hugely to the professionalism of its work. As membership of the CIE is part-time and the members typically have other full-time posts, it would be impossible in many cases for them to do the research and drafting that is undertaken by the Secretariat. It is also the case that membership of the CIE changes and the institutional memory of the Secretariat plays an important part in the continued high quality of the CIE's output.

UN human rights treaty body membership, too, is part-time and these bodies are subject to similar pressures of work and changes in composition.

The experience of the CIE suggests that UN treaty bodies would benefit enormously from an increase in the size of the permanent secretariat provided for them. Although the CIE is always arguing, with justification, for more secretariat staff, the provision made for it is much better than that made within the UN system, which in most cases appears woefully inadequate.

E. Technical assistance to states

Another important feature of the ESC arrangements at Strasbourg is the budgetary provision made to assist states that are considering ratifying the Charter. This is important at present in connection with the move to encourage the new Council of Europe member states from Central and Eastern Europe to become ESC parties. These states now amount to almost half of the total membership of the Council of Europe.

Assistance mainly takes the form of a team composed of independent experts and members of the Governmental Committee, and the ESC Secretariat visiting the state concerned and taking part in one or more seminars on the Charter with civil servants and other interested parties, particularly representatives of the social partners and human rights NGOs. A part of these seminars is devoted to technical questions concerning the preparation of national reports. In addition to such seminars, it is also possible for a state to prepare a mock, or draft report which will be reviewed by the ESC Secretariat. This assistance has been greatly appreciated by the governments concerned and has given them a sense of the seriousness and extent of the commitment involved in ratification of the ESC. It also helps to prepare a state for the task of submitting national reports of good quality. These and other initiatives[22] are now bearing fruit, with the first new Council member – Poland – ratifying the Charter in 1997 and Hungary, Romania, Slovakia and Slovenia following suit since then. Other ratifications are expected to follow.

It might be that an increase in similar assistance within the UN would serve the same purpose for states not yet parties to human rights treaties. In addition, regional or national seminars or other forms of instruction for states that have already ratified UN human rights treaties, to advise them

---

[22] Another important practice is that of allowing a state that has taken the first step of signing the ESC to attend meetings of the Governmental Committee as an observer. This brings home to it very clearly how the reporting system actually works.

further on the preparation of national reports and the human rights standards involved, could be of great value, as would seminars for national NGOs, academics and others. The experience of the ESC is that much still needs to be done to publicise nationally both the existence and the meaning of the human rights treaty obligations that states have accepted, or might accept.

F. Cooperation with the International Labour Organisation

The ILO has always been closely involved with the ESC. It played an active and constructive role in the drafting of the Charter, with the result that the ESC text contains extensive and detailed guarantees of economic rights that often mirror ILO standards. Moreover, article 26 of the ESC provides for the involvement of the ILO in the enforcement machinery of the ESC by its participation in a consultative capacity in meetings of the CIE. In practice, the ILO makes available to the ESC Secretariat its own direct requests to ILO members who are ESC parties, and its views on their compliance with their ILO treaty obligations. This is not to say that ILO standards are followed in the interpretation or application of the ESC in every case. For example, the ESC has been interpreted as prohibiting the 'closed shop' in the context of present day Europe, whereas the ILO takes a neutral position on the matter, given the great variation in practice worldwide. Clearly, UN human rights treaty bodies could take similar advantage of the expertise of UN specialised agencies.

G. The value of petition systems for a reporting system

As with a number of UN human rights treaties, the ESC was until recently enforced solely through the examination of state reports. However, the Additional Protocol to the European Social Charter Providing for a System of Collective Complaints of 1995[23] (the Collective Complaints Protocol), which entered into force in July 1998, provides for the bringing of complaints by international and national employers and trade union organisations and social rights NGOs. The complaints must be collective in the procedural sense that they may not be brought by individuals and in the

---

[23] ETS No. 158. The Collective Complaints Protocol has been ratified by Cyprus, Finland, France, Greece, Italy, Norway, Portugal and Sweden.

substantive sense that they must relate to general situations rather than to individual cases, although there is likely to be some overlap in practice between the two categories.

It may be anticipated that the Collective Complaints Protocol will benefit the ESC reporting system, as well as providing an additional means for the ESC's enforcement.[24] A serious limitation of the ESC's reporting system has been the difficulty of knowing how a law actually operates in practice, particularly in light of the almost entirely written procedure. National reports prepared by governments do not necessarily give a rounded picture. Information from trade union organisations and social rights NGOs can be of assistance, but in the case of the ESC, little information has been forthcoming from these sources. In any event, there is unlikely to be a full and balanced argument by the government and its critics of the kind that will occur during the consideration of a petition. It can be predicted that much that the CIE learns about a state's law and practice from the hearing of complaints under the Collective Complaints Protocol will also be of benefit to it for reporting purposes. This is a consideration that may be relevant to the arguments being put for the 'missing' petition systems within the UN family of human rights treaties.

H. The value of reporting systems

A thought that sometimes occurs to members of treaty monitoring bodies and others is whether all the time, effort and money that goes into the operation of a reporting system is worthwhile. From the standpoint of the ESC, the answer must be positive, although not one that can be given as loudly and clearly as one would like. States do take their reporting obligations seriously and there is evidence that they have changed their law in order to become parties to the ESC, or to accept more of its provisions. They have also at times corrected their law or practice as a result of determinations against them by the CIE.

On the last point, however, there are also many cases where states have not reacted positively, the more so the more central the issue to the political agenda of the government of the day or the more problematic the changes

---

[24] Aspects of the relationship between the reporting and complaints systems are considered in the first complaint case: *International Commission of Jurists v. Portugal*, 6 *IHRR*, 1999, p. 1142, admiss. decn.

required from a financial point of view. Faced with a situation where a state has not changed its law or practice in response to an adverse finding, the CIE, and more recently the Committee of Ministers, has in subsequent reporting cycles only been able to record and comment adversely upon this lack of response and repeat their previous determinations or recommendations. The lesson of the ESC reporting system in this regard is that a system of supervision that does not result in a legally binding decision can suffer from problems of compliance.

Unfortunately, states are not prepared, within either the Council of Europe or the UN, to agree to a reporting system that results in legally binding decisions. If one reason for this is that the purpose of such a system is to achieve improvement through constructive dialogue rather than confrontation, the general experience to date does not make this a wholly convincing argument.

17

THE ROLE OF REPORTING IN INTERNATIONAL
ENVIRONMENTAL TREATIES: LESSONS FOR
HUMAN RIGHTS SUPERVISION

DANIEL BODANSKY*

A. Introduction

Apparently, the grass often looks greener across a disciplinary fence. International environmental lawyers, if asked what lessons they can teach human rights lawyers, might well respond that the inquiry gets the matter backwards: they tend to look with envy on human rights implementation mechanisms.[1] Thus, it comes as a surprise to be asked whether there is anything to be learnt in that regard from international environmental law.

Certainly, many of the problems that plague human rights reporting are present in international environmental regimes: national reports that are inaccurate, incomplete, tardy or not prepared at all;[2] superficial reviews by international bodies; and a proliferation of reporting requirements, leading to fears of treaty congestion. A 1992 report by the US General Accounting Office (GAO) concluded that close to half of the reports required by the Montreal Protocol on Substances that Deplete the Ozone Layer (Montreal Protocol) – perhaps the most successful of all international environmental agreements – were incomplete, and for many important agreements, fewer than half of the parties have ever filed a report.[3] Even when reports

---

* The author is indebted to Joan Fitzpatrick and David Victor for many helpful comments.
[1] See, e.g., E. Barratt-Brown, 'Building a Monitoring and Compliance Regime under the Montreal Protocol', 16 *YJIL* 2, 1991, pp. 519–70.
[2] US General Accounting Office, 'International Environment: International Agreements are not Well Monitored', Report. No. GAO/RCED-92–43, January 1992, p. 3.
[3] Ibid., at pp. 3–4. The General Accounting Office (GAO) figures, however, should not be accepted uncritically. For example, data from the World Conservation Monitoring Centre, which is responsible for processing the national reports submitted under the Convention

---

are submitted, they may be inaccurate, even deliberately deceptive. The disintegration of the Soviet Union brought to light two blatant cases of misreporting, one relating to whaling and the other to the dumping of radioactive waste at sea.[4] So there should be no illusion that reporting systems generally work well in environmental regimes.

Indeed, in some important respects, international environmental law lags far behind human rights law, particularly in creating individual complaint procedures, which are virtually non-existent in the environmental arena.[5] In relation to climate change, the very idea of an obligation to 'report' was felt by some states to suggest an intrusive, heavy-handed process. Hence the more neutral phrase 'communication of information' was used instead.[6]

But international environmental law can count some successes in the area of reporting, including devices to promote timely reporting and procedures for in-depth review of reports and for consideration of compliance. To provide perspective, I begin with certain general comparisons between international environmental law and human rights law. There follows a brief description of international environmental reporting systems, and to conclude, the drawing of some possible lessons for human rights regimes.

on International Trade in Endangered Species of Wild Flora and Fauna (CITES), indicates that the percentage of parties that ultimately file reports is considerably higher than the figures reported by the GAO (82 per cent in 1989 versus 24 per cent reported by the GAO). On the other hand, even when reports are filed, they may be incomplete or inaccurate. According to Simon Lyster, a study prepared for the CITES Secretariat revealed that 'the content of annual reports has generally been so inadequate that the value of those reports which are submitted is highly dubious', and that 'at least 45 per cent of all CITES transactions involving animals and 79 per cent of those involving plants go unreported even when the transactions are between Parties which have submitted annual reports'. S. Lyster, *International Wildlife Law*, Cambridge, 1985, p. 269; see also C. Harcourt and R. Luxmoore, *The Implementation of CITES in 1986 and 1987 as Demonstrated by the Trade Statistics in the Annual Reports Submitted by the Parties*, Cambridge, 1989.

[4] In the case of whaling, 'the USSR's false reporting was so drastic and pervasive that some experts believe it accounts for the persistent inaccuracy of the IWC Scientific Committee's forecasts of whale populations'. A. and A. H. Chayes, *The New Sovereignty: Compliance with International Regulatory Agreements*, Cambridge, Mass., 1995, p. 155.

[5] Article 14 of the 1992 North American Agreement on Environmental Cooperation of the North American Free Trade Agreement (also known as the NAFTA Side Agreement) is one of the few exceptions. Under this provision, individuals may file complaints alleging that a party is failing to enforce its environmental laws effectively.

[6] D. Bodansky, 'The United Nations Framework Convention on Climate Change: A Commentary', 18 *YJIL* 2, 1993, pp. 451–558, at p. 544.

B. Some differences between international environmental and human rights law

Virginia Leary once commented that comparing the International Labour Organisation to human rights agreements was like comparing apples with oranges.[7] Here it is questionable whether we are even in the same food group. Let us briefly consider a few relevant differences.

First, international environmental law is grounded in the need for mutual action. Most international environmental problems – certainly all global ones – cannot be addressed by individual states acting alone; they require collective effort. In contrast, human rights obligations do not depend on reciprocity in the same way.[8] States owe obligations not to one another, but to individuals; moreover, one state's respect for human rights does not depend on, and may not be conditioned on, compliance by other states. This has an important implication for reporting: in international environmental law, unlike human rights law, one of the principal functions of reporting is to provide assurances to states that their own efforts to protect the environment are being reciprocated. Otherwise, those efforts may count for nothing; indeed they may give non-complying states a competitive advantage.

Second, international environmental law is typically directed at the control of private rather than governmental conduct. To be sure, environmental duties fall in the first instance on governments, and some are aimed at governmental behaviour (for example, environmental impact assessments are usually required only for governmental actions). But most environmental harm results from the behaviour of private actors and will be solved only through changes in private behaviour. In contrast, human rights have traditionally been conceived as rights *vis-à-vis* governments which can be violated only, or at least primarily, by governmental conduct.[9] In the

---

[7] V. Leary, 'Lessons from the Experience of the International Labour Organization', in *The United Nations and Human Rights: A Critical Appraisal* (ed. P. Alston), Oxford, 1992, pp. 580–619.

[8] An exception may be labour rights, which have trade implications and hence may be politically acceptable only if a state's trading partners (and competitors) undertake comparable obligations.

[9] For example, the definition of torture has a 'colour of law' requirement. See article 1(1) of the Convention against Torture which defines torture as severe pain or suffering when 'inflicted by or at the instigation of or with the consent or acquiescence of *a public official or other person acting in an official capacity*' (emphasis added).

parlance sometimes used in connection with economic, social and cultural rights, international environmental law consists primarily of duties to 'protect', while human rights law has tended to focus on duties to 'respect'. Again, this difference has an important implication for reporting: in international environmental regimes, reports must often address not only governmental actions, but individual and business behaviour.

Third, human rights treaty regimes tend to be more legalistic in nature than international environmental regimes. Once an issue is conceived in terms of rights, it is removed from the political arena of competing interests and policies. Perhaps for this reason, the paradigmatic institution established by human rights treaties is the expert committee, composed largely of lawyers. In contrast, the central institution established by international environmental agreements is the conference of the parties, whose primary task is political, namely to direct the implementation and evolution of the regime. Even the more specialised implementation committees established by some international environmental agreements are generally composed of government rather than independent experts, and take a political rather than a strictly legal approach to compliance questions.[10]

The more obviously 'political' character of international environmental regimes is reflected not only in institutional and procedural arrangements, but also in substantive obligations, which often reflect political compromises struck in order to achieve agreement. Of course, human rights agreements also are the product of negotiation, but with an important difference. In human rights agreements, the end point of the negotiations is

[10] For example, the Implementation Committee that administers the Montreal Protocol's non-compliance procedure is composed of representatives of states parties rather than independent experts. Cf. M. Koskenniemi, 'Breach of Treaty or Non-Compliance? Reflections on the Enforcement of the Montreal Protocol', *Yearbook of International Environmental Law – 1992*, vol. 3, London, 1993, pp. 123–62. Nonetheless, in some cases expert committees play an important role in the operation of international environmental agreements. For example, the Montreal Protocol's Technological and Economic Assessment Panels (TEAPs) have helped to assess the technical feasibility and cost of various proposals to adjust the Protocol's regulatory commitments. TEAPs have also assisted in identifying options and costs for projects to help former Soviet bloc countries comply with the Protocol. In that sense they have been a vital part of the process of reporting and review for the most difficult compliance cases handled to date. Expert committees have also played important roles under CITES (e.g., in assessing the status of species for listing purposes), the prior-informed-consent regimes for trade in chemicals and pesticides, and the Long-Range Transboundary Air Pollution Convention (LRTAP). See generally D. Victor, K. Raustiala and E. Skolnikoff, *The Implementation and Effectiveness of International Environmental Commitments: Theory and Practice*, Cambridge, Mass., 1998.

a common core of human rights to be respected. In contrast, international environmental negotiations often involve a process of outright horse-trading that, on the one hand, results in different requirements for different countries, but, by virtue of that fact, allows more stringent and specific requirements to be adopted than would otherwise be possible.[11]

C. An overview of international environmental reporting systems

1. FUNCTIONS OF REPORTING

Most international environmental agreements contain at least some reporting requirement. Indeed, in the case of a few agreements, reporting is the *only* specific action required of states.[12] Why is reporting such a perva-sive obligation?

A cynic might reply that reporting obligations are a substitute for sub-stantive action. States can claim they are addressing a problem, gathering information and preparing reports, when in reality they are continuing business as usual. This is one view of the emerging climate change regime, where states, facing political gridlock over the issue of how to limit their emissions of greenhouse gases, initially made substantial progress only with regard to reporting and review.

But reporting may serve a number of important functions.[13] The most obvious is to facilitate evaluation of a state's performance, in particular whether it is fulfilling its international commitments (the evaluation/com-pliance function). Self-reporting might seem a curious, even poor, means of evaluating compliance. The cynic would no doubt claim that it is naïve to expect states to admit their deficiencies; they will simply report that all is, more or less, well. And this is certainly true to some degree. For this reason, international environmental agreements have tried to develop other sources of information, including monitoring networks (for example, the

---

[11] P. Sand, *Lessons Learned in Global Environmental Governance*, Washington DC, 1990, pp. 6–9.

[12] See, e.g., LRTAP, article 8 (exchange of information). LRTAP, however, was intended to be, and has been, supplemented by protocols establishing substantive commitments to limit various long-range pollutants, including sulphur, nitrogen oxides, and volatile organic compounds.

[13] See generally P. Alston, 'The Purposes of Reporting', in United Nations, *Manual on Human Rights Reporting*, UN Doc. HR/PUB/91/1 (Rev. 1) (1997), pp. 19–24.

EMEP network to monitor the precursors and deposition of acid rain),[14] international inspections (authorised, for example, by the Antarctic marine conservation regime), and reporting by non-governmental organisations (NGOs) (for example, on trafficking in wildlife). But the cynic overstates the case. In many situations states seek to comply with their commitments and act, if not in good faith, at least not in bad faith.[15] Reporting encourages a process of self-examination; the evaluative function is played by the state itself, rather than by the public or an international body. Moreover, mis-reporting is difficult in states with open and participatory political pro-cesses and with professional bureaucracies, relatively insulated from political pressures.[16] For a mixture of these reasons, in the climate change regime the industrialised countries in their initial reports virtually all admitted that they were not on track to meet their commitments.[17]

Even when states are less than forthright, national reports can facilitate evaluation by providing a focal point for others (NGOs, intergovernmental bodies, and other observers) to assess the information provided and to criticise it. Of course, a state's performance can be evaluated even in the absence of a national report. But the formal presentation of a national report to an international body presents NGOs and other critics with a convenient occasion and target. And even incomplete or inadequately ana-lysed information may be better than none at all – for example, supplying raw data that NGOs can use in their own analyses of policy options and compliance.

A second, related function of reporting is to bring about a change in the policies and ultimately the behaviour of states (the policy reform function). Reporting can promote such change in a range of more or less coercive ways. At the more coercive end of the spectrum, the evaluative process focuses pressure on states to perform better – peer pressure from other states, public pressure, and internal bureaucratic and political pressure. Less coercively, the process of preparing a report – by mobilising and em-powering groups within and outside the government – may have a catalytic effect in promoting a process of internal policy reform. Finally, through the sharing of information in reports, states may learn about policy options

[14] EMEP refers to the 'Co-operative Programme for Monitoring and Evaluation of the Long-Range Transmission of Air Pollutants in Europe' established under LRTAP.

[15] See generally Chayes and Chayes, *supra*, note 4.   [16] Ibid., pp. 162–6.

[17] 'Second Compilation and Synthesis of First National Communications from Annex I Parties', UN Doc. FCCC/CP/1996/12, 10 June 1996.

(or, in the case of environmental reporting, technologies) not previously considered.

Both the compliance and policy reform functions concern the performance of individual states. These seem to be the primary functions of human rights reporting, focusing on compliance by individual states with existing norms.[18] Environmental reporting is also concerned to a substantial degree with the performance of individual states, although, as noted earlier, in contrast to human rights reporting, verification has as its primary function the provision of assurance to the members of the regime that other states are fulfilling their end of the bargain. In this respect what counts is not so much a state's absolute efforts to protect the environment or to comply with existing norms as its efforts relative to other states, since this is what affects competitiveness.

However, environmental reporting has an additional function, apart from individual compliance: reporting contributes to the factual basis for decisions about whether to develop new or amended norms, and thus subserves a legislative function. A notable feature of environmental regimes is their dynamic quality.[19] In contrast to human rights agreements, which tend to be relatively stable, environmental regimes need to evolve, often quite rapidly, in response to changes in the nature of environmental problems and our understanding of them. Environmental reporting contributes to this essentially legislative process in two ways, first, by contributing to scientific understanding of a problem (for example, national inventories of greenhouse gas emissions give a better picture of what is actually taking place in the atmosphere), and second, by allowing an assessment of the overall progress of states towards achieving the objectives of an agreement. Under the Montreal Protocol, for example, reporting by states on their existing use of ozone-depleting substances has helped produce more informed decisions about whether additional regulatory measures are needed.[20]

[18] See K. Partsch, 'Reporting Systems in International Relations', in *Encyclopedia of Public International Law* (ed. R. Bernhardt), vol. 9, Amsterdam, 1986, p. 330 (main function of reporting is 'to show whether and to what extent a State is fulfilling its international obligations').

[19] T. Gehring, 'International Environmental Regimes: Dynamic Sectoral Legal Systems', in *Yearbook of International Environmental Law – 1990*, Vol. 1, London, 1991, pp. 35–56.

[20] S. Oberthür, *Production and Consumption of Ozone-Depleting Substances, 1986–1995: The Data Reporting System under the Montreal Protocol*, Gesellschaft für technische Zusammenarbeit, 1997.

2. CONTENT OF REPORTS

The functions of compliance, national policy reform, and standard-setting call for information of several types.[21] Compliance review requires information about the measures adopted in response to a problem, including measures to implement the relevant international agreement, as well as about the effectiveness of those measures. National policy reform can be stimulated by more general information about how human activities contribute to a problem. The standard-setting process also requires basic scientific information about the environmental problem itself (rates of temperature change, sea-level rise, species loss, and so forth).

In terms of verifying compliance, the more specific the obligation the better the reporting and review process will typically work. When an agreement imposes only very general obligations, the reporting requirement is likely to be correspondingly general. For example, the Vienna Convention on the Protection of the Ozone Layer (Vienna Convention) requires simply that parties 'take appropriate measures . . . to protect human health and the environment against adverse effects resulting or likely to result from human activities which modify or are likely to modify the ozone layer'. And it imposes only a general reporting requirement to transmit information 'on the measures adopted . . . in implementation of this Convention'.[22] In contrast, environmental agreements that contain more specific obligations warrant correspondingly more specific reporting requirements.[23] The 1985 Sulphur Protocol to the Long-Range Transboundary Air Pollution Convention (LRTAP) requires states to reduce their sulphur emissions by 30 per cent between 1980 and 1993, and requires them to report on their 'levels of national annual sulphur emissions and the basis upon which they have been calculated'.[24]

[21] Cf. J. Ausubel and D. Victor, 'Verification of International Environmental Agreements', 17 *Annual Review of Energy & Environment*, 1992, pp. 1–43, at pp. 14–15.

[22] Vienna Convention for the Protection of the Ozone Layer, articles 2(1), and 5. For similar reporting requirements, see the Barcelona Convention for the Protection of the Mediterranean Sea Against Pollution, article 20; Kuwait Regional Convention for Cooperation on the Protection of the Marine Environment from Pollution, article XXIII.

[23] Here, a contrast could be drawn with human rights law, which typically sets forth general principles rather than specific rules. The generality of most human rights norms means that reporting obligations must also be framed in general terms – and states generally respond by reporting on the content of their laws, rather than on their actual practice.

[24] Protocol on the Reduction of Sulphur Emissions or Their Transboundary Fluxes by At Least 30 per cent, article 4. The UN Framework Convention on Climate Change (Climate

Other environmental agreements focus on procedural obligations, requiring parties to establish and report on specific implementation mechanisms. For example, article VI(1)(c) of the London (Ocean Dumping) Convention requires states to establish a permit system for the dumping of wastes at sea. Accordingly, its reporting requirement (article VI(4)) focuses on information about the nature and quantities of wastes permitted to be dumped. Similarly, the Convention on International Trade in Endangered Species of Wild Flora and Fauna (CITES) requires parties to establish a permit system for imports and exports of listed species, and to submit annual reports detailing the number and types of permits and certificates granted.[25]

Other agreements impose obligations on states to punish infractions, and require parties to provide reports detailing each infraction as well as the penalties imposed.[26] In general, when an agreement sets forth these kinds of specific requirements, although states may still submit incomplete or inaccurate reports, the specificity of the obligation makes misreporting easier to detect and hence less appealing as an option.

In terms of what has been described as the legislative function of environmental reporting, information about how human activities contribute to an environmental problem, rather than about implementation *per se*, tends to be most important. Information about the environmental problem itself is also essential to the law-making process. However, such information is mostly acquired through means other than national reporting, e.g. through ground-based or satellite monitoring systems. One of the few treaties requiring states to report information of this general kind is the 1971 Convention on Wetlands of International Importance, which obliges parties to report on changes in 'the ecological character of any wetland

Change Convention) imposes a more elaborate reporting requirement in connection with its quasi-commitment by industrialised countries to limit greenhouse gas emissions. Each industrialised party is required to provide not only a national inventory of greenhouse gas emissions, but also 'a detailed description of the policies and measures that it has adopted to implement its commitments', as well as a 'specific estimate of the effects that the policies and measures . . . will have on . . . [greenhouse gas] emissions', article 12(2).

[25] CITES, article VIII(7).

[26] See, e.g., International Convention for the Regulation of Whaling, article IX(4) (requiring details of each infraction, including 'a statement of measures taken for dealing with the infraction and of penalties imposed'); International Convention for the Prevention of Pollution from Ships (MARPOL), as modified by Protocol of 1978, article 11(1)(f) (requiring annual statistical reporting of penalties actually imposed for infringement of the Convention).

in its territory and included in the List [of Wetlands of International Importance]'.[27] More commonly, reporting obligations contribute to the lawmaking process by focusing on the human activities that contribute to a problem. For example, the inventories of greenhouse gas emissions required by the Climate Change Convention have been part of the basis for the continuing negotiations to develop more specific obligations to limit greenhouse gas emissions.

In many cases, agreements provide for the development of standardised formats and methodologies for reporting, usually by the conference of the parties or the treaty secretariat. This promotes uniformity in reporting and facilitates comparisons among and aggregation of data contained in national reports. In the case of the Climate Change Convention, the parties have adopted very detailed methodologies for the preparation of greenhouse gas inventories, developed jointly by the Organisation for Economic Cooperation and Development (OECD) and the International Energy Agency. As a rule, these common formats and methodologies have been more successful in promoting comparability among reports when the reports contain specific data (for example, emission rates) rather than more general information about implementation measures.

3. REVIEW OF REPORTS

Comparatively few international environmental agreements have specific arrangements for the review of national reports. Reports are typically processed and, in some cases, summarised by the treaty secretariat, and then forwarded to the conference of the parties. Typical is LRTAP, which provides that the Executive Body (the equivalent of the conference of the parties) shall 'review the implementation of the present Convention', but does not authorise the Executive Body to review individual reports or to request additional information.[28] As a result, reviews of reports tend to focus on the aggregate performance of the parties in achieving treaty objectives, rather than on compliance by individual countries. Such reviews play a primarily legislative function. By indicating how countries are currently

---

[27] Convention on Wetlands of International Importance, Especially as Waterfowl Habitat, article 3(2).

[28] LRTAP, article 10(2)(a). See P. Széll, 'The Development of Multilateral Mechanisms for Monitoring Compliance', in *Sustainable Development and International Law* (ed. W. Lang), London, 1995, pp. 97–109.

performing, they suggest whether adjustments or amendments are needed.[29] For example, the statistical data in reports submitted under CITES can be used to calculate the total volume of trade in a species, which in turn can be used in assessments of the species' status and the need for additional conservation measures.

In a few cases, environmental regimes involve review of individual countries' performance. Beginning in 1979, the CITES Secretariat has submitted Infraction Reports to the Conference of the Parties. Based on these Reports, the CITES Standing Committee has occasionally recommended sanctions against persistent violators.[30] However, given the incompleteness (and in some cases inaccuracies) of national reports, information about infractions has come in large part from other sources, including the NGO TRAFFIC,[31] as well as from country visits by high level delegations of the Standing Committee.

Until recently, practically the only other mechanism for focusing on an individual party's compliance with an environmental agreement was formal dispute settlement, which in practice was never used. Several recent agreements have attempted to fill the 'space between . . . traditional reporting and dispute settlement articles'[32] through two complementary mechanisms: in-depth reviews of individual country reports and non-compliance procedures. The climate change regime involves perhaps the most elaborate example of the former approach, although parties are currently considering whether to utilise the second mechanism as well, by establishing a 'multilateral consultative process to resolve questions regarding implementation'.[33] The Montreal Protocol is the leading example of the second approach. Its non-compliance procedure has already been replicated in the 1994 Sulphur Protocol to the LRTAP, and may serve as the model for the Climate Change Convention's multilateral consultative process, which has not yet been finalised.

[29] K. Sachariew, 'Promoting Compliance with International Environmental Legal Standards: Reflections on Monitoring and Reporting Mechanisms', *Yearbook of International Environmental Law 1991*, London, 1992, pp. 31–52, at p. 41.

[30] P. Sand, 'Commodity or Taboo? International Regulation of Trade in Endangered Species', *Green Globe Yearbook 1997*, Oxford, 1997, pp. 19–36.

[31] TRAFFIC (Trade Records Analysis of Fauna and Flora in Commerce) was established in 1976 as a joint programme of the World Conservation Union and the World Wide Fund for Nature, and currently has a worldwide network of eighteen offices. It works in close cooperation with the CITES Secretariat, providing information and advice on wildlife legislation and conservation policies, and investigating, monitoring and reporting on illegal trade in wild plants and animals.

[32] Széll, *supra*, note 28, p. 99.   [33] Climate Change Convention, article 13.

Both in-depth reviews and non-compliance procedures are intended to be facilitative, non-confrontational, and forward-looking. The difference between them is that in-depth reviews do not address the specific legal question of whether or not a state is in compliance with its obligations, whereas the Montreal Protocol non-compliance procedure, by its terms, is a means 'for determining non-compliance with the provisions' of the Protocol.[34] However, even the Montreal Protocol Implementation Committee acts in a pragmatic, forward-looking manner: it aims not so much to identify past problems with non-compliance as to secure solutions for the future. Accordingly, it is composed of state representatives rather than individual experts, and complements rather than supersedes the traditional methods for determining state responsibility.[35] Recently, the Montreal Protocol procedure was used to address the problem of non-compliance by the Russian Federation. As a result of pressure from the West and the offer of funding from the Global Environment Facility, Russia cooperated with the Implementation Committee to negotiate a pragmatic plan, with milestone reviews, intended to bring Russia back into compliance with the Protocol by 2000.[36]

D. Lessons for human rights law

1. HOW TO PROMOTE TIMELY REPORTS?

Like human rights reports, international environmental reports are often filed late or not at all. To counteract this tendency, international environmental regimes have adopted a number of strategies:

(i) *Establishing precise reporting deadlines.* Some treaty bodies have established precise deadlines for the submission of reports[37] in the belief

---

[34] Montreal Protocol, article 8.

[35] The Implementation Committee ordinarily meets twice a year and consists of representatives of ten parties, elected by the meeting of the parties for two-year terms, based on equitable geographic distribution. See UN Doc. UNEP/OzL.Pro.4/15, 25 November 1992, Annex IV (terms of reference of the non-compliance procedure).

[36] J. Werksman, 'Compliance and Transition: Russia's Non-Compliance Tests the Ozone Regime', 56 *Heidelberg Journal of International Law*, 1996, pp. 750–73 (discussing non-compliance proceedings involving former Soviet republics); Victor, *et al.*, *supra*, note 10, chapters 3 and 4.

[37] For example, LRTAP's Executive Body mandates that parties to the 1985 Sulphur Protocol 'report not later than 1 May of each year on their annual sulphur emissions'. Sachariew, *supra*, note 29, p. 43.

that states will be more likely to comply with a specific date than with a general requirement to report 'regularly'.[38]

(ii) Imposing costs on non-reporting states. A more potent mechanism is to threaten non-complying states with a penalty or sanction of some kind. The Executive Body of the LRTAP, for example, has said that, if reports are not filed in a timely manner, it may consider other, non-official sources of information.[39] Under the Montreal Protocol, if a state does not report data on its per capita consumption, it may lose its eligibility for preferential treatment as a developing country under article 5. This threat – against one country in 1995 and seventeen in 1996 – produced immediate results (in the form of reported data) in every instance.[40] The CITES Conference of the Parties has used a third approach, deciding in 1994 that failure to report is a possible ground for trade sanctions against the party concerned.[41]

(iii) Providing financial and technical assistance. On the assumption that the failure of developing countries to meet their reporting requirements results from inadequate resources (rather than a lack of political will or bad faith), some agreements provide financial assistance to developing countries to assist them in preparing reports. The Climate Change Convention goes furthest, requiring OECD countries to pay the 'agreed full costs incurred by developing country Parties' in meeting their reporting obligations (article 4(3)). The Montreal Protocol does not specifically provide for financial assistance. But in 1991, in response to poor reporting rates by developing countries, the implementing agencies associated with the Protocol's Multilateral Fund (MLF) began financing projects to build reporting capacity in developing countries. Many developing countries still failed to submit reports – over forty as of mid-1994 still had not submitted baseline data[42] – but these non-reporting countries were principally countries that had not yet fully implemented MLF-funded projects to build the administrative capacity to report.

(iv) Focusing political pressure on delinquent states. In the case of the ozone regime, what ultimately proved most successful in encouraging

---

[38] Ibid., p. 42.   [39] Ibid., p. 43.

[40] D. Victor, 'The Early Operation and Effectiveness of the Montreal Protocol's Non-Compliance Procedure', in Victor, *et al.*, *supra*, note 10, chapter 4.

[41] Sand, *supra*, note 30, p. 25.

[42] O. Greene, 'The Montreal Protocol: Implementation and Development in 1995', in *Verification 1996: Arms Control, Peacekeeping and the Environment* (eds J. Poole and R. Guthrie), Boulder, 1996, pp. 407–26, at p. 412.

reporting was the focused attention of the Implementation Committee, established under the Montreal Protocol's non-compliance procedure. Beginning in 1993, the Committee requested specific states to appear before it to explain their failure to report. Although a few of the named states failed to appear, most did and since then reporting has apparently improved.[43] Overall, as of September 1997, 113 of 152 parties to the Montreal Protocol had reported data for 1995 and forty-three parties had reported data for 1996.[44]

(v) *Establishing different reporting schedules for different classes of states.* No matter what is done in terms of assistance or sanctions, it may be unrealistic to expect developing countries to submit reports as frequently as developed countries. Bowing to this reality, the Climate Change Convention establishes different reporting schedules for industrialised and developing countries.[45]

2. PERMITTING INFORMATION FROM NON-GOVERNMENTAL SOURCES

Most international environmental regimes do not attempt to verify the information in national reports independently. In some cases, NGOs produce their own reviews of state performance, as they do in the human rights field. The Climate Action Network, a coalition of environmental NGOs active on the climate change issue, has produced several detailed reports on national plans to mitigate climate change, which are informally distributed at inter-governmental meetings.[46] However, these have no official status in the climate change regime. The same is true of Greenpeace studies of the hazardous waste trade in connection with the Basel Convention on the Control of Transboundary Movements of Hazardous Wastes, and of

[43] Ibid., p. 412. In contrast, efforts under CITES to stigmatise non-reporting countries have proved less successful. Despite a conference resolution in 1992 characterising the failure to submit reports as a 'major problem' and referring such failures to the Standing Committee (CITES Resolution Conf. 8.7), late reports have continued to be common.

[44] Report of the Ninth Meeting of the Parties to the Montreal Protocol, UN Doc. UNEP/OzL.Pro.9/12, 25 September 1997.

[45] Article 12(5) of the Climate Change Convention requires industrialised countries to submit their initial report within six months of the Convention's entry into force, while developing countries have three years in which to file their initial report.

[46] See, e.g., Climate Action Network, *Independent NGO Evaluations of National Plans for Climate Change Mitigation: OECD Countries*, 3rd review, January 1995.

whaling infractions under the International Convention for the Regulation of Whaling. In the International Whaling Commission, Greenpeace has needed to enlist the help of a sympathetic government that is willing formally to introduce evidence of an infraction, hardly a satisfactory state of affairs.

An exception to the general rule limiting the role of non-governmental information is CITES, which was in large part drafted by a quasi-NGO, the International Union for the Conservation of Nature (IUCN), and initially designated the IUCN as its secretariat.[47] Even though CITES contains very specific requirements on the import and export of endangered species, many states have done a 'woefully inadequate' job keeping records and reporting about wildlife transactions.[48] That is why it has been vital to develop alternative sources of information, which can be used to assess, supplement and in some cases correct the information in national reports. CITES uses one NGO (the World Conservation Monitoring Unit) to compile and maintain a computerised database of the information contained in national reports, and allows another (TRAFFIC)[49] to provide information on illegal trafficking in wildlife.

TRAFFIC has been able to play this role because governments tend to regard it as a technical rather than a political group – as a source of accurate, objective data. According to one commentator, 'NGO oversight of Parties' implementing actions under CITES has been a key variable in achieving whatever success CITES has achieved'.[50] Perhaps because of its NGO origins, CITES is also unusual in giving its Secretariat a wide variety of powers, including authority to request additional information from a country if it believes that a species is being adversely affected by trade or that the provisions of the Convention are not being implemented,[51] to offer

---

[47] See generally Lyster, *supra*, note 3, pp. 239–77.

[48] J. Heppes and E. McFadden, 'The Convention on International Trade in Endangered Species of Wild Fauna and Flora: Improving the Prospects for Preserving Our Biological Heritage', 5 *Boston University International Law Journal*, 1987, pp. 229–46, at p. 233.

[49] See *supra*, note 31.

[50] L. Kosloff and M. Trexler, 'The Convention on International Trade in Endangered Species: Enforcement Theory and Practice in the United States', 5 *Boston University International Law Journal*, 1987, pp. 327–61, at p. 336.

[51] Lyster reports that the Secretariat 'has implemented this requirement vigorously, drawing the attention of a total of 39 Parties to a total of 274 cases of alleged violations of the Convention during 1979 and 1980 and maintaining a similar level in 1981–2'. Lyster, *supra*, note 3, p. 271.

assistance, to refer matters to the Standing Committee, and to identify parties with inadequate authority to implement the Convention. Such powers differentiate the CITES Secretariat from other environmental secretariats, which generally play a simple clearing-house role.

3. IN-DEPTH REVIEWS OF NATIONAL REPORTS

A frequent complaint about human rights supervision is that for a variety of reasons (lack of time, or money, or staff, or authority), human rights treaty bodies cannot meaningfully review national reports. While the same could be said of many international environmental regimes, one exception is the Climate Change Convention, which has a highly-developed review process that has been called 'one of the pillars of the Convention'.[52] The Climate Change review process begins with a number of advantages, which might not be replicable elsewhere. Most importantly, the regime is exceptionally well-funded and staffed, with a substantial budget and five full-time professional staff for the reporting and review process alone. Moreover, only industrialised countries have been required thus far to file reports and, with relatively few exceptions, they have done so in a timely manner, producing a much better record of compliance than under any other environmental treaty regime. It is still an open question whether developing countries will have a similar record in meeting their reporting obligations.[53]

As of April 1998, all of the industrialised states parties had submitted their initial communication and the Secretariat had completed twenty-nine in-depth reviews, with another three nearly finalised.[54] The reviews have

---

[52] R. Kinley, 'Communication and Review under the Framework Convention on Climate Change', in *The Emerging International Regime for Climate Change: Structures and Options after Berlin* (eds. M. Grubb and D. Anderson), London, 1995, pp. 45–50.

[53] Pursuant to article 12(5) of the Climate Change Convention, developing countries must file their initial report within three years of the Convention's entry into force (i.e., 21 March 1997) or 'of the availability of financial resources'. Financial resources were not made available to most developing countries until 1997. As of 28 April 1998, only seven developing countries had submitted their initial communication and, of these, 'most . . . appear to require further elaboration'. UN Doc. FCCC/SBI/1998/INF.3, 28 April 1998. The Secretariat expects to receive an additional twenty-six developing country reports by the end of 1998, twenty-five in 1999, and the remainder in 2000.

[54] UN Doc. FCCC/SBI/1998/INF.1, 27 April 1998. As of the same date, twenty-three of the twenty-five industrialised states whose second national communications were due on 15 April 1997 had submitted their reports.

been conducted by teams of four to six experts, chosen by the Secretariat from names provided by governments and intergovernmental organisations. Although the review process is still only a couple of years old, in the first round of reviews alone, seventy-two experts from fifty parties took part, including twenty-eight experts from twenty-three developing countries, as well as six experts from three intergovernmental organisations.[55] An effort has been made to involve as many parties as possible, and to include at least one developing country expert on each review team, so that they gain experience in the reporting and review process.

The purpose of the review process is essentially the same as in the human rights arena, namely to enter into a constructive dialogue with the government concerned. A key means of promoting this dialogue has been the country visit. Although these visits were initially controversial and were dependent on an invitation from the state concerned, such invitations have been forthcoming (at least from industrialised states) and all the in-depth reviews to date have involved a country visit. In contrast to the reviews of national reports by human rights bodies, which last at most a couple of days (and in some cases only a few hours) and may involve the questioning of only a single official, country visits have typically been one week long and have involved meetings with a variety of government officials as well as NGOs. Each report is between ten and twenty pages long, and is reviewed and commented on by the country concerned before being finalised and made public.

The in-depth review procedure under the Climate Change Convention is still relatively new and untested and it remains to be seen whether it will yield significant results. Nevertheless, the early experience suggests several lessons for other review processes:

(i) *Keep the review process flexible.* Compared to human rights review processes, the climate change reviews are highly flexible. Instead of holding one or two formal sessions where a single government representative is questioned, the review teams engage in an unofficial give-and-take with a number of government officials and with other important stakeholders (including industry representatives and environmentalists). This back-and-forth approach continues after the country visit, as the review team

---

[55] UN Doc. FCCC/SBI/1997/20, 29 August 1997. As of August 1997, fifty-nine parties had nominated 205 national experts to participate in the in-depth reviews.

asks follow-up questions and the country concerned provides additional information and documentation.

(ii) Use ad hoc *teams of experts, rather than a single commission or committee.* The use of *ad hoc* teams rather than a single committee has allowed substantial time to be devoted to each in-depth review. A single committee or commission, even if it met year-round, would have had difficulty completing the more than thirty reviews undertaken thus far.

(iii) Disseminate the results of the reviews widely. The influence of the in-depth reviews is maximised through widespread distribution of the results. A summary of each review is available in the six official languages of the United Nations, with the full text available in its original language. The reports are published on the World Wide Web, as well as through an NGO Internet network.[56]

(iv) Look beyond simple compliance and assess the effectiveness more generally of a country's policies and measures. The more complex the international commitment, the greater the need to be able to assess whether a country is likely to comply in the future and not only whether it has complied in the past. This makes it possible to anticipate assistance needed, possible penalties, and adjustments to commitments. The Climate Change Convention in-depth review process examines not only present emissions but also national policies and forecasts of future emissions.

E. Conclusions

The differences between human rights and international environmental law give rise to differences in the functions and techniques of reporting. In drawing lessons between fields, we must be careful not to wrench an experience from one context and simply transplant it into another. Nonetheless, cross-fertilisation between fields is possible. Over time, as international law develops its range of procedures and institutional arrangements further, these can provide useful models for dealing with shared problems such as reporting.

[56] See http://www.unfccc.de/fccc/docs/idr.htm.

Appendix, chapter 17 *Reporting Obligations in International Environmental Agreements*

Agreement	Reporting requirements	Notes
• 1946 International Convention for the Regulation of Whaling	• Catch data. • Permits granted for scientific research, and information resulting from research. • Details on infractions and penalties imposed.	• Data maintained by Bureau of International Whaling Statistics, established by industry and the Norwegian Government in the 1920s. • Massive misreporting of catch data by Soviet Union in 1960s. • NGOs an unofficial source of information on infractions.
• 1972 London (Ocean Dumping) Convention	• Annual reports of permits issued and actual amounts of wastes dumped or incinerated at sea.	• 1991 Secretariat study concluded that approximately 50% of parties had never submitted a report, 30% report on a routine basis, and the remainder report intermittently.[1]
• 1972 World Heritage Convention	• Information on legislative and administrative provisions implementing the Convention. • Parties invited to submit reports every 5 years on state of conservation in World Heritage sites in their territory.	
• 1973 Convention on International Trade in Endangered Species (CITES)	• Annual report on trade permits granted, due by 31 October. • Biennial report on legislative, regulatory and administrative measures to enforce the Convention.	• Extensive reliance on NGO information about status of species and illegal trading. • Secretariat may identify instances of non-compliance. • 1994 Conference of Parties identified over 30% of parties as having failed to submit reports on time.[2]
• 1973 Marine Pollution Convention (MARPOL)	• Texts of relevant laws, orders, decrees and regulations. • Annual statistical report on penalties imposed for violations of the Convention.	• 1992 Friends of the Earth Study indicated that only six parties have submitted reports for each year since entry into force; 30 parties have never filed a report.[3]

Appendix, chapter 17 (*cont'd*)

Agreement	Reporting requirements	Notes
• 1979 Long-Range Transboundary Air Pollution Convention (LRTAP)	• Emissions data; information on major changes in national policies, control technologies.	• 'Major reviews' of implementation prepared by Secretariat.
• 1985 Sulphur Protocol to LRTAP	• Annual national sulphur emissions, due by 1 May.	
• 1985 Vienna Ozone Convention	• Biennial summary of implementation measures.	
• 1987 Montreal Protocol on Substances that Deplete the Ozone Layer	• Baseline data on production, imports and exports of controlled substances. • Annual statistical data on same, due by 30 September. • Biennial summary of research and development activities.	• Non-compliance procedure adopted in 1990. • Technical assistance to developing countries for reporting. • As of September 1997, 113 of 152 parties had reported data for 1995, and 43 for 1996.[4]
• 1989 Basel Convention on Hazardous Wastes	• Annual report detailing transboundary movements of hazardous wastes. • Information on implementation measures.	• As of October 1997, 49 of 111 parties had submitted information concerning 1994 activities with some submitting incomplete data.[5]
• 1992 UN Framework Convention on Climate Change	• National inventories of greenhouse gas emissions. • Steps taken to implement the Convention. • Detailed description of policies and measures, and estimate of their effects on emissions (industrialised countries only).	• In-depth reviews by expert teams assembled by Secretariat. • Differential reporting requirements for industrialised and developing countries.

[1] International Maritime Organisation, Doc. LDC 14/7/4, 15 October 1991.
[2] Sand, *supra*, note 30, p. 24.
[3] Chayes and Chayes, *supra*, note 4, p. 156.
[4] Report of the Ninth Meeting of the Parties to the Montreal Protocol, UN Doc. UNEP/OzL.Pro.9/12, 25 September 1997.
[5] UN Doc. UNEP/CHW.4/18 and Corr.1.

D

COMMON CHALLENGES FOR THE
TREATY BODIES

18

THE PROBLEM OF OVERLAPPING AMONG DIFFERENT TREATY BODIES

ERIC TISTOUNET

A number of human rights instruments which provide for the setting up of monitoring mechanisms and, consequently, the establishment of treaty bodies, have been adopted at the international level. Given the political difficulties of the years that followed the adoption of the Universal Declaration of Human Rights (UDHR) in 1948, the founding member states of the United Nations were unable to adopt a treaty to supplement the Declaration. Almost twenty years passed before the international community was able to agree on the International Covenant on Economic, Social and Cultural Rights (ICESCR) and the International Covenant on Civil and Political Rights (ICCPR), and a further decade before these instruments entered into force. It is no surprise that those responsible for drafting subsequent human rights instruments found it more convenient to adopt new texts rather than face the challenge of convincing states parties to the Covenants to adhere to additional protocols. This sheds some light on the reasons for the coexistence of numerous human rights instruments and, more particularly, seven human rights conventions dealing with universal rights and freedoms that overlap to a certain extent.[1]

The following discussion analyses the effect of the existence of overlapping guarantees in various human rights instruments on their interpretation and on the operation of their respective examination regimes. The discussion will be limited to those six instruments that led to the establishment of monitoring bodies, namely ICESCR, ICCPR, the Convention on

---

[1] For detailed information on this issue as well as on matters relating to the effective functioning of human rights treaty bodies see UN Docs. A/44/668, A/CONF.157/PC/Add.11/Rev.1 and E/CN.4/1997/74 (successive reports on the long-term effectiveness of the United Nations human rights treaty system prepared by Professor Philip Alston).

the Elimination of Racial Discrimination (CERD), the Convention on the Elimination of Discrimination against Women (CEDAW), the Convention against Torture (CAT), and the Convention on the Rights of the Child (CRC). The Convention on the Protection of the Rights of All Migrant Workers and Members of Their Families, which has not yet entered into force, remains outside the scope of this chapter.[2]

The first issue to be considered is the coexistence of related provisions in different instruments. There are numerous instances of the overlapping of related or similar provisions in various instruments: one of the consequences is the obligation for states parties to submit reports to and engage in discussion with different bodies with respect to similar rights, freedoms or principles. That there exist related provisions in various instruments also gives rise to certain implicit or explicit discrepancies. Since there is no single body entrusted with the task of monitoring the implementation of all the instruments, it follows that there may be differences in the interpretation given by different bodies to similar provisions, either in their general comments, their recommendations or in the concluding observations adopted following the consideration of reports. These issues are discussed in section A below.

A further issue relates to the effect of reservations made by states parties. Reservations may be made by a state party to a particular provision of a specific convention even in circumstances where no similar reservations exist to a related provision in the Covenants or in another instrument. Similarly, problems arise where a reservation to a provision in an Optional Protocol purports to effect a reservation to a specific provision in another instrument. These issues are discussed in section B below.

A. Issues as to the coexistence of related provisions in different instruments

1. IMPLICIT OR EXPLICIT DISCREPANCIES BETWEEN RELATED PROVISIONS IN DIFFERENT INSTRUMENTS

Human rights instruments, following the pattern of all treaties, proceed from discussions within the political organs of the United Nations. The result of a consensual approach towards rights or freedoms, they very much

---

[2] International Convention on the Protection of the Rights of All Migrant Workers and Members of Their Families, 18 December 1990, Doc. A/RES/45/158; 30 *ILM*, 1991, 1517.

depend on the state of international relations at any given moment. If there is a general trend in favour of a more 'progressive' approach towards human rights, the end result may be rights or freedoms expressed in a liberal way with very few limitative or restrictive clauses. The converse is also true: a situation of open conflict between delegations as to the content of even already clearly identified human rights provisions will result in rights or freedoms being expressed in a narrower way and the flourishing of limitative or restrictive clauses.

Historical and political developments which motivate the adoption of a human rights instrument necessarily impact on the interpretation given in the treaty to certain rights. There may well be discrepancies, explicit or implicit, between related provisions in different instruments, adopted at different times. Indeed these differences may go unremarked, at least at the drafting stage.

Clear instances of such discrepancies can be found between, for instance, the European Convention on Human Rights (ECHR) and the ICCPR. As an example, one may refer to article 25 (the right to participate in the conduct of public affairs), article 26 (general non-discrimination clause) and 27 (rights of persons belonging to minorities) of the ICCPR, which do not find counterparts in the ECHR, adopted more than fifteen years earlier.

Other instances of such implicit or explicit discrepancies can be found between legally and non-legally binding instruments. The significance of such a discrepancy depends on whether the legally binding instrument comes earlier or later in time. If later, the difficulties are less: the binding instrument can simply be represented as a withdrawal, or perhaps an extension, of a right first articulated in non-binding form. For example, article 15(1) of the UDHR asserts that 'everyone' has the right to a nationality. Article 24(3), its equivalent in the ICCPR, a legally binding text, extends that right only to 'every child'. The problem is more acute where the non-binding instrument is the later one. In this context one may mention, for example, a number of unwelcome developments resulting from the adoption of certain principles or rules by various United Nations congresses on the prevention of crime and the treatment of offenders. The Body of Principles for the Protection of All Persons under Any Form of Detention or Imprisonment adopted in 1988 contains provisions relating to contacts between detained persons and their lawyers or, more generally, regarding the rights of detained or imprisoned persons that raise serious issues under articles 9 and 14 of the ICCPR.

As far as United Nations instruments are concerned, there are also implicit discrepancies. For example the underlying philosophy of the CAT led to its ambit being limited under article 1 to acts committed 'by or at the instigation of or with the consent or acquiescence of a public official or other person acting in an official capacity'. As a result, the CAT Committee is not normally in a position to identify issues and make appropriate comments regarding ill-treatment by individuals. It was therefore unable to discuss issues of corporal punishment in private schools in the United Kingdom. In contrast, this particular problem was discussed at length by the CRC Committee and resulted in appropriate recommendations, including an expression of concern with regard to reasonable chastisement within the family and corporal punishment in privately-funded schools.[3] Concerns were also expressed by the HRC with regard to corporal punishment in private schools.[4] It may be rather difficult for an outside observer to understand why the CAT Committee is denied the possibility of raising questions on this issue unlike other bodies with no direct authority under CAT.

In the drafting of CRC, an extremely cautious approach was taken. As part of this approach, the draft was subject to a technical review which recommended the inclusion of a non-limitative clause. Subsequently, article 41 was included:

> Nothing in the present Convention shall affect any provisions which are more conducive to the realization of the rights of the child and which may be contained in (a) the law of the State Party; or (b) international law in force for that State.

The CRC Committee has interpreted this particular provision as authorising it to refer, if necessary, to more favourable or clearer provisions contained in other international instruments to which the reporting state is party.

Meetings of chairpersons of the treaty bodies have repeatedly called for a leading role to be played by existing bodies in the drafting of new instruments, in particular to draw attention to the possibility of overlapping between instruments and the need for consistency in standards when drafting new instruments. One cannot but mention the work being carried out on a draft Optional Protocol to the Convention on the Rights of the Child

---

[3] UN Doc. CRC/C/15/Add.34. [4] UN Doc. CCPR/C/79/Add.55.

which relates to the sale of children, child prostitution and child pornography. The CRC Committee – which was consulted together with a large number of organs and institutions, states, and non-governmental organisations (NGOs) – adamantly opposed such a trend on the assumption that these situations were already covered by the existing Convention and that an Optional Protocol would only serve to undermine the Convention itself.[5] Unfortunately, despite this expressed position, a Working Group of the Commission is now drafting a text that will eventually be adopted by the Commission and the General Assembly.[6]

A similar misfortune almost befell the Human Rights Committee (HRC) regarding a draft proposal currently being studied by the Commission on Human Rights.[7] The draft called for a third Optional Protocol to the ICCPR that would extend the list of non-derogable provisions in article 4, paragraph 2 to include articles 9, paragraphs 3 and 4 and article 14 (the rights of those arrested and standing trial). As interpreted by the HRC – and made clear to the Sub-Commission on Prevention of Discrimination and Protection of Minorities and later to the General Assembly through its Annual Report – such a step would have undermined the Covenant itself, in that it would have implicitly invited states parties to feel free to derogate from the provisions in article 9 during states of emergency if they did not ratify the proposed Optional Protocol. Thus the Optional Protocol might have had the undesirable effect of *diminishing* the protection of detained persons during states of emergency.[8] Thanks to a number of contacts at the Secretariat level and between members of the Committee and the Sub-Commission, the matter was taken up again by the Sub-Commission with the result that it no longer insists on the adoption of a Protocol but recently invited the Committee to update its General Comment No. 5 on article 4 of the Covenant.[9]

It remains to be seen whether, and how, such unfortunate developments may be avoided in the future. Meetings of chairpersons should probably enter into some sort of formal relationship with the Sub-Commission which is, after all, the main initiator of standard-setting activities in the human rights field. This will not necessarily mean that recommendations

---

[5] UN Docs. CRC/C/29; E/CN.4/1994/WG.14/2/Add.1.
[6] CHR Res.1995/78, 8 March 1995.
[7] Sub-Comm Res.1993/26; CCPR Annual Report A/49/40 Annex XI.
[8] UN Doc. A/49/40, paras. 22–3.   [9] UN Doc. A/53/40, July 1998.

by treaty bodies are immediately acted upon, but it might lead to the treaty bodies being duly consulted in the course of the preparation of Sub-Commission studies, and their views given some preference. In this regard it is interesting to note that in both cases mentioned above, the views of the respective committees on the draft Optional Protocols were requested by a resolution at the very last stage of the process and that the committees simply appeared in a very long list of bodies, alongside institutions or organs that had no say whatsoever in the implementation or monitoring of the Covenant or Convention.

Apart from conflicting provisions, there exist a relatively large number of related or similar provisions in different treaties. One may, for instance, mention children's rights, covered specifically by CRC but also envisaged by CEDAW insofar as they concern the situation of the girl child, by CERD with regard to discrimination faced by children belonging to different groups or minorities, by the CAT Committee concerning cases of ill-treatment of minors, by the ICESCR Committee regarding the impact of economic and social difficulties on the situation of children and their access to education, and by the ICCPR on forced labour, corporal punishment or juvenile justice.

Other examples could be multiplied, such as women's rights or cases of discrimination or ill-treatment of the person. The question therefore arises of the possibility of consolidating reports submitted by states parties to various instruments into one single document, or merging the supervisory bodies. Although at the present time one cannot realistically see these proposals being agreed to, a more modest approach may be feasible. One could envisage a request that states parties submit their various reports on the same date and issue them in a single UN document.[10] This would allow states to make appropriate cross-references, since developments on any given subject would be covered in the same document. Similarly, treaty bodies would have a full picture of the implementation of all rights protected under international instruments to which the reporting state is party. They would, however, retain the right to deal with all rights or principles contained in their own instruments.

---

[10] At present, reports submitted to different treaty bodies by the same country bear different symbols and are issued at different times depending on when the report is to be considered by the relevant body. Procuring copies of all reports in a short space of time is extremely difficult.

2. DIVERGENT INTERPRETATIONS GIVEN BY DIFFERENT BODIES TO RELATED PROVISIONS

(a) Concluding observations or comments

All treaty bodies now adopt some form of conclusions following the consideration of states' reports. These documents, whether they are called concluding observations, comments or concluding comments, follow to a certain extent the same pattern, although those of the CAT and CEDAW Committees are not yet as detailed and exhaustive. This common pattern is a much welcomed and long-awaited development, initiated by the HRC in March 1992.[11] At the time of writing, more than 150 separate concluding observations have been adopted. Observers, and in particular NGOs, have welcomed these documents, which detail matters of concern in a rather direct way and which often include (or appear to include) observers' own criticisms. What remains to be analysed is to what extent these documents are consistent with one another and form a coherent overall account of the human rights situation in the countries under consideration.

Given the fact that states parties increasingly submit reports due under several instruments around the same time, the situation of human rights in particular countries is often addressed by several bodies during the same year. For the purposes of this study, ten situations concerning reports considered by committees between 1995 and 1997 have been selected.[12] The author's basic intention was to ascertain:

(a) the extent to which the message sent to reporting states by each committee reflected a unified approach; and

(b) consequently, whether the interpretations by different bodies of related provisions as they applied to the same country remained complementary and not conflicting.

It is reassuring to note that, in most cases, concluding observations or comments by different treaty bodies on the same country present a comprehensive and rounded picture of the situation of human rights in that country, each committee focusing on the implementation of their

---

[11] UN Doc. A/44/40, paras. 18 and 45.

[12] Brazil, China, Denmark, Germany, Guatemala, Peru, Portugal, the Russian Federation, Spain, and the United Kingdom. The relevant documents can be retrieved from the Office of the UN High Commissioner for Human Rights (UNHCHR) website (http://www.unhchr.ch).

treaty with appropriate cross-referencing when necessary. In a few cases, committees mention concluding observations adopted by other bodies in order to reinforce their own. This is particularly true of the CRC Committee. In turn, this implies that readers of those texts, whether governmental officials, non-governmental activists or researchers, will find a unified approach by treaty bodies towards implementation issues related to provisions in different instruments.

However, there remain a number of situations where the opinions expressed and the interpretation given to rights or practices differed slightly from one body to another, perhaps because the attention of committee members was diverted to different issues. Some examples are set out below.

(i) Brazil

Concluding observations adopted on Brazil by the CERD Committee and the HRC focused on the specific situation of indigenous persons, blacks and other persons belonging to minorities. The HRC used much stronger terms to condemn summary and arbitrary executions of such persons and went into more detail as regards the process of demarcation of indigenous lands. The CERD Committee on the other hand, raised an issue regarding the prohibition on illiterates being elected in political elections that was not mentioned by the HRC.[13]

(ii) China

When considering the implementation of CRC in China, the CRC Committee concurred with the observations adopted by the CAT Committee. It went much further, however, by dealing with the ill-treatment of children in welfare institutions and the imposition of suspended death sentences on children that constitute, according to the Committee, cruel, inhuman or degrading treatment or punishment. The CERD Committee expressed particular concern regarding the ill-treatment of persons in Xinjiang which was not mentioned at all in the CAT Committee's observations. Lastly, the CRC Committee referred at length to discrimination faced by Tibetan and other minority children in the education system which went unnoticed in the observations of the CERD Committee.[14]

---

[13] UN Docs. CERD/C/304/Add.11; CCPR/C/79/Add.66.
[14] UN Docs. CRC/C/15/Add.56; A/51/44 paras. 138–50; CERD/C/304/Add.15.

(iii) Denmark

When considering Denmark, both the CAT Committee and the HRC expressed concern over methods of crowd control including the use of dogs, but the HRC discussed this issue in far more detail. The CEDAW Committee listed many concerns regarding women's rights which went unnoticed by the HRC.[15]

(iv) Germany

In considering Germany, both the HRC and the CERD Committee referred to the problem of police brutality against foreigners. However, while the HRC recommended the establishment of an independent body to investigate such problems, the CERD Committee merely recommended better training and stricter disciplinary action against perpetrators.[16]

(v) Guatemala

Significant discrepancies in the attention of committees towards the same country were noticed in the case of Guatemala. The HRC focused its attention, as far as children's rights were concerned, on the situation of street children who were subjected to serious violations of their human rights, particularly their right to life and the right not to be subjected to torture and ill-treatment. It further deplored the intensity of abuse against them by persons in authority. Similar concerns were not expressed by the CRC Committee which, as far as the problem of ill-treatment was concerned, decided to make specific recommendations as to the particular impact of the armed conflict on children, an issue which in return was not raised by the HRC.[17]

(vi) Peru

Although the HRC and the CEDAW Committee shared similar concerns with regard to the situation of women in Peru, particularly as far as their physical rights were concerned, the CAT Committee made no mention whatsoever of these issues. Moreover, the HRC addressed issues left almost untouched by the CEDAW Committee, namely widespread sexual abuse

---

[15] UN Docs. CRC/C/15/Add.33; CCPR/C/79/Add.68; A/51/44 paras. 33–41; CERD C/304/Add.2; CEDAW/C/1997/L.1/Add.7.

[16] UN Docs. CRC/C/15/Add.43; E/C.12/1993/17; CCPR/C/79/Add.72.

[17] UN Docs. CRC/C/15/Add.58; E/C.12/1/Add.3; CCPR/C/79/Add.63; A/51/44 paras. 42–57.

against women detainees, the existence of discriminatory provisions in the Civil Code, and serious shortcomings in the legislation relating to divorce that was discriminatory towards women. On the contrary, the CEDAW Committee deplored the reports of rape and gang rape occurring in the emergency zones and affecting indigenous and peasant women, an issue which was raised neither by the HRC nor by the CAT Committee. The HRC was also concerned about the use of socio-economic criteria for grouping convicted and unconvicted prisoners, an issue which was not discussed by the ICESCR Committee.[18]

(vii) Portugal

During its consideration of Portugal and, in particular its territory of Macau, the ICESCR Committee expressed its concern that the majority of the population was not familiar with the judicial system of the territory. When the HRC considered the same state party, this was not raised as an issue although it clearly falls under article 14 of the Covenant.[19]

(viii) Russian Federation

In the case of the Russian Federation's reports there again appear to be slight discrepancies between the focus of the CEDAW Committee and that of the HRC. While the latter deplored the extent of rape and domestic violence, this phenomenon was not mentioned in the comments of the former. It may be noted, however, that both the HRC and the CERD Committee expressed very similar concerns as far as racial discrimination and discriminatory attitudes towards persons belonging to minorities were involved.[20]

(ix) Spain

In the case of Spain, the CERD Committee expressed numerous and strongly worded concerns relating to instances of racism, xenophobia and discrimination against foreigners, asylum seekers and members of the roma (gypsy) community. These concerns were not addressed by the HRC.

---

[18] UN Docs. CRC/C/15/Add.8; E/C.12/1/Add.14; CCPR/C/79/Add.67 and 73; A/50/44 paras. 62–73.

[19] UN Docs. CRC/C/15/Add.45; E/C.12/1/Add.9; CCPR/C/79/Add.77; A/49/44 paras. 106–17.

[20] UN Docs. CRC/C/15/Add.5; E/C.12/1/Add.13; CCPR/C/79/Add.54; CAT/C/XVIII/CRP.1/Add.3.

The CERD Committee also raised specific concerns with regard to difficulties faced by children of the Castilian-speaking minority living in Spain's autonomous communities in receiving education in their mother tongue, an issue which the CRC Committee did not address.[21]

(x) United Kingdom

When considering the report of the United Kingdom, the ICESCR Committee expressed its concern over the insufficient efforts undertaken to ensure school placement for children of immigrants and to protect them from discrimination. A further issue raised was the absence of a broad-based policy for the protection of children from all forms of abuse. The CRC Committee did not mention any of these problems.[22]

The examples outlined above suggest that committees on the whole assume a common approach towards related provisions, although a number of discrepancies appear among the concluding observations. Such differences may derive from the committees' respective methods of work and, in particular, the format of the concluding observations or comments themselves. Extremely succinct concluding observations – as in the case of the CAT or CEDAW Committees – may convey the feeling that important issues are left out or insufficiently explored. On the other hand, overly-detailed observations may be criticised if they fail to emphasise important issues. Additionally, they run the risk of containing technical or legal considerations which may not accurately reflect the legal or practical situation in the state concerned, thus providing the government with grounds for attacking the report.

Another problem arises when a committee decides to deal at length with a particular matter in circumstances where the matter was not raised by other bodies dealing with related provisions. In these circumstances, states parties might use the apparent discrepancy to undermine the concerns which have been raised, using one committee's comments against those of the other.

It is also apparent that there is a general tendency for many committees to range beyond their terms of reference, sometimes to the detriment of their own monitoring function. One can find stronger condemnation of

---

[21] UN Docs. CRC/C/15/Add.35; CERD/C/304/Add.8; E/C.12/1/Add.2; CCPR/C/79/Add.61.
[22] UN Docs. CRC/C/14/Add.34; E/C.12/1994/Add.19; CCPR/C/79/Add.55; A/51/44 paras. 58–65; CERD/C/304/Add.9.

violations of particular rights by treaty bodies which do not deal specifically with these rights, than by the committee actually charged with monitoring these rights. This may prompt states parties to complain that they were unfairly treated by a committee on the grounds that the committee responsible for monitoring the respect of particular rights did not express similar concerns.

Hence there is an increasing need to respond to the calls of the meetings of chairpersons for better coordination between the committees. Relevant texts and documents are already circulated between committee members together with an increasingly large number of reports from special rapporteurs and NGOs. Even so, there is a limit to the number of pages of documentation that may be digested concerning a particular country, and this limit may have been reached. The situation is aggravated by the fact that committee members often receive these documents shortly before the consideration of the state party's report and at a time when they are already deeply involved in committee matters. For this reason, the profusion of information stemming from non-governmental partners may be detrimental to the coherence of the treaty bodies system.

A further factor in explaining discrepancies among concluding observations may be found in their *raison d'être*, namely, to provide at the end of a session a written document containing all issues raised during the discussion. Time constraints, as well as the necessity to obtain a consensual approach on texts that may have a serious impact at national and international level, necessarily affect the compilation of such a document.

Lastly, the main reason underlying the discrepancies between various committees' observations arises from the treaty bodies' unavoidable tendency to encompass in their consideration of states' reports all explicit or implicit issues that may arise in the implementation of the relevant treaty. Whether or not an issue has already been efficiently dealt with by another treaty body then becomes a secondary concern compared with the overriding necessity to monitor fully all issues raised under the treaty.

(b) General comments or recommendations

Among the six bodies established under UN human rights instruments, four adopt general comments or recommendations, namely the HRC and the ICESCR, CERD and CEDAW Committees. No less than seventy-seven such observations or recommendations have been adopted. Together, they form a reasonably comprehensive and detailed interpretation of provisions of human rights law by treaty bodies.[23] Obviously, the underlying philosophy of these documents has changed over the years and the texts have significantly matured. The first observations by the HRC were – at the time of the Cold War – of a rather descriptive nature whereas the latest provide a comprehensive interpretation of certain of the Covenant's provisions. The comments of the ICESCR Committee which were developed more recently have from the very beginning followed the same pattern. The recommendations of the CEDAW Committee were, at first, similar to those of the CERD Committee in that they more closely resembled resolutions than legal interpretations of the Convention. Following a decision taken a few years ago, the Committee has attempted to follow the pattern developed by the other bodies.

Most of the shortcomings outlined above as far as the examination of country reports is concerned do not arise in the case of general comments or observations. This is mainly due to the fact that, being theoretical exercises based on lengthy and technical discussion, they necessarily rely on documents and interpretations stemming from the work of other bodies. Those drafting these comments begin by surveying their own body's jurisprudence and practice, together with existing standards and the experience gained by other treaty bodies. The time factor does not play as crucial a role as in the case of concluding observations: committees are not bound to produce a text by a given date. Instead they can take several sessions to concentrate on a text and adopt the most sophisticated document possible. The latest comment by the HRC on article 25 of the ICCPR took several years before it was adopted.

As mentioned earlier, a difference may appear between certain texts, not on the basis of any discrepancies, but due to differences of approach towards them. Although the recommendations by the CERD Committee have changed noticeably over the years, they remain more descriptive than analytical and continue to take the form of pseudo-resolutions. This is why, for instance, General Recommendation No. XI on non-citizens fell short of General Comment No. 15 of the HRC on the position of aliens under the Covenant.

On the whole, general comments or recommendations adopted by various bodies do not overlap, with the exception of those texts dealing with

---

[23] Compiled in UN Doc. HRI/GEN/1/Rev.3.

non-substantive issues such as reporting obligations, overdue reports or technical assistance. Should problems of compatibility occur, there would always remain a possibility to undertake a revision of that particular text. One may, for instance note that General Comment No. 4 of the HRC on the rights of women, which was adopted in 1981, is largely outdated and compares unfavourably with both its own practice and jurisprudence and that of the CEDAW Committee. The Committee has decided to update the text to enable it to take into account all developments in the area.[24]

The future may see the various committees' general observations and recommendations providing the best illustration of the coordination between the treaty bodies and of the coherence of their views. To this end it would appear timely for the CRC and CAT Committees to face the challenge of building on their own experience and sharing with other bodies their views on the interpretation of treaty provisions. Similarly the general recommendations of both the CERD and CEDAW Committees would also gain from being more comprehensive and analytical than has been the case until now. Eventually this approach would provide a comprehensive interpretation of human rights provisions by independent bodies and would assist in the formulation of international human rights law.

B. The impact of reservations under a particular instrument on the integrity of other instruments

The impact of reservations under a particular instrument for the integrity of other instruments deserves special attention. For various reasons, states tend to enter reservations to the provisions of human rights instruments upon ratification or accession. It is not necessary in the context of this particular study to analyse why they do so and to what extent this is legitimate under international human rights law.[25] What must be stressed is that while international human rights instruments (at least those studied here) form a comprehensive and coherent corpus of legal provisions, states are rarely consistent in making the same reservation to analogous or overlapping provisions in different instruments.[26] Against that background,

---

[24] UN Doc. A/51/40, March/April 1996, para. 366.

[25] For a guide to the issues and the literature see J. P. Gardner (ed.), *Human Rights as General Norms and a State's Right to Opt Out*, London, 1997.

[26] See, however, chapter 14 of this volume concerning US practice of making reservations to human rights treaties.

attempts by a state, legitimately or otherwise to avoid the application of one particular provision in one specific instrument may conflict with obligations under another instrument. Such an action may breach the homogeneity and legal coherence of the international obligations of that state, quite apart from its implications for the international human rights system as a whole.

1. RESERVATION TO PROVISIONS OF A NEW INSTRUMENT WITH NO RESERVATION TO A RELATED PROVISION IN ANOTHER INSTRUMENT

When studying reservations to UN human rights bodies, one is struck by two concordant trends. First, new states parties tend to make more reservations than those who acceded or ratified at an earlier stage. This is probably due to the fact that they have had the opportunity to witness the activities of the relevant supervisory bodies and prefer to avoid them having a say on particular matters of interest to them. Second, states generally enter more reservations to specific conventions (those dealing with torture, women's discrimination, and children) than to those that are generic (the two Covenants). The result is that a significant number of states acceded to the Covenants without any reservations but then acceded to the Conventions (in particular those on the child and discrimination against women) with reservations on provisions already enshrined in the Covenants.

Of particular significance here is the situation of CEDAW, which is characterised by a large number of reservations. Reservations have often been made to a group of provisions which correspond to provisions in the Covenants. For instance, several states[27] expressed reservations on specific provisions in articles 9(2) (equal rights with regard to the nationality of children) and 16(1) (discrimination against women in all matters relating to marriage and family relations) whereas they did not enter reservations on related provisions in the Covenants (that is, article 3 of each of the Covenants together with articles 23(4) and 24(3) of the ICCPR).

It appears from the discussion of the reports of these states by the HRC that substantive issues in these areas have indeed been raised and, in appropriate cases, have led to expressions of concern. During the consideration

---

[27] Cyprus, Egypt, Iraq, Ireland, Jamaica, Jordan, the Libyan Arab Jamahiriya, Malta, Mauritius, Morocco, Republic of Korea and Tunisia.

of the Egyptian report,[28] for instance, a number of questions were raised and comments made on the issue of discrimination between men and women in respect of transmission of nationality to children. One may conclude that in these specific cases the monitoring of the implementation of provisions in CEDAW to which reservations were made was *de facto* transmitted or delegated to a certain extent to the HRC.

In more general terms, treaty bodies display a clear tendency towards requesting reporting states to engage in a discussion of the rationale of their reservations, especially in cases where they seem to go beyond what should be reasonably admissible in contemporary international human rights law. In 1994 the HRC adopted General Comment No. 24 on Reservations,[29] thus making its position clear with regard to the latter point. The ICESCR Committee and the HRC each regularly raise questions as to why reservations were not made in respect of the Covenants' provisions. Despite this, the two Committees do not always inquire into the rationale of reservations entered in respect of related provisions in other Conventions. It may be argued that since both committees have to consider a wide range of issues within a limited time frame, they are not disposed to look into a matter that may be perceived as being essentially theoretical and not directly connected to their supervisory activities. On the other hand, a committee whose Convention has been the object of a reservation is not well placed to engage in that sort of discussion. Obviously, such a committee may be tempted to address the issue of reservations in a general way and make appropriate recommendations with a view to the withdrawal of some or all of them. Moreover, committee members may not be aware of the issues raised by other bodies when dealing with similar issues.

This problem calls for an appropriate exchange of information about reservations entered by each reporting state to related provisions in other human rights instruments. Similarly, information should be shared which relates to the precise factors or difficulties that led the state party to enter such a reservation as well as its impact on the practical human rights situation in that country. This would allow committee members – particularly those of the ICESCR Committee and the HRC – to raise issues and make appropriate comments. Furthermore, the body supervising the Convention to which reservations have been entered should at a later stage receive these comments together with the response of the state party concerned. In

---

[28] See UN Doc. CCPR/C/79/Add.23.   [29] Reproduced in UN Doc. HRI/GEN/1/Rev.3.

the light of time constraints, it remains to be seen to what extent treaty bodies will be prepared to, or will be in a position to, undertake an analysis of all the issues involved.

Coordination between treaty bodies has not yet reached the level advocated in successive meetings of chairpersons' reports. What is undoubtedly missing – among other things – is a clear policy of treaty bodies designed to overcome some of the problems connected to the extensive practice of states parties resorting to reservations. Such a policy would allow a parallel consideration of reservations entered by reporting states to related provisions in other human rights instruments.

2. RESERVATION TO A PROVISION IN AN OPTIONAL PROTOCOL WITH NO RESERVATION TO SUBSTANTIVE PROVISIONS OF THE 'PARENT' CONVENTION

Problems also arise, for example, when a state party enters a reservation to a provision in the Optional Protocol to the ICCPR that prohibits an individual raising an issue under a specific provision of the Covenant. This issue arose in relation to Germany's reservation to article 5, paragraph 2, of the Optional Protocol under which the competence of the Committee would not extend to communications 'by means of which a violation of Article 26 of the Covenant is reprimanded, if and in so far as the reprimanded violation refers to rights other than those guaranteed under the Covenant'.

The Committee raised this issue with Germany at its fifty-eighth session on 4–5 November 1996[30] and expressed concern in its Concluding Observations.[31] In future there may very well be similar reservations to the anticipated Optional Protocols to the ICESCR and those to CEDAW. These types of reservations would lead to a disruption in the coherence of legal obligations under one particular instrument and render the operation of treaty bodies seriously dysfunctional. It would be possible, for instance, for an NGO to draw attention to a particular situation under the reporting procedure whereas the same situation could not be raised under the optional procedure. This unfortunate situation would make matters even more complex for real and potential victims of human rights abuses.

---

[30] UN Doc. CCPR/C/SR.1551–1553.   [31] See UN Doc. CCPR/C/79/Add.72.

C. Conclusions

For international human rights law to become universal does not simply require that all states become parties to all human rights instruments. It also implies that there should be a certain uniformity in the obligations undertaken by the states parties as well as a certain uniformity in the interpretation given to related provisions by different treaty bodies. Although systematic discrepancies do not appear to exist in the way committees deal with related provisions, there is clearly insufficient cross-referencing and coordination between these bodies. Concrete steps should be taken to streamline the format of concluding observations or comments as well as of general comments or recommendations. In addition, direct contacts should be established between bodies through which specific issues of concern would be drawn to the attention of bodies dealing with related issues in order to avoid any misreading or lack of coherence in the monitoring process.

Nevertheless, proposals to make treaty bodies' supervisory functions more sophisticated and efficient have to be balanced against the need to take the interests of all partners in the process fully into account. Expert members of treaty bodies, professors specialised in the activities of such bodies and staff directly in charge of the committees' secretariat are well aware of the specificities of each committee. They know the reasons for differing procedures between committees and other variations in the operation of the treaty bodies. The nuances of each regime are respected and valued as underlining the differences and particularities of the individual treaties. Those proposing reform must take account of their views and experience.

Nor should the particular interest of other partners be forgotten. Government officials or non-governmental activists coming before a particular committee increasingly tend to be aware of questions raised before other bodies and their comments. They expect certain issues to be raised and prepare themselves accordingly. Coherence of approach is therefore imperative and discrepancies should be avoided as it is the credibility of the entire treaty body system which is ultimately at stake.

Ways and means should thus be found to ensure that observations and comments adopted by other treaty bodies are used as a primary source of information by all experts. This exercise should be undertaken by either the country rapporteurs themselves or by the secretariat or both. Committee members should be systematically alerted to the extent to which a particular issue has already been dealt with in another treaty body's conclusions. Discrepancies should then be the result of a conscious decision to depart from another body's conclusions rather than of a lack of time or insufficient analysis of available documents.

Efforts should also be made to harmonise the format of concluding observations further. The CEDAW, CERD and CAT Committees should seek to develop their conclusions with a view to bringing them more into line with those of the other bodies. However the trend in the HRC, the CRC and ICESCR Committees towards including every aspect of the discussion as well as comments made in documents submitted by NGOs or specialised agencies (whether or not put forward in public session) should be restrained.

Furthermore, steps should be taken to ensure that the ICESCR Committee and the HRC do not try systematically to deal with all aspects of their generic Covenant, but should leave a number of non-urgent questions to the specific treaty body concerned. The CEDAW, CERD and CAT Committees should also attempt to limit themselves to those issues they are best equipped to deal with and avoid, where possible, dealing with other general issues that would in any case be better studied by either the ICESCR Committee or the HRC.

Finally, states should be held responsible for whatever incoherence results from their reservation policy, which can often be far from easy to understand. Treaty bodies should not miss the opportunity to criticise states parties that do not maintain a strict policy towards reservations. Again, a single UN document containing all reports from each state party would allow readers – including committee members – to grasp more easily the extent of each state party's obligations as well as any instances of incoherence or discrepancy in that regard.

19

BODIES OF KNOWLEDGE: A DIVERSITY
PROMOTION ROLE FOR THE UN HIGH
COMMISSIONER FOR HUMAN RIGHTS

CRAIG SCOTT*

A. Introduction: consolidation and diversity

In his 1997 final report on the human rights treaty bodies, Philip Alston proposed an expert group study of the modalities for consolidating the six treaty bodies.[1] But neither in his final report nor in the interim report submitted to the World Conference on Human Rights in 1993 did Alston specifically discuss the consolidation issue.[2] Instead he referred to the discussion in an earlier (1989) report in which he had presented consolidation into 'one or perhaps two new treaty bodies' as '[t]he most radical option' that had yet been put forward to address mounting problems such as system overload, resource constraints, and the burdensome proliferation of reporting duties on states.[3] In that 1989 report, Alston signalled that

---

* The author wishes to acknowledge the generous research support provided by the Social Sciences and Humanities Research Council of Canada. The author also wishes to thank Martin Scheinin, Ronald St. John Macdonald and Philip Alston for helpful comments.

[1] P. Alston, 'Final Report on Enhancing the Long-term Effectiveness of the United Nations Human Rights Treaty System', UN Doc. E/CN.4/1997/74, 7 March 1997, at para. 94 ('Alston Report 1997').

[2] For the 1993 interim report, see P. Alston, 'Interim Report of Study on Enhancing the Long-term Effectiveness of the United Nations Human Rights Treaty Regime', UN Doc. A/CONF.157/PC/62/Add.11/Rev.1, 22 April 1993.

[3] P. Alston, 'Report on Effective Implementation of International Instruments on Human Rights, Including Reporting Obligations under International Instruments on Human Rights', UN Doc. A/44/1989, 8 November 1989, at para. 179 ('Alston Report 1989'). Alston does not assume consolidation means merger into a single body nor does he presuppose anything about the structure, functions, or formal powers of such a body. But he does discuss the consolidation issue in terms of its more radical version, what he styles a single 'super-committee'. Anne Bayefsky has also raised the issue of consolidation in her 'Report on the UN Human Rights Treaties: Facing the Implementation Crisis' which was prepared

long-term consolidation may eventually warrant serious consideration,[4] but the general focus of his discussion at that time was that consolidation might well prove retrogressive. Without taking a position, he addressed some potentially problematic aspects of consolidation in the following terms:

> many of the advantages [of consolidation] can equally well be portrayed as disadvantages, and vice versa, depending on the assumptions and perspectives of the observer . . . It can be argued that the super-committee would, by virtue of its extensive purview and probably almost permanent sessions, develop enormous expertise. The counter-argument is that the variety of expertise represented on the existing range of committees is greater than could ever be captured on a single committee . . . Or, it can be argued that a single committee would facilitate the effective integration of different concerns such as racial and sex-based discrimination, children's and migrant workers' rights, and economic, social and cultural rights. The counter-argument is that some of those concerns might simply be glossed over and that the supervisory process would no longer serve to galvanize those sectors of the Government and of the community dealing with, or interested in, a specific issue.[5]

While Alston's 1997 recommendation to study the 'modalities' of consolidation could be read as a call to study only the legal and procedural means to achieve a preordained goal, it is clear enough that, in 1997 as in 1989, Alston was not advocating any particular model of consolidation.[6] This is as it should be. Even if Alston now seems, on the whole, to take the view that some form of consolidation is necessitated by the current and growing systemic crisis, the disadvantages identified in 1989 are presumably as relevant now as they were then.

The tensions canvassed by Alston can be presented in terms of consolidation's threats to diversity of knowledge. One of the benefits of the current pluralistic structure (six treaty bodies for six treaties) is the diversity of vantage points it brings to bear on any state's human rights performance. Several forms of diversity of knowledge are at stake. *Diversity of expertise*

---

for the meeting of the International Law Association (ILA) Committee on International Human Rights Law and Practice at the 1996 Helsinki Conference of the ILA. In two brief references, the Bayefsky study recommends consolidation into two new bodies, one dealing with state reports and one dealing with petitions: International Law Association, *First Report, Committee on International Human Rights Law and Practice*, Helsinki Conference, 1996, at pp. 2, 14 and 22.

[4] Alston Report 1989, *supra*, note 3, at para. 180.

[5] Ibid., at para. 182.

[6] Alston indicates the role of the expert study group would be to explore 'the contours of such a reform': Alston Report 1997, *supra*, note 1, at para. 94.

concerns the range of professional disciplines that can be relevant to the interpretation of human rights. Depending on the treaty and specific issue at hand, several fields of knowledge can fruitfully cast light on relevant dimensions of a situation or normative debate – for example, law, medicine, social work, penology and law enforcement, development economics, nutritional science, health administration, architecture, and environmental studies. *Diversity of experience* concerns the relevance of the diverse lived experience, both negative and positive, of different social groups. Many of the social markers that are the central concern of non-discrimination norms (such as gender, race, ethnicity, religion, sexuality, economic class and social status) coincide at some level with different experiences that provide different insights into what is of value, how values relate to each other, and how the world functions so as to advance or suppress those values. Some experiences can be widely shared, so much so that we might call them cultural, while others are much more specific to a particular geographical and temporal context; others again represent something closer to what we would want to call universal experience. In some middle ground between expertise and experience, there is also something we might call *diversity of normative focus*, a rather awkward way to categorise the 'different concerns' that are associated with various categories of rights, such as those mentioned by Alston in the passage quoted.

This chapter will first summarise the benefits of diversity of knowledge and make a case for why it is important to collective decision-making bodies. It will next discuss some dimensions of the current state of affairs with respect to representation of diversity of knowledge within the UN human rights committees, with a view to suggesting why there is reason for concern. Proceeding from the premise that the harnessing of diversity must be central to any consolidation reforms, the chapter then goes on to develop its central proposal that an international candidate identification process be organised by the Office of the UN High Commissioner for Human Rights (UNHCHR) who would be assisted by an eminent persons group which she would establish. This reform proposal is put forward on the twin assumptions that the human rights treaty bodies will continue to have a separate existence for some time yet and that practical experience with attempts to promote diversity will provide valuable lessons for any eventual consolidation project. UNHCHR's involvement would be designed to enhance the collective insight of each treaty body (and of the treaty bodies when they act in concert) through coordinated attention to both diversity of expertise and diversity of experience as relevant criteria for election to those bodies.

In the conclusion, brief mention will be made of a second proposal which could complement this election proposal. This is for the human rights committees, through pragmatic acts of institutional cooperation, to consider their six treaties as interconnected parts of a single human rights 'constitution' and thereby to consider themselves as partner chambers within a *consolidating* supervisory institution. Through such acts of pragmatic imagination, each committee would be encouraged to place itself within a network of dialogue with the other committees; all would seek to expand their horizons through harnessing the pool of diverse knowledge represented by their large collective membership and the diversity of normative mandates of the six treaties.

B. Valuing diversity of knowledge

We need to build into the institutional design of any consolidated treaty body what might be called a principle of interactive diversity. Such a principle is premised on the idea that superior collective judgment is exercised when multiple perspectives are encouraged to interact with each other in coming to grips with any given normative issue or decision. In order for diverse perspectives and actors to interact, there must first be a commitment to ensuring diversity is represented. Institutionalisation of this principle in the international human rights realm is justified by the imperative need to transcend limitations of knowledge and perspective, limitations that may compromise any claims to universal validity of conclusions reached by interpretive practice. Interactive diversity thus facilitates universalism. The rest of this section presents a brief justification of the foregoing claims.

A host of critical missions within and outside legal scholarship (among others, feminist theory, critical race theory, and post-colonial studies) have succeeded in unsettling the legitimacy of legal institutions, especially the domestic judiciary.[7] They have done this by demonstrating the pervasiveness of choice in the operation of legal judgment, the contingency of

---

[7] See, e.g., K. Crenshaw, N. Gotanda, G. Peller and K. Thomas (eds.), *Critical Race Theory: The Key Writings That Formed the Movement*, New York, 1995; B. Ashcroft, G. Griffiths and H. Tiffin (eds.), *The Post-colonial Studies Reader*, New York, 1995; R. Delgado and J. Stefancic (eds.), *Critical White Studies: Looking Behind the Mirror*, Philadelphia, 1997.

the criteria any given judge may find congenial to her or his choice, and the influence of what one sociologist has called the *habitus* of a judge on the relative appeal of various criteria.[8] One result of such critiques has been to show how current legal systems produce norms that are populated by some social groups more than by others. It is not simply a question of explicit exclusion. It is also a case of an abundance of implicit norms generated by dominant perspectives on and experiences of the social world, for example those which reflect male experiences.[9] These accounts have identified the absence of other social groups from participation in shaping the law as a central reason for such explicit and implicit exclusion. In short, they have demonstrated the pervasive partiality of the law.[10] Thus, Jennifer Nedelsky explains two interlinked senses of partiality that result from a lack of diversity of representation in the judiciary:

> The dispute over demands for diversity on the bench . . . could be under-stood as a dispute over the conditions of impartiality. In these terms, we can see one group claiming that a judiciary composed very largely of white, middle class men cannot be impartial. They will inevitably be biased,

[8] Pierre Bourdieu's idea of *habitus* can be paraphrased as a reference to the constellation of dispositions, baseline assumptions and world views that are embodied in a group of persons, such *habitus* being structured, *inter alia*, by a person's present location in social hierarchies as well as by formative influences such as social group experience and educational upbringing (notably professional elite formation). While we can speak of each person as having a unique *habitus*, the primary sense is of *habitus* as a shared phenomenon, '[t]he conditionings associated with a particular class of conditions of existence' that operate at some sub-conscious level on the behaviour of those imbued with such *habitus*; they are 'structured structures predisposed to function as structuring structures': see P. Bourdieu, *The Logic of Practice*, Cambridge, UK, 1990, at p. 53.

[9] See D. Réaume, 'What's Distinctive About Feminist Analysis of Law?: A Conceptual Analysis of Women's Exclusion from Law', 2 *Legal Theory*, 1996, pp. 265–99 especially at pp. 278–9.

[10] A universal extrapolation is made here. Unless shown otherwise, it is assumed that this body of critical work is relevant to every legal system. This is not to say that attention to diversity matters in the same degree or operates in the same way, only that it matters in some degree and in some way. It is also important to note that, when we focus on the diversity of juridical bodies like courts or UN human rights committees as institutions charged with supervising the state (and, in varying degrees, non-state actors), the concern is not only with the law interpretively created by those bodies. The concern is also with the law made by other organs of state that suffer their own, often more serious, problems of social group domination. But, in the context of human rights which act in part as institutional devices allocating power to courts (or committees) to judge the acts or omissions of states, lack of diversity within these supervisory juridical bodies results in both failures to perceive and unwillingness to address affronts to human rights that to some degree stem from diversity deficits in non-juridical state organs.

whether consciously or unconsciously, by the partiality of their limited perspective. Here I think it is interesting to note that the term 'partial' has two different meanings. One is partial in the sense of partial to something, liking it. The other is partial in the sense of being only a part. Both are of concern here, and both are thought to require diversity as a remedy. If the judiciary is drawn from only one group in society, there is a worry that they may be only partial to their own kind in their decision. Diversity on the bench eases that concern. And in the second sense of partiality, the inevitable limitation of one group's experience, perspective and understanding can be remedied by ensuring that judges come from all parts of society.[11]

Other critical theorists have developed similar arguments as to why impartiality should be understood in terms of a kind of fullness or enlargement of thought, and as to how such impartiality would be fostered by 'the creation of institutions and practices whereby the voices and the perspectives of others, often unknown to us, can become expressed in their own right'.[12] For example, Tanya Coke, in the context of a discussion of the salience of experience of race in the United States, succinctly explains the need for racially diverse juries:

> One fundamental reason why the racial composition of juries matters, quite apart from the issue of in-group partiality, is that a jury that draws upon the varied experiences of its members is less likely to rely upon complacent but uninformed assumptions in its deliberations. This view admits that impartiality is not embodied in a single 'ideal' juror but achieved through the cross-pollination of a range of views and experiences. The issue is not whether whites, blacks or Latinos have a greater or lesser capacity for impartial decision-making, but whether the optimum conditions for that deliberative process exist. Given the experiential boundaries of neighbourhood, job, race, gender, sexual orientation, and social station, most of us fail to recognize the false assumptions that underlie racism, sexism, and homophobia until others challenge them.[13]

Thus juries lacking in diversity of social experience are less likely to be impartial in their decision-making than are more diverse juries. As a consequence, what is affected is not (or, not just) political or societal legitimacy but also juridical validity. The fundamental insight is that an amalgamation

---

[11] J. Nedelsky, 'Judgment, Diversity and Relational Autonomy', J. A. Corry Lecture, Queen's University, Canada, October 1995 (unpublished manuscript).

[12] S. Benhabib, *Situating the Self: Gender, Community and Postmodernism in Contemporary Ethics*, New York, 1992, at pp. 140–1.

[13] T. Coke, 'Lady Justice May Be Blind, But is She a Soul Sister? Race-Neutrality and the Ideal of Representative Juries', 69 *New York University Law Review*, 1994, p. 327 at p. 357.

of limited individual perspectives produces a limited collective perspective; judgment is enhanced when we increase the angles of vision that go into the judgment.[14] Diversity in the context of a decision-making body composed of more than one person makes it more likely that all salient aspects of a normative problem, and all dimensions of a factual situation, will be perceived and factored into the deliberative process. Diversity multiplies perspectives while the need for collective decision necessitates that those perspectives engage each other. Diversity makes it less likely that reasoning will take place within the four corners of a single person's limited knowledge, and more likely that it will take place in the context of the necessity to test one's assumptions and intuitions against those of others. One could identify this as the difference between reasoning monologically and reasoning dialogically.

It might be objected that discourses of representation either entail, or degenerate into, a problematic essentialisation of identity and perspective because of a supposed underlying assumption that a given individual can also be a general representative of a social group. For example, it might be asked how any woman can be expected to represent the perspectives of women generally, especially when the relevant community for the legal order in question (here, a transnational community of women) is incredibly diverse across many other dimensions of experience (culture, race, class, place and so on). But the choice is not between communitarian essentialism (you *are* your group) or hyperindividualism. Groups emerge and change in a process of social and historical construction from within and from without. Groups may be treated as real in that sense but they are also highly contingent. Contingency includes the extent to which members have (and think of themselves as having) common experience and the extent to which such shared experience is positive or negative. Probably the key variable in determining the constructions that produce both group experience and members' identity is that of power.[15] If we accept this, then

---

[14] The phrase 'angles of vision' is Nedelsky's: 'The more angles of vision we are capable of taking into account in our judgment, the more we can free ourselves of the limitations of our private conditions. When we are locked into one perspective, whether through fear, anger, ignorance, or even through our notions of virtues such as duty, courage, or responsibility, we are not judging freely.' Nedelsky, *supra*, note 11.

[15] The argument here is, of necessity, skeletal. The abstract reference to 'power' could, instead, have been a reference to something like 'the complex interaction of different power relations'. Power cannot be considered a simple variable. There are several dimensions and manifestations of power ranging from classical exercises of coercion (police power and

we have no choice but to start somewhere in the middle of 'the' story of 'the' world as we know it. We must make judgments about our social world and what we know about the experience of different social groups, and then decide what experiential variables or demographic characteristics are *likely* to generate a certain commonality of understanding amongst people with such experience or characteristics. Here again, Coke provides insight:

> Mono-racial juries (like juries of a single gender) will . . . summon only a limited range of social experiences to interpret the facts before them. One can accept this intuitive premise without adhering to essentialist generalizations about the sympathies of different races. African-Americans, Latinos, Asian and Native Americans are not merely citizens 'who happen to be' racial minorities but are members of historically-defined communities that more often than not retain a cultural specificity.[16]

However, it is not just commonality we are looking for. It is *relevant* commonality. Relevance cannot be determined other than through some appeal to purpose – why do we want to make *this* institution more diverse? We must always ask in what ways we should be concerned with diversity in a given normative field. When we bring purpose into the picture, we are able to ask specific questions in relation to the primary justification for inter-active diversity, namely the thesis that qualitatively superior deliberation and outcomes are produced in relation to an institution's normative focus.

As soon as a given institution such as a UN human rights committee has, as any part of its mandate, a duty to counteract, remedy, or be sensitive to the harmful effects of various forms of domination that help constitute and perpetuate disadvantaged or vulnerable groups, this requires us to develop criteria of salience about which groups' experiences most need to be represented adequately in institutional dialogue if the institution's normative mandate is to be taken seriously. The fundamental issue is the extent to which dominant social groups are currently represented in a way that makes it very difficult for the perspective of less dominant social groups to be recognised, let alone acted upon, as a basis for judgment. Thus, structuring diversity of representation cannot be concerned only with multiplying perspectives; multiplicity must also be imbued with a sense of purpose. What is required is that perspectives which are salient for full deliberation

---

economic power) to pervasive forms of structural power associated with social and cultural domination. All are relevant. All also tend to be mutually reinforcing and to contribute to similar results in terms of the relative position of power of a given group of persons.
[16] Coke, *supra*, note 13 at pp. 353–4.

should be provided for through procedures that allow these perspectives to have a chance to contribute to the collective wisdom, rather than being ignored or submerged.

How might all this be relevant to the question of composition of the human rights treaty bodies? It seems evident enough that these bodies need to be diversity-sensitive in a strong sense, given that one of the central normative functions of international human rights supervision is to understand, reveal and help counteract exercises of power that produce oppression for dominated social groups. This function will be undermined without the insight of lived experience being part of the internal institutional dialogue. As such, the judgment exercised by the institution risks being systematically impaired if the perspectives of such groups are not adequately represented. This is so even when it is squarely acknowledged that diversity of social experience within an institution does indeed only produce an increased probability, not a guarantee, of meaningful understanding. The absence of guarantee is hardly a reason for not seeking to enhance diversity, within the constraints of a given institutional situation.[17]

C. Representation in the UN human rights treaty system

It is useful to outline current philosophies and practices of representation relating to the human rights committees. What follows is indicative only, but it is intended to suggest that there is reason to be concerned about diversity of knowledge, both experiential and disciplinary.

1. DIVERSITY OF SOCIAL EXPERIENCE

The criteria for the composition of the human rights committees are governed by the text of each treaty except for the Committee of the International Covenant on Economic, Social and Cultural Rights (ICESCR).[18]

---

[17] In a similar vein, while no single person filling a vacancy on a multi-person institution can embody all the diversity needs of that institution, this does not mean that it is illegitimate to factor one or more pressing diversity needs of the institution (and the capacity of a given candidate to meet those needs) into one's assessment of whose election or selection would most enhance the collective excellence of the institution.

[18] That treaty provides for the Economic and Social Council (ECOSOC) to be the supervisory body and provides no criteria for the composition of any subsidiary organ it establishes to perform that task. However, ECOSOC has adopted a resolution which sets out the criteria: ESC Res.1985/17, UN ESCOR, Supp. (No. 1), at p. 15, UN Doc. E/1985/85, 1985. Para. (b) of ESC Res.1985/17 provides that the ESCR Committee . . .

In contrast to elections to the European Court of Human Rights, election to the committees is not as dominated by statist considerations, although there are important vestiges of such considerations.[19] States elect the members of the committees.[20] All five treaties other than the ICESCR require states to nominate only their own nationals.[21] While the ICESCR Committee is not subject to this limitation, organisational practice in electing members has been no different from that under the other five treaties; to the author's knowledge, there has not as yet been any nomination of anyone other than a state's own national.[22] Four of the treaties (the Convention against Torture (CAT), the Convention on the Rights of the Child

> shall have 18 members who shall be experts with recognized competence in the field of human rights, serving in their personal capacity, due consideration being given to equitable geographical distribution and to the representation of different forms of social and legal systems; to this end, 15 seats will be equally distributed among the regional groups, while the additional three seats will be allocated in accordance with the increase in the total number of states parties per regional group.

ECOSOC's filling of the gap in the ICESCR text will be treated as akin to treaty-authorised subsidiary rules and thus ESC Res.1985/17 will be regarded as if it were part of the ICESCR text. ESC Res.1985/17 refers to 'the regional groups'. The five regional groups within the UN are: Western European and Others Group (WEOG), Middle East and Asia, Africa, Latin America and Eastern Europe.

[19] Some will find this characterisation of the European Court of Human Rights puzzling given that its judges are elected by an indirectly-elected body (the Parliamentary Assembly of the Council of Europe) from a pool of candidates nominated by each state (three nominees per state). However, under the European Convention on Human Rights (ECHR), each state is entitled to have one of its three nominees elected and the practice to date has been for the first person on each state's list to be elected, except in a few exceptional cases: H. Kruger, 'Selecting Judges for the New European Court of Human Rights', 17 *HRLJ*, 1996, p. 401 at pp. 401–2. Thus, the election procedure under the ECHR has to date operated more as an appointments procedure, albeit with a fitful checking mechanism that has resulted on rare occasions in the Parliamentary Assembly electing someone further down the list.

[20] Except for the ICESCR Committee which, being a creature of ECOSOC, is elected by the membership of ECOSOC. For all the committees, election is by secret ballot and a nominee must obtain an absolute majority.

[21] Article 29(2), International Covenant on Civil and Political Rights (ICCPR); article 17(2), Convention on the Elimination of Discrimination against Women (CEDAW); article 43(3), Convention on the Rights of the Child (CRC); article 8(2), Convention on the Elimination of Racial Discrimination (CERD); article 17(2), Convention against Torture (CAT).

[22] The depth of the practice is such that, if a state were to act in an uncharacteristically altruistic manner by nominating a non-national, '. . . the chances of election would probably be slight'. P. Alston, 'The Committee on Economic, Social and Cultural Rights', in *The United Nations and Human Rights: A Critical Appraisal* (ed. P. Alston), Oxford, 1992, p. 473 at p. 488.

(CRC), the Convention on the Elimination of Discrimination against Women (CEDAW), the Convention on the Elimination of Racial Discrimination (CERD)) allow each state to nominate only one person, thereby indirectly preventing 'over-representation' of any one state.[23] While the International Covenant on Civil and Political Rights (ICCPR) does permit nomination of two nationals,[24] it stipulates that the 'Committee may not include more than one national of the same state'.[25] There are no formal limitations for the ICESCR Committee in ESC Res.1985/17 except that implicit in the ceiling of four persons from any one regional grouping; in practice, the other five treaties' rule of one national per committee is read into the ICESCR as well. Thus statism is accommodated in a relatively limited way, its most significant element being the negative requirement that no one state can have more than one national on a committee.[26]

None of the human rights treaties refers to representational diversity related to social experience as distinct from nationality.[27] Yet, the various treaties do express some concern with diversity of representation beyond nationality. In elections to all the treaty bodies, 'equitable geographic distribution' must be considered.[28] In addition, four of the treaty texts use some variation of the formula borrowed from the Statute of the

---

[23] *Supra*, note 21. [24] Article 31(1), ICCPR. [25] Article 30(2), ICCPR.

[26] If one is to have regard to the representation of a given state across all six committees, the picture would be more complicated. For example, Egypt and the Russian Federation each currently have nationals on four of the committees.

[27] The only attention states appear to have shown matters of representation outside the treaty-based criteria has been the concern voiced by some states that, with 100 per cent of the membership of the twenty-three-person CEDAW Committee, women are unduly represented on that Committee. These states succeeded in having ECOSOC call upon states parties not to nominate only women, but the CEDAW Committee's resistance to this has resulted in no change to date. See H. Charlesworth, C. Chinkin and S. Wright, 'Feminist Approaches to International Law', 85 *AJIL*, 1991, p. 613 at p. 624; A. Byrnes, 'The "Other" Human Rights Treaty Body: The Work of the Committee on the Elimination of Discrimination Against Women', 14 *YJIL*, 1989, p. 1 at p. 9, note 27.

[28] While the common ground for all six treaty bodies is thus the 'equitable geographic distribution' formula, it is only with respect to the ICESCR Committee that the standard UN regional grouping formula is the *official* basis for election to the body: *supra*, note 18. The Convention on the Protection of the Rights of All Migrant Workers and Members of Their Families (the Migrant Workers' Convention), which is not yet in force, adds an interesting spin on geographical diversity by calling for 'due consideration [to] be given to equitable geographic distribution, *including both States of origin and States of employment*': article 72(2)(a) (emphasis added). The inclusion of this added guideline shows a concern with interstate reciprocity that partly distinguishes migrant workers' issues from many other human rights issues.

International Court of Justice (ICJ), which makes 'representation of the main forms of civilisation and of the principal legal systems of the world' constraining factors in elections to the Court.[29]

Interestingly, the two newest instruments, CAT and CRC, seem less inclined to accept that societal or civilisational differences are relevant to the collective competence of their committees. CRC drops entirely the reference to either civilisations or social systems while retaining the criterion of representation of 'principal legal systems'.[30] CAT omits any reference at all to either different social systems or different legal systems.[31] It may have been assumed that geographical diversity was a sufficient surrogate for diversity amongst societies and legal systems. Moreover each of the two committees is significantly smaller, at ten members;[32] it may have been felt that there was less room for manoeuvre to accommodate multiple representational criteria beyond geographic origin. It may also have been thought that experiential diversity is less relevant (even less legitimate) in the areas covered by the two treaties. CAT refers to legal knowledge not in terms of diversity (as do all five of the other treaties) but in terms of some implicit notion of universal legal expertise when it says that consideration should be given to the 'usefulness of the participation of some persons having legal experience'.[33] Such bracketing of diversity seems highly tendentious given what we know, for instance, about debates over different cultural and religious perspectives on children's rights. Even for one of the most universal of norms, the prohibition of torture, bracketing diversity is not without its problems, as Andrew Byrnes has noted:

> [I]n view of the possible divergence of views as to whether various punishments ordained or lawful under Islamic law which would otherwise amount to torture or other ill treatment constitute 'lawful sanctions' within the

---

[29] Article 9, Statute of the ICJ. The 'representation of the different forms of civilisation and . . . the principal legal systems' formula applies to three treaty bodies: article 31(2), ICCPR; article 8(1), CERD; and article 17(1), CEDAW. Note that these human rights treaties refer to the *different* forms of civilisation while the ICJ Statute refers more archaically to the *main* forms of civilisation. A more modern formulation, which can be treated as the equivalent, applies to the ICESCR Committee which substitutes the words 'representation of different forms of social and legal systems'. The Migrant Workers' Convention drops any reference to civilisations.

[30] Article 43(2), CRC.   [31] Article 17(1), CAT.

[32] The CERD and ICESCR Committees, and the HRC, all have eighteen members while the CEDAW Committee has twenty-three.

[33] Article 17(1), CAT.

meaning of article 1, the presence of a member with some expertise in relation to Islamic laws and culture would seem highly desirable.[34]

These criteria operate in a diffuse fashion because there is no system or
procedure by which they are given effect. The various texts require only
that 'consideration' be given to these criteria.[35] At most, the criteria act as
guidelines in a process of unofficial coordination amongst states. Predict-
ably enough, some coordination of voting in terms of the 'equitable geographic distribution' criterion has taken place by tapping into the standard
UN practice of using regional groups to some degree as a stand-in for
geographic diversity. Despite vast differences amongst states within each
group, one rationale for reliance on the regional groups in the human
rights context would seem to be a certain rough commonality of historical
and modern experience.[36] Moreover, distribution along the lines of regional
groups at least prevents a certain form of domination by any one group of
countries and thereby promotes some diversity of perspective.[37]

Most accounts of diversity of representation on the committees focus on
the regional group system.[38] In practice, despite the reference to equitable

---

[34] A. Byrnes, 'The Committee Against Torture', in Alston (ed.), *supra*, note 22, at pp. 509,
511–12, note 10.

[35] For the ICESCR, the phrase used is 'due consideration'.

[36] M. Craven, *The International Covenant on Economic, Social and Cultural Rights: A Perspective on its Development*, Oxford, 1995, p. 43. Craven goes on to make clear that he does not
see the regional groupings as reflecting the most relevant geographical considerations,
especially as they are first and foremost regional categories constructed with commonality
of *state* interest in mind: ibid., p. 44.

[37] It is recognised that the anti-domination function breaks down the greater the extent to
which the regional groups are internally diverse with respect to political and economic
systems and the greater the extent to which some of these systems are significantly shared
by states outside the regional group. It is likely, for example, that 'Western' (or Western-
oriented) states exist within the different regional groups to such a great extent that Western perspectives will not be confined to WEOG (Western European and Others Group)
members alone.

[38] See for example Craven, *supra*, note 36, at pp. 43–4; T. Opsahl, 'The Human Rights Committee', in Alston (ed.), *supra*, note 22, p. 512; and Byrnes, *supra*, note 34, p. 475, respect-
ively. On the HRC, see also D. McGoldrick, *The Human Rights Committee: Its Role in the
Development of the International Covenant on Civil and Political Rights*, Oxford, 1991,
pp. 44–7; and M. Nowak, *UN Covenant on Civil and Political Rights: CCPR Commentary*,
Kehl/Strasbourg/Arlington, 1993. The practice in electing the HRC seems to be to use the
UN regional groups as the basis for categorising states parties but to vary the standard
UN requirement of equal (i.e. the same) representation according to the proportionate
representation amongst states parties, thus justifying some regional groups having
more members than others without this being perceived as over-representation: see
McGoldrick, ibid., p. 47.

geographic distribution, geographic imbalances are not uncommon even when attempts have been made to secure a pre-vote consensus.[39] For example, the most recent election to the CEDAW Committee resulted in no member from the Eastern Europe regional group.[40]

Most attention has been focused on geographical disparities within the Human Rights Committee (HRC). Writing in the early 1990s, Opsahl noted that '[t]he geographical distribution of elected members has only roughly corresponded to the "electorate", so that, for example, Africa was under-represented until 1984'.[41] Nowak, writing in 1993, noted that, since 1986, both 'the Western and socialist industrialised [Eastern European] countries were over-represented and, above all, the Latin American States somewhat under-represented' and that, after the 1992 election, 'the Western group [was] ... the only region clearly over-represented'.[42] After the elections in early 1997, the 'clear' over-representation of Western countries on the HRC has become even more problematic: close to 50 per cent (eight of eighteen members) are now from the Western group of countries. Perhaps more serious is the fact that this coincides with a complete absence of

[39] This is well depicted in Byrnes' account of how the 1987 CAT Committee elections resulted in four WEOG members being elected but only one African member 'despite a consensus reached in preliminary consultations that there would be 3 Western European members and 2 African members': Byrnes, *supra*, note 34, at p. 512. It is important to note that a pre-vote consensus can be guaranteed only if each regional group limits the number of nominees from states which are part of that regional group to the precise number allocated in the pre-vote negotiations. The rules for election are that the candidates receiving the largest number of votes and an absolute majority of votes are elected. The exception is the ICESCR Committee. Given the guarantee of three seats per group plus a proportionate share of the remaining three seats, it is possible for any regional group, if it were inclined, to organise itself so as to pre-elect the number of candidates which it was entitled to have elected and then nominate only that exact number of persons. In this way, other states would have no choice but to vote for those nominees with the result that the idea of a general election to the committee would be thwarted. This is not to say that this has happened, only that it could happen. Such a possibility would be very unlikely if the regional groups were not entitled to a fixed number of seats but, instead, to a minimum (say, two) and a maximum (say, five).

[40] Of the twenty-three members, not one is from a state in that group. To appreciate why this is a problem, one need only note the special insight of women from Eastern Europe on the effects of transitional political and economic situations on women as well as on revivalist politics pushing traditional values: see N. Funk and M. Mueller (eds.), *Gender Politics and Post-Communism: Reflections from Eastern Europe and the Former Soviet Union*, New York, 1993. Note also that there is only one Eastern Europe member on the HRC. The list of members of all six human rights committees can be found in the 'Treaty Body Database' on the Internet website of the High Commissioner at http://www.unhchr.ch.

[41] Opsahl, *supra*, note 38, at p. 374.   [42] Nowak, *supra*, note 38, at p. 517.

representation of sub-Saharan Africa, even though the Africa group does have two nationals.[43]

While these problematic results have occurred even at the level of state-oriented geography, the 1997 election to the HRC did produce better results from a trans-societal perspective, with the highest representation yet of women, five of eighteen up from three previously.[44] The CEDAW Committee continues to be composed entirely of women (twenty-three of twenty-three). However, three of the other committees have very few women members.[45] On the other hand, interestingly, 70 per cent of the CRC Committee are currently women.[46] The representation of women across all six committees is 41.2 per cent (forty of ninety-seven members), but that figure is pushed upwards by the CEDAW Committee; on the other five committees, only 23 per cent (seventeen of seventy-four) of members are women. If one focuses on the four treaties whose mandate is to focus on rights not defined in relation to membership in a particular social group, only 15.6 per cent (ten of sixty-four) of members are women.

2. DIVERSITY OF DISCIPLINARY EXPERTISE

This discussion suggests the limited extent to which diversity of social experience is accommodated by the treaties.[47] Some diversity of knowledge

---

[43] The island state of Mauritius and the North African state of Egypt did have nominees elected. If only to show the strained nature of regional categories, it might be noted that both countries could easily be considered part of another region, namely the 'Middle East and Asia' which is itself an agglomeration without a principled basis other than geographical proximity and some sort of shared constructed identity in opposition to historical and ongoing encounters with the West.

[44] Although articles 33 and 34 of the ICCPR stipulate that a vacancy due to death is to be filled by election after nominations by any state, the practice appears to be to allow the state whose national died to be the sole state to nominate a replacement. In this way, that nominee's 'election' is assured. The female HRC member from Lebanon was replaced under this process by a male. Thus the HRC currently has four female members. However, the election results (five of eighteen) will continue to be used as the reference point in this chapter.

[45] The ICESCR Committee (two of eighteen, using last election results as the measure despite the departure of one member); the CERD Committee (two of eighteen); and the CAT Committee (one of ten).

[46] Seven out of ten members are women.

[47] Information is virtually non-existent on many other fronts. For example, most committees may appear to have considerable racial, ethnic, cultural, and religious diversity because members are drawn from around the globe (this being a surrogate benefit of some

of different legal systems was deemed desirable in all the texts except CAT. A focus on legal systems overlaps to some extent with diversity of experience, as legal systems are in many ways bound up in social systems and cultural traditions. Furthermore, there is something to be said for seeing experience with legal systems as valuable, at least potentially, for understanding how oppression occurs and is perpetuated.[48] But it may be that the focus on the need for representation of the legal profession (however broadly defined) was based more on the assumption that law is the most relevant discipline for the treaty bodies. While attention to including different legal systems reflects some commitment to diversity, it simultaneously elevates one discipline above all others. In terms of textual signals, CAT's reference to the need to consider including '*some* persons having legal experience'[49] might imply that the CAT Committee was not intended to be dominated by lawyers. It is only the absence of *some* members with knowledge of law that CAT seems to treat as a problem. Article 17(1) can be read as intended to ensure only that a critical mass of lawyers is elected to the committee ('some as distinct from none', rather than 'some as distinct from all'). However, it has probably had the somewhat perverse effect of causing priority to be given in the nomination and election process to lawyers, law being the only discipline deemed worthy of express mention.[50] Andrew Byrnes noted with regret that, in the first term of the CAT Committee (1988–1991), as many as seven of the ten members were

adherence to a distributive scheme organised around the regional groups). However, further information would be needed to determine whether any significant number of members come from non-dominant groups within their own societies. Furthermore, no information is available on social and economic status, although it may fairly be assumed that the committee members disproportionately represent more economically privileged sectors of national societies. Also, there are no openly gay women or men on any of the committees to this author's knowledge.

[48] Lawyers may not always be the best at understanding this social dimension of the operation of legal systems. Recognition of this would open the door to seeing the usefulness of having a person on a committee who, for example, has been an anti-poverty activist or a mental health advocate and knows the Kafkaesque ways in which the law deals with the poor or the mentally ill. Or, it would suggest that having the experience, from the inside, of prison conditions and regimes could provide a vital insight for treaties such as the ICCPR and CAT. Such examples would be easy to multiply. A broader insight may be that there is a value in having persons on the committees who have directly experienced serious human rights violations.

[49] Article 17(1) (emphasis added). However, note that the body most dominated by lawyers, the HRC, also includes this phrase.

[50] Byrnes, *supra*, note 34, at p. 512.

lawyers; the other three had backgrounds in medicine, public health and communications.[51]

By contrast Byrnes welcomes the '[p]rofessional diversity [which] is [a] . . . distinguishing characteristic of CEDAW', adding:

Only about half of the experts who have served as CEDAW members are lawyers. Other members come from such areas as medicine, public health and hospital administration, political science, geography, trade union and labor relations, education, social work and engineering. This diversity of experience has been reflected in the Committee's questions and has been valuable in the areas of economic and social rights and development.[52]

Writing in 1995 with similar concerns in mind, Matthew Craven has been critical of the fact that 'the vast majority of current members [of the ICESCR Committee] have a predominantly legal background', suggesting that there is a 'need for wider knowledge particularly as regards the rights to food, housing, clothing, and health'.[53] Comparatively little criticism can be found of the fact that the HRC is heavily dominated by the legal profession,

---

[51] Ibid. Lessons can be drawn from the Council of Europe human rights system. It is generally recognised that one reason for the effectiveness of the European Committee for the Prevention of Torture is that non-lawyer members of the Committee have been central to the process. This has proven especially beneficial with respect to on-site visits conducted by the committee: conversation with Judge R. St. J. Macdonald of the European Court of Human Rights, Toronto, 17 September 1997. It is worth noting that article 4(1) of the European Convention for the Prevention of Torture and Inhuman or Degrading Treatment or Punishment specifies 'professional expertise in the areas covered by the Convention'. Thus, clear recognition of non-legal professional expertise is actually written into the treaty text.

[52] Byrnes, *supra*, note 27, at p. 9.

[53] Craven, *supra*, note 36, at p. 46. A survey of the current composition of the ICESCR Committee reveals that half of the Committee (nine of eighteen) have legal backgrounds. Writing in 1995, Craven does not indicate what year he was assessing as the basis for his conclusion on the over-representation of lawyers, but the current 50 per cent is hardly the 'vast majority' to which he refers. Note that this evaluation by Craven is partly informed by his conception of the ICESCR Committee as having 'limited' functions that are 'strictly legal', ibid. Karl Joseph Partsch, in his account of the composition of the CERD Committee, appears to lament the fact that 'only half of the Committee members have had a legal background': K. Partsch, 'The Committee on the Elimination of Racial Discrimination', in Alston (ed.), *supra*, note 22, at pp. 339, 340. He juxtaposes what he sees as the under-representation of lawyers to the over-representation of 'diplomats who may have been chosen more on the basis of their rank than of their professional qualifications'. If the issue is the comparative merits of the CERD Committee having the expertise of lawyers versus diplomats (especially currently-serving diplomats), then Partsch's point is impeccable. However, the force of his concern is diminished if the comparison is between law and other relevant disciplines.

suggesting an implicit conception of 'civil and political' rights that is oriented towards the idea of a mature body of norms that need to be applied in legally expert fashion as much as developed through creative acts of interpretation.[54]

It is apparent that law has all but covered the treaty field as the discipline of choice. No mention is made of any other single field of knowledge. There is, however, an argument to be made that several of the treaties conceive their normative focus as interdisciplinary. Both the ICESCR and the ICCPR require that *each* committee member have 'recognised competence in the field of human rights';[55] CAT adopts the same formula.[56] Furthermore, the two conventions most closely associated with protecting rights of particular social groups conceptualise their respective fields in terms of a sub-discipline within the field of human rights. Both CRC and CEDAW presuppose the fields of 'children's rights' and 'women's rights', respectively, by requiring that each committee member have 'competence in the field covered by the Convention'.[57] CERD is conspicuous by its silence on the subject of expertise.

Thus, except for CERD, each text expressly presents itself as being about human rights, or a sub-discipline of human rights, *qua* field of knowledge. That being so, it is hard to maintain that law *per se* can map directly onto the treaty field, even if individual lawyers with interdisciplinary knowledge can do so. Instead, the treaty fields need to be seen as involving various distinct disciplinary bodies of knowledge *and* as interdisciplinary; the bridge between these two conceptions would seem to be that of mutual education and shared consideration through cross-disciplinary dialogue. To require that each committee member be expert in the field of the treaty is in effect to require that each member engage in a process of professional self-education through mutual education.[58]

---

[54] A quick count suggests fifteen of the eighteen members after the 1997 elections to the HRC are lawyers, Yalden, El-Shafei, and Gaitan de Pombo not being trained in law. It is to be noted that article 28(2) of the ICCPR contains an identical provision to the CAT in noting the 'usefulness of the participation of *some* persons having legal experience' (emphasis added). We have moved from the idea of some lawyers to a world of virtually all lawyers.

[55] ESC Res. 1985/17, para. (b), *supra*, note 18, and article 28(2), ICCPR.

[56] Article 17(1), CAT.

[57] Article 17(1), CEDAW; article 43(2), CRC. The CRC actually refers to 'recognized' competence while CEDAW leaves out this qualifier.

[58] For a conception of dialogue as mutual education, see G. Warnke, *Justice and Interpretation*, Cambridge, Mass., 1993 pp. 154–7, 164.

I have argued that both the legitimacy and quality of official acts of judgment are improved when institutions are composed so as to enhance interactive diversity of experience. Something similar can be claimed for interactive diversity of expertise. Whatever necessary skills they bring to the interpretive enterprise, lawyers cannot claim a monopoly of knowledge of the interpretive *content* to be given to human rights. In this regard, a recent proposal for reform of the practice of nominating and electing judges to the European Court of Human Rights is of interest. In the 1998 elections to the new, merged European Court of Human Rights, states had, as before, the right to nominate three persons. Hans Christian Kruger, Secretary to the European Commission of Human Rights, suggested a new approach to nomination, albeit one that would still stay within the constraints of the treaty requirement that 'candidates . . . must either possess the qualifications required for appointment to high judicial office or be jurisconsults of recognised competence':[59]

> Three candidates are to be proposed and it would seem appropriate that they should come from different 'worlds' of the legal profession in the land. In many of our countries one can identify three different groups making up the legal profession: the academic, the judicial service, and the practising or company lawyer. In order to avoid that the Court is composed of too many judges coming from only one of these groups, the candidates should be selected from all three of them, but only one person should be proposed from each group . . . The idea is that the eminent legal personalities proposed for election as judges to the European Court of Human Rights should be representative of the legal profession as a whole.[60]

As Kruger notes, abandonment of the Parliamentary Assembly's practice of only 'electing' the first person on each state's list would be a necessary adjunct of such a system of nomination. Kruger's proposal sees value in a diversity of sub-disciplinary perspectives within the law. But it may be, for example, that his proposal would create more intergenerational diversity in the pool of nominees. If so, this would probably also have a beneficial impact on gender diversity. On the latter score, Kruger goes on to supplement his three-estates proposal with a diplomatically-crafted proposal designed to confront the serious under-representation of women on the Court:

---

[59] Article 39(3), ECHR; article 21(1), Protocol 11 to the ECHR (ETS 155).

[60] Kruger, *supra*, note 19, at pp. 403–4. It does not appear that Kruger's proposal, an unofficial one at this stage, was actually taken up by most states as a basis for deciding on their lists of nominees for the 1998 elections to the new Court.

It goes without saying that due regard should also be paid to the need to ensure gender equality. As three candidates are to be proposed it should be clear that one candidate must be of a gender which is different from the other two.[61]

Diversity is thus on the agenda in the Council of Europe and some institutional steps are gingerly being taken to further interactive diversity.

D. The proposal: An affirmative election process

Diversity is valuable for what it contributes to dialogical reasoning. However, the dialogue cannot be merely formal: dialogue as process must be conditioned by dialogics as critical substance. The processes must not be tainted by power imbalances and the flattening effect of universalising 'neutrality'. Accordingly, there needs to be a more affirmative, proactive approach to diversity within the human rights committees.

[61] Ibid., p. 404. Prior to the 1998 elections to the Court, only one of the forty judges was a woman. On this aspect of Kruger's proposal, some action has been taken. In early October 1997 a letter was circulated to all states by the Secretary-General of the Council of Europe drawing their attention to the problem of lack of gender diversity on the Court and asking them to take this into account in their nominations for the first elections to the new Court. See D. Tarshys, Letter to Ministers in the Committee of Ministers of the Council of Europe, Strasbourg, 6 October 1997, on file with the author. Secretary-General Tarshys attaches as Appendix 5 to his letter an 'invitation' to states parties to the ECHR extended by the Ministers' own Deputies. The invitation is entitled 'Balanced representation of women and men in the new European Court of Human Rights'. Information from the Council of Europe Press Service is available on the nominees for thirty-one of the thirty-nine places on the new Court. Of the ninety-three candidates nominated from these thirty-one states (three candidates per state), thirteen were women. Two countries (the Slovak Republic and Albania) nominated two women, meaning that twenty states did not nominate any women to be amongst the three candidates from each of those states. Of the eleven states nominating women, only three states (Estonia, the Netherlands, and Slovakia) indicated their preference for their female candidate by listing her first; see *supra*, note 19 on the significance of the practice of listing a candidate at the top of a state's non-alphabetical list of three candidates, a practice which appears to have been carried over to the lists of candidates to the new Court (although a few states, like Switzerland, appear to have listed their nominees alphabetically). Elections for those thirty-one places took place at the end of January 1998 with the result that six women were elected (from Belgium, the Netherlands, Norway, the Slovak Republic, Sweden, and the Former Yugoslav Republic of Macedonia). Of those six elected, four were elected from either the second place on her state's list (Tulkens of Belgium, Greve of Norway, and Palm of Sweden) or third place (Nikolovska-Caca of Macedonia). By way of comparison, the Parliamentary Assembly also elected three men from further down the list (Maruste of Estonia, Baka of Hungary, and Wildhaber of Switzerland). In the elections for the remaining eight places, which took place in April 1998, three more women were elected – from Belgium, Croatia and Ireland.

1. GENERAL OUTLINES

The UN High Commissioner for Human Rights seems institutionally best-situated to assume the task of diversity promotion. It is proposed that she consider establishing a global search process for potential candidates. To this end, she could set up an Eminent Persons' Group (EPG) to act in an advisory capacity and to assist, as needed, in interactions with governments. She would receive suggestions of potential candidates from any person, group, or organisation. A small number would be identified as desirable candidates based on their individual capabilities and also on their contribution to institutional diversity of experience and expertise.[62] Once a person has been approached to see if she or he would stand for election if nominated, the UNHCHR, alone or in association with members of the EPG, would approach the national state of the identified candidate and ask if that country would consider nominating its national. The UNHCHR could sound out support from other states both in the regional group (or a relevant sub-region) and globally in order to present to the national state a picture of potential support. The UNHCHR may wish to consult closely with states which are influential in the UN human rights process to ask them to indicate directly to the potential nominating state their willingness not only to vote for the state's candidate but also to encourage other states to do the same.

This proposal would not require any amendment to any treaty. Nor would it, I believe, represent any excess of mandate on the part of the UNHCHR: the treaty-based rules for nomination and election of committee members would still have to be followed.[63] National states would still nominate candidates and states parties to each treaty would still do

---

[62] The politics of elections to the committees suggests that it would not be surprising if the elections process not only resulted in problems of diversity but also problems of threshold qualifications (what might be termed baseline competence) for being on a committee. As Opsahl says in a classic understatement, the UN politics of committee elections means that 'a high premium is not always placed on the individual qualities which are most important from the Committee's viewpoint, such as competence, energy, ability to co-operate, negotiating skill, and propensity to attend meetings': Opsahl, *supra*, note 38, at p. 374. Seasoned observers of the UN human rights committees may feel that the preceding discussion has leapt to the question of diversity of knowledge when basic competence is as much, or more, a concern. The proposed process would address threshold expertise concerns simultaneously with diversity concerns.

[63] The High Commissioner's mandate can be found in GA Res.48/141, 7 January 1994, reproduced in 33 *ILM*, 1994, p. 303.

the electing.[64] The UNHCHR's role would be a legitimate expression of the international public interest in the outcome of what would remain state-controlled processes.[65] Her role would be complementary to that of states parties.

2. SEEKING THE COMMITTEES' VIEWS ON DIVERSITY CRITERIA AND NEEDS

As I have argued, diversity deserves attention as one element of reform of the treaty bodies. Substantive guidelines as to the diversity criteria which the UNHCHR might apply in relation to all the committees would be useful, but cannot be laid down *a priori*. Ideally, the UNHCHR should establish such criteria by consulting with states, observers of the committees, and the committees themselves. In the process, she would gain a sense both of the receptivity to her proposed role and of the most effective means to make a difference despite the coordination problems inherent in six diffuse election processes.

Each committee could be asked by the UNHCHR to consider including as part of its agenda each year or so a consideration of the most serious gaps, i.e. the most pressing needs, in its collective expertise and experience.[66] It is recognised that this suggestion may prove ill-advised. Especially if no work is done to prepare the ground, some committee members may resist frank discussion of diversity issues, particularly in relation to social group 'representation'. Gender diversity may be an exception, given the inroads into general awareness made in the wake of the World Conference on Human Rights, held in Vienna in 1993, and the Fourth World Conference on Women, held in Beijing in 1995. UN human rights discourse is gradually coming to accept as self-evident the need to include the

---

[64] The rules differ for the ICESCR Committee in that nominations are not limited to states parties and election is by the entire ECOSOC membership.

[65] Clause 3(a) of GA Res.48/141, *supra*, note 63, builds on the language of the 1993 Vienna Declaration of Human Rights by directing that the High Commissioner 'shall . . . [f]unction . . . in the recognition that, in the framework of the purposes and principles of the Charter, the promotion and protection of all human rights is a legitimate concern of the international community'. It would probably be more accurate to refer to this as the transnational public interest, to the extent that 'international' risks being understood as a synonym for 'interstate'.

[66] See Craven, *supra*, note 36, p. 44, who proposes that ICESCR Committee engage in such an exercise.

perspectives of women more systematically. It is significant in this respect that specific and potentially far-reaching recommendations to integrate gender perspectives into the work of all the human rights committees were addressed to all six committees, in 1995 and 1996, by the Annual Meeting of the Chairpersons of the Human Rights Treaty Bodies.[67]

It might be thought that disciplinary diversity may be as much as most committees can contemplate discussing, without an undercurrent of resistance to the social 'politics' of diversity taking hold. However, given a strong view that the committees should become more, not less, juridical in character, similar resistance could also exist in relation to disciplinary pluralism.[68] In any event there will be serious constraints on how far any committee will go in making needs known, if by doing so, some current members may be voted out in the next elections. This of course applies equally to social diversity.

The committees might find that the best course is to search for some general consensus about the ideal medium-term profile of the committee. This would not preclude any committee from seeking to reach consensus on a more specific analysis of gaps and needs. In this way, some indicative guidelines could emerge to help guide the candidate identification process.

It might be thought that there is also something cumbersome about a process for consulting with each committee as a whole. It may be better simply to have the UNHCHR consult informally with the committees, welcoming submissions from any committee members and discussing matters of composition with the chairs at the time of their annual meeting. This would allow the diversity needs of any committee to be considered in terms of that committee's relations with the other committees. The more effectively and pervasively the six committees begin to interact as one *de facto* body by engaging in cooperative inter-treaty dialogue, the more it

---

[67] UN Doc. A/50/505, 4 October 1995, at para. 34; UN Doc. A/51/482, 11 October 1995, at para. 58. See also Report of the Secretary-General, 'Follow-up Action on the Conclusions and Recommendations of the Sixth Meeting of Persons Chairing the Human Rights Treaty Bodies', UN Doc. HRI/MC/1996/2 (15 August 1996) at paras. 100–8, especially on the Commission on Human Rights (para. 103), on the HRC, the ICESCR, CERD, and CRC Committees (paras. 105–8) and on the CEDAW Committee (para. 101).

[68] In this regard, note the following 1996 recommendation of Bayefsky in her study for the ILA Committee on International Human Rights Law and Practice: 'States parties should nominate to the treaty bodies individuals having the capacity to handle individual communications, *namely, persons with legal qualifications.*' ILA Committee Report, *supra*, note 3, p. 22 (emphasis added).

may be possible to consider diversity within the combined membership of ninety-seven persons as a shared pool of knowledge, thus expanding the possibilities for different combinations and recombinations of experience and expertise.

3. THE ROLE OF THE EPG

The role of the proposed Eminent Persons' Group would be to give moral and political backing to the UNHCHR. Preliminary work would be undertaken by the staff of the Office of the UNHCHR. A list of the identified potential candidates would be passed by the EPG for discussion, modification and approval and for indications of willingness to assist in approaching governments. Beyond their advisory function, the members of the EPG could be more or less active as circumstances and dispositions permit. They could actively seek out candidates to recommend to the group and they could make known their support for candidates once states have nominated them.[69]

4. THE 'KISS OF DEATH' OBJECTION

One objection to this proposal is that any process that publicly identified nominees as qualified, both in terms of indices of competence and in terms of relevant experiential and disciplinary knowledge related to human rights, could well spell the 'kiss of death' for those candidates. The underlying point is that there may be a sufficient number of states parties with little commitment to making the human rights committees effective. There is a possibility that such states might deliberately vote against very good candidates, perhaps even coordinating bloc voting against such candidates. A linked premise may be that, in the current election processes, many state representatives do not focus on the qualifications of the candidates, but cast votes for all sorts of reasons, including the pervasive 'trading' of votes

---

[69] The persons themselves should combine high moral stature on the international stage with a life that has involved some struggle in the cause of human rights. While complete lack of connection to current governments or to human rights NGOs might be an overly strong requirement, each person should nonetheless be widely recognised as someone who transcends his or her associations. The kinds of persons contemplated include people of the stature of Nelson Mandela, Rigoberta Menchu, Aung San Suu Kyi and Vaclav Havel.

across the whole UN electoral slate. The current electoral system is unedifying; even good candidates may be elected for reasons unrelated to their qualifications and willingness to serve.[70]

The sober realism of the objection must be recognised. There is indeed evidence of resentment on the part of some governments who feel that international human rights bodies are pursuing their mandate too zealously. One example was the campaign of the United Kingdom for pre-screening of nominees for the new European Court of Human Rights. On 27 February 1996, the then UK Secretary of State of Foreign and Commonwealth Affairs made the following proposal in a letter to the Secretary-General of the Council of Europe:

> Governments should agree now on an arrangement for exchanging informally the names of any new nominees as judges for the present Court before they are tabled. Part of the arrangement would be an understanding that account would be taken of the views of other governments . . .[71]

This attempt at orchestrating a more deferential European Court was not pursued, but the lesson of the UK initiative is that similar, perhaps less public, strategies could well be mounted in the UN arena by a range of states.[72]

On the other hand, the 'kiss of death' phenomenon does not seem to have been, to date, a major feature in elections to the committees. The strongest and most committed members of the various committees have been sufficiently well-known over the years, and, at the very least, do not seem to have been prejudiced by that commitment at the point of re-election. This applies to certain committee members felt by some

---

[70] It is no secret that lobbying in UN elections does not come without a certain amount (even a high degree) of horse-trading. Opsahl understates the matter when he notes that '[b]loc voting and general diplomatic bargaining may also play their roles': Opsahl, *supra*, note 38, at p. 374. There is a general consensus amongst inside observers that this practice is prevalent, perhaps in part because elections to human rights committees are held in New York where diplomats are used to UN system-wide voting politics. In that regard, Michael Reisman's observation that 'elections to the [International] Court of [Justice] are largely political' has some relevance for elections to UN juridical bodies more generally: M. Reisman, 'Redesigning the United Nations', 1 *Singapore Journal of International and Comparative Law*, 1997, p. 1 at p. 24.

[71] As quoted in Kruger, *supra*, note 19, at p. 401.

[72] One saving grace is the formally non-binding character of the committees' normative acts. Effectiveness is thus not quite the same threat.

governments to have been leaders in the process by which a particular committee may have 'overstepped its mandate'. From time to time there are rumblings about a disgruntled state contemplating targeting a committee member in a re-election, but full-scale challenges do not seem to have materialised.[73]

Moreover, to focus on the *realpolitik* of vote-trading and the desire of some governments to rein back the committees does not quite capture the complexity of the situation. For instance, states known to have concerns about the growing 'sovereignty-encroaching' dimensions of the work of some of the committees have nonetheless nominated strong candidates.[74] It seems that a good percentage of states wish to be perceived on the relevant international stage as good citizens at least as much as they wish to pursue hard-nosed foreign policy agendas. Even if such conduct is partly a tribute paid by vice to virtue, it cannot be ignored that states see much to be gained by acting in good faith in both their nomination and voting behaviour. It is arguable that the more the profile of the committees is enhanced, including through the supportive involvement of the UNHCHR and even the UN Secretary-General, the more states will see it as prestigious to have nationals nominated to some of the committees. If in turn they know that there is some institutional pressure for strong candidates to be highlighted and weak candidates (or, at least, very weak candidates) to become known as such (even if less publicly), there may even be a dynamic favouring persons who can be presented as strong candidates.

Insiders to the diplomatic process of UN electoral politics suggest another angle, the so-called 'chuff factor'. States that are less influential in interstate politics and may even have problematic human rights records

---

[73] This does not mean that one should attribute the longevity of such members to a good faith voting process. One need assume no more than that good candidates make it to the committees because some states take the process seriously enough to nominate such persons and potentially obstructionist states are not willing to spend energy amassing blocking coalitions to vote down such candidates.

[74] One example that comes to mind is Justice Bhagwati, the successful nominee from India to the HRC. His record as the pioneer of activist Supreme Court of India jurisprudence could hardly have been unknown to the Government of India. Another example might be the election of Thomas Buergenthal to the HRC. Buergenthal's pioneering role on the Inter-American Court of Human Rights and his role in pushing the UN Truth Commission for El Salvador are also well-known to most states, including the USA. Of course, the USA and India are powerful states that presumably backed their nominations with effective lobbying. Good candidates coming from less powerful countries might be more easily the targets of a blocking coalition.

may nonetheless respond favourably when approached to nominate a national who would make a superb nominee for a certain committee.[75] Apart from the sense of prestige that may be elicited, states will see benefits associated with relative cost savings in terms of the election campaign itself, given the prospect of influential support.

Surely one cannot organise reform strategies entirely around short-term realism. There are longer term system-building goals to be valued, and risks must be taken to promote those goals. One such goal is to encourage a different kind of political rationality in elections to UN human rights treaty bodies than is generally practised in most spheres of international politics. There is value in the UNHCHR promoting a process that contributes to elevating the debate. There may be some ugly politics and some short-term defeats. Some states may react negatively to what they might see as meddling in their treaty-sanctioned prerogatives; others may exploit the transparency of the process in order to try to target a candidate for defeat. That is the risk of electoral politics everywhere.

However, the effect of elevating the discourse could make it more likely that states will present their case in terms of values and less in terms of the *realpolitik* of state interest. In a more rational climate, the terms of debate may become such as to invite both public responses and some inchoate form of community judgment. Diversity itself may prove an ally. If some states object to a person as being too 'Western' or too 'Asian', too 'liberal' or too 'conservative', too 'activist' or too 'deferential', others can respond with the argument that one person does not a committee make and that diversity itself points to the importance of including different perspectives on human rights, albeit with the bottom-line requirement that all candidates have a good faith commitment to the protection of the human rights which are the focus of the committee in question.

---

[75] It may be conceded that less influential states may feel chuffed in this way, but it may still be objected that states that are either concerned about sovereignty or about their own human rights records are unlikely to elevate 'chuff' over hard calculus of political interest, especially if it is expected that a candidate who has been identified is not likely to go easy on her or his own state any more than on other states. It is possible that the trend towards the committees forbidding a national from being involved in cases or reports which concern her or his state (see 1996 Chairpersons' Report, *supra*, note 67 para. 29) will decrease states' worries that a strong candidate will boomerang on them. Some states will still probably need to be convinced that their nationals will not play some behind-the-scenes informational role which will make the committee's appraisal of the state more effective than it otherwise would be if the national were not on the committee.

It must be acknowledged that the emergence of a new kind of public rationality will be contingent on a combination of two things, neither of them certain – noble politics and gifted diplomacy. As to the former, the attempt to change the governing mode of electoral politics should benefit from high-profile states acting in a spirit of altruism. It has already been suggested that conceptions of self-interest can be flexible and that states are inclined to some extent toward thinking of their own interests in terms of aligning themselves with the community-oriented behaviour of the good citizen and with corresponding long-term goals associated with strengthening the community's institutions. This is the normative glue for much multilateral cooperation. Even within a standard interstate paradigm that revolves around the interaction of mutual self-interest under the guidance of the invisible hand of reciprocity, there has long been evidence of states operating under assumptions of what has been called 'diffuse reciprocity'.[76] Short-term benefits based on immediate and tangible mutual interests need not be all that motivate state behaviour. States do see virtue in acting in less self-regarding ways such as by promoting something as intangible as a rule of law ethic in international relations. And in some fields (of which human rights may be the prime example), some state elites wish to find ways in their international relations for them to think of themselves, and be recognised, as moral actors.

Accordingly, the UNHCHR could consider encouraging states to engage in strategically altruistic behaviour designed to show a general commitment to international human rights institution-building and a specific commitment to the system of human rights treaty bodies. By way of illustration only, three examples of behaviour to be encouraged in the election process could be suggested. First, states might consider starting a *de facto* practice of co-nominating nationals of other states along with the national state.[77] Second, and more altruistically, states could forswear nominations of their own nationals for a period of several election rounds in order to make space for and support excellent nominees from other states,

---

[76] R. Keohane, 'Reciprocity in International Relations', 40 *International Organisation*, 1986, p. 1 at p. 20. The idea of diffuse reciprocity has its parallel in theories of treaty law (especially treaty interpretation) which emphasise the relational nature of treaties and the desire of states to foster and maintain a sustainable, good faith relationship: on this, see I. Johnstone, 'Treaty Interpretation: The Authority of Interpretive Communities', 12 *Michigan Journal of International Law*, 1991, p. 371.

[77] Co-nomination would have no formal status, but nor is it specifically prohibited by the treaties.

especially less powerful states. Third, states could be encouraged to nominate persons to the committees who have been independent observers, and even perhaps strong critics, of that state's own human rights record.

In terms of gifted diplomacy, the involvement of the UNHCHR will need to be marked by strategic prudence and diplomatic acumen, not to mention charisma. The questions Robinson will have to address include: how to solicit recommendations of potential nominees; how much to encourage public debate as to the merits of candidates; how public to make it known that certain state nominees have emerged with the assistance of this process; how to approach a government whose national has been identified, including whether to call on members of the EPG to assist the UNHCHR in this regard or whether to ask some key states to make representations to the government in question; how many persons to seek to nominate through this process so as to maximise chances of election while minimising states' discomfort; whether to encourage states to make an intended nomination known to the UNHCHR so that it may be factored into the UNHCHR's overall picture of diversity needs; how to take into account the fact that, in any given election, a number of candidates may be current committee members standing for re-election whom the UNHCHR will not wish to be seen as directly challenging; and how the process will interact with regional or sub-regional groups' coordination of nominations.

Careful judgment will need to be exercised. For example, it may be justified to seek nomination and election of only one or two members to one committee. For another committee, a strategy of one nomination per regional group may make more sense. Or it may be justified to focus on the representation of, and within, an entire regional group or sub-region. In some cases it might be desirable to let the process run its course if there are a large number of good current committee members and several good and diverse challengers nominated. Overall, the UNHCHR must not be perceived to be seeking to control the current process so much as stimulating and, to some extent, helping to coordinate it.

5. A MORE RADICAL PROPOSAL FOR GREATER TRANSPARENCY

A more ambitious proposal has recently been put forward for enhancing the election process with respect to certain international human rights bodies. Reisman has proposed an international 'advise and consent' procedure modelled somewhat on practice in the United States. In that practice, bar associations and non-governmental organisations (NGOs) appraise the qualifications of candidates nominated for the federal judiciary and these appraisals then feed into the confirmation hearings held by the US Congress. Reisman's central proposal is for the NGO community (along with national bar associations) to create an unofficial procedure that would influence General Assembly voting for the ICJ. He adds that there is no reason not to extend this procedure to other bodies such as the International Law Commission as well as 'the Human Rights Committee . . . and other inter-governmental human rights institutions'.[78] As Reisman puts it, '[b]y exploiting the available network of international communications, NGOs, if they worked together, could develop an international "advise and consent" procedure that could improve the quality of candidates for international posts'.[79] Alternatively the General Assembly might consider creating a Judicial Review Committee which would hold hearings on the qualifications of candidates to the ICJ and UN Administrative Tribunal, inviting candidates to appear before the Committee and allowing submissions from interested actors, such as NGOs. Unless there is a UN Charter amendment, the Committee's powers would only be recommendatory, but the idea would be to enhance the election process by promoting a kind of participatory transparency. Reisman recommends experimenting with this procedure for five years and then extending it to other bodies if it proves successful.

Even if sufficient support could be garnered, it would not seem desirable to consider such a judicial review committee for the committees. Admirable as the desire for transparency may be, the proposal will, with some justification, be viewed as being premised on a very American practice that has been known to descend into a nationally-televised spectacle.[80] Such

---

[78] Reisman, *supra*, note 70, at pp. 25–6.   [79] Ibid., p. 26.

[80] The Legal Affairs and Human Rights Committee of the Parliamentary Assembly of the Council of Europe has adopted a resolution according to which the Assembly is to 'call upon candidates [to the European Court of Human Rights] to participate in a personal interview': Resolution 1082 (1996) of 22 April 1996 (ninth sitting), cited in Kruger, *supra*, note 19, at p. 402, note 4. Kruger notes that '[w]hilst the idea to hold such interviews probably comes from the proceedings in the United States Senate Committee relating to the appointment of judges to the United States Supreme Court, *it is of course understood that the European exercise should not take that dimension*. But the interviews should give an opportunity for the parliamentarians electing the judges to get to know the candidates a little', ibid. (emphasis added). The Council of Europe's Parliamentary Assembly organised personal interviews with all the candidate judges nominated for the new permanent

official advice and consent processes lend themselves too easily either to sensationalist and selective targeting of occasional candidates or bland endorsements of everyone who satisfies a relatively mediocre threshold of basic competence. A more serious objection is that, in the international human rights context, the General Assembly is not necessarily the right forum for addressing questions of merit and diversity in a depoliticised fashion. In contrast, the UNHCHR's office may be viewed as an official institution that is at arm's length from states and that is mandated to seek to represent a kind of transnational interest in the protection and promotion of human rights. This most emphatically does not mean that the UNHCHR is not caught up in and seriously constrained by the realities of the interstate diplomacy evident elsewhere in the UN, but it does give her both the moral and the institutional space to seek to represent the public interest in the strengthening of the UN human rights committees.

There are strategic benefits in associating a candidate identification process with the UNHCHR. The UNHCHR, as a single institution, can better approximate the centralised coordination function that the current diffuse election process lacks. Accordingly, she can develop a more coherent view of the needs of each committee. She can act on her appraisal in what she judges to be the most strategically effective way. She will of course herself be a diplomatic actor who must avoid being seen to intrude in treaty-based processes that have states and nationality at their centre. For that reason, she will undoubtedly need to carve out some creative middle ground in which she acts both as agent of the transnational order and as a kind of friend of states. In this latter capacity, she would make it clear that she views her role as secondary to that of states who must still do the nominating and the electing. Legitimacy on both dimensions would be heightened if it were known that some priority is given to looking for candidates from poorer or otherwise less influential states.

European Court of Human Rights 'to take place within a special sub-committee of the Assembly's Committee on Legal Affairs and Human Rights . . . at the Council of Europe's offices in Paris, in two periods from 17–19 December 1997 and from 7–9 January 1998'. See Tarshys, *supra*, note 61. This interviewing process may have had some impact on the eventual vote for the first thirty-one places on the new Court, which was described *supra*, in note 61. It will be recalled that, despite the fact that most states continued with their practice of putting their preferred candidate at the top of their list of three candidates, the Parliamentary Assembly elected seven of the thirty-one new judges from further down the list, including four women; see *supra*, note 19 on how, in the past, the Assembly has only rarely second-guessed states' preferred candidates.

In the UN context, transparency must be viewed instrumentally rather than as an intrinsic value to be pursued at all costs. As such, the UNHCHR, the closest thing we have to a centralised agency for considering merit and diversity in a global perspective, will have to exercise much tact and judgment. Further, her role does not exclude Reisman's main suggestion, the unofficial formation of an association of NGOs to appraise candidates in some publicly accessible manner, perhaps in concert with professional associations. This is something that could be done now as an independent initiative designed to try to influence the committee election process.[81]

The question remains of the extent to which the UNHCHR initiative should be connected to any NGO process. NGOs are probably better placed to engage in the kind of frank evaluation and assessment of candidates that Reisman recommends. The more diversity of representation within the NGO coalition that might seek to formalise such an evaluation process, the more legitimate the contribution would be. Yet, however legitimate any NGO process, it should still take into account the UNHCHR's views on the most constructive role for NGOs. For instance, it would not seem desirable for the UNHCHR to disfavour candidates unless, for some reason, the very integrity of the process was at risk. Her role should be positive – designed to promote excellent candidates who will also make a distinct contribution to diversity of knowledge. While poorer candidates may lose out, this will be a by-product, not the goal, of the UNHCHR's involvement. In contrast, the role of NGOs might be to draw attention to clearly unworthy candidates and to take a more assertive stand on problems of diversity in a given committee or the committees as a whole. However, many states will react differently to an assessment of a candidate by an NGO coalition and to an assessment by the UNHCHR. In the end, the most constructive involvement of NGOs, at least during a transitional period, might be for them to interact with the UNHCHR's process by initiating NGO-based searches for candidates who can then be suggested to the UNHCHR.

Finally, it must be acknowledged that with NGO involvement comes a potential danger of NGO influence reproducing the patterns of dominance

---

[81] There is much evidence in other spheres, notably environmental law and the law of the sea, that NGOs can help resource-strapped and thinly-spread delegations of poorer states to coordinate and represent their interests better: see e.g. J. Clapp, 'Africa, NGOs, and the International Waste Trade', 3 *Journal of Environment and Development*, 1994, p. 17.

already found in interstate and transnational society.[82] It is still the case that the most prominent and influential NGOs are Western-based and, to a significant extent, Western-oriented, although, in Geneva, there is arguably a greater degree of networking with grassroots NGOs from around the world and even a greater physical presence of those NGOs from time to time. All of this relates to the possibility that the UNHCHR might consider urging states parties to move the elections to Geneva. This could be a merely cosmetic move. Heads of mission in Geneva, whether or not more steeped in human rights issues than their colleagues in New York, are not necessarily less inclined to the baser forms of politics. Paradoxically, having elections in Geneva could create an even greater politicisation than exists in New York if states' missions in Geneva see elections to the committees as an extension of their annual battles in the Commission on Human Rights. Nonetheless, moving to Geneva would at least place elections in the right normative context and begin to lay the groundwork for a more deliberative, good faith election process than may be possible in New York.

E. Conclusion: Future explorations

In this chapter, I have not engaged in any detailed discussion of what are the most salient diversity criteria for each committee. I have rather sought to make the case for the relevance of such criteria to the work of the committees, leaving it to others to take up the further task of articulating criteria.

There has also been no discussion of a second proposal which ideally would accompany the candidate identification proposal. This second proposal would advocate a deepening of the emerging forms of cooperation amongst the committees so as to place the committees in dialogue with one another. One might achieve many of the benefits of interactive diversity by considering the potential of the committees to share their knowledge and to engage in a process of mutual education. There are many possibilities as to the forms such institutional cooperation could take.[83] The principle of

---

[82] See C. Scott, 'Commentary on Part IV – Human Rights', in *United Nations Reform: Looking Ahead after Fifty Years* (eds. E. Fawcett and H. Newcombe), Toronto, 1995, p. 168; L. Weisberg, 'The Vienna World Conference on Human Rights', in ibid., p. 173 at pp. 177–8.

[83] For example: joint drafting of general comments; overlapping sessions designed to exchange views; development of a kind of Council of the Committees through evolution of the annual meeting of the chairpersons; vigorous pursuit of bilateral relationships between

interactive diversity involves bringing to bear multiple angles of vision on normative questions. Due to the diverse normative mandates of the six treaties, there are many ways in which interaction amongst the committees could be promoted.

For example, the CEDAW Committee and the CRC Committee could interact intersectionally[84] to create a combined mandate focusing on the 'girl child'. The CEDAW Committee and the CERD Committee would intersect so as to produce the potential for an analysis in which gender is brought to race and race to gender.[85] It is through interactive institutional relations that the treaty bodies which focus on particular social groups (the CEDAW Committee, the CRC Committee as well as the CERD Committee, to the extent that minority groups are its primary concern) can increase the understanding of the ICESCR Committee and the HRC of the special and complex forms of human rights violations that might otherwise be overlooked. When the ICESCR Committee and the CEDAW Committee engage in dialogue, women's poverty should become more visible to *both*. A few years of experience with a conscious agenda of promoting dialogical engagement not only within but also amongst the human rights treaty regimes could be instructive as to the shape any long-term consolidation should take.[86]

different committees (including joint preparation of general comments and joint scrutiny of state reports); and promotion of some degree of overlapping membership across the committees.

[84] On the concept of intersectionality in the context of the social experience of black women in the United States see, for example, K. Crenshaw, 'Whose Story is it Anyway', in *Race-ing Justice, Engendering Power: Essays on Anita Hill, Clarence Thomas and the Construction of Social Reality* (ed. T. Morison), New York, 1992, p. 402 especially at pp. 404–5. Other ideas such as the concept of interdependence would point to other axes of inter-treaty dialogue: see C. Scott, 'The Interdependence and Permeability of Human Rights Norms: Towards a Partial Fusion of the International Covenants on Human Rights', *Osgoode Hall L. Jl.*, 1989, p. 769 especially at pp. 848–50.

[85] Because of a certain diversity along ethnic and racial lines, the CEDAW Committee already has its own intersectional dynamic, however unarticulated, resulting from women from different backgrounds conversing across their differences. For some sense of dialogues across difference within the field of women's rights, see the many chapters in R. Cook (ed.), *Human Rights of Women: National and International Perspectives*, Philadelphia, 1994.

[86] For example, it might become apparent that a single consolidated body is justified, but that it should be structured so as to have expert chambers with primary responsibility for specific treaties. It might then make sense to have one member from each of the UN's five regional groups associated with each chamber. If we think in terms of seven treaties (adding the Migrant Workers' Convention), that would result in a body of thirty-five persons,

Finally, there is the difficult case of the CEDAW Committee. Can we really justify a committee made up entirely of women any more than we could tolerate committees made up entirely of men? This is a more complex question than it looks, especially if we recall the centrality of questions of power to a purposive analysis of the need for diversity. Much depends on what the CEDAW Committee's current function is and what its ideal function should be. One plausible account of the CEDAW Committee is that a central function is to produce, over time, a rich account of women's rights that seeks to achieve common understandings across the radical diversity of women's experience. In that sense, the CEDAW Committee might be seen as having a complex representational function. Yet, the CEDAW Committee, too, must engage in acts of judgment that are persuasive beyond women themselves. It is hard to avoid the conclusion that, at some point, it will be desirable for the CEDAW Committee to have some gender diversity. On the timing of such a transition, much will depend on the CEDAW Committee's relationship to the other committees and on the extent to which it is the central mechanism by which women's experiences can be made known throughout the treaty body system. If and when the other committees begin consistently to contain a critical mass of women, the CEDAW Committee will have to rethink its opposition to states nominating men to the committee. This only underlines the need for further reflection, by the UNHCHR and others, on what diversity requires of us in relation to all the committees.

approximately one-third of the current ninety-seven members. This is not an unreasonable size if one notes that there are presently forty judges on the European Court of Human Rights.

20

TREATY BODIES RESPONDING TO STATES OF EMERGENCY: THE CASE OF BOSNIA AND HERZEGOVINA

MICHAEL O'FLAHERTY*

A. Introduction

The 1990s have been years of innovation for the UN human rights treaty bodies. Though the extent and nature of the developments differ from committee to committee, there is a clear pattern of effort towards greater effectiveness in implementing their respective mandates. This activism, however, creates new expectations as to the capacity and will of the committees to move forward.

In the same period, the crises of the former Yugoslavia and of Bosnia and Herzegovina[1] in particular have served as a measure by which the treaty bodies could evaluate their effectiveness in addressing emergency situations.[2]

* I am grateful to Professor T. van Boven, Professor M. Banton, Ms S. Kapferer and Ms M. Stavropoulou for their comments on drafts of this chapter.

[1] For the former Socialist Federal Republic of Yugoslavia (SFRY), of which the republics of Serbia and Montenegro later became the Federal Republic of Yugoslavia (FRY), and for Bosnia and Herzegovina the various instruments came into effect as follows: International Covenant on Civil and Political Rights (ICCPR), 23 March 1976 for Yugoslavia; 6 March 1992 for Bosnia and Herzegovina. Ratification of the First Optional Protocol to the ICCPR: 1 June 1995 for Bosnia and Herzegovina. International Covenant on Economic, Social and Cultural Rights (ICESCR), 3 January 1976 for Yugoslavia; 6 March 1992 for Bosnia and Herzegovina. Convention on the Elimination of Racial Discrimination (CERD), 4 January 1969 for Yugoslavia; 16 July 1993 for Bosnia and Herzegovina. Convention on the Elimination of Discrimination against Women (CEDAW), 28 March 1982 for Yugoslavia; 1 October 1993 for Bosnia and Herzegovina. Convention against Torture (CAT), 10 October 1991 for Yugoslavia; 6 March 1992 for Bosnia and Herzegovina. CAT petition procedure (article 22) and the article 20 procedure were accepted by Yugoslavia on 10 September 1991. Convention on the Rights of the Child (CRC), 2 February 1991 for Yugoslavia; 6 March 1992 for Bosnia and Herzegovina.

[2] Each of the procedures is described in the periodic reports issued by the treaty bodies. A brief overview of each procedure can be found in M. O'Flaherty, *Human Rights and the*

The region has provided the occasion for some of the more significant of the committees' procedural developments. The challenge represented by Bosnia and Herzegovina for the treaty bodies has by no means ended with the Dayton-Paris Agreement.[3] The present chapter examines the interaction between the treaty bodies and Bosnia and Herzegovina, identifying and evaluating innovative actions while noting some of the unmet challenges. In each case, the focus of attention is on issues of systemic significance for the work of the treaty bodies.

B. Reporting procedures

Routine application of the reporting process clearly has little to offer as a contribution to the resolution of emergency situations. The process should either be disregarded as irrelevant or refashioned. Among those treaty bodies which have addressed emergency situations some have chosen the second option. Their refashioning, in the context of former Yugoslavia and Bosnia and Herzegovina, has focused on four principal issues.

The first concerns periodicity and the tabling of reports. Emergencies must be addressed while they occur and not according to the accidental application of a reporting cycle. Moreover, reports on crisis situations, once submitted, should not be expected to take their turn on the list of reports pending consideration. The second issue relates to the state party's role as the only interlocutor. In a war situation the state party will usually control only part of its territory. Are proceedings then only to concern persons and authorities subject to its *de facto* jurisdiction? What of circumstances in which another state (perhaps also a state party) is a belligerent or supports an opposing belligerent? Who should be responsible for addressing the international community, including UN and other peace brokers and peace-keepers? A third issue is how the reporting procedure should interact with other UN human rights monitoring mechanisms which are

UN: Practice Before the Treaty Bodies, London, 1996. For the Human Rights Committee (HRC) see, S. Joseph, 'New Procedures Concerning the Human Rights Committee's Examination of State Reports', 13(1) Netherlands Quarterly of Human Rights, 1995, pp. 5–23; and I. Boerfijn, 'Towards a Strong System of Supervision: The Human Rights Committee's Role in Reforming the Reporting Procedure under Article 40 of the Covenant on Civil and Political Rights', 17 HRQ, 1995, pp. 766–93. For CERD, see M. Banton, International Action Against Racial Discrimination, Oxford, 1996, at chapter 8.

[3] Bosnia and Herzegovina-Croatia-Yugoslavia, General Framework Agreement for Peace in Bosnia and Herzegovina with Annexes, Paris, 14 December 1995, 35 ILM, 1996, 75 (hereafter GFA).

actively addressing the situation. Finally, what can and should be said in any concluding observations or comments? What recommendations might usefully be made and to whom? How can appropriate attention and publicity be drawn in a timely way to the proceedings and their outcome? Each of these areas is discussed below.

1. PERIODICITY AND THE TABLING OF REPORTS

The former Yugoslavia and Bosnia and Herzegovina have afforded treaty bodies opportunities to advance the procedures for requesting special reports. In April 1991 the HRC requested an urgent report from Iraq.[4] In November of that year it decided that such requests could, exceptionally, be made of other states parties. The first state to receive such a request was Yugoslavia; it was given some two months to table a report.[5] The report was delivered on 10 March 1992,[6] and considered during the next committee session in April 1992.[7]

In October 1992, another occasion was provided for development of the procedure when Bosnia and Herzegovina, Croatia and the Federal Republic of Yugoslavia were invited by the Chairperson of the Human Rights Committee (HRC), inter-sessionally, to submit reports within a period of three weeks.[8] Provision for such inter-sessional calling for reports was only subsequently inserted into the HRC's Rules of Procedure. It is noteworthy that at the time of the request, Bosnia and Herzegovina had not yet even indicated its intention to accede or succeed to the International Covenant on Civil and Political Rights (ICCPR). The reports[9] were submitted and considered[10] in early November 1992.

Other committees have been less swift in adopting a procedure for urgent reports and they have not provided for the making of requests inter-sessionally. Thus for instance, the Committee of the Convention on the Elimination of Racial Discrimination (CERD), during its session

---

[4] See UN Doc. CCPR/C/SR.1062/Add.1.
[5] See UN Doc. CCPR/C/SR.1112. The request was subsequently reported to be a request for submission, within the same time-frame, of the state's already overdue third periodic report: UN Doc. A/47/40 at Annex VII.
[6] UN Doc. CCPR/C/52/Add.9. [7] UN Doc. A/47/40 at paras. 431–69.
[8] UN Doc. A/48/40 at para. 311.
[9] Report of Bosnia and Herzegovina: UN Doc. CCPR/C/89 Croatia: UN Doc. CCPR/C/87; Yugoslavia UN Doc. CCPR/C/88.
[10] See UN Doc. A/48/40 at paras. 311–32.

in March 1993 requested a special report from, *inter alia*, Bosnia and Herzegovina, to be submitted in time for the August session of that year.[11] The reports arrived on time[12] but were only considered by the Committee in the third week of the session.[13]

Requesting special reports can not, of course, overcome the fact that treaty bodies are not standing bodies and can only operate during their sessions. The inappropriateness of a session-based approach to crisis situations was demonstrated in January 1993, when the Committee of the Convention on the Elimination of Discrimination against Women (CEDAW) requested urgent reports from states of former Yugoslavia, to be considered at its next session – exactly one year later![14]

Though the HRC has developed the practice of routinely indicating the subjects it wishes to see addressed in special reports,[15] it had no control over their content. Experience with Bosnia and Herzegovina would, in any case, suggest that content is largely irrelevant. It is noteworthy that the summary record of consideration by treaty bodies of special reports indicates that members pay little attention to the content of the reports themselves; their concern is with the actual situation on the ground. This is well illustrated by the CERD Committee's consideration of a special report of Bosnia and Herzegovina, submitted in 1995.[16] That committee has led the way in developing urgent procedures which do not depend on the reporting process and these are surveyed later in this chapter.

Unfortunately, the treaty bodies did not apply their procedures for the requesting of urgent reports in a consistent manner. Thus, despite the ongoing crisis in Bosnia and Herzegovina, the HRC withdrew its attention after 1992 and the CEDAW Committee after 1994.

2. THE STATE PARTY AS THE ONLY INTERLOCUTOR

In the same context, the treaty bodies have scrupulously maintained the position of the state under consideration as their interlocutor. They have, however, in respect of Bosnia and Herzegovina, developed methods for addressing other parties to the conflicts.

---

[11] The request is contained in Decision 1(42). See UN Doc. A/48/18 at Annex VIII.
[12] Report of Bosnia and Herzegovina, UN Doc. CERD/C/247.
[13] See UN Doc. CERD/C/SR. 1001.   [14] UN Doc. A/49/38 at para. 730.
[15] Its request to Bosnia and Herzegovina of 1992 made reference to articles 6, 7, 9, 10, 12 and 20 ICCPR.
[16] UN Doc. CERD/C/SR. 1082.

Both the HRC[17] and the CERD Committee have taken the opportunity during the examination of reports of Croatia and the Federal Republic of Yugoslavia to criticise their behaviour in and concerning Bosnia and Herzegovina, thereby acknowledging the extent to which they exercised control over warring factions. For instance, it was in the context of the examination of a report of the Federal Republic of Yugoslavia that the CERD Committee voiced its concern that 'the Serbs of Bosnia and Herzegovina frustrate the efforts of the Government of that State to implement the Convention'.[18] Unfortunately, the innovative manner in which the treaty bodies were willing to confront both the Federal Republic of Yugoslavia and Croatia with responsibility for actions in Bosnia and Herzegovina was not fully exploited. Hence, even during periods of obvious aggression and violation of international human rights standards and of humanitarian law, neither state was ever requested to submit an urgent report on the subject of its actions directed against Bosnia and Herzegovina.

In 1993, the CERD Committee inserted into its concluding observations on Bosnia and Herzegovina an appeal to end human rights violations. That appeal was directed to 'the Government of Bosnia and Herzegovina and all the parties concerned'.[19] The same committee, in its 1995 concluding observations, turned its attention to the Security Council with the recommendation for the application of enforcement measures regarding Bosnia and Herzegovina.[20] By contrast the HRC has not used the reporting process to address international institutions with regard to Bosnia and Herzegovina, despite precedents such as its own 1993 concluding comments on Burundi which included a recommendation addressed to the UN High Commissioner for Refugees (UNHCR).[21] For its part, the CEDAW Committee in its concluding comments of 1994 exhorted 'all of the women of Bosnia and Herzegovina not to remain passive'.[22]

3. INTERACTION WITH OTHER UN HUMAN RIGHTS MONITORING MECHANISMS

In the period from 1992 to 1995 the Commission on Human Rights' first Special Rapporteur on the situation of human rights in the former

---

[17] See, for instance, UN Doc. A/48/40 at para. 386.   [18] UN Doc. A/48/18 at para. 541.
[19] Ibid., at para. 470.   [20] UN Doc. A/50/18 at para. 224.
[21] UN Doc. A/49/40 at para. 368.   [22] UN Doc. A/49/38 at para. 757.

Yugoslavia, Tadeusz Mazowiecki, issued eighteen reports. By April 1997 his successor, Elisabeth Rehn, had issued nine. These constitute a rich source of information on exactly those matters which concern the treaty bodies. It is not surprising that the special rapporteurs have interacted in a number of ways with the treaty bodies. During a 1995 session in which the CERD Committee examined reports from former Yugoslavia, it met with Special Rapporteur Mazowiecki.[23] This encounter was the first in which the Committee met and debated with a 'country' rather than 'thematic' rapporteur of the non-conventional mechanisms. The discussion had a subversive tone in that the Special Rapporteur asked whether the conflict in the former Yugoslavia was not primarily political rather than racial or ethnic. The Committee members, their competency to comment on the situation under threat, were stung into vehemently contesting this point of view. Members also expressed unease that their analysis seemed to attract so little attention and to have such marginal influence, in contrast with positions taken by the Special Rapporteur who 'had the ear of the highest policy-making bodies in the United Nations'.[24]

Surprisingly, given the sharpness of the exchange, the concluding observations on the Federal Republic of Yugoslavia, adopted a few days later, stated that '[t]he important role played by the Special Rapporteur . . . is acknowledged and his findings of fact are endorsed'.[25] While the acknowledgement is a useful indication of the enhanced role of such *ad hoc* mechanisms in the consideration of states parties' reports, it does raise questions as to the process, if any, by which the Committee was able to determine the veracity of his findings.

Other important UN information sources seem to have been neglected in the deliberations of the treaty bodies. Thus, no attention seems to have been paid to the voluminous findings of the Commission of Experts established pursuant to Security Council Resolution 780 (1992), which issued its interim report[26] on 26 January 1993 and its final report on 27 May 1994.[27] Nor can reference be found to the findings of individuals such as the Commission on Human Rights' Special Rapporteur on Summary Executions or the Expert on Internally Displaced Persons.

---

[23] See UN Doc. CERD/C/SR. 1071.   [24] Ibid., at para. 46.

[25] UN Doc. A/50/18 at para. 235.

[26] Contained in UN Doc. S/25274 of 10 February 1993.

[27] UN Doc. S/1994/674.

4. THE DRAFTING AND PUBLICISING OF CONCLUDING OBSERVATIONS OR COMMENTS

(a) Content

Elements promoting action contained in the concluding observations or comments on the reports of Bosnia and Herzegovina fall into six categories: first, declarations of the binding applicability of the provisions of the instrument in question even in times of war and grave crisis (in the reports of the HRC and the CERD Committee); second, general exhortations to the state (and sometimes 'the parties') to respect human rights (the HRC, the CERD and CEDAW Committees); third, focused recommendations for the undertaking of certain actions, such as to release prisoners, cease 'ethnic cleansing', cooperate with the International Criminal Tribunal for the former Yugoslavia, etc. (the HRC, the CERD and CEDAW Committees); fourth, expressions of solidarity with victims and exhortations directed to the people (the CEDAW Committee); fifth, offers of technical cooperation, including the undertaking of missions to the territory (the CERD Committee), and finally, recommendations for action by the international community (the CERD Committee).

The decision on what to include in concluding observations or comments is especially problematic. A primary concern is that of staying within the treaty body's mandate. Difficulties in this regard have engaged at least one committee, the CERD Committee. During its discussion of Bosnia and Herzegovina's 1993 report,[28] a number of members indicated an anxiety about making recommendations concerning such matters as an appropriate form of political settlement in Bosnia and Herzegovina. Others felt, in the words of one member, that, 'it was not the Committee's role to make proposals about the internal ordering of Bosnia and Herzegovina: that was a political issue, which was now being discussed in another forum'.[29] A preponderance of members supported the former position on the basis that issues of ethnicity suffused the conflict and that models for its resolution were clearly within the Committee's competence. One member expressed the view that, issues of competence aside, the Committee should consider where its contribution might be most useful. In this regard he noted that whereas many international bodies were engaged with Bosnia and Herzegovina, very few were addressing the situation in Kosovo.[30]

[28] See UN Doc. CERD/C/SR. 1001.   [29] Ibid., at para. 32.   [30] Ibid., at para. 52.

What of the situation where a recommendation is clearly within a mandate but hopelessly optimistic or ambitious? Various condemnations of the war and pleas to the parties for peace and reconciliation have fallen into this category. That they had to be made, if only out of considerations of the integrity of the treaty bodies, seems incontestable. However, there were recommendations which were clearly inappropriate and over-ambitious. An example of this category was the CERD Committee's offer to Bosnia and Herzegovina of a technical cooperation mission at the height of the war, when its capital city was under siege.[31] There were also naïve recommendations with little relationship to the realities of the situation. An example was the CEDAW Committee's call to the women of Bosnia and Herzegovina to become activist in order that they might generate the political will required for change, and its urging of an end to the 'fratricidal' war.[32]

(b) Exceptional publication actions

The crisis in the former Yugoslavia prompted certain exceptional measures in the otherwise routine distribution of and publicity accorded to concluding observations or comments. The concluding comments of the HRC on Yugoslavia, adopted in April 1992, were brought to the attention of the special session of the Commission on Human Rights which met in August of that year.[33] The HRC's concluding observations on states of former Yugoslavia, including Bosnia and Herzegovina, adopted in November 1992, were on the request of the Committee Chairperson brought to the attention of the Third Committee of the General Assembly on 20 November 1992.[34] The interim report of the Committee of Experts established pursuant to Security Council Resolution 780 (1992) indicates that concluding comments of the HRC were among its sources of information.[35] These exceptional measures in relation to the HRC's comments were always undertaken on an *ad hoc* basis, and the concluding observations of other treaty bodies did not receive such distribution. The CERD Committee did, however, draw the attention of the UN Secretary-General to its 1993 concluding observations in its letter of transmittal of its annual report.[36]

---

[31] An offer made to all three states of the former Yugoslavia whose reports were considered in 1993. See UN Doc. A/48/18 at para. 472. The offer was accepted by Croatia and the Federal Republic of Yugoslavia.

[32] UN Doc. A/49/38 at para. 730.   [33] UN Doc. A/48/40 at para. 14.

[34] UN Doc. A/C.3/47/CRP.1.   [35] UN Doc. S/25274.   [36] UN Doc. A/48/18 at p. vii.

Neither the treaty bodies nor their secretariats took exceptional action to bring these findings to the attention of the general public in Bosnia and Herzegovina, or to the warring parties. Thus, for instance, advantage was not taken of the resources of the UN Centre for Human Rights' field operation in the former Yugoslavia, which from March 1994 had an office in Sarajevo.

The lack of a systematic procedure for distribution to relevant parties of concluding observations or comments meant that many of those addressed by the treaty bodies will never even have been aware of their existence. In this regard one thinks, for instance, of the Security Council, which was the subject of a 1995 CERD Committee recommendation, and of the women of Bosnia and Herzegovina, who were directly addressed by the CEDAW Committee in 1994.

5. EVALUATION OF EFFECTIVENESS OF RECOMMENDATIONS: THE EXTENT TO WHICH THE REPORT CONSIDERATION PROCESS IMPACTED ON THE SITUATION OF HUMAN RIGHTS IN BOSNIA AND HERZEGOVINA

A number of modest achievements can be attributed to the report examination process. These include:

(i) the occasion which they provided for the committees to draw attention to the applicability of the various instruments and for the Government of Bosnia and Herzegovina to indicate its commitment to honour its obligations. In this regard, the author has been informed by members of the Foreign Ministry of Bosnia and Herzegovina[37] that the proceedings before the treaty bodies motivated the drafters of the 1994 Constitution of the Federation of Bosnia and Herzegovina to make direct reference to instruments such as CERD in the Constitution;

(ii) the important statement by the CERD Committee, in its 1993 concluding observations, that efforts to create ethnically pure states are, 'totally contrary to the spirit and principles of the Convention',[38] a remark with profound implications in the post-Dayton period;

(iii) the creation of documents of record which will remain of value as sources of information on the situation of human rights in Bosnia and Herzegovina at the time. The CERD Committee proceedings are particularly useful in this regard because of, *inter alia*, the exhaustive

---

[37] Discussions in Sarajevo, March 1996.   [38] UN Doc. A/48/18 at para. 468.

analysis presented by the Committee's then rapporteur for reports of Bosnia and Herzegovina, Ms S. Sadiq Ali; and

(iv) the occasional support and empowering encouragement accorded to human rights initiatives. An example can be found in the concluding comments of the CEDAW Committee which, in their expression of solidarity with the women victims of the conflict, gave considerable encouragement to at least one women's group in central Bosnia (which received a copy of the concluding comments from a visiting member of an international NGO).[39]

For the remainder it is difficult to assess effectiveness. Certainly, the treaty bodies had no effect on the passage of the war, and there is no evidence that their findings were taken into account by any of the peace negotiators. It is also notable that they are not referred to in the findings of the Commission of Experts[40] nor addressed in the substantive sections of reports of the Special Rapporteur on the situation of human rights in the former Yugoslavia.

Could more have been achieved? An answer to that question requires examination of a broad range of issues concerning the place of the treaty bodies and of law itself within the international system. On a more modest level of analysis it can, however, be posited that the treaty bodies might have had more impact if they had applied their range of innovative procedures in a more consistent manner, through, for instance, persistently requesting urgent reports whenever required, directing requests to belligerent states and developing ongoing mutually useful relations with the Special Rapporteur for the former Yugoslavia. The possibility of enhanced effectiveness would also have been increased had there been a coherent methodology for the bringing of treaty body findings to the attention of those to whom they were addressed.

C. Procedures not based on the submission of reports

No amount of honing can make up for the range of limitations which inhibit development of the reporting process as an effective tool to address urgent or crisis situations. The most active of the committees in developing

---

[39] Stated to the author during 1996 by members of women's groups in central Bosnia.
[40] The final report contains no reference to any use being made by the Commission of the findings of the Treaty Bodies – see UN Doc. S/1994/674.

alternative strategies is the CERD Committee. Already in 1992, it sent a communication through its chairperson to the Commission on Human Rights, making recommendations for action at the forthcoming special session on the former Yugoslavia, and offering its services within the context of its mandate.[41] Nothing seems to have come of this initiative. Later, the situation in Bosnia and Herzegovina, along with Rwanda and Burundi, was to become one of the most frequent subjects of the Committee's evolving procedures, with three special decisions adopted as of the end of 1996. A brief examination of these three decisions is revealing in terms of the evolution of the procedures. It also indicates the extent to which the innovative practices of the CERD Committee remain subject to many of the problems besetting the reporting procedures.

1. DECISION 2(47) OF 1995[42]

The CERD Committee's discussion took place against the background of such events as the fall of Srebrenica and Zepa, as well as the displacement of Serbs from the Krajina region of Croatia. The CERD Committee's conclusion is noteworthy for both its forthrightness and its lack of reference to the provisions of CERD. Among the key elements were: a statement that 'any attempt to change or to uphold a changed demographic composition of an area against the will of the original inhabitants, by whatever means, is a violation of international law'; a call to the international community to both assist refugees and cooperate fully with the International Criminal Tribunal for the Former Yugoslavia; and an urgent call 'for the provision to Bosnia and Herzegovina of all means to protect itself in accordance with article 51 of the Charter of the United Nations and to live within safe and secure borders'.[43] Curiously, for a decision described in its title as addressing the situation in Bosnia and Herzegovina, the body of the text includes repeated references to the situation in the Krajina region of Croatia.

In an attempt to overcome past problems of poor distribution of its proceedings, the CERD Committee instructed that the decision be transmitted immediately to the Secretary-General of the United Nations for his

---

[41] UN Doc. A/47/18 at Annex VII.

[42] Decision 2(47), reported in UN Doc. A/50/18 at para. 26.

[43] Inclusion of this paragraph necessitated adoption of the decision by vote. In explanations after the vote a number of members indicated their unease with the paragraph: see UN Doc. A/50/18 at note 3.

attention and, through him, to the General Assembly and the Security Council. The decision was also conveyed to the Government of Bosnia and Herzegovina but, despite references to Krajina, not to the Government of Croatia.

Decision 2(47) raises legitimate concerns of committee competence and mandate and its adoption, by vote, was accompanied by a lengthy debate and protracted 'explanations after the vote'. It does, however, constitute one of the most forceful attempts of any treaty body to engage and influence international efforts to resolve the conflict in Bosnia and Herzegovina. Whether it had any effect is another matter. In this regard it may be noted that none of the UN addressees even acknowledged its receipt.[44]

2. DECISION 1(48) OF 1996[45]

The CERD Committee marked the signing of the General Framework Agreement for Peace in Bosnia and Herzegovina (GFA) by deciding at its session in March 1996 to authorise its chairman to consult with the UN High Commissioner for Human Rights (UNHCHR), the Special Rapporteur and others in order to make recommendations for action. It also decided to consult with the Government of Bosnia and Herzegovina and others on how the Committee's good offices might be put to best use. The Government was also invited to arrange a meeting between the Committee and the Commission on Human Rights of Bosnia and Herzegovina.

Decision 1(48) of 1996 includes no analytical references to the GFA and instead seems to simply endorse it. This is somewhat surprising given that the CERD Committee had, in earlier decisions, expressed itself forthrightly on the necessity of compliance of political solutions with international standards. In this regard it might be noted that the establishment within the state of two entities along ethnic lines and the reserving of some high offices of state for members of certain ethnic groups to the exclusion of others, at least raises questions of consistency with CERD.[46]

---

[44] Personal knowledge of the author in his capacity as Secretary of the Committee during the period until early 1996.

[45] Decision 1(48) reported in UN Doc. A/51/18 at chapter II.

[46] See, 'Introduction', Z. Pajic, 'An Overview of the Substantive Human Rights Regime After Dayton: A Critical Appraisal of the Constitution of Bosnia and Herzegovina', and N. Milicivic, 'The Role and Relationship of the Constitutional and non-Constitutional Domestic Human Rights Enforcement Mechanisms', in *Post-war Protection of Human Rights in Bosnia and Herzegovina* (eds. M. O'Flaherty and G. Gisvold), Dordrecht, 1998.

Though the decision lacked a sense of urgency, in that it would appear not to have given the chairperson any particular inter-sessional author-ity and to have precluded any further action until the next committee session,[47] it did rely largely for its effectiveness on inter-sessional consulta-tions. As far as the present writer is aware, the committee chairperson did not undertake the requested consultations.

3. DECISION 1(49) OF 1996[48]

Decision 1(49) of 1996 refers to but does not build upon Decision 2(47) of 1995. Among its key elements are the manner in which it is addressed, not just to the state party but to all parties to the GFA. In addition it expresses concern regarding the appropriateness of the holding of the forthcoming national elections; reiterates a willingness to assist in implementation of the GFA from the perspective of CERD; and offers assistance regarding imple-mentation of articles 4 and 7 of the CERD. The decision concludes with an invitation to the Security Council, through the Secretary-General, to decide on establishment of a successor force to the international implementation force in Bosnia and Herzegovina (IFOR).

Unlike Decision 2(47), this decision included no special instructions for its transmittal through the Secretary-General to the Security Council. The Committee also took no particular action to have this decision transmitted to parties to the GFA or to the general public in Bosnia and Herzegovina. The Office of the High Representative in Bosnia and Herzegovina did, however, seek out Decision 1(49) and ensured its wide distribution within Bosnia and Herzegovina, as a result of which it also received some local press coverage. It was also made available to the quasi-judicial body[49] adju-dicating on alleged violations of the electoral rules, and was consulted by it in its adjudication of matters which appeared to raise issues under CERD.[50]

---

[47] The Committee, '[e]ntrusts its Chairman, in close communication with its officers, to consult, in close coordination with the United Nations High Commissioner for Human Rights and other United Nations bodies, notably the Special Rapporteur on the situation of human rights in the former Yugoslavia, as well as competent regional bodies, with a view to making recommendations for follow-up action by the Committee on the Elimina-tion of Racial Discrimination' (Decision 1(48), para. 1).

[48] Reported in UN Doc. A/51/18 at chapter II.

[49] The Election Appeals Sub-Commission (EASC) established pursuant to the provisions of Annex III of the GFA.

[50] Discussion held by the author with members of the EASC legal team.

4. THE CRC COMMITTEE

Actions of the Committee of the Convention on the Rights of the Child (CRC) can be considered in the context of a review of non-report based procedures. The Committee neither sought nor received a report of Bosnia and Herzegovina during the war period. However, at its third session in January 1993, it adopted Recommendation 3 (Third Session) in which it, *inter alia*, 'request[ed] the Special Rapporteur of the Commission on Human Rights on the situation of human rights in the territory of the former Yugoslavia to take the CRC into full consideration in the fulfilment of his mandate and in his future reports'.[51] In direct response to this request, the Special Rapporteur included a lengthy examination of the situation of children in his sixth periodic report.[52] This analysis provided not only an important document of record but also a significant contribution to an overall understanding of the impact of armed conflict on children.

D. Experience with Bosnia and Herzegovina as an indicator of the appropriateness of the committees addressing situations of war

This survey indicates the profound impact which the situation of Bosnia and Herzegovina had on the practice of a number of the treaty bodies with regard to emergency or urgent situations. The question remains of the extent to which it offers guidance as to the appropriateness of such action.

1. EFFECTIVENESS OF THE ACTIONS TAKEN WITH REGARD TO THE SITUATION IN THE STATE CONCERNED

It appears that modest but real results can be detected from both the reporting and other procedures. The treaty bodies were afforded opportunities to address important statements of principle to the various belligerent parties, the Government of Bosnia and Herzegovina was afforded opportunities to affirm its commitment to honour its obligations and the very consideration of the issues by the treaty bodies allowed for the creation of valuable documents of record. It is also clear that more could probably have been achieved through consistent application of procedures, more focused and internally consistent findings and rigorous attention to issues of distribution, publicity and follow-up.

---

[51] Reported in UN Doc. A/49/41 at Section 1(E).
[52] UN Doc. E/CN.4/1994/110 at Section VII.

2. IMPACT ON THE IMAGE OF THE TREATY BODIES

Image does matter and it is important that confidence in the procedures be encouraged and enhanced. The ambition and inevitable failure of many recommendations regarding Bosnia and Herzegovina, even if unavoidable for reasons of integrity, probably reflected badly on the treaty bodies. Some of the more eccentric comments or recommendations may have also done them damage. The lack of consistency and of follow-up to earlier actions was certainly disadvantageous. Of course, issues such as these argue for improving and focusing rather than abandoning the procedures. One can also argue that, had the treaty bodies stayed entirely silent, they would have been accused of neglect. On the other hand one may ask to what extent, if any, damage was done to the image of the two treaty bodies which did not address issues arising in Bosnia and Herzegovina, the Committees of the Convention against Torture (CAT) and the International Covenant on Economic, Social and Cultural Rights (ICESCR). In addition, was the HRC negatively affected by its silence since 1992 regarding Bosnia and Herzegovina?

3. IMPACT ON THE WORK PROGRAMME OF THE TREATY BODIES

The committees are over-loaded with work and have great difficulties in giving adequate time to primary tasks such as the consideration of periodic reports. It is in this context that the new procedures were introduced and have to be considered. The impact on the work programme is most obvious in the case of the CERD Committee which, in its forty-seventh session (1995) devoted two entire meetings to a decision concerning Bosnia and Herzegovina. The problem of over-burdened treaty body schedules is such that were they to attempt to further develop the practice of addressing urgent situations or even to apply existing practices in a consistent and considered way, they would quickly be overwhelmed.

4. CAPACITY OF THE SECRETARIAT TO PERFORM ITS FUNCTIONS

At its present staffing and resource levels the secretariat is barely able to carry out its tasks in respect of the regular activities of the treaty bodies. It has not been and is not now in a position to provide an appropriate level of services for emergency procedures or even to assist in addressing current deficiencies. It does not have the resources to identify and gather pertinent documentation, liaise with non-conventional mechanisms, provide useful political advice or professionally to assist in the drafting of decisions and concluding observations. Nor has it yet put the machinery in place to ensure the speedy and appropriate distribution of these documents. This was often apparent with regard to Bosnia and Herzegovina. Thus, for instance, during 1996 the CERD Committee secretariat had neither the human and physical resources to prepare an analysis of the GFA nor even to have the text distributed in its entirety to committee members.[53]

E. Present challenges

The fighting in Bosnia and Herzegovina has ended and some progress is being made towards the creation of conditions for peace. In this context it is difficult for treaty bodies to find compelling reasons to address it in preference to other emergency situations worldwide. It would be unfortunate if this were to mean that the committees now allow Bosnia and Herzegovina simply to take its place in the regular periodic reporting and other procedures. The situation there still needs focused attention, and it also continues to afford the treaty bodies opportunities for important developments in practice and procedure.

A starting point for an examination of the range of activities which the treaty bodies might now undertake is the invitation extended to them by the GFA. Annex 6, article XIII, paragraph 4 of the GFA states that 'all competent authorities in Bosnia and Herzegovina shall cooperate with and provide unrestricted access to [*inter alia*] . . . the supervisory bodies established by any of the international agreements listed in the appendix to the Annex'. The six UN human rights instruments which have functioning treaty bodies are to be found in the Appendix. The Annex is signed for Bosnia and Herzegovina, and its two constituent Entities the Federation of Bosnia and Herzegovina and Republika Srpska, and it entered into force upon signature. This provision is reinforced within the Federation of Bosnia and Herzegovina by virtue of the Constitution of the Federation, article 7, which states that '[a]ll competent authorities in the Federation shall co-operate with [*inter alia*] . . . the supervisory bodies established by any of the instruments listed in the Annex'. The six UN instruments are so listed.

---

[53] Direct knowledge of the author.

The principal characteristics of these invitations under the GFA and the Federation's Constitution[54] are:

(i) their 'open-ended' nature, whereby the treaty bodies may become involved whenever they wish;

(ii) the granting of prior authorisation to the involvement of the treaty bodies; thus no further invitation is required;

(iii) the lack of any specification of the types of action which might be undertaken by treaty bodies, thus allowing for such activities as the conducting of missions, provision of technical cooperation, etc.; and

(iv) the standing instruction to 'all competent authorities' to cooperate with the treaty bodies. In the case of the GFA it is significant that the parties include not only Bosnia and Herzegovina but also, severally, Republika Srpska and the Federation of Bosnia and Herzegovina.

The invitation contained in the GFA is unprecedented in the experience of the treaty bodies and affords an opportunity for direct and useful participation in the process of the establishment of the peace. It can also be understood as a test of the willingness and capacity of the treaty bodies to seize opportunities as they are presented. Successful involvement by the treaty bodies in implementation of the peace agreement may lead to repeated invitations for similar participation elsewhere.

Treaty bodies which choose to address the situation of Bosnia and Herzegovina will be confronted with a wide range of needs. One of the most pressing is the provision of technical cooperation in implementing the human rights aspects of the GFA. The parties to the GFA assume extensive obligations regarding the various international human rights instruments.[55] The manner in which the obligations and interrelationship of instruments is set out in the various annexes is, however, confusing and creates significant interpretative uncertainty.[56] Of particular concern is the need for clarification of the status of the UN instruments with regard to the European Convention on Human Rights (ECHR) in a context where there is a strong tendency to afford supremacy to the ECHR even in situations

---

[54] For examination of article XIII, see M. O'Flaherty, 'The International Human Rights Monitoring Operations in Bosnia and Herzegovina', in *Honouring Human Rights: From Peace to Justice* (ed. A. Henkin), New York, 1998, pp. 71–96.

[55] See, especially, the terms of Annexes 4 and 6.

[56] See various chapters in O'Flaherty and Gisvold, *supra*, note 46.

where a UN instrument affords greater protection.[57] A willingness by the treaty bodies to address such matters would present a timely opportunity to address the important and potentially problematic issue of the relationship between human rights instruments belonging to the regional and universal regimes.

No less useful would be the provision by treaty bodies of technical co-operation regarding practical implementation of the obligations through law reform, administrative action, effective functioning of the human rights mechanisms of the GFA and the Federation of Bosnia and Herzegovina, etc. Such technical cooperation might include the provision of expert advice, training and the undertaking of missions to the territory.[58] It might be directed, as appropriate, to all levels of government officials, the judiciary, lawyers, non-governmental organisations (NGOs) and members of the various human rights mechanisms and institutions. It may well be that such services would more appropriately be provided by the UNHCHR or other UN agencies, in which case the role of the treaty bodies would be to actively promote the timely taking of action and to monitor the development and implementation of programmes. It should also be expected that such activities be accompanied by initiatives of the UN to promote general knowledge of the human rights instruments including reporting and individual procedures.

Treaty bodies might also wish to turn their attention to an analysis and commentary of elements of the GFA which are problematic from the point of view of the protection of international human rights. One of the main issues, the introduction of ethnic criteria into the elaboration of new state structures, has already been commented upon. Another concerns the nature of the new central government.[59] An essential prerequisite for the honouring by a state of its international human rights obligations is its capacity to ensure compliance with the obligations throughout its territory and by all its servants. The Government of Bosnia and Herzegovina, with enfeebled 'rump' powers and without control over police or army, does not have this capacity. Instead the effective authority lies with each of the

---

[57] For instance, the UN instruments against torture, racial discrimination and discrimination against women, as well as the CRC. Note also that the Second Optional Protocol to ICCPR contains an absolute prohibition on the death penalty whereas the European instruments only provide for a partial abolition.

[58] In a manner analogous to that of the Council of Europe, which has been active in Bosnia and Herzegovina since early 1996.

[59] GFA at Annex 4, Constitution of Bosnia and Herzegovina.

Entities.[60] Furthermore, experience since the appointment of the members of the central government indicates that there is no political will to strengthen or even support any form of national institution.[61]

The form of central government created by the GFA will impede implementation of the various instruments and obstruct the treaty bodies in carrying out any tasks in respect of Bosnia and Herzegovina. It also has systemic significance to the extent that it represents an undermining of the system on which the human rights treaty system is based. Treaty bodies may wish to draw attention to the problem and let it be known that such political settlements are to be discouraged. Of more immediate practical use, the committees may wish to explore ways to strengthen what national human rights institutions there are[62] and to make modest recommendations such as that periodic reports be largely drafted in the Entities and that Entity governments be represented in state delegations which present the reports.

It should be noted that the treaty bodies have, so far, shown little enthusiasm in taking up the opportunities offered. No treaty body has reacted in any way to the invitation contained in the Federation's Constitution. Since the GFA, two have considered Bosnia and Herzegovina, only one of which, the CERD Committee, has taken any form of action.

1. THE CERD COMMITTEE

The CERD Committee's Decision 1(48), described above, neither refers to nor takes advantage of Annex 6, article XIII of the GFA. It is expressed in traditional terms and couches its range of options in forms which both focus on and depend upon the further consent and cooperation of the state party. Subsequently and in anticipation of a further decision at the following session, the present writer, in his capacity as a human rights adviser to the High Representative in Bosnia and Herzegovina, made an informal submission to the Committee members[63] inviting them to direct their comments not just to the state party but to all parties to GFA, as well as to international actors such as the Organisation for Security and Cooperation

---

[60] The Federation of Bosnia and Herzegovina and Republika Srpska.

[61] As useful source material in this regard, see, for instance, *The Human Rights Report*, issued regularly by the Office of the High Representative in Sarajevo. This and other related publications can be viewed at http://www.ohr.int.

[62] Such as the Office of the Ombudsman for Bosnia and Herzegovina and the Human Rights Chamber (GFA, Annex 6).

[63] On file with the author.

in Europe and the Special Rapporteur. It was also suggested, *inter alia*, that the CERD Committee offer technical cooperation and assistance on implementation of the provisions of CERD regarding expressions of racial and ethnic hatred (article 4) and education against racism (article 7, CERD). Though Decision 1(49)[64] does contain most of these elements, it does not make reference to or exploit the range of options open to the Committee.

2. THE CRC COMMITTEE

The CRC Committee was invited to become involved when, on 25 September 1996, the Special Rapporteur, Ms Rehn, wrote to it requesting that it immediately address the situation in Bosnia and Herzegovina on an exceptional basis.[65] She based her request on the acute problems facing the hundreds of thousands of displaced and marginalised children and on her view that 'the Committee's capacity to influence the State's development of policy is greatly increased at the present time by virtue of the fundamental review and reform of institutions which is already underway'. With her letter she submitted a brief report on the situation of children, prepared by the Office of the UNHCHR, the Organisation for Security and Cooperation in Europe, the World Health Organisation, the office of the UNHCR and the Office of the High Representative.

The intervention of the Special Rapporteur and submission of the multi-agency report were unprecedented in the experience of the Committee. Its reaction, however, was extremely muted. No action was taken at the next committee session and, instead, Ms Rehn was invited to meet informally with the members during the session in January 1997.[66] At that session the Committee declined to take any particular action. It did, however, invite Ms Rehn to compile a special report on the situation of children in the former Yugoslavia.[67]

Reasons for the timidity of the CRC Committee are not immediately apparent. Some current and former members of the committee and its secretariat have, however, intimated to the writer that Ms Rehn's inter-

---

[64] *Supra*, note 48.   [65] Letter and attached report on file with the author.

[66] Letter to Ms Rehn from the Chairperson of the Committee on file with the author.

[67] There are no official records of Ms Rehn's informal meeting with the Committee, on 20 January 1997, though it is referred to in the Committee's Session Report: UN Doc. CRC/C/62 at para. 6. There is no reference to the request made of Ms Rehn to compile the special report.

vention came at a time when the Committee had recently gained a number of new members with little experience of the interplay of the conventional and non-conventional human rights protection procedures and little taste for developing innovative procedures. The Committee may also have been concerned not to disturb the rhythm of its consideration of periodic reports.

F. Conclusion

This chapter has addressed the actual and potential interaction of the treaty bodies and Bosnia and Herzegovina during two periods: the years of the war and the present moment. With regard to both, the focus has been on identifying and assessing actual and possible procedural innovation and to place it within the context of general treaty body activity.

The war in Bosnia and Herzegovina was a catalyst for considerable innovation. With regard to reporting procedures, it freed the process from many of those restraints which had so greatly limited its application to crisis situations. Thus, for instance, the practice of requesting urgent reports was refined and they came to be considered more speedily. Importantly, Bosnia and Herzegovina provided the context for the treaty bodies to address various parties involved in or relevant to a conflict, including non-state actors and the international community. Also, uniquely in committee practice, other states (Croatia and the Federal Republic of Yugoslavia) were addressed regarding their behaviour in Bosnia and Herzegovina when their own reports were being considered. Another significant development was the manner in which certain treaty bodies engaged the attention of the Commission on Human Rights Special Rapporteur for former Yugoslavia. Some measures were also adopted for the better referral and distribution of concluding observations and comments. Bosnia and Herzegovina also provided an opportunity for the CERD Committee to develop its non-report-based procedures for addressing emergency situations.

Application of the various procedures can be demonstrated to have had some positive, if modest, impact on issues of human rights within Bosnia and Herzegovina. It is probable also that had the innovations been pursued in a methodical and consistent fashion (and been appropriately referred and published), more might have been accomplished. Any assessment of actual or potential accomplishment must, however, take into account the debilitating effect of overloaded programmes of work and extremely limited secretariat support.

459

The current circumstances in Bosnia and Herzegovina afford new and different challenges. They invite still further procedural innovation and afford occasions for the committees to take strong positions on important principles of system-wide significance. Criteria for engagement with these matters must be somewhat distinct from those applicable to the emergency procedures, not least given the significant possibility for making constructive contributions. Treaty bodies also have the opportunity to play a central role in implementation of a peace agreement in a manner which may bode well for similar future engagement elsewhere and for consequent enhancement of both their visibility and effectiveness.

Already the CERD Committee has shown some willingness to address the post-GFA situation. It and the other treaty bodies have yet, however, to show whether they intend to exploit the full range of possibilities. Notwithstanding their limited time and resources, it is to be hoped that the treaty bodies will so do. Energetic timely action will ensure that benefit continues to be rendered both to themselves and to Bosnia and Herzegovina.

21

ENSURING EFFECTIVE SUPERVISORY PROCEDURES: THE NEED FOR RESOURCES

ELIZABETH EVATT

A. Introduction

Maintaining the supervisory procedures of the human rights treaty bodies calls for a certain sleight of hand – to turn less into more. At a period when the treaty bodies are seeking to make the monitoring system more effective, and when the demands on them are increasing (more parties, more reports, more individual communications), the resources available to support their work seem to be diminishing.[1]

Insufficient resources have been a constant problem for the treaty bodies. Despite provisions in some instruments that 'the Secretary-General of the United Nations shall provide the necessary staff and facilities for the effective performance of the functions of the Committee'[2] it has long been

---

[1] See generally P. Alston, 'Interim Report of Study on Enhancing the Long-Term Effectiveness of the United Nations Human Rights Treaty Bodies' UN Doc. A/CONF.157/PC/62/Add.11/Rev.1, 22 April 1993; P. Alston, 'Final Report on Enhancing the Long-term Effectiveness of the United Nations Human Rights Treaty System', UN Doc. E/CN.4/1997/74, 7 March 1997. A. F. Bayefsky, 'Making the Human Rights Treaties Work', in *Human Rights: An Agenda for the Next Century* (eds. Louis Henkin and J. L. Hargrove), American Society of International Law, Washington DC, 1994, p. 229; *Plan of Action to Strengthen the Implementation of the Convention on the Rights of the Child Prepared by the UN High Commissioner for Human Rights*, November 1996. See also the Report on the July 1996 meeting of the members of the Human Rights Committee to discuss reform of the procedures of the Committee, and the reports of the meeting of persons chairing the human rights treaty bodies, convened pursuant to General Assembly Resolution 49/178 of 23 December 1994.

[2] International Covenant on Civil and Political Rights (ICCPR), article 36. See also Convention on the Elimination of Discrimination against Women (CEDAW), article 17.9; Convention against Torture (CAT), article 18.3; Convention on the Rights of the Child (CRC), article 43.11. Different arrangements apply to the International Covenant on Economic, Social and Cultural Rights (ICESCR) and to the Convention on the Elimination of Racial Discrimination (CERD).

recognised that the funding of the treaty bodies and their resources are inadequate to allow them to carry out their mandate effectively.[3] Too few professional staff have been assigned to treaty body work, and even those staff who have been assigned to this work have sometimes been seconded to other work. Some meetings have been cancelled, interpreting has sometimes been restricted and summary records are sometimes not prepared.

Far from improving, this situation threatens to get worse. Limits have been imposed on documentation and delays in translations have been chronic. Petty restrictions on the distribution of documents have frustrated the work of the Human Rights Committee (HRC). These demoralising restrictions have come at a time when the increase in ratifications, in the number of communications and in the length of reports, together with the Committee's attempts to make its procedure more effective, have increased the workload of the Secretariat. In an effort to ensure that the quality of its work is not jeopardised, the Committee has asked that in the restructuring of the Office of the UN High Commissioner for Human Rights (UNHCHR), provision be made to increase the specialised staff assigned to it, in relation both to the monitoring of reports and to the consideration of communications under the Optional Protocol to the International Covenant on Civil and Political Rights (ICCPR).[4]

Against this background, the natural tendency on the part of the treaty bodies is to deal with the problem through techniques of crisis management, making minor savings here and there, working only from one session to the next. However understandable, this tends to obscure the real long-term problem. If effectiveness meant no more than efficiency in the use of existing resources, we could simply focus on how to do what is being done more efficiently. But effectiveness should also look to the goals and outcome of the process. The question then is different – what kind of servicing and resources are needed by the treaty bodies to make the monitoring system effective, that is, to enhance the level of compliance. This 'optimum effectiveness' may require further resources. In a context of diminishing United Nations resources, such effectiveness could not be achieved without seeking new sources of support. Thus it is necessary to ask not only how the level of resources historically available can best be used, but what level of

---

[3] Alston, *supra* note 1, pp. 197–206.
[4] See e.g. 'Report of the Human Rights Committee', Vol. 1, UN Doc. A/52/40 (1997), para. 19.

resources is required, as a minimum, if the treaty bodies are effectively to discharge their mandates, and how such resources might be obtained. Only when these questions have been answered is it possible to assess possible or proposed reforms.

B. Effectiveness as a function of the goals of the treaty system

The effectiveness of the treaty system, in terms of its intermediate and long-term goals, entails a number of different things.

1. EFFECTIVE MONITORING AND FOLLOW-UP

Human rights instruments create legally binding obligations for state parties to implement: they must respect and ensure the rights protected by the instrument, and also take part in the supervisory, or monitoring system established by it. States parties have voluntarily assumed these obligations and must be taken to have the intention to fulfil them. To do so in good faith, they must at the minimum present reports as required by the treaty, consider and respond to the treaty bodies' observations on the report, take follow-up action, cooperate in any communications procedure, and make appropriate responses to the views of the treaty body.

The monitoring system contributes to the effectiveness of the treaty in that the treaty body is able to assess how far states have fulfilled their legal obligations and to encourage and assist states to take corrective action when necessary.[5] The role of the treaty bodies is especially important in the context of multilateral treaties, in that the states themselves have not made use of other mechanisms to secure compliance by other parties.[6]

For monitoring to be effective, the treaty bodies need to have an adequate understanding of the current law and practice in each reporting state, of the institutional framework for protecting rights, of the extent to which rights are enjoyed in practice and the deficiencies in the implementation of rights. State reports seldom, if ever, provide the kind of information and analysis needed for such an understanding. Members of treaty bodies may do their own research, but this work is not consolidated into a working

---

[5] Though its discontinuance has been suggested: Bayefsky, *supra* note 1, p. 264.

[6] The procedure under article 41 ICCPR, under which a state may make a complaint against another state party (if both states have accepted the procedure) has not been used. Some states have, however, objected to reservations made by other states parties.

document. No provision has been made for corporate memory in regard to the situation in states parties, even though the monitoring process is intended to extend over generations. There is a need for continuing analytical studies in respect of the states parties covering the issues mentioned, studies which should be undertaken by qualified personnel. They should be updated and kept available as reference documents within the Office of the UNHCHR.

Since implementation of treaty obligations within national systems is a major goal of human rights instruments, the monitoring process should use whatever means are available to encourage states to introduce the laws, policies and institutions necessary to comply, to prepare quality reports and to take part in discussion with the treaty body. It should monitor follow-up action taken after the discussion by the state in order to implement the recommendations of the treaty body. Both the reporting process and the communications procedure should have adequate follow-up mechanisms.

2. EFFECTIVE TREATY BODIES

A number of initiatives have been taken by the treaty bodies towards greater effectiveness. For example, the HRC established a Working Group in 1995 with the task of finding ways to expand on the resources of the Committee.[7] The Working Group secured independent funds to hold a one-week meeting, followed by a special out-of-session meeting of the whole Committee immediately following the July 1996 session. The result was a detailed examination of the working methods of the Committee, agreement on some significant procedural changes and an attempt to define aspects of the work which could be undertaken as projects funded by outside agencies. Rules have been drafted to implement some of the proposals, for example, to provide for communications to be dealt with in a one-step procedure, rather than in two stages of admissibility and merits, as then the practice.

The fact that the treaty bodies seek improvements in their methods of work should give some impetus to reform. But there are constraints on

---

[7] The special Working Group was chaired by T. Buergenthal. The impetus for the Working Group came from a concern that there had been delays in considering some communications because of problems over translation and lack of resources available to the Communications Division of the Office of the UNHCHR.

what those bodies can achieve within the existing structures, especially when it comes to proposals which would require the members to give more time to the work of the HRC. Most have other full-time professional commitments, and carry out their functions in the treaty body on an essentially honorary basis. Secretariat support is essential to the introduction of new procedures. Inevitably, where reforms would make additional demands on resources, their introduction will require either additional staff or resources provided from outside the UN budget.

Another constraint on the treaty bodies is their isolation from each other. Apart from the annual meetings of chairpersons of the human rights treaty monitoring bodies they have little contact, and little opportunity to discuss the kind of reforms which would make the system more effective. If they could work more closely together they might have more influence on those who decide on the allocation of resources and they might be able, for example, to help resolve the problems caused by overlapping mandates, and the plethora of instruments and reports. In the long term it would be desirable to amalgamate the treaty bodies into a single monitoring mechanism, by consolidating the instruments.[8] This would strengthen the monitoring bodies as well as overcoming the difficulties caused to states by overlapping provisions and the fragmentation of the reporting process.

3. EFFECTIVE SECRETARIAT SUPPORT FOR TREATY BODIES

The proper functioning of the treaty bodies depends to a very great extent on the existence of a strong professional staff in the Secretariat, with specialised skills and experience. Consolidation of the treaties and the ultimate creation of a single monitoring body would call for a unified Secretariat, with a significant responsibility to work with an essentially full-time independent treaty body. Other, intermediate, proposals outlined below would also need an expansion of professional staff.

C. Possible reforms and their impact on resources

Human rights issues are assuming a growing importance in international relations. If the UN human rights system is to maintain its place in the

---

[8] This might be achieved for those states which have ratified all six instruments, leaving others to the present system. See also chapter 19 of this volume.

vanguard of the development of human rights, it needs to be reshaped. The treaty body system, as the main independent agency within the UN human rights system, should be recognised as having a significant role in the interpretation of standards, as a significant resource to assist states in compliance, and as a source of information to the whole UN system about the situation in particular states. In all this, it should make full use of modern technology.

1. MULTIPLE REPORTING PROCEDURES AND OVERLAPPING INSTRUMENTS

The reality is that human rights violations occur within individual national systems, and states parties can only comply with their treaty obligations by attending to the content and administration of their own legal systems. At that level there is a need for a unitary approach. By contrast, the existence of separate treaties, each with a separate monitoring body, and the need for separate consideration of the same issues by several different bodies, imposes unnecessary burdens on states and could lead to inconsistency and confusion.

A single treaty body considering a single comprehensive report has been suggested as a way of overcoming overlapping mandates and reducing the burden of reporting under many instruments. A single treaty body would almost certainly require full-time paid members. It would need considerably more staff resources. Though this proposal may not be practicable as an immediate solution, it should be kept in mind as a possible long-term solution, and planning for the development of the system should be done in a way that would make the transition to a single mechanism easier. For example:

- A member of one treaty body could sit as an observer at all or part of the session of another treaty body, for example when the same state is to have its reports considered in both bodies. This might help to prevent the same issues being raked over unnecessarily.
- Joint working groups, consisting of members of more than one treaty body, could be established to prepare guidelines for states explaining clearly how to deal with areas of overlap between the different instruments.
- Thematic working groups of representatives of several treaty bodies could be called together by the Office of the UNHCHR or by UN agencies

to develop guidelines for states in preparing reports on particular areas of human rights covered by more than one instrument.

• Arrangements could be made to bring the Convention on the Elimination of Discrimination against Women (CEDAW) into the same servicing structure as the other treaty bodies.

2. PREPARATION AND CONSIDERATION OF REPORTS

It is generally accepted that the programme of state reports should be set by the treaty body at least two sessions ahead, and a list of questions or issues given to the state party one session ahead. In addition, the country rapporteur, with the assistance of the Secretariat, should prepare an analysis of the human rights situation in each state whose report is to be considered, as the basis for requesting further information on laws, decisions, etc. from the state and for selecting the issues and questions to be discussed.

Such an analysis would, however, have value beyond the first consideration of a report. It would become part of an ongoing study of that state and its human rights situation. It would bring together, at Secretariat level, the reports of that state under each of the instruments, as well as information from UN agencies and non-governmental organisations (NGOs). Such continuous analysis seems essential if the treaty body system is to engage seriously in assessing state compliance. It would make the monitoring system a valuable source of information about human rights in the member states. It would open the way to a quicker and more selective examination of some states, and would enable the treaty body to focus on significant issues with other states. It might even make the process of report writing simpler for the state.

An authoritative analysis of this kind would be resource intensive. It would require high level researchers with suitable experience and qualifications. The treaty bodies could determine the priorities for this work, that is, which countries and which issues should first be studied. They might cooperate in setting the ambit of this work, through a joint working group or rapporteurs nominated for the purpose.

While this work would be done primarily by Secretariat staff, under the direction of the treaty body, it could also be a potential area of work for interns attached to the treaty bodies (with knowledge of the appropriate languages and legal systems), provided that they have a sufficient length of time to carry out useful work, for example, a minimum of one or two years.

It might be possible to seek specific funding from foundations, or support from universities for interns or post-graduate students. Perhaps a proposal could be put forward for a pilot scheme to assess the value of the proposal.

3. FOLLOW-UP TO THE REPORTING PROCESS

Follow-up to the reporting process is not well developed, at least in the HRC. Procedures should be developed to ensure that requests by treaty bodies for states to provide further information are complied with, that the information has in fact been provided and that it has been considered by the treaty body. Otherwise there seems little point in asking for it. The state might also be requested to provide information as to whether the observations and recommendations made by the treaty body were considered at state level and what response was made. Other matters which may need to be confirmed are recommendations to give publicity to concluding observations.

A comprehensive follow-up programme needs to be instituted as a necessary part of the reporting process. It should be placed under the responsibility of the country rapporteur or a general rapporteur for follow-up, with assistance of the Secretariat. The possibility of a visit to the state party to discuss aspects of the follow-up should be included in the procedure.

4. COMMUNICATIONS

In the HRC, too few professional staff are available for communications work, and serious delays are developing. Nevertheless, the reforms which are contemplated do not all involve a reduction in the workload for the communications procedures.

For example, the possibility of hearings at the request of the parties, now under consideration, would add to the time taken by some cases, though this could be offset by the new one-stage procedure (combining both admissibility and merits issues), and other changes which might speed up the handling of other cases. The follow-up to communications is gradually being made more effective and is taking up more time of the rapporteur and the Secretariat. This could increase further, especially if visits to states, or extended discussions with states are considered necessary. The new practice of assigning each communication to a case rapporteur involves an even greater commitment of time from individual members.

5. GENERAL COMMENTS

The HRC has adopted twenty-seven General Comments and more are planned. Those adopted in recent years appear to be more detailed; the result is that more time is spent in their drafting and consideration in the Working Group and in the Committee. The practice has been for these comments to be drafted by members, not by the Secretariat, although the Secretariat may provide some input. By contrast other treaty bodies may rely to a greater extent on the assistance of their Secretariat to draft general comments.

In any event, there is certainly a potential role for Secretariat staff or specialist interns to assist in the preparatory work of drafting comments. With the expansion of work and the need for members to undertake more and more tasks, there could be problems for members to find time to prepare draft comments. However, if some of this work is to be done other than by members, the responsible officer should work closely with one or more members who might form a working group for that purpose. It is envisaged that a member would always be responsible for introducing the draft to the Committee and leading the discussion.

6. BETTER USE OF INFORMATION TECHNOLOGY

The cost of going electronic is a cost that must be incurred if the treaty monitoring system is to remain viable. All material produced in the Office of the UNHCHR should be available on electronic database and, if possible on the Internet. Adequate search mechanisms should be provided. The cost of providing a modem, or even a lap top personal computer with modem for each member during their term, with access to the Internet, would be minor, and would be offset by savings in paper, copying, storage, distribution and postage. Outside organisations such as foundations could perhaps be approached to support specific parts of this transition.

D. Resource implications of these reforms

The proposals outlined above would require additional staff and additional funds to carry out the further activities intended to make the system more effective. The following section outlines the kind of resources needed.

1. MEMBERS OF TREATY BODIES

Resources would need to be available for members of treaty bodies, and support staff for the Secretariat, in a number of areas:

- additional working groups, including joint working groups and thematic working groups with members of other treaty bodies;
- greater contact with members of other treaty bodies, including attendance of members at sessions of other committees;
- visits to states parties (for technical assistance and follow-up activities in connection with reports and communications);
- access to technology, email and the Internet.

Increases in duties would require appropriate honoraria to be paid, especially to members of treaty bodies which at present have no provision for this.[9] It might also require education seminars to assist new members and enhance professional development.

Treaty bodies probably take the view that more time is needed to deal with their workload of reports. This would certainly be true if all overdue reports were presented by states. At present there are considerable backlogs. In the case of the Human Rights Committee some reports wait eighteen months to two years before consideration. Extending sessions or allocating additional sessions would require extra resources, not just to meet the cost, but also in terms of secretariat staff. It would add significantly to the time which members would need to commit to their work on the treaty body.

The functions that treaty bodies have taken on, and those contemplated here, suggest an expanding role for the members, one which will become increasingly difficult to perform on a part-time honorary basis. States need to recognise the actual demands on members, and should ensure that adequate support services are available. The proposals made here are based on a belief that there must inevitably be a consolidation of the whole system. Moving CEDAW to the Office of the UNHCHR would be just one step in this process.

2. THE SECRETARIAT

In general, the professional staff of the Secretariat are highly competent. Nevertheless, the Secretariat is understaffed, and needs to be strengthened

---

[9] See also chapter 8 of this volume, note 42, for further details.

by additional professional staff, able to respond to the growing needs of the treaty bodies. The professional staff should be able to work for more than one treaty body. Their functions should include:

- preparing in-depth evaluation of state reports and analysis of the human rights situation in a particular country, as working documents for the committees;
- working with joint working groups and thematic working groups to prepare guidelines for states parties relating to overlapping instruments;
- preparing draft lists of issues and questions;
- dealing with communications, preparation of drafts, etc.;
- follow-up to reporting and communications;
- preparing drafts of annual reports;
- preparation of draft general comments in association with one or more members of the treaty body;
- technical advice and assistance to states.

Some of these tasks might be performed by special interns or research fellows.

3. TECHNICAL ASSISTANCE

The provision of enhanced technical assistance to states, to improve the quality and regularity of reports, and to assist with the follow-up to the reporting process, would require a further commitment of professional resources at the Office of the UNHCHR. Nevertheless some of these extra costs might be offset by savings, if the result made the reporting process easier to manage.

4. CONSULTATION BETWEEN TREATY BODIES AND SECRETARIAT

Major decisions about the level of funding of treaty bodies and about the reform of the whole system will be made at the higher political levels of the UN. Nevertheless, impetus could be given to reform proposals by a common commitment of members of treaty bodies and of the Secretariat. Regrettably there is often tension between these two groups, and this has been added to by the way in which restructuring has proceeded. There is some disagreement as to how far the Secretariat should consult with members of treaty bodies about priorities and structures in the Office of the UNHCHR.

In the longer term, it is easy to foresee that there will be growing pressure to develop a more integrated system, a system which consolidates the monitoring system, with a more or less permanent independent monitoring body. Steps along the way include increasing interaction between the treaty bodies themselves and closer working relationships between the treaty bodies and the Secretariat. It makes sense to prepare now by establishing appropriate consultation mechanisms between the Secretariat and the treaty bodies about the structure of the Office of the UNHCHR.[10]

E. Increasing resources

Increasing the resources of the treaty bodies by securing a greater allocation from the UN General Budget might seem the simplest approach, but it is also the most difficult. Other alternatives include outside funding for specific projects to be carried out for and under the direction of the treaty bodies or the Secretariat. This could prove to be a flexible way to expand resources if the UN does not take up its responsibilities in this area. On this basis, potential sources of direct funding, servicing and other support for treaty bodies should include the following:

- the general budget of the UN;
- states parties;
- specialised agencies and UN bodies;
- independent private bodies;
- interns and externs;
- fellowships in human rights;
- NGOs.

These will be discussed in turn.

1. FUNDING OF THE TREATY BODIES BY THE UN

The financing of the treaty bodies is, with some exceptions, provided from the General Budget of the UN. The actual servicing of all bodies other than

---

[10] This was called for by the annual meeting of chairpersons of the human rights treaty monitoring bodies, 1996, para. 40.

CEDAW is provided by the Office of the UNHCHR. The Division for the Advancement of Women, based in New York, provides servicing for CEDAW. In the past the Convention on the Elimination of Racial Discrimination (CERD) and the Convention against Torture (CAT) were funded by the states parties in accordance with their Conventions. This proved unsuccessful, and amendments to the instruments provide for these treaty bodies to be funded from the General Budget.

The treaty bodies are dependent on the funding of the Office of the UNHCHR and on the decisions made by the Secretariat as to the staff structure and the allocation of funds. As is well known, the UN is perennially short of funds, due to the failure of many states (most notably the United States) to pay their dues. Various proposals have been made to persuade states to do so, or to secure an adequate financial base for the UN in other ways, including private endowment funds, international taxation schemes and an annual UN lottery.[11] Until this problem is solved, the funding of treaty bodies from the General Budget will likely remain inadequate.

The World Conference on Human Rights held in Vienna in 1993 called for a substantial increase in the resources for the human rights programme from within existing resources and for 'urgent steps to seek increased extra budgetary resources'.[12] It also called for an increased proportion of the regular budget to be allocated to the Centre for Human Rights (now the Office of the UNHCHR), to cover its work including that related to the treaty bodies, and for sufficient funds to be provided to the Centre to enable it to be effective. There is, however, a large gap between the rhetoric and the reality. Indeed it is not at all clear that any additional resources have been made available to the treaty bodies as a whole since 1993. Nevertheless, though the funds available generally have not been increased, recent proposals from the Office of the UNHCHR, and devoted to the improvement of the implementation of the Convention on the Rights of the Child (CRC), call for a considerable increase in the resources allocated by the Office to the work of the Committee.[13] This suggests that it may be possible

---

[11] Brian Urquhart and Erskine Childers, *Renewing the United Nations System*, Dag Hammarskjold Foundation, Uppsala, Sweden, 1994, pp. 142, 208.

[12] Vienna Declaration and Programme of Action, World Conference on Human Rights, Vienna, 14–25 June 1993, A/CONF.157/23, 12 July 1993, Plan of Action, paras. 9, 10, 11, 12.

[13] *Supra*, note 1, *Plan of Action*. The amount called for was US$ 549,000 for five substantive officers, plus rather more for technical cooperation, training courses, missions and workshops, making a total of US$ 1,390,239 to come from extra-budgetary, voluntary contributions by governments.

to augment resources, and that similar plans could be developed for other treaty bodies.

Some might argue that the treaty bodies, as independent agencies, should have their own dedicated budget, to manage in accordance with their own decisions. This possibility should certainly be on the agenda for the consultations envisaged above. If a consolidation of treaty bodies were to occur, a dedicated budget for a consolidated body would have to be given serious consideration.

2. THE STATES PARTIES

The unfortunate experience of CERD and CAT suggests that it would be unwise to develop plans which made the treaty bodies dependent on direct funding by the states parties. The need to maintain the independence of the treaty bodies further underlines the point that the core activities of those bodies should not depend on direct contributions by states.

States might, however, be invited to provide resources for particular projects of benefit to the treaty bodies. For example, the Japanese Government provided funds for the editing and publication of the *Yearbook of the Human Rights Committee*.[14] States might also contribute to the support of regional seminars to advance awareness of the conventions and the work of the treaty bodies.[15] The voluntary fund for technical cooperation and assistance is another means by which states can support the human rights programme.[16] A voluntary fund could be a way to support an expanded intern programme.

3. SPECIALISED AGENCIES AND OTHER UN BODIES

The treaty bodies have developed working relationships with the specialised agencies, and there is potential to build further on this. The agencies provide information to the treaty bodies about issues falling within their

[14] Now called the *Official Records of the Human Rights Committee*.

[15] For example, a South Pacific Women's Seminar was supported by the Australian and New Zealand Governments, as well as by the Division for the Advancement of Women in 1991.

[16] The Vienna Plan of Action called for 'generous contributions' to the voluntary funds. Vienna Declaration and Programme of Action, *supra*, note 12, I, para. 10.

mandate which are relevant to the particular instrument. Much of this information is state specific. Agencies take part in Working Group discussions on states whose reports are to be considered. The CRC makes provision for the UN Children's Fund (UNICEF) and other agencies to be represented at the consideration of reports and to provide advice and information.[17] In fact the CRC Committee has received considerable support from UNICEF.[18] The other treaty bodies do not have this kind of support.

UN agencies such as the International Labour Organisation (ILO) are responsible for monitoring treaty obligations which may overlap with the human rights instruments. More could be done to examine these areas of overlap, especially as the ILO Conventions may also include reporting obligations. A cooperative approach might help to ease the burden of reporting for the states, treaty bodies and the agencies.

The specialised agencies could be encouraged to do more to support the work of the treaty bodies, by promoting wider knowledge of the human rights system where it has special relevance to their work.[19] Where particular human rights standards in one or more states are relevant to the work of an agency, that agency could undertake studies in consultation with the treaty bodies of the application of those standards in those countries. Agencies such as the World Bank might be encouraged to commission background papers dealing with the extent of implementation of specific human rights standards in states in which they have development programmes.

Agencies concerned with a particular area of human rights could bring treaty bodies together to discuss how the issues could best be dealt with in accordance with their mandate. In 1996 the Glen Cove Roundtable[20] made many recommendations about improving cooperation between the treaty bodies and the specialised agencies. Agencies were encouraged to integrate human rights concerns into their work and to be more involved in the work of the treaty bodies.

---

[17] CRC, article 45 (special recognition of agencies); cf. CEDAW, article 22.
[18] *Supra*, note 10, para. 19.
[19] Ibid., paras. 31, 51, 52.
[20] Glen Cove Roundtable, 'Briefing Note and Final Recommendations of the Roundtable of Human Rights Treaty Bodies on the "Human Rights Approach to Women's Health with a Focus on Reproductive and Sexual Health Rights"', Glen Cove, New York State, 9–11 December 1996, WHG/97/3/8.

4. INDEPENDENT PRIVATE BODIES, FOUNDATIONS ETC.

It would be difficult for the treaty bodies to receive direct funding from private sources, due to the lack of any entity, such as a trust, to control the allocation of these funds.[21] However, the treaty bodies could ask private agencies, foundations or academic institutions to fund specific research projects which would directly or indirectly advance their work. The role of the treaty bodies (in association with the Office of the UNHCHR) would be limited to a consultant or overseeing role. A Projects Committee could devise or approve projects which might then be funded externally. Examples might include the following:

- research fellowships for persons attached to an academic institution to carry out a defined project in the Secretariat for one or more treaty bodies, under the general guidance of representatives of a Projects Committee;
- long-term interns, who could be assigned to specific projects;
- providing travel costs for special experts, e.g. former members of treaty bodies, approved by the Projects Committee to carry out specific projects;
- direct support to the work of the Office of the UNHCHR, such as that provided by the Netherlands Institute of Human Rights (SIM) in providing access to its database of human rights decisions.

While there could be a danger of over-dependency on outside support, it would be worthwhile for the treaty bodies to establish a pilot project to test the viability of this proposal.

5. INTERNS AND EXTERNS

Interns are a valuable additional resource for the professional officers in the Secretariat and for the treaty bodies. Their use is, however, limited by the short duration of their appointment (generally three months) and by the fact that one professional officer cannot easily supervise the work of more than one or two interns. To make more and better use of interns, a special scheme could be devised to provide for terms of up to one or two

---

[21] The Working Group of the Human Rights Committee, mentioned earlier, also foresaw that if other funds were available, the allocation from the UN budget might be cut.

years. This might reduce the burden on the professional staff and enable interns to take on a wider range of responsibilities.

The Special Working Group of the Human Rights Committee discussed the role and use of interns. A number of points were later agreed in principle by the Committee: first, the responsibility of the Secretariat for the selection and supervision of interns; secondly, the need for them to have at least a basic professional degree and preferably two working languages, and thirdly a minimum term of service of at least one year. This would require a waiver of current Secretariat rules. Funding would be needed to support an intern for such a period, and the Committee should explore the possibility of funding from independent sources (under conditions which maintain the Committee's independence). But the number of interns would still be limited by the ability of the Secretariat staff to provide supervision.

The term 'extern' would be used when the person concerned did not work at the Office of the UNHCHR, but possibly under the supervision of one or more members of a treaty body or other person. They could, perhaps, help case rapporteurs or country rapporteurs.

6. FELLOWSHIPS IN HUMAN RIGHTS

Private foundations and academic institutions could be encouraged to establish Fellowships in Human Rights to be held by persons chosen in consultation with one or more treaty bodies, to undertake research projects approved by and for the benefit of the relevant bodies, for example, a draft general comment. The treaty bodies could set up a joint committee (in association with the Secretariat) to explore this idea, as well as those mentioned earlier, with private foundations and academic institutions.

Former members of treaty bodies willing to volunteer their time might also be recognised as fellows or special experts, so that their expertise could be used to augment the resources of the Secretariat and the committees. For example, certain tasks related to communications could be performed by former members, such as assisting the rapporteur on follow-up by analysing the relevant material, or by carrying out research on current communications. A recognised status within the Office would ensure that these former members could have appropriate access to files. However, while former members may give their time freely, not many would be able or willing to cover their fares to Geneva or accommodation for the period necessary. Funding would thus need to be secured to support this idea.

7. CONTRIBUTION OF NGOS

The treaty bodies value highly the input from both international and national NGOs.[22] Most treaty bodies receive information and briefings from NGOs. CEDAW receives 'alternative reports' on the states whose reports are being examined, provided by International Women's Rights Action Watch (IWRAW). The NGO, Defence of Children International, organises national groups to prepare alternative country reports under the Convention on the Rights of the Child. Other treaty bodies do not have a support group of this kind which brings in material from national organisations on a regular basis. Ideally, one would like the state party to consult with national and local NGOs at the time the report is being prepared, but this is rare.

International NGOs such as Amnesty International, Human Rights Watch and Lawyers' Committee for Human Rights provide considerable material to the Committees, but these organisations do not have the resources to coordinate their work, and there is often duplication.

National NGOs generally have few resources, they do not necessarily know when the meetings of treaty bodies are to be held, they do not have copies of the reports, and they do not know how to prepare material for the Committees. The quality of their material is uneven. There is often far too much material from NGOs in affluent states.[23] For others, where the need may be great, nothing is provided, because nothing is known about the treaty monitoring system. With few exceptions, the national NGOs have little ability to coordinate their efforts or to contribute to the resources of the Committees beyond the material they have compiled.

A well-organised NGO movement would make the work of the treaty bodies easier. It would be less time-consuming for those bodies if the submissions of NGOs, especially national NGOs, were coordinated. The treaty bodies could lend their support to proposals for strengthening the work of

---

[22] The HRC has, since July 1996, invited NGOs to meetings with the pre-sessional Working Group. Participants include Amnesty International, Organisation mondiale contre la torture (OMCT), International Commission of Jurists (ICJ), International Federation of Human Rights (IFHR), International Alliance Against Torture (IAAT). In New York, the Lawyers' Committee for Human Rights (LCHR) and Human Rights Watch (HRW), would be expected to be present.

[23] The most active national NGOs in supporting the work of the Human Rights Committee in recent years have been those of Hong Kong, Ireland, Japan, the United Kingdom and the United States – voluminous, but uncoordinated.

national and international NGOs and to the funding submissions they may make to foundations. NGOs could consider establishing a single liaison group to work with the treaty bodies. Such a group might be able to attract further funding, perhaps from foundations.

A new initiative of the International Federation for Human Rights (Fédération internationale des droits de l'homme-FIDH) would help member organisations to come to the UNHCHR office in Geneva and to receive training on their means of actions in the treaty monitoring bodies and to participate in the sessions of treaty bodies when their country report is being considered. Funding is being sought by FIDH for this initiative. The treaty bodies should encourage and support proposals of this kind.

F. Conclusion

Any independent observer of the present system would conclude that the treaty body system needs a complete overhaul. But is there any commitment to do this, and to provide the necessary resources? It is extremely doubtful.

22

SERVICING AND FINANCING HUMAN
RIGHTS SUPERVISORY BODIES

MARKUS SCHMIDT

A. The background

Since their inception in the 1970s, UN treaty-based procedures in the field of human rights have become gradually better known. The number of states parties to the major UN human rights instruments has risen dramatically since 1989: with 191 ratifications the Convention on the Rights of the Child (CRC) has become the most widely ratified of any UN convention. Human rights education campaigns and programmes in many countries provide information about the various procedures, and encourage citizens to avail themselves of these mechanisms. But as always, exposure and success have their price: as more and more states ratify the various UN human rights instruments, the respective supervisory bodies have experienced increasing difficulties in coping with a growing workload under the periodic state reporting and individual complaints procedures. They must examine more periodic state reports and more complaints every year if they are to avoid an unacceptable backlog of complaints and reports, opening themselves to the charge that 'justice delayed is justice denied'.

At the same time, the meeting time allotted to the treaty bodies in the UN conference calendar and by UN conference services has remained by and large unchanged; treaty bodies hold two to three sessions totalling six to twelve weeks of meetings each year. Requests by treaty bodies to be allotted more meeting time have met with limited success. While the workload of supervisory bodies has more than doubled over the past decade, the UN Secretariat staff resources available to service their work have, in real terms, been reduced over the same period of time.

Of the UN treaty bodies, the Human Rights Committee (HRC) has drawn attention to this unsatisfactory situation in its Annual Report to the General Assembly for many years. Thus, in 1990, it noted that its 'increased workload means that the Committee will not be able to examine communications at the same speed or to maintain the same level of quality unless the Secretariat staff is reinforced'.[1] In 1994, it became more specific, noting that with its increased workload under the Optional Protocol to the International Covenant on Civil and Political Rights (ICCPR), it could no longer examine communications expeditiously; this highlighted 'the urgent need to reinforce the Secretariat staff'. The HRC called upon the UN Secretary-General 'to ensure a substantial increase in the number of staff, specialised in the various legal systems, assigned to service the Committee', and reiterated that its work under the Optional Protocol 'continues to suffer as a result of insufficient Secretariat resources'.[2] The HRC's request was politely noted, but little if anything was done in real terms to remedy the situation, and the financial crisis which has plagued the UN since 1995 has led to further retrenchment in the Secretariat.

Other treaty bodies, such as that of the Convention on the Elimination of Racial Discrimination (CERD) Committee, have similarly complained about the fact that lack of financial resources has resulted in sessions being simply cancelled. In mid-1994, the Committee devoted part of a meeting to the issue of its available logistics and resources. In response to the experts' concerns, the Assistant Secretary-General outlined a number of measures designed to improve the situation, including regularisation of professional posts and improvement of electronic communications.[3] But two years later, identical problems persisted, and the UN financial crisis prompted another reduction in documentation services to the Committee.[4]

B. Financing of UN treaty bodies

The budget for the activities of UN human rights treaty bodies is determined through the normal biennial budget cycles: the proposed biennial

---

[1] See Annual Report of the HRC for 1990, UN Doc. A/45/40, vol. I, para. 595.
[2] Annual Report of the HRC for 1994, UN Doc. A/49/40, vol. I, para. 383.
[3] See UN Doc. CERD/C/SR.1050, 25 September 1996, pp. 7–15. It should be noted that this summary record was produced more than two years after the meeting, which took place on 5 August 1994. Serious delays in the production of official and summary records are another factor which may hamper the efficiency of the treaty bodies' work.
[4] See UN Doc. CERD/C/SR.1158, 9 August 1996, para. 3.

budget of the Office of the UN High Commissioner for Human Rights (UNHCHR) is submitted to the UN's budgetary authorities and is subject to negotiations in the Fifth Committee of the General Assembly.[5] Usually, a biennial budget is discussed and adopted sufficiently in advance for human rights supervisory bodies to be able to assess realistically what will be available to them over the next two-year budget cycle, both in terms of meeting time, travel allocations, secretariat staff resources, and other activities.

The major UN budgetary authorities, in particular the Programme Planning Budget Board and the Advisory Committee on Administrative and Budgetary Questions (ACABQ) have been reluctant in recent years to appropriate the funds necessary for the proper discharge of all of the mandated activities of the Office of the UNHCHR. Treaty body activities have not been spared in this process.[6] Thus, in the context of the financial crisis which hit the UN in 1995–1996, the HRC was urged to agree to economies in the servicing of its fifty-sixth session in March 1996, held in New York. The Committee Chairperson agreed to reduce the number of staff servicing the Optional Protocol procedure, and only a limited number of cases were examined as a result during this session. That such concessions are subsequently interpreted as final and not only temporary, and that they may prompt further requests for economies, became evident during preparations for the Committee's fifty-ninth session in March-April 1997 and its sixty-second session in March-April 1998. Similar considerations apply to the limitation of documentation decreed as a measure of economy.

Urgent or new activities which have not been budgeted for the ongoing biennium are always difficult to approve *ex post facto*, however necessary they may be. Thus, it took several *démarches* by the HRC before a one-week extension of its summer session in 1994 was approved, which allowed it to reduce its deplorable backlog of pending complaints under the Optional Protocol to the ICCPR.[7] As noted before, the CERD Committee could only schedule one annual meeting for many years because of financial

---

[5] See chapter 23 of the organisation's budget.

[6] The composition of the ACABQ in recent years has not always been propitious for the approval of higher budgetary appropriations for the human rights programme.

[7] During this extra week, the HRC adopted sixteen Views (i.e. decisions on the merits) under article 5, para. 4, of the Optional Protocol, and declared eleven cases inadmissible. In its Annual Report for 1994, the HRC notes, however, that failure to provide more staff for the preparation of the extended session resulted in a bigger backlog in the Secretariat's handling of incoming complaints and thus in a smaller number of newly registered cases – Annual Report, *supra*, note 2, para. 384.

difficulties and because there were no appropriations for its meetings in the regular budget of the UN.

The political realities of the UN, the unwillingness of major contributors to the UN budget to approve substantial budget increases, as well as the current reorientation of priorities within the UN human rights programme justify the following unpalatable but sober conclusion: the treaty bodies will have to live with the *status quo* in terms of services available in the foreseeable future. At worst, they may have to accept another reduction in Secretariat services available to them. It is clear that the treaty bodies must oppose a reduction in services, but they should consider alternative mechanisms for the financing of their activities.

In the long term, the financing of treaty body activities through the regular budget of the UN alone will not suffice. Financing of activities through extra-budgetary resources and voluntary contributions must be considered seriously in the short term. Through voluntary contributions, in particular, the resources at the disposal of the Secretariat may be improved over and above what can be done within the regular budget. The equipment of the Secretariat with up-to-date information technology and computers, the creation of web sites, the design and implementation of new databases, etc., are among improvements that could be effected through voluntary contributions. While some might object on principle to such voluntary contributions because they open the activities of the human rights supervisory bodies to all kinds of external influences, the likelihood of influence-peddling is small. In some respects, voluntary contributions may be likened to private sector sponsoring of activities; and such 'sponsoring' is becoming increasingly important in the activities even of international and regional organisations. Imaginative fund-raising activities are obviously a serious alternative way of alleviating the treaty bodies' plight in the short term.

One device to strengthen substantive support to treaty bodies which *may* – and the emphasis is on the conditional – help them discharge their mandates more effectively in the short term is the adoption and implementation of so-called Plans of Action, under which voluntary contributions from states parties earmarked for a treaty body will finance the activities of additional staff – consultants, experts, etc. – assigned specifically to that treaty body's activities. The CRC Committee was the first to discuss and adopt such a Plan of Action and to secure the necessary voluntary contributions. It summarised the rationale for the Plan as follows:

[3] The CRC through its innovative methods of work has become an international focal point in identifying problems in protecting the rights of the child, suggesting appropriate solutions and, when necessary, helping to mobilize the intellectual and material resources of the international community to help implement these solutions. It is important to explore ways of strengthening the operation of the Committee in order to maximize its impact on the effective enjoyment by children of their rights. Based on the recommendations and requests of the Committee made in the first five years of activity, two types of support will be necessary. First, the substantive support for the Committee's work with States parties reports should be significantly strengthened. Second, follow-up mechanisms will be devised to transform recommendations into reality. This will necessitate resources and coordination.[8]

The Plan envisages a support team of four staff members who would primarily carry out research and prepare the preliminary analysis of states parties' reports for consideration by the Committee, collect and analyse information on the follow-up of the Committee's recommendations, and assist the Committee in the preparation of substantive background papers.[9] The support team for the Committee assumed its duties in the second half of 1997. Although an assessment of the effectiveness of its work is perhaps premature, there are indications that the *support team* has worked primarily as a *servicing team*; several of the team's duties as envisaged in the Plan of Action have not been carried out because of lack of funds.

Other treaty bodies, notably the Committee on Economic, Social and Cultural Rights, have equally formulated a Plan of Action, but the voluntary contributions for the effective implementation of the Plan have not lived up to expectations. The implementation of Plans of Action is indeed costly – the CRC Committee estimated the resources required from voluntary contributions, on an annual basis, to be approximately US$1.25 million.[10]

Useful as they are, Plans of Action designed to help strengthen the activities of treaty bodies present major problems. First, they rely entirely on voluntary contributions from states parties to the relevant instruments, and if contributions are not pledged or not paid in time, the plan may have to be reduced in scope, shortened in its life span, or simply abandoned. Second, they shift the emphasis from financing of treaty body activities through the regular budget of the UN to financing such activities from

---

[8] UNHCHR, *Revised Plan of Action to Strengthen the Implementation of the Convention on the Rights of the Child*, Geneva, 1996, para. 3.
[9] Ibid., para. 19.   [10] This figure excludes 13 per cent of UN programme support costs.

outside the regular budget. Third, they could open the door to influence-peddling on the part of the major contributors to such plans.

These considerations have prompted a number of states parties to the conventions to voice strong reservations about the desirability and practicality of Plans of Action. They argue, with much justification, that such plans seem to belie the fact that treaty bodies' activities are a core element of the UN human rights programme and one which by any reckoning should be financed through the organisation's regular budget. Furthermore, Plans of Action are seen as a stopgap measure for the long-term problems faced by all treaty bodies. As a Plan's life span is limited and entirely dependent on voluntary contributions, it may be terminated at any time, and jeopardise the successful implementation of the activities of the treaty body concerned. Some treaty bodies, therefore, have been reluctant to engage in any substantive discussion about tailor-made Plans of Action.[11]

A second possibility which might benefit the activities of treaty bodies in the short term would be for states parties to the various UN human rights instruments to consider the financing of so-called junior professional officers (JPOs), who would be specifically assigned to the work of the treaty bodies and based in the Office of the UNHCHR. At present, many states in the Western group finance programmes for JPOs, but they are generally assigned to technical cooperation projects, or to field offices of the UN Development Programme, and then usually for a two-year period.

Treaty bodies could request states parties to assign JPOs to the regular UN Secretariat, but it would be preferable to do so for a three-year period, so as to give them the opportunity to acquire the necessary experience to become a fully operative and effective member of the Secretariat team.[12] The cost-benefit ratio for assignments of a lesser duration is questionable, as past experience has shown that new staff members may take up to twelve months before they are familiar with all the subtleties of the treaty bodies' procedures. JPOs who are assigned to the treaty bodies' work for a sufficiently long duration would assist the Secretariat in reducing the

---

[11] The HRC was a case in point – a preliminary draft for a Plan of Action was prepared but not discussed by the experts for a considerable time. By mid-1999 the Committee agreed to the adoption of the Plan of Action.

[12] By mid-1997, there were indications that between four and six JPOs funded by Western European states might be assigned to the Support Services Branch of the Office of the UNHCHR, which services the activities of treaty bodies.

backlog in processing of periodic reports and individual complaints. Subject to sufficient budgetary resources, JPOs might subsequently be employed on a regular basis. This option, if pursued with vigour, could yield positive results quickly. It is a positive sign that two Scandinavian JPOs were assigned to the treaty bodies' activities in 1998.

Reliance on the work of competent JPOs would be useful, but their services would not constitute a panacea to the problems faced by treaty bodies. Another, third, possibility is to tap into the resources of large academic institutions and, or alternatively, European or North American foundations (notably those in Germany, the United States, the United Kingdom, Canada and Scandinavia). These institutions could finance long-term internships of flexible duration (six to twelve months) with the Secretariat of the treaty bodies. Informal arrangements under which academic institutions have sent promising graduate students in law, political science or international relations for internships of between three and twelve months to the Office of the UNHCHR have existed in the past. On balance, they have worked well and have helped the Secretariat to cope with increasing backlogs in individual complaints.

Some academic institutions and foundations have provided financial assistance to interns working in the Office of the UNHCHR. An informal survey among treaty body experts who are either affiliated with academic institutions or maintain links with large foundations indicates that several such institutions or foundations would consider funding or endowing scholarships for longer-term internships with human rights supervisory bodies. For the UN, this opportunity of assistance to treaty bodies is almost cost-free (only office space and data processing equipment would have to be provided) and it is one that can be activated with minimal lead times.

C. Servicing activities of the supervisory bodies

Experience has shown that all measures taken so far by treaty bodies to cope with growing backlogs both under periodic state reporting and complaints procedures are palliatives which amount to good medicine but not to a cure for the major ills of the system. An innovative approach is required. If the treaty bodies do not radically alter their decision-making mechanisms and streamline their procedures in the near future, they will run up backlogs of such proportions that their activities may well become irrelevant to states parties. It must be added that the regional human rights organisations, and in particular the Council of Europe and the Organization of American States (OAS), are facing similar problems and have either adopted or are in the process of considering radical reform proposals.[13]

Jamaica was the first state party to react to the backlog in the examination of individual complaints under the Optional Protocol to the ICCPR when it denounced the Optional Protocol on 23 October 1997. Its Solicitor-General deplored the fact that the HRC had failed to find ways to examine the numerous capital punishment cases pending against Jamaica under the Optional Protocol more expeditiously.[14]

It is unrealistic to expect a substantial increase in the staffing or financial resources available to treaty bodies in the near or medium-term future. So far, the impact of appeals to this effect by the HRC and the now annual meetings of the chairpersons of the treaty bodies has been negligible. On the contrary, the slogans that all activities have to be serviced 'from within existing resources' and that 'more has to be done with less', carry the day. This has become particularly obvious during the process of restructuring which the UN human rights programme has undergone since 1996. In relation to the servicing of treaty bodies, the following measures should be considered.

1. STREAMLINING AND SIMPLIFICATION OF PROCEDURES

Treaty body procedures should be streamlined and simplified considerably. In the decision-making processes, it would be desirable to abandon the time-honoured but time-consuming practice of deciding by consensus. The time has come to have all decisions of treaty bodies adopted by majority vote, which would save the treaty bodies considerable time. The difficulties experienced by the HRC in adopting consensus decisions on many difficult Optional Protocol cases in recent years demonstrates that

---

[13] Thus, Protocol 11 to the European Convention on Human Rights, which entered into force in November 1998, provides for a merger of the European Commission of Human Rights and the European Court of Human Rights, and envisages a complex 'chamber system' for the Court. Within the OAS, a seminar convened in Washington, DC, in December 1996 discussed reform proposals for the Inter-American Human Rights System – see Document OEA/Ser. G, CP/doc.2828/96 ('Toward a New Vision of the Inter-American Human Rights System').

[14] See UN Doc. CCPR/C/SR.1623, 23 October 1997; *Journal de Genève*, 4 November 1997.

consensus decision-making, while well suited for the *treaty-making process*, is less appropriate for the *treaty interpretation process* of human rights supervisory bodies with a quasi-judicial mandate. Moreover, deciding by consensus is not only time-consuming but actually *lowers* the quality of decisions, as it suffices for one expert to challenge a text otherwise acceptable to all other committee members for there to be another round of discussion. Majority voting generally improves the quality of decisions and, far from eroding their authority, contributes to the enhancement of their standing.[15] Resort to majority voting is a solution that is easy to implement and is actually provided for in the rules of procedure of the bodies concerned.

Some treaty bodies, in particular the HRC and the CERD Committee, are acutely aware of the need to adapt their procedures to a context of shrinking Secretariat resources. In July 1996, the HRC discussed a detailed report from its Working Group on Procedures, which proposed far-reaching changes in the examination of periodic reports and individual communications. It envisages, for example, authorising the Committee's Working Group on Communications to declare complaints inadmissible and that the Committee might join the consideration of the admissibility and the merits of a complaint.[16] The CERD Committee has similarly amended its rules of procedure to allow the joinder of admissibility and merits decisions.[17] Between November 1996 and July 1997, the HRC amended its rules of procedure to reflect many of the proposals of the Working Group on Procedures.[18] The revised rules will enable the HRC to examine individual complaints under the Optional Protocol more expeditiously, such that the average gain of time in the examination of a complaint should be approximately one year. As a rule, the admissibility and the merits of complaints will be considered jointly in the future.

---

[15] On this point see M. Schmidt, 'Individual Human Rights Complaints Procedures Based on UN Treaties and the Need for Reform', 41 *International and Comparative Law Quarterly*, 1992, pp. 645–59, at pp. 657–8.

[16] The report of the Working Group on Procedures was not made public; the Committee's rules of procedure were subsequently amended during the fifty-eighth, fifty-ninth and sixtieth sessions.

[17] Rule 94, para. 7, reads: 'The Committee may, in appropriate cases and with the consent of the parties concerned, decide to deal jointly with the question of admissibility and the merits of a communication.' See Annual Report of the CERD Commitee for 1994, UN Doc. A/48/18, Annex V, pp. 138–9.

[18] The amended Rules of Procedure are reproduced in UN Doc. CCPR/C/3/Rev. 5, 11 August 1997. The changes concern Rules 91 to 97.

Parallel to the streamlining of treaty body procedures, the Secretariat can and should simplify the handling of periodic reports and individual communications. Treaty bodies should agree to the rule that communications under individual complaints procedures must be submitted in one of the official languages of the UN or, preferably, in the Secretariat working languages of English, French or Spanish. The current practice which allows for the submission of complaints in all languages is impractical and extremely resource-intensive. In the past, this has led to situations in which complaints submitted in a language other than a Secretariat working language were left unattended for months and ultimately filed away.[19] Until now, the treaty bodies have not required complaints to be submitted in one of the Secretariat working languages. In 1995, the HRC expressed concern at the long-known fact that an increasing number of cases are submitted in languages other than the Secretariat's working languages, and at the consequent delay in the examination of such complaints.[20]

With the reduction of translation services within the UN, the handling of complaints in non-UN languages becomes increasingly problematic. For at least one official UN language, Russian, the backlog that has built up over the years has reached alarming proportions, especially after the accession of most of the former Soviet republics to the existing human rights instruments. Financial implications notwithstanding, a lawyer proficient in Russian must be added to the Secretariat.

In respect of periodic reporting procedures, the current practice of preparation of country profiles and comparative analyses is time-consuming and labour-intensive. In their current format, their benefit to experts is limited and does not outweigh the strain placed on scarce resources. It is submitted here that alternative reports, prepared by NGOs and submitted to treaty bodies as a counterweight to a state's official periodic report, are of more use to experts. Alternatively, one might devise an altogether new format for comprehensive country profiles and analyses, which would rely on country data collected by other UN departments and specialised agencies, and which could be prepared by the Research and Right to Development Branch of the Office of the UNHCHR.

---

[19] Thus the HRC expressed concern over the perceived Secretariat practice of informing prospective complainants that they had to submit their cases in one of the Secretariat working languages.

[20] Annual Report of HRC for 1995, UN Doc. A/50/40, vol. I, para. 491.

2. TOWARDS BETTER USE OF THE MEETING TIME
OF TREATY BODIES

Treaty body experts have, within the time available to them during meetings, been making considerable efforts to apply their legal experience and skills to the drafting and fine-tuning of decisions under the complaints procedures, to the formulation of compromise proposals, of general comments and of concluding observations on periodic state reports. Several committees now regularly form small 'drafting groups' during their sessions. This is a positive development which, though admittedly placing an added burden on the experts, provides undeniable benefits. Many decisions and documents which would have been referred to subsequent committee sessions in previous years have been adopted in a more timely fashion on the basis of such 'drafting group' texts.

An appeal can be made to treaty bodies to exercise more discipline in their deliberations. At present, there is still too much duplication in questions addressed by experts to states parties during the examination of periodic reports, as well as unnecessarily prolonged debates over comparatively small procedural details in the examination of individual complaints.[21] If time is a scarce commodity for treaty bodies, they must use it in the most rational manner possible. On the other hand, it makes little sense to confine the examination of a report to one meeting or even parts thereof, or to schedule several reports per day, as has been done by the CERD Committee on past occasions. A meaningful exchange of views between treaty body experts and state party representatives would simply become impossible in such a situation.

Several proposals for a more effective use of the treaty bodies' time have been formulated recently. Buergenthal suggests that in order to increase the number of complaints decided under the Optional Protocol to the ICCPR, the HRC should set up chambers consisting of seven or nine members, which would be allowed to make final decisions on the merits of complaints. In the absence of a formal amendment to the Optional Protocol, the committee plenary would retain formal authority to endorse the decisions of the chambers.[22] Such proposals deserve support, but for the

---

[21] For periodic reports, this point is made by T. Buergenthal, 'The Human Rights Committee', in *The United Nations and Human Rights: A Critical Appraisal* (ed. P. Alston), 2nd edn, Oxford, 1999.

[22] Ibid.

Secretariat, they are not without their problems. If two committee chambers decide on the merits of complaints, this would imply that, at least in theory, the Secretariat would be required to prepare double the number of case files or drafts. At the very least, the Secretariat would require databases with powerful search engines, and ultimately an increase in staff would be necessary.

If each of the chambers requires simultaneous interpretation and the translation of all documents in all or several working languages, matters become more complicated. Also, given the costs of interpretation and translation services in the UN system,[23] a chamber system would require a sizeable increase in budgetary appropriations. Given the UN's precarious financial situation, a chamber system may therefore be envisaged only if at least one chamber works without simultaneous interpretation facilities and without translation of most of its documents. Whether this is acceptable to the experts concerned is an open question.

Another possibility for treaty bodies to use their time more effectively would be to move towards some form of discretionary jurisdiction, insofar as examination of complaints under the individual complaints procedures is concerned. It has become evident that as these procedures have gradually become better known, the treaty bodies concerned have been running up increasing backlogs in the handling of complaints. The life span of complaints under the Optional Protocol to the ICCPR now averages between three and four years. Assume, for a moment, that large and populous states parties to the Optional Protocol encourage their citizens to have recourse to the procedure before the HRC. The HRC would be flooded with complaints and could not be expected to do justice to each and every individual complaint. In such circumstances it should take the bold step of accepting for consideration only those cases which raise serious issues of interpretation of the ICCPR (or other relevant instrument), or cases which lend themselves to elucidating the scope of the substantive provisions of the ICCPR. This proposal is formulated forcefully by Professor Steiner in chapter two of this volume. Admittedly, his proposal would require an amendment to the Optional Protocol, but it deserves serious discussion and support.

Finally, the inter-sessional periods (that is, the time between sessions of treaty bodies) should be used more effectively than they have been until

---

[23] It is estimated, for example, that the translation and editing of a single page of a document into all official UN languages costs approximately US$1,100.

now. For example, follow-up to decisions adopted under individual complaints procedures and to concluding observations on periodic reports should be undertaken. In respect of the former, the inter-sessional activities of a former Special Rapporteur for Follow-Up on Views of the HRC illustrate what can be done between sessions.[24]

Although treaty bodies have historically been hesitant about delegating more authority to the Secretariat than is required by the routine of daily activities, it is ultimately unavoidable that they agree to do so. Delegation of authority should extend to the adoption of routine decisions by the Secretariat, especially for simple procedural issues or cases which fall clearly outside the remit of the treaty body concerned. One could even envisage that ultimately, routine inadmissibility decisions are made by the Secretariat, after consultation with the treaty bodies concerned. While creating additional work for the Secretariat, this would take pressure off the agenda of treaty body plenary sessions.

3. RELIANCE ON MODERN INFORMATION TECHNOLOGY

Better use of existing information technology may help the Secretariat to perform its duties more effectively. If all available technological possibilities were to be used, the need for additional staff resources could be reduced significantly. If the existing databases are improved or updated and new ones created, this would make the day-to-day handling of individual complaints and periodic reports by the Secretariat far more efficient. The development of electronic information systems – recommended by the Commission on Human Rights as early as 1989 – was not a priority for the Office of the UNHCHR until recently.[25] It was not until 10 December 1996 that the High Commissioner's website was launched,[26] but since then it has been upgraded and expanded on a continuous basis and become a valuable source of information for treaty bodies.

---

[24] On the activities of the Special Rapporteur for Follow-Up on Views, see M. Schmidt, 'Portée et suivi des constatations du Comité des droits de l'homme de l'ONU', in *La protection des droits de l'homme par le Comité des droits de l'homme des Nations Unies*, Actes du colloque de Montpellier, 6–7 March 1995, pp. 157–69. The Committee's Annual Reports for 1996 (UN Doc. A/51/40, vol. I), 1997 (UN Doc. A/52/40, vol. I) and 1998 (UN Doc. A53/40, vol. I) contain a separate chapter on follow-up activities.

[25] This point was made forcefully by the chairpersons of the UN treaty bodies during their seventh meeting in September 1996 – see UN Doc. A/51/482, 10 October 1996, para. 37.

[26] The site address is: http://www.unhchr.ch.

A full text database for CRC was developed by the UN Children's Fund (UNICEF) in collaboration with the Office of the UNHCHR.[27] The High Commissioner has indicated that full text databases for the other treaty bodies would be developed as quickly as possible. In October 1997, information technology consultants began to design a comprehensive database and electronic information retrieval system for the individual complaints procedures implemented by three treaty bodies. Apart from enabling the Secretariat to research issues quickly, the availability of such a database (including possibly comparative jurisprudence in the field of civil and political rights or racial discrimination) would greatly benefit the experts during their meetings. A prototype of this database is being tested; the database is now operative but is thus far accessible only within the Office of the UNHCHR.

Lastly, the UN Secretariat and treaty bodies should rely more on human rights databases developed for the World Wide Web, notably by the human rights programmes and libraries of the University of Minnesota, University of Cincinnati, Yale Law School, etc., whose administrators regularly meet in the context of the so-called 'DIANA' project.[28] One cannot but endorse the recent recommendation of chairpersons of the UN human rights treaty bodies that the Office of the UNHCHR should make particular efforts to cooperate with the development of these academic databases.[29]

4. IMPROVING PROFESSIONAL FLEXIBILITY IN THE SECRETARIAT

Finally, there should be a move towards much more flexibility *within* the Secretariat. Experience with the servicing of treaty bodies in recent years suggests that the current hyper-specialisation of Secretariat staff may lead to bottlenecks in the servicing of supervisory procedures. If staff are

---

[27] See UNHCHR, *supra*, note 8, para. 24.

[28] For a general overview of DIANA, see N. Finke et al., 'DIANA: A Human Rights Database', 16 *Human Rights Quarterly*, 1994, pp. 753–6; remarks by H. Koh, American Society of International Law, Proceedings of the eighty-ninth Annual Meeting, 5–8 April 1995, pp. 13–14. Apart from DIANA, the European Coordination Committee on Human Rights Documentation also regularly discusses human rights information technology issues.

[29] UN Doc. A/51/482, para. 37; see also the updated report by Philip Alston, 'Final Report on Enhancing the Long-term Effectiveness of the United Nations Human Rights Treaty System', UN Doc. E/CN.4/1997/74, 7 March 1997, paras. 60–6, also discussed in C. Scott, chapter 19, above.

responsible *only* for individual complaints or *only* for periodic reports, the ensuing specialisation creates more difficulties than it *a priori* solves. In the event of staff movements, suitable replacements are difficult to find, and treaty body activities may be held in abeyance because qualified staff are unavailable.

Under the new structure of the Office of UNHCHR, approved in 1996, staff are required to be more flexible for assignments within sections of the Office. Thus, it is envisaged that staff members of the two treaty implementation teams in the Office's Support Services Branch have responsibility for all treaty body activities: reports, complaints, and general comments. The job descriptions for professional posts have been redesigned to reflect the need for more professional versatility and flexibility. It makes eminent sense to have staff members responsible for individual complaints procedures, who have acquired particular expertise on particular countries, contribute to the drafting of concluding observations on periodic reports of these countries.

The move towards a better integrated servicing of supervisory procedures deserves full support. It should be incremental, so that the 'institutional memory' of the procedures can be disseminated evenly throughout the system. The lead times for making integrated teams fully operative are, however, longer than expected: the restructuring of the Office of UNHCHR has taken much longer than even its detractors had prophesied. Some treaty bodies have also expressed concern about the new structure, but this relates more to the absence of consultation of treaty bodies during the restructuring process. The seventh meeting of the chairpersons of UN treaty bodies in September 1996 did, however, rightly point out that if the restructuring process leads to the elimination of the posts of committee secretaries, this would be 'inefficient, counter-productive and ultimately unworkable'.[30] Without the function of committee secretaries who, in many ways, become the institutional memory of the treaty bodies over time, the work of the treaty bodies would face considerable disruptions.

D. The outlook for the future

In the years 1994–1998, there have been major reorientations within the UN human rights programme. The first UN High Commissioner for

---

[30] See UN Doc. A/51/482, paras. 40–2.

Human Rights, Mr Ayala Lasso, placed major emphasis on the development of technical cooperation programmes, of preventive mechanisms and on human rights field presence, either in the form of field operations or field offices. With this recent emphasis on field activities, the UN human rights programme has, in the first High Commissioner's own words, 'gained a new dimension, one which will be an important part of its future'.[31]

It is a fact that this reorientation of priorities was effected 'from within existing resources', and that the activities of supervisory bodies suffered as a result, since Secretariat resources have been taken away from the treaty bodies in recent years. With some degree of simplification, it can be said that they have been reallocated to technical cooperation and field activities. There is little reason for treaty bodies to expect an improvement of this situation in the short term. The blame for this situation cannot be placed only at the door of the current High Commissioner, Ms Mary Robinson. In most respects, she merely seeks to implement the 1993 Vienna Declaration and Programme of Action. Furthermore, it is undeniable that human rights field presence is both necessary and desirable.

The restructuring of the Office of UNHCHR, completed in 1998, should result in the more effective delivery of programmes, which should in principle also benefit the activities of the UN treaty bodies, though on longer lead times than had been anticipated. It is undeniable that more emphasis will have to be placed in the future on a more effective *management* of the Office. A combination of imaginative and charismatic leadership and effective management might not be easy to achieve in a highly politicised environment, but it would incite those working towards the implementation of human rights supervisory procedures to face new challenges with renewed vigour and determination. The management adage coined by Warren Bennis, that 'managers do things right; leaders do the right thing', is not out of context here.[32]

From a longer-term perspective, increased cooperation between the UN supervisory bodies and their regional counterparts is another *desideratum*.

---

[31] See the High Commissioner's 1996 Report to the General Assembly, UN Doc. A/51/36, 18 October 1996, chapter IV, para. 51.

[32] During the restructuring of the Office of the UNHCHR in 1996–1997, the management consulting firm hired to coordinate and lead the restructuring process emphasised the need to introduce sounder management practices. For an illustrative example of the management literature, see W. Bennis and B. Nanus, *Leaders – The Strategies for Taking Charge*, New York, 1985.

The first High Commissioner, Mr Ayala Lasso, indicated that he was anxious to encourage horizontal cooperation between the treaty bodies and parallel regional bodies, for example, those of the Council of Europe.[33] At the Secretariat level, regular exchanges of professional staff members between the UN and regional organisations would help both parties to familiarise themselves with the other's procedures. They may further prompt or catalyse improvements in procedures and programmes on either side, on the basis of the experiences gained in a different institutional environment. Such cross-over secondments are procedurally possible and could be effected 'from within existing resources'.

Finally, one does well not to forget the following dilemma: if the Secretariat were to operate with maximum efficiency in the servicing of all of the treaty bodies' activities, the treaty bodies would not be in a position to examine, within the meeting time allotted to them, all the periodic reports and individual communications presented to them. The same situation would obtain if all states always submitted their periodic reports within the imparted deadlines, which is far from being the case.[34] Over time, the backlog of reports would simply assume unmanageable proportions.

A reduction of overlapping reporting requirements could be achieved if the reporting guidelines of the treaty bodies were harmonised and consolidated, though because of the different mandates of the bodies concerned, harmonisation can only go so far. Ultimately, consolidation would not address the far broader problem of duplication, which is inherent in the structure of the UN human rights protection system itself. Over time, the UN has adopted increasingly specialised and narrowly focused instruments, which by and large supplement the two Covenants of 1966 and deal in more detail with issues already covered by the Covenants.[35]

Some experts have advocated that for states parties to more than one UN human rights convention, treaty bodies might replace the current plurality of reports by one comprehensive, 'global' report which would enable at

---

[33] See UN Doc. CERD/C/SR.1151, 15 March 1996, at para. 63.

[34] As of 1 December 1998 there were 1,160 overdue reports to the six treaty bodies, as Table 2 in Chapter 1 of this volume illustrates. The trend shows no sign of abating as illustrated by the Human Rights Committee's observation in July 1999 that two-thirds of states parties to the ICCPR had not submitted their reports in time, and that thirty-seven of those states were five or more years overdue in submitting reports. UN Press Release HR/CT/99/26, 29 July 1999, p. 1.

[35] This point is rightly made by E. Tistounet in 'Reporting Procedures and Related Issues', 61/62 *Nordic Journal of International Law*, 1994, pp. 233–8, at p. 235.

least those states to deal with all their reporting obligations jointly.[36] Yet, during the last meetings of the treaty body chairpersons, the issue of 'global reports' was not discussed in any meaningful detail, and the participants focused on revision of the treaty bodies' methods of work instead. Nonetheless, the submission of 'global reports' by states parties to the various instruments deserves serious consideration and encouragement. It would reduce both the recurrent duplication in reporting requirements and enable the Secretariat to streamline its servicing of the examination of periodic reports.

'Great necessities call forth great leaders.' This old saying may well apply to the UN human rights programme. In the current financial situation of the UN, it will require imaginative and far-sighted leadership if all mandated activities are to be serviced effectively in a context of stagnant or diminishing resources. To this end, the cooperation and the commitment of all concerned – states parties to the relevant treaties, concerned citizens, non-governmental organisations, the UN Secretariat and UN treaty and supervisory bodies – will be required.

---

[36] Cf. F. Pocar, 'Codification of Human Rights Law by the United Nations', in *Festschrift in Honor of Judge Manfred Lachs*, The Hague, 1995, pp. 139–58, at p. 158.

E

LOOKING TO THE FUTURE

23

BEYOND 'THEM' AND 'US': PUTTING TREATY BODY REFORM INTO PERSPECTIVE

PHILIP ALSTON*

The contributors to this volume have adopted approaches which are essentially empirical and critical. They are empirical in that most of the authors have been actively involved in the work of the treaty bodies, either as members of the treaty bodies, non-governmental organisation (NGO) participants, Secretariat members, or close observers. While there is a great deal of work that needs to be done from both theoretical and conceptual perspectives to explain the reasons for the successes and failures of the system,[1] this is not the task the contributors to this volume have set themselves. Their approaches are critical in the sense that the main focus is on the demonstrated shortcomings and failures of the monitoring activities of the expert, independent committees established to monitor government compliance with obligations voluntarily accepted under each of the six principal UN human rights treaties.

A. Considering alternative approaches

The volume as a whole covers the gamut of problems and challenges, ranging from such petty but demoralising restrictions as the removal of pencils

---

* I am grateful to James Crawford for his very helpful comments on an earlier draft.

[1] For all the sophistication and volume of the analyses that have been devoted to the work of the United Nations in the human rights field, there is a surprising paucity of analyses of the type that have been undertaken either in relation to international law in general or to international environmental law in particular. See for example B. Kingsbury, 'The Concept of Competing Conceptions of International Law', 19 *Michigan Journal of International Law*, 1998, p. 345, and other contributions to the same symposium, ibid., pp. 303–579; and E. Brown Weiss and H. Jacobson (eds.), *Engaging Countries: Strengthening Compliance with International Environmental Accords*, Cambridge, Mass., 1998.

and paper from the meeting rooms in Geneva (in the wake of the financial crisis precipitated by the United States withholding of its assessed dues to the UN), through artificial Secretariat-enforced delays in making language translations of documents available, to much larger issues which rightly preoccupy most of the contributors. These larger issues include the wholly inadequate funding of the system, the reluctance of most governments to increase the effectiveness of the procedures, the use of reservations in an effort to ensure the domestic marginality of the treaties, the lack of expertise and the questionable independence of some committee members, and the inadequate follow-up which occurs in relation to many of the outcomes produced by the treaty bodies, whether in the form of 'concluding observations' on country reports or 'final views' on individual complaints. There is ample room for criticism and it is difficult to disagree with Elizabeth Evatt's assessment that '[a]ny independent observer would conclude that the treaty body system needs a complete overhaul'.[2]

For those who are looking for a diagnosis of the system as it is, and for prescriptions as to how it might be improved, the foregoing chapters provide a rich resource. The purpose of the present chapter is not to replicate those analyses, nor to summarise them. The problems they address are too diverse for a synthesis of the type which purports to discern an emerging consensus from a multiplicity of diagnoses.

Nevertheless, there appears to be a shared belief on the part of the contributors to the volume that the basic assumptions upon which the treaty body system is based are valid. In particular, the assumption of the desirability of universal participation in the system is not contested by any of them. Indeed, this assumption is now a reality, given that there is no state in the world which is not a party to at least one of the six treaties and that the vast majority of states are a party to many of them. There are some commentators, however, who have questioned the validity of this assumption. The most persistent critic in this respect has been Anne Bayefsky. Since her critique is typical of an approach that is not represented in the present volume it seems appropriate to compare the assumptions broadly shared by the contributors to this volume with her diagnoses and prescriptions. In particular, her work provides an important point of comparison since it has been more systematic and comprehensive, and has continued over a longer period of time, than any other comparable scholarly work on the subject.

---

[2] E. Evatt, chapter 21 *supra*.

Over the past five years Bayefsky has published several detailed critiques of the system. The first was published in 1994 in the wake of the Vienna World Conference on Human Rights and was part of a major initiative by the American Society of International Law to identify a human rights agenda for the next century.[3] The second, published in 1996, was a detailed report prepared for the Committee on International Human Rights Law and Practice of the International Law Association.[4] Another, published in 1998, consisted of a paper presented at the previous year's Annual Conference of the American Society of International Law.[5]

The analysis which follows will focus first on the diagnosis offered by Bayefsky and secondly on her prescriptions, which emphasise, among other things, the unworkability of a treaty system which counts 'non-democratic' states among its participants. In brief, my contention is that her criticism of the system is based on highly unrepresentative examples and does not provide an accurate or balanced picture and that her diagnosis is based on a fundamental misunderstanding of the nature and objectives of the system. Those problems appear to result from a greatly oversimplified contrast between 'us' (the liberal democratic states) and 'them' (the 'extreme delinquents' who have 'no democratic aspirations'),[6] which seems to be the golden thread that runs through all of the analyses.

B. The perceived shortcomings of the system

Bayefsky begins her most recent analysis by suggesting that those who question the optimism of international lawyers in relation to the work of the treaty bodies are 'frequently branded as disloyal or cynical'.[7] Perhaps there have been such responses, although I am unaware of them. In any event,

---

[3] A. Bayefsky, 'Making the Human Rights Treaties Work', in *Human Rights: An Agenda for the Next Century* (eds. L. Henkin and J. L. Hargrove) Washington DC, 1994, pp. 229–95 (hereinafter referred to as 'Bayefsky (1994)').

[4] A. Bayefsky, 'Report on the UN Human Rights Treaties: Facing the Implementation Crisis', contained in Committee on International Human Rights Law and Practice, First Report of the Committee (International Law Association, Helsinki Conference (1996)) (hereinafter referred to as 'Bayefsky (1996)').

[5] 'Remarks by Anne F. Bayefsky', Panel discussion entitled: 'The UN Human Rights Regime: Is it Effective?', 91 *Proceedings of the Annual Meeting of the American Society of International Law 1997*, Washington DC, 1998, p. 460, at pp. 466–72 (hereinafter referred to as 'Bayefsky (1998)').

[6] Ibid., p. 472.   [7] Ibid., p. 466.

the contributions to this volume, written though they are by a group which is essentially supportive of what the present system seeks to achieve, are, as already noted, almost uniformly critical of various aspects of the current functioning of the system.

Bayefsky's analysis is based upon the identification of seven 'unfortunate details' or shortcomings of the system. The first three focus on: (i) non-reporting and late reporting by states; (ii) the existence of a large backlog of reports awaiting examination by the treaty bodies; and (iii) the ineffectual working methods used by the treaty bodies. Most commentators are in agreement that these present real problems, and that there is much room for improvement. The shortcomings of existing practices and possible means by which to remedy them have been detailed in the three reports I prepared for the UN General Assembly as an 'independent expert',[8] in the various reports adopted in recent years by the Meetings of the Chairpersons of the Human Rights Treaty Bodies,[9] as well as in the analyses contained in the present volume. In short, none of these shortcomings is disputed by most observers of the system, even though their prescriptions vary to a degree.

The remaining four issues identified by Bayefsky also pertain to matters in relation to which most commentators would be in agreement. They concern: (iv) publicity and accessibility; (v) the fact-finding capacities of the system; (vi) the weakness of complaints systems; and (vii) the inadequacy of measures to follow up on the work of the treaty bodies. In my view, however, her analysis of most of these matters is based on a selection of one-sided and unrepresentative examples which, rather than providing an accurate reflection of the overall situation, paints an unduly bleak picture. This in turn makes the radical solutions proposed seem both more justifiable and more politically acceptable than they are. Underlying both the critique and the solutions is a highly debateable set of assumptions as to the functions and objectives of the treaty system and its monitoring

---

[8] 'Long-term Approaches to Enhancing the Effectiveness of United Nations Human Rights Treaty Bodies: Expert Study Prepared by Mr Philip Alston', UN Doc. A/44/668 (1989); 'Interim Report on Updated Study by Mr Philip Alston', UN Doc. A/CONF.157/PC/62/ Add.11/Rev.1 (22 April 1993); and 'Final Report on Enhancing the Long-Term Effectiveness of the United Nations Human Rights Treaty System', UN Doc. E/CN.4/1997/74 (7 March 1997).

[9] For the most recent reports see UN Docs. A/53/432 (1998) [tenth session]; A/53/125 (1998) [ninth session]; A/52/507 (1997) [eighth session]; and A/51/482 (1996) [seventh session].

apparatus. I shall deal in turn with each of the three matters that affect the reporting system, leaving aside point (vi), which is adequately dealt with in chapter 2 of this volume.[10]

1. PUBLICITY AND ACCESSIBILITY

The fourth shortcoming of the work of the treaty bodies, according to Bayefsky, is that it is conducted in isolation from the media and NGOs. She identifies four constituencies that she considers especially important in this context, all of which she portrays as being uninvolved or marginalised.

> Normally only a handful of individuals, if any, from the country concerned observe the dialogue on the country report. National news media rarely attend. One or two representatives of international nongovernmental organizations (NGOs) are usually present. International news media are almost never there.[11]

The first two groups are nationals from the reporting state and international NGOs. In relation to the first group, she cites the example of the Canadian report considered by the Committee of the Convention on the Elimination of Discrimination against Women (CEDAW) in 1997. 'National NGOs learned of the date of the consideration of the Canadian report by the Committee only weeks in advance, and not one attended.'[12] But this is rather unusual by the standards of most of the treaty bodies. When Canadian reports were presented to the Committee supervising the International Covenant on Economic, Social and Cultural Rights (ICESCR) in both 1993 and 1998, there was standing room only in the conference room. A large number of national NGOs participated in the process and attended the dialogue between the Government and the Committee, and many hundreds of pages of information (indeed, thousands of pages in 1998) were submitted to the Committee by post, email, fax and in person. The reports dealing with Hong Kong, submitted to the Human Rights Committee by the United Kingdom on various occasions in the late 1980s and 1990s, were also observed by a very large number of NGO representatives and other

---

[10] See H. Steiner, chapter 2, *supra*. In essence, Bayefsky's critique focuses on her view that existing petitions systems are an inadequate alternative to faulty reporting systems because of their low rate of acceptance by states, the small number of complaints lodged, the slow handling of complaints, and the minimal contribution made by the committees in cases involving complexity and legal subtlety. See Bayefsky (1998), p. 469.

[11] Ibid., p. 467.   [12] Ibid., p. 468.

observers,[13] and many other such examples could be cited. Even if these could be considered to be exceptional cases, it is clear that the average is much closer to the middle than to the single extreme case cited by Bayefsky.

Nor is there any hard and fast rule according to which only the reports of developed countries attract significant NGO attention. In her 1996 report Bayefsky noted that '[w]hile dozens of people may attend the reports of the United States, the United Kingdom or Japan, there is often a sole representative of Amnesty International or one or two other persons from international NGOs watching the reports of developing countries'.[14] Again, to take the case of the ICESCR Committee, reports from states as diverse as the Dominican Republic, Nigeria, Hong Kong, Israel and Sri Lanka have all drawn large numbers of both national observers and international NGOs.

It is important in any event not to accept what might be termed a 'conference-room head count' as the sole criterion for assessing the degree of interest and participation in the work of these committees. One of the principal problems confronted by the members of most committees today is how to cope with an ever-expanding volume of information submitted by an increasingly diverse set of actors at both the national and international levels. This raises many questions: how to ensure the transparency of the process; how to evaluate the credibility of the information; how to do justice to the enormous efforts made by many NGOs; how to communicate with these often distant partners; how to enable governments to have sufficient notice of the critiques in order to be able to respond to them; and how to structure the overall process so as to profit from these inputs without allowing them to dominate the agenda or control the dialogue as a whole? One thing is clear, however. This overwhelming trend is not consistent with the suggestion that the monitoring process is isolated from civil society.

The other two constituencies which are said to be relatively uninvolved in the process are the national and international media. Bayefsky cites the example of the examination of the US report to the Human Rights Committee in 1995, an event which she notes 'went unreported, except by the *Washington Post . . .*'.[15] Leaving aside the notorious lack of interest by the US media in news of this type, the example is not at all representative of the reaction of national news media. The involvement of a wide range of Irish NGO representatives in the process involving the Human Rights

---

[13] These are described in some detail in this volume by A. Byrnes, chapter 13, *supra*.
[14] Bayefsky (1996), p. 8. [15] Bayefsky (1998), p. 467.

Committee's 1993 examination of that country's report was accompanied by considerable media interest within the country, and resulted in an *Irish Times* correspondent going to Geneva.[16] Reports by Canada to the ICESCR Committee drew heavy media coverage in both 1993 and 1998. The Canadian media were represented in Geneva and newspaper, television and radio coverage was extensive. A report by the United Kingdom to the same Committee in 1998 resulted in a front page story in *The Guardian* and a range of other media stories. Nor is media coverage limited to the developed countries. Assuming even a moderately free media, UN treaty bodies often attract what might even be considered to be disproportionately high media attention in many developing countries. The media in Nigeria, the Dominican Republic, Panama, Hong Kong and elsewhere have devoted very extensive coverage to the activities of the ICESCR Committee in relation to national reports.[17]

It is true, of course, that the work of the treaty bodies rarely provides grist for the mills of the British Broadcasting Corporation's *BBC World*, Cable News Network (CNN), and their like in other languages. Nor can it be said that the media coverage attracted by most treaty bodies in most cases is as strong as it should be. But the situation is not at all accurately portrayed by saying that '[n]ational news media rarely attend [and] . . . international news media are almost never there'.[18]

More importantly, such statements are of limited value since they proceed on the basis of the wrong criteria. For the most part, for reasons of cost, the media rarely seek to provide direct coverage of events that extend over the course of several days and which, by their very nature, have few defining, dramatic, especially photogenic or telegenic, moments. Such events are inevitably covered at arm's length, through reliance upon UN press releases or interviews outside the conference room, or on the basis of press conferences by NGO representatives or by the chairperson of the relevant committee. For example, Madame Christine Chanet, as Chairperson of the Human Rights Committee in 1997–1998, succeeded in

[16] This dimension is chronicled in some detail in M. O'Flaherty and L. Heffernan, *International Covenant on Civil and Political Rights: International Human Rights Law in Ireland*, Dublin, 1995, pp. 69–82.
[17] The Department of Public Information, at the UN Office in Geneva, collects newspaper clippings from around the world and makes them available from time to time to the treaty body concerned.
[18] Bayefsky (1998), p. 467.

significantly raising the media profile of that committee. Nor is media coverage the sole test against which to measure the impact of the treaty bodies. The US case mentioned by Bayefsky is revealing in that respect. It drew great interest from human rights and other interest groups around the USA,[19] and attracted scholarly attention as far afield as India.[20] In this respect it gave substance to the complaint sometimes voiced, at least in private, by US diplomats to the effect that their participation in such monitoring exercises comes at a higher price than that of most other countries because of the particular vigilance of the organs of civil society in their country.

A reaction by the government concerned is, in most respects, the most desirable outcome of the relevant procedures, but such responses are particularly hard to track and the causal link is usually impossible to demonstrate. Two illustrations must suffice. The first concerns the issue of fees for tertiary education in the canton of Zürich, Switzerland, an issue which arose in the context of the work of the ICESCR Committee. On the basis of detailed information presented to it, and in anticipation of its examination of the report of Switzerland, the ICESCR Committee wrote a letter to the Swiss Government in 1997 outlining some considerations which it believed should be taken into account in the ongoing consideration of budget policy options in relation to university fees. This was a classic exchange of letters – *notes verbales* in the arcane language of diplomacy – which journalists could not have seen and were unlikely to discover. Nevertheless, the exchange became an important part of the public debate and the Committee's letter was widely publicised in the Swiss news media.

The second example comes from an Australian newspaper report of March 1999 which began:

> The Government filled the position of Aboriginal Social Justice Commissioner after a 14-month delay – on the eve of a United Nations committee hearing into Australia's recent record on Aboriginal rights. The Committee of the Convention on the Elimination of Racial Discrimination (CERD) issued an 'early warning' notice to Australia in August [1998] ... [The] move will take some heat off the Government in Geneva next week, when it will face detailed questioning from the UN committee.[21]

---

[19] See generally *supra* S. Grant, chapter 14.

[20] U. Baxi, '"A Work in Progress": The United States Report to the United Nations Human Rights Committee', 36 *Indian Journal of International Law*, 1996, pp. 34–53.

[21] M. Kingston, 'Aboriginal Justice Job Filled after UN Warning', *Sydney Morning Herald*, 4 March 1999, http://www.smh.com.au/news/9903/04/text/national1.html.

In such a context the formal proceedings in Geneva may be of more symbolic value. They act as a catalyst to action taken far from any UN committee room. For that reason, counting the number of media or NGO representatives sitting in the conference room does not capture the impact of the exercise. Nor would one expect any government to acknowledge that it had taken any initiative with a view to heading off criticism from the CERD Committee. The real impact of the work can only emerge from a more nuanced and in-depth analysis.

2. THE FACT-FINDING CAPACITIES OF THE SYSTEM

Bayefsky's fifth criticism focuses on the fact that 'the treaty bodies do not engage in fact-finding'.[22] Because she considers neither NGOs nor the experts themselves to be entirely reliable, this implies that the information base is flawed and that political considerations can subvert the process. In order to overcome these difficulties she proposes the following solutions:

> The treaty bodies should visit states parties in order to engage in fact-finding prior to the scheduled consideration of state reports. Fact-finding for every state party should be carried out on a routine, non-discriminatory basis. It would not be necessary for all members of the treaty bodies to visit every state.
> The treaty bodies should visit state parties which have not reported for an unreasonable length of time, in order to engage in fact-finding and facilitate the production of a report or solicit alternative sources of information.
> The General Assembly should ensure that the treaty bodies have sufficient resources and administrative support to engage in fact-finding.[23]

She notes further that NGOs 'are not without their political agendas', and that the information submitted 'is often highly selective'.[24] But this goes to the very nature of NGOs. They are political organisations in the sense that the heart-felt advocacy of specific policies is their very *raison d'être*. To expect an NGO lobbying, for example, in favour of greater per capita expenditure on prisons, or on child vaccinations, to submit a comprehensive picture of all the relevant budgetary considerations as well as the counter-arguments against their own positions would be entirely unrealistic – though they can be expected to be honest and not to attempt to mislead by suppressing relevant information.

---

[22] Bayefsky (1998), p. 468.   [23] Bayefsky (1996), pp. 15–16.   [24] Bayefsky (1998), p. 468.

In any case the treaty bodies are protected in various ways from being misled. First, NGOs cover a very broad spectrum of political views and a submission by one is very often juxtaposed against a submission by another which provides a significantly different perspective or interpretation. Second, the weight to be accorded to information provided by a given NGO inevitably reflects the track record – in terms of reliability, accuracy and balance – the NGO has achieved in the past, thus providing NGOs with an incentive to meet basic standards of probity. Third, it is highly likely that the government in question will provide a detailed refutation of any information which may be wrong or unbalanced. Fourth, the role of Committee members is precisely to exercise their informed judgment, on the basis of a multiplicity of sources, as to which allegations appear to be well-founded and which do not.

Nevertheless, Bayefsky believes that the treaty bodies have often 'been unduly driven by such limited [NGO] contributions'.[25] It is true that most of the treaty bodies now take extensive account of information provided by NGO sources and there may have been cases in which undue weight has been accorded to such information, although Bayefsky does not provide any examples. But such occasional errors must be placed in perspective. All available official sources of information are used, as are media reports and any other credible sources. NGO information is thus taken into a balance and weighed against those other sources. It is sometimes found wanting, but this is as it should be. The process of information gathering can be greatly improved, but it can never be rendered 'scientific' in any full sense,[26] and, having regard to resource constraints, the exclusion or downgrading of NGO information would certainly not improve the process. Indeed, 'fact-finding', by which Bayefsky seems to mean *in situ* missions to the country concerned, is usually only useful if it takes full account of information provided by NGO sources, both within and outside the country concerned.

A second argument for abandoning government reports and relying instead upon *in situ* fact-finding missions is that 'treaty body members

---

[25] Ibid.

[26] See, for example, the extensive writings of Majone on the interplay between science and politics, even in areas such as the setting of health, safety and environmental standards. He notes that such standard-setting exercises are 'in reality a microcosm in which conflicting epistemologies, regulatory philosophies, national traditions, social values and professional attitudes are faithfully reflected'. G. Majone, 'Science and Trans-Science in Standard Setting', 9 *Science, Technology and Human Values*, 1984, p. 15.

often are nominated by governments concerned to ensure state representation in the guise of independent experts', a practice which is said to provide
'opportunities for straying from the legal framework for implementation'.[27]
This may well be true, but it is unclear how fact-finding missions conducted at considerable expense by those very same members will obviate
the problem. The only example given concerns the treatment of Israel, by
both the CERD and the ICESCR Committees, 'under conditions that have
not been applied to any other state party'.[28] No details are provided in
relation to the CERD Committee's alleged unfair treatment, but in relation
to the ICESCR, the Committee is said to have permitted NGO oral criticism of Israel at two sessions in 1996 'on non-Covenant subjects such as the
implementation of the Oslo agreements, in the absence of having scheduled
a dialogue with the state party or the consideration of a state report'.[29]
Leaving aside the questions of whether a Committee can censor NGO statements in advance, and of whether the 1993 Oslo Accords between the Israeli
Government and the Palestine Liberation Organisation could be said to
have no bearing upon the very wide range of issues covered in the ICESCR,
these assertions are simply wrong. The initial report of Israel under the
ICESCR was already overdue in 1996 and the Committee had previously
received representations from NGOs containing information which, if correct, would have provided grounds for serious concern in terms of Israel's
obligations under the Covenant. Under the circumstances, the Committee
followed a procedure which had previously been applied in a number of
cases (e.g. Canada, Nigeria and the Philippines) and invited the Government of Israel to submit its overdue report, thus providing it with the
opportunity to refute the allegations made.

As to the proposed solution of universal and compulsory *in situ* fact-
finding missions to the territory of every state which is a party to each of the
six human rights treaties (recall, for example, that the Convention on
the Rights of the Child has 191 parties), such an approach would indeed
transform the system. However, it flies directly in the face of all indications
from virtually all states as to what they consider to be the acceptable limits
of the treaty supervisory system. Such missions are extremely expensive, involving interpreters, staff members and committees composed of
between ten and twenty-three members. The grossly inadequate funding
currently provided would need to be multiplied perhaps fifty times over,

---

[27] Bayefsky (1998), p. 468.   [28] Ibid.   [29] Ibid., note 10.

a remote prospect at a time of incessant budget-cutting in international organisations. Moreover, the nature of the system would be transformed beyond recognition and certainly beyond anything which governments could be said to have accepted under the terms of the existing treaty texts. The governments of developed countries would be every bit as averse to such a transformation as would those of the developing countries.

3. THE INADEQUACY OF FOLLOW-UP MEASURES

Bayefsky correctly notes that successful implementation is, to a significant extent, a function of follow-up. But she considers this to be especially weak in the case of the treaty bodies. This is manifested in various ways. The first problem is: 'States parties often fail to answer questions put by the treaty body members, for lack of time, ability or inclination . . . Written responses are usually not requested, and if received are almost never published.'[30] The latter point is indeed a problem. In principle, all of the documentation forming part of the exchange between the Committee and the state should be accessible in some way, as I pointed out in my 1997 report to the Commission on Human Rights.[31] It is also the case that information sought is often not provided, but this does not mean that the most appropriate or productive response is to engage in a form of never-ending paper warfare.

In most cases, the dialogue with states is best seen as the culmination rather than the mid-point of a lengthy process. In terms of the dialogue itself, the exchange between the committee and the government is designed to provide the governmental representatives with the opportunity to respond to all issues raised by the committee. To the extent that they do so to the satisfaction of the committee, the dialogue has served its purpose. To the extent that some issues are left unaddressed, or that the replies provided are unconvincing, it is for the committee to draw the appropriate conclusions, but again the dialogue may well have served its purpose. Moreover, it is a continuing dialogue, which will be resumed on the occasion of the next periodic report. In the case of second or subsequent reports, there will be an existing agenda of unresolved issues, and a state party may after reflection respond in ways it refused to do earlier. The process can be frustrating, and takes time. But it is a process, and its strengths need to be appreciated as well as its weaknesses.

---

[30] Ibid., p. 470.   [31] UN Doc. E/CN.4/1997/74, *supra* note 8, paras. 55–6.

The second problem highlighted goes to transparency:

> Follow-up also requires access to the process. Since attendance at the treaty body meetings is so difficult, a comprehensible, timely, written account of the proceedings is essential. However, it is also virtually impossible to obtain.[32]

As noted earlier, attendance at the meetings occurs to a much greater extent than this characterisation would suggest. Nevertheless, it is clear that the vast majority of those who are potentially interested in the process will never be able to attend. The question then is whether they can obtain access to the relevant information which they require. Bayefsky's analysis focuses entirely on the availability of 'summary records' which can indeed take a long time to appear even in a single language. This is, again, a result of the financial 'crisis' which has been inflicted upon the UN by those states which have failed to pay their assessed dues. But the focus on summary records again leaves us with a distorted picture of the issue. In the first place, the summary records are, in fact, available in either English or French within a reasonably short space of time. Requiring an interested individual to speak one or more foreign languages or obtain assistance with a translation is burdensome, but it is a burden with which most of those appearing before, or aspiring to work with, the committees have long had to cope.

Second, the UN issues 'press releases' which appear within hours of every meeting of a treaty body (except where confidentiality applies) and are available on the Internet. These too tend to alternate in French or English, but this need not be too much of a deterrent when automatic translation software is available free on the Internet and at low cost commercially. Such software programmes leave much to be desired, but the essence of a document is usually captured. Until recently, press releases were remarkably detailed and provided a reliable record of the meeting, despite their formally 'unofficial' status. The latter is a diplomatic nicety which enables instant news reports to be generated without holding up the process so governments can approve or disapprove the content, as is theoretically the case with the summary records. The latter may be 'corrected' by those concerned within a specified time of their issuance, but happily such corrections usually only serve to draw attention to the disputed report and they are thus resorted to mainly as a formality to pacify foreign ministries.

---

[32] Bayefsky (1998), p. 470.

But for the purposes of NGOs and almost anyone else wanting to know what has transpired in treaty body discussions, the press releases which are available worldwide on the Internet within hours are important resources.[33]

Third, the most important outcome of the 'dialogue' is the 'concluding observations' adopted by each committee at the end of its consideration of every governmental report. These observations are available as soon as they are adopted and are usually posted very soon thereafter on the Internet. In this respect, Bayefsky's sole focus on the summary records is unjustified and accords undue importance to one document, while ignoring the far more important one (the concluding observations) and a reasonable substitute for the summary records (the press releases).

Finally, there is a rapidly growing network of NGO-organised information services which make the details of the consideration of any given report widely and quickly available to many of the most interested constituencies. Indeed, it is not unknown for diplomats to complain to the UN secretariat that NGOs in their home country were disseminating copies of the concluding observations before the diplomatic mission had been able to send them back to the government.

Overall, the suggestion that 'it is . . . virtually impossible to obtain' an adequate record of treaty body proceedings is misleading.

Bayefsky draws a further conclusion. In her view '[f]ollow-up of concluding observations by potentially interested non-governmental sources in a state party is consequently often very weak, if done at all'.[34] Again, while much remains to be done in this regard, it is clear from the examples identified in this volume alone that this statement is a considerable overstatement, and is not supported by the facts.

The further suggestion is that bodies such as the General Assembly and the Commission on Human Rights, 'which have a responsibility to follow up treaty body conclusions', do not do so because 'they are driven by political considerations'.[35] Political organs are usually driven by political considerations but a great variety of factors can go into the political calculations

---

[33] Sadly, since this analysis was written, it needs to be said as the volume goes to press, that the quality of the press releases being produced in Geneva appears to have dropped dramatically in late 1998 and in 1999. Recent press releases have been excessively brief, lacking in essential detail and filled up with standard information which should not be included in an average press release purporting to report news. This is a particularly lamentable development which should be reversed.

[34] Bayefsky (1998), p. 470.   [35] Ibid., pp. 470–1.

that are made in any given case. Moreover, the relationship between the treaty bodies and the political organs is an issue which is far more complex than such simplifications would suggest. The independence of the treaty bodies *per se* has in fact been respected to a remarkable extent by the political organs of the UN. They have not intervened when they think that a treaty body has got it wrong. Nor, happily, have they sought to intervene at the behest of states parties looking for a way of overturning the conclusions reached by a committee. For the political organs to become more involved *vis-à-vis* 'delinquents' would be, at best, a double-edged sword.

While the involvement of the political organs in relation to financial and administrative matters is inevitable given the structure of the UN system, drawing the line between the substantive matters in relation to which they might reasonably and constructively intervene and those on which they should not is extremely difficult. In addition, the intervention of the political organs risks removing the matter from the effective realm of the treaty body. Yet a measure of continued cooperation is needed if the system is to function, and there will usually be no point in pressing an issue immediately, and risking a rupture of relations with the government concerned. There is of course much more that could be done (resources permitting) in terms of follow-up, but this is a far more complex question than Bayefsky suggests.

C. The overall assessment

It is hardly surprising that, on the basis of the various assessments and judgments described above, Bayefsky arrives at a rather negative view of the system as a whole. Thus, in her 1994 study, she characterised the UN human rights system as being dominated by a solid 'front of rejection'. Since the end of the Cold War, '[s]erious efforts at implementation and behavioral changes [have been] thwarted at every opportunity'. The human rights treaty mechanisms 'remain as relics of the past' which 'contain gigantic loopholes that are taken up with new zeal by large numbers of holdouts'.[36]

Her 1996 study was equally pessimistic in its outlook. The centrepiece of the work of the treaty bodies – the dialogue between states and the committees – 'frequently amounts to a series of unclear, incomplete, misleading,

---

[36] Bayefsky (1994), p. 231.

or dishonest representations, on the one hand, and a series of polite, but sceptical responses, on the other hand'.[37] She concluded that, 'on a procedural level the enforcement regime [sic] associated with the treaty bodies is seriously flawed' and that the 'system of implementation . . . is riddled with major deficiencies'.[38] In sum, there is an 'implementation crisis . . . of dangerous proportions'.[39]

By the time of her 1998 study, neither the overall assessment nor the outlook had improved:

> . . . the information available is not comprehensive; input is not obtained from all interested parties; the dialogue, for these reasons as well as constraints upon time, accessibility, and follow-up, is often marginally constructive, and with those states that need it most, frequently never takes place.[40]

Clearly some of this is true; the system does suffer from some serious weaknesses. But, as an overall assessment, Bayefsky's analysis is unbalanced and unrealistic (a) in its assessment of what the committees, within the constraints of existing or foreseeable resources, might do; and (b) in its image of what form an international human rights implementation mechanism might reasonably take.

D. Identifying the underlying causes of the weaknesses

Having identified the principal weaknesses in the system of treaty supervision, the next step is to seek to identify the underlying causes for the inadequacies of the 'seriously flawed' system. In so far as it proves possible to isolate such factors, and particularly if a limited group of countries can be seen to be responsible for them, it makes sense to seek to counter them. Bayefsky's choice of targets, however, is highly selective and her choice of means (penalising those responsible, and if this does not work, expelling them from the system) impractical and counter-productive.

In her analysis, the culprits, it seems, are developing countries in general and non-democratic ones in particular. Thus, the fact that the dialogue frequently consists of 'a series of unclear, incomplete, misleading, or dishonest representations' is demonstrated by examples taken from replies given by Tunisia, Algeria, Mexico, Nigeria, Jamaica, Senegal, Pakistan and Libya.[41] Not a single example is given in relation to a Western country, but

---

[37] Bayefsky (1996), p. 6.   [38] Ibid., p. 10.   [39] Ibid., p. 11.
[40] Bayefsky (1998), p. 471.   [41] Bayefsky (1996), pp. 6–7.

this is not for want of possible examples. Similarly 'States having the largest number of overdue reports frequently include those with extremely poor human rights records, such as: Togo, Liberia, the Central African Republic, Somalia, Afghanistan, Cambodia and Lebanon'.[42] Five of those seven have in fact been immersed in devastating civil wars for a rather long period of time. But instead of this being seen as some sort of explanation for a poor record of compliance with rather demanding and bureaucratic reporting mechanisms, it is simply translated into their having dreadful human rights records.

The reporting process itself is also seen to be particularly marginal and ineffective in relation to most developing countries. Thus, Bayefsky observes that while 'dozens of people' may attend when the reports of developed countries are presented, the reports of developing countries are often watched only by 'a sole representative of Amnesty International or one or two other persons from international NGOs . . .'.[43] Individual petition procedures are also undermined, or at least condemned to a level of superficiality, by the record of a range of developing countries, most of which would presumably qualify under Bayefsky's criteria as 'non-democracies'. Thus, the complaints procedure under the Optional Protocol to the International Covenant on Civil and Political Rights (ICCPR) is flawed because '[n]ot even a single case has been registered from . . . such states as Algeria, Bulgaria, Chad, Congo, El Salvador, Malawi, Namibia, Nepal, Romania, Somalia and Uganda'.[44] The fact that the United States has refused to permit its citizens to lodge such complaints, or that the United Kingdom, Ireland, the United States and various others have refused to make the declaration which would permit the CERD Committee to examine complaints relating to those countries, is nowhere mentioned. The presence of developing countries within the regime also seems to explain why the Optional Protocol process 'has been of little assistance in the context of the human rights problems of Western democratic states'.[45]

> The cases decided . . . relate to states with widely differing human rights conditions. The members of the Committee also come from states with substantially different human rights records. These circumstances appear to result in a number of instances in which the Committee handles egregious violations of the Covenant more easily than others.[46]

---

[42] Bayefsky (1998), p. 467.   [43] See *supra* note 14.   [44] Bayefsky (1998), p. 469.
[45] Bayefsky (1996), p. 11.   [46] Bayefsky (1998), p. 469.

The non-involvement of the General Assembly and the Commission on Human Rights is criticised. This is attributed to the fact that 'they are driven by political considerations, which almost always exclude taking action on specific states'. In particular, they are criticised for having failed to take up the negative assessments of relevant treaty bodies in relation to Egypt and Syria.[47] As noted earlier, it is hardly surprising that political bodies take full account of political considerations in their work, but it is certainly not the case that this has precluded either of them from singling out a large number of specific states for criticism. While it is true that they have usually not done so in response to treaty body reports, there may well be strong prudential reasons for the political organs not opting to take up every case of a violation identified by the treaty bodies. Even taking up only the more serious cases, on an individual basis and specifically in response to a finding by one treaty body, raises major policy issues which need to be carefully considered.

Overall then, virtually every specific example Bayefsky chooses to cite points consistently to developing countries as the cause of the system being so 'seriously flawed', although in fact the point on the democratic spectrum at which they would be placed by most observers would seem to differ greatly within the group of those she names.

E. The prescriptions that follow from the diagnosis

Bayefsky's recommendations for reform follow from her diagnosis. Her 1994 report proposed, *inter alia*, denial of access to, or expulsion from, the treaty regime of:

- 'those states that do not adhere to a set of minimum requirements';
- 'those states that fail to withdraw incompatible reservations';
- 'any state that does not allow individual communications'; and
- any 'states that disallow . . . media events' such as press conferences and media interviews linked to the work of the treaty bodies.[48]

In her 1998 report she concluded that one of the major problems with the treaty monitoring system is that it 'includes many states that share no common democratic aspirations'. In her view, 'extensive resistance to [the types of reform that she advocates] comes from nondemocratic states'. This, she says, gives rise to two further questions:

---

[47] Ibid., p. 471.   [48] Bayefsky (1994), pp. 264–5.

(1) What is the best method for securing democratic reform? Through the equal participation of nondemocracies within the treaty system? Or through alternative venues for interchange outside the treaty system, such as the marketplace – that is, economic pressure for reform? (2) Who is the system for? Is it aimed at assisting democracies, or aspiring democracies, to adjust and calibrate their laws and practices? Or is it aimed at the unrepentant social deviant, and intended to expose the depravity and provide a tool for critics everywhere? [49]

Her conclusion, in effect, is that 'unrepentant social deviants' or 'extreme delinquents', by which she apparently means 'non-democracies', should be excluded from the treaty system by one means or another. This is mainly because the continuing participation of such states depends on 'continued low levels of resources, tolerance of illegitimate reservations, and feeble institutional methodologies'.[50]

There are, however, a number of major problems with this conclusion. First, as already suggested earlier, the difference between the behaviour of democratic and non-democratic states, or of developed and developing states, is, in many respects, one of degree. There are Western states which have a poor reporting record and there are developed states with poor human rights records which have been assiduous in the submission of reports. There are certainly some developing states which are disdainful of the process and deaf to the suggestions of the committees. There are also Western states which barely react to criticism from a treaty body because they find it hard to comprehend how fault could have been found. This stems from an implicit assumption that, even if their record is imperfect, it is so much better than that of Bayefsky's 'non-democracies' that no criticism could be justified. Similarly, the reservations lodged by some Islamic states to certain treaties are lamentably sweeping and imprecise, but those put forward by the United States have also been widely criticised.[51] Nonetheless key Western states, even when they criticise such reservations, are hostile to the idea that the committees have an autonomous competence to invalidate reservations and even more so to the idea that committees are competent to 'expel' states parties.[52]

When it comes to financial and political support for the system as a whole there are certainly major differences from one country to the next, but it is not at all clear that these attitudes closely mirror the extent to which

---

[49] Bayefsky (1998), pp. 471–2.   [50] Ibid., p. 472.
[51] See *supra* S. Grant, chapter 14.   [52] Bayefsky (1998), p. 472.

a state is democratic or not. The United States, for example, has consistently opposed the payment of an honorarium (currently $3,000 per year) to the members of the three treaty bodies which do not currently receive them, despite the fact that independence and expertise are even less likely to be attracted where no remuneration at all is provided. In general then, it would seem both unwise and not consistent with the record to base a set of prescriptions on the assumption that there are clear cut and fundamental differences between the two groups of states in their relationship to the treaty system.

Second, the basis upon which a country qualifies as democratic or not is never spelled out by Bayefsky, but the implicit definition is evidently a wide one. Indeed it seems to encompass any state party which would resist the radically transformed system advocated by Bayefsky. The problem with this sort of analysis is that many of the democratic states which she sees as ideal citizens in this respect have steadfastly resisted the strengthening of the system in the ways she advocates (or indeed in any other ways), have refused to withdraw reservations subject to sustained challenges, have prevented additional resources flowing to the system, have themselves failed to report for a decade or longer, have refused to heed all of the recommendations directed at them, or have refused to accept some or all of the various international complaints procedures.

Third, Bayefsky effectively refuses to take any account of the differences in capacity between rich and poor countries in terms of their ability and preparedness to participate fully in the treaty system. It is one thing to insist that respect for basic human rights cannot be contingent upon per capita gross national product (GNP, or any other comparable economic indicator); it is quite another to demand that poor countries will be able or willing to devote the same level of resources to reporting and complaints procedures as some developed states with strong internal human rights constituencies. It is precisely for this reason that considerable emphasis has been placed upon the need for technical assistance to such states. As I noted in my 1997 report, in relation to the question of whether the international community should be providing resources to facilitate the ratification of treaties by such states and to assist them in meeting the subsequent reporting burden, at least initially:

> Curiously, it has yet to be acknowledged that such activities, which are essential to laying the foundations for a stable and peaceful world in which human rights are respected, should be funded adequately within the United Nations

framework. It almost seems to be thought that efforts to promote the acceptance of human rights norms would somehow be tainted if progress were purchased at a price, in terms of the necessary technical assistance. In contrast, the principle was recognized long ago in the environmental area in which many of the arrangements made in relation to key treaties provide for financial and other forms of assistance to help States to undertake the necessary monitoring, to prepare reports and to implement some of the measures required in order to ensure compliance with treaty obligations.[53]

Yet Bayefsky is dismissive of the role of technical assistance,[54] and makes no provision for it in a list of recommendations covering ten pages.[55]

Fourth, Bayefsky proposes that economic sanctions of some unspecified type should be brought to bear against any state which is not prepared to accept the approach that she proposes. Democratic reform, she says, is best achieved through 'economic pressure for reform'.[56] Her 1994 report was more explicit: '. . . at bottom, tying economic interests to improving human rights protection is the only message rejectionists are likely to understand'.[57] Leaving aside the very unsatisfactory track record of most human rights-linked economic sanctions, it is entirely unclear who would impose them, what triggers would be used, or what form they might take. Presumably a *coup d'état* or other setback on the road to democracy would lead to an ultimatum being issued by one or more of the treaty bodies (what if they disagreed in their assessments?) to the state concerned and failure to comply would lead to expulsion. It is, to say the least, rather difficult to see how such a system would function. No doubt linking sanctions in this way to the treaty supervisory system would transform the nature of the system, but it seems highly unlikely that it would be for the better.

What would remain in the aftermath of such a revolution? First, a much smaller system: 'membership would be limited to those states sharing democratic aspirations' (more probably, to a sub-set of such states).[58] It would then presumably look very much like the membership of existing regional human rights organisations, thus putting into stark relief the question as to what is to be gained from a universal system? This result contradicts Bayefsky's perception that there are certain states who need to benefit from the system more than others.[59] However great the shortcomings of the

---

[53] UN Doc. E/CN.4/1997/74, 1997, *supra* note 8, para. 25. See also *supra* D. Bodansky, chapter 17.
[54] Bayefsky (1996), p. 10.   [55] Ibid., pp. 12–22.   [56] Bayefsky (1998), p. 472.
[57] Bayefsky (1994), p. 265.   [58] Ibid.   [59] *Supra*, note 40.

existing system might be, 'improvements' of the type advocated would be regressive.

F. Conclusion

The human rights treaty supervisory system has come a very long way in a relatively short time. As recently as 1969 there was not a single human rights treaty body in existence. States were extremely reluctant to subject their human rights record to any sort of scrutiny. The terms agreed in the text of the several treaties that had been adopted envisaged a minimalist approach to monitoring. No treaty-based individual complaints system existed and the prospects for any coming into force were not considered good. The only human rights reporting exercise that had been tried had yielded almost nothing. [60]

Thirty years later the system has developed so rapidly that it has problems of which human rights proponents in earlier eras could only have dreamed. Those problems are certainly considerable, but they must be viewed against the background of the historical evolution of the system as a whole and in light of a range of other factors. The latter include the determined gradualism which inevitably characterises developments in the human rights field, the reluctance of all governments to facilitate the emergence of a truly effective international human rights monitoring regime, and the shrinking resources available to the United Nations for such activities. In addition, it is inevitably difficult to achieve flexible institutional and substantive changes in the context of a regime which has its foundations in a range of treaties, each of which was, to some extent, drafted in such a way as to limit the possibilities of dramatic change from within, by processes of interpretation and application as distinct from amendment.

For these and other reasons there are no short cuts to the development of an effective monitoring system and there are no magic formulae (such as the expulsion of non-democratic states) which will transform the capacity of

---

[60] The system established in 1956 and disbanded in 1981 called upon states to report to the Commission on Human Rights, on the basis of the Universal Declaration of Human Rights. The reports were expected to describe 'developments and the progress achieved during the preceding three years in the field of human rights, and measures taken to safeguard human liberty'. CHR Res. 1 (XII) (1956), para. 1. See generally P. Alston, 'The Commission on Human Rights', in *The United Nations and Human Rights: A Critical Appraisal* (ed. P. Alston), 1992, pp. 183–4.

the system to promote compliance with human rights norms. What is needed instead is a systematic examination of the possibilities that exist to strengthen each of the individual elements that together determine whether the system as a whole works and how effectively it does so. International human rights treaty supervision cannot usefully be seen as an all or nothing proposition.

The value of a book such as this is, as Jacobson and Brown Weiss have pointed out in their study of factors affecting compliance with environmental treaties, that it can focus on those factors 'that can be manipulated in the relatively short run through policy interventions'.[61] In that context the situation of developing countries is of particular interest, although not because more of them may be undemocratic by comparison with their developed country counterparts. As Jacobson and Brown Weiss note, 'it would not be very surprising or particularly helpful to those interested in improving compliance for us to discover that rich countries are more likely to comply with treaties than are poor countries . . .'.[62]

The more interesting challenge is to identify the measures which are capable of encouraging, enabling and as necessary pressuring, those countries to comply with their human rights treaty obligations. Democratisation is certainly a key factor, but it is not a result which is ever likely to be brought about solely by measures taken within a human rights treaty system. Condemnation by a treaty body can contribute to pressures towards democratisation by reinforcing and legitimising opposition demands and even by helping to call into question, both internally and externally, the legitimacy of the government. At the end of the day, it remains the case that no set of concluding observations, no matter how trenchant or incisive, can bring about a transition to democracy. But neither will expulsion from the treaty system.

The treaty supervisory process should not be viewed in monochrome. It is not a case of either a committee or a government 'winning' in the sense that a failure by a committee to elicit any meaningful response from a government means that it has 'failed'. The process itself is much more complex than such a one-dimensional snapshot in black and white can capture. The principle of accountability can be furthered merely by the act of submitting a report. In the case of states which are notably reluctant to accept meaningful international scrutiny, and examples vary from the

---

[61] See *supra* Brown Weiss and Jacobson, note 1, p. 9.
[62] Ibid.

United States to China, the very act of reporting is significant, as is the process of defending the report and responding to questioning. Similarly, even where the position of a government remains clearly unmoved by the entire process, the government itself should not be seen as the sole actor of importance. Opposition groups, civil society in general, the media, regional and international organisations and other states can all draw significant inferences from the critical conclusions drawn by the treaty bodies.

Where states fail to report at all, the situation is admittedly much less satisfactory. But again, the process must be seen in a longer-term perspective as one in which persistently delinquent governments will eventually have a price to pay, if only in the sense that their delinquency is one more factor in justifying the taking of other measures.

Moreover, the treaty body system should not be considered in isolation. An excessive emphasis on the condemnatory or punitive aspects of the treaty supervisory process only serves to obscure the fact that a large part of the overall international human rights regime is far better equipped than the treaty bodies to undertake such activities. The Commission on Human Rights, the General Assembly and even the Security Council, are all able to respond to serious violations in a more nuanced, tailored, and potentially effective manner than is an expert committee that meets two or three times a year and has a very limited range of options available to it. Ironically, the legal foundations of any measures taken by the political organs would in fact be significantly weakened by the expulsion of the states in question from the individual treaty regimes. Such expulsions would also be likely to give a dramatic impetus to a thus far reasonably well repressed urge on the part of some governments to withdraw from treaty regimes which they feel have subjected them to excessive criticism.

Thus, rather than focusing on expulsion, the treaty bodies should continue to develop the quality and depth of their analyses and conclusions while also exploring the development of the encouraging and enabling functions which they are able to perform. Recent studies of compliance with environmental treaty reporting obligations have highlighted the crucial importance of administrative capacity. In order to produce strong reports and to maximise responsiveness to the process as a whole, states need to have an adequate number of personnel available for the task. Those personnel in turn need to have sufficient expertise, be adequately supported in financial terms, and have a strong domestic legal mandate to do the job properly. In many (but perhaps not all) respects, 'administrative capacity correlates with total GNP and GNP per capita'.[63] For these reasons, environmental treaties have placed increasing emphasis on positive incentives to encourage compliance. They might take the form of 'special funds for financial or technical assistance, training programmes and materials, access to technology, or bilateral or multilateral assistance outside the framework of the Convention, from governments, multilateral development banks, or, in some cases, the private sector'.[64]

It is striking that so few of these techniques have been developed in any serious and systematic fashion in relation to the human rights treaties. In addition to the many other incremental recommendations for reform which are canvassed in this volume, much more needs to be done to explore the ways in which compliance with human rights treaty obligations can be both facilitated and encouraged through the provision of positive incentives. It is time for governments and international organisations to put their money where their mouths are by investing in the long-term future of the human rights treaty monitoring system which they have put in place and upon which so many expectations have been placed.

[63] Ibid., p. 531.   [64] Ibid., p. 546.

INDEX